IN THE NAME OF

ALLAH

THE ALL-COMPASSIONATE, ALL-MERCIFUL

The Concise Presentation of the

FIQH

Of the Sunnah and the Noble Book

- Title: The Concise Presentation of the FIQH
  of the Sunnah and the Noble Book
- Author: Dr. Abdul-Azeem Badawi
- English Edition 1 (2007)
- Translated from the Arabic Edition 3 (2001)
- Translator: Jamaal al-Din M. Zarabozo
- Layout Design: IIPH, Riyadh, Saudi Arabia
- Filming and Cover Designing: Samo Press Group

The Concise Presentation of the FIQH

Of the Sunnah and the Noble Book

الوجيز في فقة السنة والكتاب العزيز

Dr. Abdul-Azeem Badawi

Translated by

Jamaal al-Din M. Zarabozo

INTERNATIONAL ISLAMIC PUBLISHING HOUSE

King Fahd National Library Cataloging-in-Publication Data

Badawi, Abdul Azeem

The Concise Presentation of the Fiqh of the Sunnah and the Noble Book / Abdul-Azeem Badawi .- Riyadh, 2007

...p ; ...cm

ISBN Hard Cover: 9960-9827-8-5
ISBN Soft Cover: 9960-9827-9-3

1- Islamic fiqh 2- Fiqh Sunnah I - Title

250 dc 1427/6000
1427/6001

ISBN Hard Cover: **9960-9827-8-5** Legal Deposit no. **1427/6000**
ISBN Soft Cover: **9960-9827-9-3** Legal Deposit no. **1427/6001**

International Islamic Publishing House (IIPH)
P.O.Box 55195 Riyadh 11534, Saudi Arabia
Tel: 966 1 4650818 - 4647213 - Fax: 4633489
E-Mail: iiph@iiph.com.sa - www.iiph.com.sa

Transliteration Chart

أ	a
آ - ى	â
ب	b
ت	t
ة	h or t (when followed by another Arabic word)
ث	th
ج	j
ح	ḥ
خ	kh
د	d
ذ	dh
ر	r
ز	z
س	s
ش	sh
ص	ṣ
ض	ḍ
ط	ṭ

ظ	<u>dh</u>
ع	‘
غ	gh
ف	f
ق	q
ك	k
ل	l
م	m
ن	n
هـ - ه - ـه	h
و	w
و (as a long vowel)	oo
ي	y
ي (as a long vowel)	ee
ء	’ (Omitted in initial position)

ـَ	Fatḥah	a
ـِ	Kasrah	i
ـُ	Ḍammah	u
ـّ	Shaddah	Double letter
ـْ	Sukoon	Absence of vowel

Symbols Directory

(سبحانه وتعالى) : *Subhânahu wa Ta'âla* — "The Exalted."

(ﷺ) : *Ṣalla-Allâhu 'Alayhi wa Sallam* — "Blessings and peace be upon him."

(عليه السلام) : *'Alayhis-Salâm* — "May peace be upon him."

(رضي الله عنه) : *Raḍia-Allâhu 'Anhu* — "May Allah be pleased with him."

(رضي الله عنها) : *Raḍia-Allâhu 'Anha* — "May Allah be pleased with her."

بسم الله الرحمن الرحيم

Introduction

By the Esteemed Shaykh Muhammad Ṣafwat Noor ad-Deen

In the name of Allah. All praise be to Allah and the blessings and peace be upon the Messenger of Allah.

Bukhari and Muslim have recorded in their *Ṣaḥeeḥs* from Mu'âwiyah ibn Abu Sufiyân that the Messenger of Allah (ﷺ) stated, "For whomever Allah wants good, He gives him understanding of the faith."

They also recorded from Abu Moosa al-Ash'ari that the Prophet (ﷺ) said, "The guidance and knowledge which Allah has sent to me are like abundant rain falling on a land. A part (of the land) had fertile soil that absorbed the rainwater and sprouted vegetation and a lot of grass. Other parts were hard, so they held (but did not absorb) the rainwater. Allah made the people benefit from it so that they drank, watered (their animals), and cultivated (their fields). The rain fell on another part. It was barren, so it neither held water nor sprouted vegetation. These are the examples of whoever understood the religion of Allah, and benefited from what Allah revealed to me, by learning it and teaching it to others, and whoever did not pay attention to it. (Thus), he (the latter) did not accept the guidance of Allah with which I have been sent."

To proceed:
Dear Reader,

"The character of the Messenger of Allah (ﷺ) was the Qur'an,"[1] as his wife 'Âishah (رضي الله عنها) described him. Another words, he was a practical example and embodiment of the revelation. For that reason, the Prophet (ﷺ) would tell the people, "Pray in the manner that you have seen me praying."[2]

During the pilgrimage, he said, "Take your rites of pilgrimage from me."[3]

About the ablution, he stated, "Whoever makes ablution like this ablution of mine..."[4]

On another occasion he said, "Don't you have in me an example?"[5]

The Lord of Power, Perfect is He, has stated:

﴿لَقَدْ كَانَ لَكُمْ فِي رَسُولِ اللَّهِ أُسْوَةٌ حَسَنَةٌ لِمَنْ كَانَ يَرْجُوا اللَّهَ وَالْيَوْمَ الْآخِرَ وَذَكَرَ اللَّهَ كَثِيرًا ﴿٢١﴾﴾ (سورة الأحزاب: ٢١)

﴾Indeed in the Messenger of Allah you have an excellent example to follow for him who hopes in [the Meeting with] Allah and the Last Day and remembers Allah much.﴿ *(Qur'an 33: 21)*

Therefore, it becomes incumbent upon every Muslim to learn what the Prophet (ﷺ) did with respect to his acts of worship and worldly interactions such that he can emulate the Prophet (ﷺ) — that is, in fact, the religion of Islam.

---

[1] *Ṣaheeḥ al-Jâmi'*, no. 4811.
[2] *I'rwâ' al-Ghaleel*, no. 262.
[3] *I'rwâ' al-Ghaleel*, no. 1074.
[4] *Ṣaheeḥ al-Jâmi'*, no. 6175.
[5] *Mukhtasar Ṣaheeḥ Muslim*, no. 229.

This concise work in your hands encompasses, in the briefest manner, the proper manner of following the Prophet (ﷺ) in acts of worship, worldly dealings and other topics of fiqh. So that the soul of the reader may be convinced to put these words into practice, the author has beautified his words with proper evidence. The author, may Allah reward him, was very careful to ensure that his evidences were such that were accepted by the scholars of hadith. Hence, he presents authentic and other accepted hadith. He refrains from that which is defective because the religion of Allah is not in need of such rejected reports.

Shaykh 'Abdul 'Adheem ibn Badawi has compiled with briefness in wording the evidences that can satisfy the truth seeker. This book, albeit small in comparison with the larger works, has combined together two books. First, it is a book containing fiqh that takes the hand of the reader and shows him what he should do. Second, it is a book of hadith that displays the statements and actions of the Prophet (ﷺ). The combination of these two is a great blessing. The book is sufficient for the one seeking to travel to Allah's pleasure and will also satisfy the knowledge seekers thirst for knowledge. Thus, it is a book that the people need. I hope that the reader will ponder over it, starting with its introduction and not neglecting its final words, while acting upon what it contains between these two.

I have read the book from its beginning to the end of the section on the pilgrimage and I have found that it is very simple and straightforward, free of exhaustive differences of opinions, easy for the one who wishes to succeed by righteous deeds and wishes to know the beneficial knowledge. We ask Allah to bless the Noble Shaykh by allowing him to continue to produce such beneficial output and we ask that his knowledge be benefited from. We ask Allah (ﷻ) to grant him success. We also ask that every reader be given the ability to act upon this work and be provided with purity of intention in statement and action, in both private and open deeds.

Written by the one in need of the forgiveness and pleasure of his Lord,

Muhammad Ṣafwat Noor ad-Deen

General President,
Anṣâr as-Sunnah al-Muhammadiyah,
Egypt

Author's Introduction

Verily, all praise is to Allah. We praise Him, seek His help and seek His forgiveness. We seek refuge in Allah from the evils within our souls and the harm of our deeds. Whomever Allah guides, there is none to misguide. And whomever He sends astray, there is none to guide. I bear witness that there is none worthy of worship except Allah alone, with no partner, and I bear witness that Muhammad is His servant and Messenger.

﴿يَـٰٓأَيُّهَا ٱلَّذِينَ ءَامَنُوا۟ ٱتَّقُوا۟ ٱللَّهَ حَقَّ تُقَاتِهِۦ وَلَا تَمُوتُنَّ إِلَّا وَأَنتُم مُّسْلِمُونَ ﴿١٠٢﴾﴾

(سورة آل عِمرَان: ١٠٢)

﴿O' you who believe! Fear Allah as He should be feared and die not except in a state of Islam [as Muslims] with complete submission to Allah.﴾ *(Qur'an 3: 102)*

﴿يَـٰٓأَيُّهَا ٱلنَّاسُ ٱتَّقُوا۟ رَبَّكُمُ ٱلَّذِى خَلَقَكُم مِّن نَّفْسٍ وَٰحِدَةٍ وَخَلَقَ مِنْهَا زَوْجَهَا وَبَثَّ مِنْهُمَا رِجَالًا كَثِيرًا وَنِسَآءً ۚ وَٱتَّقُوا۟ ٱللَّهَ ٱلَّذِى تَسَآءَلُونَ بِهِۦ وَٱلْأَرْحَامَ ۚ إِنَّ ٱللَّهَ كَانَ عَلَيْكُمْ رَقِيبًا ﴿١﴾﴾

(سورة النِّسَاء: ١)

﴿O' mankind! Be dutiful to your Lord, Who created you from a single person [Adam], and from him He created his wife, and from them both He created many men and women and fear Allah through Whom you demand your mutual [rights], and [do not cut the relations of] the kinship. Surely, Allah is Ever an All-Watcher over you.﴾

(Qur'an 4: 1)

﴿يَـٰٓأَيُّهَا ٱلَّذِينَ ءَامَنُواْ ٱتَّقُواْ ٱللَّهَ وَقُولُواْ قَوْلًا سَدِيدًا ﴿٧٠﴾ يُصْلِحْ لَكُمْ أَعْمَـٰلَكُمْ وَيَغْفِرْ لَكُمْ ذُنُوبَكُمْ ۗ وَمَن يُطِعِ ٱللَّهَ وَرَسُولَهُۥ فَقَدْ فَازَ فَوْزًا عَظِيمًا ﴿٧١﴾﴾

(سورة الأحزاب: ٧٠-٧١)

﴿O' you who believe! Keep your duty to Allah and fear Him, and speak [always] the truth. He will direct you to do righteous good deeds and will forgive you your sins. And whosoever obeys Allah and His Messenger he has indeed achieved a great achievement.﴾ *(Qur'an 33: 70-71)*

To proceed:

Verily, the truest speech is the book of Allah. The best guidance is the guidance of Muhammad. The worst of matters are the newly-invented ones. Every newly-invented matter is an innovation. Every innovation is a misguidance and every misguidance is in the Hell-fire.[1]

The knowledge of fiqh is one of the most virtuous and noble fields of learning. Through this knowledge, the acts of worship are made sound — and this worship is the ultimate goal of the creation of humankind, as Allah (ﷻ) has said,

﴿وَمَا خَلَقْتُ ٱلْجِنَّ وَٱلْإِنسَ إِلَّا لِيَعْبُدُونِ ﴿٥٦﴾﴾ (سورة الذاريات: ٥٦)

﴿And I [Allah] created not the jinn and humans except they should worship Me [Alone].﴾ *(Qur'an 51: 56)*

The foundation of success is not achieved by the human except by correcting his belief in monotheism and making it devoid of any

---

[1] This is known as *khuṭbah al-ḥâjah* by which the Prophet (ﷺ) may begin his sermons, lessons and admonitions. The great scholar Shaykh al-Albâni has written a beneficial treatise on this preamble.

form of associating partners with Allah. However, the success is not completed except by making one's worship sound and making it, as well, devoid of any form of innovation. The Prophet (ﷺ) has stated that the sign of Allah wanting good for a person is that he has understanding of the faith. The Prophet (ﷺ) said, "For whomever Allah wants good, He gives them understanding of the religion."[2]

> "The greatness and nobility of this knowledge is beyond description and mastering. This is so because it contains the rules by which a Muslim acts and adheres in all of the deeds of his life concerning him and his Lord. It also covers his acts between him and the other humans. By it, the tie between the worship of his Lord in public and private is strengthened through actions of purity, prayer, zakah, fasting and pilgrimage. By it, the banner of Islam is spread and the light of the Qur'an is held high. This is via the fiqh of jihad, battles, warfare, security, treaties and so forth. By it, one seeks permissible wealth and sustenance and stays distant from the sources of sin and harm. This is via the fiqh of social interactions, such as buying, selling, options, interest, money exchange and other similar acts concerning the financial interactions among humans. It also includes rules for the wealth used for religious functions, such as foundations, bequests and other financial issues. It also covers the fiqh of inheritance by which the wealth is distributed to its rightful owners in the most just distribution and system of inheritance. Similarly, the blessings of marital life and related laws are also found via this knowledge. By this knowledge of fiqh, Islam protects the necessities of life via the criminal and penal laws. Thus, people live in safety and security. Similar benefits accrue from the laws related to food, animal slaughter, vows, oaths, judicial laws and

---

[2] Bukhari, no. 3316; Muslim, no. 1037 and Ibn Mâjah, no. 220.

principles by which justice, resolution of disputes, supporting of rights and repelling of injustice are accomplished."[3]

For this and other reasons, the poet has said,

"If the possessor of knowledge is not always honoured by his knowledge
Then the people of fiqh are most deserving of being honoured
How many perfumes give off a good odour but not like musk?
And how many birds fly but not like a hawk"

"All of points of Islamic law actually boil down to one view. This is so even in the secondary issues, although there may be lots of differences of opinion. This is also the case with respect to the foundational issues. No other view would be feasible. The evidences for this are numerous, including:

First, evidence from the Qur'an: For example, Allah (ﷻ) says:

﴿... وَلَوْ كَانَ مِنْ عِندِ غَيْرِ ٱللَّهِ لَوَجَدُوا۟ فِيهِ ٱخْتِلَـٰفًا كَثِيرًا ﴿٨٢﴾﴾

(سورة النِّساء: ٨٢)

﴾... Had it been from other than Allah, they would surely have found therein many contradictions.﴿ *(Qur'an 4: 82)*

Here, Allah denies that there should be any contradiction. If there was anything in the Qur'an that lead to two contradictory conclusions, the words of this verse would certainly not be truthful. Allah (ﷻ) also says:

﴿... فَإِن تَنَـٰزَعْتُمْ فِى شَىْءٍ فَرُدُّوهُ إِلَى ٱللَّهِ وَٱلرَّسُولِ إِن كُنتُمْ تُؤْمِنُونَ بِٱللَّهِ وَٱلْيَوْمِ ٱلْـَٔاخِرِ ۚ ذَٰلِكَ خَيْرٌ وَأَحْسَنُ تَأْوِيلًا ﴿٥٩﴾﴾

(سورة النِّساء: ٥٩)

---

[3] From Abu Bakr Zayd's introduction to *at-Taqreeb li-Fiqh Ibn Qayyim al-Jawziyah*, vol.. 1, Pp. 6-7.

﴾... [And] if you differ in anything among yourselves, refer it to Allah and His Messenger, if you believe in Allah and in the Last Day. That is better and more suitable for final determination.﴿ *(Qur'an 4: 59)*

This verse is explicit in indicating the removal of disputes and differences of opinion. The disputants should take their issue to the Shari'ah, and this is to remove the difference of opinion. But the difference of opinion cannot be removed except by referring it to one source. If this one source also creates differences of opinion, then it cannot be referred to to put an end to such disputes. This would be fallacious. Another verse states:

﴿وَلَا تَكُونُوا۟ كَٱلَّذِينَ تَفَرَّقُوا۟ وَٱخْتَلَفُوا۟ مِنۢ بَعْدِ مَا جَآءَهُمُ ٱلْبَيِّنَٰتُ ... ﴿١٠٥﴾﴾

(سورة آل عِمرَان: ١٠٥)

﴾And be not as those who divided and differed among themselves after the clear proofs had come to them...﴿ *(Qur'an 3: 105)*

The clear proofs make up the Shari'ah. If it were not for the fact that these clear proofs do not lead to differences and do not admit to them at all, how would it be said, ﴾after the clear proofs had come to them﴿. Otherwise, they would have the greatest excuse for their differences of opinion. This is not the case. Hence, the Shari'ah has no contradictions to it.

The verses that censure division and differences and which order returning to the Shari'ah are many. All of them are definitive concerning the fact that there is no contradiction in the Shari'ah. It is all from one source and upon one view. Al-Mazani, the companion of ash-Shafi'i, stated, "Allah has censured division and differences and has ordered, in circumstances of differences of opinion, to refer to the Book and the Sunnah."

Second, the majority of the scholars of the Shari'ah have affirmed that in the Qur'an and the Sunnah there are abrogated and abrogating commands in general. They have warned about being ignorant about them and making mistakes concerning them. It is known that abrogation occurs between contradicting evidences that cannot be reconciled at all. Otherwise, one would not be abrogating and the other abrogated. If differences in the religion were allowed, why would there be any benefit to affirming abrogation, even without a definitive text? In that case, there would be no benefit in discussing such a topic because people would be able to act upon both of the pieces of evidence continually, based on the fact that divergence and difference of opinion is a part of the faith. But all of that is fallacious by consensus. This indicates that there is no room or basis for such differences of opinion in the Shari'ah. This is also the case with every type of evidence for which there is a shade of conflict, such as the general and the particular, the unrestricted and restricted and so on. All of these principles would be demolished if such differences would be allowed. Such is an improper view.

<u>Third</u>, if the Shari'ah did allow divergent conclusions then it would mean that it would require the human to perform what is beyond his means. This is so because if we assume two conflicting pieces of evidence and we also assume that both of them are requested by the Lawgiver, then the person is required to perform, one, what both pieces of evidence demand or, two, perform what one of them demands and not the other. Both of these hypotheses are not sound. The first hypothesis would mean, for example, that if the Shari'ah says both "do" and "do not" a single act at a single time, he would be obliged to implement both of these commands which would be impossible. The second hypothesis is also false as it goes against the hypothesis [that both of them are requested by the Lawgiver]. The same is true for the

third hypothesis because both are demanded. Thus, only the first is left and what has been previously stated has been confirmed.

Fourth, the legal theorists agree that in confirming the principle of weighing which evidence is stronger when faced with two contradictory pieces of evidence that cannot be reconciled. They also agree that it is not sound to ignore one of the conflicting pieces of evidence without determining which is stronger. To say that contradictory views are acceptable in the Shari'ah removes this science of weighing between the evidences as there would be no benefit to it and no need for it even with the assumption that there are contradictions in the Shari'ah. But that is not proper and what the conclusion it leads to is also not sound."[4]

Therefore, I say, since all points of Islamic law actually boil down to one view, in the primary issues as well as in the secondary issues and even if there are lots of differences of opinion, I wished to write a book on fiqh which would restrict itself to the strongest opinion that are supported by the sound evidence. At the same time, I follow the path of the people of *ijtihâd* and verification with in-depth research, those who determine the reality and make clear the new issues, providing for it various evidence from the light of the Prophet (ﷺ). They follow the Sunnah wherever it leads its followers, providing for the people a great knowledge, built upon the most guiding of principles.

This form of fiqh is what was passed on by the Companions of the Prophet (ﷺ) to those who followed them in goodness throughout the generations. They then recorded the fiqh according to this noble and sound methodology.[5]

---

[4] Ash-Shâṭibi, *al-Muwâfaqât*, vol. 4, Pp. 118-122, with some abridgement.

[5] This paragraph is based on what is found in the introduction to *at-Taqreeb*, op cit.

I have entitled by book *The Concise Presentation of the Fiqh of the Sunnah and the Noble Book.*

I have arranged the book in the following order: purification, prayer, fasting, zakah, pilgrimage, marriage, business transactions, vows, food, bequests, inheritance, penal punishments, judicial principles, jihad and slave emancipation.

The secret behind this ordering is: Allah has created humans to worship Him alone and since the foundation of worship and the pillar of the faith is the prayer, I began with it. However, I put purification before it since it is a prerequisite of the prayer and the prerequisite should come prior to that for which it is a prerequisite.

Since the fast is something that Allah especially rewards, as stated in the hadith, I have connected it with the prayer. I put the fast before the zakah in order to put the act of worship of the body before act of worship related to wealth only, which is the zakah, and the act of worship of the body and the wealth, which is the pilgrimage. Since marriage is the cause behind the existence of the worshippers, I have made it the first topic after the acts of worship. I have followed this with business transactions because those people that are the result of marriage are continually buying and selling. It is customary for people to swear and make oaths a lot while involved in business, so I conjoined vows and oaths after business transactions to explain what is proper and improper concerning such swearing. I followed these with food, bequests, inheritance and criminal punishment. Since it is the judiciary that usually distributes issues of inheritance and always implements the fixed prescribed punishments — as it is not permissible to establish the fixed prescribed punishments unless one is the ruler or his representative — I followed those up with the book on judicial principles.

Since Muslims are obliged, after establishing the religion of Allah in themselves, to strive to establish the religion of Allah upon

Allah's earth and to call people to the worship of Allah, it normally occurs in all times and places that there are people who try to block the path of Allah and prevent the callers to Allah from propagating Allah's faith. Thus, I spoke about jihad and its rulings. Since the present of combatant slaves is sometimes a result of fighting, as they are the prisoners of the disbelievers and polytheists, I put slave emancipation after jihad in order to show that Islam encourages the freeing of slaves and blesses the prisoners of the war with freedom.

The wisdom behind putting slave emancipation at the end of this book, *The Concise Presentation,* is the hope that Allah will make this deed a cause for emancipating me from the Hell-Fire, for verily He is the All-Powerful, the Oft-Forgiving.

By Allah, the Great, I ask that I have been blessed with what is correct, that He reward me for it and that He forgive me concerning what it contains of mistakes.

I also ask Him to make the Muslims benefit from it.

And all praise and thanks are for Allah.

'Abdul 'Adheem ibn Badawi

Chapter One — Purity

Lexically, the word *ṭahârah* means cleaning and being free from impurity. As a technical term, it means lifting spiritual impurity and removing physical impurity.[1]

Water and Its Various Categories

All water that falls from the sky or comes from the earth is pure, as Allah (ﷻ) has said:

﴿... وَأَنزَلْنَا مِنَ ٱلسَّمَآءِ مَآءً طَهُورًا ﴿٤٨﴾﴾ (سورة الفرقان: ٤٨)

﴿... We send down purifying water from the sky.﴾ *(Qur'an 25: 48)*

Also, the Prophet (ﷺ) said about the water in the ocean, "Its water is pure and its (animals that have died) are permissible (to eat)."[2] Furthermore, the Prophet (ﷺ) also said about well water, "Verily, water is pure and nothing makes it impure."[3]

Thus, it remains in a state of purity, even if someone pure mixes with it, as long as it still considered water. For example, the Prophet (ﷺ) told the women who were preparing his daughter for

---

[1] *Al-Majmoo' Sharḥ al-Muhadhdhib*, vol. 1, p. 79.

[2] This hadith is *ṣaḥeeḥ*. See Nâṣir ad-Deen al-Albâni, *Ṣaḥeeḥ al-Jâmi'*, no. 309. Recorded by Mâlik, Abu Dawood, Tirmidhi, Ibn Mâjah and Nasâ'i.

[3] This hadith is *ṣaḥeeḥ*. See Nâṣir ad-Deen al-Albâni, *al-I'rwâ' al-Ghaleel*, no. 14. Recorded by Abu Dawood, Tirmidhi and Nasâ'i.

burial, "Wash her three, five or more times, as you see fit. (Wash her) with water [mixed with] lotus leaves and make the last one with camphor or with some camphor."[4]

Water would not be considered impure, even if something impure should mix with it, unless the impurity changes it quality. This is based on the hadith of Abu Sa'eed who narrated: "It was said to the Messenger of Allah, 'Shall we make ablution from the well of Budhâh. This is the well in which the filth of menstruating women, dogs and putrid things were thrown.' The Prophet (ﷺ) replied, 'Verily, water is pure (and purifying) and nothing makes it impure.' "[5]

Impurities

In Arabic, the word for impurity is *najâsah* (pl., *najâsât*). It refers to everything that is repulsive to people of sound nature. They protect themselves from such things and they wash their garments whenever such things fall upon them. Thus, such things include filth, urine and so forth.[6]

---

[4] Recorded by Bukhari and Muslim.

[5] This hadith is *ṣaḥeeḥ*. See Nâṣir ad-Deen al-Albâni, *I'rwâ' al-Ghaleel*, 14. Recorded by Abu Dawood, Tirmidhi and Nasâ'i. In *Tuhfaḥ al-Aḥwadhi*, vol. 1, p. 204, al-Mubârakfoori wrote, "aṭ-Ṭeebi said, 'The meaning of '(filth of) were thrown' is that the well was in a channel wherein the water flowed from some of the lands where the Bedouins would camp. They would throw their garbage on the steps of their households and the water flow would take it into the well. The way the question was put made it seem like the people themselves would throw such filth into the well due to a lack of piety. This is something a Muslim would not do. How could anyone think that the best and most pious of the generations would do something of that nature.' Such has been stated by more than one scholar. It is the apparent, specific meaning of what occurred."

[6] *Ar-Rawḍah an-Nadiyah*, vol. 1, p. 12.

The principle ruling concerning any kind of matter is that of permissibility and purity (That is, they are to be considered permissible and pure unless proven otherwise). If someone, therefore, claims that an object is impure, then the burden of proof is upon him to bring forth some evidence for the impurity of that object. If he does, his conclusion will be followed. If he is not able to bring forth such proof or if he does not present an acceptable proof, then our judgment will be according to the original principle and it being free of any impurity.[7] Since declaring something to be impure is an obligation that concerns all people, it is not permissible to make such a declaration unless a proof has been established for it.

Those items for which there is proof that they are impure include the following:

1. and 2. Human urine and feces

As for feces, its impurity is proven by the hadith narrated by Abu Hurayrah (رضي الله عنه) that the Messenger of Allah (ﷺ) said, "If one of you steps with his sandals into something filthy (*al-adhâ*), then dirt is the purification for it."[8] *Al-Adhâ* refers to everything that harms someone, such as impure things, filth, rocks and thorns.[9] Its meaning in this particular hadith, though, as is clear, is impurities.

Concerning urine there is the hadith narrated by Anas (رضي الله عنه) in which a Bedouin was urinating in the mosque and the people got up to stop him. The Messenger of Allah (ﷺ) then said, "Leave him and do not cut him off (from his act)." Anas continued by narrating that when he had finished urinating, the Prophet (ﷺ) asked for a container of water to pour over the urine.[10]

---

[7] *As-Sail al-Jarâr*, vol. 1, p. 31.
[8] This hadith is *saheeh*. Recorded by Abu Dawood.
[9] *'Awn al-Ma'bood*, vol. 2, p. 44.
[10] Recorded by Bukhari and Muslim.

3. and 4. al-Madhi and al-Wadi

The *madhi* is a thin, clear, sticky fluid that is produced during amorous stimulation but it does not come out like an ejaculation or gush out and it also does not cause any type of exhaustion afterwards. In fact, a person may not even realize that he has excreted it. It occurs both for men and women.[11] It is impure. Thus, the Prophet (ﷺ) ordered that the private part should be washed due to it. 'Ali ibn Abi Ṭâlib stated, "I was a person who would have *madhi* come out often but I was too shy to ask the Prophet (ﷺ) about it, due to my relationship with his daughter. Thus, I requested al-Miqdâd ibn al-Aswad to ask him. (He did) and the Prophet (ﷺ) said, 'He should wash his private part and make ablution.'"[12]

Al-Wadi is a white, thick fluid that comes out after urination[13] (usually due to an infection or something of that nature). It is also impure. Ibn 'Abbâs stated, "(There is) semen, *al-wadi* and *al-madhi*. As for semen, it is the thing due to which one must make *ghusl*. As for *al-wadi* and *al-madhi*, he said, 'Wash your private part or (he said private parts) and make the ablution like that for the prayer.'"[14]

5. Dung of animals that cannot be eaten

'Abdullâh ibn Mas'ood said, "The Messenger of Allah (ﷺ) went to relieve himself and said, 'Bring me three stones.' I brought him two stones and a piece of dung. He took the two stones and discarded the dung, saying, 'It is filth.'"[15]

---

[11] An-Nawawi, *Sharḥ Ṣaḥeeḥ Muslim*, vol. 3, p. 213.

[12] Recorded by Bukhari and Muslim. This is Muslim's wording.

[13] As-Sayyid Sâbiq, *Fiqh as-Sunnah*, vol. 1, p. 24.

[14] This hadith is *ṣaḥeeḥ*. See Shaykh al-Albâni, *Ṣaḥeeḥ Sunan Abi Dawood*, 190. Recorded by al-Bayhaqi.

[15] This hadith is *ṣaḥeeḥ*. See Nâṣir ad-Deen al-Albâni, *Ṣaḥeeḥ Ibn Mâjah*, no. 253. With different wording it is recorded by Bukhari, Ibn Mâjah and Tirmidhi.

6. Menstrual blood

Asmâ' bint Abi Bakr stated that a woman came to the Prophet (ﷺ) and said, "We get menstrual blood on our clothing, so what should we do?" He replied, "Rub it, then scratch it off with water and then wet it and then (you can) pray in it."[16]

7. Dog saliva

Abu Hurayrah (ﷺ) narrated that the Messenger of Allah (ﷺ) said, "The purifying of one of your bowls that a dog licked in is for it to be washed seven times, the first time being with dirt."[17]

8. Carrion

This refers to the animal that has died without being slaughtered in the legally sanctioned manner. The Prophet (ﷺ) said, "If the pelt is tanned, it becomes pure."[18]

The exceptions for the skin or pelt of carrion being impure are the following:

8.1. Dead fish and locusts are considered pure. This is based on the hadith from Ibn 'Umar who said that the Prophet (ﷺ) said, "Two types of dead animals and two types of blood have been made permissible for us. The two dead animals are fish and locusts. The two types of blood arc the liver and the spleen."[19]

---

[16] Recorded by Bukhari and Muslim. This is Muslim's wording.

[17] This hadith is *ṣaḥeeḥ*. See Nâsir ad-Deen al-Albâni, *Ṣaḥeeḥ al-Jâmi'*, no. 3933. It is recorded by Muslim.

[18] This hadith is *ṣaḥeeḥ*. See Nâṣir ad-Deen al-Albâni, *Ṣaḥeeḥ al-Jâmi'*, no. 511. Recorded by Muslim and Abu Dawood.

[19] This hadith is *ṣaḥeeḥ*. See Nâṣir ad-Deen al-Albâni, *Ṣaḥeeḥ al-Jâmi'*, no. 210. Recorded by Aḥmad and al-Bayhaqi.

8.2. Animals that do not have circulating blood in them, such as flies, ants, bees and so on. Abu Hurayrah (ﷺ) narrated that the Messenger of Allah (ﷺ) said, "If a fly falls into a bowl of yours, then immerse it into it completely and then throw it out for in one of its wings is a disease and in the other is the antidote."[20]

8.3. Bones, horns, nails, hairs and feathers of dead animals are all pure based on the basic ruling of purity (unless there is proof otherwise). Bukhari recorded, without a complete chain, that az-Zuhri said about the bones of dead animals, such as an elephant and others, "I have met some of the earlier scholars who use to use those for combing or applying oil and they did not see any harm in that."[21] Ḥamâd said, "There is no harm concerning the feathers of the dead animals."

How to Clean Impurities

> "The Lawgiver who has informed us of the impure items has also informed us of the manner by which they are to be purified. Thus, it is obligatory upon us to follow what He (ﷻ) has stated and fulfill His commands. Therefore, if it is narrated that something should be washed until the color, smell or taste of the impurity no longer persists, (this is how it must be purified). If it is narrated that something is supposed to have water poured over it, sprinkled with water, scrubbed, wiped over the earth (to be made pure) or that by simply walking over the ground (it is made pure), then such is how it is to be purified. One should also realize that water is the basic agent to be used for purifying impurities, as the

[20] This hadith is *ṣaḥeeḥ*. See Nâṣir ad-Deen al-Albâni, *Ṣaḥeeḥ al-Jâmi'*, no. 837. Recorded by Bukhari and Muslim.

[21] Bukhari, vol. 1, p. 342.

Lawgiver has described it by saying, 'Allah has created water purifying.'[22] When the purifying agent is confirmed by the Lawgiver, then no other choice should be made. If one does so, then he is going from what is known to purify the object to something concerning which it is not known if it will purify the object. This is going against what is the sanctioned way."[23]

Based on this point, below are presented the sanctioned ways of purifying specific impure objects or objects made impure:

1. Purifying of animal skin by tanning it

Ibn 'Abbâs narrated that the Prophet (ﷺ) said, "Any pelt that is tanned has been made pure."[24]

2. Purifying the bowl in which a dog has licked

Abu Hurayrah (رضي الله عنه) narrated that the Messenger of Allah (ﷺ) said, "The purifying of one of your bowls that a dog licked in is for it to be washed seven times, the first time being with dirt."[25]

3. Purifying the garment which has had menstrual blood on it

Asmâ' bint Abi Bakr (رضي الله عنها) stated that a woman came to the Prophet (ﷺ) and said, "We get menstrual blood on our clothing, so

---

[22] Ash-Shawkâni, *as-Sail al-Jarâr*, vol. 1, p. 42. As for the statement, "Allah has created water purifying," Ibn Ḥajar stated in *at-Talkheeṣ*, vol. 1, p. 14, "I have not found it narrated in this fashion." Actually, the hadith of Abu Sa'eed was mentioned earlier, which states, "Verily, water is pure (and purifying) and nothing makes it impure."

[23] Ash-Shawkâni, *as-Sail al-Jarâr*, vol. 1, p. 47.

[24] This hadith is *ṣaḥeeḥ*. See Nâṣir ad-Deen al-Albâni, *Ṣaḥeeḥ Sunan Ibn Mâjah*, no. 2907. Recorded by Aḥmad, Tirmidhi and Ibn Mâjah.

[25] This hadith is *ṣaḥeeḥ*. See Nâṣir ad-Deen al-Albâni, *Ṣaḥeeḥ al-Jâmi'*, no. 3933. It is recorded by Muslim.

what should we do?" He replied, "Rub it, then scratch it off with water and then wet it and then (you can) pray in it."[26]

There is no harm if some traces of the blood are left after that. Abu Hurayrah narrated that Khawlah bint Yasâr said, "O' Messenger of Allah, I only own one garment and I (wear it) while menstruating. (What should I do?)" He replied, "When you become pure (from your menses), wash the place of the blood and then pray in it." She then said, "Even if its traces are not removed?" He replied, "The water is sufficient for you and its traces will not harm you."[27]

4. Purifying the bottom of the woman's dress

An ex-slave of Ibrâheem ibn 'Abdur-Raḥmân ibn 'Awf asked Umm Salama (ﷺ), the wife of the Prophet (ﷺ), "I am a woman who lets her dress drag and I walk in filthy places (so what should I do)?" Umm Salamah said that the Prophet (ﷺ) replied, "What comes after it purifies it."[28]

5. Purifying the garment upon which a nursing baby boy has urinated

Abu as-Samḥ, the servant of the Prophet, narrated that the Prophet (ﷺ) said, "The urine of the baby girl is to be washed while that of the baby boy is to be sprinkled over."[29]

---

[26] Recorded by Bukhari and Muslim. This is Muslim's wording.

[27] This hadith is *ṣaḥeeḥ*. See Nâṣir ad-Deen al-Albâni, *Ṣaḥeeḥ Sunan Abi Dawood*, no. 351. Recorded by Abu Dawood, Aḥmad and al-Bayhaqi.

[28] This hadith is *ṣaḥeeḥ*. See Nâṣir ad-Deen al-Albâni, *Ṣaḥeeḥ Ibn Mâjah*, no. 430. Recorded by Mâlik, Abu Dawood, Tirmidhi and Ibn Mâjah.

[29] This hadith is *ṣaḥeeḥ*. See Nâṣir ad-Deen al-Albâni, *Ṣaḥeeḥ Sunan Nasâ'i*, no. 293. Recorded by Abu Dawood and Nasâ'i.

6. Purifying the garment from al-Madhi

Sahl ibn Ḥunayf said, "I used to suffer a lot from having *madhi* and used to wash a lot due to it. I mentioned that to the Messenger of Allah (ﷺ) and he said, 'It is sufficient for you to make ablution from that.' I said, 'What should I do about what falls upon my clothing?' He replied, 'It is sufficient for you to take a handful of water and wet your clothing wherever you see any place on which it has fallen.' "[30]

7. Purification of the bottom of sandals

Abu Sa'eed narrated that the Prophet (ﷺ) said, "When one of you comes to the mosque, he should turn his sandals over and look at them. If he finds any filth on them, he should wipe them on the ground and then pray in them."[31]

8. Purification of the ground and earth

Abu Hurayrah (رضي الله عنه) narrated that a Bedouin started to urinate in the mosque. The people tried to get to him and the Prophet (ﷺ) said to them, "Leave him and pour over his urine a large bowl or container of water. Certainly, you have been sent to make things easy and you have not been sent to make things difficult."[32] The Prophet

---

[30] This hadith is *ḥasan*, See Nâṣir ad-Deen al-Albâni, *Ṣaḥeeḥ Ibn Mâjah*, no. 409. Recorded by Abu Dawood, Tirmidhi and Ibn Mâjah.

[31] This hadith is *ṣaḥeeḥ*. See Shaykh al-Albâni, *Ṣaḥeeḥ Sunan Abi Dawood*, no. 605. Recorded by Abu Dawood. (Translator's note: This is what the author has written but, in reality, the hadith with the above wording has been recorded by Aḥmad. Abu Dawood has the same meaning but different wording, simply saying to wipe the shoes but not saying to wipe the shoes on the ground.)

[32] This hadith is *ṣaḥeeḥ*. See Shaykh al-Albâni, *I'rwâ' al-Ghaleel*, no. 1710. Recorded by Bukhari and Nasâ'i. Abu Dawood and Tirmidhi have lengthier versions. (Translator's note: Perhaps it should be noted that the Prophet's mosque was not carpeted nor did it have a roof. Hence, he urinated on the dirt and ground.)

ordered that to be done immediately in order to purify the grounds. If he had left it until it become dry and its remains disappeared, the place would be considered pure. This conclusion is based on the hadith of Ibn 'Umar who said, "Dogs used to urinate and pass through the mosque during the lifetime of the Prophet and they would not pour water over it."[33]

Sunan al-Fiṭra (The Natural Practices)

Abu Hurayrah (رضي الله عنه) narrated that the Messenger of Allah (ﷺ) said, "Five are from the natural practices: circumcision, shaving the pubic hairs, plucking the armpit hairs, clipping the nails and trimming the moustache."[34]

Zakariya narrated from Abu Zâ'idah on the authority of Muṣ'ab ibn Shaybah from Ṭalq ibn Ḥabeeb from 'Abdullâh ibn az-Zubayr on the authority of 'Â'ishah (رضي الله عنها) who said that the Messenger of Allah (ﷺ) said, "Ten are from the natural practices: trimming the moustache, leaving the beard to grow, using the toothstick, (cleaning) by putting water in the nose, clipping the nails, washing the knuckles and finger joints, plucking the underarm hairs, shaving the pubic hairs, using water the clean the private part (after urinating)." Zakariya then said, "Muṣ'ab said, 'I have forgotten the tenth, unless it is rinsing one's mouth.'"[35]

---

[33] This hadith is *ṣaḥeeḥ*. See Shaykh al-Albâni, *Ṣaḥeeḥ Sunan Abi Dawood*, no. 368. Recorded by Bukhari without its complete chain and recorded by Abu Dawood.

[34] Recorded by Bukhari, Muslim, Abu Dawood, Tirmidhi, Nasâ'i and Ibn Mâjah.

[35] This hadith is *ḥasan*. See Shaykh al-Albâni, *Mukhtasar Ṣaḥeeḥ Muslim*. Recorded by Muslim, Abu Dawood, Tirmidhi, Nasâ'i and Ibn Mâjah.

Circumcision

Circumcision is obligatory with respect to both men and women as it is from the outward signs of Islam. The Prophet (ﷺ) said to a man who embraced Islam, "Cut off the hairs of (the time of) unbelief and get circumcised."[36]

It is from the way of the Prophet Abraham (عليه السلام). Abu Hurayrah (رضي الله عنه) narrated that the Prophet (ﷺ) said, "Abraham was circumcised after he had become eighty years old."[37] Allah said to His prophet Muhammad (ﷺ):

﴿ثُمَّ أَوْحَيْنَآ إِلَيْكَ أَنِ ٱتَّبِعْ مِلَّةَ إِبْرَٰهِيمَ حَنِيفًا ...﴿١٢٣﴾﴾ (سورة النّحل: ١٢٣)

﴿Then, We have inspired you [Muhammad]: 'Follow the religion of Abraham, the pure monotheist...'﴾ *(Qur'an 16: 123)*

It is recommended that the circumcision take place on the seventh day after the birth. Jâbir narrated that the Prophet (ﷺ) had the *'aqeeqah*[38] for al-Ḥasan and al-Ḥusayn and he had them circumcised on the seventh day (after their birth).[39] Ibn 'Abbâs stated, "Seven are Sunnah acts for the seventh day of a child's life: naming the child, circumcision..."[40] Although each of these hadith have some weakness to it, they strengthen each other since they come from

---

[36] This hadith is *ḥasan*. See Shaykh al-Albâni, *Ṣaḥeeḥ al-Jâmi'*, no. 1251. Recorded by Abu Dawood and al-Bayhaqi.

[37] Recorded by Bukhari and Muslim. (Translator's Note: However, with the wording quoted by the author, it was recorded by Aḥmad.)

[38] (This refers to the slaughtering of one or two sheep after the birth of a child.)

[39] Recorded by aṭ-Ṭabarâni in *aṣ-Ṣagheer*. See Shaykh al-Albâni, *Tamâm al-Minnah*, p. 68.

[40] Recorded by aṭ-Ṭabarâni in *al-Awsaṭ*. See Shaykh al-Albâni, *Tamâm al-Minnah*, p. 68.

different sources and contain no narrators who are suspect with respect to their integrity.[41]

Leaving the Beard to Grow

Leaving the beard to grow is obligatory. Shaving it is forbidden as it is changing the creation of Allah, which is an action of Satan, as Allah (ﷻ) has said:

﴿... وَلَآمُرَنَّهُمْ فَلَيُغَيِّرُنَّ خَلْقَ ٱللَّهِ ... ﴿١١٩﴾﴾ (سورة النّساء: ١١٩)

﴿... [Satan has said,] 'Indeed I will order them to change the nature created by Allah.'...﴾ *(Qur'an 4: 119)*

By shaving the beard, one is impersonating women, while "The Messenger of Allah (ﷺ) cursed the men who impersonate women."[42]

The Prophet (ﷺ) has ordered the beard to left to grow. His order implies obligation, as is well-known. Abu Hurayrah (رضي الله عنه) narrated that the Messenger of Allah (ﷺ) said, "Cut the moustache and leave the beard, being different from the Magians."[43] Ibn 'Umar also narrated that the Prophet (ﷺ) said, "Differ from the polytheists, leave the beard to grow and trim the moustache."[44]

---

[41] Shaykh al-Albâni, *Tamâm al-Minnah*, p. 68.

[42] This hadith is *ṣaḥeeḥ*. See Shaykh al-Albâni, *Ṣaḥeeḥ al-Jâmi'*, no. 5100. Recorded by Bukhari and Tirmidhi.

[43] This hadith is *ṣaḥeeḥ*. See Shaykh al-Albâni, *Mukhtasar Ṣaḥeeḥ Muslim*, no. 181. Recorded by Muslim.

[44] Recorded by Bukhari and Muslim.

The Toothstick

The use of the toothstick is a recommended act in general but in certain circumstances it is given even greater emphasis and preference. These are:

1. When making ablution: Abu Hurayrah (رضي الله عنه) narrated that the Prophet (ﷺ) said, "If it were not to be a hardship on my Nation, I would order them to use the toothstick when making ablution."[45]

2. At the time of the prayer: Abu Hurayrah narrated that the Prophet said, "If it were not to be a hardship on my Nation, I would order them to use the toothstick at every prayer."[46]

3. Upon reciting the Qur'an: 'Ali said, "We were ordered to use the toothstick." He also said, "When the human stands to pray, an angel comes to him and stands behind him, listening to the Qur'an and coming closer to him. He continues to listen and come close to him until he put his mouth upon (the person's) mouth. He does not read a verse except that it goes into the angel."[47]

4. Upon entering the house: Al-Miqdâd ibn Shurayḥ narrated from his father who said, "I asked 'Â'ishah, 'What did the Prophet do first when he entered his house?' She said, 'Use the toothstick.' "[48]

5. Upon getting up at night: Ḥudhayfah said, "When the Messenger of Allah (ﷺ) would get up to perform the late night prayers, he would

---

[45] This hadith is *ṣaḥeeḥ*. See Shaykh al-Albâni, *Ṣaḥeeḥ al-Jâmi'*, no. 5416. Recorded by Aḥmad.

[46] Recorded by Bukhari, Muslim, Tirmidhi and Nasâ'i. However, Bukhari's wording is, "with every prayer."

[47] This hadith is *ṣaḥeeḥ* due to supporting evidence. See Shaykh al-Albâni, *Silsilat al-Aḥâdeeth aṣ-Ṣaḥeeḥah*, no. 1213. Recorded by al-Bayhaqi.

[48] This report is *ṣaḥeeḥ*. See Shaykh al-Albâni, *Ṣaḥeeḥ Sunan Ibn Mâjah*, no. 235. Recorded by Muslim, Abu Dawood, Ibn Mâjah and Nasâ'i.

clean his teeth with a toothstick."[49]

The Disapproval of Removing Gray Hairs

'Amr ibn Shu'ayb narrated from his father on the authority of his grandfather that the Messenger of Allah (ﷺ) said, "Do not pluck out gray hairs. No Muslim gets a gray hair in Islam except that it will be a light for him on the Day of Resurrection."[50]

Dying gray hair with henna, katam[51] *or other plants and the prohibition of dying them black*

Abu Dharr narrated that the Prophet (ﷺ) said, "The best thing to change these gray hairs is by henna and *katam*."[52] In addition, Abu Hurayrah narrated that the Messenger of Allah (ﷺ) said, "The Jews and the Christians do not dye (their beards), so differ from them."[53] Jâbir also narrated that Abu Quḥâfah was brought to the Prophet (ﷺ) on the day of the conquering of Makkah and his beard was white from its gray hair. The Messenger of Allah (ﷺ) then said, "Change this (color) but avoid black."[54] Finally, Ibn 'Abbâs narrated

---

[49] Recorded by Bukhari, Muslim, Abu Dawood and Nasâ'i. This is Muslim's wording. The wording of the other three is, "When he would get up at night."

[50] This hadith is *ṣaḥeeḥ*. See Shaykh al-Albâni, *Ṣaḥeeḥ al-Jâmi'*, no. 7463. Recorded by Abu Dawood and Nasâ'i.

[51] [*Katam* refers to the leaves of a tree that commonly grows in Yemen, having a black-reddish color to it. The technical name for the tree, according to Aḥmad Ḥasan, is mimosa flava. See Aḥmad Ḥasan, trans., *Sunan Abu Dawood* (Lahore, Pakistan: Sh. Muhammad Ashraf, 1984), vol. 3, p. 1168.] - Translator

[52] This hadith is *ṣaḥeeḥ*. See Shaykh al-Albâni, *Ṣaḥeeḥ al-Jâmi'*, no. 1546. Recorded by Abu Dawood, Tirmidhi, Ibn Mâjah and Nasâ'i.

[53] Recorded by Bukhari and Muslim.

[54] This hadith is *ṣaḥeeḥ*. See Shaykh al-Albâni, *Ṣaḥeeḥ al-Jâmi'* no. 4170. Recorded by Muslim, Abu Dawood, Nasâ'i and Ibn Mâjah.

that the Messenger of Allah (ﷺ) also said, "At the end of time there will be a people who will dye with black dye like the crops of doves and they (therefore) will not smell the scent of Paradise."[55]

The Etiquette of Relieving Oneself

1. It is recommended for the one entering the bathroom to say, "In the name of Allah. O' Allah, I seek refuge in you from the male and female devils." This is based on the hadith from 'Ali (رضي الله عنه) who said that the Prophet (ﷺ) said, "The barrier between the eyes of the jinn and the private parts of humans when one of them enters the place to relieve oneself is by saying, 'In the name of Allah.' "[56] Additionally, Anas (رضي الله عنه) stated, "When the Prophet (ﷺ) would enter the place to relieve himself, he would say, 'O' Allah, I seek refuge in you from the male and female devils.' "[57]

2. Upon leaving the place, it is recommended to say, "(I seek) Your forgiveness." 'Â'ishah (رضي الله عنها) said, "When the Prophet (ﷺ) would leave from the place of relieving oneself he would say, '(I seek) Your forgiveness.' "[58]

3. It is also recommended to enter the place first with one's left foot and to step out first with one's right foot. This is in keeping with the principle of beginning noble things with the right and non-noble acts with the left, for which there is a general evidence.[59]

---

[55] This hadith is *ṣaḥeeḥ*. See Shaykh al-Albâni, *Ṣaḥeeḥ al-Jâmi'* no. 8153. Recorded by Abu Dawood and Nasâ'i.

[56] Ibid, no. 3611. Recorded by Tirmidhi and Ibn Mâjah.

[57] This hadith is *ṣaḥeeḥ*. Recorded by Bukhari, Muslim, Abu Dawood, Ibn Mâjah, Tirmidhi and Nasâ'i.

[58] This hadith is *ṣaḥeeḥ*. See Shaykh al-Albâni, *Ṣaḥeeḥ al-Jâmi'* no. 4714. Recorded by Abu Dawood, Tirmidhi and Ibn Mâjah.

[59] Ash-Shawkâni, *as-Sail al-Jarâr*, vol. 1, p. 64.

4. In open spaces (such as the desert), it is recommended to go such a distance that one is not seen. Jâbir said, "We went with the Messenger of Allah on a journey and whenever he wished to relieve himself, he would go away until he could not be seen."[60]

5. It is also recommended that one not raise one's clothing until one is close to the ground. Ibn 'Umar said, "When the Prophet (ﷺ) wished to relieve himself, he would not raise his garment until he was close to the ground."[61]

6. It is not allowed to face or have one's back to the *qiblah*, either while in the desert or in a building. Abu Ayyoob al-Anṣâri (رضي الله عنه) narrated that the Prophet (ﷺ) said, "If you go to relieve yourselves, do not face or put your back to the *qiblah* upon urinating or defecating. Instead, face the East or the West."[62]

Abu Ayyoob stated, "When we came to ash-Shâm, we found the bathrooms within the buildings facing the *qiblah*, so we would turn ourselves away and ask Allah for forgiveness."[63]

7. It is forbidden to relieve oneself in the paths of the people or in the places of shade. Abu Hurayrah (رضي الله عنه) narrated that the Prophet (ﷺ) said, "Avoid the acts causing cursing." They asked, "What are the acts causing cursing, O' Messenger of Allah?" He replied, "It is the one who relieves himself in the paths of the people or in their places of shade."[64]

---

[60] This hadith is *ṣaḥeeḥ*. See Shaykh al-Albâni, *Ṣaḥeeḥ Ibn Mâjah*, no. 268. Recorded by Ibn Mâjah and Abu Dawood.

[61] This hadith is *ṣaḥeeḥ*. See Shaykh al-Albâni, *Ṣaḥeeḥ al-Jâmi'*, no. 4652. Recorded by Abu Dawood. Also recorded by Tirmidhi from Anas.

[62] This hadith is *ṣaḥeeḥ*. See Shaykh al-Albâni, *Mukhtasar Ṣaḥeeḥ Muslim*, 109.

[63] Recorded by Bukhari, Muslim and Tirmidhi.

[64] This hadith is *ṣaḥeeḥ*. See Shaykh al-Albâni, *Ṣaḥeeḥ al-Jâmi'*, no. 110. Recorded by Abu Dawood and, with a slightly different wording, Muslim.

8. It is disliked to urinate in one's bathing place. Ḥumayd al-Ḥimeeri said, "I met a man who accompanied the Prophet (ﷺ) like Abu Hurayrah accompanied him. And he said, 'The Messenger of Allah (ﷺ) prohibited that one should comb (our hair) daily or that one should urinate in his bathing place.'"[65]

9. It is forbidden to urinate in stagnant water. Jâbir (رضي الله عنه) narrated from the Messenger of Allah (ﷺ) that, "He (ﷺ) prohibited urinating in stagnant water."[66]

10. It is permissible to urinate while standing but to do so sitting is preferred. Ḥudhayfah said, "I was with the Prophet (ﷺ) and he went to the garbage dump of the people and urinated while standing. I moved away and he said, 'Come closer.' I came closer until I stood behind him and he then made ablution and wiped over his slippers."[67]

We said that sitting is preferred because that was the Prophet's most common practice, In fact, 'Â'ishah (رضي الله عنها) even said, "If someone tells you that the Messenger of Allah (ﷺ) urinated while standing, do not believe him. He would only urinate while sitting."[68] This statement of hers does not negate what Ḥudhayfah said, as she was reported what she had seen while Ḥudhayfah narrated what he saw. It is known that one who affirms something takes precedence over one who negates an act, as the first has some additional knowledge.

11. It is obligatory to keep clean of the urine. Ibn 'Abbâs narrated, "The Prophet (ﷺ) passed by two graves (whose inhabitants) were being punished. He said, 'They are being punished but they are not

---

[65] This hadith is *ṣaḥeeḥ*. See Shaykh al-Albâni, *Ṣaḥeeḥ al-Jâmi'*, no. 322. Recorded by Nasâ'i and Abu Dawood.

[66] This hadith is *ṣaḥeeḥ*. See Shaykh al-Albâni, *Ṣaḥeeḥ al-Jâmi'*, no. 6814. Recorded by Muslim and Nasâ'i.

[67] Recorded by Muslim, Bukhari, Tirmidhi, Nasâ'i and Ibn Mâjah.

[68] This hadith is *ṣaḥeeḥ*. See Shaykh al-Albâni, *Ṣaḥeeḥ al-Jâmi'*, no. 29. Recorded by Nasâ'i and Tirmidhi.

being punished for a great matter. As for one of them, he did not keep himself clean of his urine and, as for the other, he used to spread tales among the people (to cause harm).' "[69]

12. The person should not hold his private part with his right hand while urinating nor should he clean it with his right hand. Abu Qatâdah narrated that the Messenger of Allah (ﷺ) said, "When one of you urinates, he is not to hold his private part with his right hand and he should also not clean (his private part) with his right hand."[70]

13. It is permissible to clean the private part with water, stone or similar items. However, to use water is best. Anas (رضي الله عنه) narrated, "The Messenger of Allah (ﷺ) would go to relieve himself and I and a young boy would carry a leather waterskin of water and a spear and he would wash his private part with water."[71] 'Â'ishah (رضي الله عنها) narrated that the Messenger of Allah (ﷺ) said, "If one of you goes to relieve himself, he should take with him three stones and clean himself with them, as those will suffice him."[72]

14. It is not permissible to use less than three stones. Salmân al-Fârisi (رضي الله عنه) said: "It was said to him, 'Your Prophet teaches you everything, even how to defecate!' He replied, 'Certainly. He has prohibited us from facing the *qiblah* while defecating or urinating, from cleaning the private parts with the right hand, from cleaning with less than three stones and from cleaning by using dung or a bone.' "[73]

---

[69] Recorded by Bukhari, Muslim, Tirmidhi and Nasâ'i.

[70] This hadith is *ṣaḥeeḥ*. See Shaykh al-Albâni, *Ṣaḥeeḥ al-Jâmi'*, no. 325. Recorded, with this wording, by Ibn Mâjah. Bukhari, Muslim, Abu Dawood, Tirmidhi and Nasâ'i also all recorded it but with different wordings.

[71] Recorded by Bukhari, Muslim and Nasâ'i.

[72] This hadith is *ṣaḥeeḥ*. See Shaykh al-Albâni, *Ṣaḥeeḥ Sunan Nasâ'i*, no. 43. Recorded by Nasâ'i and Abu Dawood.

[73] This hadith is *ṣaḥeeḥ*. See Shaykh al-Albâni, *Ṣaḥeeḥ al-Jâmi'*, no. 255. Recorded by Muslim, Tirmidhi, Abu Dawood, Ibn Mâjah and Nasâ'i.

15. It is not allowed to wipe with bones or dung. Jâbir said, "The Messenger of Allah (ﷺ) prohibiting wiping with a bone or dung."[74]

Containers and Utensils

It is permissible to use all types of containers and utensils save for gold and silver ones, as it is specifically forbidden to use them for eating or drinking, while they may be used for other purposes.

Ḥudhayfah narrated that the Prophet (ﷺ) said, "Do not drink from gold or silver containers and do not wear silk or brocade garments as they are for them in this world and for you in the Hereafter."[75]

Umm Salamah narrated that the Messenger of Allah (ﷺ) said, "The one who drinks from a silver container only gargles into his stomach the fire of Hell."[76] Recorded by Bukhari and Muslim; however, another narration in Muslim states, "The one who eats or drinks from a silver or gold container..." Muslim noted that none of the narrators made any mention of eating or gold except in the narration of Ibn Mus-hir. Shaykh al-Albâni stated, "This additional information contradicts what has been narrated in a stronger form, although it is correct in its meaning based on what can be derived from the hadith. This is because eating and gold are greater and more serious issues than drinking and silver, as is obvious."[77]

---

[74] This hadith is *ṣaḥeeḥ*. See Shaykh al-Albâni, *Ṣaḥeeḥ al-Jâmi'*, no. 6827. Recorded by Muslim and Abu Dawood.

[75] Recorded by Bukhari, Muslim, Tirmidhi, Abu Dawood, Ibn Mâjah (without the mention of silk or brocade) and Nasâ'i.

[76] Recorded by Bukhari, Muslim and Ibn Mâjah.

[77] Shaykh al-Albâni, *I'rwâ' al-Ghaleel*, vol. 1, p. 69.

Purification for the Prayer

Ibn 'Umar narrated that he heard the Prophet (ﷺ) say, "The prayer is not accepted without purification."[78] There are two forms of such purification: purification by using water and purification by using soil. As for the purification with water, it is either ablution (*wuḍoo'*) or "bathing" (*ghusl*).

Ablution

Its characteristics

Humrân, the ex-slave of 'Uthmân (رضي الله عنه), stated that 'Uthmân called for a pitcher of water and he made ablution. He washed his hands three times. Then he rinsed his mouth and inserted water into his nose (and breathed it out). Then he washed his face three times. Then he washed his right arm until the elbows three times. Then he washed his left arm until his elbows three times. Then he wiped his head. Then he washed his right foot until the ankles three times. Then he did similarly with the left foot. He then said, "I saw the Messenger of Allah make ablution like this ablution of mine. The Messenger of Allah (ﷺ) then said, 'Whoever makes ablution like this ablution of mine and then stands and prays two units (*rak'ahs*) of prayer with no other thoughts coming to his mind, then his previous sins will be forgiven.'" Ibn Shihâb added, "Our scholars would say that that is the most complete form of ablution one can make for the prayer."[79]

---

[78] This hadith is *ṣaḥeeḥ*. See Shaykh al-Albâni, *Mukhtasar Ṣaḥeeḥ Muslim*, no. 104. Recorded by Muslim and Tirmidhi.

[79] Recorded by Bukhari, Muslim, Abu Dawood and Nasâ'i.

Conditions for the correctness of the ablution

1. The intention

The Prophet (ﷺ) said, "Verily, all actions are based on intention."[80] It is not sanctioned to actually state the intention, as such has not been confirmed from the Prophet (ﷺ).

2. Mentioning the Name of Allah

The Prophet (ﷺ) said, "There is no prayer for the one who does not have ablution and there is no ablution for one who did not mention the name of Allah upon it."[81]

3. To perform the acts one after the other (without a lengthy break between the different acts)

Khâlid ibn Ma'dân narrated: "The Prophet (ﷺ) saw a man pray while there was a spot about the size of a coin on his foot that he had not washed. So the Prophet (ﷺ) ordered him to repeat his ablution and prayer."[82]

The obligatory components of the ablution

1. and 2. Washing the face, this includes rinsing the mouth and the nose

3. Washing the arms until the elbows[83]

---

[80] Recorded by Bukhari, Muslim, Tirmidhi, Ibn Mâjah and Nasâ'i.

[81] This hadith is *ḥasan*. Recorded by Abu Dawood and Ibn Mâjah.

[82] This hadith is *ṣaḥeeḥ*. See Shaykh al-Albâni, *Ṣaḥeeḥ Sunan Abi Dawood*, no. 161. Recorded by Abu Dawood.

[83] Ash-Shafi'ee wrote in *al-Umm*, vol. 1, p. 25, "It never suffices in washing one's arms unless one washes from the fingertips until the elbows. It will not suffice unless one washes the top, bottom and sides of the hands, until both are washed, not leaving any part of them. Even if a small part is left, it will not suffice."

4. and 5. Wiping all of the head. And the ears are considered part of the head (and are not considered part of the face while making ablution)

6. Washing both feet until the ankles

Some of these are based on the Qur'anic verse:

﴿يَـٰٓأَيُّهَا ٱلَّذِينَ ءَامَنُوٓاْ إِذَا قُمْتُمْ إِلَى ٱلصَّلَوٰةِ فَٱغْسِلُواْ وُجُوهَكُمْ وَأَيْدِيَكُمْ إِلَى ٱلْمَرَافِقِ وَٱمْسَحُواْ بِرُءُوسِكُمْ وَأَرْجُلَكُمْ إِلَى ٱلْكَعْبَيْنِ ... ﴿٦﴾﴾

(سورة المائدة: ٦)

﴾O' you who believe! When you intend to offer the prayer, wash your faces and your arms up to the elbows, rub [by passing wet hands over] your heads, and [wash] your feet up to the ankles...﴿ *(Qur'an 5: 6)*

Rinsing the mouth and the nose are obligatory because, in the Qur'an, Allah has ordered the washing of the face and it is confirmed that the Prophet (ﷺ) would always rinse the nose and mouth in every ablution. Everyone who narrated and described how he made ablution made mention of rinsing these two. It can be concluded that the washing of the face ordered in the Qur'an includes rinsing the mouth and nose.[84] Furthermore, the command to rinse these two are also found in the following statements of the Prophet (ﷺ): "When one of you makes ablution, he should put water up his nose and then blow it out."[85]

"(In ablution,) you should put water well up your nose, unless you are fasting."[86]

---

[84] Ash-Shawkâni, *as-Sail al-Jarâr*, vol. 1, p. 81.

[85] This hadith is *ṣaḥeeḥ*. See Shaykh al-Albâni, *Ṣaḥeeḥ al-Jâmi'*, no. 443. Recorded by Abu Dawood and Nasâ'i.

[86] This hadith is *ṣaḥeeḥ*. See Shaykh al-Albâni, *Ṣaḥeeḥ Sunan Abi Dawood*. no. 129 and 131. Recorded by Abu Dawood.

"When you make ablution, rinse the mouth."[87]

Concerning the obligation of wiping the entire head, the command for wiping in the Qur'an is actually ambiguous. Hence, one turns to the Sunnah to explain it. It is confirmed in the *Ṣaḥeeḥs* of Bukhari and Muslim, as well as in other works, that the Prophet wiped his entire head. This is evidence of the obligation of wiping the entire head. Here, one might argue that in the hadith of al-Mugheerah, it is narrated that the Prophet wiped over his forehead only and his turban. The response to this is that the Prophet (ﷺ) wiped only over his forehead because he completed the rest of his head by wiping over his turban. And this is what we are saying. Thus, in that hadith, there is no evidence for one simply to wipe over the forehead or only part of the head without completing it by wiping over the turban.[88] The result is that it is obligatory to wipe the entire head. The one wiping the head does this by wiping over his (entire) head only or by wiping over his turban only or by wiping over his head and turban. All of them are correct and confirmed.

As for the ears being considered from the head and therefore obligatory to be wiped, it is based on the Prophet's statement, "The two ears are part of the head."[89]

7. Running the fingers through the beard

Anas ibn Mâlik (رضي الله عنه) stated: When the Messenger of Allah (ﷺ) would make ablution, he would take a handful of water and put it below his jaw and run his fingers through his beard. And he said, 'This is how my Lord has ordered me to do.'"[90]

---

[87] Op. cit.

[88] *Tafseer Ibn Katheer*, vol. 2, p. 24, with some abridgement.

[89] This hadith is *ṣaḥeeḥ*. See Shaykh al-Albâni, *Ṣaḥeeḥ Ibn Mâjah*, no. 357. Recorded by Ibn Mâjah.

[90] This hadith is *ṣaḥeeḥ*. See Shaykh al-Albâni, *I'rwâ' al-Ghaleel*, no. 92.=

8: Washing between the fingers and the toes

The Prophet said, "Complete the ablution, run waters between your fingers and toes, and put water well up your nose, unless you are fasting."[91]

The recommended (Sunan) acts related to ablution

1. Using the toothstick

Abu Hurayrah narrated that the Prophet (ﷺ) said, "If it were not to be a hardship on my Nation, I would order them to use the toothstick when making every ablution."[92]

2. Washing the hands three times at the beginning of the ablution

This is confirmed in the narration from 'Uthmân in which he was describing the ablution of the Prophet (ﷺ), wherein he washed his hands three times.[93]

3. Combining together the rinsing of the mouth and the nose three times, each time with one handful of water

In the hadith of 'Abdullâh ibn Zayd in which he was teaching the ablution of the Messenger of Allah (ﷺ), he stated that the Prophet (ﷺ) would rinse his mouth and nose from one handful of water and he would do such rinsing three times.[94]

=Recorded by Abu Dawood and al-Bayhaqi.

[91] This hadith is *ṣaḥeeḥ*. See Shaykh al-Albâni, *Ṣaḥeeḥ Sunan Abi Dawood*, nos. 129 and 131. Recorded by Abu Dawood.

[92] This hadith is *ṣaḥeeḥ*. See Shaykh al-Albâni, *Ṣaḥeeḥ al-Jâmi'*, no. 5416. Recorded by Aḥmad.

[93] Recorded by Bukhari, Muslim, Abu Dawood and Nasâ'i.

[94] This hadith is *ṣaḥeeḥ*. See Shaykh al-Albâni, *Mukhtasar Ṣaḥeeḥ Muslim*, no. 125. Recorded by Muslim.

4. To rinse extensively unless one is fasting

The Messenger of Allah (ﷺ) said, "(In ablution,) you should put water well up your nose, unless you are fasting."[95]

5. Starting with the right before the left side

'Â'ishah (رضي الله عنها) stated, "The Prophet (ﷺ) would like to begin with the right in putting on his shoes, combing his hair, acts of purification and in all of his affairs."[96] Furthermore, in the hadith of 'Uthmân in which he described the ablution of the Prophet (ﷺ), he mentioned that he washed the right side first and then the left.[97]

6. Rubbing the forearm

'Abdullâh ibn Zayd narrated, "The Prophet (ﷺ) was brought two-thirds of a *mudd*[98] of water and he started to rub his forearms."[99]

7. Washing each part three times

In the hadith of 'Uthmân (رضي الله عنه), he stated that the Prophet (ﷺ) washed each part three times. However, it is also verified that the Prophet (ﷺ) would wash each part only once or twice.[100]

It is also recommended to sometimes wipe the head more than once. This is because it has been authentically narrated from 'Uthmân

---

[95] This hadith is *ṣaḥeeḥ*. See Shaykh al-Albâni, *Ṣaḥeeḥ Sunan Abi Dawood*, nos. 129 and 131. Recorded by Abu Dawood.

[96] Recorded by Bukhari, Muslim and Nasâ'i.

[97] Recorded by Bukhari, Muslim, Abu Dawood and Nasâ'i.

[98] A *mudd* is equivalent to what a person with average sized hands holds with his hands cupped together.

[99] The chain of this hadith is *ṣaḥeeḥ*. See *Ṣaḥeeḥ Ibn Khuzaymah*, 1/62/118.

[100] This hadith is *ḥasan* ṣaḥeeḥ. See Shaykh al-Albâni, *Ṣaḥeeḥ Sunan Abi Dawood*, no. 124. Recorded by Bukhari from the hadith of 'Abdullâh ibn Zayd and by Abu Dawood and Tirmidhi from the hadith of Abu Hurayrah.

that he wiped his head three times and said, "I saw the Messenger of Allah (ﷺ) make ablution like this."[101]

8. The proper order while making ablution

The Prophet (ﷺ) would usually perform the ablution in the known order. However, it has also been authentically narrated from al-Miqdâm ibn Ma'ad Yakrib who said, "The Messenger of Allah (ﷺ) was brought water and he made ablution. He washed his hands three times and then rinsed his mouth and his nose three times and then washed his face three times and then washed his forearms three times and then wiped his head and his ears, the outside and inside of them."[102]

9. Supplications afterwards

The Prophet (ﷺ) said, "None of you makes ablution and completes the ablution properly and then says, 'I bear witness that there is none worthy of worship except Allah and that Muhammad is the servant of Allah and His Messenger,' except that the eight gates of Paradise will be opened for him and he enters from any he wishes."[103] Tirmidhi's narration adds to say, "O' Allah, make me from those who repent and make me from those who purify themselves."[104]

Abu Sa'eed narrated that the Prophet (ﷺ) said, "Whoever makes ablution and then says, 'Perfect and exalted are you, O' Allah,

---

[101] This hadith is *ḥasan* ṣaḥeeḥ. See Shaykh al-Albâni, *Ṣaḥeeḥ Sunan Abi Dawood*, no. 101. Recorded by Abu Dawood.

[102] This hadith is *ṣaḥeeḥ*. See Shaykh al-Albâni, *Ṣaḥeeḥ Sunan Abi Dawood*, no. 112. Recorded by Abu Dawood.

[103] This hadith is *ṣaḥeeḥ*. See Shaykh al-Albâni, *Ṣaḥeeḥ Mukhtasar Ṣaḥeeḥ Muslim*, no. 143. Recorded by Muslim.

[104] This hadith is *ṣaḥeeḥ*. See Shaykh al-Albâni, *Ṣaḥeeḥ Sunan Tirmidhi*, no. 48. Recorded by Tirmidhi.

and with Your praise. There is none worthy of worship except You. I seek Your forgiveness and repent to you,' it will be written for him on a white scroll and sealed with a seal that will not be broken until the Day of Resurrection."[105]

10. Performing two units (*rak'ahs*) of prayer afterwards

After explaining the manner of the Prophet's ablution, 'Uthmân said, "I saw the Prophet (ﷺ) before ablution like this ablution of mine. And the Prophet said, 'Whoever makes ablution like this ablution of mine and then stands and prays two units (*rak'ahs*) of prayer with no other thoughts coming to his mind, then his previous sins will be forgiven.'"[106]

Abu Hurayrah also narrated: "The Prophet (ﷺ) said to Bilâl at the time of the Morning Prayer, 'Inform me of a deed you performed in Islam concerning which you have the most hope for as I heard your footsteps in front of me in Paradise.' He replied, 'There is no deed concerning which I am more hopeful except that I never purify myself during the night or day but that I pray with that purification whatever has been recorded for me to pray.'"[107]

What negates the ablution

1. Whatever comes out of the private parts of urine, fetus or wind

Allah has said:

﴿... أَوْ جَآءَ أَحَدٌ مِّنكُم مِّنَ ٱلْغَآئِطِ ... ﴿٦﴾﴾ (سورة المائدة: ٦)

[105] This hadith is *ṣaḥeeḥ*. See Shaykh al-Albâni, *Ṣaḥeeḥ at-Targheeb wa at-Tarheeb*, no. 22. Recorded by al-Ḥâkim. Note that none of the reports concerning making supplications during the making of ablution are authentic.

[106] Recorded by Bukhari, Muslim, Abu Dawood and Nasâ'i.

[107] Recorded by Bukhari and Muslim.

﴾... If any of you comes from answering the call of nature...﴿ *(Qur'an 5: 6)*

The Prophet (ﷺ) also said, "The prayer of whoever discharges *ḥadath* not accepted until he performs ablution again." A person from Ḥaḍramawt asked, "What is *ḥadath*, Abu Hurayrah?" Abu Hurayrah replied, "Passing wind with or without sound."[108]

This also includes the release of *al-madhi* and *al-wadi* from the private parts. The following report was recorded earlier: Ibn 'Abbâs stated, "(There is) semen, *al-wadi* and *al-madhi*. As for semen, it is the thing due to which one must make *ghusl*. As for *al-wadi* and *al-madhi*, he said, 'Wash your private part or (he said private parts) and make the ablution like that for the prayer.' "[109]

2. A deep sleep

This is a sleep in which the person is left with no sense of awareness, regardless if he is fully lying down or not. This point is based on the hadith from Ṣafwân ibn A'ssâl who said, "The Messenger of Allah (ﷺ) ordered us to, while we were travelling, not to remove our leather socks for three days and nights except in the case of sexual defilement. But from defecation, urination and sleep (we did not have to remove them).[110] Thus, the Prophet (ﷺ) made no distinction between sleeping, urinating and defecating.

Furthermore, 'Ali (رضي الله عنه) narrated that the Messenger of Allah (ﷺ) said, "The eye is the drawstring of the anus. So whoever sleeps

---

[108] Recorded, with various wording, by Bukhari, Muslim, Abu Dawood, Tirmidhi, Aḥmad and al-Bayhaqi.

[109] *Ṣaḥeeḥ*. See Shaykh al-Albâni, *Ṣaḥeeḥ Sunan Abi Dawood*, no. 190. Recorded by al-Bayhaqi.

[110] This hadith is *ḥasan*. See Shaykh al-Albâni, *Ṣaḥeeḥ Sunan Nasâ'i*, no. 123. Recorded by Tirmidhi and Nasâ'i.

must make ablution."[111] What this hadith means is that when one is awake, he is aware of any gas that he may pass and thus his being awake is termed the drawstring concerning gassing.[112]

3. Losing consciousness due to intoxication or illness

This invalidates the ablution because the loss of awareness is greater in this case than it is in sleep.

4. Touching one's private part, without any barrier (such as a garment), a touch of lust

The Prophet (ﷺ) said, "Whoever touches his private part should then make ablution."[113] The Prophet (ﷺ) also said (about touching one's private part), "Isn't it just a part of you?"[114] It is just a part of you if the touch does not contain any lust. In that case, it is just like touching any other body part. However, if it is touched with lust, then the touch is not similar to touching any other part of the body, as the other parts are not usually touched with lust. And this is a matter that can clearly be noted.[115]

5. Eating camel's meat

Al-Barâ' ibn 'Âzib narrated that the Messenger of Allah (ﷺ) said, "Make ablution from camel meat and do not make ablution from goat (or sheep) meat."[116] Jâbir ibn Samurah also narrated: "A

---

[111] This hadith is *ḥasan*. See Shaykh al-Albâni, *Ṣaheeḥ Ibn Mâjah*, no. 386. Recorded by Ibn Mâjah and Abu Dawood has something similar.

[112] Ash-Shawkâni, *Nail al-Awṭâr*, vol. 1, p. 242.

[113] This hadith is *ṣaḥeeḥ*. See Shaykh al-Albâni, *Ṣaḥeeḥ Ibn Mâjah*, no. 388. Recorded by Abu Dawood, Ibn Mâjah, Nasâ'i and Tirmidhi. Some narrations state, "He should not pray until he makes ablution."

[114] This hadith is *ṣaḥeeḥ*. See Shaykh al-Albâni, *Ṣaḥeeḥ Ibn Mâjah*, no. 392. Recorded by Abu Dawood, Ibn Mâjah, Nasâ'i and Tirmidhi.

[115] Shaykh al-Albâni, *Tamâm al-Minnah*, p. 103.

[116] This hadith is *ṣaḥeeḥ*. See Shaykh al-Albâni, *Ṣaḥeeḥ Ibn Mâjah*, no. 401.=

man asked the Messenger of Allah (ﷺ), 'Shall I make ablution from sheep's meat?' He replied, 'If you wish make ablution and if you do not wish to do so, do not make ablution.' Then he asked, 'Do I make ablution from camel's meat?' He replied, 'Yes, make ablution from camel's meat.' '"[117]

The Acts for Which Ablution is Required (Or What is Forbidden for One not in a State of Ablution)

1. The prayer

Allah (ﷻ) has said:

﴿يَٰٓأَيُّهَا ٱلَّذِينَ ءَامَنُوٓاْ إِذَا قُمۡتُمۡ إِلَى ٱلصَّلَوٰةِ فَٱغۡسِلُواْ وُجُوهَكُمۡ وَأَيۡدِيَكُمۡ إِلَى ٱلۡمَرَافِقِ وَٱمۡسَحُواْ بِرُءُوسِكُمۡ وَأَرۡجُلَكُمۡ إِلَى ٱلۡكَعۡبَيۡنِۚ ... ٦﴾

(سورة المائدة: ٦)

﴾O' you who believe! When you intend to offer the prayer, wash your faces and your hands [forearms] up to the elbows, rub [by passing wet hands over] your heads, and [wash] your feet up to ankles...﴿

(Qur'an 5: 6)

And the Prophet (ﷺ) also said, "Allah does not accept a prayer without purification."[118]

2. Circumambulation of the House of Allah (Ka'bah) in Makkah

The Prophet (ﷺ) said, "Circumambulation of the House is a

=Recorded by Abu Dawood, Tirmidhi and Ibn Mâjah.

[117] This hadith is *ṣaḥeeḥ*. See Shaykh al-Albâni, *Mukhtasar Ṣaḥeeḥ Muslim*, no. 146. Recorded by Muslim.

[118] This hadith is *ṣaḥeeḥ*. See Shaykh al-Albâni, *Mukhtasar Ṣaḥeeḥ Muslim*, no. 104. Recorded by Muslim and Tirmidhi.

type of prayer except that Allah has permitted speaking during it."[119]

The acts for which ablution is recommended

1. Mentioning the name of Allah

Al-Muhâjir ibn Qunfudh narrated that he greeted the Messenger of Allah (ﷺ) but the Prophet (ﷺ) did not respond to him until he had made ablution. Then he said, "Nothing prevented me from responding to you except that I disliked mentioning Allah except while in a state of purification."[120]

2. Sleep

Al-Barâ' ibn 'Âzib narrated that the Prophet (ﷺ) said: "When you go to bed, perform ablution like you do for prayer. Then lie on your right side and say (the following), 'O' Allah, I submit my soul to You, I entrust all my affairs to You and I rely upon You for protection out of hope and fear of You. There is neither resort nor safety but with You. I believe in Your Book that You have revealed and in Your Prophet that You have sent.' If you die that night, you will die with *fiṭrah* (i.e., Islam). Make them (these words) the last you say (before you sleep)."[121]

3 While in a state of sexual defilement

If a person in this state wishes to eat, drink, sleep or repeat the act of sexual intercourse, it is recommended that he make ablution. 'Â'ishah (رضي الله عنها) said, "When the Messenger of Allah (ﷺ) was sexually

---

[119] This hadith is *ṣaḥeeḥ*. See Shaykh al-Albâni, *Ṣaḥeeḥ al-Jâmi'*, no. 3954. Recorded by Tirmidhi.

[120] This hadith is *ṣaḥeeḥ*. See Shaykh al-Albâni, *Ṣaḥeeḥ Ibn Mâjah*, no. 280. Recorded by Abu Dawood, Ibn Mâjah and Nasâ'i, but in Nasâ'i's case it is not narrated back to the Prophet (Blessings and peace of Allah be upon him).

[121] Recorded by Bukhari and Muslim.

defiled and he wished to eat or drink, he would make ablution like the ablution for the prayer."[122] Ammâr ibn Yâsir stated, "The Prophet (ﷺ) allowed the one who is sexually defiled who wished to eat, drink or sleep to make ablution like the ablution for the prayer."[123] In addition, Abu Sa'eed narrated that the Prophet (ﷺ) said, "If one of you has (had intercourse) with his wife and wishes to repeat it, he should make ablution."[124]

4. Before making *ghusl* (the complete bathing), regardless of whether it be obligatory or recommended *ghusl*

'Â'ishah stated, "When the Messenger of Allah would bathe from sexual defilement, he would begin by washing his hands and then pour water from his right hand to his left and wash his private parts and then make ablution like the ablution for the prayer."[125]

5. (After) Eating what has been cooked over fire

Abu Hurayrah (رضي الله عنه) narrated that he heard the Messenger of Allah (ﷺ) say, "Make ablution from what the fire has touched (that is, what has been cooked over a fire)."[126] This is interpreted to imply recommendation due to the hadith of 'Amr ibn Umayyah aḍ-Ḍamari who said, "I saw the Prophet (ﷺ) cut off a piece of the shoulder of a sheep and eat from it. Then he was called to the prayer, he stood, put down the knife and prayed without making ablution."[127]

---

[122] This hadith is *ṣaḥeeḥ*. See Shaykh al-Albâni, *Mukhtasar Ṣaḥeeḥ Muslim*, no. 162. Recorded by Muslim, Nasâ'i and Abu Dawood.

[123] This hadith is *ṣaḥeeḥ*. Recorded by Abu Dawood.

[124] This hadith is *ṣaḥeeḥ*. See Shaykh al-Albâni, *Ṣaḥeeḥ al-Jâmi' aṣ-Ṣagheer*, no. 263. Recorded by Muslim, Abu Dawood, Tirmidhi, Nasâ'i and Ibn Mâjah.

[125] This hadith is *ṣaḥeeḥ*. See Shaykh al-Albâni, *Mukhtasar Ṣaḥeeḥ Muslim*, no. 155. Recorded by Muslim.

[126] This hadith is *ṣaḥeeḥ*. See Shaykh al-Albâni, *Mukhtasar Ṣaḥeeḥ Muslim*, no. 147. Recorded by Muslim and Nasâ'i.

[127] This hadith is *ṣaḥeeḥ*. See Shaykh al-Albâni, *Mukhtasar Ṣaḥeeḥ Muslim*,=

6. For every prayer

Buraydah said, "The Prophet used to make ablution for every prayer. On the day of the Conquering of Makkah, he made ablution, wiped over his socks and prayed the prayers with one ablution. 'Umar then said to him, 'O' Messenger of Allah, you have done something that you did not use to do.' He replied, 'I did it intentionally, O' Umar.' "[128]

7. After every act of negating the ablution

This point is based on the hadith narrated by Abu Buraydah who said: "One morning the Messenger of Allah (ﷺ) called Bilâl and said, 'O' Bilâl, how is it that you were ahead of me in Paradise. I entered Paradise last night and I heard your footsteps in front of me?' Bilâl replied, 'O' Messenger of Allah, I do not commit a sin except that I pray two units (*rak'ahs*) of prayers and I never pass wind (or any other such act that negates ablution) except that I make ablution due to it.' The Messenger of Allah (ﷺ) then said, 'It is due to these two.' "[129]

8. Due to vomiting

Ma'dân ibn Abu Ṭalḥah narrated from Abu ad-Dardâ' who stated, "The Messenger of Allah (ﷺ) vomited and broke his fast and then made ablution. I met Thawbân in the mosque of Damascus and mentioned that to him and he said, 'He told the truth. I poured the water for him (for his ablution).' "[130]

=no. 148. Recorded by Muslim with this wording and by Bukhari.

[128] This hadith is *ṣaḥeeḥ*. See Shaykh al-Albâni, *Mukhtasar Ṣaḥeeḥ Muslim*, no. 142. Recorded by Muslim, Abu Dawood, Tirmidhi and Nasâ'i.

[129] This hadith is *ṣaḥeeḥ*. See Shaykh al-Albâni, *Ṣaḥeeḥ al-Jâmi' aṣ-Ṣagheer*, no. 7894. Recorded by Tirmidhi. (There is some abridgement to the original wording of Tirmidhi.)

[130] The chain of this hadith is *ṣaḥeeḥ*. See Shaykh al-Albâni, *Tamâm al-*=

9. After carrying the deceased

The Prophet (ﷺ) said, "Whoever washes the deceased should make the complete bathing (*ghusl*). And whoever carries him should make ablution."[131]

Wiping Over the "Leather Socks"

Imam an-Nawawi wrote in his commentary to *Ṣaheeḥ Muslim*, vol. 3, p. 164:

> "Those whose opinions are respected in consensus all agree that it is permissible to wipe over the leather socks while travelling or non-travelling, regardless of whether it is out of need or not. Even the woman who stays in her house or the cripple who cannot walk is allowed to do so. Only the Shi'tes and Kharijites reject this concept but their opposing view need not be taken into consideration. Al-Ḥasan al-Basri stated, 'Seventy of the Companions of the Messenger of Allah narrated to me that the Messenger of Allah (ﷺ) used to wipe over his socks.'"[132]

The best proof for the permissibility of this form of wiping is what Muslim recorded from al-A'mash on the authority of Ibrâheem

=*Minnah*, p. 111. Recorded by Tirmidhi. It was also recorded by Abu Dawood but without the mention of making ablution.

[131] This hadith is *ṣaḥeeḥ*. See Shaykh al-Albâni, *al-Janâiz*, p. 53. Recorded by Aḥmad, Ibn Ḥibbân and al-Bayhaqi. Tirmidhi has a similar meaning, "The apparent meaning implies obligation. However, we do not come to this conclusion due to the hadith of Ibn 'Abbâs in which the Prophet has said, 'If you wash the dead, you do not have to make *ghusl* for your deceased are not impure. It is sufficient for you to wash your hands.' This was recorded by al-Ḥâkim and al-Bayhaqi." This is a slightly abridged quote from Shaykh al-Albâni, *Aḥkâm al-Janâ'iz*, p. 53.

[132] An-Nawawi, *Sharḥ Ṣaḥeeḥ Muslim*, vol. 3, p. 164.

from Hamâm who said, "Jareer urinated and then he wiped over his leather socks. It was said to him, 'Do you do that?' He replied, 'Yes. I saw the Messenger of Allah (ﷺ) urinate and then make ablution and wipe over his leather socks.'" Al-A'mash added, "Ibrâheem liked that hadith because Jareer embraced Islam after the revelation of *Soorah al-Mâ'idah*."[133]

An-Nawawi wrote,

> "Its meaning is that Allah has said in *Soorah al-Mâ'idah* (verse 6), 'Wash your faces and your forearms up to the elbows, rub (by passing wet hands over) your heads, and (wash) your feet up to ankles,' and, therefore, if Jareer's Islam would have been before the revelation of *al-Mâ'idah*, it could be understood that his hadith concerning wiping the socks was abrogated by the verse in *al-Mâ'idah*. Since his embracing of Islam was after that fact, we know that his hadith is to be acted upon and it clarifies that the verse applies to the one who is not wiping. Thus, the Sunnah here particularizes the verse. And Allah alone knows best."[134]

The conditions for wiping over leather socks

The permissibility of wiping over socks is conditioned by the fact that one has put on the socks while in a state of purity. Al-Mugheerah ibn Shu'bah said, "We were with the Prophet (ﷺ) one night while travelling. I poured water for him from a container and he washed his face and arms and wiped his head and then I moved to remove his leather socks and he said, 'Leave them for I put them on while they (the feet) were in a state of purity.' Then he wiped over them."[135]

---

[133] This hadith is *ṣaḥeeḥ*. See Shaykh al-Albâni, *Mukhtasar Ṣaḥeeḥ Muslim*, no. 136. Recorded by Muslim and Tirmidhi.

[134] An-Nawawi, *Sharḥ Ṣaḥeeḥ Muslim*, vol. 3, p. 164.

[135] Recorded by Bukhari, Muslim and Abu Dawood.

The length of time in which one can simply wipe

'Ali ibn Abi Ṭâlib (ﷺ) stated (about wiping over the socks), "The Messenger of Allah (ﷺ) set the limit of three days and nights for the traveller and one day and night for the resident (non-travelling person)."[136]

What is to be wiped and the manner of wiping

The portion to be wiped is the top of the socks. 'Ali ibn Abi Ṭâlib (ﷺ) said, "If the religion were built upon personal opinion, it would be considered more correct to wipe the bottom of the socks instead of the top of the socks. But I saw the Messenger of Allah (ﷺ) wipe over the top of the socks."[137]

What is obligatory concerning the manner of wiping is anything that meets the definition of the word "wiping".

Wiping over non-leather socks (such as woollen socks) and sandals or shoes

In the same way that it is permissible to wipe over leather socks, it is also permissible to wipe over woollen socks or shows. Al-Mugheerah ibn Shu'bah stated, "The Prophet (ﷺ) made ablution and wiped over the leather socks and sandals."[138]

'Ubayd ibn Jurayj said, "It was said to Ibn 'Umar, 'We have seen you do something that we have not seen anyone other than you do.' He asked, 'What is that?' They said, 'We have seen you where

[136] This hadith is *ṣaḥeeḥ*. See Shaykh al-Albâni, *Mukhtasar Ṣaḥeeḥ Muslim*, no. 139. Recorded by Muslim and Nasâ'i.

[137] This hadith is *ṣaḥeeḥ*. See Shaykh al-Albâni, *I'rwâ' al-Ghaleel*, no. 103. Recorded by Abu Dawood.

[138] This hadith is *ṣaḥeeḥ*. See Shaykh al-Albâni, *I'rwâ' al-Ghaleel*, no. 101. Recorded by Abu Dawood, Tirmidhi and Ibn Mâjah.

these tanned sandals.' He replied, 'I saw the Messenger of Allah (ﷺ) wear them and make ablution with them on and wipe over them.' "[139]

What Invalidates the Wiping

The wiping is invalidated by one of three things

1. The time period has come to an end, this is because it is known that there is a time limit and it is not permissible to exceed the determined amount.

2. Sexual defilement

This point is based on the hadith from Ṣafwân ibn Assâl who said, "The Messenger of Allah (ﷺ) ordered us to, while we were travelling, not to remove our leather socks for three days and nights except in the case of sexual defilement. But from defecation, urination and sleep (we did not have to remove them)."[140]

3. Removing what has been wiped over from the feet

If one removes what has been wiped over and then (negates the ablution and) wears them again, one would not have put them on while the feet were still in a state of purity.

Note: The ending of the time period and removing what has been wiped over only negate the act of wiping. It is no longer permissible to wipe until one makes ablution, washes the feet and then wears the article again. However, if the person remained in a state of purity when he removed the article of clothing or when the period came to an end, he remains in his state of purity and can continue to pray as

[139] [This hadith is *ṣaḥeeḥ* according to Shaykh al-Albâni. It is recorded by Nasâ'i and others. See Shaykh al-Albâni, *Ṣaḥeeḥ Sunan Nasâ'i.*] - Translator

[140] This hadith is *ḥasan*. See Shaykh al-Albâni, *Ṣaḥeeḥ Sunan Nasâ'i*, no. 123. Recorded by Tirmidhi and Nasâ'i.

long as he wills until he does something to invalidate his ablution.

<u>A Second Note</u>: If someone wears two sets of socks and wipes over both of them and then removes the upper pair after wiping over them, it is permissible for him to continue during the set time period to wipe over his lower socks, because he had entered into them while his feet were in a state of purity. However, if he is wearing just one pair and wipes over them and then puts on another pair, he cannot wipe over them as he did not meet the condition of wearing them while in a state of purity.[141]

The Complete Bathing (Ghusl)

What makes the ghusl obligatory

1. The ejaculation of semen, regardless of whether one is awake or asleep

The Prophet (ﷺ) said, "The liquid (that is, the *ghusl*) is due to the liquid (that is, the semen)."[142] Umm Salamah narrated that Umm Sulaym said,"O' Messenger of Allah! Allah does not shy away from the truth. Does the woman have to make *ghusl* if she has a wet dream?" He replied, "Yes, if she sees the liquid."[143]

When one is awake, as opposed to when one is sleeping, the emerging of the semen has to be due to lust for it to require *ghusl*. The Prophet (ﷺ) said, "If the liquid is ejaculated, one must make *ghusl* due to sexual defilement. If it was not ejaculated, there is no *ghusl*."[144] Ash-Shawkâni stated, "*Ḥadhaf* (the word used in the

---

[141] This is what Shaykh al-Albâni has informed me.

[142] This hadith is *ṣaḥeeḥ*. See Shaykh al-Albâni, *Mukhtasar Ṣaḥeeḥ Muslim*, no. 151. Recorded by Muslim and Abu Dawood.

[143] Recorded by Bukhari, Muslim and Tirmidhi.

[144] The chain is *ḥasan* ṣaḥeeḥ. See Shaykh al-Albâni, *I'rwâ' al-Ghaleel*, vol.=

hadith) means to shoot and this will only occur if there is lust involved. Thus the author (of the book ash-Shawkâni was commenting upon) has said, 'If the semen is emitted not out of lust, such as due to illness or a malady (causing dripping of urine), then it is not obligatory to make *ghusl*.' "[145]

If someone experiences a wet dream but sees no fluids, then *ghusl* is not obligatory. However, if one finds the fluids but does not recall the wet dream, it is obligatory to make *ghusl*. 'Â'ishah (ﷺ) said, "The Messenger of Allah (ﷺ) was asked about a man who found wetness but did not recall experiencing a wet dream. The Prophet stated, 'He must make *ghusl*.' Then he was asked about a man who experienced such a dream but found no fluids and he said, '*Ghusl* is not obligatory upon him.' "[146]

2. Sexual intercourse even if one does not ejaculate

Abu Hurayrah (ﷺ) reported that the Prophet (ﷺ) said, "If one places himself between her four parts (that is, thighs of his wife) and has intercourse with her, then *ghusl* is obligatory whether or not he ejaculated."[147]

3. A non-Muslim embracing Islam

Qays ibn 'Âṣm stated that when he embraced Islam, the Prophet (ﷺ) ordered him to make *ghusl* with water and lotus leaves.[148]

=1, p. 162. Recorded by Aḥmad.

[145] Ash-Shawkâni, *Nail al-Awṭâr*, vol. 1, p. 275.

[146] This hadith is *ṣaḥeeḥ*. See Shaykh al-Albâni, *Ṣaḥeeḥ Sunan Abi Dawood*, no. 216. Recorded by Tirmidhi and Abu Dawood.

[147] This hadith is *ṣaḥeeḥ*. See Shaykh al-Albâni, *Mukhtasar Ṣaḥeeḥ Muslim*, no. 152. Recorded by Muslim.

[148] This hadith is *ṣaḥeeḥ*. See Shaykh al-Albâni, *I'rwâ' al-Ghaleel*, no. 128. Recorded by Nasâ'i, Tirmidhi and Abu Dawood.

4. When the menses and post-partum bleeding come to an end

'Â'ishah (ﷺ) narrated that the Prophet (ﷺ) said to Fâṭimah bint Abi Ḥubaysh, "When the menses come upon you, leave the prayers. And when the (menses) leave you, then make *ghusl*."[149] Post-partum bleeding carries the same ruling as menstruation in this manner according to the consensus of the scholars.

5. On Fridays

Abu Sa'eed al-Khudri narrated that the Prophet (ﷺ) said, "*Ghusl* on the day of Friday is obligatory on every post-puberty (person)."[150]

The essential components of the ghusl

1. The intention

The Prophet (ﷺ) said, "Verily, all actions are based on intention."[151]

2. Reaching the entire body with water.

The preferred way to perform the ghusl

'Â'ishah said, "When the Prophet (ﷺ) would perform *ghusl* because of sexual defilement, he used to begin by washing his hands. Then he would pour water from his right hand to his left and wash his private part. He would then perform the ablution of the prayer. Then he would take some water and put his fingers down to the roots of his hair. When he saw that he fulfilled that part, he would pour three

---

[149] Recorded by Bukhari, Muslim, Abu Dawood, Tirmidhi and Nasâ'i. Other than Bukhari, they have, "And wash the blood from you."

[150] Recorded by Bukhari, Muslim, Abu Dawood, Nasâ'i and Ibn Mâjah.

[151] Recorded by Bukhari, Muslim, Tirmidhi, Ibn Mâjah and Nasâ'i.

handfuls of water over his head using both hands. (Finally) he would pour water over all his body and then was his feet."[152]

Note: It is not required for a woman to unbraid her hair when she makes *ghusl* due to sexual defilement. However, she must due so when making *ghusl* after her menses. Umm Salamah said, "O' Messenger of Allah! I am a woman with tightly braided hair on my head, do I need to undo them for making the *ghusl* due to sexual defilement?" He replied, "No, it will be sufficient for you to pour three handfuls of water over your head and then pour water over yourself and you will be purified."[153]

'Â'ishah narrated that Asmâ' asked the Prophet (ﷺ) about the *ghusl* after the menses. He replied, "She should take her water mixed with lote-tree leaves and purify herself well with it and then pour water over her head, and rub it in well until it reaches the roots of her hair. Then she should pour water over herself. Then she should take a piece of cotton with musk on it and purify herself with it." Asmâ' asked, "How shall she purify herself with it?" He said, "Exalted by Allah, she should purify herself with it." 'Â'ishah then kind of whispered to her, "She should apply it to the traces of blood." She (Asmâ') then asked him about *ghusl* due to sexual defilement. He replied, "She should take water and purify herself well with it or complete the purification and then pour water over her head and rub it in till it reaches the roots of her hair and then pour water over herself."

This hadith is explicit in demonstrating that the *ghusl* of the woman after menses differs from that due to sexual defilement. In one case, the Prophet (ﷺ) emphasized that the woman must rub vigorously and

---

[152] Recorded by Bukhari and Muslim.

[153] This hadith is *ṣaḥeeḥ*. See Shaykh al-Albâni, *I'rwâ' al-Ghaleel*, no. 136. Recorded by Muslim, Abu Dawood, Nasâ'i, Tirmidhi and Ibn Mâjah.

purify herself in way that was not emphasized while describing the *ghusl* due to sexual intercourse. Similarly, the hadith of Umm Salamah is evidence that it is not obligatory to unbraid one's hair for the *ghusl* due to sexual defilement.[154] The basic ruling would be for her to undo her braids in order to ensure that the water reaches what is below them. However, she is excused from doing so due to the number of times she would have to do that and the hardship that she would encounter, as opposed to the case of the *ghusl* after the menses which occurs only once in a month.[155]

Note: It is permissible for a husband and wife to perform the *ghusl* together in one place, wherein one can see the private parts of the other. 'Â'ishah said, "I would make *ghusl* with the Messenger of Allah (ﷺ) from one bowl while were both sexually defiled."[156]

Occasions in which it is recommended to make ghusl

1. Performing *ghusl* for every separate act of sexual intercourse

Abu Râfi' narrated that the Prophet (ﷺ) would visit his different wives during one night and make *ghusl* for each one. Abu Râfi' said to him, "O' Messenger of Allah, can't you just make it one?" He replied, "This is purer, better and more purifying."[157]

2. Performing *ghusl* for every prayer by the woman who is *mustaḥâḍah*[158]

She can perform *ghusl* for every prayer or for the Noon and Afternoon prayers together with one *ghusl* and the Sunset and Night

---

[154] Cf., Ibn al-Qayyim, *Tahdheeb Sunan Abi Dawood*, vol. 1, Pp. 166-167.

[155] Ibid.

[156] Recorded by Bukhari, Muslim and Nasâ'i.

[157] This hadith is *ḥasan*. See Shaykh al-Albâni, *Ṣaḥeeḥ Sunan Ibn Mâjah*, no. 480. Recorded by Abu Dawood and Ibn Mâjah.

[158] [This is where a woman suffers from metrorrhagia or uterine hemorrhaging,=

prayer with one *ghusl* and the Morning prayer with another *ghusl*. This is based on the report from 'Â'ishah (ﷺ) who said, "Umm Ḥabeebah had continuous bleeding during the time of the Messenger of Allah (ﷺ) and he ordered her to make *ghusl* for every prayer."[159] In another narration, she stated, "A woman had continuous bleeding during the time of the Prophet (ﷺ) and he ordered her to pray the Afternoon prayer earlier while delaying the Noon prayer and to perform one *ghusl* for the both of them. (He also ordered that she) delay the Sunset prayer and pray the Night prayer earlier and make one *ghusl* for the both of them. (He also ordered that she) make one *ghusl* for the Morning prayer."[160]

3. Performing *ghusl* after being unconscious

'Â'ishah said, "(In his last days), the Prophet (ﷺ) became grievously ill. He asked whether the people had performed the prayer. We replied, 'No, Messenger of Allah. They are waiting for you.' He said, 'Put water in the tub for me.'" 'Â'ishah added, "We did so. He made *ghusl* and tried to stand up, but he fainted. When he recovered, he again asked whether the people had performed the prayer. We said, 'No, they are waiting for you, Messenger of Allah.' He again said, 'Put water in the tub for me.' He sat down, made *ghusl*, and tried to stand up, but he fainted again. Then he recovered and asked, 'Have the people performed the prayer?' We replied, 'No, they are waiting for you, Messenger of Allah.' He said, 'Put water in the tub for me.' He sat down, made *ghusl*, and tried to stand up, but he fainted. Then he recovered and asked, 'Have the people performed the prayer?' We

---

=a condition where the woman has a continual blood flow not related to menstruation.]

[159] This hadith is *ṣaḥeeḥ*. See Shaykh al-Albâni, *Ṣaḥeeḥ Sunan Abi Dawood*, no. 269. Recorded by Abu Dawood.

[160] This hadith is *ṣaḥeeḥ*. See Shaykh al-Albâni, *Ṣaḥeeḥ Sunan Abi Dawood*, no. 273. Recorded by Abu Dawood and Nasâ'i.

replied, 'No, they are waiting for you, Messenger of Allah.'" In the remainder of the hadith, he sends for Abu Bakr (رضي الله عنه) to lead the prayer.[161]

4. Performing *ghusl* after burying a polytheist

'Ali ibn Abi Ṭâlib (رضي الله عنه) narrated that he came to the Prophet (ﷺ) and said, "Abu Ṭâlib has passed away." The Prophet (ﷺ) told him, "Go and bury him." 'Ali then said that he did so and when he came back to the Prophet (ﷺ), the Prophet told him, "Perform *ghusl*."[162]

5. Performing *ghusl* for the two *'Eids* and the Day of 'Arafah

Al-Bayhaqi recorded from ash-Shafi'ee on the authority of Zâdân who said, "A man asked 'Ali about *ghusl* and he said, 'Make *ghusl* every day if you wish.' The man replied, 'No, I am talking about the washing that is a (virtuous) *ghusl*.' 'Ali then told him, '(That is) on Friday, the Day of 'Arafah, the *'Eid* of the Sacrifice and the *'Eid* of the Breaking of the Fast.'"

6. Performing *ghusl* due to washing a deceased person

The Prophet (ﷺ) said, "Whoever washes the deceased should make *ghusl*."[163]

7. Performing *ghusl* in order to enter the inviolable state of the Major Pilgrimage (Hajj) or the Minor Pilgrimage (*'Umrah*)

Zayd ibn Thâbit (may Allah be pleased with him) stated that he saw the Messenger of Allah (ﷺ) remove any sewn garments for his

---

[161] Recorded by Bukhari and Muslim.

[162] The chain of this report is *ṣaḥeeḥ*. See Shaykh al-Albâni, *al-Janâ'iz*, p. 134. Recorded by Nasâ'i and Abu Dawood.

[163] This hadith is *ṣaḥeeḥ*. See Shaykh al-Albâni, *Ṣaheeḥ Ibn Mâjah*, no. 1195. Recorded by Ibn Mâjah.

inviolable state and make *ghusl* for such.[164]

8. Performing *ghusl* prior to entering Makkah

It is narrated that Ibn 'Umar would not enter Makkah unless he would spend the night at Dhu Ṭuwâ until the morning and then make *ghusl* and then enter Makkah during the daytime. He narrated that the Prophet (ﷺ) had done that.[165]

Purification with the Use of Soil (Tayammum or "Dry Purification")

The proof for its validity

Allah (ﷻ) says:

﴿... وَإِن كُنتُم مَّرْضَىٰٓ أَوْ عَلَىٰ سَفَرٍ أَوْ جَآءَ أَحَدٌ مِّنكُم مِّنَ ٱلْغَآئِطِ أَوْ لَـٰمَسْتُمُ ٱلنِّسَآءَ فَلَمْ تَجِدُوا۟ مَآءً فَتَيَمَّمُوا۟ صَعِيدًا طَيِّبًا فَٱمْسَحُوا۟ بِوُجُوهِكُمْ وَأَيْدِيكُم مِّنْهُ ... ﴿٦﴾﴾ (سورة المائدة: ٦)

﴿But if you are ill or on a journey or any of you comes from answering the call of nature, or you have been in contact with women [i.e. sexual intercourse] and you find no water, then perform *tayammum* with clean earth and rub therewith your faces and hands...﴾ *(Qur'an 5: 6)*

The Prophet (ﷺ) also said, "The pure ground is the ablution for the Muslim even if he does not find water for ten years."[166]

---

[164] This hadith is *ḥasan*. See Shaykh al-Albâni, *I'rwâ' al-Ghaleel*, no. 149. Recorded by Tirmidhi.

[165] Recorded by Bukhari, Muslim (and this is his wording), Abu Dawood and Tirmidhi.

[166] This hadith is *ṣaḥeeḥ*. See Shaykh al-Albâni, *Ṣaḥeeḥ Sunan Abi Dawood*,=

The causes that make it permissible

Tayammum is permissible when one is not able to use water, due to its being unavailable or out fear that using it would be harmful due to an illness in the body or extreme cold.

'Imrân ibn Ḥusayn (رضي الله عنه) said, "We were with the Messenger of Allah (ﷺ) on a journey and he led the people in prayer while there was a man who did not join the people. The Prophet said, 'What prevented you from praying with the people?' He said, 'I became sexually defiled and there is no water.' The Prophet (ﷺ) then told him, 'You should use the ground as that will be sufficient for you.' "

Jâbir (رضي الله عنه) said, "We went out on a journey and one of us was struck by a rock and injured in his head. He had a wet dream and he asked his companions, 'Do you see that I have an exemption to make *tayammum* (instead of *ghusl*)?' They replied, 'We do not find any exemption for you while you have the ability to use water.' Thus, he made *ghusl* and died (due to it). When we came to the Messenger of Allah (ﷺ) we informed him of what had happened. He said, 'They killed him and may Allah destroy them. Should they not have asked if they did not know? Truly, the cure for the one who is lost is in asking. It would have been sufficient for him to make *tayammum*.' "[167]

=no. 322. Recorded by Tirmidhi, Abu Dawood and Nasâ'i with very similar wordings.

[167] This hadith is *ḥasan*. See Shaykh al-Albâni, *Ṣaḥeeḥ Sunan Abi Dawood*, no. 326. Recorded by Abu Dawood. However, it has a rejected additional portion to it which states, "[It would have been sufficient for him to make *tayammum* and simply to wipe over it with some drops of water or apply a rag and then wipe over that while washing the rest of the body." In *'Aun al-Ma'bood* (vol. 1, p. 535), Shams al-Ḥaqq said, "The narration that combines *tayammum* with washing is only narrated by Zubayr ibn Khurayq. In addition to him not being strong in hadith, he has contradicted the rest of the narrators=

'Amr ibn al-'Âṣ (رضي الله عنه) said about when he was sent for the Battle of Dhât al-Salâsil, "I had a wet dream during a terribly cold night. I feared that if I were to make *ghusl* I would die. Thus, I made *tayammum* and led my companions in the Morning prayer. When the Messenger of Allah (ﷺ) came to us I mentioned that to him. The Prophet (ﷺ) said, 'O' 'Amr, did you lead your companions in prayer while you were sexually defiled?' I said, 'I recalled Allah's statement:

﴿... وَلَا تَقْتُلُوٓا۟ أَنفُسَكُمْ ۚ إِنَّ ٱللَّهَ كَانَ بِكُمْ رَحِيمًا ﴿٢٩﴾﴾ (سورة النِّسَاء: ٢٩)

﴿... Do not kill yourselves. Surely, Allah is Most Merciful to you.﴾ *(Qur'an 4: 29)*'

The Messenger of Allah (ﷺ) just laughed and did not say anything further."[168]

What is the "ground" that can be used

[The word used in the Qur'an is *aṣ-Ṣa'eed* (الصعيد)]. In *Lisân al-'Arab*,[169] it states, "*Aṣ-Ṣa'eed* is the earth. It is also said that it is the clean earth. It is also said that it is any clean soil. In the Qur'an, it states:

﴿... فَتَيَمَّمُوا۟ صَعِيدًا طَيِّبًا ... ﴿٦﴾﴾ (سورة المَائدة: ٦)

﴿... Perform *tayammum* with clean earth...﴾ *(Qur'an 5: 6)*

Abu Isḥâq said, '*aṣ-Ṣa'eed* is the face of the earth. The person is

---

=who narrated from 'Aṭâ ibn Abi Ribâḥ. Therefore, the narrations that combines together *tayammum* and washing is a weak narration by which rulings cannot be affirmed." Make a note of this for a point that shall come up shortly.

[168] This hadith is *ṣaḥeeḥ*. See Shaykh al-Albâni, *Ṣaḥeeḥ Sunan Abi Dawood*, no. 323. Recorded by Abu Dawood, Aḥmad and al-Ḥâkim.

[169] *Lisân al-'Arab*, vol. 3, p. 254.

supposed to strike his hands on the face of the earth (that is, the ground). It does not matter if there is soil or not at that spot. This is because *aṣ-Ṣa'eed* is not simply soil, it is the face of the earth, whether it is soil or not.' He also said, 'If the whole earth where a rock with no soil on it and the person struck that rock that would be purifying for him if he were to wipe his face with it.'"

The manner in which it is to be performed

'Ammâr ibn Yâsir (ﷺ) said, "I was sexually defiled and I did not find water. So I rolled myself on the ground and I prayed. I mentioned that to the Prophet (ﷺ) and he said, 'It would have been sufficient for you to do like so,' and the Prophet (ﷺ) struck the earth with his palms, blew in them, then wiped his face and palms with them."[170]

Note: The ruling concerning *tayammum* is that it takes the place of ablution. Hence, it makes permissible whatever ablution makes permissible. Furthermore, it is permissible to perform it before the time of prayer begins in the same way that one may make ablution before the time of prayer begins. Similarly, one may pray as much as one wish after performing *tayammum* in the same way that one may pray as much as one wills after making ablution.

What invalidates it

Everything that invalidates ablution also invalidates *tayammum*. Furthermore, the presence of water for one who did not have access to water or the ability to use water for one who was previously incapable also invalidates the *tayammum*. However, all the prayers prayed previously with the *tayammum* are valid and need not be repeated.

---

[170] Recorded by Bukhari, Muslim, Abu Dawood and Nasâ'i.

Abu Sa'eed al-Khudri (ﷺ) narrated: "Two men went out on a journey. The time for prayer came and they did not have water with them. Thus, they made *tayammum* with pure earth and they both prayed. Later they came across water during the time of the same prayer. One of them repeated his prayer and ablution while the other did not. Then they came to the Messenger of Allah (ﷺ) and mentioned that to him. He said to the one who did not repeat his prayer, 'You have captured the Sunnah and your prayer suffices.' Then he told the one who made ablution and repeated (the prayer), 'For you is the reward twice.'"[171]

Note: If someone has an injury that he has bandaged or a break that he has put a cast on, then he is no longer obliged to wash that portion of his body. At the same time, it is not necessary for him to wipe over it or make *tayammum* for it. The proof for this is Allah's statement:

﴿لَا يُكَلِّفُ ٱللَّهُ نَفْسًا إِلَّا وُسْعَهَا ... ﴿٢٨٦﴾﴾ (سورة البَقَرَة: ٢٨٦)

﴾Allah burdens not a person beyond his scope...﴿ *(Qur'an 2: 286)*

Furthermore, the Messenger of Allah (ﷺ) said, "If I order you something, do as much of it as you are capable."[172] Thus, the Qur'an and Sunnah have dropped anything that a person is not able to do. To say that something else must be done as a substitute is a Shari'ah ruling that cannot be mandated except by the Qur'an or Sunnah. Since there is no verse or Sunnah stating wiping as a substitute washing over the casts and other things that one cannot was over, that view cannot be upheld.[173]

---

[171] This hadith is *ṣaḥeeḥ*. See Shaykh al-Albâni, *Ṣaḥeeḥ Sunan Abi Dawood*, no. 327. Recorded by Abu Dawood and Nasâ'i.

[172] This hadith is *ṣaḥeeḥ*. See Shaykh al-Albâni, *Mukhtasar Ṣaḥeeḥ Muslim*, no. 639. Recorded by Muslim and Nasâ'i.

[173] Ibn Ḥazm, *al-Muḥalla*, vol. 2, p. 74.

The permissibility of making tayammum with a wall[174]

Ibn 'Abbâs (ﷺ) narrated, " 'Abdullâh ibn Yasâr, the client of Maymoonah (ﷺ) the wife of the Prophet (ﷺ) and I went to Abu Juhaym ibn al-Ḥârith ibn aṣ-Ṣimmah al-Anṣâri. Abu al-Juhaym said, 'The Prophet (ﷺ) was returning from Bir Jamal (close to Madeenah) and a man met him and greeted him. The Prophet (ﷺ) did not return the greetings until he turned to a wall (with his hands) and wiped his face and hands and then he returned his greetings.' "[175]

Menstruation and Post-partum Bleeding

Menstruation is the well-known bleeding that women have. In Islamic Law, there is no established maximum or minimum time limit. That is determined by what is customarily found among the women.

Post-partum bleeding is the bleeding that occurs due to giving birth. Its maximum length is forty days. Umm Salamah said, "During the lifetime of the Prophet (ﷺ), the post-partum women would wait[176] for forty days."[177]

If the blood stops flowing before forty days, the woman should make *ghusl* and purify herself. If it continues beyond forty days, she

---

[174] It matters not if the wall is made of clay or stone, plastered with oil or not. This is what our Shaykh al-Albâni has concluded to me. Then he said, "And your Lord does not forget."

[175] Recorded by Bukhari (without its complete chain), Muslim, Abu Dawood and Nasâ'i.

[176] [That is, not to pray, not have sexual intercourse and so on.]

[177] This hadith is *ḥasan ṣaḥeeḥ*. See Shaykh al-Albâni, *Ṣaḥeeḥ al-Jâmi'*, no. 530. Recorded by Abu Dawood, Tirmidhi and Ibn Mâjah.

should make *ghusl* for the completion of forty days and be considered pure.

What is Prohibited for the Menstruating and Post-partum Bleeding Women

All the actions (discussed earlier) prohibited for the one who is not in a state of ablution are also prohibited for menstruating and post-partum bleeding women. However, the following are additionally prohibited:

1. Fasting

She must make up the fasts after she becomes pure. Mu'âdhah said, "I asked 'Â'ishah, 'Why does the menstruating woman make up her fasts but not her prayers?' She replied, 'We experienced these things during the time of the Messenger of Allah (ﷺ) and he ordered us to make up our fasts and he did not order us to make up our prayers.' "[178]

2. Sexual intercourse

Allah (ﷻ) says:

﴿وَيَسْـَٔلُونَكَ عَنِ ٱلْمَحِيضِ ۖ قُلْ هُوَ أَذًى فَٱعْتَزِلُوا۟ ٱلنِّسَآءَ فِى ٱلْمَحِيضِ ۖ وَلَا تَقْرَبُوهُنَّ حَتَّىٰ يَطْهُرْنَ ۖ فَإِذَا تَطَهَّرْنَ فَأْتُوهُنَّ مِنْ حَيْثُ أَمَرَكُمُ ٱللَّهُ ... ﴿٢٢٢﴾﴾

(سورة البقـرة: ٢٢٢)

﴿They ask you concerning menstruation. Say: that is an *adha* [a harmful thing for a husband to have a sexual intercourse with his wife while she is having her menses], therefore keep away from women

---

[178] Recorded by Bukhari, Muslim (and this is his wording), Tirmidhi, Abu Dawood and Ibn Mâjah.

during menses and go not unto them till they have purified [from menses and have taken a bath]. And when they have purified themselves, then go in unto them as Allah has ordained for you...》

(Qur'an 2: 222)

Concerning this issue, the Prophet said, "(You may) do everything (with the menstruating woman) except for sexual intercourse."[179]

The ruling concerning one who has sexual intercourse with a menstruating woman

An-Nawawi wrote in his commentary to *Ṣaḥeeḥ Muslim*, "If a Muslim believes it is permissible to have sexual intercourse with a menstruating woman, he becomes a disbelieving, apostate. If he commits such an act while not believing it is permissible but out of forgetfulness, ignorant that she was having her menses, ignorant that it is forbidden or being coerced to do so, then there is no sin or expiation due from him. But if he did so intentionally, knowing that she was menstruating, knowing that is forbidden and out of choice, then he has committed a major sin. Ash-Shafi'ee explicitly stated that it is a major sin. It is a must that he repent. There are two opinions as to whether he must expiate for that act."[180]

The stronger opinion is that the expiation is obligatory. This is based on the hadith narrated by Ibn 'Abbâs from the Prophet (ﷺ) who said concerning a man who had sexual intercourse with his menstruating wife, "He is to give a *dinâr*[181] or half a dinar in charity."[182]

---

[179] This hadith is *ṣaḥeeḥ*. See Shaykh al-Albâni, *Ṣaḥeeḥ al-Jâmi' aṣ-Ṣagheer*, no. 527. Recorded by Muslim, Abu Dawood, Tirmidhi, Ibn Mâjah and Nasâ'i.

[180] An-Nawawi, *Sharḥ Ṣaḥeeḥ Muslim*, vol. 3, p. 204.

[181] [A *dinâr* was the common gold coin in currency at that time.]

[182] This hadith is *ṣaḥeeḥ*. See Shaykh al-Albâni, *Ṣaḥeeḥ Ibn Mâjah*, no. 523. Recorded by Abu Dawood, Nasâ'i and Ibn Mâjah.

The option stated in the hadith is related to whether the act occurred in the first days of the menses or in the later days. It is narrated that Ibn 'Abbâs said, "If he had relations with her at the beginning of the (days of) bleeding, then he is to give a *dinâr*. If it were toward the end of (the days) of bleeding, he gives half a *dinâr*."[183]

Istiḥâḍah (Metrorrhagia or uterine hemorrhaging, a condition where the woman has a continual blood flow)

Specifically this refers to bleeding at times other than the menses or post-partum bleeding or the bleeding is connected to those times but continues beyond them. If it is the first case, where the bleeding occurs other than at the time of menses or post-partum bleeding, the case is clear. If it is the latter case, then if the woman has a regular pattern (for the length of her menses), then anything which is beyond that norm would be considered *istiḥâḍah*. The Prophet (ﷺ) said to Umm Ḥabeebah, "Abstain (from the prayer) for the time that your menses used to keep you (from the prayer) and then wash and pray."[184]

The woman may also recognize her case by distinguishing the characteristics of the blood flow. In the case of menstruation, the blood is dark and recognizable. In *istiḥâḍah*, it will be different. Thus, the Prophet (ﷺ) said to Fâṭimah bint Abi Ḥubaysh, "If it were the blood of the menses, which is dark and known, then refrain from the prayers. If it were the other (blood), then make ablution, for it is only a vein."[185]

---

[183] This is *ṣaḥeeḥ* as a statement of Ibn 'Abbâs. See Shaykh al-Albâni, *Ṣaḥeeḥ Sunan Abi Dawood*. Recorded by Abu Dawood.

[184] This hadith is *ṣaḥeeḥ*. See Shaykh al-Albâni, *I'rwâ' al-Ghaleel*, no. 202. Recorded by Muslim.

[185] This hadith is *ṣaḥeeḥ*. See Shaykh al-Albâni, *I'rwâ' al-Ghaleel*, no. 204. Recorded by Nasâ'i and Abu Dawood.

If a girl with this condition reaches puberty and cannot distinguish (her regular menses or the different nature of the blood), then she should follow what is the customary pattern for her women. The Prophet (ﷺ) said to Ḥamnah bint Jaḥsh, "This is just a strike from the strikes of Satan (in order to try to cause you harm and confusion). Therefore, have your menses for six or seven days by Allah's knowledge. Then make *ghusl*. After you have purified and cleaned yourself, pray for twenty-four nights and twenty-three days and fast as well (during that time). That will be sufficient for you. Do that every month, just like the women menstruate and just like they purify themselves based on the timing of their periods of menses and purity."[186]

Rulings for istiḥâḍah

The matters that are forbidden for the menstruating women are not forbidden for the woman with *istiḥâḍah*. However, she must perform ablution for every prayer, as the Prophet (ﷺ) told Fâṭimah bint Abu Ḥubaysh, "Make ablution for every prayer."[187]

As discussed earlier, in addition, it is also recommended for her to make *ghusl* for every prayer.

---

[186] This hadith is *ḥasan*. See Shaykh al-Albâni, *I'rwâ' al-Ghaleel*, no. 205. Recorded by Abu Dawood, Tirmidhi and Ibn Mâjah (who has this meaning but not this wording).

[187] This hadith is *ṣaḥeeḥ*. See Shaykh al-Albâni, *Ṣaḥeeḥ al-Jâmi' aṣ-Ṣagheer*, no. 507. Recorded by Abu Dawood and Ibn Mâjah.

Chapter Two — The Prayers

𝒯he obligatory prayers are five: the Noon (الظهر *adh-dhuhr*), Afternoon (العصر *al-'aṣr*), Sunset (المغرب *al-maghrib*), Night (العشاء *al-'ishâ'*) and Dawn (الفجر *al-fajr*).

Anas ibn Mâlik (رضي الله عنه) said, "The prayers were made obligatory on the Night of Ascension and they were set at fifty. They were continually reduced until they reached five. Then it was called out, 'O' Muhammad, the statement has not been replaced to Me. For those five prayers, you will (get the reward) of fifty.' "[1]

Ṭalḥah ibn 'Ubaydullâh (رضي الله عنه) said that a Bedouin, with dishevelled hair, came to the Messenger of Allah (ﷺ) and said, "O' Messenger of Allah inform me as to what Allah has obligated of the prayers." The Prophet (ﷺ) replied, "The five (daily) prayers, unless you also do some voluntarily."[2]

Its Place in the Religion

'Abdullâh ibn 'Umar (may Allah be pleased with him) narrated that the Messenger of Allah (Blessings and peace be upon him) said, "Islam is built upon five (pillars): testifying that there is none worthy of worship except Allah and that Muhammad is the Messenger of Allah, establishing the prayers, giving the zakah,

---

[1] Recorded by Bukhari, Muslim and Nasâ'i. The above wording is from Tirmidhi.

[2] Recorded by Bukhari, Muslim, Abu Dawood and Nasâ'i.

making the pilgrimage to the House and fasting the month of Ramaḍân."[3]

Ruling Concerning One Who Does not Pray

The Muslims are in agreement that if one denies the obligation of the prayer, he has committed disbelief and has left the fold of Islam. However, they differ about one who does not pray while believing that it is obligatory. The cause for this difference of opinion is the fact that in some hadith, the Messenger of Allah (ﷺ) called the one who abandoned the prayer a disbeliever, without distinguishing between the one who denied the prayer and the one who was simply lackadaisical. Jâbir narrated that the Messenger of Allah (ﷺ) said, "Between a man and polytheism (*shirk*) and disbelief (*kufr*) is the abandoning of the prayer."[4] Buraydah narrated that the Prophet (ﷺ) also said, "The covenant that is between us and them (the disbelievers) is the prayer. Whoever abandons it has committed an act of unbelief."[5]

However, the strongest of the opinions of the scholars is that what is meant by *kufr* (disbelief) here is the "lesser *kufr*" that does not take one out of the fold of Islam. This conclusion is made in order to reconcile the meaning of the above hadith with other hadith, such as the following: "Allah, blessed and exalted be He, has prescribed five prayers upon His servants. Whoever performs them without missing anything out of belittling their rights has a promise from

---

[3] Recorded by Bukhari, Muslim (and this is his wording), Tirmidhi and Nasâ'i.

[4] This hadith is *ṣaḥeeḥ*. See Shaykh al-Albâni, *Ṣaḥeeḥ al-Jâmi'*, no. 2848. Recorded by Muslim (and this is his wording), Abu Dawood, Tirmidhi and Ibn Mâjah.

[5] This hadith is *ṣaḥeeḥ*. See Shaykh al-Albâni, *Ṣaḥeeḥ Ibn Mâjah*, no. 884. Recorded by Ibn Mâjah, Nasâ'i and Tirmidhi.

Allah that He will enter him into Paradise. And whoever does not perform them has no promise from Allah. He may either punish him or He may forgive him."[6] Since the Prophet (ﷺ) said about the issue of he who does not perform them is up to Allah, we know that leaving the prayers is something less than disbelief and associating partners with Allah. This is because Allah has said:

﴿إِنَّ ٱللَّهَ لَا يَغْفِرُ أَن يُشْرَكَ بِهِۦ وَيَغْفِرُ مَا دُونَ ذَٰلِكَ لِمَن يَشَآءُ ... ﴿٤٨﴾﴾

(سورة النِّسَاء: ٤٨)

﴿Verily, Allah forgives not that partners should be set up with him in worship, but He forgives anything else to whom He pleases...﴾ *(Qur'an 4: 48)*

Abu Hurayrah reported that the Messenger of Allah (ﷺ) said, "The first deeds for which the Muslim servant (of Allah) will be held accountable on the Day of Judgment will be the obligatory prayers. If he fulfilled them, (he will have prospered and been successful). But if not, it will be said, 'See if he has any voluntary prayers with which may be completed that which was wanting in his obligatory prayers.' Then the rest of his obligatory deeds will be judged in like fashion."[7]

Ḥudhayfah ibn al-Yamân narrated that the Messenger of Allah (ﷺ) said, "Islam will be effaced in the same way that the colors of a garment fade away, to the point that the fasts, prayers, pilgrimage and charity will not be known and the Book of Allah will be taken up in the night and not one verse of it will be left on earth. A group of people will be left, old men and women. They will say, 'We found

---

[6] This hadith is *ṣaḥeeḥ*. See Shaykh al-Albâni, *Ṣaḥeeḥ Ibn Mâjah*, no. 115. Recorded by Mâlik, Aḥmad, Abu Dawood, Ibn Mâjah and Nasâ'i.

[7] This hadith is *ṣaḥeeḥ*. See Shaykh al-Albâni, *Ṣaḥeeḥ Ibn Mâjah*, no. 1172. Recorded by Ibn Mâjah (and this is his wording), Tirmidhi and Nasâ'i.

our fathers upon this statement, 'There is none worthy of worship except Allah,' and we also say the same.' " Ṣilah said to Ḥudhayfah, "What good will the statement, 'None is worthy of worship except Allah,' do them when they do not know the prayers, fasting, pilgrimage and charity?" Ḥudhayfah turned away from him. He repeated the question three times and each time Ḥudhayfah turned away from him. Finally, Ḥudhayfah turned to him and said three times, "O' Ṣilah, it will save them from the Hell-Fire."[8]

Upon Whom is the Prayer Obligatory?

The prayer is obligatory upon every adult,[9] sane Muslim

'Ali (ﷺ) narrated that the Prophet (ﷺ) said, "The pen (recording the deeds) has been raised (and is not recording) for three: the one who is sleeping until he awakens, the child until he reaches the age of puberty and the insane one until he becomes sane."[10]

The guardian of the child must order the child to perform the prayers, even if they are not obligatory on the child, in order to get him used to perform them regularly. 'Amr ibn Shu'ayb narrated from his father on the authority of his grandfather who said that the Messenger of Allah (ﷺ) said, "Order your children to pray at the age of seven and beat them to do so at the age of ten and separate them in their bedding."[11]

---

[8] This hadith is *ṣaḥeeḥ*. See Shaykh al-Albâni, *Ṣaḥeeḥ Ibn Mâjah*, no. 3273. Recorded by Ibn Mâjah.

[9] [What is translated as "adult" here actually means anyone who has reached the age of puberty.] - Translator

[10] This hadith is *ṣaḥeeḥ*. See Shaykh al-Albâni, *Ṣaḥeeḥ al-Jâmi'*, no. 3513. Recorded by Abu Dawood.

[11] This hadith is *ḥasan*. See Shaykh al-Albâni, *Ṣaḥeeḥ al-Jâmi'*, no. 5868. Recorded by Abu Dawood, Aḥmad and al-Ḥâkim.

The times of the prayers

Jâbir ibn 'Abdullâh reported: "The Angel Gabriel came to the Prophet (ﷺ) and said, 'Stand and pray.' He prayed the Noon prayer when the sun had passed its zenith. Then he came in the afternoon and said, 'Stand and pray.' Then he prayed the Afternoon prayer when every object and its shadow had become the same length. Then he came at sunset and said, 'Stand and pray.' He prayed when the sun had disappeared. Then he came in the night and said, 'Stand and pray.' He prayed when the twilight had disappeared. Then he came at dawn and said, 'Stand and pray.' He prayed when the dawn had lit up — or he said became brightened. Then he came on the next day for the Noon prayer and said, 'Stand and pray.' He prayed the Noon prayer when an object and its shade were the same length. Then he came for the Afternoon prayer and said, 'Stand and pray.' He prayed the Afternoon prayer when the shadow of an object was twice the object's length. Then he came for the Sunset prayer, and it has only one time. Then he came for the Night prayer and it was when half or one third of the night had passed and he prayed the Night prayer. Then he came in the dawn when it was very light and said, 'Stand and pray,' and he prayed the Dawn prayer. Then he said, 'The time (for the prayers) are between these two,' (that is, between the two sets of times in which he prayed with him)."[12] Tirmidhi said, "Muhammad (that is, Bukhari) said, 'The most authentic report concerning the times of the prayers is the hadith of Jâbir.'"

The times are:

1. The Noon prayer is from the sun passing its zenith until the shadow of an object is equal to the object's length.

2. The Afternoon prayer is from when the shadow of an object is

---

[12] This hadith is *ṣaḥeeḥ*. See Shaykh al-Albâni, *I'rwâ' al-Ghaleel*, no. 250. Recorded by Aḥmad, Nasâ'i and Tirmidhi.

equal to the object's length until sunset.

3. The Sunset prayer is from sunset until the twilight disappears. The Prophet (ﷺ) said, "The time for the Sunset prayer is as long as the twilight has not left."[13]

4. The Night prayer is from the disappearance of the twilight until half of the night. This is based on the Prophet's statement, "The time of the Night prayer is until half the night."[14]

5. The Morning prayer is from the break of dawn until sunrise, based on the Prophet's statement, "The time for the Morning prayer is from the break of dawn as long as the sun has yet to rise."[15]

Which is the "Middle prayer"

Allah (ﷻ) says:

﴿حَـٰفِظُواْ عَلَى ٱلصَّلَوَٰتِ وَٱلصَّلَوٰةِ ٱلْوُسْطَىٰ وَقُومُواْ لِلَّهِ قَـٰنِتِينَ ﴿٢٣٨﴾﴾

(سورة البقرة: ٢٣٨)

---

[13] This hadith is *ḥasan*. See Shaykh al-Albâni, *I'rwâ' al-Ghaleel,* vol. 1, p. 268. Recorded by Muslim with this wording and by Abu Dawood and Nasâ'i. [Note: This is what the author has stated however there does not seem to be any hadith with such wording. The reference that he has given from Shaykh al-Albâni does not contain such a hadith. The author is most likely referring to a hadith that Shaykh al-Albâni refers to on p. 271. In this hadith, from *Ṣaḥeeḥ Muslim*, a person asked the Prophet (Blessings and peace of Allah be upon him) about the timing of the prayers and, instead of giving him a verbal reply immediately, the Prophet demonstrated the timing of the prayers during the next two days and then he told the man, "The prayer is between these two timings (I have just demonstrated for you)." The mistake this author has made is to change those actions into actual statements of the Prophet. And Allah alone knows best.] - Translator

[14] [See previous note.]

[15] [See previous note but one.]

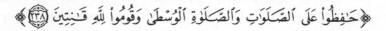

﴾Guard strictly the prayers, especially the middle prayer [i.e., the best prayer]. And stand before Allah with obedience.﴿ *(Qur'an 2: 238)*

'Ali (رضي الله عنه) reported that the Messenger of Allah (ﷺ) said during the Battle of al-Aḥzâb, "They have preoccupied us from the middle prayer, the Afternoon prayer. May Allah fill their homes and graves with Fire."[16]

It is preferred to pray the noon prayer earliest in its proper time as long as it is not excessively hot

Jâbir ibn Samurah said, "The Prophet (ﷺ) used to perform the Noon prayer when the sun moved passed its zenith."[17]

It is preferred to let it cool down before praying the noon prayer when it is excessively hot

Abu Hurayrah (رضي الله عنه) narrated that the Prophet (ﷺ) said, "If it is very hot, perform the prayer after it has cooled off as the intensity of the heat is from the exhalation of Hell."[18]

It is preferred to pray the afternoon prayer early (in its time)

Anas (رضي الله عنه) narrated that the Messenger of Allah (ﷺ) used to pray the Afternoon prayer while the sun was high and bright in the sky. A person could then go to the outskirts of Madeenah and arrive there while the sun was still high in the sky.[19]

---

[16] This hadith is *ṣaḥeeḥ*. See Shaykh al-Albâni, *Mukhtasar Ṣaḥeeḥ Muslim*, no. 217. Recorded by Muslim.

[17] This hadith is *ṣaḥeeḥ*. See Shaykh al-Albâni, *I'rwâ' al-Ghaleel*, no. 254. Recorded by Muslim.

[18] Recorded by Bukhari, Muslim, Abu Dawood, Tirmidhi, Nasâ'i and Ibn Mâjah.

[19] Recorded by Bukhari, Muslim, Abu Dawood, Nasâ'i and Ibn Mâjah.

The sin of one who misses the afternoon prayer

Ibn 'Umar narrated that the Messenger of Allah (ﷺ) said, "The one who misses the Afternoon prayer is like one deprived of his family and wealth."[20] Buraydah narrated that the Prophet (ﷺ) said, "The one who abandons the Afternoon prayer has had his deeds voided."[21]

The sin of the one who delays the afternoon prayer until the sun is yellow (and low toward the horizon)

Anas narrated that he heard the Messenger of Allah (ﷺ) say, "That is the prayer of the hypocrite: He sits watching the sun until it is between the two horns of the Devil and then he stands, praying four (*rak'ahs*) quickly like the pecking of a bird, not remembering Allah but little."[22]

It is preferred to pray the sunset prayer immediately and it is disliked to delay it

'Uqbah ibn 'Âmir (may Allah be pleased with him) narrated that the Prophet (ﷺ) said, "My Nation shall continue to be in a good state — or he said upon the natural way — as long as they do not delay the Sunset prayer until the (numerous) stars appear together."[23] Salamah ibn al-Akwa' (may Allah be pleased with him) narrated that the Messenger of Allah (ﷺ) would pray the Sunset prayer when the

---

[20] Recorded by Bukhari, Muslim, Abu Dawood, Tirmidhi and Nasâ'i.

[21] This hadith is *ṣaḥeeḥ*. See Shaykh al-Albâni, *Ṣaḥeeḥ Sunan Nasâ'i*, no. 497. Recorded by Bukhari and Nasâ'i.

[22] This hadith is *ṣaḥeeḥ*. See Shaykh al-Albâni, *Ṣaḥeeḥ Sunan Abi Dawood*, no. 399. Recorded by Muslim (and that is his wording), Abu Dawood, Tirmidhi and Nasâ'i.

[23] This hadith is *ḥasan ṣaḥeeḥ*. See Shaykh al-Albâni, *Ṣaḥeeḥ Abi Dawood*, no. 403. Recorded by Abu Dawood.

sun would set and disappear (behind the horizon).[24]

It is preferred to delay the night prayer as long as there is no causing of hardship

'Â'ishah said, "One night the Prophet (ﷺ) waited until most of the night had passed and the people in the mosque were sleeping and then he went out and prayed. He said, 'This would be its time if it were not to be a hardship upon my Nation.'"[25]

The disapproval of sleeping before the night prayer and of conversing afterwards without any true need or benefit

Abu Barzah (رضي الله عنه) stated that the Messenger of Allah (ﷺ) disliked sleeping before the Night prayer or conversing afterwards.[26] Anas said, "We waited for the Prophet one night until half the night had been reached. He came and led the people in prayer and then addressed us, saying, "Certainly, the people have prayed and gone to sleep while you (here) are continually in prayer as long as you are waiting for the prayer."[27]

It is preferred to perform the morning prayer early in its time

'Â'ishah (رضي الله عنها) said, "The believing women used to attend the Morning prayer with the Messenger of Allah (ﷺ) completely

---

[24] Recorded by Bukhari (without the words, "the sun would set"), Muslim and Tirmidhi, while Abu Dawood and Ibn Mâjah have something similar.

[25] This hadith is *ṣaḥeeḥ*. See Shaykh al-Albâni, *Mukhtasar Ṣaḥeeḥ Muslim*, no. 223. Recorded by Muslim.

[26] Recorded by Bukhari, Muslim, Abu Dawood and Nasâ'i.

[27] Recorded by Bukhari (and this is his wording), Muslim, Abu Dawood and Nasâ'i.

covered in their garments. Then they would go back to their houses after finishing the prayer and no one could recognize them due to the darkness."[28]

When does the person actually catch the time of the prayer?

Abu Hurayrah reported that the Messenger of Allah (ﷺ) said, "Whoever catches a *rak'ah* of the Morning prayer before the sun rises has caught the Morning prayer. Whoever catches a *rak'ah* of the Afternoon prayer before the sun sets has caught the Afternoon prayer."[29] This ruling is not particular for only the Morning and Afternoon prayers but is general for every prayer. Abu Hurayrah reported that the Prophet (ﷺ) said, "Whoever has caught a *rak'ah* of the prayer has caught the prayer."[30]

Making up missed prayers

Anas reported that the Prophet of Allah (ﷺ) said, "Whoever forgets a prayer or sleeps through it, then the expiation is to perform it when he remembers it."[31]

Does the one who intentionally leaves a prayer until its time finishes make-up the prayer?

Ibn Ḥazm said,

> "Allah has made for every prayer an appointed time with set limits. It begins at a specified time and becomes void at a

[28] Recorded by Bukhari, Muslim, Abu Dawood, Nasâ'i, Tirmidhi and Ibn Mâjah.

[29] Recorded by Bukhari and Muslim, while Nasâ'i has something similar.

[30] Recorded by Bukhari, Muslim, Abu Dawood, Tirmidhi and Nasâ'i.

[31] This hadith is *ṣaḥeeḥ*. See Shaykh al-Albâni, *Mukhtasar Ṣaḥeeḥ Muslim*, no. 229. Recorded by Muslim.

specified time. There is no difference between one who prays it before its time and one who prays it after its time — as each one of them has prayed it outside of its time. In addition, the making-up of a prayer is a legal issue and such legal rulings are not permissible except by Allah upon the tongue of His Messenger (ﷺ). If making up an obligatory prayer that the one who intentionally has abandoned the prayer did not perform until its time was finished, neither Allah nor His Messenger would have failed to point that out, they also would not have forgotten to mention it and they also would not intentionally leave us without explaining the issue. (Allah says,)

﴿... وَمَا كَانَ رَبُّكَ نَسِيًّا ﴿٦٤﴾﴾ (سورة مَريَم: ٦٤)

﴾... Your Lord is never forgetful.﴿ *(Qur'an 19: 64)*

Every law that has not been brought in the Qur'an or Sunnah is void."[32]

The times in which it is prohibited to pray

'Uqbah ibn 'Âmir (ﷺ) said, "There are three times (of the day) concerning which the Messenger of Allah (ﷺ) prohibited us from praying or from burying our dead: when the sunrise first occurs until it rises (above the horizon), during high noon until the sun goes past its zenith, when the sun is leaning toward sunset until it sets."[33]

The Prophet (ﷺ) explained the reason for such prohibition when he said to 'Amr ibn 'Abasah, "Pray the Morning prayer and then refrain from praying until the sunrise and it is above (the

---

[32] Ibn Ḥazm, *al-Muḥalla*, vol. 2, p. 235.

[33] This hadith is *ṣaḥeeḥ*. See Shaykh al-Albâni, *Ṣaḥeeḥ Ibn Mâjah*, no. 1233. Recorded by Muslim, Abu Dawood, Tirmidhi, Nasâ'i and Ibn Mâjah.

horizon), for it rises between the two horns of the Devil and at that time the disbelievers prostrate to it. Then pray for the prayer is witnessed and attended (by angels) until the shadow is the length of a lance (which is high noon) and then refrain from prayer, for at that time Hell is heated up. Then when the shadows start appearing, pray, for the prayer is witnessed and attended (by angels), until you pray the Afternoon prayer. After that refrain from praying until the sun sets for it sets between the two horns of the Devil and the disbelievers prostrate to it at that time."[34]

Times and places that are exempted from the prohibition

As for the time that it is exempted, it is high noon on Fridays. This is based on the statement of the Prophet (ﷺ), "No man makes *ghusl* on Friday and purifies what he can and puts on some oil of his oil and applies some perfume from his house, and then goes out without coming between two people, and then prays what has been written for him to pray, then remains quiet while the Imam speaks, but he will be forgiven for what he did between that Friday and the previous one."[35] In this hadith, the Prophet (ﷺ) is encouraging praying what has been recorded for the person and nothing prevents him from praying except the arrival of the Imam. This view (that said time is exempted on Friday) was the opinion of more than one of the pious predecessors, including 'Umar ibn al-Khaṭṭâb. Aḥmad ibn Ḥanbal followed his view, saying, "The arrival of the Imam prohibits prayers and his speech (*khuṭbah*) prohibits speaking." Thus, he has made the cause of the prohibition for prayer the arrival of the Imam and not high noon.

---

[34] This hadith is *ṣaḥeeḥ*. See Shaykh al-Albâni, *Mishkât al-Maṣâbiḥ*, no. 1042. Recorded by Muslim.

[35] This hadith is *ṣaḥeeḥ*. See Shaykh al-Albâni, *Ṣaḥeeḥ at-Targheeb wa at-Tarheeb*, no. 689. Recorded by Bukhari.

As for the place which is exempted, it is Makkah, may Allah increase its honour and esteem. At none of the above times is it disliked to pray in Makkah. This is based on the Prophet's statement, "O' Tribe of 'Abdu-Manâf, do not prevent anyone from circumambulating this house or praying (herein) at any time of the day or night."[36]

The prayers that are prohibited at the aforementioned times are only the purely voluntary prayers that have no specific reason for their performance. It is permissible, for example, to make up missed obligatory or voluntary prayers during those times. This is based on the Prophet's statement, "Whoever forgets a prayer should pray it when he remembers it and there is no expiation for it other than that."[37]

It is also permissible to prayer right after performing ablution at whatever time it may be. This is based on the narration from Abu Hurayrah: "The Prophet (ﷺ) said to Bilâl at the time of the Morning prayer, 'Inform me of a deed you performed in Islam concerning which you have the most hope for as I heard your footsteps in front of me in Paradise.' He replied, 'There is no deed concerning which I am more hopeful except that I never purify myself during the night or day but that I pray with that purification whatever has been recorded for me to pray.'"[38]

Also, the "prayer for greeting the mosque" is permissible at any time. This is because the Prophet (Blessings and peace be upon him) said, "When one of you enters the mosque, he should not sit

---

[36] This hadith is *ṣaḥeeḥ*. See Shaykh al-Albâni, *Ṣaḥeeḥ Sunan Ibn Mâjah*, no. 1036. Recorded by Ibn Mâjah, Tirmidhi and Nasâ'i.

[37] Recorded by Bukhari, Muslim and Abu Dawood. Without the sentence, "There is no expiation," it is also recorded by Nasâ'i, Tirmidhi and Ibn Mâjah.

[38] Recorded by Bukhari and Muslim.

until he prays two *rak'ahs*."[39]

The impermissibility of performing voluntary prayers after dawn and before the morning prayer

Yasâr, the client of Ibn 'Umar said, "Ibn 'Umar saw me praying after dawn. He said, 'O' Yasâr, the Messenger of Allah (ﷺ) came to us and we were praying this prayer and he said, 'Those of you who are present should inform those who are absent: You are not to pray after dawn begins except two *rak'ahs*.' '"[40]

The impermissibility of performing voluntary prayers once the obligatory prayer has been commenced

Abu Hurayrah reported that the Prophet (ﷺ) said, "If the prayer has been commenced, there is not to be any prayer except the obligatory one."[41]

The places in which one is not permitted to pray

Abu Hurayrah (رضي الله عنه) narrated that the Messenger of Allah (ﷺ) said, "I have been given excellence over the prophets by six matters: I have been given the most comprehensive speech, I have been supported by fear (in the enemy's hearts), the spoils of war have been

---

[39] Recorded by Bukhari, Muslim, Abu Dawood, Tirmidhi, Ibn Mâjah and Nasâ'i.

[40] This hadith is *ṣaḥeeḥ*. See Shaykh al-Albâni, *Ṣaḥeeḥ al-Jâmi' aṣ-Ṣagheer*, no. 5353. Recorded by Abu Dawood. Tirmidhi has it with the wording, "There is no prayer after dawn except two *rak'ahs*." [Note: Literally the Prophet (Blessings and peace of Allah be upon him) said, "Two prostrations," but he was referring to the two *rak'ahs* of Sunnah that one performs before the obligatory Morning prayer.] - Translator

[41] This hadith is *ṣaḥeeḥ*. See Shaykh al-Albâni, *Ṣaḥeeḥ Ibn Mâjah*, no. 945. Recorded by Muslim, Tirmidhi, Abu Dawood, Nasâ'i and Ibn Mâjah.

made permissible for me, the earth has been made a source of purification and place for prayer for me, I have been sent to all of the creation and the (line of) prophets has been sealed by me."[42]

The whole earth is place for prayer (lit., *masjid*) except for the places excluded in the following hadith:

Jundab ibn 'Abdullâh al-Bajali said that he heard the Prophet (ﷺ) saying just five days before his death, "Those who came before you used to take the gravesites of their prophets and pious people as places of prayer. Indeed, do not take gravesites as places of prayer — I forbid you that."[43]

Abu Sa'eed al-Khudri said that the Prophet (ﷺ) said, "The whole earth is a place for prayer except a graveyard and a bathroom."[44]

Al-Barâ' ibn 'Âzib said, "The Messenger of Allah (ﷺ) was asked about praying in camel pastures and he replied, 'Do not pray in the camel pastures for they are from devils.' He was then asked about praying in the sheep pastures and he replied, 'Pray therein for they are blessings.' "[45]

---

[42] This hadith is *ṣaḥeeḥ*. See Shaykh al-Albâni, *Mukhtasar Ṣaḥeeḥ Muslim*, no. 257. Recorded by Muslim.

[43] This hadith is *ṣaḥeeḥ*. See Shaykh al-Albâni, *I'rwâ' al-Ghaleel*, no. 286. Recorded by Muslim.

[44] This hadith is *ṣaḥeeḥ*. See Shaykh al-Albâni, *Ṣaḥeeḥ Ibn Mâjah*, no. 606. Recorded by Abu Dawood, Ibn Mâjah and Tirmidhi.

[45] This hadith is *ṣaḥeeḥ*. See Shaykh al-Albâni, *Ṣaḥeeḥ al-Jâmi' aṣ-Ṣagheer*, no. 7351. Recorded by Abu Dawood.

The Call to Prayer

The Ruling Concerning It

The call to prayer is the announcement of the beginning of the time of prayer, said with specific words.[46] It is obligatory. Mâlik ibn al-Ḥuwayrith narrated that the Prophet (ﷺ) said, "If the prayer time comes, one of you should make the call to prayer and the eldest of you should lead you in prayer."[47] The Prophet (ﷺ) ordered them to make the call to prayer and an order implies obligation, as is well-known.

Anas said, "If the Prophet (ﷺ) would lead us in a military expedition against a people, he would not start the encounter until the morning. He would wait and if he heard the call to payer, he would refrain (from attacking). If he did not hear the call to prayer, he would attack them."[48]

Its Virtues

Mu'âwiyah narrated that the Prophet (ﷺ) said, "The callers to the prayer will have the longest necks on the Day of Resurrection."[49]

'Abdur-Raḥmân ibn 'Abdullâh ibn 'Abdur-Raḥmân ibn Abu Ṣa'ṣa'h al-Anṣâri al-Mâzini narrated from his father that Abu Sa'eed

---

[46] As-Sayyid Sâbiq, *Fiqh as-Sunnah*, vol. 1, p. 94.

[47] Recorded by Bukhari and Muslim.

[48] Recorded by Bukhari with this wording while Muslim has something similar.

[49] This hadith is *ṣaḥeeḥ*. See Shaykh al-Albâni, *Mukhtasar Ṣaḥeeḥ Muslim*, no. 6645. Recorded by Muslim.

al-Khudri said to him, "I see that you are a person who loves goats and the open spaces. If you are with your goats or in the open spaces and you make the call to prayer, raise your voice for everything within the sound of the caller, including the humans, jinn and anything else, will be a witness to it on the Day of Resurrection. I heard that from the Messenger of Allah (ﷺ)."[50]

The Description of the Call

'Abdullâh ibn Zayd ibn 'Abdur-Rabbihi said, "While the Messenger of Allah was intending to strike a bell (to call the people to prayer), although he did not like it as it was the practice of the Christians, a visitor came to me in my sleep at night. It was a man wearing two green garments and in his hand was a bell he was carrying. I said to him, 'O' servant of Allah, do you want to sell the bell?' He said, 'What will you do with it?' I said, 'We will call the people to the prayer.' He said, 'Shall I not tell you about something that is better than that?' I said, 'Certainly.' He said, '(Instead,) say: Allah is great, Allah is great, Allah is great, Allah is great. I bear witness that none is worthy of worship except Allah. I bear witness that none is worthy of worship except Allah. I bear witness that Muhammad is the Messenger of Allah. I bear witness that Muhammad is the Messenger of Allah. Come to the prayer. Come to the prayer. Come to the success. Come to the success. God is great, God is great. There is none worthy of worship except Allah.' Then he went back a little and he said, 'Then say when you are commencing the prayer: Allah is great, Allah is great. I bear witness that none is worthy of worship except Allah. I bear witness that Muhammad is the Messenger of Allah. Come to the prayer. Come to the success.

---

[50] This hadith is *ṣaḥeeḥ*. See Shaykh al-Albâni, *Ṣaḥeeḥ Sunan Nasâ'i*, no. 625. Recorded by Bukhari and Nasâ'i.

The prayer has commenced. The prayer has commenced. God is great, God is great. There is none worthy of worship except Allah.' When the morning came, I went to the Messenger of Allah (ﷺ) and informed him of what I had seen. The Messenger of Allah (ﷺ) said, 'That vision is true, Allah willing.' Then he ordered for the call to be made. Bilâl, the ex-slave of Abu Bakr, made the call with those words.' "[51]

It is preferred for the caller to pronounce two sayings of "Allah is Great" together

'Umar ibn al-Khaṭṭâb (رضي الله عنه) narrated that the Messenger of Allah (ﷺ) said, "When the caller says, 'Allah is great, Allah is great,' you should say, 'Allah is great, Allah is great.' "[52] This is a clear indication that the caller to the prayer combines these two sentences together and the listener responds in the same way.[53]

It is recommended to make Tarjee'

Tarjee' is to repeat the two testimonies of faith in a louder voice after stating them in a quieter voice.[54] Abu Maḥdhoorah stated that the Prophet (ﷺ) taught him to make the call to prayer in the following fashion:

اللَّهُ أَكْبَرُ اللَّهُ أَكْبَرُ أَشْهَدُ أَنْ لا إِلَهَ إِلاَّ اللَّهُ أَشْهَدُ أَنْ لا إِلَهَ إِلاَّ اللَّهُ أَشْهَدُ أَنَّ
مُحَمَّدًا رَسُولُ اللَّهِ أَشْهَدُ أَنَّ مُحَمَّدًا رَسُولُ اللَّهِ ثُمَّ يَعُودُ فَيَقُولُ أَشْهَدُ أَنْ لا

---

[51] This hadith is *ḥasan* ṣaḥeeḥ. See Shaykh al-Albâni, *Ṣaheeḥ Sunan Abi Dawood*, no. 469. Recorded by Aḥmad, Abu Dawood and Tirmidhi, while Ibn Mâjah recorded an abridged version.

[52] This hadith is *ṣaḥeeḥ*. See Shaykh al-Albâni, *Ṣaḥeeḥ Sunan Abi Dawood*, no. 527. Recorded by Muslim and Abu Dawood.

[53] An-Nawawi, *Sharḥ Ṣaḥeeḥ Muslim*, vol. 3, p. 79.

[54] Ibid, p. 81.

إِلَهَ إِلاَّ اللَّهُ أَشْهَدُ أَنْ لا إِلَهَ إِلاَّ اللَّهُ أَشْهَدُ أَنَّ مُحَمَّدًا رَسُولُ اللَّهِ أَشْهَدُ أَنَّ مُحَمَّدًا رَسُولُ اللَّهِ حَيَّ عَلَى الصَّلاةِ مَرَّتَيْنِ حَيَّ عَلَى الْفَلاحِ مَرَّتَيْنِ اللَّهُ أَكْبَرُ اللَّهُ أَكْبَرُ لا إِلَهَ إِلاَّ اللَّهُ

"Allah is great, Allah is great. I bear witness that none is worthy of worship except Allah. I bear witness that Muhammad is the Messenger of Allah. Then one repeats that and says again: I bear witness that none is worthy of worship except Allah. I bear witness that Muhammad is the Messenger of Allah. Twice one says: Come to the prayer. Twice one says: Come to the success. Then: God is great, God is great. There is none worthy of worship except Allah."[55]

The saying, "prayer is better than sleep," in the first call for the morning prayer

Abu Maḥdhoorah stated that the Prophet (ﷺ) taught him to make the call to prayer and it included the following words: "Come to the prayer. Come to the prayer. Come to the success. Come to the success. Prayer is better than sleep. Prayer is better than sleep — and that was in the first call[56] to the Morning prayer. God is great, God is great. There is none worthy of worship except Allah."[57]

Al-Ameer aṣ-Ṣan'âni stated, "Ibn Raslân said, 'It is sanctioned to make this extra statement in the first call to prayer for the Morning prayer in order to wake those who are sleeping. As for the second

---

[55] This hadith is *ṣaḥeeḥ*. See Shaykh al-Albâni, *Mukhtasar Ṣaḥeeḥ Muslim*, no. 191. Recorded by Muslim.

[56] [The Morning prayer has two calls to prayer. One is before dawn - the actual time of the beginning of the prayer time - while the second is at the beginning of dawn.]

[57] This hadith is *ṣaḥeeḥ*. See Shaykh al-Albâni, *Ṣaḥeeḥ Sunan Nasâ'i*, no. 628. Recorded by Nasâ'i.

call, it is to inform as to the beginning of the time (of the prayer) and to call the people to the prayer.' "[58]

It is preferred to make the call at the earliest time of the prayer and to pronounce it before its time only for the morning prayer

Jâbir ibn Samurah said, "Bilâl used to make the call to prayer when the sun passed its zenith and he did not leave any of the words of the call. However, he would not make the announcement of the commencing of the prayer until the Prophet (ﷺ) would go out to (the mosque). When the Prophet (ﷺ) went out (to the mosque), he would announce the commencement of the prayer as soon as he saw him."[59]

Ibn 'Umar narrated that the Prophet (ﷺ) said, "Bilâl makes the call while it is (still) night. So eat and drink until Ibn Umm Maktoom makes the call to prayer."[60]

The Prophet (ﷺ) explained the wisdom behind making the call to the Morning prayer before its time. He said, "The call of Bilâl should not prevent anyone from his pre-dawn meal. He makes the call during the night so that the one who is praying may return and so he may alert the one who is sleeping."[61]

What one should say upon hearing the call to prayer and the call of the commencing of the prayer

It is recommended for the one who hears the call to prayer to repeat what the caller has stated. Abu Sa'eed al-Khudri narrated that

---

[58] Aṣ-Ṣan'âni, *Subul as-Salâm*, vol. 1, p. 120.

[59] This hadith is *ṣaḥeeḥ*. See Shaykh al-Albâni, *Ṣaḥeeḥ Sunan Abi Dawood*, no. 503. Recorded by Aḥmad (and this is his wording), Muslim and Abu Dawood.

[60] Recorded by Bukhari and Muslim.

[61] Recorded by Bukhari, Muslim and Abu Dawood.

the Prophet (ﷺ) said, "If you hear the call (to prayer), say similar to what the caller is saying."[62]

'Umar ibn al-Khaṭṭâb narrated that the Prophet (ﷺ) said, "When the caller to prayer says, 'Allah is great, Allah is great,' you say, 'Allah is great, Allah is great.' When he says, 'I bear witness that none is worthy of worship except Allah,' you say, 'I bear witness that none is worthy of worship except Allah.' When he says, 'I bear witness that Muhammad is the Messenger of Allah,' you say, 'I bear witness that Muhammad is the Messenger of Allah.' When he says, 'Come to the prayer.' You say, 'There is no power and might except in Allah.' When he says, 'Come to the success,' you say, 'There is no power and might except in Allah.' When he says, 'God is great, God is great,' you say, 'God is great, God is great.' When he says, 'There is none worthy of worship except Allah,' you say, 'There is none worthy of worship except Allah.' Whoever says that sincerely from his heart will enter Paradise."[63]

When the caller says, "Come to the prayer", or "Come to the success", if one repeats what he says or says, "There is no power and might except in Allah," or if he says both of these statements, then he has acted correctly.

When the caller is done with the call to the prayer or the announcement of the commencing of the prayer while the listener responding, the listener should then say what is stated in the following two hadith: 'Abdullâh ibn 'Amr narrated that the heard the Prophet (ﷺ) say, "If you hear the caller to prayer, repeat similar to what he says and then state prayers for me, for whoever prays for me once will have Allah (ﷻ) bless him ten times. Then ask Allah to

---

[62] Recorded by Bukhari, Muslim, Abu Dawood, Tirmidhi, Ibn Mâjah and Nasâ'i.

[63] Recorded by Muslim.

grant me the position of *al-waseelah* as it is a rank in Paradise that is only becoming one of Allah's servants and I hope that it will be me. Whoever asks for me to have *al-waseelah* will be permitted (my) intercession."[64]

Jâbir (ﷺ) reported that the Messenger of Allah (ﷺ) said, "Whoever says upon hearing the call to prayer,

"اللَّهُمَّ رَبَّ هَذِهِ الدَّعْوَةِ التَّامَّةِ وَالصَّلاةِ الْقَائِمَةِ آتِ مُحَمَّدًا الْوَسِيلَةَ وَالْفَضِيلَةَ وَابْعَثْهُ مَقَامًا مَحْمُودًا الَّذِي وَعَدْتَهُ "

'O' Allah, Lord of this perfect call[65] and the prayer about to be performed, grant Muhammad *al-waseelah* and *al-faḍeelah*,[66] and resurrect him to the praiseworthy position that You had promised him,' will be granted my intercession on the Day of Resurrection."[67]

Note: It is recommended for a Muslim to supplicate often between the call to prayer and the announcement of the commencement of the prayer for the supplications at that time are responded to. Anas (ﷺ) said that the Messenger of Allah (ﷺ) said, "The supplication between the call to prayer and the announcement of the commencement of the prayer is not rejected."[68]

---

[64] This hadith is *ṣaḥeeḥ*. See Shaykh al-Albâni, *Mukhtasar Ṣaḥeeḥ Muslim*, no. 198. Recorded by Muslim, Abu Dawood, Tirmidhi and Nasâ'i.

[65] This is in reference to the call of *Tawḥeed* and the belief in the Prophet Muhammad (Blessings and peace be upon him). JZ

[66] [This is a position that is greater than the rest of creation or it could be considered a kind of description of the place of *al-waseelah*. Allah knows best.] - Translator

[67] This hadith is *ṣaḥeeḥ*. See Shaykh al-Albâni, *I'rwâ' al-Ghaleel*, no. 243. Recorded by Bukhari, Abu Dawood, Tirmidhi, Nasâ'i and Ibn Mâjah.

[68] This hadith is *ṣaḥeeḥ*. See Shaykh al-Albâni, *Ṣaḥeeḥ Sunan Abi Dawood*, no. 489. Recorded by Tirmidhi and Abu Dawood.

What is recommended for the one making the call to prayer [69]

It is recommended for the caller to prayer to fulfill the following:

1. He should desire the pleasure of Allah by his making the call

Thus, he should not accept any wages for his deed. 'Uthmân ibn al-'Âṣ once said to the Messenger of Allah (ﷺ), "O' Messenger of Allah, appoint me the Imam of my people." He responded, "You are their Imam and lead them according to the ability of the weakest among them. Appoint a caller to prayer who does not accept any wages for his making the call."[70]

2. He should be free of both the minor and major forms of spiritual impurity

This was discussed earlier while discussing for whom the ablution is recommended.

3. He should be standing, facing the *Qiblah* (the direction of Makkah)

Ibn al-Mundhir stated, "There is a consensus that standing while saying the call to prayer is a Sunnah for his voice can then reach a further distance. It is also from the Sunnah that he face the *qiblah* while making the call, as the callers of the Messenger of Allah (ﷺ) would make the call while facing the *qiblah*."

4. He should turn his head and neck to the right while saying, "Come to the prayer", and to the left while saying, "Come to the salvation"

Abu Juḥayfah narrated that he saw Bilâl making the call, adding, "I would watch his mouth move from here to there while

---

[69] Cf., as-Sayyid Sâbiq, *Fiqh as-Sunnah*, vol. 1, p. 99.

[70] This hadith is *ṣaḥeeḥ*. See Shaykh al-Albâni, *Ṣaḥeeḥ Sunan Abi Dawood*, no. 497. Recorded by Abu Dawood, Nasâ'i and Ibn Mâjah.

making the call."[71]

5. He should place his finger tips into his ears

Abu Juḥayfah said, "I saw Bilâl making the call and he would turn, his mouth would move from here to there, and (the tips of) his fingers were in his ears."[72]

6. He should raise his voice while making the call

The Prophet (ﷺ) said, "Everything within the sound of the caller, including the humans, jinn and anything else, will be a witness to it on the Day of Resurrection."[73]

What is the interval between the call to prayer and the announcement of the commencement of the prayer?

Between the call to prayer and the announcement of the commencement of the prayer there should be enough time for people to prepare for the came and to come to it as the call has been established for this purpose — otherwise the purpose would be lost. Ibn Baṭṭâl said, "There is no specified limit for that except for the beginning of the time and the gathering of the worshippers."[74]

---

[71] Recorded by Bukhari, Muslim, Abu Dawood, Tirmidhi and Nasâ'i. As for turning the chest to each side, there is no evidence for that in the Sunnah. None of the hadith about turning the neck mention the chest as well. This comment is from Shaykh al-Albâni, *Tamâm al-Minnah*, p. 150.

[72] This hadith is *ṣaḥeeḥ*. See Shaykh al-Albâni, *Ṣaḥeeḥ Sunan Tirmidhi*, no. 164. Recorded by Tirmidhi who said, "It is a *ḥasan* ṣaḥeeḥ hadith. The people of knowledge act based on this hadith: they prefer for the caller to put his fingertips into his ears while giving the call."

[73] This hadith is *ṣaḥeeḥ*. See Shaykh al-Albâni, *Ṣaḥeeḥ Sunan Nasâ'i*, no. 625. Recorded by Bukhari and Nasâ'i.

[74] Quoted by Ibn Ḥajar, *Fatḥ al-Bâri*, vol. 2, p. 106.

It is prohibited to leave the mosque after the call has been given

Abu Sha'thâ' said: "We were sitting in the mosque with Abu Hurayrah and the caller made the call to prayer. A man in the mosque stood and starting walking. Abu Hurayrah watched him until he left the mosque. Abu Hurayrah then said, 'That man has disobeyed Abu al-Qâsim [meaning the Prophet (ﷺ)].' "[75]

The call to prayer and the announcement of the commencement of the prayer for those who have missed the prayer time

If someone sleeps through the prayer or forgets a prayer, it is sanctioned for him to make the call to prayer and the announcement of the commencement. Abu Dawood recorded that on the occasion when the Prophet and his Companions slept through the time of the Morning prayer while they were travelling, the Prophet told Bilâl to give the call to prayer and the announcement of the commencement of the prayer.[76]

If a number of prayers have been missed, then only one call to prayer is made but a separate announcement of the commencing of the prayer is given for each prayer. This is based on the statement of Ibn Mas'ood who said, "The polytheists preoccupied the Messenger of Allah from four of the prayers during the Battle of the Trench, until whatever Allah had willed of the night had passed. He told Bilâl to make the call to prayer. Then he made the announcement of the

[75] This hadith is *ṣaḥeeḥ*. *Mukhtasar Ṣaḥeeḥ Muslim*, no. 249. Recorded by Muslim, Nasâ'i, Abu Dawood and Tirmidhi. Abu Dawood's and Tirmidhi's narration clarify that such as for the Afternoon prayer.

[76] This hadith is *ṣaḥeeḥ*. See Shaykh al-Albâni, *Ṣaḥeeḥ Sunan Abi Dawood*, no. 420. Recorded by Abu Dawood.

commencing of the prayer and he prayed the Noon prayer. Then he made the announcement again and the prayed the Afternoon prayer. Then he made the announcement again and he made the Sunset prayer. Then he made the announcement again and he prayed the Night prayer."[77]

The Conditions for the Soundness of the Prayer

The following conditions and prerequisites must be met for the prayer to be sound:

1. One must have knowledge that the time of the prayer has begun Allah (ﷻ) says:

﴿... إِنَّ ٱلصَّلَوٰةَ كَانَتْ عَلَى ٱلْمُؤْمِنِينَ كِتَٰبًا مَّوْقُوتًا ﴿١٠٣﴾﴾

(سورة النِّساء: ١٠٣)

﴾... Verily, the prayer is enjoined on the believers at fixed hours.﴿ *(Qur'an 4: 103)*

The prayer is not valid before its time begins nor after its time has ended, unless one has an excuse.

2. Being in a state of purity, free of the major and minor defilements Allah (ﷻ) says:

﴿يَٰٓأَيُّهَا ٱلَّذِينَ ءَامَنُوٓاْ إِذَا قُمْتُمْ إِلَى ٱلصَّلَوٰةِ فَٱغْسِلُواْ وُجُوهَكُمْ وَأَيْدِيَكُمْ

[77] This hadith is *ṣaḥeeḥ*. See Shaykh al-Albâni, *Ṣaḥeeḥ Sunan Nasâ'i*, no. 638. Recorded by Tirmidhi and Nasâ'i.

إِلَى ٱلْمَرَافِقِ وَٱمْسَحُوا۟ بِرُءُوسِكُمْ وَأَرْجُلَكُمْ إِلَى ٱلْكَعْبَيْنِ ۚ وَإِن كُنتُمْ جُنُبًا فَٱطَّهَّرُوا۟ ... ﴿٦﴾ (سورة المائدة: ٦)

﴾O' you who believe! When you intend to offer prayer, wash your faces and your forearms up to the elbows, rub [by passing wet hands over] your heads, and [wash] your feet up to ankles. If you are in a state of sexual defilement, purify yourself...﴿ *(Qur'an 5: 6)*

Furthermore, Ibn 'Umar narrated that the Prophet (ﷺ) said, "The prayer is not accepted without purification."[78]

3. Purity of the clothes, body and place in which one prays

Concerning the purity of the clothing, Allah (ﷻ) says:

﴿وَثِيَابَكَ فَطَهِّرْ ﴿٤﴾﴾ (سورة المدّثر: ٤)

﴾And your garments purify.﴿ *(Qur'an 74: 4)*

The Prophet (ﷺ) also said, "When one of you comes to the mosque, he should turn his sandals over and look at them. If he finds any filth on them, he should wipe them on the ground and then pray in them."[79]

Concerning the purification of the body, the Prophet (ﷺ) had said in response to 'Ali's question about *al-madhi*, "He should wash his private part and make ablution."[80]

---

[78] This hadith is *ṣaḥeeḥ*. See Shaykh al-Albâni, *Mukhtasar Ṣaḥeeḥ Muslim*, no. 104. Recorded by Muslim and Tirmidhi.

[79] This hadith is *ṣaḥeeḥ*. See Shaykh al-Albâni, *Ṣaḥeeḥ Sunan Abi Dawood*, no. 605. Recorded by Abu Dawood. [Translator's note: This is what the author has written but, in reality, the hadith with the above wording has been recorded by Aḥmad. Abu Dawood has the same meaning but different wording, simply saying to wipe the shoes but not saying to wipe the shoes on the ground.]

[80] Recorded by Bukhari and Muslim. This is Muslim's wording.

Furthermore, he said to the woman with a prolonged flow of blood, "Remove the blood from you and pray."[81]

As for the purification of the place in which one prays, the Prophet (ﷺ) had told his Companions when the Bedouin urinated in the mosque, "Pour over his urine a large bowl of water."[82]

Note: If someone prays and unknowingly he had some impurity on him or his clothing, the prayer is still valid and he does not repeat the prayer. If he discovers it during the prayer and he is able to, if it is for example on his shoes or a garment that is not covering his private parts, remove it while praying, he removes it and continues praying. If he is not able to remove it, he just continues praying and does not repeat his prayer. This is based on the hadith narrated by Abu Sa'eed in which the Prophet (ﷺ) was praying and he removed his sandals. Therefore, the people also removed their sandals. When he had finished and turned to the people, he asked them why they had removed their sandals. They replied, "We saw you remove yours, so we removed ours." Then he told them, "Gabriel came to me and informed me that they had some filth on them. When one of you comes to the mosque, he should turn his sandals over and look at them. If there is some filth on them, he should wipe them on the ground and then pray in them."[83]

4. Covering of the *'awrah* (that is, the parts of the body that are meant to be covered, as explained below)

Allah (ﷻ) says:

---

[81] Recorded by Bukhari, Muslim, Tirmidhi, Ibn Mâjah and Nasâ'i.

[82] This hadith is *ṣaḥeeḥ*. See Shaykh al-Albâni, *al-I'rwâ' al-Ghaleel*, no. 1710. Recorded by Bukhari and Nasâ'i. Abu Dawood and Tirmidhi have lengthier versions. [Translator's note: Perhaps it should be noted that the Prophet's mosque was not carpeted nor did it have a roof. Hence, he urinated on the dirt and ground.]

[83] Recorded by Abu Dawood.

﴿ يَٰبَنِيٓ ءَادَمَ خُذُواْ زِينَتَكُمۡ عِندَ كُلِّ مَسۡجِدٖ ... ﴿٣١﴾ ﴾ (سورة الأعراف: ٣١)

﴾O' Children of Adam, take your adornment [that is, wear your clothing] at every mosque...﴿ *(Qur'an 7: 31)*

The meaning is, "Cover your private parts", because the reference is to the fact that they used to circumambulate the Ka'bah in the nude. Additionally, the Prophet (ﷺ) said, "The prayer of an adult woman is not accepted unless she is wearing a headcovering."[84]

For the man, the *'awrah* is what is between the navel and the knees. It is stated in a hadith, narrated by 'Amr ibn Shu'ayb from his father on the authority of his grandfather, that the Prophet (ﷺ) said, "What is between the navel and the knee is *'awrah.*"[85] Jarhad al-Aslami said, "The Messenger of Allah (ﷺ) passed by me while I was wearing a cloak and my thigh became exposed. He said, 'Cover your thigh, for verily the thigh is *'awrah.*' "[86]

In the case of the woman, all of her in the prayer is *'awrah* save for the face and hands. The Prophet (ﷺ) said, "The woman is (all) *'awrah.*"[87] The Prophet (ﷺ) said as well, "The prayer of an adult woman is not accepted unless she is wearing a headcovering."[88]

---

[84] This hadith is *ṣaḥeeḥ*. See Shaykh al-Albâni, *Ṣaḥeeḥ Sunan Ibn Mâjah*, no. 534. Recorded by Abu Dawood, Tirmidhi and Ibn Mâjah.

[85] This hadith is *ḥasan*. See Shaykh al-Albâni, *I'rwâ' al-Ghaleel*, no. 271. Recorded by ad-Dâraquṭni, Aḥmad and Abu Dawood. [Actually, with this wording it was recorded only by ad-Dâraquṭni. Aḥmad and Abu Dawood only have similar meanings in their narration.] - Translator

[86] This hadith is *ṣaḥeeḥ* due to supporting evidence. See Shaykh al-Albâni, *I'rwâ' al-Ghaleel*, no. 269. Recorded by Tirmidhi and Abu Dawood. See Ibn al-Qayyim's important comments on this issue in *Tahdheeb as-Sunan*, vol. 6, p. 17.

[87] This hadith is *ṣaḥeeḥ*. See Shaykh al-Albâni, *Ṣaḥeeḥ al-Jâmi' aṣ-Ṣagheer*, no. 669. Recorded by Tirmidhi.

[88] This hadith is *ṣaḥeeḥ*. See Shaykh al-Albâni, *Ṣaḥeeḥ Sunan Ibn Mâjah*, no. 534. Recorded by Abu Dawood, Tirmidhi and Ibn Mâjah.

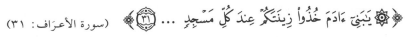

5. Facing the *Qiblah*

Allah has said:

﴿وَمِنْ حَيْثُ خَرَجْتَ فَوَلِّ وَجْهَكَ شَطْرَ ٱلْمَسْجِدِ ٱلْحَرَامِ ۚ وَحَيْثُ مَا كُنتُمْ فَوَلُّوا۟ وُجُوهَكُمْ شَطْرَهُۥ ... ﴿١٥٠﴾﴾ (سورة البَقَرَة: ١٥٠)

﴾And from wheresoever you start forth [for prayers], turn your face in the direction of *al-Masjid al-Ḥarâm* [at Makkah], and wheresoever you are, turn your faces towards it...﴿ *(Qur'an 2: 150)*

In addition, the Prophet (ﷺ) told the one who had not performed his prayer properly, "When you are going to prayer, complete the ablution and then face the *qiblah*..."[89]

It is permissible not to face the *qiblah* if one is in great fear or performing voluntary prayers while travelling and riding on a means of transportation. Allah has said:

﴿فَإِنْ خِفْتُمْ فَرِجَالًا أَوْ رُكْبَانًا ... ﴿٢٣٩﴾﴾ (سورة البَقَرَة: ٢٣٩)

﴾And if you fear [an enemy], perform prayer on foot or riding...﴿ *(Qur'an 2: 239)*

In 'Umar said (in relation to this verse), "Facing the *qiblah* or not facing it." Nâfi' commented, "I do not believe that Ibn 'Umar stated that except that it came from the Prophet (ﷺ)."[90] Ibn 'Umar also said, "The Prophet (ﷺ) used to pray while riding his animal in any direction it faced. He would also perform the *Witr* prayer on it. However, he would not perform the obligatory prayers upon it."[91]

---

[89] Recorded by Bukhari and Muslim.

[90] This hadith is *ṣaḥeeḥ*. Recorded by Mâlik and Bukhari.

[91] Recorded by Bukhari (without its complete chain) and Muslim.

Note: If someone tries to determine the direction of the *qiblah* and prays in the direction he thinks proper, discovering later that he was mistaken, he does not repeat his prayer. 'Âmir ibn Rabee'ah said, "We were with the Prophet (ﷺ) during a journey on a dark night. We could not know the direction of the *qiblah* so everyone prayed in his direction. In the morning we mentioned that to the Messenger of Allah (ﷺ) and then the following verse was revealed:

﴿... فَأَيْنَمَا تُوَلُّوا فَثَمَّ وَجْهُ اللَّهِ ... ﴿١١٥﴾﴾ (سورة البقرة: ١١٥)

﴿... So wherever you turn yourselves or your faces there is the Face of Allah...﴾ *(Qur'an 2: 115)*."[92]

6. Intention

This is where the person intends in his heart the specific prayer that he is about to pray, such as the obligatory Noon prayer or Afternoon prayer and so on. It is not sanctioned to actually state the intention, as the Prophet (ﷺ) never stated it. When the Prophet (ﷺ) would stand to pray, he would say, "*Allâhu Akbar* (God is Great)", and would not say anything beforehand. He would never state the intention. He would not say, for example, "I am praying for the sake of Allah, such and such prayer, while facing the *qiblah*, four *rak'ahs* as Imam or follower." Nor would he say, "In fulfilling the prayer on time or making the prayer up." All of those statements are innovations. None of them have ever been recording from him, not with a sound or a weak chain, an unbroken or broken chain. Nor has any of them been narrated by from any of his Companions or approved by any of the Followers or the four famous Imams.[93]

---

[92] This hadith is *ḥasan*. See Shaykh al-Albâni, *Ṣaḥeeḥ Sunan Ibn Mâjah*, no. 835. Recorded by Tirmidhi and Ibn Mâjah while al-Bayhaqi has something similar.

[93] Cf., Ibn al-Qayyim, *Zâd al-Ma'âd*, vol. 1, p. 51.

The Description of the Prayer[94]

When the Messenger of Allah (ﷺ) would stand for prayer, he would face the *qiblah*, standing close to the *sutrah*.[95] He used to say, "Verily, all actions are based on intention and for every person is what he intended."[96]

Then he would begin his prayer by saying, "*Allâhu Akbar*" and would raise his hands with this saying. Then he would put his right hand over his left above his chest. He would put his sight towards the ground. He would begin the prayer by reciting various supplications, praising and extolling Allah therein. Then he would seek refuge in Allah from the accursed Satan. Then he would recite, "In the name of Allah, the One Full of Mercy, the Ever Merciful," but he would not recite this aloud. Then he would recite *Soorah al-Fâtiḥah*, reciting each verse separately. When he reached the end of *Soorah al-Fâtiḥah*, he would say *Âmeen*. He would say that aloud and lengthen its pronunciation. Then he would recite another *Soorah* after *Soorah al-Fâtiḥah*, sometimes making a lengthy reading while other times a short one.

---

94 This is a summary of what Shaykh al-Albâni has mentioned in *Ṣifat aṣ-Ṣalâh an-Nabi*.

95 [The *sutrah* is a "barrier" between the one praying and any one who passes in front of him. It should be something at least the size of a camel saddle and the person should pray close to it, not leaving a big distance between him and his *sutrah*.] - Translator

96 [The way this is written in the original Arabic makes it seem like the Prophet (Blessings and peace of Allah be upon him) would say these words before the prayer. However, that could not possibly be its meaning and such is not what is stated in Shaykh al-Albâni's reference. Hence, the author means to emphasize that the intention must be in the heart at the beginning of the prayer. And Allah alone knows best.] - Translator

The Prophet (ﷺ) would recite the Qur'an audibly in the Morning prayer, the first two units (*rak'ahs*) of both the Sunset and the Night prayers. He would recite it silently in the Noon and the Afternoon prayers as well as in the last two units of the Sunset and Night prayers. He would also recite it audibly in the Friday prayer, the two *'Eid* prayers, the Prayer for Rain and the Eclipse prayers.

He would make the last two *rak'ahs* about half as short as the first two, the length of about fifteen verses or sometimes he would only recite *Soorah al-Fâtiḥah* in them.

When he would finish the entire reciting, he would pause a little, raise his hands, say the *takbeer* ("Allah is Great") and then bow. He would put his hands on his knees and separate his fingers. Sometimes he would put his hands on his knees as if he were grasping them. He would keep his arms away from his side and would stretch out his back and keep it straight, such that if one were to pour water on his back it would settle there.

He would be very calm and still in his bow. He used to say, "*Subḥanna Rabbiyal-'Adheem* (Exalted and Perfect is my Lord, the Great)", three times. Also while bowing, he would state a number of words of remembrance and supplications, sometimes one and sometimes another. He also prohibited the reciting of the Qur'an while bowing or prostrating.

Then he would raise his back from the bowing position and saying, "*Sami'-Allâhu liman ḥamidah* (Allah has heard him who praises Him)". He would also raise his hands while moving to stand straight. While standing, he would say, "*Rabbanâ wa lakal-ḥamd* (Our Lord and to You is the praise)". Sometimes he would say more than simply that. Then he would say the *takbeer* and go down to prostrate. He would put his hands on the ground before his knees. He would lean on his hands and spread them out. He would bring his fingers together and direct them towards the *qiblah*. He would place them parallel to his shoulders or, sometimes, parallel to his ears. He would firmly place his nose and forehead on the ground. He used to say, "I have been ordered to prostrate on seven bones: the forehead — and he pointed to his nose (as well) —, the two hands, the two knees and the ends (toes) of the two feet." He also said, "There is no prayer for the one whose nose does not touch the ground in the manner that the forehead does." He would remain calm and still in the prostration. He would say, "*Subḥanna Rabbiyal-'Adheem* (Exalted and Perfect is my Lord, the Great)", three times. He would also recite a number of words of remembrance and supplications in this position, varying the different supplications that he would make. He stated that one should exert himself in making numerous supplications in this position. Then he would raise his head while pronouncing the *takbeer*. Then he would spread out his left leg and sit on it, resting his bones and being still. His right leg would remain erect on the foot, with the toes pointing toward the *qiblah*. At this juncture, he would say, "O' Allah, forgive me, have mercy on me, strengthen me, raise me (in rank), guide me, pardon me and provide for me." Then he would state the *takbeer* and make a second prostration like the first one. Then he would raise his head while making the *takbeer* and sit straight on his left leg, until all his bones returned to the sitting position, and then he would get up, pushing up off the ground. In the second *rak'ah* he would do the same that he did in the first but he would make this *rak'ah* shorter than the previous one.

At the send of the second *rak'ah*, he would sit for the saying of the *tashahhud*. If it were a two-*rak'ah* prayer, he would sit on his left leg like he did so in between the two prostrations. He would sit similarly in the first *tashahhud* of the three and four-*rak'ah* prayers. While sitting for the *tashahhud*, he would put his right hand on his right thigh and his left hand on his left thigh. He would spread out his left hand and make a fist with his right, pointing with his right index finger and fixing his gaze upon it. When he raised his finger, he would move it while supplicating. He would say, "It is stronger than iron against Satan," meaning the index finger.

He would recite after each two *rak'ahs*, the *tahiyyat*[97] and the Prophet (ﷺ) would also state the prayers upon himself in the first *tashahhud* as well as later, and he established that for his Nation as well. The Prophet (ﷺ) used to make various different types of supplications during his prayer.

Then he would make the salutations to his right, saying, "Peace be upon you and the mercy of Allah," and to his left as well. Occasionally, during the first greeting he would add, "and His blessings" at the end of the phrase.

The Necessary Components of the Prayer

The prayer is composed of obligatory and necessary components that combined together make up its true form. If any of these obligatory aspects are not performed, its true form is not met and it is not considered the prayer from a Shari'ah perspective. The necessary components of the prayer are the following:

1. The opening *Takbeer*

'Ali ibn Abi Ṭâlib (رضي الله عنه) narrated that the Prophet (ﷺ) said, "The key to the prayer is the purification. The act that puts on into the inviolable state (of prayer) is the *takbeer*. And the act that ends the inviolable state is the salutation."[98] Abu Hurayrah also reported that

---

[97] [This is the portion beginning with *at-tahiyyâtu li-llâh*.]

[98] This hadith is *ḥasan* ṣaḥeeḥ. See Shaykh al-Albâni, *Ṣaḥeeḥ Ibn Mâjah*, no. 222. Recorded by Tirmidhi, Abu Dawood and Ibn Mâjah.

the Prophet (ﷺ) said to the one who did not perform his prayer properly, "When you stand to perform the prayer, state the *takbeer*."[99]

2. The act of standing in the obligatory prayers for the one who has the ability to do so

Allah (ﷻ) says:

﴿... وَقُومُوا لِلَّهِ قَانِتِينَ ﴿٢٣٨﴾﴾ (سورة البَقـرَة: ٢٣٨)

﴿... And stand before Allah with obedience.﴾ *(Qur'an 2: 238)*

The Prophet (ﷺ) used to pray standing and he ordered 'Imrân ibn Ḥuṣayn to do so. He told him, "Pray standing. If you are not able to do so, then sitting. And if you are not able to do that, then on your side."[100]

3. Reciting *Soorah al-Fâtiḥah* in every *rak'ah*

'Ubâdah ibn aṣ-Ṣâmit (رضي الله عنه) narrated that the Messenger of Allah (ﷺ) said, "There is no prayer for the one who did not read the Opening of the Book (that is, *Soorah al-Fâtiḥah*)."[101] The Prophet also ordered the one who did not perform his prayer properly to recite and then said at the end, "And do such throughout your entire prayer."[102]

4. and 5. The act of bowing and having calmness and stillness while bowing

Allah (ﷻ) says:

---

[99] Recorded by Bukhari and Muslim.

[100] This hadith is *ṣaḥeeḥ*. See Shaykh al-Albâni, *Ṣaḥeeḥ al-Jâmi' aṣ-Ṣagheer*, no. 3778. Recorded by Bukhari, Abu Dawood and Tirmidhi.

[101] Recorded by Bukhari, Muslim, Tirmidhi, Nasâ'i, Ibn Mâjah & Abu Dawood. Abu Dawood alone has the additional words, "and then some other portion."

[102] Recorded by Bukhari and Muslim.

﴿يَـٰٓأَيُّهَا ٱلَّذِينَ ءَامَنُوا۟ ٱرْكَعُوا۟ وَٱسْجُدُوا۟ ... ﴿٧٧﴾﴾ (سورة الحج: ٧٧)

﴿O' you who believe! Bow down, and prostrate yourselves...﴾ *(Qur'an 22: 77)*

Furthermore, the Prophet (ﷺ) told the one who had not prayed properly, "Then bow until you are calm and still while bowing."[103]

6. and 7. Standing up straight after bowing and having calmness and stillness while standing

Abu Mas'ood al-Anṣâri narrated that the Messenger of Allah (ﷺ) said, "The prayer of a person does not count unless he makes his back straight in the bowing and prostration."[104] The Prophet (ﷺ) also told the one who did not perform his prayer properly, "Then arise (from the bowing position) until you are standing straight."[105]

8. and 9. The act of prostrating and having calmness and stillness while prostrating

The Prophet (ﷺ) told the man who did not perform his prayer properly, "Then prostrate until you are still and calm while prostrating. Then rise up until you are sitting, still and calm. And then prostrate until you are still and calm while prostrating."[106]

The limbs that one is supposed to prostrate on are described in the following hadith: Ibn 'Abbâs narrated that the Prophet (ﷺ) said, "I have been ordered to prostrate on seven bones: the forehead — and he pointed to his nose (as well) —, the two hands, the two knees and the ends (toes) of the two feet."[107] He also said, "There is no prayer

---

[103] Recorded by Bukhari and Muslim.

[104] This hadith is *ṣaḥeeḥ*. See Shaykh al-Albâni, *Ṣaḥeeḥ Ibn Mâjah*, no. 710. Recorded by Nasâ'i, Tirmidhi, Abu Dawood and Ibn Mâjah.

[105] Recorded by Bukhari and Muslim.

[106] Ibid.

[107] Recorded by Bukhari, Muslim and Nasâ'i.

for the one whose nose does not touch the ground in the manner that the forehead does."[108]

10. and 11. The act of sitting between the two prostrations and having calmness and stillness during said sitting

The Prophet (ﷺ) said, "The prayer of a person does not count unless he makes his back straight in the bowing and prostration."[109] Furthermore, the Prophet (ﷺ) ordered the one who did not pray properly to do this, as was mentioned above under the obligation of the prostration.

12. The final *Tashahhud*

Ibn Mas'ood said, "Before it was made obligatory to say the *tashahhud*, we used to say, 'Peace be upon Allah, peace be upon Gabriel and Michael.' Then the Messenger of Allah (ﷺ) said, 'Do not say that but say, 'All compliments are to Allah...''"[110]

Note: The most authentic narration concerning the wording of the *tashahhud* is that narrated by Ibn Mas'ood who said: "The Messenger of Allah (ﷺ) taught me the *tashahhud*, while my two hands were between his, like he would teach me a chapter of the Qur'an. (The wording was,)

التَّحِيَّاتُ لِلَّهِ وَالصَّلَوَاتُ وَالطَّيِّبَاتُ السَّلامُ عَلَيْكَ أَيُّهَا النَّبِيُّ وَرَحْمَةُ اللَّهِ وَبَرَكَاتُهُ السَّلامُ عَلَيْنَا وَعَلَى عِبَادِ اللَّهِ الصَّالِحِينَ أَشْهَدُ أَنْ لا إِلَهَ إِلاَّ اللَّهُ وَأَشْهَدُ أَنَّ مُحَمَّدًا عَبْدُهُ وَرَسُولُهُ

---

[108] This hadith is *ṣaḥeeḥ*. Recorded by ad-Dâraquṭni. Shaykh al-Albâni has mentioned it in *Ṣifat aṣ-Ṣalâh*, p. 123.

[109] This hadith is *ṣaḥeeḥ*. See Shaykh al-Albâni, *Ṣaheeḥ Ibn Mâjah*, no. 710. Recorded by Nasâ'i, Tirmidhi, Abu Dawood and Ibn Mâjah.

[110] This hadith is *ṣaḥeeḥ*. See Shaykh al-Albâni, *I'rwâ' al-Ghaleel*, no. 319. Recorded by Nasâ'i, ad-Dâraquṭni and al-Bayhaqi.

'All compliments, prayers and pure words are due Allah. Peace be upon you, O' Prophet, and the mercy of Allah and His blessings. Peace be upon us and upon the righteous servants of Allah. I bear witness that none is worthy of worship except Allah and I bear witness that Muhammad is His servant and messenger.' "[111]

A Second Note: As for the statement, "Peace be upon you, O' Prophet, and the mercy of Allah and His blessings," Ibn Ḥajar wrote,

> "In some of the chains of this hadith of Ibn Mas'ood there is an indication that these words are changed as during his time they were said in the second person while after his death they are said in the third person. In the Book of Asking Permission in *Ṣaḥeeḥ al-Bukhari* from the chain of Abu Ma'mar from Ibn Mas'ood, after narrating the hadith of the *tashahhud*, Ibn Mas'ood says, 'That was while he was among us. After he died, we would say, 'Peace...,' meaning upon the Prophet.' This is how it is found in Bukhari. Abu 'Awânah in his *Ṣaḥeeh*, as-Sirâj, al-Jawziqi, Abu Na'eem al-Aṣbahâni and al-Bayhaqi record through numerous chains back to Abu Na'eem, the teacher of Bukhari, the wording, 'After he died, we would say, 'Peace be upon the Prophet', that is, without saying, 'meaning...'.' In this manner, Abu Bakr ibn Abi Shaybah also narrated it from Abu Na'eem.
>
> As-Subki stated in his commentary to *Sharḥ al-Minhâj*, after mentioning just the narration of Abu 'Awânah, 'If that is authentic from the Companions, it indicates that addressing him in the salutation after the (death of) the Prophet is not obligatory. Instead, one says, 'Peace be upon the Prophet'.' I (Ibn Ḥajar) add: It is definitely authentic. I have found strong corroborating evidence for it. 'Abdur-Razzâq said: Ibn Jurayj narrated to us saying: 'Aṭâ' informed me that the Companions used to say while

[111] Recorded by Bukhari and Muslim.

the Prophet (ﷺ) was alive, 'Peace be upon you, O' Prophet', and when he died, they would say, 'Peace be upon the Prophet'. And that chain is sound."[112]

Shaykh al-Albâni said in *Ṣifat aṣ-Ṣalâh*, "That must have been learned from the Prophet (ﷺ). It is supported by the fact that when 'Â'ishah (رضي الله عنها) would teach the *tashahhud*, she would say, 'Peace be upon the Prophet'. This has been recorded by as-Sirâj in his *Musnad* and al-Mukhliṣ in *al-Fawâ'id*, with two authentic chains from her."[113]

13. Saying prayers for the Prophet (ﷺ) after the final *Tashahhud*

Faḍâlah ibn 'Ubayd al-Anṣâri narrated that the Messenger of Allah (ﷺ) saw a man praying. (During the final sitting,) that man did not praise or glorify Allah nor did he state prayers for the Prophet (ﷺ) and then he went away. The Prophet (ﷺ) said, "He has been hasty." Then he called for him and said to him and to another, "When one of you prays, he should begin by praising his Lord and exalting Him, then he should say prayers for the Prophet (ﷺ) and then he can supplicate whatever he wishes."[114]

Ibn Mas'ood said, "A man came until he sat in front of the Messenger of Allah (ﷺ) while were with him. The man said, 'O' Messenger of Allah, as for invoking peace upon you, that we know, but how are we to say prayers for you when you pray for you in the prayers?' The Prophet (ﷺ) remained silent until we wished that the man had not asked him. Then he said, 'If you are praying, say, 'O' Allah, bestow blessings upon Muhammad, the illiterate Prophet, and

---

[112] Ibn Ḥajar, *Fatḥ al-Bâri,* vol. 2, p. 314.

[113] Shaykh al-Albâni, *Ṣifah aṣ-Ṣalât*, p. 126.

[114] The chain of this report is *ṣaḥeeḥ*. See Shaykh al-Albâni, *Ṣifat aṣ-Ṣalâh* (Maktabah al-Mârif edition), p. 182. Recorded by Tirmidhi and Abu Dawood.

upon the family of Muhammad...' ' "[115]

Note: The best manner of praying for the Prophet (ﷺ) is what has been reported by K'ab ibn 'Ujrah who said: "We said, 'O' Messenger of Allah, we know how to invoke peace for you but how shall we pray for you?' He replied,

اللَّهُمَّ صَلِّ عَلَى مُحَمَّدٍ وَعَلَى آلِ مُحَمَّدٍ كَمَا صَلَّيْتَ عَلَى آلِ إِبْرَاهِيمَ إِنَّكَ حَمِيدٌ مَجِيدٌ اللَّهُمَّ بَارِكْ عَلَى مُحَمَّدٍ وَعَلَى آلِ مُحَمَّدٍ كَمَا بَارَكْتَ عَلَى آلِ إِبْرَاهِيمَ إِنَّكَ حَمِيدٌ مَجِيدٌ

'Say, O' Allah send prayers upon Muhammad and on the family of Muhammad as you sent prayers upon the family of Abraham, for You are Worthy of Praise, Full of Glory. O' Allah, pour blessings upon Muhammad and upon the family of Muhammad as you poured blessings upon the family of Abraham, for You are Worthy of Praise, Full of Glory.' "[116]

14. The salutations

The Prophet (ﷺ) said, "The key to the prayer is the purification. The act that puts on into the inviolable state (of prayer) is the *takbeer*. And the act that ends the inviolable state is the salutation."[117]

---

[115] The chain of this report is *ḥasan*. See *Ṣaḥeeḥ Ibn Khuzaymah*, vol. 1, Pp. 252, 351 and 711.

[Actually, Bukhari has virtually the same report but the wording of the prayer is slightly different, not having the words, "the illiterate Prophet," for example.] - Translator

[116] Recorded by Bukhari, Muslim, Abu Dawood, Tirmidhi, Ibn Mâjah and Nasâ'i.

[117] This hadith is *ḥasan* ṣaḥeeḥ. See Shaykh al-Albâni, *Ṣaḥeeḥ Ibn Mâjah*, no. 222. Recorded by Tirmidhi, Abu Dawood and Ibn Mâjah.

The Obligatory Acts of the Prayer

1. The saying of the *takbeer* for the movements in the prayers and the saying of, "Allah hears him who praises Him. Our Lord, for You is the praise"

Abu Hurayrah (رضي الله عنه) said, "When the Prophet (ﷺ) would go to pray, he would say the *takbeer* when he stood, say the *takbeer* when he bowed, then he would say, 'Allah hears him who praises Him,' when he raised his back from the bowing. Then he would say while standing, 'Our Lord, for You is the praise.' Then he would state the *takbeer* upon going down (to prostrate). Then he would state the *takbeer* upon raising his head (from the prostration) and then state the *takbeer* upon prostrating. He would again state the *takbeer* when raising his head (from the prostration). He would do that during the entire prayer until he finished. He would also state the *takbeer* when standing from the sitting after the (first two) *rak'ahs*."[118] The Prophet has also said, "Pray in the manner that you have seen me praying."[119]

The Prophet (Blessings and peace of Allah be upon him) ordered the one who had not performed the prayer properly to pray in that manner. The Prophet (ﷺ) said, "No one completes the prayer until he washes the places of ablution and then says the *takbeer* and praises and extols Allah. He should also recite what he wishes of the Qur'an and then say the *takbeer*. Then he bows until his bones come to rest and then he says, 'Allah hears him who praises Him,' until his back is straight. Then he says the *takbeer* and then he prostrates until his bones come to rest... Then he raises his head and says the *takbeer*.

---

[118] Recorded by Bukhari, Muslim and Nasâ'i.
[119] This hadith is *ṣaḥeeḥ*. See Shaykh al-Albâni, *I'rwâ' al-Ghaleel*, no. 262. Recorded by Bukhari.

If he does that, he has completed his prayer."[120]

2. The first *Tashahhud*

Ibn Mas'ood narrated that the Prophet Muhammad (ﷺ) said, "When you sit after every two *rak'ah*, say, 'All compliments, prayers and pure words are due Allah. Peace be upon you, O' Prophet, and the mercy of Allah and His blessings. Peace be upon us and upon the righteous servants of Allah. I bear witness that none is worthy of worship except Allah and I bear witness that Muhammad is His servant and messenger.' Then he may choose whatever supplication he likes and supplicate to his Lord with it."[121]

The Prophet (ﷺ) also told the one who had not performed the prayer properly, "When you sit in the middle of the prayer, come to rest, sit upon your left thigh and then say the *tashahhud*."[122]

3. It is obligatory upon the person when he prays to put a *sutrah* (barrier) in front of him that prevents people from passing by in front of him and he should not look beyond the *sutrah*

Sahl ibn Abi Ḥathmah narrated that the Messenger of Allah (ﷺ) said, "When you pray, you should pray toward a *sutrah* and come close to it, and not allow the Devil to cut off his prayer."[123] Ibn 'Umar also narrated that the Messenger of Allah (ﷺ) said, "Do not pray except towards a *sutrah*, and do not let anyone pass in front of

---

[120] This hadith is *ṣaḥeeḥ*. See Shaykh al-Albâni, *Ṣaḥeeḥ Sunan Abi Dawood*, no. 763. Recorded by Abu Dawood.

[121] This hadith is *ṣaḥeeḥ*. See Shaykh al-Albâni, *I'rwâ' al-Ghaleel*, no. 336. Recorded by Nasâ'i.

[122] This hadith is *ṣaḥeeḥ*. See Shaykh al-Albâni, *Ṣaḥeeḥ Sunan Abi Dawood*, no. 766. Recorded by Abu Dawood.

[123] This hadith is *ṣaḥeeḥ*. See Shaykh al-Albâni, *Ṣaḥeeḥ Sunan Nasâ'i*, no. 722. Recorded by al-Ḥâkim (and this is his wording) and by Abu Dawood and Nasâ'i, with the wording, "When one of you prays towards a *sutrah*".

you. But if someone refuses but to try to pass in front of you, you should fight him for he has a devil with him."[124]

The requirement of the *sutrah* may be fulfilled by a wall, a pillar, a camel stirrup or a saddle that is place in the direction of the prayer. The minimum that is sufficient is the wooden portion of a camel saddle that the rider leans on. This is based on the hadith of Moosa ibn Ṭalḥah from his father who narrated that the Messenger of Allah (ﷺ) said, "If you place in front of you something like the wooden portion at the back of a camel saddle and you pray toward it, then nothing that passes beyond it will be of any concern."[125]

The worshipper being close to the sutrah

Bilâl narrated that the Prophet (ﷺ) would pray and the distance between him and the wall would be about three forearms length.[126] Sahl ibn S'ad said, "The distance between the place of prayer of the Messenger of Allah and the wall would be sufficient for a sheep to pass."[127]

When the person is praying towards a *sutrah*, he must not allow anything to pass between him and his *sutrah*. Ibn 'Abbâs said, "The Prophet (ﷺ) was once praying and a sheep started to pass in front of him, so he rushed toward the *qiblah* and pressed its belly against the wall (so that it would pass on the other side)."[128] Abu

---

[124] This hadith is *ṣaḥeeḥ*. See Shaykh al-Albâni, *Ṣifat aṣ-Ṣalâh*, p. 72. Recorded by Ibn Khuzaymah.

[125] This hadith is *ṣaḥeeḥ*. See Shaykh al-Albâni, *Mukhtasar Ṣaḥeeḥ Muslim*, no. 339. Recorded by Muslim, Tirmidhi and Abu Dawood.

[126] This hadith is *ṣaḥeeḥ*. See Shaykh al-Albâni, *Ṣifat aṣ-Ṣalâh*, p. 62. Recorded by Bukhari.

[127] Recorded by Bukhari, Muslim and Abu Dawood.

[128] This hadith is *ṣaḥeeḥ*. See Shaykh al-Albâni, *Ṣifat aṣ-Ṣalâh*, p. 64. Recorded by Ibn Khuzaymah.

Sa'eed al-Khudri narrated that the Messenger of Allah (ﷺ) said, "When one of you is praying, he should not allow anyone to pass in front of him and he should prevent him to the best of his ability. If he refuses (but to pass), he should fight him for he is a devil."[129]

If the person does not have a *sutrah*, then his prayer is cut off by a donkey, woman or black dog. 'Abdullâh ibn aṣ-Ṣâmit narrated from Abu Dharr that the Prophet (ﷺ) said, "If one of you stands to prayer, then if he has like the back of a saddle in front of him, that will act like a barrier. If he has nothing like the back of a saddle in front of him, then his prayer is cut off by a donkey, a woman and a black dog." 'Abdullâh said, "O' Abu Dharr, what is the difference between a black dog from a reddish dog or a yellowish dog?" He replied, "O' son of my brother, I asked the Messenger of Allah (ﷺ) what you asked me and he said, "The black dog is a devil."[130]

It is forbidden to pass in front of one who is praying

Abu Juhaym narrated that the Messenger of Allah (ﷺ) said, "If the one who passes in front of the one who is praying knew what was upon him (of sin), it would be better for him to wait for forty than to pass in front of him."[131]

The sutrah of the Imam is the sutrah for the followers

Ibn 'Abbâs said, "I came riding on a female donkey, while I was on the threshold of puberty, and the Prophet (ﷺ) was leading the

---

[129] This hadith is *ṣaḥeeḥ*. See Shaykh al-Albâni, *Mukhtasar Ṣaḥeeḥ Muslim*, no. 338. Recorded by Muslim.

[130] This hadith is *ṣaḥeeḥ*. See Shaykh al-Albâni, *Ṣaḥeeḥ al-Jâmi' aṣ-Ṣagheer*, no. 719. Recorded by Muslim, Nasâ'i, Tirmidhi and Abu Dawood.

[131] Recorded by Bukhari, Muslim, Abu Dawood, Tirmidhi, Nasâ'i and Ibn Mâjah.

people in prayer at Mina. I passed in front of the row and got off the animal, leaving it free to graze. Then I entered the row and no one objected to what I had done."[132]

The Recommended Acts of the Prayer

The recommended or *sunan* acts of the prayer are of two types, statements and actions. As for the recommended statements, they are:

1. The opening supplication

The most virtuous form is that narrated by Abu Hurayrah (may Allah be pleased with him) who said, "When the Messenger of Allah (Blessings and peace be upon him) would make the opening *takbeer* and then he would remain silent before begin the reciting. I said, 'O' Messenger of Allah, for whom I would sacrifice my mother and father, I see that you are silent between the *takbeer* and the reciting. What do you say?' He said, 'I say: 'O' Allah, put a distance between me and my sins like the distance between the East and the West. O' Allah, cleanse me from my sins like a white garment is cleansed from filth. O' Allah, wash me of my sins by water, ice and snow.''"[133]

2. Seeking refuge in Allah

Allah (ﷻ) says:

﴿فَإِذَا قَرَأْتَ الْقُرْءَانَ فَاسْتَعِذْ بِاللَّهِ مِنَ الشَّيْطَانِ الرَّجِيمِ ﴿٩٨﴾﴾ (سورة النّحل: ٩٨)

﴿When you want to recite the Qur'an, seek refuge with Allah from

---

[132] Recorded by Muslim and Abu Dawood. Bukhari has also recorded it with the words, "And he was not praying towards a wall." This narration only negates the presence of a wall. It is known that it was the Prophet's custom not to pray in the open spaces except with a spear set in front of him (to act as a *sutra*).

[133] Recorded by Bukhari, Muslim, Ibn Mâjah and Abu Dawood.

Satan, the cursed one.﴿ *(Qur'an 16: 98)*

Abu Sa'eed al-Khudri narrated that when the Prophet would begin his prayer, he would start with the opening supplication and then he would say, "I seek refuge in Allah, the All-Hearing, the All-Knowing, from the accursed Satan, from his madness, his arrogance and his poetry."[134]

3. The saying of *Âmeen*

Wâ'il ibn Ḥujr said, "When the Messenger of Allah (ﷺ) would recite (at the end of *al-Fâtiḥah*), 'Nor (the path) of those who have gone astray,' he would then say, *Âmeen*, and raise his voice in doing so."[135] Abu Hurayrah (رضي الله عنه) narrated that the Messenger of Allah (ﷺ) said, "If the Imam says *Âmeen*, say *Âmeen*, for if one's *Âmeen* corresponds with the *Âmeen* of the angels, all of his previous sins will be forgiven."[136]

4. Reciting portions of the Qur'an
after reciting *Soorah al-Fâtiḥah*

Abu Qatâdah said: "The Prophet (ﷺ) would recite in the first two *rak'ahs* of the Noon prayer the Opening (*Soorah*) of the Book and two *Soorahs*. He would lengthen first and make the second shorter. Sometimes one could hear some of the verses. During the Afternoon prayer, hc would recite the Opening (*Soorah*) of the Book and two *Soorahs*. He used to make the first *rak'ah* of the Morning prayer long and make the second shorter."[137] He also stated, "The

---

[134] This hadith is *ṣaḥeeḥ*. See Shaykh al-Albâni, *I'rwâ' al-Ghaleel*, no. 342. Recorded by Abu Dawood and Tirmidhi.

[135] This hadith is *ṣaḥeeḥ*. See Shaykh al-Albâni, *Ṣifat aṣ-Ṣalâh*, p. 83. Recorded by Abu Dawood and Tirmidhi.

[136] Bukhari, Muslim, Nasâ'i, Abu Dawood, Tirmidhi and Ibn Mâjah.

[137] This hadith is *ṣaḥeeḥ*. See Shaykh al-Albâni, *Ṣaḥeeḥ Sunan Nasâ'i*, no. 932. Recorded by Bukhari.

Prophet (ﷺ) would, in the first two *rak'ahs* of the Noon and the Afternoon prayers, recite the Opening of the Book and a *Soorah*. We would hear a verse sometimes. Then in the last two *rak'ahs*, he would just recite the Opening (*Soorah*) of the Book."[138]

It is also Sunnah to sometimes recite portions of the Qur'an in the final two *rak'ahs* of the prayer. Abu Sa'eed said, "In each of the first two *rak'ahs* of the Noon prayer, the Prophet (ﷺ) would recite about thirty verses length. In the last two, he would recite about fifteen verses length — or he said: half of that. In each of the first two *rak'ahs* of the Afternoon prayer, he would recite about fifteen verses length and about half of that in the last two *rak'ahs*."[139]

The Sunnah is to make the recitation audible in the Morning Prayer as well as in the first two *rak'ahs* of the Sunset and *'Isha'* prayer, while one recites inaudibly in the Noon and Afternoon prayers, in the third *rak'ah* of the Sunset prayer as well as the last two *rak'ahs* in the Night prayer.

5. Saying the *Tasbeeḥ* (Exalting Allah)
in the bowing and prostration

Ḥudhayfah said, "I prayed with the Prophet and he used to say while bowing, '*Subḥanna Rabbiyal-'Adheem* (Exalted and perfect is my Lord, the Great)', and in his prostration, '*Subḥanna Rabbiyal-A'lâ* (Exalted and perfect is my Lord, the All-High)'."[140] 'Utbah ibn 'Âmir said, "The Prophet used to say three times while bowing, '*Subḥanna Rabbiyal-'Adheem wa bi-Ḥamdi* (Exalted and perfect is

---

[138] This hadith is *ṣaḥeeḥ*. See Shaykh al-Albâni, *Mukhtasar Ṣaheeḥ Muslim*, no. 286. Recorded by Muslim.

[139] This hadith is *ṣaḥeeḥ*. See Shaykh al-Albâni, *Mukhtasar Ṣaheeḥ Muslim*, no. 287. Recorded by Muslim.

[140] This hadith is *ṣaḥeeḥ*. See Shaykh al-Albâni, *Ṣaheeḥ Sunan Nasâ'i*, no. 1001. Recorded by Nasâ'i, Abu Dawood and Tirmidhi.

my Lord, the Great and He is Praised)', and in his prostration he would say three times, '*Subḥanna Rabbiyal-A'lâ wa bi-Ḥamdihi* (Exalted and perfect is my Lord, the All-High and He is Praised)'."[141]

6. Upon standing up from bowing

Upon standing up from bowing, in addition to saying, "Our Lord and to You is the Praise", one also adds,

مِلْءُ السَّمَاوَاتِ وَمِلْءُ الأَرْضِ وَمَا بَيْنَهُمَا وَمِلْءُ مَا شِئْتَ مِنْ شَيْءٍ بَعْدُ

"Filling the heavens and filling the earth and what is between them, and filling what You will in addition."[142] If one wishes, he may just say that portion. Otherwise, he may also wish to complete it by the following words:

أَهْلَ الثَّنَاءِ وَالْمَجْدِ أَحَقُّ مَا قَالَ الْعَبْدُ وَكُلُّنَا لَكَ عَبْدٌ اللَّهُمَّ لا مَانِعَ لِمَا أَعْطَيْتَ وَلا مُعْطِيَ لِمَا مَنَعْتَ وَلا يَنْفَعُ ذَا الْجَدِّ مِنْكَ الْجَدُّ

"Possessor of Praise and Majesty. The truest thing a servant can say, and we are all servants to you. O' Allah, no one can withhold what You grant and no one can give what You withhold. And one's possessions cannot benefit him in front of You."[143]

رَبَّنَا وَلَكَ الْحَمْدُ حَمْدًا كَثِيرًا طَيِّبًا مُبَارَكًا فِيهِ مُبَارَكًا عَلَيْهِ كَمَا يُحِبُّ رَبُّنَا وَيَرْضَى

"Our Lord and to You is the Praise, much pure praised, blessed in

---

[141] This hadith is *ṣaḥeeḥ*. See Shaykh al-Albâni, *Ṣifat aṣ-Ṣalâh*, p. 127. Recorded by Abu Dawood and al-Bayhaqi.

[142] This hadith is *ṣaḥeeḥ*. See Shaykh al-Albâni, *Mukhtasar Ṣaḥeeḥ Muslim*, no. 296. Recorded by Muslim, Abu Dawood and Nasâ'i.

[143] This hadith is *ṣaḥeeḥ*. See Shaykh al-Albâni, *Mukhtasar Ṣaḥeeḥ Muslim*, no. 296. Recorded by Muslim, Abu Dawood and Nasâ'i.

Himself, blessed upon them, as our Lord loves and is pleased with."[144]

7. Supplications between the two prostrations

Ḥudhayfah said, "The Prophet (ﷺ) used to say between the two prostrations,

رَبِّ اغْفِرْ لِي رَبِّ اغْفِرْ لِي

"My Lord, forgive me. My Lord, forgive me."[145] And Ibn 'Abbâs narrated that the Prophet (ﷺ) used to say between the two prostrations:

اللَّهُمَّ اغْفِرْ لِي وَارْحَمْنِي وَاجْبُرْنِي وَاهْدِنِي وَارْزُقْنِي

"O' Allah, forgive me, have mercy on me, strengthen me, guide me and provide for me."[146]

8. Making prayer for the Prophet (ﷺ) during the first *Tashahhud* as the Prophet did so

'Â'ishah (رضي الله عنها) said, "We used to prepare for the Messenger of Allah (ﷺ) his toothstick and water for purification. Allah would wake him during the night for as much as He willed. He would use the toothstick and make ablution. Then he would pray nine *rak'ahs* and he would not sit during any of them except the eight one. He would supplicate to his Lord and invoke prayers upon His Prophet.

---

[144] This hadith is *ṣaḥeeḥ*. See Shaykh al-Albâni, *Ṣifat aṣ-Ṣalâh*, p. 119.

[145] This hadith is *ṣaḥeeḥ*. See Shaykh al-Albâni, *Sunan Ibn Mâjah*, no. 731. Recorded by Ibn Mâjah.

[146] This hadith is *ṣaḥeeḥ*. See Shaykh al-Albâni, *Sunan Ibn Mâjah*, no. 732. Recorded by Tirmidhi, Abu Dawood and Ibn Mâjah.

Note: Abu Dawood records, "Pardon me," instead of "Strengthen me." Ibn Mâjah records, "Exalt my rank," instead of "Guide me." It is recommended to combine them all together and to add, "Pardon me and exalt my rank."

Then he would rise and not make the salutation. Then he would pray the ninth *rak'ah*, sit and then praise his Lord, pray for His prophet, supplicate and then make the salutations..."[147]

9. Supplicating after the first and the second *Tashahhud*:

As for supplicating after the first *tashahhud*, Ibn Mas'ood narrated that the Prophet Muhammad (ﷺ) said, "When you sit after every two *rak'ah*, say,

التَّحِيَّاتُ لِلَّهِ وَالصَّلَوَاتُ وَالطَّيِّبَاتُ السَّلامُ عَلَيْكَ أَيُّهَا النَّبِيُّ وَرَحْمَةُ اللَّهِ وَبَرَكَاتُهُ السَّلامُ عَلَيْنَا وَعَلَى عِبَادِ اللَّهِ الصَّالِحِينَ أَشْهَدُ أَنْ لا إِلَهَ إِلاَّ اللَّهُ وَأَشْهَدُ أَنَّ مُحَمَّدًا عَبْدُهُ وَرَسُولُهُ

'All compliments, prayers and pure words are due Allah. Peace be upon you, O' Prophet, and the mercy of Allah and His blessings. Peace be upon us and upon the righteous servants of Allah. I bear witness that none is worthy of worship except Allah and I bear witness that Muhammad is His servant and messenger.' Then he may choose whatever supplication he likes and supplicate to his Lord with it."[148]

As for supplicating after the second *tashahhud*, Abu Hurayrah narrated that the Messenger of Allah (ﷺ) said, "When you are finished with the final *tashahhud*, you should seek refuge in Allah from four matters:

مِنْ عَذَابِ جَهَنَّمَ وَمِنْ عَذَابِ الْقَبْرِ وَمِنْ فِتْنَةِ الْمَحْيَا وَالْمَمَاتِ وَمِنْ شَرِّ الْمَسِيحِ الدَّجَّالِ

---

[147] This hadith is *ṣaḥeeḥ*. See Shaykh al-Albâni, *Mukhtasar Ṣaḥeeḥ Muslim*, no. 390. Recorded by Muslim.

[148] This hadith is *ṣaḥeeḥ*. See Shaykh al-Albâni, *I'rwâ' al-Ghaleel*, no. 336. Recorded by Nasâ'i.

'From the punishment in Hell, the punishment in the grave, the trials of life and death and from the evils of the False Messiah'."[149]

10. The second salutation

The Prophet (ﷺ) used to make two salutations. Ibn Mas'ood said, "The Prophet used to make the salutations to the right and to the left, (saying,) 'Peace be upon you and the mercy of Allah', and 'Peace be upon you and the mercy of Allah', (turning in such a way) that the whiteness of his cheeks could be seen."[150] Sometimes he would make just one salutation. 'Â'ishah (رضي الله عنها) said, "The Prophet (ﷺ) would make one salutation in the prayer, towards the front with his head slightly tilted to the right."[151]

In addition to the recommended statements, there are also the following recommended acts in the prayer:

1. Raising one's hands when saying the opening *takbeer*, when bowing and rising from the bowing and when standing from the *tashahhud*

Ibn 'Umar said, "The Messenger of Allah (ﷺ) used to raise his hands parallel his shoulders when he begin the prayer, when he made the *takbeer* to start his bow, when raising his head from bowing as well."[152]

Nâfi' said, "When Ibn 'Umar would begin his prayer, he would say

---

[149] This hadith is *ṣaḥeeḥ*. See Shaykh al-Albâni, *Mukhtasar Ṣaḥeeḥ Muslim*, no. 306 and *Ṣaḥeeḥ Sunan Ibn Mâjah*, no. 741. Recorded by Muslim and Ibn Mâjah.

[150] This hadith is *ṣaḥeeḥ*. See Shaykh al-Albâni, *Ṣaḥeeḥ Sunan Abi Dawood*, no. 878. Recorded by Abu Dawood, Nasâ'i, Ibn Mâjah and also by Tirmidhi but without the last portion.

[151] This hadith is *ṣaḥeeḥ*. See Shaykh al-Albâni, *Sunan Tirmidhi*, no. 242. Recorded by Tirmidhi.

[152] Recorded by Bukhari, Muslim, Tirmidhi and Nasâ'i.

the *takbeer* and raise his hands. When he went to bow, he would raise his hands. When he said, 'Allah hears him who praises Him', he would raise his hands. When he stood after two *rak'ahs*, he would raise his hands. And he attributed all of those acts to the Prophet of Allah (ﷺ)."[153]

It is also Sunnah to sometimes raise them at every movement, whether going down or coming up. This is based on the hadith of Mâlik ibn al-Ḥuwayrith who said that he saw the Prophet (ﷺ) raise his hands in the prayer when he bowed, when he raised his head from bowing, when he prostrated and when he raised his head from prostration. He would raise them parallel to the end of his ears.[154]

2. Putting the right hand over the left upon the chest

Sahl ibn S'ad said, "The people were ordered to place the right hand on the left forearm while praying." Abu Ḥâzim said, "I knew that Sahl had attributed this (precept) to the Prophet (ﷺ)."[155] Wâ'il ibn Ḥujr said, "I prayed with the Messenger of Allah (ﷺ) and he put his right hand over his left hand upon his chest."[156]

3. Looking at the place of prostration

'Â'ishah (رضي الله عنها) said, "When the Messenger of Allah (ﷺ) entered the Ka'bah, his sight did not leave the place of his prostration until he exited from it."[157]

---

[153] This hadith is *ṣaḥeeḥ*. See Shaykh al-Albâni, *Ṣaḥeeḥ Sunan Abi Dawood*, no. 663. Recorded by Bukhari and Abu Dawood.

[154] This hadith is *ṣaḥeeḥ*. See Shaykh al-Albâni, *Ṣaḥeeḥ Sunan Nasâ'i*, no. 1040. Recorded by Nasâ'i and Aḥmad.

[155] This hadith is *ṣaḥeeḥ*. See Shaykh al-Albâni, *Mukhtasar Ṣaḥeeḥ Bukhari*, no. 402. Recorded by Bukhari and Mâlik.

[156] This hadith is *ṣaḥeeḥ*. See Shaykh al-Albâni, *I'rwâ' al-Ghaleel*, no. 352. Recorded by Ibn Khuzaymah.

[157] This hadith is *ṣaḥeeḥ*. See Shaykh al-Albâni, *Ṣifat aṣ-Ṣalâh*, p. 69. Recorded by al-Ḥâkim.

4. Doing the acts in the bowing that are described in the following hadith

'Â'ishah said, "While bowing, the Messenger of Allah (ﷺ) would not leave his head to droop nor raise it but it would be in between those two." Abu Ḥumayd said while describing the prayer of the Prophet (ﷺ), "When he would bow, he would lean his hands on his knees and spread out his back."[158] Wâ'il ibn Ḥujr said, "When the Prophet (ﷺ) was bowing, he would spread out his fingers."[159] Abu Ḥumayd also said, "When the Prophet was bowing, he would put his hands on his knees as if he were grasping them, spreading his fingers out and he would keep his arms away from his sides."[160]

5. Putting one's hands on the floor before one's knees when going down to prostrate

Abu Hurayrah narrated that the Messenger of Allah (ﷺ) said, "When one of you goes to prostrate, he should not kneel like a camel kneels, but he should put his hands down before his knees."[161]

6. Doing the acts in the prostration that are described in the following hadith

While describing the prayer of the Prophet (ﷺ), Abu Ḥumayd said, "When he prostrated, he would not put his hands stretched out nor would he clench them. His toes would be facing the *qiblah*."[162]

---

[158] This hadith is *ṣaḥeeḥ*. See Shaykh al-Albâni, *Ṣifat aṣ-Ṣalâh*, p. 110. Recorded by Bukhari and Abu Dawood.

[159] This hadith is *ṣaḥeeḥ*. See Shaykh al-Albâni, *Ṣifat aṣ-Ṣalâh*, p. 110. Recorded by Ibn Khuzaymah.

[160] This hadith is *ṣaḥeeḥ*. See Shaykh al-Albâni, *Ṣaḥeeḥ Sunan Tirmidhi*, no. 214. Recorded by Abu Dawood and Tirmidhi.

[161] This hadith is *ṣaḥeeḥ*. See Shaykh al-Albâni, *Ṣaḥeeḥ Sunan Abi Dawood*, no. 746. Recorded by Abu Dawood, Nasâ'i and Aḥmad.

[162] This hadith is *ṣaḥeeḥ*. See Shaykh al-Albâni, *Ṣaḥeeḥ Sunan Abi Dawood*,=

Al-Barâ' narrated that the Messenger of Allah (ﷺ) said, "When you prostrate, put your palms (on the ground) and raise your forearms."[163] 'Abdullâh ibn Mâlik ibn Buḥaynah said, "When praying the Prophet would separate his arms such that one could see the whiteness of his armpits."[164] 'Â'ishah said, "I noticed the Messenger of Allah (ﷺ) missing from the bed. I found him prostrating with his heels together and his toes facing the *qiblah.*"[165] Wâ'il ibn Ḥujr said, "I came to Madeenah to see the prayer of the Messenger of Allah (ﷺ)..." Among the aspects he mentioned was, "He would then go down and prostrate, and his head would be between his two palms."[166] Wâ'il ibn Ḥujr also said, "When the Prophet (ﷺ) prostrated, he would put his fingers together."[167] Al-Barâ' said, "When the Messenger of Allah (ﷺ) prostrated, he would put his hands on the ground and have his palms and fingers facing the *qiblah.*"[168]

7. The sitting between the two prostrations should be as described in the following hadith

'Â'ishah (رضي الله عنها) said, "He (ﷺ) would spread out his left leg and keep his left leg erect."[169] Ibn 'Umar said, "It is from the Sunnah of

---

=no. 672. Recorded by Bukhari and Abu Dawood.

[163] This hadith is *ṣaḥeeḥ*. See Shaykh al-Albâni, *Ṣifat aṣ-Ṣalâh*, p. 126. Recorded by Muslim.

[164] Recorded by Bukhari, Muslim and Nasâ'i.

[165] This hadith is *ṣaḥeeḥ*. See Shaykh al-Albâni, *Ṣifat aṣ-Ṣalâh*, p. 126. Recorded by Ibn Khuzaymah and al-Bayhaqi.

[166] The chain of this report is *ṣaḥeeḥ*. Recorded by Ibn Khuzaymah.

[167] This hadith is *ṣaḥeeḥ*. See Shaykh al-Albâni, *Ṣifat aṣ-Ṣalâh*, p. 123. Recorded by Ibn Khuzaymah and al-Bayhaqi.

[168] The chain of this report is *ṣaḥeeḥ*. See Shaykh al-Albâni, *Sifat al-Salât*, p. 123. Recorded by al-Bayhaqi.

[169] This hadith is *ṣaḥeeḥ*. See Shaykh al-Albâni, *Mukhtasar Ṣaḥeeḥ Muslim*, no. 302. Recorded by Muslim and Abu Dawood.

the prayer to make the right foot erect, with its toes facing the *qiblah*, while sitting on the left."[170] Ṭâwus said, "We asked Ibn 'Abbâs about sitting on the heels and feet (between the two prostrations). He said, 'It is Sunnah.' We said to him, 'We find it harsh on the leg.' Ibn 'Abbâs said, 'But it is the Sunnah of your Prophet (ﷺ).' "[171]

8. Not getting up from the prostration until one has sat straight

Abu Qulâbah said that Mâlik ibn al-Ḥuwayrith al-Laythi narrated that he saw the Prophet (ﷺ) praying and when he was in the odd-numbered *rak'ahs*, he would not stand up until he first sat straight."[172]

9. To push up off the ground when going to stand again

Ayyoob narrated that Abu Qulâbah said, "Mâlik ibn al-Ḥuwayrith came and led us in prayer in this mosque of ours. He said, 'I am not leading you in prayer nor do I intend to prayer, am I only trying to show you how I saw the Prophet praying.' " Ayyoob said, "I asked to Abu Qulâbah, 'What was the manner of his prayer?' He said, 'It was like the prayer of our Shaykh in this mosque of ours,' that is 'Amr ibn Salamah." Ayyoob then said, "That Shaykh would complete the *takbeer* and when he raised his head from the second prostration, he would sit and then push up off the ground and then stand."[173]

---

[170] This hadith is *ṣaḥeeḥ*. See Shaykh al-Albâni, *Ṣaḥeeḥ Sunan Nasâ'i*, no. 1109. Recorded by Nasâ'i.

[171] This hadith is *ṣaḥeeḥ*. See Shaykh al-Albâni, *Mukhtasar Ṣaḥeeḥ Muslim*, no. 303. Recorded by Muslim, Abu Dawood and Tirmidhi.

[172] This hadith is *ṣaḥeeḥ*. See Shaykh al-Albâni, *Mukhtasar Ṣaḥeeḥ Bukhari*, no. 437. Recorded by Bukhari and Abu Dawood.

[173] This hadith is *ṣaḥeeḥ*. See Shaykh al-Albâni, *Mukhtasar Ṣaḥeeḥ Bukhari*, no. 437. Recorded by Bukhari and al-Bayhaqi. It was also recorded by ash-Shafi'ee who further said, "This is what we follow. We tell the one who stands from the prostration or sitting in the prayer that he should push off=

10. The sitting between the two prostrations should be as described in the following hadith

While describing the prayer of the Prophet (ﷺ), Abu Ḥumayd said, "When sitting after the two *rak'ahs*, he would sit on his left leg and keep his right straight (with the foot erect). When sitting during the fourth *rak'ah*, he would bring his left foot all the way across, keep his right leg straight (and foot erect) and sit on his buttocks."[174] Ibn 'Umar said, "When the Messenger of Allah (ﷺ) would sit during the prayer, he would put his right hand upon his right thigh, clench all of his fingers and point with his index finger. He would put his left hand upon his left thigh."[175] Nâfi' said, "When 'Abdullâh ibn 'Umar would sit during the prayer, he would put his hands on his knees and point his finger and fix his glaze on that. Then he said that the Messenger of Allah (ﷺ) had said, "It is stronger than iron against Satan," meaning the index finger.[176]

The Words of Remembrance and Supplications to Be Said After the Prayers

1. Thawbân said, "When the Messenger of Allah (ﷺ) would finish his prayer, he would seek forgiveness three times and then say,

---

=from the ground with his both hands together, following the sunnah. This is more humble and more helpful for the person in the prayer and better to keep him from turning away. To stand in any other fashion is disliked but he need not repeat it nor must he make a prostration of forgetfulness due to it." Ash-Shafi'ee, *Kitâb al-Umm*, vol. 1, p. 117.

174 This hadith is *ṣaḥeeḥ*. See Shaykh al-Albâni, *Mukhtasar Ṣaḥeeḥ Bukhari*, no. 448. Recorded by Bukhari.

175 This hadith is *ṣaḥeeḥ*. See Shaykh al-Albâni, *Ṣaḥeeḥ Sunan Abi Dawood*, no. 851. Recorded by Muslim and Abu Dawood.

176 This hadith is *ḥasan*. See Shaykh al-Albâni, *Ṣifat aṣ-Ṣalâh*, p. 140. Recorded by Aḥmad.

اللَّهُمَّ أَنْتَ السَّلامُ وَمِنْكَ السَّلامُ تَبارَكْتَ يا ذا الْجَلالِ وَالإِكْرام

'O' Allah, You are the One Who is free from any shortcoming or vice and from You comes peace. Blessed You are, O' One of Grandeur and Honour.' Al-Waleed said that he asked al-Awzâ'ee, "How is the asking of forgiveness." He replied, "It is to say,

أَسْتَغْفِرُ اللَّه أَسْتَغْفِرُ اللَّه

'I seek Allah's forgiveness, I seek Allah's forgiveness.'"[177]

2. Abu az-Zubayr said: Ibn az-Zubayr would say after finishing the prayer by saying the salutations,

لا إِلَهَ إِلاَّ اللَّهُ وَحْدَهُ لا شَرِيكَ لَهُ لَهُ الْمُلْكُ وَلَهُ الْحَمْدُ وَهُوَ عَلَى كُلِّ شَيْءٍ قَدِيرٌ لا حَوْلَ وَلا قُوَّةَ إِلاَّ بِاللَّهِ لا إِلَهَ إِلاَّ اللَّهُ وَلا نَعْبُدُ إِلاَّ إِيَّاهُ لَهُ النِّعْمَةُ وَلَهُ الْفَضْلُ وَلَهُ الثَّنَاءُ الْحَسَنُ لا إِلَهَ إِلاَّ اللَّهُ مُخْلِصِينَ لَهُ الدِّينَ وَلَوْ كَرِهَ الْكَافِرُونَ

"There is none worthy of worship except Allah, alone, without any partner, to Him is the dominion and to Him is the praise. And He has power over all things. There is no power and no might except in Allah. There is none worthy of worship except Allah. We do not worship but Him. To Him belongs all bounties. To Him belongs all grace. And to Him is all worthy praise. There is none worthy of worship except Allah, to whom we are pure in devotion, even if the disbelievers are averse." He said that the Prophet (ﷺ) would recite these words after every prayer.[178]

---

[177] This hadith is *ṣaḥeeḥ*. See Shaykh al-Albâni, *Ṣaheeḥ Sunan Ibn Mâjah*, no. 756. Recorded by Muslim, Tirmidhi, Nasâ'i, Abu Dawood and Ibn Mâjah.

[178] This hadith is *ṣaḥeeḥ*. See Shaykh al-Albâni, *Ṣaḥeeḥ Sunan Nasâ'i*, no. 1272. Recorded by Muslim, Abu Dawood and Nasâ'i.

3. Warrâd, the ex-slave of al-Mugheerah ibn Shu'bah, said, "Al-Mugheerah ibn Shu'bah wrote to Mu'âwiyah telling him that when the Messenger of Allah would finish his prayer, he would then say,

لا إِلَهَ إِلاَّ اللَّهُ وَحْدَهُ لا شَرِيْكَ لَهُ لَهُ المُلْكُ وَلَهُ الحَمْدُ وَهُوَ عَلَى كُلِّ شَيْءٍ قَدِيْرٌ اللَّهُمَّ لا مَانِعَ لِمَا أَعْطَيْتَ وَلا مُعْطِيَ لِمَا مَنَعْتَ وَلا يَنْفَعُ ذَا الْجَدِّ مِنْكَ الْجَدُّ

'There is none worthy of worship except Allah, alone, without any partner, to Him is the dominion and to Him is the praise. And He has power over all things. O' Allah, there is none who can withhold what You have given. And there is none who can give when You have withheld. And one's possessions cannot benefit him in front of You.' "[179]

4. K'ab ibn 'Ujrah narrated that the Messenger of Allah (ﷺ) said, "There are expressions to be said after every obligatory prayer the repeaters of which or the performers of which will never cause disappointment: saying *Subḥânallâh* ('Exalted and perfect is Allah') thirty three times, *al-Ḥamdulillâh* ('All praise are to Allah alone') thirty three times and *Allâhu akbar* ('Allah is the Greatest') thirty-four times."[180]

Abu Hurayrah narrated that the Messenger of Allah (ﷺ) said,

مَنْ سَبَّحَ اللَّهَ فِي دُبُرِ كُلِّ صَلاةٍ ثَلاثًا وَثَلاثِينَ وَحَمِدَ اللَّهَ ثَلاثًا وَثَلاثِينَ وَكَبَّرَ اللَّهَ ثَلاثًا وَثَلاثِينَ فَتْلِكَ تِسْعَةٌ وَتِسْعُونَ وَقَالَ تَمَامَ الْمِائَةِ "لا إِلَهَ إِلاَّ اللَّهُ وَحْدَهُ لا شَرِيكَ لَهُ لَهُ الْمُلْكُ وَلَهُ الْحَمْدُ وَهُوَ عَلَى كُلِّ شَيْءٍ قَدِيرٌ"

[179] Recorded by Bukhari, Muslim and Abu Dawood.

[180] This hadith is *ṣaḥeeḥ*. See Shaykh al-Albâni, *Ṣaḥeeḥ Sunan Nasâ'i*, no. 1278. Recorded by Muslim, Tirmidhi and Nasâ'i.

غُفِرَتْ خَطَايَاهُ وَإِنْ كَانَتْ مِثْلَ زَبَدِ الْبَحْرِ

"For whoever, at the end of every prayer, extols Allah's perfection thirty-three times, praises Allah thirty-three times and declares Allah's greatness thirty-three times[181], that will be ninety-nine and to complete one hundred he should then say, 'There is none worthy of worship except Allah, alone, without any partner, to Him is the dominion and to Him is the praise. And He has power over all things,' then his previous sins will be forgiven if they were (in amount) like the foam on the sea."[182]

5. Mu'âdh ibn Jabal narrated that once the Messenger of Allah (ﷺ) took him by his hand and said to him: "O' Mu'âdh, by Allah I love you, by Allah I love you." Then he said, "I advise you, O' Mu'âdh, to always say at the end of every prayer, 'O' Allah, help me in establishing Your remembrance, giving You thanks and excelling in worship of You.' "[183]

6. Abu Umâmah narrated that the Prophet (ﷺ) said, "For whoever recites the Verse of the Throne (*Qur'an 2: 255*) after every obligatory prayer, nothing is preventing him from entering Paradise except dying."[184] In the narration of Muhammad ibn Ibrâheem there is also

---

[181] Note: It is also reported that one may say each expression ten times each, eleven times each, fifteen times each or twenty-five times each, adding the statement, "There is none worthy of worship except Allah." The worshipper should sometimes say it one amount and on other occasions a different amount. These amounts have been recorded by, respectfully, Bukhari, Muslim and Nasâ'i (*Ṣaḥeeḥ Sunan Nasâ'i*, no. 1279).

[182] This hadith is *ṣaḥeeḥ*. See Shaykh al-Albâni, *Mukhtasar Ṣaḥeeḥ Muslim*, no. 314. Recorded by Muslim.

[183] This hadith is *ṣaḥeeḥ*. See Shaykh al-Albâni, *Ṣaḥeeḥ al-Jâmi' aṣ-Ṣagheer*, no. 7969. Recorded by Abu Dawood and Nasâ'i.

[184] This hadith is *ṣaḥeeḥ*. See Shaykh al-Albâni, *Ṣaḥeeḥ al-Jâmi' aṣ-Ṣagheer*, no. 6464. Recorded by aṭ-Ṭabarâni.

the addition of reading, "Say: He is Allah, (the) One."

7. 'Uqbah ibn 'Âmir said, "The Messenger of Allah (ﷺ) told me to recite the two *Soorahs* of seeking refuge[185] after every prayer.[186]

8. Umm Salamah narrated that the Prophet (ﷺ) used to say after the salutations of the Morning prayer,

اللَّهُمَّ إِنِّي أَسْأَلُكَ عِلْمًا نَافِعًا وَرِزْقًا طَيِّبًا وَعَمَلاً مُتَقَبَّلاً

"O' Allah, I ask you for beneficial knowledge, excellent provisions and accepted deeds."[187]

Disliked Actions During the Prayer

1. Fidgeting with one's clothing or body without any need

Mu'ayqeeb narrated that the Prophet (ﷺ) said about a man levelling the dirt when he prostrated, "If you must do so, then do it only once."[188]

2. Placing one's hands on one's waist during the prayer

Abu Hurayrah (رضي الله عنه) said the he [the Prophet (ﷺ)] forbade that one should pray with his hands on his waist.[189]

---

[185] These are the last two *Soorahs* of the Qur'an, *Soorah al-Falaq* and *Soorah an-Nâs*.

[186] This hadith is *ṣaḥeeḥ*. See Shaykh al-Albâni, *Ṣaḥeeḥ Sunan Nasâ'i*, no. 1268. Recorded by Abu Dawood and Nasâ'i.

[187] This hadith is *ṣaḥeeḥ*. See Shaykh al-Albâni, *Ṣaḥeeḥ Sunan Ibn Mâjah*, no. 753. Recorded by Ibn Mâjah and Aḥmad.

[188] Recorded by Bukhari, Muslim, Abu Dawood, Tirmidhi, Ibn Mâjah and Nasâ'i.

[189] Recorded by Bukhari, Muslim, Abu Dawood, Tirmidhi and Nasâ'i.

3. Looking towards the sky

Abu Hurayrah narrated that the Messenger of Allah (ﷺ) said, "People should stop looking towards the sky while supplicating in prayer or their sight may be taken away from them."[190]

4. Looking around with any need to do so

'Â'ishah said, "I asked the Messenger of Allah (ﷺ) about looking around while praying and he said, 'This is a part that is stolen swiftly by Satan from the prayer of the servant.'"[191]

5. Looking at something distracting

'Â'ishah said, "The Prophet (ﷺ) had prayed in a shirt that had some markings on it. He then said, 'These markings distracted me in the prayer. Take it to Abu Jahm and bring me a heavy garment with no markings.'"[192]

6. Prohibition of *as-Sadl* and covering the mouth

Abu Hurayrah said, "The Messenger of Allah forbade *as-sadl* in the prayer and he forbade the man from covering the mouth."[193] In *'Awn al-Ma'bood*, Shams al-Ḥaq wrote, "Al-Khaṭṭâbi said that leaving one's garment too long (*as-sadl*) is where a garment stretches down all the way to the ground."[194] In *Nail al-Awtâr*, ash-Shawkâni

---

[190] This hadith is *ṣaḥeeḥ*. See Shaykh al-Albâni, *Mukhtasar Ṣaḥeeḥ Muslim*, no. 343. Recorded by Muslim and Nasâ'i.

[191] This hadith is *ṣaḥeeḥ*. See Shaykh al-Albâni, *Ṣaḥeeḥ al-Jâmi' aṣ-Ṣagheer*, no. 7047. Recorded by Bukhari, Abu Dawood and Nasâ'i.

[192] This hadith is *ṣaḥeeḥ*. See Shaykh al-Albâni, *Ṣaḥeeḥ al-Jâmi' aṣ-Ṣagheer*, no. 2066. Recorded by Bukhari, Muslim, Abu Dawood, Nasâ'i and Ibn Mâjah.

[193] This hadith is *ḥasan*. See Shaykh al-Albâni, *Ṣaḥeeḥ Sunan Ibn Mâjah*, no. 966. Recorded by Abu Dawood. Tirmidhi recorded the first part only while Ibn Mâjah recorded the second part only.

[194] *Awn al-Ma'bood*, vol. 2, p. 347.

stated, "Abu 'Ubaydah stated in his work on rare words, '*As-Sadl* is where the man lets his garment fall loose without bringing in the sides of it to his front. If he brings the sides of the garment together it is not *as-sadl*.' The author of *an-Nihâyah* stated, 'It is where the person envelopes himself with his garment, putting his arms within the garment, and bows and prostrates in that state.' He also said, 'It is also said that it is where one puts the middle of his body-length garment upon his head, letting fall its two ends upon his right and left without making it to be upon his two shoulder-blades.' Al-Jawhari said, 'To make *sadl* with one's garment is to let it flow long.' There is no prohibition to understanding the hadith in all of these senses as a homonym can be understood in all of its senses and *as-sadl* has all of these meanings to it. To understand a homonym in all of its senses is a very strong approach."

7. Yawning

Abu Hurayrah narrated that the Prophet (ﷺ) said, "Yawning in the prayer is from Satan. Therefore, if one of you yawns, he should restrain it to the best of his ability."[195]

8. Spitting in the direction of the *qiblah* or one one's right side

Jâbir said that the Messenger of Allah (ﷺ) had said, "When you stand to prayer, Allah is front of you. Therefore, do not spit in front of yourself or towards your right side. But spit towards your left, underneath your left foot. But if you are compelled to do so suddenly, he should spit in his garment like his," then he folded part of his garment over another part of it.[196]

---

[195] This hadith is *ṣaḥeeḥ*. See Shaykh al-Albâni, *Ṣaḥeeḥ al-Jâmi' aṣ-Ṣagheer*, no. 3013. Recorded by Tirmidhi and Ibn Khuzaymah.

[196] This hadith is *ṣaḥeeḥ*. Recorded by Muslim and Abu Dawood.

9. Intertwining one's fingers

Abu Hurayrah narrated that the Messenger of Allah (ﷺ) said, "If one of you makes ablution in his house and then comes to the mosque, he is in the prayer until he returns. Therefore he should not do like this," and he intertwined his fingers.[197]

10. Folding or tucking back the hair or the garment

Ibn 'Abbâs narrated that the Prophet (ﷺ) said, "I have been ordered to prostrate on seven bones and not to fold back garments or hair."[198]

11. Putting the knees down before the hands when going into prostration

Abu Hurayrah narrated that the Messenger of Allah (ﷺ) said, "When one of you goes to prostrate, he should not kneel like a camel kneels, but he should put his hands down before his knees."[199]

12. Spreading the forearms out (like a dog) in the prostration

Anas narrated that the Prophet (ﷺ) said, "Be level in the prostration and you should not spread your forearms out like a dog does."[200]

13. Praying after the food has arrived or is ready or while one needs to relieve himself

'Â'ishah (may Allah be pleased with her) said that she heard the Prophet (ﷺ) say, "There is to be no prayer when the food is

---

[197] This hadith is *ṣaḥeeḥ*. See Shaykh al-Albâni, *Ṣaḥeeḥ al-Jâmi' aṣ-Ṣagheer*, no. 445. Recorded by al-Ḥâkim.

[198] Recorded by Bukhari, Muslim and Nasâ'i.

[199] This hadith is *ṣaḥeeḥ*. See Shaykh al-Albâni, *Ṣaḥeeḥ Sunan Abi Dawood*, no. 746. Recorded by Abu Dawood, Nasâ'i and Aḥmad.

[200] Recorded by Bukhari, Muslim, Tirmidhi, Abu Dawood and Ibn Mâjah. Nasâ'i has something similar.

presented or when one needs to relieve himself."[201]

14. Preceding the Imam in any action of the prayer

Abu Hurayrah narrated that the Prophet (ﷺ) said, "Don't you fear that if you raise your head before the Imam that Allah may make your head the head of a donkey or give him the appearance of a donkey?"[202]

Permissible Acts During the Prayer

1. Taking some steps due to need

'Â'ishah said, "The Messenger of Allah (ﷺ) was praying in the house and the door was locked. I came and asked for the door to be opened. He walked and opened it for me and then he returned to his place of prayer." She described that the door was in the direction of the *qiblah*.[203]

2. Carrying a child

Abu Qatâdah narrated that the Messenger of Allah (ﷺ) was praying while carrying Umâmah the daughter of Zaynab the daughter of the Messenger of Allah (ﷺ) and of Abu al-'Âṣ ibn ar-Rabee'. When he stood, he carried her and when he prostrated, he put her down."[204]

---

[201] This hadith is *ṣaḥeeḥ*. See Shaykh al-Albâni, *Ṣaḥeeḥ al-Jâmi' aṣ-Ṣagheer*, no. 7509. Recorded by Muslim and Abu Dawood.

[202] Recorded by Bukhari (with this wording), Muslim, Abu Dawood, Nasâ'i and Ibn Mâjah.

[203] This hadith is *ḥasan*. See Shaykh al-Albâni, *Ṣaḥeeḥ Sunan Nasâ'i*, no. 1151. Recorded by Tirmidhi, Abu Dawood and Nasâ'i.

[204] Recorded by Bukhari, Muslim, Abu Dawood and Nasâ'i.

3. Killing a scorpion or a snake

Abu Hurayrah narrated that the Messenger of Allah (ﷺ) ordered the killing of the two black creatures during the prayer, that is, the scorpion and the snake.[205]

4. Turning and indicating some meaning due to need

Jâbir said, "The Messenger of Allah (ﷺ) was in pain and we prayed behind him while he was sitting. He turned to us and saw us standing, so he motioned to us and we also sat as well."[206]

5. Spitting into one's clothing or taking out a handkerchief from one's pocket

The permissibility of this action is based on the hadith of Jâbir mentioned earlier, in which he spoke of the prohibition of spitting in the direction of the *qiblah*.

6. Signalling to indicate a response to one who has greeted the praying person

'Abdullâh ibn 'Umar said that the Messenger of Allah (ﷺ) went out to the village of Quba' to pray there. Some of the Anṣâr came to him and greeted him by while he was praying. 'Abdullâh ibn 'Umar asked Bilâl, "How did you see the Messenger of Allah return their greeting and they would greet him while he was praying?" He replied, "He would do like this," and he opened his palm, and Ja'far ibn 'Awn (the narrator did the same demonstrating it), with the inside of the palm facing down and the top of the hand facing up.[207]

---

[205] This hadith is *ṣaḥeeḥ*. See Shaykh al-Albâni, *Ṣaḥeeḥ al-Jâmi' aṣ-Ṣagheer*, no. 1147. Recorded by Ibn Khuzaymah.

[206] This hadith is *ṣaḥeeḥ*. See Shaykh al-Albâni, *Ṣaḥeeḥ Sunan Nasâ'i*, no. 1145. Recorded by Muslim, Nasâ'i and Abu Dawood.

[207] This hadith is *ḥasan* ṣaḥeeḥ. See Shaykh al-Albâni, *Ṣaḥeeḥ Sunan Abi Dawood*, no. 82. Recorded by Abu Dawood.

7. The men saying *Subḥânallâh* and the women clapping (their hands against their thighs) due to something that has occurred in the prayer

Sahl ibn S'ad narrated that the Messenger of Allah (ﷺ) said, "O' people, why is it that when something happened in the prayer you clapped. Clapping is only for women. If something happens to one of you in the prayer, he should say, *Subḥânallâh* (Exalted and perfect is Allah),' for no one will hear *Subḥânallâh* except that it will capture his attention..."[208]

8. Correcting the Imam

Ibn 'Umar said, "The Prophet was reciting during the prayer and he got confused (in the recital). When he finished he said to Ubayy, 'Didn't you pray with us?' He replied in the affirmative, so the Prophet (ﷺ) asked him, 'What prevented you (from correcting me)?' "[209]

9. Touching the leg of a sleeping person

'Â'ishah said, "I would stretch my leg out in the direction of the *qiblah* while the Prophet (ﷺ) was praying. When he prostrated, he touched me and I would pull my leg. When he stood, I would stretch it back out again."[210]

10. Opposing the one who wants to pass in front of the praying person

Abu Sa'eed narrated that he heard the Messenger of Allah (ﷺ) say, "If you are praying towards something as a barrier from the people and sometimes tries to pass in front of it, repel him in is chest.

[208] Recorded by Bukhari, Muslim and Abu Dawood.

[209] This hadith is *ṣaḥeeḥ*. See Shaykh al-Albâni, *Ṣaḥeeḥ Sunan Abi Dawood*, no. 803. Recorded by Abu Dawood.

[210] Recorded by Bukhari (with this wording) while Muslim has something similar.

If he refuses, then fight him for he is a devil."[211]

11. Crying

'Ali said, "There were no horsemen among us on the Day of Badr except al-Miqdâd. I could see that we were all sleeping except the Messenger of Allah (ﷺ) who was beneath a tree praying and crying until the morning."[212]

Acts that Invalidate the Prayer

1. Being certain that one has invalidated the ablution

'Ibbâd ibn Tameem narrated from his uncle that a man complained to the Messenger of Allah (ﷺ) about feeling something (in his abdomen) in the prayer. The Prophet (ﷺ) said, "Do not turn away (from the prayer) unless you hear a sound or notice a smell."[213]

2. Intentionally not performing a pillar or prerequisite of the prayer without a valid excuse

This point is based on the statement of the Prophet (ﷺ) to the one who did not pray properly, "Go back and pray for you have not prayed."[214] Similarly, the Prophet (ﷺ) told the one who had not washed a portion of the top of his feet to repeat the ablution and the prayer.[215]

---

[211] This hadith is *ṣaḥeeḥ*. See Shaykh al-Albâni, *Ṣaḥeeḥ al-Jâmi' aṣ-Ṣagheer*, no. 638. Recorded by Muslim.

[212] The chain of this report is *ṣaḥeeḥ*. Recorded by Ibn Khuzaymah.

[213] Recorded by Bukhari, Muslim, Abu Dawood, Ibn Mâjah and Nasâ'i.

[214] Recorded by Bukhari, Muslim, Abu Dawood, Tirmidhi and Nasâ'i.

[215] This hadith is *ṣaḥeeḥ*. See Shaykh al-Albâni, *Ṣaḥeeḥ Sunan Abi Dawood*, no. 161. Recorded by Abu Dawood.

3. Intentionally eating or drinking during the prayer

Ibn al-Mundhir said, "The people of knowledge all agree that one who intentionally eats or drinks during an obligatory prayer must repeat the prayer."[216] For the majority of the scholars, it also invalidates a voluntary prayer as the same things that invalidate an obligatory prayer invalidate a voluntary prayer.

4. Intentionally speaking something not
due to what is needed for the prayer

Zayd ibn al-Arqam said, "We used to speak during the prayer, a person would speak to the person to his side during the prayer. This was until:

﴿ ... وَقُومُوا لِلَّهِ قَانِتِينَ ﴿٢٣٨﴾ ﴾ (سورة البَقَرَة: ٢٣٨)

﴿... Stand before Allah with obedience.﴾ *(Qur'an 2: 238)*

— was revealed. We were then ordered to remain silent and forbidden to speak."[217]

5. Ibn al-Mundhir has reported that there is a consensus that laughing invalidates the prayer.[218]

6. An adult woman, donkey or black dog passing in front
of the praying person within the distance of his prostration

The Prophet (ﷺ) said, "If one of you stands to prayer, then if he has like the back of a saddle in front of him, that will act like a barrier. If he has nothing like the back of a saddle in front of him, then his prayer is cut off by a donkey, a woman and a black dog."[219]

---

[216] Ibn al-Mundhir, *al-Ijmâ'*, p. 40.

[217] Recorded by Bukhari, Muslim, Tirmidhi, Abu Dawood and Nasâ'i. Bukhari and Nasâ'i do not have the final words, "We were forbidden to speak."

[218] Ibn al-Mundhir, *al-Ijmâ'*, p. 40.

[219] This hadith is *ṣaḥeeḥ*. See Shaykh al-Albâni, *Ṣaḥeeḥ al-Jâmi' aṣ-Ṣagheer*, no. 719. Recorded by Muslim, Nasâ'i, Tirmidhi and Abu Dawood.

Voluntary Prayers

Their Virtues

Abu Hurayrah reported that the Prophet (ﷺ) said, "The first deeds for which the servant (of Allah) will be held accountable on the Day of Judgment will be his prayers. If they are sound, he will have prospered and been rescued. If they are rotten, he will be miserable and be at loss. If there were some deficiency in his obligatory prayers, the Lord will say, 'See if he has any voluntary prayers with which may be completed that which was wanting in his obligatory prayers.' Then the rest of his obligatory deeds will be judged in like fashion."[220]

It is preferred for them to be performed at home

Jâbir narrated that the Messenger of Allah (ﷺ) said, "If one of you performs the prayers in his mosque, he should reserve a portion of his prayers for his house as then Allah will make in his house, due to his prayer, goodness."[221] And Zayd ibn Thâbit narrated that the Prophet (ﷺ) said, "You should pray in your houses for the best prayer of a man is that in his house, save for the obligatory prayers."[222]

---

[220] This hadith is *ṣaḥeeḥ*. See Shaykh al-Albâni, *Ṣaḥeeḥ Sunan Nasâ'i*, nos. 451 and 452. Recorded by Tirmidhi and Nasâ'i.

[221] This hadith is *ṣaḥeeḥ*. See Shaykh al-Albâni, *Mukhtasar Ṣaḥeeḥ Muslim*, no. 375. Recorded by Muslim.

[In the original Arabic text, the author put the word, "light" instead of "goodness." It seems that this was simply a typographical error as this translator could not find said hadith with that wording in *Ṣaḥeeḥ Muslim* or in other works of hadith. Allah knows best.] - Translator

[222] Recorded by Bukhari, Muslim, Abu Dawood and Nasâ'i.

The Types of Voluntary Prayers

Voluntary prayers are of the "specific" variety or of the unrestricted variety

The "specific" or "restricted" voluntary prayers are what are known as the regularly performed Sunnah prayers, before and after the obligatory prayers. They are further subdivided into emphasized and non-emphasized.

The ten rak'ahs of emphasized sunnah prayers

Ibn 'Umar said, "I (learned and) preserved from the Prophet (ﷺ) ten *rak'ahs*: two *rak'ahs* before the Noon prayer as well as two after it, two *rak'ahs* after the Sunset Prayer, two *rak'ahs* after the Night prayer and two *rak'ahs* before the Morning prayer. The latter was a time in which no one would meet the Prophet (ﷺ) but Ḥafṣah (رضي الله عنها) (Ibn 'Umar's sister and the Prophet's wife) informed me that when the caller to prayer made the call and dawn had appeared, he would pray two *rak'ahs*."[223] 'Â'ishah said, "The Prophet (ﷺ) would not miss four *rak'ahs* before the Noon prayer and two before the Morning prayer."[224]

Non-emphasized sunnah prayers

These are two *rak'ahs* before the Afternoon, Sunset and Night prayers. 'Abdullâh ibn Mughaffal narrated that the Prophet (ﷺ) said, "Between the two calls,[225] there is a prayer. Between the two calls,

---

[223] This hadith is *ṣaḥeeḥ*. See Shaykh al-Albâni, *I'rwâ' al-Ghaleel*, no. 44. Recorded by Bukhari with this wording while Tirmidhi has something similar.

[224] This hadith is *ṣaḥeeḥ*. See Shaykh al-Albâni, *Ṣaḥeeḥ Sunan Nasâ'i*, no. 1658. Recorded by Bukhari, Abu Dawood and Nasâ'i.

[225] [This is in reference to, first, the call to prayer and then, second, the=

there is a prayer." Upon saying that a third time, he said, "For whoever wills (to pray it)."[226]

It is preferred to perform four rak'ahs before the afternoon prayer

'Ali said, "The Prophet (ﷺ) used to pray four *rak'ahs* before the Afternoon prayer. He would separate between them by (during the *tashahhud*) giving salutations upon the angels near (to Allah) and those who followed them of the Muslims and the believers."[227] Ibn 'Umar narrated that the Prophet (ﷺ) said, "May Allah have mercy on a person who prays four (*rak'ahs*) before the Afternoon prayer."[228]

What has been reported concerning the Prophet's reciting in some of these prayers

'Â'ishah narrated that the Prophet (ﷺ) had said: "Excellent are the two *Soorahs* that are read in the two *rak'ahs* before the Morning prayer, ﴾Say, O' you who disbelieve,﴿ and ﴾Say, He is Allah, [the] One.﴿"[229] Abu Hurayrah also said, "The Messenger of Allah (ﷺ) would recite in the two *rak'ahs* (before) the Morning prayer, ﴾Say, O' you who disbelieve,﴿ and ﴾Say, He is Allah, [the] One.﴿"[230] Ibn 'Abbâs narrated that the Messenger of Allah (ﷺ) used to recite in the

---

=pronouncement of the commencement of the prayer.]

[226] Recorded by Bukhari, Muslim, Abu Dawood, Tirmidhi, Nasâ'i and Ibn Mâjah.

[227] This hadith is *ḥasan*. See Shaykh al-Albâni, *Ṣaḥeeḥ Sunan Tirmidhi*, no. 353. Recorded by Tirmidhi.

[228] This hadith is *ḥasan*. See Shaykh al-Albâni, *Ṣaḥeeḥ Sunan Tirmidhi*, no. 354. Recorded by Tirmidhi and Abu Dawood.

[229] This hadith is *ṣaḥeeḥ*. See Shaykh al-Albâni, *Ṣaḥeeḥ Sunan Ibn Mâjah*, no. 944. Recorded by Ibn Khuzaymah, Aḥmad and Ibn Mâjah.

[230] This hadith is *ṣaḥeeḥ*. See Shaykh al-Albâni, *Mukhtasar Ṣaḥeeḥ Muslim*, no. 360. Recorded by Muslim, Abu Dawood, Nasâ'i and Ibn Mâjah.

two *rak'ahs* (before) the Morning prayer, ﴾Say [O' Muslims], 'We believe in Allah and that which has been sent down to us'﴿ from *al-Baqarah (Qur'an 2: 136)* and in the last (*rak'ah*) of them, ﴾We believe in Allah, and bear witness that we are Muslims﴿ *(Qur'an 3: 52)*."[231]

Ibn Mas'ood said, "I could not count the number of times I heard the Messenger of Allah (ﷺ) recite in the two *rak'ahs* after the Afternoon prayer and in the two *rak'ahs* before the Morning prayer, ﴾Say, O' you who disbelieve,﴿ and ﴾Say, He is Allah, [the] One.﴿"[232]

The *Witr* Prayer (The Prayer Made Up of an Odd Number of *Rak'ahs*)

The ruling and excellence of the witr prayer

The *witr* prayer is an emphasized Sunnah that the Prophet (ﷺ) strongly encouraged. Abu Hurayrah narrated that the Messenger of Allah (ﷺ) said, "Verily, Allah is odd (in number, that is only one) and He loves the odd in number."[233] 'Ali said, "The *witr* prayer is not mandatory, like your obligatory prayers but the Messenger of Allah (ﷺ) used to perform the *witr* prayer and he then said, 'O' People of the Qur'an, verily, Allah is odd (in number, that is only one) and He loves the odd in number.'"[234]

---

[231] This hadith is *ṣaḥeeḥ*. See Shaykh al-Albâni, *Ṣaḥeeḥ al-Jâmi' aṣ-Ṣagheer*, no. 905. Recorded by Muslim, Nasâ'i and Abu Dawood.

[232] This hadith is *ḥasan* ṣaḥeeḥ. See Shaykh al-Albâni, *Ṣaḥeeḥ Sunan Tirmidhi*, no. 355. Recorded by Tirmidhi.

[233] Recorded by Bukhari and Muslim.

[234] This hadith is *ṣaḥeeḥ*. See Shaykh al-Albâni, *Ṣaḥeeḥ Sunan Ibn Mâjah*, no. 959. Recorded by Ibn Mâjah, Tirmidhi and Nasâ'i. For the last two hadiths,=

The timing of the witr prayer

It is permissible to perform the *witr* prayer any time from after the Night prayer until the break of dawn. However, it is preferred to be said during the last third of the night. 'Â'ishah said, "The Prophet (ﷺ) would make *witr* during every part of the night, the beginning, middle or last portion of the night. He would finish his *witr* close to dawn."[235]

It is preferred to perform the *witr* prayer in the first portion of the night for one who fears that he will not get up in the later portion of the night. Similarly, it is preferred to perform the *witr* prayer at the end of the night for the one who believes that he will be able to get up at that time. Abu Qatâdah narrated that the Prophet (ﷺ) said to Abu Bakr, "At what time do you pray *witr*?" He replied, "I pray *witr* before I sleep." He then asked 'Umar, "What time do you pray *witr*?" He replied, "I sleep then I pray *witr*." The Prophet (ﷺ) then said to Abu Bakr, "You have taken the safe way," and he said to 'Umar, "You have taken the strong way."[236]

'Â'ishah (رضي الله عنها) said, "The Prophet (ﷺ) used to pray while I would be sleeping across the bed. When he intended to perform the *witr* prayer, he would wake me and I would also pray *witr*."[237]

=Abu Dawood only quoted the portions containing the words of the Prophet (Blessings and peace of Allah be upon him).

[235] Recorded by Bukhari (in an abridged fashion) and by Muslim (with this wording). Also recorded by Nasâ'i, Abu Dawood and Tirmidhi, with Abu Dawood and Tirmidhi having additional text at the end of the hadith.

[236] This hadith is *ḥasan ṣaḥeeḥ*. See Shaykh al-Albâni, *Ṣaḥeeḥ Sunan Ibn Mâjah*, no. 988. Recorded by Ibn Khuzaymah, Abu Dawood and Ibn Mâjah.

[237] Recorded by Bukhari and Muslim.

The number of rak'ahs and the description of the witr prayer

The minimum for the *witr* prayer is one *rak'ah*. Ibn 'Umar narrated that the Prophet (ﷺ) said, "The night prayer is to be in two *rak'ah* sets. If one of you fears the coming of the morning, he should pray one *rak'ah* making all that he prayed an odd number."[238]

It is also permissible to perform the *witr* prayer as three, five, seven or nine *rak'ahs*. 'Â'ishah said, "The Prophet (ﷺ) did not used to pray more than eleven *rak'ahs*, not during Ramaḍân or at other times. He would pray four *rak'ahs*, and do not ask about how excellent and lengthy they were, and then he would pray four *rak'ahs*, and do not ask about how excellent and lengthy they were, and then he would pray three."[239] She also said, "The Messenger of Allah (ﷺ) used to pray thirteen *rak'ahs* during the night. Out of that, he would make *witr* with five *rak'ahs* and he would not sit but in the last of them."[240] 'Â'ishah also said, "We used to prepare the toothstick and water for him. Allah would awaken him during the night whenever He had willed. Then he would use the toothstick and make ablution. Then he would pray nine *rak'ahs* and not sit except in the eighth of them, wherein he would mention Allah, praise Him and supplicate to Him. Then he would stand and not make the salutation. He would stand and pray the ninth *rak'ah* and then sit, remember Allah, praise Him and supplicate to Him, and then make the salutation such that we could hear him. Then he would pray two *rak'ahs* while sitting after he had made the salutations. O' my son,

---

[238] Recorded by Bukhari, Muslim, Nasâ'i while Tirmidhi has something similar.

[239] Recorded by Bukhari, Muslim, Abu Dawood and Tirmidhi.

[240] This hadith is *ṣaḥeeḥ*. See Shaykh al-Albâni, *Mukhtasar Ṣaḥeeḥ Muslim*, no. 382. Recorded by Muslim, Abu Dawood and by Tirmidhi with additional text at the end.

those are eleven *rak'ahs*. When the Prophet of Allah (ﷺ) aged and became heavier, he would perform *witr* in seven *rak'ahs* and do two *rak'ahs* like what he did before. O' my son, that makes nine."[241]

If one performs the *witr* prayer in three *rak'ahs*, then one should read what is described in the following hadith: Ibn 'Abbâs said, "The Messenger of Allah (ﷺ) used to recite in the *witr* prayer, ﴾Read! In the Name of your Lord, Who has created﴿ (*Soorah al-'Ala*), ﴾Say, O' you who disbelieve,﴿ and ﴾Say, He is Allah, [the] One.﴿ respectively in each *rak'ah*."[242]

The Qunoot (special supplication) during the witr prayer

Al-Ḥasan ibn 'Ali said, "The Messenger of Allah (ﷺ) taught me what statements to say in the *witr* prayer. (He taught me to say:)

اللَّهُمَّ اهْدِنِي فِيمَنْ هَدَيْتَ وَعَافِنِي فِيمَنْ عَافَيْتَ وَتَوَلَّنِي فِيمَنْ تَوَلَّيْتَ وَبَارِكْ لِي فِيمَا أَعْطَيْتَ وَقِنِي شَرَّ مَا قَضَيْتَ فَإِنَّكَ تَقْضِي وَلا يُقْضَى عَلَيْكَ وَإِنَّهُ لا يَذِلُّ مَنْ وَالَيْتَ تَبَارَكْتَ رَبَّنَا وَتَعَالَيْتَ

'O' Allah, guide me along with those whom You have guided. Pardon me along with those whom You have pardoned. Be an ally to me along with those for whom You are an ally. Bless for me that which You have bestowed on me. Protect me from the evil that You have decreed, for verily You decree and none can decree over You. Certainly, he whom You show allegiance to is never to be abased. And he whom You take as an enemy is never to be honoured. O' our Lord, blessed and exalted are You.' "[243]

---

241 This hadith is *ṣaḥeeḥ*. See Shaykh al-Albâni, *Ṣaḥeeḥ Sunan Nasâ'i*, no. 1510. Recorded by Muslim, Abu Dawood and Nasâ'i.

242 This hadith is *ṣaḥeeḥ*. See Shaykh al-Albâni, *Ṣaḥeeḥ Sunan Nasâ'i*, no. 1607. Recorded by Tirmidhi and by Nasâ'i with additional text at the beginning of the hadith.

243 This hadith is *ṣaḥeeḥ*. See Shaykh al-Albâni, *Ṣaḥeeḥ Sunan Nasâ'i*, no.=

The Sunnah is to make this supplication before bowing. This point is based on the hadith of Ubayy ibn K'ab who said, "The Messenger of Allah (ﷺ) used to make the *qunoot* in the *witr* prayer before bowing."[244] It is not sanctioned to make the *qunoot* in the obligatory prayers unless some sort of disaster has befallen the people. In that case, it is not in only some of the prayers but may be said in all and it will be said after the bowing. Abu Hurayrah (رضي الله عنه) said, "When the Messenger of Allah (ﷺ) wanted to supplicate against anyone or for anyone, he would make the *qunoot* after the bowing."[245]

As for continually performing the *qunoot* during the Morning prayer, this is an innovation, as the Companions of the Messenger of Allah (ﷺ) explicitly stated. Abu Mâlik S'ad ibn Ṭâriq al-Ashja'ee said, "I said to my father, 'O' father, you prayed behind the Messenger of Allah (ﷺ), Abu Bakr, 'Umar, 'Uthmân and 'Ali here in Koofah for about fifty years. Did they used to make the *qunoot* in the Morning prayer?' He said, 'O' my son, it is an innovation.'"[246]

"It is inconceivable that every morning the Messenger of Allah (ﷺ) would continuously until his death say, after standing from bowing, 'O' Allah, guide me along with those whom You have guided. Be an ally to me along with those for whom You are an ally...,' saying this audibly with the Companions saying *Âmeen* behind him while such an action was not something known to the Muslim Nation, in fact most of the Muslim Nation had forgotten it,

=1647. Recorded by Abu Dawood, Tirmidhi, Ibn Mâjah and Nasâ'i.

[244] This hadith is *ṣaḥeeḥ*. See Shaykh al-Albâni, *Ṣaḥeeḥ Sunan Abi Dawood*, no. 1266. Recorded by Abu Dawood.

[245] This hadith is *ṣaḥeeḥ*. See Shaykh al-Albâni, *Ṣaḥeeḥ al-Jâmi' aṣ-Ṣagheer*, no. 4655. Recorded by Bukhari.

[246] This hadith is *ṣaḥeeḥ*. See Shaykh al-Albâni, *I'rwâ' al-Ghaleel*, no. 435. Recorded by Aḥmad and Ibn Mâjah.

including the majority — in fact, all — of the Companions, to the point that one of them would say, 'It is an innovation', as S'ad ibn Ṭâriq al-Ashja'ee said."[247]

The Late-Night Prayer

The late-night prayer is a beloved Sunnah. It is, in fact, one of the special practices of the pious. Allah (ﷻ) says:

﴿إِنَّ ٱلْمُتَّقِينَ فِى جَنَّٰتٍ وَعُيُونٍ ﴿١٥﴾ ءَاخِذِينَ مَآ ءَاتَىٰهُمْ رَبُّهُمْ ۚ إِنَّهُمْ كَانُوا۟ قَبْلَ ذَٰلِكَ مُحْسِنِينَ ﴿١٦﴾ كَانُوا۟ قَلِيلًا مِّنَ ٱلَّيْلِ مَا يَهْجَعُونَ ﴿١٧﴾ وَبِٱلْأَسْحَارِ هُمْ يَسْتَغْفِرُونَ ﴿١٨﴾ وَفِىٓ أَمْوَٰلِهِمْ حَقٌّ لِّلسَّآئِلِ وَٱلْمَحْرُومِ ﴿١٩﴾﴾ (سورة الذّاريَات: ١٥-١٩)

﴿Verily, the pious will be in the midst of Gardens and Springs [in the Paradise], taking joy in the things which their Lord has given them. Verily, they were before this doers of good. They used to sleep but little by night [invoking their Lord (Allah) and praying, with fear and hope]. And in the hours before dawn, they were [found] asking [Allah] for forgiveness, and in their properties there was the right of the beggar, and the poor who does not ask the others.﴾

(Qur'an 51: 15-19)

Abu Mâlik al-Ash'ari narrated that the Prophet (ﷺ) said, "In Paradise there is a room, from the inside you can see the outside and from the outside you can see the inside." A Bedouin stood and said, "For whom is it?" The Prophet (ﷺ) replied, "It is for the one who has good speech, gives food to others, fasts often and prays during the night when the people are sleeping."[248]

---

[247] Ibn al-Qayyim, *Zâd al-Ma'âd*, vol. 1, p. 271.

[248] This hadith is *ḥasan*. See Shaykh al-Albâni, *Ṣaḥeeḥ al-Jâmi' aṣ-Ṣagheer*,=

It is even more so recommended during Ramaḍân

Abu Hurayrah said, "The Messenger of Allah (ﷺ) would exhort people to praying at night during Ramaḍân without making it a necessary act. He would say, 'Whoever prays the (nights of) Ramaḍân with faith and hoping for reward will have his previous sins forgiven.'"[249]

Its number of rak'ahs

Its minimum is one *rak'ah* and its maximum is eleven, based on the previously quoted statement of 'Â'ishah, "The Prophet (ﷺ) did not used to pray more than eleven *rak'ahs*, not during Ramaḍân or at other times."[250]

The sanctioning of performing the night prayers of Ramaḍân in a congregation

'Â'ishah (رضي الله عنها) said, "One night the Messenger of Allah (ﷺ) prayed in the mosque and some people prayed with him. On the following night, the number of people had increased. On the third or fourth night, the Prophet (ﷺ) did not go out (to pray with them). In the morning, he said, 'I did see what you did and nothing prevented me from coming out (to pray with you) except that I feared that it would bc made obligatory upon you.' And that was during Ramaḍân."[251]

'Abdur-Raḥmân ibn al-Qâri said, "I went one night during Ramaḍân to the mosque with 'Umar ibn al-Khaṭṭâb (رضي الله عنه). The people

---

=no. 2123. [With this wording, it was recorded by Tirmidhi.] - Translator

[249] Recorded by Bukhari (but only the portion quoted from the Prophet), Muslim, Abu Dawood, Tirmidhi and Nasâ'i.

[250] Recorded by Bukhari, Muslim, Abu Dawood and Tirmidhi.

[251] Recorded by Bukhari, Muslim and Abu Dawood.

were praying in separate groups, a person praying by himself or a person leading a small group in prayer. 'Umar said, 'I think that if I were to combine all of these people behind one reciter it would be more seemly.' Then he decided to do so and gathered them all together behind Ubayy in K'ab. Then I went out with him on another night and the people were all praying behind their reciter. 'Umar said, 'What an excellent new practice this is. Those who sleep through it are better than those who are performing it' — that is, it is better to perform it at the end of the night as the people were performing it together at the beginning of the night."[252]

It is preferred for the man to pray with his wife during times other than Ramaḍân

Abu Sa'eed narrated that the Messenger of Allah (ﷺ) said: " If a man wakes his wife during the night and they pray — or he said, they pray two *rak'ahs* together — then they will be recorded among the men who remember Allah often and the women who remember Allah often."[253]

Making up missed late-night prayers

'Â'ishah (may Allah be pleased with her) said, "If the Messenger of Allah (ﷺ) would miss the late-night prayer due to pain or otherwise, he would pray twelve *rak'ahs* during the day."[254] 'Umar ibn al-Khattâb (رضي الله عنه) narrated that the Prophet (ﷺ) had said, "Whoever sleeps through his portion or part of it (during the night)

---

[252] This hadith is *ṣaḥeeḥ*. See Shaykh al-Albâni, *Mukhtasar Ṣaḥeeḥ al-Bukhari*, no. 986. Recorded by Mâlik and Bukhari.

[253] This hadith is *ṣaḥeeḥ*. See Shaykh al-Albâni, *Ṣaḥeeḥ Ibn Mâjah*, no. 1098. Recorded by Abu Dawood and Ibn Mâjah.

[254] This hadith is *ṣaḥeeḥ*. See Shaykh al-Albâni, *Ṣaḥeeḥ al-Jâmi' aṣ-Ṣagheer*, no. 1104. Recorded by Muslim, Tirmidhi, Abu Dawood, Nasâ'i and Ibn Mâjah.

and reads it between the Morning prayer and the Noon prayer shall have recorded for him as though he had read it during the night."[255]

The disapproval of leaving the late-night prayer for one who customarily performs it

'Abdullâh ibn 'Amr ibn al-'Âṣ narrated that the Messenger of Allah (ﷺ) had said to him, "O' 'Abdullâh, do not be like so-and-so. He used to get up during the night and then he abandoned performing the late-night prayer."[256]

The Forenoon prayer (*Ṣalât aḍ-Ḍuḥâ*), also known as "The Prayer of the Penitent" (*Ṣalât al-Awwâbeen*)

Its legal sanction

Abu Hurayrah said, "My dear friend [the Prophet (ﷺ)] advised me to do three (things): fast three days out of every month, pray two *rak'ahs* in the forenoon and to perform the *witr* prayer before I sleep."[257]

Its virtues

Abu Dharr narrated that the Prophet (ﷺ) said, "Every morning there is on the bones and joints of any of you a charitable act. Every

[255] This hadith is *ṣaḥeeḥ*. See Shaykh al-Albâni, *Ṣaḥeeḥ Sunan Ibn Mâjah*, no. 1104. Recorded by Muslim, Tirmidhi, Abu Dawood, Nasâ'i and Ibn Mâjah.

[256] Recorded by Bukhari and Muslim.

[257] This hadith is *ṣaḥeeḥ*. See Shaykh al-Albâni, *Mukhtasar Ṣaḥeeḥ Muslim*, no. 367. Recorded by Muslim and Abu Dawood.

saying of *Subḥânallâh* is a charitable act; every saying of 'All praise is due to Allah' is a charitable act; every saying of 'There is none worthy of worship except Allah' is a charitable act; every saying of 'Allah is greatest' is a charitable act; ordering good is a charitable act; eradicating evil is a charitable act. To fulfill that charity, it is sufficient to pray two *rak'ahs* of the forenoon."[258]

Its number of rak'ahs

The minimum number of *rak'ahs* for the Forenoon prayer is two, based on the hadith just quoted, and its maximum is eight. Umm Hâni narrated that on the day of the Conquering of Makkah, the Messenger of Allah (ﷺ) bathed in her house and then prayed eight *rak'ahs*.[259]

The best time to perform the forenoon prayer

Zayd ibn Arqam said that the Prophet (ﷺ) went out to the people of Qubâ' and they were praying the Forenoon prayer. He said, "The prayer of the penitent is when the weaned camels feel the heat of the sun," during the forenoon.[260]

Prayer Immediately After Purifying Oneself (The Sunnah of Ablution)

Abu Hurayrah (رضي الله عنه) narrated:

---

[258] This hadith is *ṣaḥeeḥ*. See Shaykh al-Albâni, *Mukhtasar Ṣaḥeeḥ Muslim*, no. 364. Recorded by Muslim and Abu Dawood.

[259] Recorded by Bukhari, Muslim, Abu Dawood, Tirmidhi and Nasâ'i.

[260] This hadith is *ṣaḥeeḥ*. See Shaykh al-Albâni, *Mukhtasar Ṣaḥeeḥ Muslim*, no. 368. Recorded by Muslim.

"The Prophet (ﷺ) said to Bilâl at the time of the Morning prayer, 'Inform me of a deed you performed in Islam concerning which you have the most hope for as I heard your footsteps in front of me in Paradise.' He replied, 'There is no deed concerning which I am more hopeful except that I never purify myself during the night or day but that I pray with that purification whatever has been recorded for me to pray.' "[261]

The Prayer of Asking for Guidance (*Ṣalât al-Istikhârah*)

It is recommended for anyone who is considering a matter to seek help from Allah in making the right choice, as described in the following hadith. Jâbir said, "The Messenger of Allah (ﷺ) used to teach us the supplication for seeking guidance in all types of matters like he would teach us a *Soorah* of the Qur'an. He would say, 'If one of you is considering a matter, he should pray two *rak'ahs*, other than obligatory prayers, and then say,

"اللَّهُمَّ إِنِّي أَسْتَخِيرُكَ بِعِلْمِكَ وَأَسْتَقْدِرُكَ بِقُدْرَتِكَ وَأَسْأَلُكَ مِنْ فَضْلِكَ الْعَظِيمِ فَإِنَّكَ تَقْدِرُ وَلا أَقْدِرُ وَتَعْلَمُ وَلا أَعْلَمُ وَأَنْتَ عَلاَّمُ الْغُيُوبِ اللَّهُمَّ إِنْ كُنْتَ تَعْلَمُ أَنَّ هَذَا الأَمْرَ خَيْرٌ لِي فِي دِينِي وَمَعَاشِي وَعَاقِبَةِ أَمْرِي — أَوْ قَالَ فِي عَاجِلِ أَمْرِي وَآجِلِهِ — فَاقْدُرْهُ لِي وَإِنْ كُنْتَ تَعْلَمُ أَنَّ هَذَا الأَمْرَ شَرٌّ لِي فِي دِينِي وَمَعَاشِي وَعَاقِبَةِ أَمْرِي — أَوْ قَالَ فِي عَاجِلِ أَمْرِي وَآجِلِهِ — فَاصْرِفْهُ عَنِّي وَاصْرِفْنِي عَنْهُ وَاقْدُرْ لِيَ الْخَيْرَ حَيْثُ كَانَ ثُمَّ رَضِّنِي بِهِ"

---

[261] Recorded by Bukhari and Muslim.

'O' Allah, I seek Your guidance by Your knowledge; I seek the ability by Your ability; and I ask of Your great bounty. For verily, You have ability and I do not have ability. And You know and I do not know. You know the world of the Unseen. O' Allah, if You know that this matter is best for me in my religion, my living and the end of my affairs — or he says: best for my near future and best for my long-term future — then decree it for me. But if You know that it is worst for me in my religion, my living and the end of my affairs — or he says: worst for my near future and worst for my long-term future — then turn it away from me, turn me away from it and decree for me the good wherever it may be and then make me pleased with it.' Then he should state his need.' "[262]

The Eclipse Prayer

If there is a solar or lunar eclipse, it is recommended to call out, "The prayer in congregation." 'Abdullâh ibn 'Amr said, "When there was a solar eclipse during the time of the Messenger of Allah (ﷺ), it was called out, 'The prayer in congregation'."[263]

When the people are gathered in the mosque, the Imam leads them in two *rak'ahs* in the manner described in the following hadith. 'Â'ishah said, "There was a solar eclipse during the lifetime of the Prophet (ﷺ). He went to the mosque and the people got in rows behind him. He made the opening *takbeer*. Then the Messenger of Allah (ﷺ) made a long Qur'anic recital. Then he made the *takbeer* and bowed a lengthy bowing. Then he said, 'Allah hears him who praises Him,' and then stood again but did not then prostrate. He

---

262 This hadith is *ṣaḥeeḥ*. See Shaykh al-Albâni, *Ṣaḥeeḥ Sunan Ibn Mâjah*, no. 1136. Recorded by Bukhari, Abu Dawood, Tirmidhi, Ibn Mâjah and Nasâ'i.

263 Recorded by Bukhari, Muslim and Nasâ'i.

recited again a lengthy recital, but shorter than the first reciting. He then made the *takbeer* and bowed a lengthy bowing, but shorter than the first. Then he said, 'Allah hears him who praises Him,' and then he prostrated. In the last *rak'ah* he did the same as in the first. Thus, he completed four bowings with four prostrations. The sun had appeared before he finished (the prayer)."[264]

A speech (khuṭbah) after the prayer

It is Sunnah for the Imam, after making the salutations of the prayer, to address the people, admonishing them, reminding them and encouraging them to do good deeds. 'Â'ishah narrated that the Messenger (ﷺ) prayed during a solar eclipse. She then described the prayer, mentioning that the Prophet (ﷺ) gave the salutations after the sun had already reappeared. Then he addressed the people, saying about solar and lunar eclipses, "They are two signs of the signs of Allah. They do not eclipse due to the life or death of anyone. So if you see them, rush to the prayer."[265] Asmâ' said, "The Prophet (ﷺ) ordered for the freeing of slaves during the solar eclipse."[266]

Abu Moosa said, "There was a solar eclipse, so the Prophet (ﷺ) got up alarmed, fearing that it may be the Hour (of Doomsday). He came to the mosque and prayed with the longest standing, bowing and prostrating that I had ever seen him perform. He then said, 'These signs that Allah sends are not due to the death or life of anyone. Instead, Allah puts the fear of Him into His slaves by such signs. If you see anything of this nature, rush to His remembrance, supplicating to Him and seeking His forgiveness.' "[267]

---

[264] Recorded by Bukhari, Muslim and Nasâ'i.

[265] Ibid.

[266] This hadith is *ṣaḥeeḥ*. See Shaykh al-Albâni, *Mukhtasar Ṣaḥeeḥ al-Bukhari*, no. 118. Recorded by Bukhari.

[267] Recorded by Bukhari, Muslim and Nasâ'i.

The apparent meaning of the Prophet's words, "Rush to..." imply obligation. Thus, the eclipse prayer is a communal obligation, as Abu 'Awânah stated in his *Ṣaḥeeḥ* (vol. 2, p. 398), wherein he entitled a chapter, "Clarifying the Obligatory Status of the Eclipse Prayer". Then he presented some of the hadith that order its performance. Ibn Khuzaymah's chapter heading has the same implication. He stated (vol. 2, p. 38), "Chapter: The Order to Pray During a Solar or Lunar Eclipse". He also mentioned some of the hadith that order its performance. Ibn Ḥajar stated in *Fatḥ al-Bâri* (vol. 2, p. 527), "The majority of the scholars state that it is an emphasized Sunnah. Abu 'Awânah explicitly stated in his *Ṣaḥeeḥ* that it is obligatory but I have not seen that from other than him, except what is related from Malik who considered it to be similar to the Friday prayer. Az-Zayn ibn al-Muneer also transmitted from Abu Ḥaneefah that he considered it obligatory. Similarly, some Ḥanafi scholars have narrated that it is obligatory."[268]

The Prayer for Rain (*Ṣalât al-Istisqâ'*)

If the rain stops and the land becomes dry, it is recommended to go to the place of the *'Eid* prayer (which is usually outside the city) to perform the prayer for rain. The Imam leads the people in two *rak'ahs*, making a lot of supplications and seeking forgiveness. He also turns his garment inside out, putting what would usually be on his right side over his left side and vice-versa. 'Ibbâd ibn Tameem narrated from his uncle 'Abdullâh ibn Zayd who said, "The Prophet (ﷺ) went out to the place of prayer and prayed for rain. Facing the

---

[268] The gist of this paragraph was taken from Shaykh al-Albâni, *Tamâm al-Minnah*, p. 261.

qiblah, he preformed two *rak'ahs* and inverted his cloak." Sufiyân said that al-Mas'oodi informed him from Abu Bakr that that meant that he would put the right side of his garment over his left side.[269] He also said, "I saw the Prophet when he went out to perform the prayer for rain. He turned his back to the people, faced the *qiblah* and supplicated. Then he inverted his cloak and led us in two *rak'ahs* of prayer, reciting the Qur'an audibly therein."[270]

The Prostration of Reciting the Qur'an

Ibn Ḥazm stated in *al-Muḥalla*, "There are fourteen places of prostration in the Qur'an: The first is at the end of *Soorah al-'Arâf*, then in *al-Ra'd*, *an-Naḥl*, *Subḥân* (*Soorah al-Isrâ'*), *Kâf Ha Ya 'Ain Ṣâd* (*Soorah Maryam*), the beginning of *al-Ḥajj*, and there is no prostration close to its end, then in *al-Furqân*, *al-Naml*, *Alif Lam Meem Tanzeel* (*Soorah as-Sajdah*), *Ṣâd*, *Ḥa Meem Fuṣṣilat*, *Wa an-Najm* at the end, then in *al-Inshiqâq* when saying, ﴾They do not prostrate,﴿ and then at the ending of *al-'Alaq*."[271]

The ruling of this prostration

Ibn Ḥazm also said, "This prostration is not obligatory but it is virtuous. This prostration is to be made during the obligatory or voluntary prayers, outside of the prayer at any time, such as when the sun rises, sets or passes the meridian. It may be done toward the

[269] Recorded by Bukhari (with this wording,) Muslim, Abu Dawood, Tirmidhi and Nasâ'i.

[270] This hadith is *ṣaḥeeḥ*. See Shaykh al-Albâni, *Ṣaḥeeḥ Sunan Abi Dawood*, no. 1029. Recorded by Bukhari with this wording. Abu Dawood recorded it but without mentioning that the Qur'anic recital was audible.

[271] Ibn Ḥazm, *al-Muḥalla*, vol. 5, Pp. 105-106.

qiblah or not toward the *qiblah*. It can be done in a state of purity or while not in a state of purity."

As for it being a virtuous act and not obligatory, one can see that the Prophet (ﷺ) read *Soorah an-Najm* and prostrated[272] while Zayd ibn Thâbit read it to him and he did not prostrate, in order to show that such is permissible, as Ibn Ḥajar noted in *Fatḥ al-Bâri* (vol. 2, p. 555).[273]

Ibn Ḥazm further said, "As for prostrating without ablution or not toward the *qiblah*, this is all because it is not a prayer. The Prophet (ﷺ) said, 'The prayers of the night and day are two *rak'ahs* each.'[274] Thus, anything less than two *rak'ahs* is not a prayer, unless there is some text stating it is a prayer, like the prayer of fear, the *Witr* prayer or the Funeral prayer. However, there is no text stating that the prostration due to reciting is a prayer."

Its virtues

Abu Hurayrah (may Allah be pleased with him) reported that the Messenger of Allah (ﷺ) said, "When the descendant of Adam recites a verse of prostration and prostrates, Satan departs crying and saying, 'O' woe, the descendant of Adam was ordered to prostrate and he prostrated and for him is Paradise while I was ordered to prostrate and I disobeyed, so for me is the Hell-fire.' "[275]

---

[272] Recorded by Bukhari, Muslim, Abu Dawood and Nasâ'i.

[273] Recorded by Bukhari, Muslim, Nasâ'i, Abu Dawood and Tirmidhi.

[274] This hadith is *ṣaḥeeḥ*. See Shaykh al-Albâni, *Ṣaḥeeḥ Sunan Abi Dawood*, no. 1151. Recorded by Abu Dawood, Tirmidhi, Ibn Mâjah and Nasâ'i.

[275] This hadith is *ṣaḥeeḥ*. See Shaykh al-Albâni, *Mukhtasar Ṣaḥeeḥ Muslim*, no. 369. Recorded by Muslim.

What one says upon prostrating

'Â'ishah said, "During the prostrating of recitation at night, the Prophet (ﷺ) would say a number of times in the prostration,

سَجَدَ وَجْهِي لِلَّذِي خَلَقَهُ وَشَقَّ سَمْعَهُ وَبَصَرَهُ بِحَوْلِهِ وَقُوَّتِهِ

'My face has prostrated to the One Who created it and brought forth its hearing and seeing by His Power and Might.'"[276] 'Ali narrated that the Prophet (ﷺ) would say the following when prostrating,

اللَّهُمَّ لَكَ سَجَدْتُ وَبِكَ آمَنْتُ وَلَكَ أَسْلَمْتُ أَنْتَ رَبِّي سَجَدَ وَجْهِيَ لِلَّذِي خَلَقَهُ فَصَوَّرَهُ وَشَقَّ سَمْعَهُ وَبَصَرَهُ فَتَبَارَكَ اللَّهُ أَحْسَنُ الْخَالِقِينَ

"O' Allah, to You I prostrate, in You I have believed and to You I submit. You are my Lord. My face has prostrated to the One Who created it, then shaped it and brought forth its hearing and seeing by His Power and Might. Blessed be Allah, the best of creators."[277]

Ibn 'Abbâs said, "I was with the Prophet (ﷺ) when a man came and said, 'Last night I saw what people see when sleeping. I saw as though I was praying toward the foot of a tree. I recited a verse of prostration and prostrated. The tree prostrated with my prostration. I heard it saying,

اللَّهُمَّ احْطُطْ عَنِّي بِهَا وِزْرًا وَاكْتُبْ لِي بِهَا أَجْرًا وَاجْعَلْهَا لِي عِنْدَكَ ذُخْرًا

'O' Allah, remove from me due to it a sin, record for me due to it a reward and store it for me with You.'" Ibn 'Abbâs further said, "I saw the Prophet (ﷺ) recite a verse of prostration and then prostrate. I

---

[276] This hadith is *ṣaḥeeḥ*. See Shaykh al-Albâni, *Ṣaḥeeḥ Sunan Abi Dawood*, no. 1255. Recorded by Abu Dawood, Tirmidhi and Nasâ'i.

[277] This hadith is *ṣaḥeeḥ*. See Shaykh al-Albâni, *Ṣaḥeeḥ Sunan Ibn Mâjah*, no. 866. Recorded by Muslim, Ibn Mâjah, Abu Dawood and Tirmidhi.

heard him saying in his prostration the same was what that man had heard the tree say."[278]

The Prostration of Thankfulness

It is recommended to make a prostration of thankfulness, following the example of the Prophet (ﷺ), for anyone who has received a blessing or has been saved from some disaster or has been given glad tidings of something that pleases him. Abu Bakrah said, "Whenever the Prophet (ﷺ) received good news or news that made him happy, he would immediately prostrate out of thankfulness to Allah, the Blessed and Exalted."[279]

The same rulings that apply to the prostration of recitation apply to this prostration.

The Prostration Due to Forgetting or Missing Something of the Prayer

It is confirmed that the Prophet (ﷺ) sometime missed something in the prayer. It is also authentically reported that he said, "I am only a human like you and I forget like you forget. Thus, if I forget, then remind me."[280]

---

[278] This hadith is *ṣaḥeeḥ*. See Shaykh al-Albâni, *Ṣaḥeeḥ Sunan Ibn Mâjah*, no. 865. Recorded by Tirmidhi and Ibn Mâjah.

[279] This hadith is *ḥasan*. See Shaykh al-Albâni, *Ṣaḥeeḥ Sunan Ibn Mâjah*, no. 1143. Recorded by Ibn Mâjah (and this is his wording), Abu Dawood & Tirmidhi.

[280] This hadith is *ṣaḥeeḥ*. See Shaykh al-Albâni, *Ṣaḥeeḥ al-Jâmi' aṣ-Ṣagheer*, no. 2339 and *I'rwâ' al-Ghaleel*, no. 339. (Recorded by Bukhari and Muslim.)

He laid down for his Nation (Ummah) certain laws that we may summarize in the following:[281]

1. When a person stands after the first two *rak'ahs* of an obligatory prayer (neglecting to perform the first *tashahhud*)

'Abdullâh ibn Buḥaynah said, "The Messenger of Allah (ﷺ) led us in two *rak'ahs* of one of the prayers and then he stood and did not sit. The people stood with him. Then when he finished the prayer and while we were waiting for him to give say the salutations, he made the *takbeer* before the salutations and made two prostrations while sitting. Then he made the salutations."[282]

Al-Mugheerah ibn Shu'ban narrated that the Messenger of Allah (ﷺ) said, "If one of you stands after two *rak'ahs* but was not completely standing, he should sit back down. However, if one stood completely, he should not sit but he should make two prostrations of forgetfulness."[283]

2. When a person prays five *rak'ahs*

'Abdullâh narrated that once the Messenger of Allah (Blessings and peace be upon him) prayed five *rak'ahs* in the Noon prayer. It was said to him, "Was the prayer increased?" He replied, "Why do you say that?" "You prayed five *rak'ahs*," was the reply.

---

[281] See as-Sayyid Sâbiq, *Fiqh as-Sunnah*, vol. 1, p. 190.

[282] Reported by Bukhari, Muslim, Nasâ'i, Abu Dawood, Tirmidhi and Ibn Mâjah.

[283] This hadith is *ṣaḥeeḥ*. See Shaykh al-Albâni, *I'rwâ' al-Ghaleel*, vol. 2, Pp. 109-110. Recorded by Abu Dawood and Ibn Mâjah. It is important to note that the hadith does not distinguish between the person being closer to standing and therefore he should continue to stand or being closer to sitting and therefore he should sit. As is apparent in the hadith, its meaning is only that if one is not completely standing, he should sit back down, even if he were close to being completely standing.

So he (ﷺ) performed two prostrations after he had given the salutations.[284]

3. When a person mistakenly gives the salutations after two or three *rak'ahs*

Abu Hurayrah (رضي الله عنه) narrated that the Messenger of Allah (ﷺ) once finished the prayer after only two *rak'ahs*. Dhu al-Yadayn said to him, "Was the prayer shortened or did you forget, O' Messenger of Allah?" The Messenger of Allah (ﷺ) asked, "Is Dhu al-Yadayn speaking the truth?" When the people answered in the affirmative, the Messenger of Allah (ﷺ) stood, prayed the last two *rak'ahs*, made the salutations, then made the *takbeer*, prostrated similar to or longer than his prostration (in prayer) and then he raised his head.[285]

'Imrân ibn Ḥuṣayn narrated that once the Messenger of Allah (ﷺ) was praying the Afternoon prayer and gave the salutations after only three *rak'ahs*. He then entered his house. One man with long hands, called al-Khirbâq, got up and told the Messenger of Allah (ﷺ) what had happened. He came out upset, dragging his cloak until he came to the people. He asked, "Is this man being truthful?" They said, "Yes." So he then prayed one *rak'ah*, then he made the salutations, then he made two prostrations and then made the salutations (again).[286]

4. When the person does not realize how much he has prayed

Ibrâheem narrated from 'Alqamah that 'Abdullâh (Ibn Mas'ood) said: The Messenger of Allah (ﷺ) prayed (and Ibrâheem was not sure if he increased or decreased the prayer).[287] When the

---

[284] Bukhari, Muslim, Abu Dawood, Tirmidhi, Ibn Mâjah and Nasâ'i.

[285] Ibid.

[286] This hadith is *ṣaḥeeḥ*. See Shaykh al-Albâni, *Ṣaḥeeḥ Ibn Mâjah*, no. 1001. Recorded by Muslim, Abu Dawood, Nasâ'i and Ibn Mâjah.

[287] Ibrâheem was in doubt but the correct view is that the Prophet (Blessings=

Prophet (ﷺ) made the salutations, it was said to him, "O' Messenger of Allah, has something changed in the prayer?" The Prophet asked why this was asked. They said, "Because you prayed such and such." The Prophet (ﷺ) then turned, faced the *qiblah* and made two prostrations. Then he turned to face us and said, "If there were some change in the prayer, I would have informed you. However, I am a human like yourselves and I forget like you forget. When I forget, remind me. When one of you becomes doubtful in the prayer, he should try to determine what is correct and finish his prayer based on that. Then he should make the salutations and perform two prostrations."[288]

Determining what is correct is by "recalling what one recited in the prayer, such as recalling that one read two specific *Soorahs* in the two *rak'ahs*, by which he will know that he had prayed two *rak'ahs* instead of only one. The person might recall that he made for first *tashahhud*, by which he would know that he had prayed two *rak'ahs* and not only one or he prayed three instead of two. He might recall that he only read *Soorah al-Fâtiḥah* by itself in one *rak'ah* and then he prayed another *rak'ah*, by which he will know that he has prayed four and not three *rak'ahs*, and so on. If he determines what is closest to what is correct, the doubt can be removed. And it makes no difference if the individual is the leader of the prayer or a follower."[289]

If he tries to determine how much he prayed but nothing becomes predominant in his mind, then he should pray based on what he is certain that he prayed, in other words the lesser amount that he has no doubt about. This is based on the hadith narrated by Abu

=and peace of Allah be upon him) made an increase in the prayer, as mentioned by Ibn al-Atheer in *Jâmi' al-Uṣool*, vol. 5, p. 541.

288 Recorded by Bukhari, Muslim, Abu Dawood, Nasâ'i and Ibn Mâjah.

289 Ibn Taymiyah, *Majmoo' al-Fatâwâ Ibn Taymiyah*, vol. 13, p. 23.

Sa'eed al-Khudri in which the Prophet (ﷺ) said, "If one of you has doubts in his prayers as to how much he has finished, three or four (*rak'ahs*, for example), he should leave and doubt and based his actions on the portion he is certain of. Then he should perform two prostrations before he says the salutations. If indeed he does pray five *rak'ahs*, these (prostrations) will make his prayer even (in its number of *rak'ahs*). If he then completes four *rak'ahs*, these two will serve to debase Satan."[290]

The status of the prostration due to forgetfulness

The prostration due to forgetfulness in obligatory, as the Prophet (ﷺ) ordered its performance, as in the aforementioned hadith, and performed it whenever he forgot something and not once did he not perform it.

The timing of the prostrations

"The apparent meaning of the statements demonstrate that there is a difference between making an increase in the prayer as opposed to missing something of the prayer as well as having doubt and being able to determine what is correct and having doubt and simply basing one's action on the minimum that one is certain of... To apply the known texts, there is an understood difference between these. It can be explained in this manner: If something was left out of the prayer, such as leaving the first *tashahhud*, the prayer needs something to restore it. This restoration is before the salutation in order to make the prayer complete, as the salutation is the ending of the prayer. However, if there were an addition to the prayer, such as an extra *rak'ah*, then there should not be another additional part in the

---

[290] This hadith is *ṣaḥeeḥ*. See Shaykh al-Albâni, *Ṣaḥeeḥ al-Jâmi' aṣ-Ṣagheer*, no. 632. Recorded by Muslim, Abu Dawood and Nasâ'i.

prayer. Thus, in this case, the prostration is after the salutations, as it is debasing to Satan. It is in the role of an independent prayer that restores what is missing in his prayer, as the Prophet (ﷺ) has made the two prostrations to be like one *rak'ah*. Similarly, if someone has doubt but is able to determine what is correct in his prayer, then the two prostrations are to debase Satan and should be after the salutations... Furthermore, if he had given the salutations and there was something left to his prayer and he completed it, it would be complete and the salutations would be extra. Thus, the prostrations have to be after the salutations as a debasement for Satan. However, if he has doubt concerning how much he prayed and nothing comes to clear to him, then he may have prayed four or five *rak'ahs*. If he ends up actually praying five, the two prostrations will make the prayer even for him, as it will be like he prayed six *rak'ahs* instead of five. Thus, in that case, it will be before the salutations. This view that we are supporting here takes into consideration all of the hadith and does not leave a single one while, at the same time, employs sound analogy in those cases not mentioned in the hadith, adjoining what is not mentioned in the texts to similar acts mentioned in the texts."[291]

The prostration of forgetfulness due to missing a sunan act of the prayer

If someone forgets a Sunnah part of the prayer, he makes the prostration of forgetfulness. The Prophet (ﷺ) said, "For everything forgotten, there are two prostrations." But this is Sunnah and not obligatory, as a related act (that is, the prostration due to what one missed) cannot be stronger than the original act (that is, the Sunnah act that was missed).[292]

---

[291] Ibn Taymiyah, *Majmoo' al-Fatâwâ*, vol. 24, p. 23.

[292] Cf., Ash-Shawkâni, *as-Sail al-Jarâr*, vol. 1, p. 275.

The Congregational Prayer

Its ruling

The congregational prayer is an obligation upon each individual who prays, unless there is some valid excuse. Abu Hurayrah (رضي الله عنه) reported that the Prophet (ﷺ) said, "By the One in Whose hand is my soul, I considered ordering a stick be lit on fire (as a torch) and then order the call to prayer to be made and then command a person to lead the prayer and myself go to the houses of those who did not attend (the congregational prayer) and burn them down. By the One in Whose hand is my soul, if one of them knew that he was to gain a bone heavy with meat or meat between two rib bones, he would have definitely attended the Night prayer."[293]

Abu Hurayrah narrated that a blind man came to the Prophet (ﷺ) saying, "O' Messenger of Allah, I have no one to guide me to the mosque." He therefore asked the Messenger of Allah (ﷺ) to excuse him from the congregation and allow him to pray in his house. The Messenger of Allah granted him permission. When the blind man had turned away, he called him back and asked, "Do you hear the call to prayer?" He replied, "Yes." He said, "Then respond to it."[294]

'Abdullâh ibn Mas'ood, the Companion of the Prophet, said, "Whoever wishes to meet Allah tomorrow as a Muslim should guard these prayers whenever he is called to them. Allah sanctioned for your Prophet the Sunnah of guidance. And part of this Sunnah is to

---

[293] Recorded by Bukhari (this is his wording), Muslim, Abu Dawood, Ibn Mâjah (without the last sentence) and Nasâ'i.

[294] This hadith is *ṣaḥeeḥ*. See Shaykh al-Albâni, *Mukhtasar Ṣaḥeeḥ Muslim* no. 320. Recorded by Muslim and Nasâ'i.

perform the prayers (in the mosques in which the call to prayer is given). If you pray in your houses like those people who stayed behind and prayed in their houses, you have left the Sunnah of your Prophet. If you leave the Sunnah of your Prophet, you will be misguided. No man purifies himself well and then goes to one of the mosques of Allah except that Allah will record for him, for every step he takes, a good deed, exalt him a degree and erase from him a sin. We have seen that no one would not attend the prayers except for someone who was well known for his hypocrisy. A man would come to the prayer being supported by two men until they placed him in the row."[295]

Ibn 'Abbâs reported that the Messenger of Allah (ﷺ) said, "Whoever hears the call to prayer and does not come to it then there is no prayer for him unless he has a valid excuse."[296]

Its virtues and excellence

'Abdullâh ibn 'Umar narrated that the Messenger of Allah (ﷺ) said, "The congregational prayer is twenty-seven times better than the prayer of a person prayed individually."[297] Abu Hurayrah also reported that the Messenger of Allah (ﷺ) said, "The prayer of a person in congregation is twenty-five levels better than the prayer of a person prayed in his house or in the market. This is because when one of you performs ablution in an excellent manner and then goes to the mosque desiring only the prayer, he will not walk a step except that he will be raised a rank and a sin will be expiated. While he

---

295 This hadith is *ṣaḥeeḥ*. See Shaykh al-Albâni, *Ṣaḥeeḥ al-Jâmi' aṣ-Ṣagheer*, no. 631. Recorded by Muslim, Nasâ'i, Abu Dawood and Ibn Mâjah.

296 This hadith is *ṣaḥeeḥ*. See Shaykh al-Albâni, *Ṣaḥeeḥ al-Jâmi' aṣ-Ṣagheer*, no. 645. Recorded by Ibn Mâjah, al-Ḥâkim and al-Bayhaqi.

297 Recorded by Bukhari, Muslim, Tirmidhi, Nasâ'i and Ibn Mâjah.

prays, the Angels invoke prayers upon him for as long as he remains seated in his place of worship, saying, 'O' Allah have mercy on him, O' Allah forgive him, O' Allah turn towards him.' And you are continually considered in the prayer as long as you are waiting for the prayer."[298]

Abu Hurayrah also narrated that the Prophet (ﷺ) said, "For whoever goes out to the mosque in the beginning of the day and at the end of the day, Allah will prepare his lodging in Paradise every time he goes in the beginning and end of the day."[299]

Do women attend the congregational prayers?

It is permissible for women to go to the mosque and attend the congregational prayers on the condition that they avoid any kind of beautification or perfume that may stir the desires or lead to temptation.[300] Ibn 'Umar narrated that the Prophet (ﷺ) said, "Do not prevent your women from attending the mosques. And their homes are better for them."[301] Abu Hurayrah narrated that the Messenger of Allah (ﷺ) said, "Any woman who has applied the fragrance of incense must not attend the Night prayer with us."[302] Abu Hurayrah also narrated that the Prophet (ﷺ) said as well, "Do not prevent the female slaves of Allah from the mosques of Allah, but let them go out without having perfumed themselves."[303]

---

[298] Recorded by Bukhari, Muslim and Abu Dawood.

[299] Recorded by Bukhari and Muslim.

[300] As-Sayyid Sâbiq, *Fiqh as-Sunnah*, vol. 1, p. 193.

[301] This hadith is *ṣaḥeeḥ*. See Shaykh al-Albâni, *Ṣaḥeeḥ Sunan Abi Dawood*, no. 530. Recorded by Abu Dawood and Aḥmad.

[302] This hadith is *ṣaḥeeḥ*. See Shaykh al-Albâni, *Ṣaḥeeḥ al-Jâmi' aṣ-Ṣagheer*, no. 2703. Recorded by Muslim, Abu Dawood and Nasâ'i.

[303] This hadith is *ḥasan* ṣaḥeeḥ. See Shaykh al-Albâni, *Ṣaḥeeḥ Sunan Abi Dawood*, no. 529. Recorded by Abu Dawood and Aḥmad.

"Their houses are better for them"

Although it is allowed for a woman to go to the mosque, her prayer in her own house is more excellent. Umm Ḥumayd al-Sâ'diyah narrated that she went to the Messenger of Allah (ﷺ) and said, "O' Messenger of Allah, I love to pray with you." He replied, "I am aware that you love to pray with me. But your prayer in your chamber is better than your prayer in your room. And your prayer in your room is better than your prayer in your house. Your prayer in your house is better than your prayer in the mosque of your people. And your prayer in the mosque of your people is better than your prayer in my mosque."[304]

The etiquette of walking to the mosque

Abu Qatâdah said, "While we were praying with the Prophet (ﷺ) when he heard some men making some noise. When he had finished the prayer, he said, 'What was going on with you?' They said, 'We hurried to get to the prayer.' So he told them, 'Do not do that. When you come to the prayer, you must have calmness. That part of the prayer that you catch, pray it and complete what you missed.'"[305]

Abu Hurayrah narrated that the Prophet (ﷺ) said, "If you hear the announcing of the commencing of the prayer, walk to the prayer with calmness and dignity and do not run. That part of the prayer that you catch, pray it and complete what you missed."[306]

K'ab ibn 'Ujrah narrated that the Messenger of Allah (ﷺ) said, "When one of you performs the ablution in an excellent manner and

---

[304] This hadith is *ḥasan*. Recorded by Aḥmad and Ibn Khuzaymah.

[305] Recorded by Bukhari and Muslim.

[306] Recorded by Bukhari (this is his wording), Muslim, Abu Dawood, Tirmidhi, Nasâ'i and Ibn Mâjah.

then leaves with the intention of going to the mosque, let him not interlace his hands because he is in prayer."[307]

What to say while leaving one's house

Anas ibn Mâlik narrated that the Prophet (ﷺ) said, "When a person leaves his home and says,

بِسْمِ اللَّهِ تَوَكَّلْتُ عَلَى اللَّهِ لا حَوْلَ وَلا قُوَّةَ إِلاَّ بِاللَّهِ

'With the name of Allah, I put my trust in Allah and there is no might or power except with Allah.' It will be said to him, 'You are guided, sufficed and protected.' The devils will go away from him."[308]

In a narration in which Ibn 'Abbâs describes spending the night at the Messenger of Allah's house and how he prayed at night, he stated that the caller made the call to prayer and the Prophet (ﷺ) went out to the prayer, saying,

اللَّهُمَّ اجْعَلْ فِي قَلْبِي نُورًا وَفِي لِسَانِي نُورًا وَاجْعَلْ فِي سَمْعِي نُورًا وَاجْعَلْ فِي بَصَرِي نُورًا وَاجْعَلْ مِنْ خَلْفِي نُورًا وَمِنْ أَمَامِي نُورًا وَاجْعَلْ مِنْ فَوْقِي نُورًا وَمِنْ تَحْتِي نُورًا اللَّهُمَّ أَعْطِنِي نُورًا

"O' Allah, make a light in my heart; and on my tongue a light; and in my hearing a light; and in my vision a light; and make behind me a light; and in front of me a light; and behind me a light; and above me a light; and below me a light; and O' Allah give me light."[309]

---

[307] This hadith is *ṣaḥeeḥ*. See Shaykh al-Albâni, *Ṣaḥeeḥ Sunan Tirmidhi*, no. 316. Recorded by Tirmidhi and Abu Dawood.

[308] This hadith is *ṣaḥeeḥ*. See Shaykh al-Albâni, *Ṣaḥeeḥ Sunan al-Jâmi' aṣ-Ṣagheer*, no. 6419. Recorded by Abu Dawood and Tirmidhi.

[309] This hadith is *ṣaḥeeḥ*. See Shaykh al-Albâni, *Mukhtasar Ṣaḥeeḥ Muslim*, no. 379. Recorded by Muslim and Abu Dawood.

What to say upon entering the mosque

'Abdullâh ibn 'Amr ibn al-'Âṣ narrated that when the Prophet (ﷺ) would enter the mosque, he would say,

أَعُوذُ بِاللَّهِ الْعَظِيمِ وَبِوَجْهِهِ الْكَرِيمِ وَسُلْطَانِهِ الْقَدِيمِ مِنَ الشَّيْطَانِ الرَّجِيمِ

"I seek refuge in Allah, the Great, and in His Noble Face and His ancient rule, from the accursed Satan."[310]

Fâṭimah (رضي الله عنها), the daughter of the Messenger of Allah (ﷺ), said that when the Messenger of Allah (ﷺ) would enter the mosque, he would say,

بِسْمِ اللَّهِ وَالسَّلَامُ عَلَى رَسُولِ اللَّهِ اللَّهُمَّ اغْفِرْ لِي ذُنُوبِي وَافْتَحْ لِي أَبْوَابَ رَحْمَتِكَ

"In the name of Allah and peace be upon the Messenger of Allah. O' Allah forgive me my sins and open for me the doors of Your Mercy." And upon leaving, he would say,

بِسْمِ اللَّهِ وَالسَّلَامُ عَلَى رَسُولِ اللَّهِ اللَّهُمَّ اغْفِرْ لِي ذُنُوبِي وَافْتَحْ لِي أَبْوَابَ فَضْلِكَ

"In the name of Allah and peace be upon the Messenger of Allah. O' Allah forgive me my sins and open for me the doors of Your Bounty."[311]

---

[310] This hadith is *ṣaḥeeḥ*. See Shaykh al-Albâni, *Ṣaḥeeḥ Sunan Abi Dawood*, no. 441. Recorded by Abu Dawood.

[311] This hadith is *ṣaḥeeḥ*. See Shaykh al-Albâni, *Ṣaḥeeḥ Sunan Ibn Mâjah*, no. 625. Recorded by Ibn Mâjah and Tirmidhi.

The prayer of "Greeting the mosque"

When a person enters the mosque, it is obligatory upon him to pray two *rak'ahs* before he sits. Abu Qatâdah narrated that the Prophet said, "When one of you enters the mosque, he should not sit until he prays two *rak'ahs*."[312] I have said that it is obligatory due to the most apparent implication of the imperative for which there is no related evidence that shows that its apparent implication is not what is meant. The only objection to this may be the hadith of Ṭalḥah ibn 'Ubaydullâh in which the Bedouin with dishevelled hair came to the Messenger of Allah (ﷺ) and said, "O' Messenger of Allah, inform me of what Allah has obligated upon me concerning the prayer?" The Prophet (ﷺ) replied, "The five (daily) prayers, unless you also do some voluntarily."[313]

"To quote this hadith as evidence that this prayer (of 'greeting the mosque') is not obligatory is problematic in my view. This is because when explaining the very basic of Islam it is not appropriate to make additional comments that are not relevant at that point. If this were not true, then all of the obligations of the Shari'ah would only be the five (pillars) mentioned [in the hadith quoted above when the Prophet (ﷺ) was speaking to the Bedouin]. This, obviously, goes against the consensus and invalidates the majority of the Shari'ah. Instead, one follows a later coming evidence if it is authenticated and abides by what it implies of obligation, recommendation and so forth. On this point there is a difference of opinion but this is the stronger of the two opinions."[314] The obligatory status of this prayer is further strengthened by the fact that the Prophet (ﷺ) ordered its performance.

---

312 Recorded by Bukhari, Muslim, Abu Dawood, Tirmidhi, Ibn Mâjah and Nasâ'i.

313 Recorded by Bukhari, Muslim, Abu Dawood and Nasâ'i.

314 Ash-Shawkâni, *Nail al-Awṭâr*, vol. 1, p. 364.

One performs this prayer even if the Imam is speaking (during the Friday prayer)

Jâbir ibn 'Abdullâh narrated that a man came while the Prophet (ﷺ) was giving the speech on Friday and the Prophet (ﷺ) said to him, "O' so and so, have you prayed?" He replied in the negative, so the Prophet (ﷺ) told him, "Stand and pray."[315]

"If this prayer is to be left, it should have been left under his circumstances because he already sat, while this prayer is supposed to be before one sits, he was ignorant of its ruling and the Prophet (ﷺ) had to cut off his speech to speak to him and order him to pray the prayer of greeting the mosque. If the prayer of greeting the mosque were not so important during other times, why would the Prophet (ﷺ) had paid so much attention to it during this time."[316]

If the beginning of the prayer is announced, there is no prayer except the obligatory prayer

Abu Hurayrah narrated that the Prophet (ﷺ) said, "When the announcement of the commencing of the prayer is said, there is no prayer except the obligatory prayer."[317]

Mâlik ibn Buḥaynah narrated that the Messenger of Allah (ﷺ) saw a man praying two *rak'ahs* after the announcement for the commencement of the prayer had been given. When the Messenger of Allah (ﷺ) finished, the people surrounded him and the Messenger of Allah (ﷺ) said to him, "Is the Morning prayer four *rak'ahs*! Is the

---

[315] Recorded by Bukhari, Muslim, Abu Dawood, Tirmidhi, Ibn Mâjah and Nasâ'i.

[316] An-Nawawi, *Sharḥ Ṣaḥeeḥ Muslim*, vol. 5, p. 226.

[317] This hadith is *ṣaḥeeḥ*. See Shaykh al-Albâni, *Mukhtasar Ṣaḥeeḥ Muslim*, no. 263. Recorded by Muslim, Abu Dawood, Tirmidhi, Ibn Mâjah and Nasâ'i.

morning prayer four *rak'ahs*!"[318]

The excellence of catching the opening takbeer with the Imam

Anas narrated that the Messenger of Allah (ﷺ) said, "Whoever prays for the sake of Allah forty days in a congregation, catching the first *takbeer*, then written for him will be freedom from two matters: freedom from the Hell-fire and freedom from hypocrisy."[319]

Whoever comes to the mosque after the Imam had finished

Sa'eed ibn al-Musayyab said, "A man from the Anṣâr was about to die and he said, 'I shall narrate to you a hadith which I am not narrating except out of hope for reward. I heard the Messenger of Allah (ﷺ) say, 'If one of you performs the ablution well and then goes out to the prayer, then he will not raise his right foot except that Allah will record for him a good deed and he will not step with his left except that Allah will remove a sin from him, whether he be close or distant (from the mosque). If he comes to the mosque and prays in a congregation, he will be forgiven. If he comes to the mosque and they had already prayed part and part is remaining and he prays what he catches and completes the rest, the (reward) will be the same. And if he comes to the mosque and they have already prayed and he completes the prayer (by himself), the (reward) will be the same.'''"[320]

---

[318] Recorded by Bukhari (this is his wording) and Muslim.

[319] This hadith is *ḥasan*. See Shaykh al-Albâni, *Ṣaḥeeḥ Sunan Tirmidhi*, no. 200. Recorded by Tirmidhi.

[320] This hadith is *ṣaḥeeḥ*. See Shaykh al-Albâni, *Ṣaḥeeḥ Sunan Abi Dawood*, no. 527. Recorded by Abu Dawood.

Abu Hurayrah narrated that the Prophet (ﷺ) said, "Whoever makes ablution well and then goes out to the mosque but finds that the people had already prayed will be rewarded by Allah a reward similar to the reward of those who prayed and were present without their reward being diminished in any way."[321]

Joining the prayer with the Imam regardless of what position he is in

'Ali ibn Abu Ṭâlib and Mu'âdh ibn Jabal (may Allah be pleased with them) both said that the Messenger of Allah (ﷺ) said, "If one of you comes to the prayer and the Imam is in a certain part (of the prayer), then he should perform whatever the Imam is performing."[322]

When should one count the rak'ah?

Abu Hurayrah narrated that the Messenger of Allah (ﷺ) said, "If you come to the prayer and we are in prostration, prostrate and do not count it as (a complete *rak'ah*). Whoever catches the bowing has caught the prayer."[323]

Whoever bows before reaching the row

Abu Bakrah narrated that he came while the Prophet (ﷺ) was bowing and, therefore, he immediately bowed before entering the row. He mentioned that to the Prophet (ﷺ) who told him, "May Allah

---

[321] This hadith is *ṣaḥeeḥ*. See Shaykh al-Albâni, *Ṣaḥeeḥ Sunan Abi Dawood*, no. 528. Recorded by Abu Dawood and Nasâ'i.

[322] This hadith is *ṣaḥeeḥ*. See Shaykh al-Albâni, *Ṣaḥeeḥ Sunan Tirmidhi*, no. 484 and *Ṣaḥeeḥ al-Jâmi' aṣ-Ṣagheer*, no. 261. Recorded by Tirmidhi.

[323] This hadith is *ṣaḥeeḥ*. See Shaykh al-Albâni, *Ṣaḥeeḥ al-Jâmi' aṣ-Ṣagheer*, no. 468. Recorded by Abu Dawood.

increase you in eagerness, do not repeat (it)."[324]

'Aṭâ' narrated that he heard Ibn az-Zubayr saying while on the pulpit, "If one of you comes to the mosque and the people are bowing, he should bow and walk while bowing until he reaches the row. That is the Sunnah."[325] And Zayd ibn Wahb said, "I went with 'Abdullâh, that is, Ibn Mas'ood, from his house to the mosque. When we reached the mosque, the Imam bowed, so 'Abdullâh made the *takbeer* and bowed, and I bowed with him. Then we walked until we reached the row, at which time the people raised their heads. When the Imam had finished the prayer, I stood up, thinking that I had not caught that prayer. 'Abdullâh took my hand and sat me back down, saying, 'You have caught (the *rak'ah*).' "[326]

The Imam is ordered to make things easy upon the people

Abu Hurayrah reported that the Prophet (ﷺ) said, "When one of you prays with the people, let him be brief for among them are the weak, the ill and the aged. When one of you prays on his own, he may lengthen the prayer as much as he likes."[327]

The Imam should lengthen the first rak'ah

Abu Sa'eed said, "The beginning of the Noon prayer was announced and a person could go to (the graveyard of) al-Baqee' and

---

[324] This hadith is *ṣaḥeeḥ*. See Shaykh al-Albâni, *Ṣaḥeeḥ al-Jâmi' aṣ-Ṣagheer*, no. 3565. Recorded by Bukhari, Abu Dawood and Nasâ'i.

[325] The chain of this report is *ṣaḥeeḥ*. See Shaykh al-Albâni, *Silsilat al-Aḥâdeeth aṣ-Ṣaḥeeḥah*, no. 229.

[326] This hadith is *ṣaḥeeḥ*. See Shaykh al-Albâni, *Silsilat al-Aḥâdeeth aṣ-Ṣaḥeeḥah*, vol. 2, p. 52. Recorded by al-Bayhaqi.

[327] Recorded by Bukhari (and this is his wording), Muslim, Abu Dawood, Tirmidhi and Nasâ'i.

fulfill his need, make ablution and then come while the Messenger of Allah (ﷺ) would still be in the first *rak'ah*, owing to how long he would make it."[328]

It is obligatory to follow the Imam and it is forbidden to precede him

Anas narrated that the Prophet (ﷺ) said, "Indeed, the Imam has only been appointed to be followed. When he says the *takbeer,* then say the *takbeer.* When he goes into prostration, then go into prostration. When he rises, then rise..."[329]

Abu Hurayrah narrated that the Prophet (ﷺ) said, "Is not the one who raises his head before the Imam afraid that Allah might transform his head into that of a donkey or disfigure his face to that of a donkey?"[330]

Who has the most right to be the Imam?

Abu Mas'ood al-Anṣâri narrated that the Messenger of Allah (ﷺ) said, "The one leading the people in prayer should be the one who is most proficient in the Book of Allah. If they are equal in that, then the one most knowledgeable of the Sunnah. If they are equal in that, then the one who made the emigration earlier. If they are equal in their emigration, then the one who became Muslim first. A man should not lead another man in prayer in the place of his authority nor sit in the seat reserved for him in his house except with his permission."[331]

---

[328] This hadith is *ṣaḥeeḥ*. See Shaykh al-Albâni, *Ṣaḥeeḥ Sunan Nasâ'i*, no. 930. Recorded by Muslim and Nasâ'i.

[329] Recorded by Bukhari, Muslim, Abu Dawood, Tirmidhi, Nasâ'i and Ibn Mâjah.

[330] Ibid.

[331] This hadith is *ṣaḥeeḥ*. See Shaykh al-Albâni, *Mukhtasar Ṣaḥeeḥ Muslim*,=

This hadith shows that the occupant of a house or the appointed Imam of a mosque has more right than others to be the Imam, unless they give said permission to others. This point is based on the later portion of the above hadith, "A man should not lead another man in prayer in the place of his authority."

A child being the Imam

'Amr ibn Salma said, "When Makkah was conquered, every tribe rushed to embrace Islam. And my father rushed to embrace Islam before (the other members of) my tribe. When my father returned, he said, 'By Allah, I have come to you from the Prophet for certain. He (ﷺ) said: 'Perform such and such prayer at such and such time. When the time for prayer comes, one of you should make the call to prayer and the one who know the most Qur'an should lead the prayer.' So the people looked and they did not find anyone who knew more Qur'an than I because I used to learn from the caravans. So they put me forward (to lead them) and at that time I was a child of six or seven years.' "[332]

The Imam praying a voluntary prayer and the follower praying an obligatory prayer and vice-versa

Jâbir narrated that Mu'âdh ibn Jabal (رضي الله عنه) used to pray with the Prophet (ﷺ) and then go to lead his people in prayer.[333]

=no. 316. Recorded by Muslim, Tirmidhi, Abu Dawood, Nasâ'i and Ibn Mâjah. In a narration by Muslim and others, it also states, "If they are equal in the time of their emigration, then the elder."

332 This hadith is *ṣaḥeeḥ*. See Shaykh al-Albâni, *Ṣaḥeeḥ Sunan Nasâ'i*, no. 761. Recorded by Bukhari, Abu Dawood and Nasâ'i.

333 This hadith is *ṣaḥeeḥ*. See Shaykh al-Albâni, *Mukhtasar Ṣaḥeeḥ al-Bukhari*, no. 387. Recorded by Bukhari, Muslim, Abu Dawood and Nasâ'i.

Yazeed ibn al-Aswad said that he had prayed with the Prophet (ﷺ) when he was a young boy. When the Prophet (ﷺ) had prayed, there were two men at the end of the mosque who had not prayed (with them). He called for them to come and they came shaking in fear. He asked them, "What prevented you from praying with us?" They said, "We prayed at our residences." The Prophet (ﷺ) then told them, "Do not do so. If you prayed in your residences and then come across the prayer with the Imam, pray with him for it will be counted as an optional prayer for you."[334]

The Imam being a traveller and the follower being a resident and vice-versa

Ibn 'Umar said, " 'Umar lead the people of Makkah in the Noon prayer and gave the salutations after two *rak'ahs*. Then he said, 'Complete your prayers, O' people of Makkah, for we are travellers.' "[335]

If a traveller is following a resident Imam, the traveller also completes the prayer

Moosa ibn Salamah al-Hudhali said, "I asked Ibn 'Abbâs, 'How shall I pray if I am in Makkah and I do not pray with the Imam?' He replied, 'Two *rak'ahs* — the Sunnah of Abu al-Qâsim [meaning the Prophet (ﷺ)].' "[336]

---

[334] This hadith is *ṣaḥeeḥ*. See Shaykh al-Albâni, *Ṣaḥeeḥ Sunan Abi Dawood*, no. 538. Recorded by Abu Dawood, Tirmidhi and Nasâ'i.

[335] This hadith is *ṣaḥeeḥ*. See al-Arnâ'oot's footnotes to *Jâmi' al-Uṣool*, vol. 5, p. 708. Recorded by 'Abdur-Razzâq.

[336] This hadith is *ṣaḥeeḥ*. See Shaykh al-Albâni, *I'rwâ' al-Ghaleel*, no. 571. Recorded by Muslim and Nasâ'i.

Abu Mijlaz said, "I said to Ibn 'Umar, 'If a traveller catches two *rak'ahs* with the people — that is, with resident, non-travellers — will those two *rak'ahs* suffice for him or does he have to pray according to their prayer?' He laughed and said, 'He prays according to their prayer.' "[337]

One who has the ability to stand following an Imam who is sitting and sitting with him

'Â'ishah (﵂) narrated, "Allah's Messenger (ﷺ) prayed sitting in his house during an illness while some people prayed behind him standing. The Prophet (ﷺ) signalled to them to sit down. On completion of the prayer he said, 'The Imam is to be followed. Bow when he bows and raise your heads (from bowing when he raises his head); and if he prays sitting, then pray sitting.' "[338]

Anas said, "Once Allah's Messenger (ﷺ) fell from a horse and injured the right side of his body. He offered one of the prayers while sitting and we also prayed behind him sitting. When he completed the prayer, he said, "Indeed, the Imam has only been appointed to be followed. When he says the *takbeer,* then say the *takbeer*. When he goes into prostration, then go into prostration. When he rises, then rise. When he says, *Sami' Allâhu liman Ḥamidah,*' say, '*Rabbana wa lakal-ḥamd.*' And if he prays sitting, then all of you pray sitting."[339]

[337] This report has a *ṣaḥeeḥ* chain. See Shaykh al-Albâni, *I'rwâ' al-Ghaleel,* no. 22. Recorded by al-Bayhaqi.

[338] Recorded by Bukhari, Muslim and Abu Dawood.

[339] Recorded by Bukhari, Muslim, Abu Dawood, Tirmidhi, Nasâ'i and Ibn Mâjah.

If there is only one follower, he prays to the right of the Imam, exactly parallel to him

Ibn 'Abbâs said, "I spent the night at my aunt Maymoonah's. The Messenger of Allah (ﷺ) prayed the Night prayer, came and prayed four *rak'ahs* and then slept. Then he got up and prayed. I came and stood to his left and he made me stand to his right."[340]

Two or more people stand in a row behind the Imam

Jâbir narrated, "The Messenger of Allah (ﷺ) stood to pray and I stood to his left. He took me by my hand and turned me until I stood to his right. Then Jâbir ibn Ṣakhr came and stood to the left of the Messenger of Allah (ﷺ). He took both of our hands and pushed us back until we stood behind him."[341]

If the follower is a woman, she stands behind the Imam

Anas ibn Mâlik narrated that the Messenger of Allah (ﷺ) prayed with him and his mother or aunt. Anas said, "He made me stand on his right side and made the woman stand behind us."[342]

The obligation of straightening the rows

It is obligatory upon the Imam not to begin the prayer until the lines have been straightened. Either he can order someone to straighten the prayers or he himself can do it. Anas reported that the Messenger of Allah (ﷺ) said, "Straighten the rows for straightening

---

[340] This hadith is *ṣaḥeeḥ*. See Shaykh al-Albâni, *I'rwâ' al-Ghaleel*, no. 540 and *Ṣaḥeeḥ Sunan Ibn Mâjah*, no. 792. Recorded by Bukhari (and this is his wording), Muslim, Abu Dawood, Tirmidhi, Nasâ'i and Ibn Mâjah.

[341] This hadith is *ṣaḥeeḥ*. See Shaykh al-Albâni, *I'rwâ' al-Ghaleel*, no. 540. Recorded by Muslim, Abu Dawood and Ibn Mâjah.

[342] Recorded by Bukhari, Muslim, Abu Dawood and Nasâ'i.

the row is part of the completion of the prayer."[343] Abu Mas'ood said, "The Messenger of Allah (ﷺ) would touch our shoulders in the prayer and say, 'Be straight and do not differ, for then your hearts will differ.'"[344]

An-Nu'mân ibn Basheer said, "The Messenger of Allah (ﷺ) used to straighten our rows in such a manner that it were as if he were going to use the rows to straighten an arrow. He continued to do that until we understood what he wanted from us. But one day he came out and was about to start the prayer when he saw a man with his chest sticking out in the row. He then said, 'Servants of Allah! You must straighten your rows or Allah will cause dissension among your faces (that is, among yourselves).'"[345]

Ibn 'Umar narrated that the Messenger of Allah (ﷺ) said, "Set the rows in order, stand shoulder to shoulder, close the gaps, be pliant in the hands of your brethren and do not leave any gaps for Satan. If anyone joins up a row, Allah will join him up. And if anyone breaks a row, Allah will break him off."[346]

Anas narrated that the Messenger of Allah (ﷺ) said,

"Stand close together in your rows and bring them near one another. Stand with your necks even to each other. By the One in whose hand is my soul, I can certainly see Satan coming in through openings in the row like little black sheep."[347]

---

[343] Bukhari, Muslim (and this is his wording), Abu Dawood and Ibn Mâjah.

[344] This hadith is *ṣaḥeeḥ*. See Shaykh al-Albâni, *Ṣaḥeeḥ al-Jâmi' aṣ-Ṣagheer*, no. 961. Recorded by Muslim.

[345] This hadith is *ṣaḥeeḥ*. See Shaykh al-Albâni, *Ṣaḥeeḥ al-Jâmi' aṣ-Ṣagheer*, no. 3972. Recorded by Muslim, Abu Dawood, Tirmidhi and Nasâ'i.

[346] This hadith is *ṣaḥeeḥ*. See Shaykh al-Albâni, *Ṣaḥeeḥ Sunan Abi Dawood*, no. 620. Recorded by Abu Dawood.

[347] This hadith is *ṣaḥeeḥ*. See Shaykh al-Albâni, *Ṣaḥeeḥ Sunan Abi Dawood*, no. 621. Recorded by Abu Dawood and Nasâ'i.

How to straighten the rows

Anas said, "The Prophet (ﷺ) said, 'Make the rows in order for I see you behind me. So each would put his shoulder clinging to the shoulder of the person next to him and his heel clinging to the heel of the person next to him.'"[348]

An-Nu'mân ibn Basheer also said, "I would see a man from among us clinging his heel to the heel of his companion."[349]

The rows of the men and the women

Abu Hurayrah reported that the Messenger of Allah (ﷺ) said, "The best rows for the men are the front ones and the worst are the last ones. The best rows for the women are the last ones and the worst are the first ones."[350]

The excellence of the front rows and being on the right side of the row

Al-Barâ' ibn 'Âzib (may Allah be pleased with him) narrated that the Messenger of Allah (Blessings and peace be upon him) would say, "Indeed Allah and His Angels invoke blessings upon those who are the first rows."[351]

---

[348] This hadith is *ṣaḥeeḥ*. See Shaykh al-Albâni, *Ṣaḥeeḥ Mukhtasar Ṣaḥeeḥ al-Bukhari*, no. 393. Recorded by Bukhari.

[349] This hadith is *ṣaḥeeḥ*. See Shaykh al-Albâni, *Ṣaḥeeḥ Mukhtasar Ṣaḥeeḥ al-Bukhari*, no. 124, p. 124. Recorded by Bukhari without its complete chain.

[350] This hadith is *ṣaḥeeḥ*. See Shaykh al-Albâni, *Ṣaḥeeḥ al-Jâmi' aṣ-Ṣagheer*, no. 331. Recorded by Muslim, Abu Dawood, Tirmidhi, Nasâ'i and Ibn Mâjah.

[351] This hadith is *ṣaḥeeḥ*. See Shaykh al-Albâni, *Ṣaḥeeḥ Sunan Abi Dawood*, no. 618. Recorded by Abu Dawood and by Tirmidhi, but with the words, "the front rows."

Al-Barâ' also said, "When we prayed behind the Messenger of Allah (ﷺ) we loved to be on his right, as he would turn his face towards us." He also said, "I heard him say, 'My Lord, protect me from Your punishment on the day that You resurrect Your servants.' "[352]

Who should stand behind the Imam

Abu Mas'ood al-Anṣâri narrated that the Messenger of Allah (ﷺ) would say, "Let those who are intelligent and prudent be nearest to me and then those who are next (in such virtue) to them."[353]

Disapproval of praying between two pillars

Mu'âwiyah ibn Qurrah narrated from his father who said, "We were prohibited from making a row between two pillars during the time of the Messenger of Allah (ﷺ) and we were completely repelled from doing so."[354] This is with respect to a congregational prayer. Otherwise, there is no harm if an individual prays between two pillars if he has a *sutra* (barrier in front of him). Ibn 'Umar narrated that the Prophet (ﷺ) entered the House (of Allah, the Ka'bah) with Usâmah ibn Zayd, 'Uthmân ibn Ṭalḥah and Bilâl. He stayed there for some time. I was the first person to enter it after him. I asked Bilâl (رضي الله عنه), "Where did he pray?" He replied, "Between the two front pillars."[355]

---

[352] This hadith is *ṣaḥeeḥ*. See Shaykh al-Albâni, *at-Targheeb*, no. 500. Recorded by Muslim.

[353] This hadith is *ṣaḥeeḥ*. See Shaykh al-Albâni, *Ṣaḥeeḥ Sunan Abi Dawood*, no. 626. Recorded by Muslim, Abu Dawood, Ibn Mâjah and Nasâ'i.

[354] This hadith is *ṣaḥeeḥ*. See Shaykh al-Albâni, *Ṣaḥeeḥ Sunan Ibn Mâjah*, no. 821. Recorded by Ibn Mâjah, al-Ḥâkim and al-Bayhaqi.

[355] This hadith is *ṣaḥeeḥ*. See Shaykh al-Albâni, *Mukhtasar Ṣaḥeeḥ Bukhari*, p. 139. Recorded by Bukhari.

Valid excuses for not attending the congregational prayers

1. Cold and rain

Nâfi' narrated that on a cold and wind day, Ibn 'Umar made the call to prayer and announced during it, "Pray in your homes." Then he said, "The Messenger of Allah (ﷺ) would tell the caller to prayer on cold and rainy nights to say, 'Pray in your homes.' "[356]

2. One's meal being presented

Ibn 'Umar narrated that the Messenger of Allah (ﷺ) said, "If your dinner is presented to you and the prayer is commenced, begin with your dinner and do not be hasty until you finish it." Thus, if the dinner was presented to Ibn 'Umar and the prayer would start, he would not go to the prayer until he had finished, even though he could hear the reciting of the Imam.[357]

3. When needing to relieve oneself

'Â'ishah (may Allah be pleased with her) narrated that she heard the Messenger of Allah (ﷺ) say, "There is no prayer when the food has been served or when one is repressing the urge to relieve himself."[358]

The Prayer of the Traveller

The shortening of the prayer is obligatory upon the traveller during the Noon, Afternoon and Night prayers. Allah (ﷻ) has said:

---

[356] Recorded by Bukhari, Muslim, Abu Dawood and Nasâ'i.

[357] Recorded by Bukhari, Muslim (without the statement about Ibn 'Umar), and Abu Dawood.

[358] This hadith is *ṣaḥeeḥ*. See Shaykh al-Albâni, *Ṣaḥeeḥ al-Jâmi' aṣ-Ṣagheer*, no. 7509. Recorded by Muslim and Abu Dawood.

﴿وَإِذَا ضَرَبْتُمْ فِي ٱلْأَرْضِ فَلَيْسَ عَلَيْكُمْ جُنَاحٌ أَن تَقْصُرُوا۟ مِنَ ٱلصَّلَوٰةِ إِنْ خِفْتُمْ أَن يَفْتِنَكُمُ ٱلَّذِينَ كَفَرُوٓا۟ ... ﴿١٠١﴾﴾ (سورة النِّساء: ١٠١)

﴿And when you [Muslims] travel in the land, there is no sin on you if you shorten your prayer if you fear that the disbelievers may attack you...﴾ *(Qur'an 4: 101)*

Ya'la ibn Umayah asked 'Umar ibn al-Khaṭṭâb about these words, ﴿If you fear that the disbelievers may attack you﴾. He said, "The people are now in security." 'Umar replied, "I wondered about the same thing that you wonder about. So I asked the Messenger of Allah (ﷺ) about it and he said, 'This is a charity that Allah has bestowed upon you, so accept it.' "[359]

Ibn 'Abbâs said, "Allah obligated the prayer upon the tongue of your Prophet (ﷺ): while resident four *rak'ahs*, while travelling two *rak'ahs* and while in fear one *rak'ah*."[360] 'Umar also said, "The prayer of the traveller is two *rak'ahs*; the Friday prayer is two *rak'ahs*; the (*'Eid* prayers) of breaking the fast and of the sacrifice are two *rak'ahs*. Each of them is complete without any shortening. This is from the tongue of Muhammad (ﷺ)."[361] And 'Â'ishah said, "When the prayers were first made obligatory, they were two *rak'ahs* each. The prayer of the traveller was affirmed as such while the prayer of the resident was lengthened."[362]

---

[359] This hadith is *ṣaḥeeḥ*. See Shaykh al-Albâni, *Ṣaḥeeḥ al-Jâmi' aṣ-Ṣagheer*, no. 3762. Recorded by Muslim, Abu Dawood, Nasâ'i, Ibn Mâjah and Tirmidhi.

[360] This hadith is *ṣaḥeeḥ*. See Shaykh al-Albâni, *Ṣaḥeeḥ Sunan Ibn Mâjah*, no. 876. Recorded by Muslim, Abu Dawood, Nasâ'i and Ibn Mâjah (but without the last phrase).

[361] This hadith is *ṣaḥeeḥ*. See Shaykh al-Albâni, *Ṣaḥeeḥ Sunan Ibn Mâjah*, no. 871. Recorded by Nasâ'i and Ibn Mâjah.

[362] Recorded by Bukhari, Muslim, Abu Dawood and Nasâ'i.

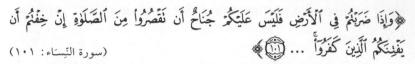

Ibn 'Umar said, "I accompanied the Messenger of Allah (ﷺ) on travels and he never prayed more than two *rak'ahs* until he died. And I accompanied Abu Bakr (on travels) and he never prayed more than two *rak'ahs* until he died. I accompanied 'Umar (on travels) and he never prayed more than two *rak'ahs* until he died. Then I accompanied 'Uthmân (on travels) and he never prayed more than two *rak'ahs* until he died. And Allah (ﷻ) has said:

﴿لَّقَدْ كَانَ لَكُمْ فِي رَسُولِ ٱللَّهِ أُسْوَةٌ حَسَنَةٌ ... ﴿٢١﴾﴾ (سورة الأحزاب: ٢١)

﴿Indeed in the Messenger of Allah you have an excellent example...﴾ *(Qur'an 33: 21)*."[363]

The distance of the journey

The scholars have differed greatly over the minimum length of a journey that allows the shortening of the prayers. Ibn al-Mundhir and others report more than twenty various opinions on this topic. The strongest view is that, "There is no limit set in principle, except for what may be described as 'travelling' in the language of the Arabs addressed by the Prophet (ﷺ). If there were a specific limit for travelling other than the point that we just mentioned, why would the Prophet (ﷺ) completely neglect to mention it and why did they neglect to ask him about it and why would they agree upon not passing on that limitation to us?"[364]

When the shortening of the prayer begins

"The majority of the scholars state that the shortening of the prayer is sanctioned in one departs from the residence and leaves the city and this condition is not met until one leaves the last of its

[363] Recorded by Bukhari, Muslim, Abu Dawood and Nasâ'i.

[364] Ibn Ḥazm, *al-Muḥalla*, vol. 5, p. 21.

houses. Ibn al-Mundhir said, 'I do not know of the Prophet (ﷺ) shortening his prayers during any of his travels until after he completely left Madeenah.' Anas said, 'I prayed the Noon prayer as four *rak'ahs* with the Prophet (ﷺ) in Madeenah and at Dhul-Ḥulayfah as two *rak'ahs*.' "[365]

If a traveller stops at a locale for a need but does not intend to remain there, he may shorten his prayer until he departs

Jâbir said, "The Prophet (ﷺ) stayed at Tabook for twenty days, shortening his prayer (all along)."[366] Ibn al-Qayyim said, "The Prophet (ﷺ) did not say to his Nation, 'A person should not shorten his prayer if he stays longer than that.' However, it is agreed that he did remain there for that period."[367] If the person intends to stay more than nineteen days, then he should do as Ibn 'Abbâs said, "The Prophet (ﷺ) stayed in a place for nineteen days and shortened his prayers. As for us, if we travel for nineteen days, we shorten our prayers. If we stay longer than that, we complete the prayers."[368]

---

[365] As-Sayyid Sâbiq, *Fiqh as-Sunnah*, vol. 1, Pp. 240-241. The statement of Anas was recorded by Bukhari, Muslim, Abu Dawood, Tirmidhi and Nasâ'i. The prayer that he was referring to at Dhul-Ḥulayfah was the Afternoon prayer, as is made explicit in narrations other than that of Bukhari.

[366] This hadith is *ṣaḥeeḥ*. See Shaykh al-Albâni, *Ṣaḥeeḥ Sunan Abi Dawood*, no. 1094. Recorded by Abu Dawood.

[367] Quoted in as-Sayyid Sâbiq, *Fiqh as-Sunnah*, vol. 1, p. 241.

[368] This hadith is *ṣaḥeeḥ*. See Shaykh al-Albâni, *I'rwâ' al-Ghaleel*, no. 575. Recorded by Bukhari, Tirmidhi, Ibn Mâjah and Abu Dawood (except that he recorded seventeen days).

Combining Prayers

The causes for combining prayers

1. Travelling

Anas said, "When the Prophet (ﷺ) would depart before high noon, he would delay the Noon prayer until the time of the Afternoon prayer, then stop and combine them. If high noon had passed be he departed, he would pray the Noon prayer and then ride off."[369]

Mu'âdh said, "The Prophet was at the Battle of Tabook (and hence he was travelling). If (at that time) he departed before high noon, he would delay the Noon prayer until he would combine it with the Afternoon prayer, praying the two together. If he departed after high noon, he would pray the Noon and Afternoon prayers together and then set off. If he departed before the Sunset prayer, he would delay the Sunset prayer until he would combine it with the Night prayer. But if he departed after Sunset, he would prayer the Night prayer early and pray it with the Sunset prayer."[370]

Mu'âdh also narrated, "They went with the Messenger of Allah (ﷺ) during the year of Tabook. The Messenger of Allah (ﷺ) used to combine the Noon and Afternoon prayers and the Sunset and Night prayers. One day he would delay the prayer. Then he would also go out and combine the Noon and Afternoon prayers and then re-enter (the place he was staying at). Then he would go out and pray the Sunset and Night prayers together."[371]

---

[369] Recorded by Bukhari, Muslim, Abu Dawood and Nasâ'i.

[370] This hadith is *ṣaḥeeḥ*. See Shaykh al-Albâni, *Ṣaḥeeḥ Sunan Abi Dawood*, no. 1067. Recorded by Aḥmad, Abu Dawood and Tirmidhi.

[371] This hadith is *ṣaḥeeḥ*. See Shaykh al-Albâni, *Ṣaḥeeḥ Sunan Abi Dawood*, no. 1065. Recorded by Abu Dawood and Nasâ'i. The first part is also recorded by Muslim and Ibn Mâjah.

2. Rain

Nâfi' said, "When the governors would combine the Sunset and Night prayers due to rain, 'Abdullâh ibn 'Umar would combine them with them." Hishâm ibn 'Urwah stated, "His father 'Urwah, Sa'eed ibn al-Musayyab and Abu Bakr ibn 'Abdur-Raḥmân ibn al-Ḥârith ibn Hishâm ibn al-Mugheerah al-Makhzoomi used to combine the Sunset and Night prayers on rainy nights if the people would combine those prayers and they did not object to that."[372] Moosa ibn 'Uqbah said, " 'Umar ibn 'Abdul-'Azeez used to combine the Sunset and Night prayers if it rained. Sa'eed ibn al-Musayyab, 'Urwah ibn az-Zubayr, Abu Bakr ibn 'Abdur-Raḥmân and the shaykhs of that time would pray them with him and would not object to that."[373]

Ibn 'Abbâs stated, "The Messenger of Allah (ﷺ) prayed the Noon and the Afternoon prayers together and prayed the Sunset and Night prayers together without there being any fear and without travelling."[374] Ibn 'Abbâs also said, "The Messenger of Allah (ﷺ) combined the Noon and Afternoon prayers and the Sunset and Night prayers in Madeenah without being in a state of fear or rain."[375] "He recognized that combining due to rain was something well-known during the time of the Prophet (ﷺ). If this were not the case, there would have been no benefit to him specifically denying rain as a cause for the combining of the prayers."[376]

---

[372] This hadith is *ṣaḥeeḥ*. See Shaykh al-Albâni, *I'rwâ' al-Ghaleel*, vol. 3, p. 40. Recorded by Mâlik.

[373] This hadith is *ṣaḥeeḥ*. See Shaykh al-Albâni, *I'rwâ' al-Ghaleel*, vol. 3, p. 40. Recorded by al-Bayhaqi.

[374] This hadith is *ṣaḥeeḥ*. See Shaykh al-Albâni, *Ṣaḥeeḥ al-Jâmi' aṣ-Ṣagheer*, no. 1068.

[375] This hadith is *ṣaḥeeḥ*. See Shaykh al-Albâni, *Ṣaḥeeḥ al-Jâmi' aṣ-Ṣagheer*, no. 1070. Recorded by Muslim and Nasâ'i, as well as by Abu Dawood with some additional text at the end.

[376] Shaykh al-Albâni, *I'rwâ' al-Ghaleel*, vol. 3, p. 40.

3. Due to some temporary need that arises

Ibn 'Abbâs stated, "The Messenger of Allah (ﷺ) prayed the Noon and the Afternoon prayers together and prayed the Sunset and Night prayers together without there being any fear and without travelling." Abu az-Zubayr asked Sa'eed, "Why did he (the Prophet) do that?" He replied, "I asked Ibn 'Abbâs the same thing that you asked me and he replied, 'He wanted it to be such that no one of his Nation would face hardship.' "[377] Again, Ibn 'Abbâs also said, "The Messenger of Allah combined the Noon and Afternoon prayers and the Sunset and Night prayers in Madeenah without being in a state of fear or rain." He was then asked, "What did he mean by that act?" Ibn 'Abbâs said, "He wanted his Nation not to face any hardship."[378]

An-Nawawi stated in his commentary to *Ṣaḥeeḥ Muslim* (vol. 5, p. 219):

> "A number of Imams are of the opinion that it is permissible to combine prayers while resident due to some need as long as one does not take that as a general practice. This is the opinion of Ibn Seereen and Aṣḥâb from the companions of Mâlik. Al-Khaṭṭâbi has also narrated it from al-Qafâl and the elder Shâshi, of al-Shafi'ee's followers, on the authority of Abu Isḥâq al-Marwazi from a number of the scholars of hadith. It is also the conclusion if Ibn al-Mundhir. This view is supported by the plain meaning of Ibn 'Abbâs' statement, 'He wanted his Nation not to face any hardship.' He did not say that it was due to illness or any other reason. And Allah alone knows best."

---

[377] This hadith is *ṣaḥeeḥ*. See Shaykh al-Albâni, *Ṣaḥeeḥ al-Jâmi' aṣ-Ṣagheer*, no. 1068.

[378] This hadith is *ṣaḥeeḥ*. See Shaykh al-Albâni, *Ṣaḥeeḥ al-Jâmi' aṣ-Ṣagheer*, no. 1070. Recorded by Muslim and Nasâ'i, as well as by Abu Dawood with some additional text at the end.

The Friday Prayer

Attending the Friday prayer is an individual obligation upon every Muslim except for five: a slave, a woman, a child, an ill person and a traveller.

Allah (ﷻ) says:

﴿يَٰٓأَيُّهَا ٱلَّذِينَ ءَامَنُوٓاْ إِذَا نُودِىَ لِلصَّلَوٰةِ مِن يَوْمِ ٱلْجُمُعَةِ فَٱسْعَوْاْ إِلَىٰ ذِكْرِ ٱللَّهِ وَذَرُواْ ٱلْبَيْعَ ۚ ذَٰلِكُمْ خَيْرٌ لَّكُمْ إِن كُنتُمْ تَعْلَمُونَ ﴿٩﴾﴾ (سورة الجُمُعَة : ٩)

﴿O' you who believe! When the call is proclaimed for the prayer on the day of Friday, come to the remembrance of Allah and leave off business [and every other thing], that is better for you if you did but know.﴾ *(Qur'an 62: 9)*

Târiq ibn Shihâb narrated that the Prophet (ﷺ) said, "The Friday prayer is a duty and obligation upon every Muslim in the community except four: a slave, a woman, a child (non-adult) or a sick person."[379] Ibn 'Umar narrated that the Prophet (ﷺ) said as well, "There is no Friday prayer upon the traveller."[380]

The encouragement to perform it

Abu Hurayrah narrated that the Prophet (ﷺ) said, "Whoever makes *ghusl* and then comes to the Friday prayer, then prays as much as (Allah has) written for him and then remains silent until the Imam finishes his *khuṭbah*, and then he prays with him, forgiven for him will be whatever he did (of minor sins) from that Friday to the

---

[379] This hadith is *ṣaḥeeḥ*. See Shaykh al-Albâni, *Ṣaḥeeḥ Sunan Abi Dawood*, no. 942 and *Ṣaḥeeḥ al-Jâmi' aṣ-Ṣagheer*, no. 3111. Recorded by Abu Dawood, ad-Dâraquṭni, al-Bayhaqi and al-Ḥâkim.

[380] Recorded by al-Dâraquṭni.

previous Friday plus an additional three days."[381] Abu Hurayrah also narrated that the Prophet (ﷺ) said, "The five daily prayers, one Friday prayer to the next Friday prayer, Ramaḍân to the next Ramaḍân, they all expiate whatever is between them as long as the person avoids the great sins."[382]

Warning about being lackadaisical concerning the Friday prayer

Ibn 'Umar and Abu Hurayrah both reported that they heard the Prophet (ﷺ) saying upon the *minbar* (pulpit), "The people must cease from not performing the Friday prayer or Allah will put a seal over their hearts and they will then become from the heedless."[383]

'Abdullâh narrated that the Prophet (ﷺ) said about people who stayed behind from the Friday prayer, "Surely, I considered appointing someone to lead the prayer, then I would go to those men who did not attend the Friday prayer and burn down their houses upon them."[384]

Abu al-Ja'd ad-Ḍamri narrated that the Messenger of Allah (ﷺ) stated, "Whoever misses three Friday prayers because he was lackadaisical concerning them, Allah will put a seal over his heart."[385] In fact, Usâmah ibn Zayd narrated that the Prophet (ﷺ)

---

[381] This hadith is *ṣaḥeeḥ*. See Shaykh al-Albâni, *Ṣaḥeeḥ al-Jâmi' aṣ-Ṣagheer*, no. 6062. Recorded by Muslim.

[382] This hadith is *ṣaḥeeḥ*. See Shaykh al-Albâni, *Ṣaḥeeḥ al-Jâmi' aṣ-Ṣagheer*, no. 3875. Recorded by Muslim and also by Tirmidhi but without the mention of Ramadhân.

[383] This hadith is *ṣaḥeeḥ*. See Shaykh al-Albâni, *Ṣaḥeeḥ al-Jâmi' aṣ-Ṣagheer*, no. 5480. Recorded by Muslim and Nasâ'i.

[384] This hadith is *ṣaḥeeḥ*. See Shaykh al-Albâni, *Ṣaḥeeḥ al-Jâmi' aṣ-Ṣagheer*, no. 5142. Recorded by Muslim.

[385] This hadith is *ḥasan* ṣaḥeeḥ. See Shaykh al-Albâni, *Ṣaḥeeḥ Sunan Abi=*

said, "Whoever leaves three Friday prayers without an excuse will be recorded among the hypocrites."[386]

The time of the Friday prayer

The time for the Friday prayer is the same as the time for the Noon prayer, although it is permissible to perform it before that time.

Anas narrated that the Messenger of Allah (ﷺ) would perform the Friday prayer when the sun would pass (the meridian).[387]

Jâbir stated, "The Messenger of Allah (ﷺ) would pray the Friday prayer and then we would go to our camels and rest them while the sun was passing the meridian."[388]

The Friday speech (Khuṭbah)

This speech is obligatory, as the Prophet did it continuously and at no time did he not do it. This point taken into consideration with the Prophet's words, "Pray in the manner that you have seen me praying,"[389] (lead to the conclusion that it is obligatory).

The Prophet's guidance concerning the khuṭbah

The Prophet (ﷺ) said, "Prolonging the prayer and shortening the *khuṭbah* is a sign of one's understanding of the religion. So,

=*Dawood*, no. 923. Recorded by Abu Dawood, Tirmidhi, Nasâ'i and Ibn Mâjah.

386 This hadith is *ṣaḥeeḥ*. See Shaykh al-Albâni, *Ṣaḥeeḥ al-Jâmi' aṣ-Ṣagheer*, no. 6144. Recorded by aṭ-Ṭabarâni.

387 This hadith is *ṣaḥeeḥ*. See Shaykh al-Albâni, *Ṣaḥeeḥ Sunan Abi Dawood*, no. 960. Recorded by Bukhari, Abu Dawood and Tirmidhi.

388 This hadith is *ṣaḥeeḥ*. See Shaykh al-Albâni, *I'rwâ' al-Ghaleel*, no. 597. Recorded by Muslim.

389 *Ṣaḥeeḥ*, (*I'rwâ' al-Ghaleel*, no. 262).

prolong the prayer and shorten the *khuṭbah* (sermon) for there is charm in (precise) expression."[390]

Jâbir ibn Samurah said, "I used to pray the prayers with the Prophet (ﷺ) and his prayer was appropriate in length and balanced and his *khuṭbahs* were appropriate in length and balanced."[391]

Jâbir ibn 'Abdullâh said, "When the Messenger of Allah (ﷺ) delivered the *khuṭbah*, his eyes became red, his voice rose, and his anger increased such that it was like one giving a warning about the enemy and saying, 'The enemy is making a morning attack on you and an evening one too.' "[392]

Khuṭbah al-Ḥâjah

The Prophet (ﷺ) used to begin his *khuṭbahs*, admonitions and lessons with what is known as *khuṭbah al-ḥâjah*. This is its wording:[393]

إِنَّ الْحَمْدَ لِلَّهِ نَحْمَدُهُ وَنَسْتَعِينُهُ وَنَسْتَغْفِرُهُ وَنَعُوذُ بِاللَّهِ مِنْ شُرُورِ أَنْفُسِنَا وَسَيِّئَاتِ أَعْمَالِنَا مَنْ يَهْدِهِ اللَّهُ فَلا مُضِلَّ لَهُ وَمَنْ يُضْلِلْ فَلا هَادِيَ لَهُ أَشْهَدُ أَنْ لا إِلَهَ إِلاَّ اللَّهُ وَحْدَهُ لا شَرِيكَ لَهُ وَأَشْهَدُ أَنَّ مُحَمَّدًا عَبْدُهُ وَرَسُولُهُ

﴿يَا أَيُّهَا الَّذِينَ آمَنُوا اتَّقُوا اللَّهَ حَقَّ تُقَاتِهِ وَلَا تَمُوتُنَّ إِلَّا وَأَنتُم مُّسْلِمُونَ ﴿١٠٢﴾﴾

(سورة آل عِمران: ١٠٢)

---

[390] This hadith is *ṣaḥeeḥ*. See Shaykh al-Albâni, *Ṣaḥeeḥ al-Jâmi' aṣ-Ṣagheer*, no. 2100 and *I'rwâ' al-Ghaleel*, no. 618. Recorded by Muslim.

[391] This hadith is *ṣaḥeeḥ*. See Shaykh al-Albâni, *Ṣaḥeeḥ Sunan Tirmidhi*, no. 418. Recorded by Muslim and Tirmidhi.

[392] This hadith is *ṣaḥeeḥ*. See Shaykh al-Albâni, *Ṣaḥeeḥ al-Jâmi' aṣ-Ṣagheer*, no. 4711 and *I'rwâ' al-Ghaleel*, no. 611. Recorded by Muslim and Tirmidhi.

[393] This hadith is *ṣaḥeeḥ*. See Shaykh al-Albâni, *Ṣaḥeeḥ Sunan Nasâ'i*, no. 1331. Recorded by Muslim and Nasâ'i.

﴿ يَٰٓأَيُّهَا ٱلنَّاسُ ٱتَّقُوا۟ رَبَّكُمُ ٱلَّذِى خَلَقَكُم مِّن نَّفْسٍ وَٰحِدَةٍ وَخَلَقَ مِنْهَا زَوْجَهَا وَبَثَّ مِنْهُمَا رِجَالًا كَثِيرًا وَنِسَآءً ۚ وَٱتَّقُوا۟ ٱللَّهَ ٱلَّذِى تَسَآءَلُونَ بِهِۦ وَٱلْأَرْحَامَ ۚ إِنَّ ٱللَّهَ كَانَ عَلَيْكُمْ رَقِيبًا ﴿١﴾ ﴾ (سورة النِّساء: ١)

﴿ يَٰٓأَيُّهَا ٱلَّذِينَ ءَامَنُوا۟ ٱتَّقُوا۟ ٱللَّهَ وَقُولُوا۟ قَوْلًا سَدِيدًا ﴿٧٠﴾ يُصْلِحْ لَكُمْ أَعْمَٰلَكُمْ وَيَغْفِرْ لَكُمْ ذُنُوبَكُمْ ۗ وَمَن يُطِعِ ٱللَّهَ وَرَسُولَهُۥ فَقَدْ فَازَ فَوْزًا عَظِيمًا ﴿٧١﴾ ﴾

(سورة الأحزاب: ٧٠-٧١)

"All praises are to Allah alone. We praise Him, seek His Help, and ask for His forgiveness. We seek refuge in Allah from the evil in our souls and from our sinful deeds. Whoever Allah guides, no one can mislead. And whoever Allah sends astray, no one can guide. I bear witness that there is none worthy of worship except Allah, One, without any partner. And I bear witness that Muhammad is His servant and messenger. ﴾O' you who have believed, fear Allah as He should be feared and die not except as Muslims﴿.[394] ﴾O' mankind, fear your Lord, Who created you from one soul and created from it its mate and dispersed from both of them many men and women. And fear Allah, through whom you ask one another, and the wombs. Indeed Allah is ever, over you, an Observer﴿.[395] ﴾O' you who have believed, fear Allah and speak words of appropriate justice. He will [then] amend for you your sins. And whoever obeys Allah and His Messenger has certainly attained a great attainment﴿.[396]

To proceed: "Verily, the best speech is the Book of Allah. The best guidance is the guidance of Muhammad. The worst affairs are the newly-introduced matters. Every newly-introduced matter is a

---

394 *(Qur'an 3: 102)*
395 *(Qur'an 4: 1)*
396 *(Qur'an 33: 70-71)*

heresy. And every heresy is misguidance. And every misguidance is in the Fire (of Hell).

(Ibn al-Qayyim stated,)

> "If anyone ponders over the *khuṭbahs* of the Prophet (ﷺ) and of his Companions he will find them filled with the explanation of the guidance, monotheism and mention of the attributes of the Lord. (They also contain) the pillars of the faith in general, calling people to Allah, reminding of the bounties of Allah that make Him beloved to His creation and His days that make them fear His punishment. There is also the command to remember Him and thank Him which make them beloved to Him. They mention Allah's greatness, attributes and names that make Him beloved to His creation. And they are ordered to obey Him, give thanks to Him and remember Him as matters that make them beloved to Him. The listeners leave and they then love Him and He loves them. The Prophet (ﷺ) would often give *khuṭbahs* by reciting the Qur'an and *Soorah Qâf* in particular."[397]

Umm Hishâm bint al-Ḥârith an-Nu'mân said, "I did not memorize (*Soorah*) *Qâf* except from the mouth of the Messenger of Allah (ﷺ) as he would to give it as a *khuṭbah* while on the pulpit."[398]

The obligation of remaining silent and the prohibition of speaking during the khuṭbah

Abu Hurayrah narrated that the Messenger of Allah (ﷺ) said, "When the Imam is delivering the *khuṭbah*, and you ask your companion to keep quiet and listen, then no doubt you have done a

---

[397] Ibn al-Qayyim, *Zâd al-Ma'âd*, vol. 1, p. 116.

[398] Recorded by Bukhari, Muslim, Nasâ'i, Ibn Mâjah, Abu Dawood (with an abridged text) and Tirmidhi (with a similar text).

purposeless act (*laghawt*)."[399]

When does one catch the Friday prayer

The Friday prayer is two *rak'ahs* in a congregation. If someone who is not obliged to pray the Friday prayer does not attend the prayer or if someone has a valid excuse not to attend it, then he will prayer the Noon prayer as four *rak'ahs* instead. However, if a person catches one *rak'ah* (meaning the act of bowing) with the Imam, he has caught the Friday prayer. Abu Hurayrah narrated that the Prophet (ﷺ) said, "Whoever catches a *rak'ah* of the Friday prayer has caught the prayer."[400]

Prayers before and after the Friday prayer

Abu Hurayrah reported that the Prophet (ﷺ) said, "Whoever makes *ghusl* and then comes to the Friday prayer, then prays as much as (Allah has) written for him and then remains silent until the Imam finishes his *khuṭbah*, and then he prays with him, forgiven for him will be whatever he did (of minor sins) from that Friday to the previous Friday plus an additional three days."[401]

The one who comes before the Friday prayer should pray as much as he wishes, without any limit, until the Imam comes. There is, however, no basis for what is commonly known today as the Sunnah prayers prior to the Friday prayer. It is well-known that "The

---

[399] This hadith is *ṣaḥeeḥ*. See Shaykh al-Albâni, *Ṣaḥeeḥ Sunan Ibn Mâjah*, no. 911. Recorded by Nasâ'i and Ibn Mâjah had something similar. [Actually, with this wording it was recorded by Bukhari.] - Translator

[400] This hadith is *ṣaḥeeḥ*. See Shaykh al-Albâni, *I'rwâ' al-Ghaleel*, no. 622 and *Ṣaḥeeḥ al-Jâmi' aṣ-Ṣagheer*, no. 5999. Recorded by Nasâ'i and Ibn Mâjah has something similar.

[401] This hadith is *ṣaḥeeḥ*. See Shaykh al-Albâni, *Ṣaḥeeḥ al-Jâmi' aṣ-Ṣagheer*, no. 6062. Recorded by Muslim.

Prophet (ﷺ) would, when Bilâl was finished making the call to prayer, start the *khuṭbah*. No one at that time would stand to pray two *rak'ahs* and yet at that time there was only one call to prayer. Therefore, when did they supposedly pray the Sunnah (before the Friday prayer)?"[402]

As for after the Friday prayer, if one wishes he may pray either four *rak'ahs* or two *rak'ahs*. Abu Hurayrah reported that the Messenger of Allah (ﷺ) said, "If one of you prays the Friday prayer, he should pray four *rak'ahs* after it."[403]

Ibn 'Umar, however, said, "The Prophet (ﷺ) would not pray after the Friday prayer until after he had left and he would then pray two *rak'ahs* in his house."[404]

The etiquette of Friday

It is recommended for anyone who intends to attend the Friday prayer to abide by what is contained in the following hadith.

Salmân al-Fârisi narrated that the Prophet (ﷺ) said, "No man makes *ghusl* on Friday and purifies what he can and puts on some oil of his oil and applies some perfume from his house, and then goes out without coming between two people, and then prays what has been written for him to pray, then remains quiet while the Imam speaks, but he will be forgiven for what he did between that Friday and the previous one."[405]

---

[402] Ibn al-Qayyim, *Zâd al-Ma'âd*, vol. 1, p. 118.

[403] This hadith is *ṣaḥeeḥ*. See Shaykh al-Albâni, *I'rwâ' al-Ghaleel*, no. 625 and *Ṣaḥeeḥ al-Jâmi' aṣ-Ṣagheer*, no. 640. Recorded by Muslim (with this wording), Abu Dawood and Tirmidhi.

[404] Recorded by Bukhari (without mentioning "in his house") and Muslim.

[405] This hadith is *ṣaḥeeḥ*. See Shaykh al-Albâni, *Ṣaḥeeḥ al-Jâmi' aṣ-Ṣagheer*, no. 7736. Recorded by Bukhari.

Abu Sa'eed narrated [that the Prophet (ﷺ) said][406], "For whoever makes *ghusl* on Friday, wears the best of his clothing, applies some perfume if he has it, then comes to the Friday prayer, without stepping over the necks of the people, then prays whatever Allah has recorded for him to pray, then remains silent when the Imam comes out until he is finished with his prayer, then it will be an expiation for whatever occurred between it and the previous Friday."[407]

Abu Hurayrah narrated that the Messenger of Allah (ﷺ) said, "When it is Friday, there are angels upon every door to the mosque recording the first (to arrive) and then the next (and so on). When the Imam sits, the scroll is rolled up and they come and listen to the reminder. The one who comes early is like one who sacrificed a camel. Next is he like one who sacrificed a cow. Then is he like one who sacrificed a sheep. Then he is like one who sacrificed a chicken. Then is he like one who sacrificed an egg."[408]

Recommended words of remembrance and supplications on Friday

1. Praying for and conveying peace upon the Prophet (ﷺ) often on Friday

Aws ibn Aws narrated that the Messenger of Allah (ﷺ) stated, "The most virtuous of your days is Friday. On that day, Adam was created and on that day he died; (on that day) the horn will be blown and the people will be the stupor. Increase your prayers upon me as

---

[406] [The words in the brackets above were missing from the Arabic text but they should have been there.] - Translator

[407] This hadith is *ṣaḥeeḥ*. See Shaykh al-Albâni, *Ṣaḥeeḥ al-Jâmi' aṣ-Ṣagheer*, no. 6066. Recorded by Abu Dawood.

[408] This hadith is *ṣaḥeeḥ*. See Shaykh al-Albâni, *Ṣaḥeeḥ al-Jâmi' aṣ-Ṣagheer*, no. 775. Recorded by Muslim, Nasâ'i and Ibn Mâjah.

your prayers will be presented to me." The people said, "O' Messenger of Allah, how will our prayers be presented to you when you have passed away?" He said, "Allah has prohibited the earth from consuming the bodies of the prophets."[409]

2. Reciting *Soorah al-Kahf* on Fridays

Abu Sa'eed al-Khudri reported that the Prophet (ﷺ) said, "For whoever recited *Soorah al-Kahf* on Friday, it will light for him a light between the two Fridays (the current and the next one)."[410]

3. Increasing one's supplications on this day hoping to catch the Special Hour of response to supplications

Jâbir reported that the Messenger of Allah said, "Friday is made up of twelve 'hours'. There is one hour in which no Muslim asks Allah except that Allah gives him what he asks. And seek that time in the last hour after the Afternoon prayer."[411]

The Friday prayer is to be in the larger communal mosques

'Â'ishah said, "The people would come on the day of Friday from their residences and from the outlying villages..."[412] Az-Zuhri said, "The people of Dhul-Ḥulayfah used to perform the Friday

---

[409] This hadith is *ṣaḥeeḥ*. See Shaykh al-Albâni, *Ṣaḥeeḥ al-Jâmi' aṣ-Ṣagheer*, no. 889. Recorded by Abu Dawood, Ibn Mâjah and Nasâ'i.

[410] This hadith is *ṣaḥeeḥ*. See Shaykh al-Albâni, *I'rwâ' al-Ghaleel*, no. 626 and *Ṣaḥeeḥ al-Jâmi' aṣ-Ṣagheer*, no. 647. Recorded by al-Ḥâkim and al-Bayhaqi.

[411] This hadith is *ṣaḥeeḥ*. Recorded by Abu Dawood, Nasâ'i (and this is his wording) and also by al-Ḥâkim who said, "This is authentic according to the criterion of Muslim." See Shaykh al-Albâni, *at-Targheeb*, no. 705.

[412] Abu Dawood records it in this fashion. It is also recorded by Bukhari and Muslim as part of a longer hadith.

prayer with the Prophet and they came from a distance of about ten kilometres from Madeenah."[413] 'Aṭâ' ibn Abi Rabâḥ said, "The people of Mina used to attend the Friday prayers in Makkah."[414]

Ibn Ḥajar stated in *Talkheeṣ* (vol. 2, p. 55), "It is not reported that the Prophet (ﷺ) ever gave permission for the performing of the Friday prayers in any of the other mosques of Madeenah or in any of the nearby villages."

'Eid and Friday falling on one day [415]

If *'Eid* falls on a Friday, then the obligation of the Friday prayer is dropped for those who attended the *'Eid* Prayer. Zayd ibn Arqam said, "The Prophet (ﷺ) prayed the *'Eid* prayer and then gave an exemption for the Friday prayer, saying, "Whoever wishes to pray (the Friday prayer) may pray it."[416]

It is preferred for the Imam to still hold the Friday prayer for those who wish to attend it and for those who did not attend the 'Eid

Abu Hurayrah reported that the Prophet (ﷺ) said, "Two festivals have occurred together on this day of yours. For whoever wishes, this will suffice for his Friday prayer. And we are going to perform the Friday prayer."[417]

---

[413] Recorded by al-Bayhaqi.

[414] Ibid.

[415] Cf., as-Sayyid Sâbiq, *Fiqh as-Sunnah*, vol. 1, p. 267.

[416] This hadith is *ṣaḥeeḥ*. See Shaykh al-Albâni, *Ṣaḥeeḥ Sunan Ibn Mâjah*, no. 1082. Recorded by Abu Dawood and Ibn Mâjah.

[417] This hadith is *ṣaḥeeḥ*. See Shaykh al-Albâni, *Ṣaḥeeḥ Sunan Ibn Mâjah*, no. 1083. Recorded by Abu Dawood and by Ibn Mâjah from the narrations of Ibn 'Abbâs.

The *'Eid* Prayers

The Status of the 'Eid Prayers

The *'Eid* prayers are obligatory upon both men and women. This is based on the fact that the Prophet (ﷺ) continually performed them and ordered the people to go out to them. Umm 'Aṭiyah (may Allah be pleased with her) said, "Our Prophet (ﷺ) ordered us to come out (on the Day of *'Eid*) with the mature girls and the virgins staying in seclusion."[418]

Ḥafṣah bint Seereen said, "We used to prevent the young ladies from going out on the Day of *'Eid*. Then a woman came and stayed in the residence of the Tribe of Khalf. We went to her and she narrated that her sister's husband had fought twelve battles alongside the Prophet (ﷺ) and her sister herself had gone along on six battles. She said, 'We use to treat the ill and the injured.' She also (once said to the Prophet), 'O' Messenger of Allah, is there any harm if one of us does not have an outer cloak that she does not go out (to the *'Eid*)?' He replied, 'Her companion should give her from her garment to wear and they should attend the good deeds and the supplications of the believers.' "[419]

The timing of the 'Eid prayers

Yazeed ibn Khumayr al-Raḥabi said, " 'Abdullâh ibn Busr, a Companion of the Prophet (ﷺ), went out with the people for *'Eid* of Breaking the Fast or of the Sacrifice and he objected to the fact that

---

[418] Recorded by Bukhari, Muslim, Abu Dawood and Tirmidhi.

[419] Recorded by Bukhari and Muslim. See Shaykh al-Albâni, *Mishkât al-Maṣâbeeḥ*, no. 1431.

the Imam was late. He said, 'We would be finished by this time now.' And that was the time of the prayer (that is, the time of the voluntary prayer which takes place after the sun has fully risen)."[420]

Going out to the place of prayer (Muṣalla)

The aforementioned hadith demonstrate that the place of the *'Eid* prayer is out in the open; it is not to be held in the mosque. The Prophet (ﷺ) went out to perform it and those who came after him did the same.

Is there a call to prayer or announcement for the beginning of the 'Eid prayer?

Ibn 'Abbâs and Jâbir ibn 'Abdullâh both said, "The call to prayer was not given on either the day of Breaking the Fast or the Day of Sacrifice."[421] Jâbir also said, "There is no call to prayer for the prayer on the Day of Breaking the Fast, not when the Imam goes out or after he goes out. There is also no announcement of the commencement of the prayer or any other form of calling. There is nothing. No call on that day or announcement of the beginning of the prayer."[422]

A description of the 'Eid prayer

The *'Eid* prayer is two *rak'ahs*. It contains twelve (extra) *takbeers*, seven in the first *rak'ah* after the opening *takbeer* and before the recital of the Qur'an and five in the second *rak'ah* before the recital of the Qur'an. 'Amr ibn Shu'ayb narrated from his father

---

[420] This hadith is *ṣaḥeeḥ*. See Shaykh al-Albâni, *Ṣaḥeeḥ Sunan Abi Dawood*, no. 1005. Recorded by Abu Dawood and Ibn Mâjah.

[421] Recorded by Bukhari and Muslim.

[422] This is part of the hadith just referred to as recorded by Muslim.

on the authority of his grandfather who said, "The Messenger of Allah would make seven *takbeers* in the first (*rak'ah*) and five in the last (*rak'ah*) in the two *'Eid* prayers."[423] 'Â'ishah (ﷺ) said, "The Messenger of Allah (ﷺ) would make seven and five (extra) *takbeers*, other than the (regular) *takbeers* for bowing, in the Breaking of the Fast and Sacrifice (*'Eid* prayers)."[424]

The Qur'anic recitation during the 'Eid prayers

An-Nu'mân ibn Basheer said, "The Messenger of Allah (ﷺ), in the two *'Eid* prayers and in the Friday prayer, used to recite, ﴿Glorify the Name of your Lord, the Most High﴾ (*Soorah al-A'lâ*) and, ﴿Has there come to you the narration of the overwhelming﴾ (*Soorah al-Ghâshiyah*)."[425]

'Ubaydullâh ibn 'Abdullâh said, " 'Umar went out on the day of *'Eid* and sent for Abu Wâqid al-Laythi, asking, 'What would the Prophet (ﷺ) recite on a day like this?' He replied, "(*Soorah*) *Qâf* and ﴿The Hour has drawn near﴾ (*Soorah al-Qamar*)."[426]

The khuṭbah is after the prayer

Ibn 'Abbâs said, "I witnessed the *'Eid* with the Messenger of Allah (ﷺ), Abu Bakr, 'Umar and 'Uthmân (may Allah be pleased

---

[423] This hadith is *ṣaḥeeḥ*. See Shaykh al-Albâni, *Ṣaḥeeḥ Sunan Ibn Mâjah*, no. 1057 and *Mishkât al-Maṣâbeeḥ*, no. 1441. Recorded by Ibn Mâjah.

[424] This hadith is *ṣaḥeeḥ*. See Shaykh al-Albâni, *I'rwâ' al-Ghaleel*, no. 639 and *Ṣaḥeeḥ Sunan Ibn Mâjah*, no. 1058. Recorded by Ibn Mâjah and Abu Dawood.

[425] This hadith is *ṣaḥeeḥ*. See Shaykh al-Albâni, *I'rwâ' al-Ghaleel*, no. 644 and *Ṣaḥeeḥ Sunan Ibn Mâjah*, no. 1281. Recorded by Muslim, Abu Dawood, Tirmidhi, Nasâ'i and by Ibn Mâjah (but without mention of the Friday prayer).

[426] This hadith is *ṣaḥeeḥ*. See Shaykh al-Albâni, *I'rwâ' al-Ghaleel*, vol. 3, p. 118 and *Ṣaḥeeḥ Sunan Ibn Mâjah*, no. 106. Recorded by Muslim, Abu Dawood, Tirmidhi, Nasâ'i and Ibn Mâjah.

with them) and they all would pray before giving the *khuṭbah*."[427]

Prayers before or after it

Ibn 'Abbâs said, "The Prophet (ﷺ) performed two *rak'ahs* on the Day of Breaking the Fast and he did not pray anything before or after it."[428]

What is recommended to be done for the day of 'Eid

1. Performing the complete bathing (*Ghusl*)

'Ali (رضي الله عنه) was asked about the complete bathing and he replied, "(It is for) Friday, the Day of 'Arafah, the Day of Breaking the Fast and the Day of the Sacrifice."

2. Wearing one's best clothing

Ibn 'Abbâs said, "The Messenger of Allah (ﷺ) used to wear a green cloak on the Day of *'Eid*."[429]

3. Eating on the day of Breaking the Fast before going out for the prayer

Anas said, "The Messenger of Allah (ﷺ) would not depart on the Day of Breaking the Fast until he had eaten some dates."[430]

---

[427] This hadith is *ṣaḥeeḥ*. Recorded by Bukhari and Muslim.

[428] Recorded by Bukhari, Muslim and Nasâ'i.

[429] The chain of this report is good (*jayid*). See Shaykh al-Albâni, *Silsilat al-Aḥâdeeth aṣ-Ṣaḥeeḥah*, no. 1279. Al-Haythami stated in *Majma' az-Zawâ'id*, vol. 2, p. 201, "It is recorded by aṭ-Ṭabarâni in *al-Awsaṭ* and its narrators are trustworthy."

[430] This hadith is *ṣaḥeeḥ*. See Shaykh al-Albâni, *Ṣaḥeeḥ Sunan Tirmidhi*, no. 448. Recorded by Bukhari and Tirmidhi.

4. Delaying eating on the Day of Sacrifice until one can eat from one's sacrificial animal

Abu Buraydah said, "The Messenger of Allah (ﷺ) would not depart on the Day of Breaking the Fast until he had eaten. And he would not eat on the Day of Sacrifice until he had slaughtered (the sacrificial animal)."[431]

5. Taking a different path (while returning from the prayer)

Jâbir said, "On the Day of *'Eid*, the Prophet (ﷺ) would take a different path (when returning from the prayer)."[432]

6. The saying of the *Takbeer* during the days of *'Eid*

Allah (ﷻ) has said:

﴿...وَلِتُكْمِلُوا۟ ٱلْعِدَّةَ وَلِتُكَبِّرُوا۟ ٱللَّهَ عَلَىٰ مَا هَدَىٰكُمْ وَلَعَلَّكُمْ تَشْكُرُونَ ﴿١٨٥﴾﴾

(سورة البَقَرَة: ١٨٥)

﴾... [He wants that you] must complete the same number [of days], and that you must magnify Allah for having guided you so that you may be grateful to Him.﴿ *(Qur'an 2: 185)*

This is concerning the *'Eid* of Breaking the Fast. About the *'Eid* of Sacrifice, Allah says:

﴿وَٱذْكُرُوا۟ ٱللَّهَ فِىٓ أَيَّامٍ مَّعْدُودَٰتٍ ... ﴿٢٠٣﴾﴾ (سورة البَقَرَة: ٢٠٣)

﴾And remember Allah during the appointed Days...﴿ *(Qur'an 2: 203)*

---

[431] This hadith is *ṣaḥeeḥ*. See Shaykh al-Albâni, *Ṣaḥeeḥ Sunan Tirmidhi*, no. 447. Recorded by Ibn Khuzaymah and by Tirmidhi but with words, "until he prayed."

[432] This hadith is *ṣaḥeeḥ*. See Shaykh al-Albâni, *Mishkât al-Maṣâbeeḥ*, no. 1343. Recorded by Bukhari.

And also:

﴿... كَذَٰلِكَ سَخَّرَهَا لَكُمْ لِتُكَبِّرُوا اللَّهَ عَلَىٰ مَا هَدَاكُمْ ... ﴿٣٧﴾﴾

(سورة الحج: ٣٧)

﴿... Thus have We made them subject to you that you may magnify Allah for His Guidance to you...﴾ *(Qur'an 22: 37)*

On the Day of Breaking the Fast, the *takbeer* is to be said from the time the person leaves to go to the place of prayer until the time that he prays. Ibn Abi Shaybah reported that Yazeed ibn Haroon had informed him on the authority of Ibn Abi Dhi'b that az-Zuhri said, "The Messenger of Allah (ﷺ) would go out on the Day of Breaking the Fast and he would make the *takbeer* until he reached the place of the prayer and until he finished his prayer. Once he finished the prayer, he discontinued the *takbeer*."[433]

Shaykh al-Albâni said,

> "This chain is *ṣaḥeeḥ*, missing the name of the Companion only. It is narrated through another way on the authority of 'Umar from the Prophet (ﷺ). Al-Bayhaqi recorded from the chain of 'Abdullâh ibn 'Umar from Nâfi' from 'Abdullâh ibn 'Umar, The Messenger of Allah (ﷺ) used to go out for the two *'Eid*s with al-Faḍl ibn 'Abbâs, 'Abdullâh ibn 'Abbâs, 'Ali, Ja'far, al-Ḥasan, al-Ḥusain, Usâmah ibn Zayd, Zayd ibn Ḥârithah and Aiman ibn Umm Aiman (may Allah be pleased with them). He would be raising his voice saying, 'There is none worthy of worship except Allah' and 'Allah is greatest'... Al-Bayhaqi said, 'This chain is better than the previous one.' I (that is, al-Albâni) say, 'Its narrators are trustworthy and are the narrators of Muslim, save for

---

433 This hadith is *ṣaḥeeḥ*. See Shaykh al-Albâni, *Silsilat al-Aḥâdeeth aṣ-Ṣaḥeeḥah*, no. 171.

'Abdullâh ibn 'Umar who is al-'Umari al-Mukabbir.' Adh-Dhahabi said about him, 'He is honest but there is some problem with his memory.' He and others put the notation that he is from the narrators of Muslim. Someone like that can be used as supporting evidence. Thus, this is a sound supporting evidence for the report of az-Zuhri which is missing the name of the Companion only. Therefore, the hadith is authentic, in my opinion, both as a statement of a Companion and as a statement of the Prophet. And Allah alone knows best."[434]

The timing for the *takbeer* during the Days of the Sacrifice is from the morning of the Day of Arafah until the afternoon of the last day of the Days of *Tashreeq*. That has been authentically narrated from 'Ali, Ibn 'Abbâs and Ibn Mas'ood (may Allah be pleased with them).[435]

As for what one should say in the *takbeer*, the matter is flexible. "It is confirmed from Ibn Mas'ood that he would make the statement of *takbeer* twice, saying during the days of *Tashreeq*:

'*Allâhu akbar, Allâhu akbar, lâ ilâha illa-Allâh* (there is none worthy of worship except Allah), *Allâhu akbar, Allâhu akbar, wa lilâhi-l-ḥamd* (to Allah belongs the praise).'

Ibn Abi Shaybah recorded this with a *ṣaḥeeḥ* chain. However, at another location, with the same chain, he mentioned that he said the *takbeer* three times. This is how al-Bayhaqi records it from Yaḥya ibn Sa'eed from al-Ḥâkim, who is Ibn Farooḥ Abu Bakâr, from 'Ikrimah

---

434 Shaykh al-Albâni, *I'rwâ' al-Ghaleel*, vol. 3, p. 123.

435 Ibn Abi Shaybah (vol. 2, p. 165) narrated it from 'Ali via two chains, one of them good. And from this means it was recorded by al-Bayhaqi (vol. 3, p. 314). Then he recorded similar from Ibn 'Abbâs with a sound chain. Al-Ḥâkim recorded it from him and from Ibn Mas'ood similarly. See Shaykh al-Albâni, *I'rwâ' al-Ghaleel*, vol. 3, p. 125.

from Ibn 'Abbâs, saying the *takbeer* three times. And the chain of that report is also *ṣaḥeeḥ*."[436]

The Prayer while in a State of Fear

Allah, Exalted be He, says:

﴿وَإِذَا كُنتَ فِيهِمْ فَأَقَمْتَ لَهُمُ ٱلصَّلَوٰةَ فَلْتَقُمْ طَآئِفَةٌ مِّنْهُم مَّعَكَ وَلْيَأْخُذُوٓا۟ أَسْلِحَتَهُمْ فَإِذَا سَجَدُوا۟ فَلْيَكُونُوا۟ مِن وَرَآئِكُمْ وَلْتَأْتِ طَآئِفَةٌ أُخْرَىٰ لَمْ يُصَلُّوا۟ فَلْيُصَلُّوا۟ مَعَكَ وَلْيَأْخُذُوا۟ حِذْرَهُمْ وَأَسْلِحَتَهُمْ ... ﴿١٠٢﴾﴾

(سورة النِّساء: ١٠٢)

﴿When you [O' Messenger] are among them, and lead them in the prayer, let one party of them stand up [in prayer] with you taking their arms with them; when they finish their prostrations, let them take their positions in the rear and let the other party come up which has not yet prayed, and let them pray with you taking all the precautions and bearing arms...﴾ *(Qur'an 4: 102)*

Description of the prayer in a state of fear

Al-Khaṭṭâbi said, "There are various forms to the prayer in a state of fear. The Prophet (ﷺ) performed it on different occasions in different manners, performing it in a way that is best for the prayer and best for safeguarding. Although they are of different forms, their meanings are in agreement."[437]

---

[436] Shaykh al-Albâni, *I'rwâ' al-Ghaleel*, vol. 3, p. 125.

[437] Quoted in an-Nawawi, *Sharḥ Ṣaḥeeḥ Muslim*, vol. 6, p. 126.

(The various forms are as follows:)

1. Ibn 'Umar said, "The Messenger of Allah (ﷺ) prayed the prayer in a state of fear with one party while the other party was facing the enemy. Then they left and stood in the place of the other party and faced the enemy. Those others then came and the Prophet (ﷺ) led them in one *rak'ah* of prayer and gave the salutations. Then they made up one *rak'ah* while the other party also made up one *rak'ah*."[438]

2. Sahl ibn Abi Ḥathmah said, "The Messenger of Allah (ﷺ) prayed with his Companions in a state of fear. He lined them up in two rows. Those closest to him prayed one *rak'ah* with him. Then he stood and remained standing until those behind him prayed a *rak'ah*. Then those in the back came forward and those in the front went back, and he prayed one *rak'ah* with (the new) group. Then he sat until those who came later prayed one *rak'ah* and then he made the salutations."[439]

3. Jâbir ibn 'Abdullâh said, "I witnessed the prayer in a state of fear with the Messenger of Allah (ﷺ). He arranged us in two lines, one behind the Messenger of Allah (ﷺ) while the enemy was between us and the *qiblah*. The Prophet (ﷺ) made the *takbeer* and everyone did so. Then he bowed and we all bowed with him. Then he raised his head from the bowing and we all raised our heads. Then he went down into prostration with the row that was closest to him while the row in the back was facing the enemy. When the Prophet (ﷺ) finished the prostration and the row next to him stood up, the row in the back went into prostration and then stood. Then the row in the

---

[438] Recorded by Bukhari, Muslim (and this is his wording), Abu Dawood, Tirmidhi and Nasâ'i.

[439] Recorded by Bukhari and Muslim. Nasâ'i and Tirmidhi have something similar.

back came forward and the row in the front went to the back. The Prophet bowed as we all did. He then raised his head and we all did the same. Then he went into prostration and the row that was now closest to him, which used to be in the back during the first *rak'ah*, also went into prostration with him while those in the other row stayed standing and facing the enemy. When the Messenger of Allah (ﷺ) and the row closest to him finished the prostration, the row in the back performed the prostration. Then the Prophet (ﷺ) made the salutations and we all did so together."[440]

[440] This hadith is *ṣaḥeeḥ*. This is Muslim's wording. See Shaykh al-Albâni, *Ṣaḥeeḥ Sunan Nasâ'i*, no. 1456. Recorded by Muslim and Nasâ'i.

Chapter Three — The Funeral Prayers [1]

If a Muslim is approaching death, it is recommended for his family to prompt him to say the testimony of faith. Abu Sa'eed al-Khudri related that the Messenger of Allah (ﷺ) said, "Prompt your deceased (that is, those about to die) to say, 'There is none worthy of worship except Allah.' "[2] The Prophet (ﷺ) ordered this prompting in the hopes that the person's last words would be, "There is none worthy of worship except Allah". Mu'âdh ibn Jabal narrated that the Messenger of Allah (ﷺ) said, "Whosoever's last words are, 'There is none worthy of worship except Allah,' will enter Paradise."[3]

If the matter is decreed and the soul is taken, then a number of steps should be followed:

1. and 2. The deceased's eyes should be closed and supplications should be made for the deceased

Umm Salamah said, "The Messenger of Allah (ﷺ) came to Abu Salamah after his gaze had become fixed (that is, after he passed away). He closed his eyes and said, 'When the soul is taken, the eyesight follows it.' Some of the members of his family started to cry. The Prophet (ﷺ) then said, 'Do not supplicate anything but good

---

[1] This is a summary of Shaykh al-Albâni's *Aḥkâm al-Janâ'iz.*

[2] This hadith is *ṣaḥeeḥ*. See Shaykh al-Albâni, *I'rwâ' al-Ghaleel*, no. 686. Recorded by Muslim, Abu Dawood, Tirmidhi, Ibn Mâjah and Nasâ'i.

[3] This hadith is *ṣaḥeeḥ*. See Shaykh al-Albâni, *Ṣaḥeeḥ Sunan Abi Dawood*, no. 2673. Recorded by Abu Dawood.

upon yourselves for the angels say *Âmeen* to what you say.' He then said, 'O' Allah, forgive Abu Salamah, raise his rank among the guided, have him followed by good successors in his family. And forgive us and him, O' Lord of the Worlds. Expand his grave and illuminate it for him.'"[4]

3. Covering the entire body with a garment

'Â'ishah said, "When the Messenger of Allah (ﷺ) died, he was covered in an embroidered garment."[5]

4. Promptly preparing the body and taking it to be buried

Abu Hurayrah reported that the Prophet (ﷺ) said, "Hurry in performing the funeral for if he were a pious person, you will take him to goodness. If he was other than that, it is evil that you are removing from you necks."[6]

5. Some or one of the people should move quickly to pay off the deceased's debt

Jâbir ibn 'Abdullâh said, "A man died and we washed, shrouded and embalmed him. We then placed him for the Messenger of Allah (ﷺ) where the deceased were usually placed, near what is known as the Place of Gabriel (next to the Prophet's mosque). Then we called the Messenger of Allah (ﷺ) to come and perform the prayer for him. He came, took a few steps and said, 'Maybe your companion has a debt.' They said, 'Yes. Two *dinars*.' So he went back and then one of us, called Abu Qatâdah said, 'O' Messenger of Allah, it is my responsibility.' The Messenger of Allah (ﷺ) said to

---

[4] This hadith is *ṣaḥeeḥ*. See Shaykh al-Albâni, *al-Janâ'iz,* p, 12. Recorded by Muslim and also by Abu Dawood but with the sentence, "When the soul is taken."

[5] Recorded by Bukhari (with a lengthier version) and Muslim (with the above abridged version).

[6] Recorded by Bukhari, Muslim, Abu Dawood and Tirmidhi.

him, 'They are your responsibility upon your wealth and the deceased is cleared of them?' He said, 'Yes.' So then the Prophet (ﷺ) prayed upon him. When the Messenger of Allah (ﷺ) would later meet Abu Qatâdah, he would say, 'What has happed to the two *dinars*?' Finally, one time Abu Qatâdah said, 'I have paid them, O' Messenger of Allah.' Then the Prophet (ﷺ) said, 'It is now, then, that his skin has finally cooled down on him.' "[7]

What is permissible for those present and others to do

It is permissible for them to uncover the face of the deceased and to kiss him. It is also allowed to cry for the deceased for a period of three days. 'Â'ishah said, "The Prophet (ﷺ) went to 'Uthmân ibn Madh'oon when he was dead. He uncovered his face, leaned over and kissed him. He also cried to the extent that I saw tears running down his cheeks."[8] 'Abdullâh ibn Ja'far stated, "The Prophet (ﷺ) allowed the family of Ja'far to mourn for three days. Then he came to them and said, 'Do not cry for your brother after today.' "[9]

What is obligatory upon the relatives of the deceased

Two things are obligatory upon the deceased's relatives when they hear about the death. The first is that they must have patience and be pleased with Allah's decree. Allah (ﷻ) has said:

﴿وَلَنَبْلُوَنَّكُم بِشَىْءٍ مِّنَ ٱلْخَوْفِ وَٱلْجُوعِ وَنَقْصٍ مِّنَ ٱلْأَمْوَٰلِ وَٱلْأَنفُسِ وَٱلثَّمَرَٰتِ ۗ

---

[7] This hadith is *ṣaḥeeḥ*. See Shaykh al-Albâni, *al-Janâ'iz,* p. 16. Recorded by al-Ḥâkim and al-Bayhaqi.

[8] This hadith is *ṣaḥeeḥ*. See Shaykh al-Albâni, *I'rwâ' al-Ghaleel*, no. 693 and *Ṣaḥeeḥ Sunan Ibn Mâjah*, no. 1191. Recorded by Ibn Mâjah, Abu Dawood and Tirmidhi.

[9] This hadith is *ṣaḥeeḥ*. See Shaykh al-Albâni, *Ṣaḥeeḥ Sunan Nasâ'i*, no. 4823 and *al-Janâ'iz*, p. 21. Recorded by Abu Dawood and Nasâ'i.

وَبَشِّرِ ٱلصَّـٰبِرِينَ ﴿١٥٥﴾ ٱلَّذِينَ إِذَآ أَصَـٰبَتْهُم مُّصِيبَةٌ قَالُوٓاْ إِنَّا لِلَّهِ وَإِنَّآ إِلَيْهِ رَٰجِعُونَ
﴿١٥٦﴾ أُوْلَـٰٓئِكَ عَلَيْهِمْ صَلَوَٰتٌ مِّن رَّبِّهِمْ وَرَحْمَةٌ وَأُوْلَـٰٓئِكَ هُمُ ٱلْمُهْتَدُونَ ﴿١٥٧﴾﴾

(سورة البَقَرَة: ١٥٥-١٥٧)

﴿And certainly, We shall test you with something of fear, hunger, loss of wealth, lives and fruits. But give glad tidings to those who are patient, who, when afflicted with calamity, say, 'Truly! To Allah we belong and truly, to Him we shall return.' They are those on whom are blessings from their Lord, and [they are those who] receive His Mercy, and it is they who are the guided-ones.﴾ *(Qur'an 2: 155-157)*

Anas (ﷺ) said, "The Messenger of Allah (ﷺ) passed by a woman at a grave who was crying. He said to her, 'Fear Allah and have patience.' She said, 'Get away from me. You have not experienced what I experienced.' She did not recognize who he was. She was then told that it was the Messenger of Allah. This fact almost killed her. She went to the door of the Messenger of Allah (ﷺ) and did not find any attendant there. She said, 'O' Messenger of Allah, I did not recognize you.' He then said, 'Truly, patience is (to be exhibited) at the beginning of the affliction.' "[10]

There is great reward for being patient upon the death of one's child

Abu Sa'eed al-Khudri narrated that the women asked the Prophet (ﷺ), "Appoint a day for us (to teach us)." So he (did so and) preached to them, saying, "If three children of a woman pass away, they will be a barrier from the Hell-fire." A woman said, "And even only two?" He replied, "And only two."[11]

---

[10] Recorded by Bukhari, Muslim (and this is his wording) and Abu Dawood.

[11] Recorded by Bukhari and Muslim.

The second matter that is obligatory on the relatives is that they must say the statement, "Truly! To Allah we belong and truly, to Him we shall return," as is mentioned in the above quoted verse. In addition, they should say,

اللَّهُمَّ أْجُرْنِي فِي مُصِيبَتِي وَأَخْلِفْ لِي خَيْرًا مِنْهَا

"O' Allah, reward me for my affliction and replace it with something better for me."

Umm Salama (ﷺ) said that she heard the Messenger of Allah (ﷺ) say, "No servant is inflicted with an infliction but if he says,

إِنَّا لِلَّهِ وَإِنَّا إِلَيْهِ رَاجِعُونَ اللَّهُمَّ أْجُرْنِي فِي مُصِيبَتِي وَأَخْلِفْ لِي خَيْرًا مِنْهَا

'We belong to Allah and to Him we are returning. O' Allah, reward me in my affliction and make what is after it better for me,' Allah will reward him for his affliction and will give him a better replacement." Umm Salama said when (her husband) Abu Salamah died, "What Muslims are better than Abu Salamah, the first household that emigrated to the Messenger of Allah? Then I said those words [the Prophet (ﷺ) taught me] and Allah replaced him for me by the Messenger of Allah (ﷺ) (whom she married)."[12]

What is forbidden upon the relatives of the deceased

1. Wailing

Abu Mâlik al-Ash'ari narrated that the Prophet (ﷺ) said, "Four matters will be in (among the people of) my Nation from the matters of the Days of Ignorance and they will not give them up: Boasting about social status, defaming lineage, seeking rain via the stars and wailing." He also said, "If the wailing woman does not

---

[12] This hadith is *ṣaḥeeḥ*. See Shaykh al-Albâni, *Ṣaḥeeḥ al-Jâmi' aṣ-Ṣagheer*, no. 5764 and *al-Janâ'iz*, p. 23. Recorded by Muslim.

repent before her death, she will be resurrected on the Day of Judgment wearing a long garment of tar and a smaller garment of scabies."[13]

2. and 3. Striking the cheeks or tearing the front of one's gown

'Abdullâh narrated that the Prophet (ﷺ) said, "The one who strikes the cheeks, tears the front of the gown or laments the lamenting of the Days of Ignorance is not from among us."[14]

4. Shaving one's head

Abu Burdah ibn Abu Moosa said, "Abu Moosa fell seriously ill and fainted while his head was in the lap of one of the women of his household. Thereupon, the woman screamed. He was not able to respond to her in any way but when he regained his consciousness he said, 'I dissociate from those people from whom the Prophet (ﷺ) disassociated himself and the Messenger of Allah (ﷺ) disassociated himself from the woman who wails, the woman who shaves her head due to a calamity and the woman who tears the front opening of her garment.'"[15]

5. Dishevelling one's hair

One of the women who gave the pledge of allegiance to the Prophet (ﷺ) said, "From the matters that we pledged to the Prophet (ﷺ) and from the matters that we vowed not to disobey him in were (as he said to us): you will not scratch your face, wail, tear one's garment nor make the hair dishevelled."[16]

---

[13] This hadith is *ṣaḥeeḥ*. See Shaykh al-Albâni, *al-Janâ'iz*, p. 27 and *Silsilat al-Aḥâdeeth aṣ-Ṣaḥeeḥah*, no. 734. Recorded by Muslim.

[14] Recorded by Bukhari, Muslim, Tirmidhi and Nasâ'i.

[15] Recorded by Bukhari, Muslim and Nasâ'i.

[16] This hadith is *ṣaḥeeḥ*. See Shaykh al-Albâni, *al-Janâ'iz*, p. 30. Recorded by Abu Dawood.

What Must be Done for the Deceased

The deceased's relatives or others must take care of four matters: washing the deceased, shrouding him, praying for him and burying him.

1. Washing the Deceased

The conclusion that this is obligatory derives from the order of the Prophet (ﷺ) to do so as found in numerous hadith, such as:

1.a. The Prophet (ﷺ) who said about a pilgrim who died when his animal threw him, "Wash him with water and lotus leaves..."[17]

1.b. The Prophet (ﷺ) stated about his daughter Zaynab, "Wash her three, five or seven times..."[18]

A description of the washing (ghusl) of the deceased

Umm 'Aṭiyyah (رضي الله عنها) narrated that the Messenger of Allah (ﷺ) said to the women when they were washing his daughter, "Start with her right side and the places of ablution of her body."[19]

Umm 'Aṭiyyah also said, "The Prophet (ﷺ) came to us while we were washing his daughter. He said, 'Wash her three, five or more times, as you see fit. (Wash her) with water (mixed with) lotus leaves and make the last one with camphor or with some camphor. And inform me when you have finished.' When we finished, we informed him and he gave us his long waist-cloth and said, 'Wrap her body in it.' "[20]

---

[17] Recorded by Bukhari, Muslim, Abu Dawood, Tirmidhi and Nasâ'i.

[18] Recorded by Bukhari and Muslim.

[19] Ibid.

[20] Recorded by Bukhari, Muslim, Abu Dawood, Tirmidhi, Ibn Mâjah and Nasâ'i.

Umm 'Aṭiyyah also said, "We braided the head of her hair into three plaits."[21] In another narration she said, "We braided her hair into three plaits and put it toward the back."[22]

Who should perform the ghusl for the deceased?

The one who has knowledge of the Sunnah of the *ghusl* is the one who should perform the *ghusl*, especially if he is a relative of the deceased. Those who took on the responsibility of washing the Prophet's body were members of his family. For example, 'Ali (ﷺ) said, "I washed the Messenger of Allah (ﷺ) and I expected to find what one finds among the deceased but I did not notice a thing. He was in a good state both alive and dead."[23]

Men should wash males and women should wash females. The exception to this are spouses, as either of them may wash the other. 'Â'ishah (ﷺ) said, "If I had a chance to do it again, none except the wives of the Prophet (ﷺ) would have washed him."[24] 'Â'ishah also said, "The Prophet (ﷺ) returned and came to me from a funeral at the al-Baqee' Cemetery. I had a headache and said, 'O' my head.' He replied, 'No, in fact, O' my head.' Then he said, 'What would it harm you if you were to die before me and I would then wash you, shroud you, pray over you and bury you?' "[25]

---

[21] Recorded by Bukhari, Muslim and Nasâ'i.

[22] Ibid.

[23] This hadith is *ṣaḥeeḥ*. See Shaykh al-Albâni, *Ṣaḥeeḥ Sunan Ibn Mâjah*, no. 1198 and *al-Janâ'iz*, p. 50. Recorded by Ibn Mâjah.

[24] This hadith is *ṣaḥeeḥ*. See Shaykh al-Albâni, *Ṣaḥeeḥ Sunan Ibn Mâjah*, no. 1196 and *al-Janâ'iz*, p. 49. Recorded by Abu Dawood and Ibn Mâjah.

[25] This hadith is *ṣaḥeeḥ*. See Shaykh al-Albâni, *Ṣaḥeeḥ Sunan Ibn Mâjah*, no. 1197 and *al-Janâ'iz*, p. 50. Recorded by Ibn Mâjah.

It is not sanctioned to wash a martyr who has died on the battlefield

Jâbir said, "The Prophet (ﷺ) said, 'Bury them with their blood,' that was on the Day of Uḥud and he did not have them washed."[26]

2. The Shroud

The conclusion that this is obligatory derives from the order of the Prophet (ﷺ) who said about a pilgrim who died when his animal threw him, "Wash him with water and lotus leaves and shroud him in two garments..."[27]

The shroud or its price is to come from the wealth of the deceased, even if he did not leave anything else behind as inheritance. Khabbâb ibn al-Aratt said, "We emigrated with the Prophet (ﷺ) seeking the pleasure of Allah. Our reward was upon Allah. Some of us passed away without consuming any of his reward (in this world). Those included Muṣ'ab ibn 'Umayr. One the other hand, some of received our rewards in this life. He (Muṣ'ab) was killed in the Battle of Uḥud and we could find nothing to shroud him with except his cloak. When we pulled it to cover his head, his feet became bare and when we wanted to cover his feet, his head became bare. Accordingly, the Prophet told us to cover his head with it and to cover his feet with *al-Idhkhir* (a special type of pleasant smelling grass)."

It is a must that the shroud be a garment that covers all of the body. If all one can find is a shorter garment that cannot cover all of

---

[26] This hadith is *ṣaḥeeḥ*. See Shaykh al-Albâni, *Ṣaḥeeḥ Sunan Nasâ'i*, no. 1893 and *al-Janâ'iz*, Pp. 54-55. Recorded by Bukhari, Abu Dawood, Nasâ'i and Tirmidhi.

[27] Recorded by Bukhari, Muslim, Abu Dawood, Tirmidhi and Nasâ'i.

the body, then one covers the head and places some grasses over the feet, as in the hadith of Khabbâb.

The following are recommended for the shroud

1. Being white in colour

The Prophet (ﷺ) said, "Wear of your clothing the white clothing for it is the best of your clothing. Also shroud your deceased in it."[28]

2. The shroud should consist of three garments

'Â'ishah stated, "The Messenger of Allah (ﷺ) was shrouded in three white Yemenite pieces of cotton cloth from Saḥool (a city in Yemen), none of which was an undergarment or a turban."[29]

3. If possible, one of the garments should have a striped pattern

Jâbir narrated that the Prophet (ﷺ) said, "If one of you dies and, if it can be found, let him be shrouded in a striped garment."[30]

Prayer for the Deceased

Prayer for the deceased Muslim is a communal obligation, as the Prophet (ﷺ) has commanded it in many hadith. Zayd ibn Khâlid al-Juhani narrated that a man from among the Companions of the Prophet (ﷺ) died on the Day of Khaybar. That was mentioned to the Prophet (ﷺ) and he said, "Pray for your companion." The people's

---

[28] This hadith is *ṣaḥeeḥ*. See Shaykh al-Albâni, *Ṣaḥeeḥ al-Jâmi' aṣ-Ṣagheer*, no. 3236 and *al-Janâ'iz*, p. 62. Recorded by Tirmidhi and Abu Dawood.

[29] Recorded by Bukhari, Muslim, Abu Dawood, Tirmidhi, Nasâ'i and Ibn Mâjah.

[30] This hadith is *ṣaḥeeḥ*. See Shaykh al-Albâni, *Ṣaḥeeḥ al-Jâmi' aṣ-Ṣagheer*, no. 455 and *al-Janâ'iz*, p. 63. Recorded by Abu Dawood.

expressions changed upon hearing that. The Prophet (ﷺ) then said, "Your companion misappropriated something from the booty." Zayd said, "We searched his belonging and found some beads of the Jews that were not even worth two *dirhams*."[31]

The exception to the obligation of the prayer is in the following two cases

First is the child who had not reached the age of puberty. 'Â'ishah (رضي الله عنها) said, "Ibrâheem, the son of the Prophet, died while he was eighteen months old and the Prophet (ﷺ) did not perform the (funeral) prayer for him."[32] Second is the martyr. Anas said, "The martyrs of the (Battle of) Uḥud were not washed but were buried with their blood. And he (the Prophet) did not pray (the Funeral prayer) for them."[33]

However, non-obligation does not deny that it is sanctioned for pray for them

'Â'ishah said, "The Messenger of Allah (ﷺ) was brought one of the children of the Anṣâr and he prayed (the Funeral prayer) for him..."[34] 'Abdullâh ibn az-Zubayr said, "On the Day of Uḥud, the Messenger of Allah (ﷺ) ordered that Ḥamzah (رضي الله عنه) be brought and he covered him in a cloak. Then he prayed for him, saying nine *takbeers*. Then he was brought those who had been killed and they

---

[31] This hadith is *ṣaḥeeḥ*. See Shaykh al-Albâni, *al-Janâ'iz*, p. 79. Recorded by Abu Dawood, Ibn Mâjah and Nasâ'i.

[32] Its chain is *ḥasan*. See Shaykh al-Albâni, *al-Janâ'iz*, p. 80 and *Ṣaḥeeḥ Sunan Abi Dawood*, no. 2729. Recorded by Abu Dawood.

[33] This hadith is *ḥasan*. See Shaykh al-Albâni, *Ṣaḥeeḥ Sunan Abi Dawood*, no. 2688. Recorded by Abu Dawood in this abridged fashion and recorded by Tirmidhi as a lengthier report.

[34] This hadith is *ṣaḥeeḥ*. See Shaykh al-Albâni, *Ṣaḥeeḥ Sunan Nasâ'i*, no. 1839. Recorded by Muslim and Nasâ'i.

were put in a row. He prayed for them and he prayed again for him (that is, he prayed again for Ḥamzah) with them."[35]

The larger the congregation, the better and more beneficial it is for the deceased

The Prophet (ﷺ) said, "No deceased is prayed for by a group of Muslims that reach one hundred in number, all of them interceding for him, except that he will be interceded for."[36] The Messenger of Allah (ﷺ) also said, "No Muslim dies and forty men who do not associate anything with Allah stand for his funeral prayer except that Allah will make them intercede for him."[37]

It is preferred that they form three rows behind the Imam, regardless of how small their numbers are

Marthad al-Yazani narrated from Mâlik ibn Hubayrah that the Messenger of Allah (ﷺ) said, "No Muslim dies and is prayed for by three rows of Muslims except that (forgiveness for him) is mandated." Thus, based on this hadith, whenever there was a funeral prayer, Mâlik would put the people into three rows.[38]

If a number of men and women are prayed for at the same time

The normal case is that each individual receives his or her own funeral prayer. However, it is permissible to perform the prayer for more than one person at one time. In such a case, the deceased males,

---

[35] Its chain is *ḥasan*. See Shaykh al-Albâni, *al-Janâ'iz*, p. 49. All of the narrators are trustworthy. It was recorded by aṭ-Ṭaḥâwi in *M'âni al-Âthâr*.

[36] This hadith is *ṣaḥeeḥ*. See Shaykh al-Albâni, *Ṣaḥeeḥ Sunan Nasâ'i*, no. 1881. Recorded by Muslim, Tirmidhi and Nasâ'i.

[37] This hadith is *ṣaḥeeḥ*. See Shaykh al-Albâni, *Silsilat al-Aḥâdeeth aṣ-Ṣaḥeeḥah*, no. 2267. Recorded by Muslim and Abu Dawood, with Ibn Mâjah having something similar.

[38] This hadith is *ḥasan*. See Shaykh al-Albâni, *al-Janâ'iz*, Pp. 99-100.

even if they are young, are placed closest to the Imam while the females are placed further from the Imam in the direction of the *qiblah*.

Nâfi' stated, "Ibn 'Umar prayed over nine deceased people at once. He put the males closest to the Imam and then the women further in front towards the *qiblah*, putting them all into a parallel row. The funeral prayer of Umm Kulthum, the daughter of 'Ali and the wife of 'Umar ibn al-Khaṭṭâb, and her son Zayd was performed together. The Imam on that day was Sa'eed ibn al-'Âṣ and in the congregation were Ibn 'Abbâs, Abu Hurayrah, Abu Sa'eed and Abu Qatâdah. The boy was placed immediately in front of the Imam. One man objected to that. I looked to Ibn 'Abbâs, Abu Hurayrah, Abu Sa'eed and Abu Qatâdah. I said, 'What is this practice?' They said, 'It is the Sunnah.' "[39]

Where should the funeral prayer be held?

It is permissible to perform the funeral prayer in the mosque

'Â'ishah (رضي الله عنها) said, "When S'ad ibn Abu Waqqâṣ died, the Prophet's wives requested that his prayer be in the mosque so that they could pray for him. The people did so and had the funeral in front of their apartments (adjoining the mosque) and they prayed for him. He was taken out through the 'door of the funeral prayers' to his final resting place." When the news of this reached the people, they found it blameworthy. They said, "A funeral prayer should not be taken into the mosque." When this reached 'Â'ishah, she said, "Why are the people so quick to level blame concerning matters that they are not knowledgeable of? They blame us for bringing the funeral prayer into the mosque and while the Prophet (Blessings and peace

---

[39] This hadith is *ṣaḥeeḥ*. See Shaykh al-Albâni, *Ṣaḥeeḥ Sunan Nasâ'i*, no. 1869 and *al-Janâ'iz*, p. 103. Recorded by Nasâ'i.

be upon him) did not pray over Suhayl ibn Bayḍâ' except in the mosque."[40]

However, it is preferable to perform the funeral prayer outside of the mosque in a place specifically designated for funeral prayers, as was the usual case during the lifetime of the Prophet (ﷺ) and what he customarily did. Thus, Ibn 'Umar said, "The Jews came to the Prophet (ﷺ) with a man from them and a woman who had committed adultery. The Prophet ordered that they be stoned and they were stoned close to the place of the funeral prayers near the mosque."[41] Abu Hurayrah reported, "The Messenger of Allah (ﷺ) announced the death of the ruler of Abyssinia on the day that he died. He then went out to the place of prayer and lined the people in rows and made four *takbeers* (in the prayer)."[42]

It is, though, not allowed to perform the prayer in the midst of the graves (that is, in a graveyard). Anas narrated that the Prophet (ﷺ) forbade the performance of the funeral prayer amidst the graves.[43]

Where should the Imam stand?

Abu Ghâlib al-Khayâṭ stated, "I saw Anas ibn Mâlik perform a funeral prayer for a male. He stood opposite his (the deceased's) head. When he was removed, the bier of a woman from the Quraysh or of the Anṣâr was brought. It was said to (Anas), 'O' Abu Ḥamzah,

---

[40] This hadith is *ṣaḥeeḥ*. See Shaykh al-Albâni, *Ṣaḥeeḥ Sunan Nasâ'i*, no. 1589. Recorded by Muslim, and this is his wording. Recorded by Abu Dawood and Nasâ'i in abbreviated form.

[41] This hadith is *ṣaḥeeḥ*. See Shaykh al-Albâni, *al-Janâ'iz*, p. 106. Recorded by Bukhari.

[42] Recorded by Bukhari, Muslim, Abu Dawood and Nasâ'i.

[43] Its chain is *ḥasan*. See Shaykh al-Albâni, *al-Janâ'iz*, p. 108. Shaykh al-Albâni stated that it is recorded by aṭ-Ṭabarâni in *al-Awsaṭ*.

this is the funeral of so and so daughter of so and so, so pray over her.' He did perform the prayer for her and he stop opposite the middle of her body. Al-'Alâ' ibn Ziyâd al-'Adawi was among us. When he saw the different places that he stood for the male and the female, he said, 'O' Abu Ḥamzah, is this where the Messenger of Allah (ﷺ) would stand as you stood and for a woman as you stood?' He replied, 'Yes.' Al-'Alâ' turned to us and said, 'You (must) remember (this).' "[44]

The Description of the Prayer

There are to be four, five and even up to nine *takbeers* made in the funeral prayer. Sometimes the Prophet (ﷺ) would do it one way and sometimes he would do it another way.

As for four *takbeers*, Abu Hurayrah reported, "The Messenger of Allah (ﷺ) announced the death of the ruler of Abyssinia on the day that he died. He then went out to the place of prayer and lined the people in rows and made four *takbeers* (in the prayer)."[45]

Regarding five *takbeers*, 'Abdur-Raḥmân ibn Abu Layla said, "Zayd ibn Arqam used to make four *takbeers* in our funeral prayers and sometimes he would make five *takbeers*. I asked him about this and he said, 'The Messenger of Allah (ﷺ) would make these *takbeers*.' "[46]

---

[44] This hadith is *ṣaḥeeḥ*. See Shaykh al-Albâni, *Ṣaḥeeḥ Sunan Ibn Mâjah*, no. 1214. Recorded by Abu Dawood, Tirmidhi and Ibn Mâjah.

[45] Recorded by Bukhari, Muslim, Abu Dawood and Nasâ'i.

[46] This hadith is *ṣaḥeeḥ*. See Shaykh al-Albâni, *Ṣaḥeeḥ Sunan Ibn Mâjah*, no. 1222. Recorded by Muslim, Abu Dawood, Tirmidhi, Ibn Mâjah and Nasâ'i.

As for six or seven *takbeers*, such was been narrated in reports coming from the Companions. However, they are considered as having their source with the Prophet (ﷺ) because some of the leading Companions did that in the presence of other Companions and none of them objected to it. 'Abdullâh ibn Ma'qil said, " 'Ali ibn Abi Ṭâlib prayed over Sahl ibn Ḥunayf and made six *takbeers*. Then he turned to us and said, 'He was from the participants at Badr.' "[47] Moosa ibn 'Abdullâh ibn Zayd said, " 'Ali prayed over Abu Qatâdah and made seven *takbeers*. He was from the participants at Badr."[48]

'Abd Khayr said, " 'Ali would make six *takbeers* over those who participated at Badr, five over the other Companions of the Prophet (ﷺ) and four over the rest of the people."[49]

'Abdullâh ibn az-Zubayr said, "The Messenger of Allah (ﷺ) prayed over Ḥamzah, saying nine *takbeers*..."[50]

The hands should be raised during the first takbeer

'Abdullâh ibn 'Abbâs said, "The Messenger of Allah (ﷺ) would raise his hands in the Funeral prayer during the first *takbeer* and then not repeat doing so."[51]

(After raising the hands,) he would put his right hand over the left hand, wrist and forearm and put them firmly upon his chest. Sahl ibn S'ad said, "The people were ordered to place the right hand on the

---

[47] Its chain is *ṣaḥeeḥ*. See Shaykh al-Albâni, *al-Janâ'iz*, p. 113. Recorded by al-Ḥâkim and al-Bayhaqi.

[48] Its chain is *ṣaḥeeḥ*. See Shaykh al-Albâni, *al-Janâ'iz*, p. 114. Recorded by al-Bayhaqi.

[49] Its chain is *ṣaḥeeḥ*. See Shaykh al-Albâni, *al-Janâ'iz*, p. 113. Recorded by ad-Dâraquṭni and al-Bayhaqi.

[50] Its chain is *ḥasan*. See Shaykh al-Albâni, *al-Janâ'iz*, p. 49. All of the narrators are trustworthy. It was recorded by at-Tahâwi in *Mâni al-Athâr*.

[51] Its narrators are trustworthy. See Shaykh al-Albâni, *al-Janâ'iz*, p. 116.

left forearm while praying."[52]

After the opening *takbeer*, he would read *Soorah al-Fâtiḥah* and another *Soorah* of the Qur'an. Ṭalḥah ibn 'Abdullâh ibn 'Awf said, "I prayed the Funeral prayer behind Ibn 'Abbâs. He read *Soorah al-Fâtiḥah* and another *Soorah*. He made it aloud until we could hear him. When he finished the prayer, I took him by his hand and asked him about that. He replied, 'I did it aloud in order to teach you that it is the Sunnah and it is proper.' "[53]

It is to be read silently, as Abu Umâmah ibn Sahl said, "The Sunnah in the Funeral prayer is to read after the first *takbeer Soorah al-Fâtiḥah* silently. Then one makes three *takbeers* and makes the salutations after the last of them."[54]

After the second *takbeer*, one states prayers for the Prophet (ﷺ), based on the aforementioned hadith of Abu Umâmah in which one of the Companions of the Prophet (ﷺ) told him, "The Sunnah in the Funeral prayer is for the Imam to make the *takbeer* and then recite *al-Fâtiḥah* silently to himself after the first *takbeer*. Then he states prayers for the Prophet (ﷺ). He then makes sincere supplications for the deceased after the third *takbeer*. And he does not recite anything in either of those two. Then he makes a silent salutation to himself."[55]

---

[52] This hadith is *ṣaḥeeḥ*. See Shaykh al-Albâni, *Mukhtasar Ṣaḥeeḥ Bukhari*, no. 402. Recorded by Bukhari and Mâlik.

[53] This hadith is *ṣaḥeeḥ*. See Shaykh al-Albâni, *al-Janâ'iz*, p. 119. Recorded by Nasâ'i. As for reciting only *Soorah al-Fâtihah*, this is narrated by Bukhari, Abu Dawood, Tirmidhi and Ibn Mâjah.

[54] Its chain is *ṣaḥeeḥ*. See Shaykh al-Albâni, *al-Janâ'iz*, p. 111. Recorded by Nasâ'i.

[55] This hadith is *ṣaḥeeḥ*. See Shaykh al-Albâni, *al-Janâ'iz*, p. 122. This is recorded in ash-Shâfi'ee's *al-Umm* and by al-Bayhaqi.

Then he states the remaining *takbeers* and he makes sincere supplications for the deceased, as the Prophet (ﷺ) stated, "If you pray over the deceased make sincere supplications for him."[56]

One should supplicate for him according to what has been affirmed from the Prophet (ﷺ). This would include what 'Awf ibn Mâlik narrated. He said that he prayed the Funeral prayer behind the Messenger of Allah (ﷺ) and he memorized the supplication that he made. It was,

اللَّهُمَّ اغْفِرْ لَهُ وَارْحَمْهُ وَعَافِهِ وَاعْفُ عَنْهُ وَأَكْرِمْ نُزُلَهُ وَوَسِّعْ مُدْخَلَهُ وَاغْسِلْهُ بِالْمَاءِ وَالثَّلْجِ وَالْبَرَدِ وَنَقِّهِ مِنَ الْخَطَايَا كَمَا نَقَّيْتَ الثَّوْبَ الأَبْيَضَ مِنَ الدَّنَسِ وَأَبْدِلْهُ دَارًا خَيْرًا مِنْ دَارِهِ وَأَهْلاً خَيْرًا مِنْ أَهْلِهِ وَزَوْجًا خَيْرًا مِنْ زَوْجِهِ وَأَدْخِلْهُ الْجَنَّةَ وَأَعِذْهُ مِنْ عَذَابِ الْقَبْرِ وَ مِنْ عَذَابِ النَّارِ

"O' Allah, forgive him; have mercy on him; pardon him and excuse him; give him an honourable reception; make his grave wide; wash him with water, snow and ice; cleanse him of sin as a white garment is cleansed of filth; exchange for him an abode that is better than his present abode, and his family for a better family and his spouse for a better spouse. Enter him into Paradise. Protect him from the punishment of the grave and the punishment of the Hell-fire." 'Awf added, "I wished that I had been that deceased person."[57]

It is also sanctioned to make supplications between the final *takbeer* and the salutations. Abu Ya'foor narrated that 'Abdullâh ibn Abi Awfa (رضي الله عنه) stated, "I witnessed it and he made four *takbeers* over the deceased. Then he stood for a while, that is, they would

---

[56] This hadith is *ṣaḥeeḥ*. See Shaykh al-Albâni, *al-I'rwâ' al-Ghaleel*, no. 732. Recorded by Abu Dawood and Ibn Mâjah.

[57] This hadith is *ṣaḥeeḥ*. See Shaykh al-Albâni, *al-Janâ'iz*, p. 123. Recorded by Muslim, Ibn Mâjah and Nasâ'i.

supplicate. Then he said, 'Do you people see me making five *takbeers*?' They said, 'No.' He said, 'Certainly, the Messenger of Allah (ﷺ) would make four *takbeers*.' "[58]

Then the person makes the two salutations similar to the salutations in the obligatory prayers, one to the right and the other to the left. This is based on the statement of 'Abdullâh ibn Mas'ood, "Three actions did the Prophet (ﷺ) perform and the people have left. One of them is the salutations in the Funeral prayer being the same as the salutations in the (obligatory) prayers."[59]

It is permissible to state the salutation only once. This is based on the narration from Abu Hurayrah who said, "The Prophet (ﷺ) performed the funeral prayer and made four *takbeers* and only one salutation."[60]

It is not allowed to perform the funeral prayer during the prohibited times of prayer except due to necessity

'Uqbah ibn 'Âmir (رضي الله عنه) said, "There are three times (of the day) concerning which the Messenger of Allah (ﷺ) prohibited us from praying or from burying our dead: when the sunrise first occurs until it rises (above the horizon), during high noon until the sun goes beyond the zenith, when the sun is leaning toward sunset until it sets."[61]

---

[58] Its chain is *ṣaḥeeḥ*. See Shaykh al-Albâni, *al-Janâ'iz*, p. 126. Recorded by al-Bayhaqi.

[59] Its chain is *ḥasan*. See Shaykh al-Albâni, *al-Janâ'iz*, p. 127. Recorded by al-Bayhaqi.

[60] Its chain is *ḥasan*. See Shaykh al-Albâni, *al-Janâ'iz*, p. 128. Recorded by al-Ḥâkim and al-Bayhaqi.

[61] This hadith is *ṣaḥeeḥ*. See Shaykh al-Albâni, *Ṣaheeḥ Ibn Mâjah*, no. 1233. Recorded by Muslim, Abu Dawood, Tirmidhi, Nasâ'i and Ibn Mâjah.

The virtue of performing the funeral prayer and following the funeral bier

Abu Hurayrah narrated that the Prophet (ﷺ) said, "Whoever prays for the deceased but does follow the funeral bier will get one *qeerât* (of reward) and the one who follows it will receive two *qeerâts*." It was said, "And what is a *qeerât* (amount)?" He replied, "The smaller of the two of them is like Mount Uḥud."[62]

This virtue of following the funeral bier is only for men and not for women. The Prophet (ﷺ) prohibited women from following the funeral prior. However, this is a prohibition of discouragement only. Umm 'Aṭiyyah stated, "We were prohibited from following the funeral bier but it was not made something strict upon us."[63]

However, it is not allowed to follow the funeral bier via any means that contradict the Shari'ah. The narrated texts mention two matters in particular: raising the voices in crying and following the bier with incense. The Prophet (ﷺ) said, "The funeral bier is not to be followed in the procession by (wailing) sounds or fire."[64]

Included in this category is the raising of one's voice by reciting words of remembrance in front of the funeral bier, as this is an innovation. This view is based on Qays ibn 'Ibâd's statement, "The Companions of the Prophet (ﷺ) would dislike for anyone to raise their voice during the funeral."[65] Furthermore, by doing such an act, one is resembling the Christians, as their raise their voices by

---

[62] This hadith is *ṣaḥeeḥ*. See Shaykh al-Albâni, *Ṣaḥeeḥ al-Jâmi' aṣ-Ṣagheer*, no. 6355. Recorded by Muslim.

[63] Recorded by Bukhari, Muslim, Abu Dawood and Ibn Mâjah.

[64] This hadith is *ḥasan*. See Shaykh al-Albâni, *al-Janâ'iz*, p. 70. Recorded by Abu Dawood.

[65] Its narrators are trustworthy. See Shaykh al-Albâni, *al-Janâ'iz*, p. 71. Recorded by al-Bayhaqi.

reciting the Gospel and words of remembrance in a melodic, mournful manner.

Worse than that is what is being commonly done today in some Muslim lands in imitation of the disbelievers wherein the funeral procession is led by people playing musical instruments in a sorrowful tone.

It is obligatory to move quickly with the funeral procession, but not to run or jog

The Prophet (ﷺ) said, "Hurry in performing the funeral for if he were a pious person, you will take him to goodness. If he was other than that, it is evil that you are removing from you necks."[66]

It is permissible to walk in front, behind, to the right or to the left of the funeral bier, all along being close to it. However, those who are riding on some mode of transportation should be behind the procession. Al-Mugheerah ibn Shu'bah narrated that the Prophet (ﷺ) said, "The rider is to be behind the funeral procession while the one walking may be wherever he wishes with respect to it."[67] However, it is best to be behind it, as implied in the Prophet's words, "Follow the funeral procession." This is also supported by 'Ali's statement when he said, "Walking behind it (the funeral procession) is preferred to walking in front of it like the prayer of a man in congregation is preferred to his prayer said alone."[68]

---

[66] Recorded by Bukhari, Muslim, Abu Dawood and Tirmidhi.

[67] This hadith is *ṣaḥeeḥ*. See Shaykh al-Albâni, *Ṣaḥeeḥ al-Jâmi' aṣ-Ṣagheer*, no. 3533. Recorded by Tirmidhi, Nasâ'i and Abu Dawood.

[68] Its chain is *ḥasan*. See Shaykh al-Albâni, *al-Janâ'iz*, p. 74. Recorded by al-Bayhaqi.

What is to be said when entering or passing by the gravesites

'Â'ishah (رضي الله عنها) said: "I said, 'What should I say to them[69], O' Messenger of Allah?' He said,

قُولِي السَّلامُ عَلَى أَهْلِ الدِّيَارِ مِنَ الْمُؤْمِنِينَ وَالْمُسْلِمِينَ وَيَرْحَمُ اللَّهُ الْمُسْتَقْدِمِينَ مِنَّا وَالْمُسْتَأْخِرِينَ وَإِنَّا إِنْ شَاءَ اللَّهُ بِكُمْ لَلَاحِقُونَ

'Say, Peace be upon the inhabitants of these places from the believers and the Muslims. May Allah have mercy on those who preceded us and those who will come after. Allah willing, we shall be joining you.' "[70]

Sulaymân ibn Buraydah narrated from his father who said, "The Messenger of Allah (ﷺ) taught us that if we go to the graves (we should say,),

السَّلامُ عَلَيْكُمْ أَهْلَ الدِّيَارِ مِنَ الْمُؤْمِنِينَ وَالْمُسْلِمِينَ وَإِنَّا إِنْ شَاءَ اللَّهُ لاحِقُونَ أَسْأَلُ اللَّهَ لَنَا وَلَكُمُ الْعَافِيَةَ

'Peace be upon you, O' inhabitants of the graves from believers and Muslims. We, Allah willing, shall be joining you. I ask Allah for us and for you well-being."[71]

---

[69] Referring to people in graves. - Translator

[70] This hadith is *ṣaḥeeḥ*. See Shaykh al-Albâni, *Ṣaḥeeḥ al-Jâmi'*, no. 4421, *al-Janâ'iz*, p. 183. Recorded by Muslim and Nasâ'i.

[71] This hadith is *ṣaḥeeḥ*. See Shaykh al-Albâni, *Ṣaḥeeḥ Sunan Nasâ'i*, no. 1928. Recorded by Muslim and Nasâ'i.

The Burial

It is obligatory to bury the deceased, even if he were a disbeliever, as the Prophet (ﷺ) said to 'Ali when Abu Ṭâlib had passed away, "Go and bury him."[72]

The Sunnah is to bury the dead in a graveyard, as the Prophet (ﷺ) used to bury the dead in the Baqee' Graveyard, as has been unquestionably narrated from him. It has not been narrated from any of the early Muslims that they would bury the deceased anywhere other than a graveyard. The only exception to this has been what was definitively narrated that the Prophet (ﷺ) himself was buried in his home. This was a particular ruling for him, as indicated by the statement of 'Â'ishah who said, "When the Messenger of Allah (ﷺ) died, they differed concerning his burial. Abu Bakr (رضي الله عنه) said, 'I heard the Messenger of Allah (ﷺ) saying something that I did not forget. (He said,) 'Allah does not take the soul of a prophet except at the place in which he loves to be buried.' "[73]

Another exception to the general rule is the case of the martyrs who die in battle. They are to be buried at the place of their martyrdom. They are not to be taken to the graveyards. This is based on the hadith of Jâbir who said, "On the Day of Uḥud, the killed were being taken to be buried at the Baqee' Cemetery. Then the announcer of the Messenger of Allah (ﷺ) proclaimed, 'The Messenger of Allah (ﷺ) orders you to bury the deceased at their places.' "[74]

---

[72] This hadith is *ṣaḥeeḥ*. See Shaykh al-Albâni, *Ṣaḥeeḥ Sunan Nasâ'i*, no. 1895. Recorded by Nasâ'i.

[73] This hadith is *ṣaḥeeḥ*. See Shaykh al-Albâni, *Ṣaḥeeḥ Sunan Tirmidhi*, no. 5649. Recorded by Tirmidhi.

[74] This hadith is *ṣaḥeeḥ*. See Shaykh al-Albâni, *Ṣaḥeeḥ Sunan Nasâ'i*, no. 1893. Recorded by Abu Dawood, Nasâ'i and Tirmidhi.

It is not permissible to bury the deceased during the following times — except due to necessity

1. 'Uqbah ibn 'Âmir said, "There are three times (of the day) concerning which the Messenger of Allah (ﷺ) prohibited us from praying or from burying our dead: when the sunrise first appears until it rises (above the horizon), during high noon until the sun goes beyond the zenith, when the sun is leaning toward sunset until it sets."[75]

2. Jâbir said, "The Messenger of Allah (ﷺ) mentioned a man from among his Companions who had died, been wrapped in a shroud not long (enough to cover his whole body) and was buried during the night. The Messenger of Allah (ﷺ) reprimanded (the people) for burying the man during the night such that he was not able to perform the prayer for him. (This should only be done) when it is a necessity."[76]

If one is forced to perform the burial at night, it is permissible — even if one has to use lamps and put those lamps into the grave to make the preparing of the grave easier. Ibn 'Abbâs said, "The Messenger of Allah (ﷺ) put a man into his grave at night and he lit lamps in his grave."[77]

It is a must to make the grave deep, wide and excellent

Hishâm ibn 'Âmir said, "During the Day of Uḥud, some Muslims died and others were wounded. We said, 'O' Messenger of

---

[75] This hadith is *ṣaḥeeḥ*. See Shaykh al-Albâni, *Ṣaḥeeḥ Ibn Mâjah*, no. 1233. Recorded by Muslim, Abu Dawood, Tirmidhi, Nasâ'i and Ibn Mâjah.

[76] This hadith is *ṣaḥeeḥ*. See Shaykh al-Albâni, *Ṣaḥeeḥ Sunan Nasâ'i*, no. 1787. Recorded by Muslim, Abu Dawood and Nasâ'i.

[77] This hadith is *ḥasan*. See Shaykh al-Albâni, *al-Janâ'iz*, p. 141. Recorded by Tirmidhi.

Allah, it is difficult for us to build proper graves for each person. What shall we do?' He replied, 'Dig, making them wide, deep and excellent. Bury two and three in one grave. Put the one who knew the most Qur'an ahead.' My father was the third of three in a grave but he knew the most Qur'an and so they put him ahead."[78]

It is permissible to make the grave a vertical hole straight down and it is also permissible to make the grave a hole with a niche cut out at the bottom to the side of the hole.[79] Both practices existed during the time of the Prophet (ﷺ) but the latter is considered preferable. Anas ibn Mâlik said, "When the Prophet (ﷺ) died, in Madeenah there was a man who dug graves with a niche to the side and another who dug straight down. They (the Companions) said, 'Let us ask our Lord for guidance. We shall send for both of them and the first one to come we will choose.' So they sent for both and the one who digs with the niche to the side came first. Thus, the Prophet (ﷺ) was buried in the niche to the side of the grave."[80]

The accepted practice is for men to lower the body into the grave, even if the deceased is a woman, as this is what was practiced during the time of the Prophet (ﷺ) and this has been the continual practice of the Muslims until today. The relatives of the deceased have the most right to place the deceased in the grave. This point is based on the generality of the verse:

---

[78] This hadith is *ṣaḥeeḥ*. See Shaykh al-Albâni, *al-Janâ'iz*, p. 146. Recorded by Nasâ'i, Abu Dawood and Tirmidhi.

[79] [In the latter manner of making a grave, the body is place into the niche and the area is covered by bricks or something similar. Then the hole is filled with dirt. In this manner, when the dirt is shoveled back into the grave, it does not fall on top of the body, which is safe in the niche to the side of the grave.] - Translator

[80] Its chain is *ḥasan*. Recorded by Ibn Mâjah.

﴿... وَأُوْلُوا ٱلْأَرْحَامِ بَعْضُهُمْ أَوْلَىٰ بِبَعْضٍ فِي كِتَٰبِ ٱللَّهِ ... ﴿٦﴾﴾

(سورة الأحزاب: ٦)

﴾... And blood relations among each other have closer personal ties in the Decree of Allah...﴿ *(Qur'an 33: 6)*

Furthermore, 'Ali narrated, "I washed the Messenger of Allah (ﷺ). I went to him and I expected to find what one normally sees among the dead but did not find any such thing. The Prophet (ﷺ) was good (in appearance) both alive and dead. Only four people took part in lowering him and burying him: 'Ali, al-'Abbâs, al-Faḍl and Ṣâliḥ, the ex-slave of the Messenger of Allah. A niche was dug for the Prophet (ﷺ) and bricks were placed next to him."[81]

It is permissible for the husband to fulfill the role of placing his wife in the grave

This is based on the hadith of 'Â'ishah who said, "The Messenger of Allah (ﷺ) came to me on the day that his illness began. I said (due to a headache I had), 'O' my head.' He replied, 'I wished that (death) would come to you while I am alive for then I would prepare you and bury you.' "[82]

However, this is conditioned upon the husband not having had sexual intercourse during that night. Otherwise, it is not proper for him to put her in the grave and it would be preferred for others to do it, even if the person is a non-relative. This condition is based on the hadith narrated by Anas who said, "We attended to funeral of the daughter of the Messenger (ﷺ). He was sitting at the grave and I could see his eyes filled with tears. He said, 'Is there any among you men who did not have intercourse last night?' Abu Ṭalḥah said, 'I, O'

---

[81] Its chain is *ṣaḥeeḥ*. Recorded by al-Ḥâkim and al-Bayhaqi.

[82] This hadith is *ṣaḥeeḥ*. Similar is recorded in Bukhari and Muslim.

Messenger of Allah.' He said, 'Then go down (into the grave),' and he went into her grave."[83]

The sunnah is to enter the body (head first) from the end of the grave (where the feet will be)

Abu Isḥâq said, "Al-Ḥârith asked that 'Abdullâh ibn Yazeed perform the prayer for him. He did so and then entered the body from the end of the grave (where the feet will eventually be placed). He then said, 'This is the Sunnah.' "[84]

The deceased is placed in the grave on his right side, with his face directed toward the *qiblah*. His head and legs, therefore, will be (perpendicular to the *qiblah*,) to the right and left of the *qiblah*. This has been the practice of the people of Islam since the time of the Messenger of Allah (ﷺ) until our times now.

The one who places the deceased into the grave should say, "In the name of Allah and upon the Sunnah of the Messenger of Allah," or "upon the way (*millah*) of the Messenger of Allah." Ibn 'Umar said, "When the Prophet (ﷺ) would put the deceased into the grave, he would say,

بِسْمِ اللَّهِ وَعَلَى سُنَّةِ رَسُولِ اللَّهِ

'In the name of Allah and upon the Sunnah of the Messenger of Allah.' "[85]

Al-Bayâḍi (رضي الله عنه) narrated that the Messenger of Allah (ﷺ) said, "When the deceased is placed into his grave, the one placing

---

[83] This hadith is *ṣaḥeeḥ*. See Shaykh al-Albâni, *al-Janâ'iz*, p. 149. Recorded by Bukhari.

[84] Its chain is *ṣaḥeeḥ*. See Shaykh al-Albâni, *al-Janâ'iz*, p. 150. Recorded by Abu Dawood.

[85] This hadith is *ṣaḥeeḥ*. See Shaykh al-Albâni, *al-Janâ'iz*, p. 152. Recorded by Abu Dawood, Tirmidhi and Ibn Mâjah.

him there, when putting him into the grave, should say, 'In the name of Allah, by Allah and upon the way (*millah*) of the Messenger of Allah.' "[86]

It is recommended for the one at the gravesite to throw three handfuls, with both hands, over the grave after the bricks have been laid to close the niche. Abu Hurayrah said, "The Messenger of Allah (ﷺ) prayed over a funeral and then came and threw three handfuls of soil towards the head of the deceased."[87]

The following are sunan acts after burying the deceased

1. The grave should be elevated from the earth about a handspan. In other words, it should not be level with the earth. This is so it can be respected and not disrespected. Jâbir said, "The Prophet's grave was made with a niche in it. Bricks were then erected behind (his body). And his grave was raised about a handspan above the earth."[88]

2. The grave should have a mound to it. Sufiyân at-Tamâr said, "I saw the grave of the Prophet (ﷺ) and it was mounded."[89]

3. The grave should be marked by a stone, rock or something of that nature, so that other family members may be buried in the same locale in the future. Al-Muṭalib ibn Abi Widâ'ah said, "When 'Uthmân ibn Madh'oon died, he was taken to his grave and buried. The Prophet (ﷺ) ordered a man to bring a rock. He was not able to carry it, so the Messenger of Allah went to him and uncovered his

---

[86] Its chain is *ḥasan*. See Shaykh al-Albâni, *al-Janâ'iz*, p. 152. Recorded by al-Ḥâkim.

[87] This hadith is *ṣaḥeeḥ*. See Shaykh al-Albâni, *I'rwâ' al-Ghaleel*, no. 751. Recorded by Ibn Mâjah.

[88] Its chain is *ḥasan*. See Shaykh al-Albâni, *al-Janâ'iz*, p. 153. Recorded by Ibn Ḥibbân and al-Bayhaqi.

[89] This hadith is *ṣaḥeeḥ*. See Shaykh al-Albâni, *al-Janâ'iz*, p. 154. Recorded by Bukhari.

forearms." Al-Muṭalib said, "The one who narrated this to me from the Messenger of Allah (ﷺ) said, 'It is as if I can now see the whiteness of his forearms of the Messenger of Allah (ﷺ) as he uncovered them." Al-Muṭalib continued saying, "The Prophet (ﷺ) carried it and placed it at the head (of the deceased). He then said, 'By this, I mark and grave and my brother and shall bury there whoever dies of his family.' "[90]

4. One should stand at the grave and supplicate for the deceased, asking him to be kept firm in his faith and to be forgiven. He should also tell those present to do the same. 'Uthmân ibn 'Affân said, "When the Prophet (ﷺ) would finish the burying of a deceased, he would stand at the grave and say, 'Seek refuge for you brother and ask for him to be made firm, for he is now being questioned.' "[91]

It is permissible to sit at the grace during the burial in order to remind those present of death and what will occur after death. This point is substantiated by the following hadith of al-Barâ' ibn 'Âzib:

"We went with the Prophet (ﷺ) during the funeral of one of the Anṣâr. We reached the grave and when the niche was dug, the Messenger of Allah (ﷺ) sat and we sat around him, silent, as if birds were upon our heads. He had a stick with which he was poking the ground. Then he raised his head and said, 'Seek refuge in Allah from the punishment of the grave.' He said that twice or three times. Then he said, 'When the believing servant is about to depart from this world and enter into the Hereafter, angels descend to him from the heaven, their faces white like the sun. They have with them a shroud from the shrouds of Paradise and embalming fluid from the fragrance of Paradise. They sit away from him at the extent of his eyesight.

---

[90] This hadith is *ḥasan*. See Shaykh al-Albâni, *al-Janâ'iz*, p. 155. Recorded by Abu Dawood.

[91] Its chain is *ṣaḥeeḥ*. See Shaykh al-Albâni, *al-Janâ'iz*, p. 156. Recorded by Abu Dawood.

Then the angel of death approaches until he sits at his head. He then says, 'O' pure soul! Come out to forgiveness from your Lord and His pleasure.' Then (the soul) comes out like water dropping from the opening of a waterskin. (The Angel of Death) then takes it. When it he takes it, it does not remain in his hands for the blinking of an eye but he immediately puts it into that shroud and fragrance. And from that soul comes out the best smell, like the best smelling musk of this world. They then ascend with the soul. They do not pass by any gathering of angels except that they would say, 'What is this beautiful soul?' They will say, 'It is so and so, the son of so and so,' calling him by the best names that he was called in this world. When they reach the lowest heaven, they ask for it to be opened and the gates are opened for them. The most exalted angels of each level escort him to the next level, until he reaches the seventh heaven. Allah (ﷻ) will then say, 'Write My servant's record in the *'Iliyeen* and return him to the earth, for from it I created them, into it I send them back and from it I shall resurrect them again.' Then his soul is placed once again into his body. Two angels come and sit next to him. They say to him, 'Who is your Lord?' He says, 'My Lord is Allah.' They then say to him, 'What is your religion?' He will say, 'My religion is Islam.' Then they say to him, 'Who is that man who was sent among you?' He will say, 'He is the Messenger of Allah.' They will say, 'What is your knowledge?' He will say, 'I read the Book of Allah, believed in it and affirmed what it said.' A caller then calls from the heaven, 'My servant has verily told the truth. So provide him with furnishing from Paradise, clothe him from Paradise and open for him a door to Paradise.' He is then brought its scent and fragrance. His grave is then expanded as far as his vision can see. Then a man with a beautiful face, excellent clothing and fine scent comes. He says, 'Have glad tidings of that which will make you happy, for this is the day that you were promised.' (The deceased) will say to him, 'Who are you? Your face is like that which comes with goodness.' He will reply, 'I am your righteous deeds.' (The deceased) will then say, 'My Lord, establish the Hour so that I may return to my family and property.' But when the disbelieving slave is about to depart from this world and enter into the Hereafter, angels with black faces descend to him from the heaven. They have with them rough fabric. They sit away from him at the extent of his eyesight. Then the angel of death approaches until he sits at his head. He then says, 'O' evil soul! Come out to wrath and anger from your Lord.' It spreads throughout the body but it is taken out like a skewer is pulled through wet wool. It is then taken and as soon as it is taken, it is not in their hands for the blinking of an eye but it is placed in that rough fabric. From this soul comes the worst scent one can find on the earth. He is then taken up and whenever they pass by any angels, they say, 'Who is this evil soul?' They will answer, 'It is so and so, the son of so and so,' and they will call him by the worst names that he was known by in this world. This will continued until they reach the lowest heaven. They will ask for permission to enter and it will not be granted." Then the Messenger of Allah (ﷺ) recited the verse:

﴿إِنَّ ٱلَّذِينَ كَذَّبُوا۟ بِـَٔايَـٰتِنَا وَٱسْتَكْبَرُوا۟ عَنْهَا لَا تُفَتَّحُ لَهُمْ أَبْوَٰبُ ٱلسَّمَآءِ وَلَا يَدْخُلُونَ ٱلْجَنَّةَ حَتَّىٰ يَلِجَ ٱلْجَمَلُ فِى سَمِّ ٱلْخِيَاطِ ... ﴿٤٠﴾﴾ (سورة الأعراف: ٤٠)

﴿Verily, those who deny Our signs and treat them with arrogance, for them the gates of heaven will not be opened, and they will not enter Paradise until the camel goes through the eye of the needle [which is impossible]...﴾ *(Qur'an 7: 40)*

[The Messenger of Allah (ﷺ) then continued,] "Allah will then say, 'Write My servant's record in the *Sijjeen*.' He will then be thrust with great force." The Messenger of Allah then read the verse:

﴿... وَمَن يُشْرِكْ بِٱللَّهِ فَكَأَنَّمَا خَرَّ مِنَ ٱلسَّمَآءِ فَتَخْطَفُهُ ٱلطَّيْرُ أَوْ تَهْوِى بِهِ

ٱلرِّيحُ فِى مَكَانٍ سَحِيقٍ ﴿٣١﴾ (سورة الحجّ : ٣١)

﴿... Whoever assigns partners to Allah, it is as if he had fallen from the sky, and the birds had snatched him, or the wind had thrown him to a far off place.﴾ *(Qur'an 22: 31)*

[Then the Prophet (ﷺ) continued,] "Return his soul to his body. Two angels come and sit next to him. They say to him, 'Who is your Lord?' He says, 'Uh, uh, I do no know.' They then say to him, 'What is your religion?' He will say, 'Uh, uh, I do no know.' Then they say to him, 'Who is that man who was sent among you?' He will say, 'Uh, uh, I do no know.' A caller than calls from the heaven, 'He lies. So provide him with furnishing from Hell and open for him a door to Hell.' He is then brought its heat and hot wind. His grave is then so constricted that his ribs are broken. Then a man with an ugly face, terrible clothing and foul scent comes. He says, 'Have tidings of that which will make you unhappy, for this is the day that you were promised.' (The deceased) will say to him, 'Who are you? Your face is like that which comes with evil.' He will reply, 'I am your evil deeds.' (The deceased) will then say, 'Do not let the hour be established.' " In another narration, it states, "A blind, deaf and dumb man is appointed for him. In his hand is a sledgehammer which if he were to strike a mountain with it, it would turn to dust. He strikes him once and he becomes dust. Then Allah returns him (the deceased) to how he was and he strikes him again. He lets out a screech that everything except humans and jinn can hear."[92]

Paying condolences

It is sanctioned to give condolences to the family of the deceased, by saying to them what one thinks will give them solace,

---

[92] This hadith is *ṣaḥeeḥ*. See Shaykh al-Albâni, *al-Janâ'iz*, p. 159. Recorded by Aḥmad and Abu Dawood.

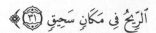

reduce their grief and encourage them to be pleased with what Allah has decreed and to be patient. If one has learned and recalls what the Prophet (ﷺ) would say, one can use those expressions. Otherwise, one may say whatever good words he thinks will achieve the purpose and which do not contradict the Shari'ah.

Usâmah ibn Zayd said, "We were with the Prophet (ﷺ) when one of his daughters called for him to come to her and informed him that her son or daughter had passed away. The Messenger of Allah (ﷺ) said, 'To Allah belongs what He takes and what He gives. Everything has an appointed term. Tell her to have patience and hope for reward.' "[93]

With respect to condolences, though, there are two aspects that should be avoided, even if the people customarily do them:

1. Gathering together in a specific place, like in a house, cemetery or mosque, for the purpose of condolences.

2. Having the family of the deceased prepare food for their visitors who are coming to make condolences.

Jareer ibn 'Abdullâh al-Bajaly (رضي الله عنه) said, "We (the Companions) would consider getting together with the family of the deceased and preparing food after the burial to be a type of wailing."[94]

The Sunnah is for the relatives of the deceased and their neighbours to prepare food and take care for the family of the deceased. This is based on the hadith narrated by 'Abdullâh ibn Ja'far who said, "When the news of Ja'far's death came, when he was killed, the Prophet (ﷺ) said, 'Prepare food for the family of Ja'far for news has come to them that shall preoccupy them.' "[95]

---

[93] Recorded by Bukhari and Muslim.

[94] This hadith is *ṣaḥeeḥ*. See Shaykh al-Albâni, *Ṣaḥeeḥ Sunan Ibn Mâjah*, no. 1308. Recorded by Ibn Mâjah.

[95] This hadith is *ḥasan*. See Shaykh al-Albâni, *Ṣaḥeeḥ al-Jâmi' aṣ-Ṣagheer*, no. 1015. Recorded by Abu Dawood, Tirmidhi and Ibn Mâjah.

What benefits the deceased

The deceased can be benefited by the deeds done by others. These actions include the following:

1. The Muslim making supplications for him

This is based on Allah's words:

﴿وَٱلَّذِينَ جَآءُو مِنۢ بَعۡدِهِمۡ يَقُولُونَ رَبَّنَا ٱغۡفِرۡ لَنَا وَلِإِخۡوَٰنِنَا ٱلَّذِينَ سَبَقُونَا بِٱلۡإِيمَٰنِ وَلَا تَجۡعَلۡ فِي قُلُوبِنَا غِلّٗا لِّلَّذِينَ ءَامَنُواْ رَبَّنَآ إِنَّكَ رَءُوفٞ رَّحِيمٌ ١٠﴾

(سورة الحشر: ١٠)

﴾And those who came after them say, 'Our Lord! Forgive us and our brethren who have preceded us in Faith, and put not in our hearts any hatred against those who have believed. Our Lord! You are indeed full of Kindness, Most Merciful.'﴿ *(Qur'an 59: 10)*

Furthermore, the Prophet (ﷺ) said, "The supplication of the Muslim for his brother in his absence is responded to. At his head is an entrusted angel every time he supplicates something good for his brother. The entrusted angel say, '*Âmeen* and for you the same.'"[96]

2. Any Muslim repaying the debt of the deceased

This point is based on the previously mentioned hadith in which Abu Qatâdah repaid two *dinars* on behalf of a deceased.

3. Any Muslim fulfilling the vow of fasting or any other type of vow on behalf of the deceased

S'ad ibn 'Ubâdah said, "I asked the Messenger of Allah (ﷺ) about my mother who had died while she had yet to fulfill a vow. He

---

[96] This hadith is *ṣaḥeeḥ*. See Shaykh al-Albâni, *Ṣaḥeeḥ al-Jâmi' aṣ-Ṣagheer*, no. 3381. Recorded by Muslim.

said, 'Fulfill it on her behalf.' "[97]

4. Righteous deeds performed by the pious son

Allah (ﷻ) says:

﴿وَأَن لَّيْسَ لِلْإِنسَٰنِ إِلَّا مَا سَعَىٰ ۝٣٩﴾ (سورة النّجم: ٣٩)

﴾And that man can have nothing but that for which he strives.﴿ *(Qur'an 53: 39)*

The Prophet (ﷺ) further stated, "The best that a person consumes is from what he has earned and his child is from his earnings."[98]

5. What the deceased left behind in the form of righteous deeds and continual charity

Abu Hurayrah reported that the Messenger of Allah (ﷺ) said, "When the human dies his deeds come to an end, except for three: a continuing act of charity, knowledge that is being benefited from and a pious son who supplicates for him."[99]

Visiting the graves

It is sanctioned to visit the graves as a kind of admonition and remembrance of the Hereafter. However this is conditioned upon the person not saying anything that is displeasing to the Lord, such as supplicating to the one in the grave and seeking his help instead of Allah's. Abu Sa'eed al-Khudri narrated that the Messenger of Allah

---

[97] Recorded by Bukhari, Muslim, Abu Dawood, Tirmidhi and Nasâ'i.

[98] This hadith is *ṣaḥeeḥ*. See Shaykh al-Albâni, *I'rwâ' al-Ghaleel*, no. 1626. Recorded by Abu Dawood, and this is his wording, and by Tirmidhi, Ibn Mâjah and Nasâ'i. [This is what is noted in the footnote but this is actually the wording of Nasâ'i and Ibn Mâjah. Abu Dawood's wording is slightly different. Allah alone knows best.] - Translator

[99] This hadith is *ṣaḥeeḥ*. See Shaykh al-Albâni, *Ṣaḥeeḥ al-Jâmi' aṣ-Ṣagheer*, no. 893. Recorded by Muslim, Abu Dawood, Tirmidhi and Nasâ'i.

(ﷺ) said, "I forbade you from visiting the graves. But (you may now) visit them for in doing so there is a lesson. But do not say anything that displeases the Lord."[100]

Women are the same as men with respect to it being recommended that they visit the graves, as they can benefit from the same reason for which it is sanctioned to visit the graves. Furthermore, the hadith of 'Â'ishah has already been presented in which she asked the Prophet (ﷺ) what she should say when she visits the graves. The Prophet (ﷺ) taught her what to say without prohibiting her from visiting them and without clarifying that women are not to visit graves.

What is forbidden to do at the gravesite

1. Sacrificing an animal for the sake of Allah

The Prophet (ﷺ) said, "There is no sacrificing (at a gravesite) in Islam." 'Abdur-Razzâq said, "(Before Islam,) they used to sacrifice a cow or a sheep at the grave."[101]

2. — 6. The actions described in the following hadith are all prohibited at the gravesite

Jâbir (رضي الله عنه) said, "The Prophet (ﷺ) forbade plastering a grave, sitting on it, building upon it, adding to its height or writing upon it."[102]

---

[100] This hadith is *ṣaḥeeḥ*. See Shaykh al-Albâni, *Janâ'iz*, p. 179. Recorded by al-Ḥâkim and al-Bayhaqi, without the last sentence which is recorded by al-Bazzâr.

[101] Its chain is *ṣaḥeeḥ*. See Shaykh al-Albâni, *Janâ'iz*, p. 203. Recorded by Abu Dawood.

[102] Its chain is *ṣaḥeeḥ*. See Shaykh al-Albâni, *Janâ'iz*, p. 204. Recorded by Abu Dawood. This is Abu Dawood's wording. Other versions, with some additions or deletions, are recorded by Muslim, Tirmidhi and Nasâ'i.

7. Praying towards the grave

The Prophet (ﷺ) said, "Do not pray towards the graves."[103]

8. Prayer at the gravesite, even if not toward the grave

Abu Sa'eed al-Khudri narrated that the Messenger of Allah (ﷺ) said, "All of the (places on the earth) are a place to pray except for a graveyard and a bathroom."[104]

9. Building mosques upon it

'Â'ishah and Ibn 'Abbâs both stated, "When the Messenger of Allah (ﷺ) was in his last illness, he kept on putting his blanket over his face. Whenever he felt hot and short of breath, he would uncover his face. During that time, he said, 'May the curse of Allah be on the Jews and the Christians. They would take the graves of their Prophets as places of worship.' The Prophet was warning (the Muslims) against doing such deeds as they did."[105]

'Â'ishah also said, "The Messenger of Allah (ﷺ) said during his illness form which he did not recover, 'May the curse of Allah be on the Jews and the Christians. They would take the graves of their Prophets as places of worship.' If it were not for that, his grave would have been made a prominent place but it was feared that it would be taken as a place of worship.'"[106]

---

[103] This hadith is *ṣaḥeeḥ*. See Shaykh al-Albâni, *Ṣaḥeeḥ al-Jâmi' aṣ-Ṣagheer*, no. 7348. Recorded by Muslim, Abu Dawood, Tirmidhi and Nasâ'i.

[104] This hadith is *ṣaḥeeḥ*. See Shaykh al-Albâni, *Ṣaḥeeḥ al-Jâmi' aṣ-Ṣagheer*, no. 2767. Recorded by Abu Dawood and Tirmidhi.

[105] Recorded by Bukhari, Muslim and Nasâ'i.

[106] Ibid.

10. Taking the gravesite as a place for festivals

This refers to going to the gravesite at specific times or festivals in order to perform acts of worship or other acts there. The Messenger of Allah (ﷺ) said, "Do not turn my grave into a place for season festivals and do not turn your houses into graves.[107] Make prayers upon me for your prayers reach me wherever you are."[108]

11. Travelling for the purpose of visiting a grave

Abu Hurayrah narrated that the Prophet (ﷺ) said, "Do not undertake a journey[109] except to three mosques: *al-Ḥarâm* Mosque (in Makkah), the Mosque of the Messenger of Allah (ﷺ) (in Madeenah) and al-Aqsa Mosque (in Jerusalem)."[110]

12. Lighting lamps on the graves

This is an innovation unknown to the pious predecessors. The Messenger of Allah (ﷺ) said, "And every heresy is misguidance. And every misguidance is in the Fire (of Hell)." Furthermore, this act is a waste of wealth which is prohibited by a clear text. The Prophet (ﷺ) said, "Allah dislikes for you three things: talking idly, wasting your wealth, and asking excessively (for charity)."[111]

13. Breaking the bones of the deceased

The Prophet (ﷺ) said, "Verily, breaking the bone of the deceased believer is like breaking it while he is alive."[112]

---

107 [By not performing voluntary prayers therein.] - Translator

108 This hadith is *ṣaḥeeḥ*. See Shaykh al-Albâni, *Ṣaḥeeḥ al-Jâmi' aṣ-Ṣagheer*, no. 7226. Recorded by Abu Dawood.

109 [That is, for the purpose of worship.] - Translator

110 Recorded by Bukhari, Muslim, Abu Dawood and Nasâ'i.

111 Recorded by Bukhari and Muslim.

112 This hadith is *ṣaḥeeḥ*. See Shaykh al-Albâni, *Ṣaḥeeḥ al-Jâmi' aṣ-Ṣagheer*, no. 2143. Recorded by Abu Dawood and Ibn Mâjah.

Chapter Four — Fasting

The Ruling of the Fast

Fasting the month of Ramaḍân is one of the pillars of Islam and one of its obligatory acts. Allah (ﷻ) says:

﴿يَٰٓأَيُّهَا ٱلَّذِينَ ءَامَنُواْ كُتِبَ عَلَيۡكُمُ ٱلصِّيَامُ كَمَا كُتِبَ عَلَى ٱلَّذِينَ مِن قَبۡلِكُمۡ لَعَلَّكُمۡ تَتَّقُونَ ﴿١٨٣﴾﴾ (سورة البَقَرَة: ١٨٣)

﴿O' you who believe! Observing the fast is prescribed for you as it was prescribed for those before you, that you may become the pious.﴾ *(Qur'an 2: 183)*

Shortly afterwards, Allah also says:

﴿شَهۡرُ رَمَضَانَ ٱلَّذِيٓ أُنزِلَ فِيهِ ٱلۡقُرۡءَانُ هُدٗى لِّلنَّاسِ وَبَيِّنَٰتٖ مِّنَ ٱلۡهُدَىٰ وَٱلۡفُرۡقَانِۚ فَمَن شَهِدَ مِنكُمُ ٱلشَّهۡرَ فَلۡيَصُمۡهُۖ ... ﴿١٨٥﴾﴾

(سورة البَقَرَة: ١٨٥)

﴿The month of Ramaḍân in which was revealed the Qur'an, a guidance for mankind and clear proofs for the guidance and the criterion [between right and wrong]. So whoever of you is resident during the month must observe fast...﴾ *(Qur'an 2: 185)*

Ibn 'Umar narrated that the Messenger of Allah (ﷺ) said, "Islam is built upon five (pillars): testifying that there is none worthy of worship except Allah and that Muhammad is the Messenger of Allah, establishing the prayers, giving the zakah, making the pilgrimage to the House and fasting the month of Ramaḍân."[1] All of the Muslim Nation has agreed that it is obligatory to fast the month of Ramaḍân and that it is one of the pillars of Islam. It is something that is known about the religion by necessity. The one who rejects it as a practice is a disbelieving apostate who has left the fold of Islam.[2]

The Virtues of the Fast of Ramaḍân

Abu Hurayrah narrated that the Messenger of Allah (ﷺ) said, "Whoever fasts the month of Ramaḍân with faith and hoping for its reward shall have all of his previous sins forgiven for him."[3]

Abu Hurayrah (رضي الله عنه) also narrated that the Messenger of Allah (ﷺ) said, "Allah has said, 'All the deeds of the human are for him except fasting. It is for Me and I shall reward it.' The fast is a shield. If it is a day in which one of you is fasting, he should avoid sexual relations and quarrelling. If any one wants to pick a fight with him, he should say, 'I am fasting.' By the One in whose hand is the soul of Muhammad, the smell coming from the mouth of a fasting person is better to Allah than the scent of musk. For the fasting person, they are two occasions of pleasure: when he breaks his fast he is pleased and when he meets his Lord he will be pleased with his fasting."[4]

Sahl ibn S'ad narrated that the Prophet (ﷺ) said, "In Paradise there is a gate called *ar-Rayyân*. Those who fast will enter through it on the Day of Resurrection and none other than them shall enter it. It

---

[1] Recorded by Bukhari and Muslim.

[2] As-Sayyid Sâbiq, *Fiqh as-Sunnah*, vol. 1, p. 366.

[3] Recorded by Bukhari, Muslim, Nasâ'i and Ibn Mâjah.

[4] Recorded by Bukhari, Muslim and Nasâ'i.

will be said, 'Where are those who fasted?' They will stand and none other than them shall enter it. When they all enter it, it will be closed and no one will then enter through it."[5]

Fasting Becomes Obligatory upon the Sighting of the New Moon

Abu Hurayrah narrated that the Prophet (ﷺ) said, "Fast due to its sighting and break your fast due to its sighting. If it is obscured to you, then reckon the month to be thirty days."[6]

How is the beginning of the month confirmed?

"The beginning of the month is established by the sighting of the crescent by one righteous person or by completing thirty days of the month of Sha'bân. Ibn 'Umar said, 'The people were looking for the new moon. I informed the Messenger of Allah (ﷺ) that I had seen it. He then fasted and ordered the people to fast.'[7]"[8] If the new moon is not seen, due to cloud cover or due to some other reason, then Sha'bân is to be completed as thirty days, based on the hadith of Abu Hurayrah above.

However, the month of Shawâl is only commenced by two witnesses. 'Abdur-Raḥmân ibn Zayd ibn Khaṭṭâb said, while delivering a speech on a day concerning which there was doubt (as to whether Ramaḍân had come to an end or not), "Verily, I sat with the

---

[5] Recorded by Bukhari, and this is his wording, Muslim, Tirmidhi, Ibn Mâjah and Nasâ'i.

[6] Recorded by Muslim, and this is his wording,, Bukhari and Nasâ'i.

[7] This hadith is *ṣaḥeeḥ*. See Shaykh al-Albâni, *I'rwâ' al-Ghaleel*, no. 908. Recorded by Abu Dawood.

[8] As-Sayyid Sâbiq, *Fiqh as-Sunnah*, vol. 1, p. 367.

Companions of the Messenger of Allah (ﷺ) and asked them. They informed me that the Messenger of Allah (ﷺ) had said, 'Fast due to its sighting, break your fast due to its sighting and performed the pilgrimage rites by it. If it is cloudy, then complete thirty days. If two Muslims bear testimony to it, fast and break the fast.'"[9]

The Governor of Makkah, al-Ḥârith ibn Ḥâṭib said, "The Messenger of Allah (ﷺ) told us to perform the rites of pilgrimage due to its sighting. And if we do not see it but two reputable witnesses say that saw it, we perform the rites according to their witness."[10]

By combining the two statements in these two reports, "If two Muslims bear testimony to it, fast and break the fast" in the hadith of 'Abdur-Raḥmân ibn Zayd and "If we do not see it but two reputable witnesses say that saw it, we perform the rites according to their witness" in the hadith of al-Ḥârith, they indicate, by implication, that it is not allowed to start the fast or break the fast due to the witness of only one person. However, since starting the fast has been exempted based on evidence (quoted above), it leaves only the issue of breaking the fast, for which there is no evidence that it may be done on the basis of one witness only. This is the abridgement of the argument as found in *Tuḥfah al-Aḥwadhi* (vol. 3, Pp. 373-374).

Note: If a person sees the new moon by himself, he does not fast until the people fast nor does he break his fast until the people also break their fast, as Abu Hurayrah (may Allah be pleased with him) narrated that the Prophet (ﷺ) said, "The fast is on the day that the people fast. Breaking the fast is on the day that the people break the fast. The

---

[9] This hadith is *ṣaḥeeḥ*. See Shaykh al-Albâni, *Ṣaḥeeḥ al-Jâmi' aṣ-Ṣagheer*, no. 3811. Recorded by Aḥmad and also by Nasâ'i but without the part, "two Muslims."

[10] This hadith is *ṣaḥeeḥ*. See Shaykh al-Albâni, *Ṣaḥeeḥ Sunan Abi Dawood*, no. 205. Recorded by Abu Dawood.

slaughtering is on the day when the people slaughter."[11]

Upon whom it is obligatory

The scholars are in agreement that the fast is obligatory upon every sane, adult, healthy, non-travelling Muslim. In addition, women must also be pure of menses and post-partum bleeding.[12]

As for the fast not being obligatory upon those are not sane or adult, the Prophet said, "The pen (recording the deeds) has been raised (and is not recording) for three: the one who is sleeping until he awakens, the child until he reaches the age of puberty and the insane one until he becomes sane."[13]

It not being obligatory upon those who are not healthy or who are not resident is based on Allah's words:

﴿... فَمَن كَانَ مِنكُم مَّرِيضًا أَوْ عَلَىٰ سَفَرٍ فَعِدَّةٌ مِّنْ أَيَّامٍ أُخَرَ ... ﴿١٨٤﴾﴾

(سورة البَقـَرَة: ١٨٤)

﴿... But if any of you is ill or on a journey, the same number [should be made up] from other days...﴾ *(Qur'an 2: 184)*

If the ill person or traveller do fast, that fast would suffice them, as the permission for them to break their fast is simply an exemption. If they following the regular non-exemption ruling, that is fine.

---

[11] This hadith is *ṣaḥeeḥ*. See Shaykh al-Albâni, *Ṣaḥeeḥ al-Jâmi' aṣ-Ṣagheer*, no. 3869. Recorded by Tirmidhi who said, "Some of the people of knowledge interpret this hadith to mean: "The fasting and breaking of the fast are to be done with the congregation and the masses of the people."

[12] As-Sayyid Sâbiq, *Fiqh as-Sunnah*, vol. 1, p. 506.

[13] This hadith is *ṣaḥeeḥ*. See Shaykh al-Albâni, *Ṣaḥeeḥ al-Jâmi'*, no. 3513. Recorded by Abu Dawood.

However, which is better for them: to break the fast or to fast?

If the ill person or traveller do not find any hardship in fasting, then fasting is preferred. If they encounter hardship, then breaking the fast is preferred. Abu Sa'eed al-Khudri stated, "We were on a military expedition with the Messenger of Allah (ﷺ) during Ramaḍân. Some of were fasting while others broke the fast. Those who were fasting did not find any fault with those who broke the fast and vice-versa. They saw it as those who had the strength to fast (would fast) and that was good. And those who had some weakness would break the fast and that was also good."[14]

The evidence that menstruating and post-partum women do not fast is the hadith of Abu Sa'eed in which the Prophet (ﷺ) said, "Is it not the case that when she menstruates, she does not pray or fast? That is the shortcoming in her religion."[15]

If a menstruating or post-partum woman does fast, her fast is not valid as being free from the impurities of menstruating and post-partum bleeding are from the prerequisites of the fast. The woman also has to make up those missed days of fasting. 'Â'ishah (رضي الله عنها) said, "We used to menstruate during the time of the Messenger of Allah (ﷺ) and we were ordered to make up the fasts and we were not ordered to make up the prayers."[16]

---

[14] This hadith is *ṣaḥeeḥ*. See Shaykh al-Albâni, *Ṣaḥeeḥ Sunan Tirmidhi*, no. 574. Recorded by Muslim and Tirmidhi.

[15] This hadith is *ṣaḥeeḥ*. See Shaykh al-Albâni, *Mukhtasar Ṣaḥeeḥ al-Bukhari*, no. 951. Recorded by Bukhari.

[16] This hadith is *ṣaḥeeḥ*. See Shaykh al-Albâni, *Ṣaḥeeḥ Sunan Tirmidhi*, no. 630. Recorded by Muslim, Abu Dawood, Tirmidhi and Nasâ'i.

What is obligatory upon the elderly and the permanently ill

One who is not able to fast, due to old age or some other reason, does not fast and instead feeds one poor person for every day. Allah has said:

﴿... وَعَلَى ٱلَّذِينَ يُطِيقُونَهُۥ فِدْيَةٌ طَعَامُ مِسْكِينٍ ... ﴿١٨٤﴾﴾

(سورة البقرة: ١٨٤)

﴾And as for those who can fast only with difficulty, they are to feed a poor person [for every day]...﴿ *(Qur'an 2: 184)*

'Aṭâ' narrated that he heard Ibn 'Abbâs read this verse and then say, "It is not abrogated. It applies to the elderly man and elderly woman who is not able to fast. They are to feed one poor person in lieu of every day (of fasting)."[17]

The pregnant or nursing woman

The pregnant or nursing woman who does not have the ability to fast or who fears for the health of her child may break the fast, feed a poor person and then she does not have to make up those days of fasting. Ibn 'Abbâs said, "An exemption was given for the elderly man and elderly women. If they found it difficult to fast, they could break their fast if they so willed and feed a poor person for every day of fasting. They would not then make up those fasts. This was then abrogated by the verse which states:

﴿... فَمَن شَهِدَ مِنكُمُ ٱلشَّهْرَ فَلْيَصُمْهُ ... ﴿١٨٥﴾﴾ (سورة البقرة: ١٨٥)

---

[17] This hadith is *ṣaḥeeḥ*. See Shaykh al-Albâni, *I'rwâ' al-Ghaleel*, no. 912. Recorded by Bukhari.

﴿... So whoever of you is present at his home must observe fast that month...﴾ *(Qur'an 2: 185)*

However, it was reaffirmed for the elderly man or elderly women, if they did not have the ability to fast, and for the pregnant or nursing woman, if they feared, that they could break their fast and feed a poor person in lieu of every day of fasting."[18] It is also recorded that he said, "If, during Ramaḍân, the pregnant woman fears for her health or the nursing woman fears for the health of her child, they may break the fast and feed one poor person in lieu of each day and they do not make up their fasts."[19] Nâfi' said, "One of Ibn 'Umar's daughters was married to a man from the Quraysh. She was pregnant and would become very thirsty during Ramaḍân. Ibn 'Umar told her to break her fast and to feed a poor person in lieu of every day."[20]
How much food is obligatory?

It is narrated that, "Anas ibn Mâlik was too weak to fast one year so he prepared a bowl of *thareed*[21] and invited thirty poor people and fed them such that they were satisfied."[22]

---

[18] Its chain is strong. Recorded by al-Bayhaqi.

[19] This hadith is *ṣaḥeeḥ*. Shaykh al-Albâni, in *I'rwâ' al-Ghaleel*, vol. 4, p. 19, ascribes it to aṭ-Ṭabari and says that its chain is *ṣaḥeeḥ* according to Muslim's criteria.

[20] Its chain is *ṣaḥeeḥ*. See Shaykh al-Albâni, *I'rwâ' al-Ghaleel*, vol. 4, p. 20. Recorded by ad-Dâraquṭni.

[21] [A dish of soaked bread, meat and broth.]

[22] Its chain is *ṣaḥeeḥ*. See Shaykh al-Albâni, *I'rwâ' al-Ghaleel*, vol. 4, p. 21. Recorded by ad-Dâraquṭni.

The Essential Components of the Fast

1. The intention

Allah (ﷻ) has said:

﴿وَمَآ أُمِرُوٓا۟ إِلَّا لِيَعْبُدُوا۟ ٱللَّهَ مُخْلِصِينَ لَهُ ٱلدِّينَ حُنَفَآءَ ... ﴿٥﴾﴾ (سورة البيّنة: ٥)

﴿And they were not commanded except to worship Allah, [being] sincere to Him in religion, inclining to truth...﴾ *(Qur'an 98: 5)*

The Prophet (ﷺ) also said, "Verily, all actions are based on intention and for every person is what he intended."[23] This intention must be present every night before the time of *Fajr*. Ḥafṣah (رضي الله عنها) stated that the Prophet (ﷺ) said, "There is no fast for the one who does not make the intention to fast before *Fajr* (dawn)."[24]

2. Refraining from anything that breaks the fast from the dawn of dawn until sunset

Allah (ﷻ) has said:

﴿... فَٱلْـَٔـٰنَ بَـٰشِرُوهُنَّ وَٱبْتَغُوا۟ مَا كَتَبَ ٱللَّهُ لَكُمْ ۚ وَكُلُوا۟ وَٱشْرَبُوا۟ حَتَّىٰ يَتَبَيَّنَ لَكُمُ ٱلْخَيْطُ ٱلْأَبْيَضُ مِنَ ٱلْخَيْطِ ٱلْأَسْوَدِ مِنَ ٱلْفَجْرِ ۖ ثُمَّ أَتِمُّوا۟ ٱلصِّيَامَ إِلَى ٱلَّيْلِ ۚ ... ﴿١٨٧﴾﴾
(سورة البقرة: ١٨٧)

---

[23] [The way this is written in the original Arabic makes it seem like the Prophet (Blessings and peace of Allah be upon him) would say these words before the prayer. However, that could not possibly be its meaning and such is not what is stated in Shaykh al-Albâni's reference. Hence, the author means to emphasize that the intention must be in the heart at the beginning of the prayer. And Allah alone knows best.] - Translator

[24] This hadith is *ṣaḥeeḥ*. See Shaykh al-Albâni, *Ṣaḥeeḥ al-Jâmi' aṣ-Ṣagheer*, no. 6538. Recorded by Abu Dawood, Tirmidhi and Nasâ'i.

﴾... So now have sexual relations with them and seek that which Allah has ordained for you [offspring], and eat and drink until the white light of dawn appears to you distinct from the black darkness [of night], then complete your fast till the nightfall...﴿ *(Qur'an 2: 187)*

Six matters break the fast

1. and 2. Intentionally eating or drinking

If a person forgetfully eats or drinks, then he does not have to make up the fast nor is there any expiation in his case. Abu Hurayrah narrated that the Prophet (ﷺ) said, "Whoever forgets while he is fasting and eats or drinks something should complete his fast, for it was Allah who fed him or gave him to drink."[25]

3. Vomiting intentionally

If a person is overcome by nausea and vomits, then he does not have to make up the fast nor is there any expiation in his case. Abu Hurayrah narrated that the Prophet (ﷺ) said, "One who is overcome and vomits does not make up the day. One who intentionally makes himself vomit must make up the day."[26]

4. and 5. Menstruation and post-partum bleeding

Even if these occur at the last moment before sundown, they break the fast according to the consensus of the scholars.

6. Sexual intercourse

The one who commits this act must perform the expiation that is described in the following hadith. Abu Hurayrah narrated: "While

[25] This hadith is *ṣaḥeeḥ*. See Shaykh al-Albâni, *Ṣaḥeeḥ al-Jâmi' aṣ-Ṣagheer*, no. 6573. Recorded by Muslim, and this is his wording, and by Bukhari, Ibn Mâjah and Tirmidhi.

[26] This hadith is *ṣaḥeeḥ*. See Shaykh al-Albâni, *Ṣaḥeeḥ al-Jâmi' aṣ-Ṣagheer*, no. 6234. Recorded by Tirmidhi, Abu Dawood and Ibn Mâjah.

we were sitting with the Prophet (ﷺ) a man came and said, 'O' Messenger of Allah, I have been destroyed.' He asked him, 'What has happened to you?' He replied, 'I had intercourse with my wife while I was fasting.' The Messenger of Allah (ﷺ) then told him, 'Do you have a slave that you can free?' He replied, 'No.' He then said, 'Can you fast two months consecutively?' he replied, 'No.' The Messenger of Allah (ﷺ) then asked him, 'Can you feed sixty poor people?' He replied, 'No.' The Prophet (ﷺ) then kept silent when a big basket full of dates was brought to him. He said, 'Where is the questioner?' The man replied, 'It is I.' The Messenger of Allah (ﷺ) told him, 'Take these dates and give them in charity.' The man said, 'To someone poorer than I, O' Messenger of Allah (ﷺ)? By Allah, there is no family between Madeenah's mountains poorer than I.' The Prophet (ﷺ) laughed to such an extent that his premolars could be seen. He then said, 'Feed your family with it.'"

The Etiquette of Fasting

It is recommended for the fasting person to abide by the following acts:

1. Pre-dawn meal

Anas narrated that the Messenger of Allah (ﷺ) said, "Have a pre-dawn meal for there is blessing in the pre-dawn meal."[27] This "pre-dawn meal" can be fulfilled simply by a sip of water. 'Abdullâh ibn 'Amr narrated that the Messenger of Allah (ﷺ) said, "Have a pre-dawn meal even if it just be a sip of water."[28]

---

[27] Recorded by Bukhari, Muslim, Tirmidhi, Nasâ'i and Ibn Mâjah.

[28] This hadith is *ṣaḥeeḥ*. See Shaykh al-Albâni, *Ṣaḥeeḥ al-Jâmi' aṣ-Ṣagheer*, no. 2945. Recorded by Ibn Ḥibbân.

It is also recommended to delay the eating of the pre-dawn meal. Anas narrated from Zayd ibn Thâbit who said, "The Prophet (ﷺ) had a pre-dawn meal and then he went to the prayer. I (Anas) asked him, 'What was the time between the call to prayer and the pre-dawn meal?' He replied, 'About the time it takes to read fifty verses.' "[29]

If the person hears the call to prayer while his food or drink is already in his hand, he can eat or drink. Abu Hurayrah narrated that the Messenger of Allah (ﷺ) said, "If one of you hears the call to prayer while his cup is in his hand, he should not put it down until he has satisfied his need from it."[30]

2. Refraining from vain speech, foul language and other acts that do not befit the fast

Abu Hurayrah narrated that the Prophet (ﷺ) said, "If it is a day in which one of you is fasting, he should avoid sexual relations and quarrelling. If any one wants to pick a fight with him, he should say, 'I am fasting.' "[31] He also narrated that the Messenger of Allah (ﷺ) said, "For whoever does not give up false speech and acting by it, Allah has no need for him to leave his food and drink."[32]

3. Generosity and studying the Qur'an

Ibn 'Abbâs said, "The Prophet (ﷺ) was the most generous of the people in doing well. He was most generous during Ramaḍân when he would meet with (the Angel) Gabriel. Gabriel would meet with him every night during Ramaḍân until the month finished. The

---

[29] Recorded by Bukhari, Muslim, Tirmidhi, Nasâ'i and Ibn Mâjah.

[30] This hadith is *ṣaḥeeḥ*. See Shaykh al-Albâni, *Ṣaḥeeḥ al-Jâmi' aṣ-Ṣagheer*, no. 607. Recorded by Abu Dawood and al-Ḥâkim.

[31] Recorded by Bukhari, Muslim and Nasâ'i.

[32] This hadith is *ṣaḥeeḥ*. See Shaykh al-Albâni, *Mukhtasar Ṣaḥeeḥ al-Bukhari*, no. 921. Recorded by Bukhari, Abu Dawood and Tirmidhi.

Prophet (ﷺ) would recite the Qur'an with him. When he would meet Gabriel, he was more generous in doing good than a beneficial fast wind."[33]

4. Hastening in breaking the fast

Sahl ibn S'ad narrated that the Messenger of Allah (ﷺ) said, "The people will continue to be in a state of goodness as long as they hasten in breaking their fast."[34]

5 Breaking the fast with what is mentioned in the hadith, if it is easy to do so

Anas said, "The Prophet (ﷺ) would break his fast with ripe dates before praying. If not ripe dates, he would break his fast with dried dates. If that were not available, he would drink some water."[35]

6. Making the supplication stated in the following hadith upon breaking one's fast

Ibn 'Umar narrated that the Messenger of Allah (ﷺ) would say the following upon breaking his fast,

ذَهَبَ الظَّمَأُ وَابْتَلَّتِ الْعُرُوقُ وَثَبَتَ الأَجْرُ إِنْ شَاءَ اللَّهُ

"The thirst has gone, the veins have become moist and the reward is confirmed, Allah willing."[36]

---

[33] Recorded by Bukhari and Muslim.

[34] Ibid.

[35] This hadith is *ḥasan ṣaḥeeḥ*. See Shaykh al-Albâni, *Ṣaḥeeḥ al-Jâmi' aṣ-Ṣagheer*, no. 2065. Recorded by Abu Dawood and Tirmidhi.

[36] This hadith is *ḥasan*. See Shaykh al-Albâni, *Ṣaḥeeḥ Sunan Abi Dawood*, no. 2066. Recorded by Abu Dawood.

Actions that are Permissible for the Fasting Person

1. Washing for the sake of getting cooler

Abu Bakr ibn 'Abdur-Raḥmân narrated from one of the Companions of the Prophet (ﷺ) who said, "I saw the Messenger of Allah (ﷺ) in al-'Arj (a village outside of Madeenah) pour water over his head while fasting due to thirst or due to the heat."[37]

2. Rinsing one's mouth and nose but without putting the water too deep

Laqeeṭ ibn Ṣabirah narrated that the Messenger of Allah (ﷺ) said, "(In ablution,) you should put water well up your nose, unless you are fasting."[38]

3. The medical practice of cupping or drawing blood

Ibn 'Abbâs stated, "The Prophet (ﷺ) was cupped while he was fasting."[39] However, this act is disliked for the person who is weak. Thâbit al-Banâni said, "Anas ibn Mâlik was asked, 'Did you (Companions) dislike the act of cupping for the fasting person?' He replied, 'No, unless due to weakness (on the part of the person who would then find difficulty fasting).'"[40]

---

[37] This hadith is *ṣaḥeeḥ*. See Shaykh al-Albâni, *Ṣaḥeeḥ Sunan Abi Dawood*, no. 2072. Recorded by Abu Dawood.

[38] This hadith is *ṣaḥeeḥ*. See Shaykh al-Albâni, *Ṣaḥeeḥ Sunan Abi Dawood*, no. 129 and 131. Recorded by Abu Dawood.

[39] This hadith is *ṣaḥeeḥ*. See Shaykh al-Albâni, *Ṣaḥeeḥ Sunan Abi Dawood*, no. 2079. Recorded by Bukhari, Abu Dawood and by Tirmidhi who added, "and he was in the inviolable state of pilgrimage."

[40] This hadith is *ṣaḥeeḥ*. See Shaykh al-Albâni, *Mukhtasar Ṣaḥeeḥ al-Bukhari*, no. 947. Recorded by Bukhari. Donating blood would have the same ruling=

4. Kissing or touching one's spouse for the one who has the ability to control his actions

'Â'ishah (ﷺ) said, "The Prophet (ﷺ) would kiss and caress while fasting. And he was the one who had most control over his desires."[41]

5. To still be in a state of sexual defilement in the morning

Both 'Â'ishah and Umm Salamah narrated that it would be *Fajr* time and the Prophet (ﷺ) would be in state of sexual defilement due to relations with his family and then he would bathe and fast.[42]

6. Continuing the fast until the pre-dawn meal

Abu Sa'eed al-Khudri narrated that he heard the Messenger of Allah (ﷺ) say, "Do not fast without breaking it. But if you insist on continuing (the fast), you may fast until the pre-dawn meal." But then they said to him, "O' Messenger of Allah (ﷺ), but you continue your fast." He replied, "I am not similar to any of you (on this matter). During the night, I have one who feeds me and gives me to drink."[43]

7. The use of a toothstick, perfume, oil, kohl, eye drops, and injections

The basic ruling concerning all of these originally permissible matters is that they are still permissible. If they were forbidden for the fasting person, Allah or His Messenger (ﷺ) would have clarified that. And Allah (ﷻ) says:

=as cupping. If the person donating blood fears that he will become very weak, he should not donate the blood during the daytime except in cases of necessity.

[41] Recorded by Bukhari, Muslim, Abu Dawood and Tirmidhi.

[42] Ibid.

[43] This hadith is *ṣaḥeeḥ*. Recorded by Bukhari and Abu Dawood.

﴿... وَمَا كَانَ رَبُّكَ نَسِيًّا ﴿٦٤﴾﴾ (سورة مَريَم : ٦٤)

﴿... Your Lord is never forgetful.﴾ *(Qur'an 19: 64)*

Voluntary Fasts

The Messenger of Allah (ﷺ) recommended the fasting of the following days:

1. Six days out of the month of Shawwâl

Abu Ayyoob al-Anṣâri narrated that the Messenger of Allah (ﷺ) said, "Whoever fasts Ramaḍân and then follows it with six days of Shawwâl will be as if he fasted the entire year."[44]

2. and 3. Fasting the day of 'Arafah for those who are not performing the pilgrimage and fasting the Day of 'Ashoora' as well as one day before it

Abu Qatâdah narrated the following: "The Messenger of Allah (ﷺ) was asked about fasting the Day of 'Arafah and he replied, 'It expiates for the previous and the upcoming year.' He was also asked about fasting the Day of 'Ashoora' and he said, 'It expiates for the previous year.'"[45]

Umm Faḍl bint al-Ḥârith said, "Some people were debating whether the Messenger of Allah was fasting on the Day of 'Arafah. Some said he was while others said he was not. So I sent him a cup of

---

[44] This hadith is *ṣaḥeeḥ*. See Shaykh al-Albâni, *Ṣaḥeeḥ Sunan Abi Dawood*, no. 2125. Recorded by Muslim, Tirmidhi, Abu Dawood and Ibn Mâjah.

[45] This hadith is *ṣaḥeeḥ*. See Shaykh al-Albâni, *I'rwâ' al-Ghaleel*, no. 955. Recorded by Muslim.

milk and, while upon his camel at 'Arafah, he drank it."[46]

Abu Ghaṭafân ibn Ṭareef al-Murri said, "I heard Ibn 'Abbâs say, 'When the Messenger of Allah (ﷺ) fasted the Day of 'Ashoora' and ordered the others to do so as well, they said, 'O' Messenger of Allah (ﷺ), it is a day which the Jews and Christians honour.' Therefore, he said, 'Next year, Allah willing, we shall fast the ninth day.' However, the following year did not come before the death of the Messenger of Allah (ﷺ).' "[47]

4. Fasting most of the sacred months

Abu Hurayrah reported that the Messenger of Allah (ﷺ) said, "The best fast after that of Ramaḍân is during Allah's sacred months and the best prayer after the obligatory prayer is the prayer of the night."[48]

5. Fasting most of the month of Sha'bân

'Â'ishah (رضي الله عنها) said, "I never saw the Messenger of Allah (ﷺ) fast a complete month except for the month of Ramaḍân. I also never saw him fast more than he did during the month of Sha'bân."[49]

6. Mondays and Thursdays

Usâmah ibn Zayd said, "The Prophet of Allah (ﷺ) used to fast Mondays and Thursdays. When he asked about it, he said, 'The deeds of the servants are presented on Monday and Thursday.' "[50]

---

[46] Recorded by Bukhari, Muslim and Abu Dawood.

[47] This hadith is *ṣaḥeeḥ*. See Shaykh al-Albâni, *Ṣaḥeeḥ Sunan Abi Dawood*, no. 2136. Recorded by Muslim and Abu Dawood.

[48] This hadith is *ṣaḥeeḥ*. See Shaykh al-Albâni, *Ṣaḥeeḥ Sunan Abi Dawood*, no. 2122. Recorded by Muslim, Abu Dawood, Nasâ'i and Tirmidhi.

[49] Recorded by Bukhari, Muslim and Abu Dawood.

[50] This hadith is *ṣaḥeeḥ*. See Shaykh al-Albâni, *Ṣaḥeeḥ Sunan Abi Dawood*, no. 2128. Recorded by Abu Dawood.

7. (Any) three days out of every month

'Abdullâh ibn 'Amr said that the Messenger of Allah (ﷺ) had said to him, "Fast three days of every month, for every good deed is rewarded ten-fold, and that will be like a perpetual fast."[51] It is recommended that those days be the thirteenth, fourteenth and fifteenth days of the month.[52] Abu Dharr narrated that the Messenger of Allah (ﷺ) said, "O' Abu Dharr, if you fast three days out of the month, then fast the thirteenth, fourteenth and fifteenth."

8. Alternating days by fasting one day and not fasting the next

'Abdullâh ibn 'Amr narrated that the Prophet (ﷺ) said, "The most beloved fast to Allah is the fast of David, he used to fast one day and then not fast the next."[53]

9. The first ten days of the month of Dhul-Ḥijjah

Hunaydah ibn Khâlid narrated from his wife from one of the wives of the Prophet (ﷺ), "The Messenger of Allah (ﷺ) used to fast the (first) nine days of Dhul-Ḥijjah, the Day of 'Ashoora', three days of every month and the first Monday of every month and Thursday."[54]

---

[51] Recorded by Bukhari, Muslim, Abu Dawood (without that middle sentence) and Nasâ'i.

[In reality, this translator could not find this wording with this exact text in any of the standard works. It seems to be a combination of a couple of texts, one found in *Musnad Aḥmad*. And Allah alone knows best.] - Translator

[52] [That is, of the lunar month. These days are the days of the full moon.] - Translator

[53] Recorded by Bukhari, Muslim, Nasâ'i, Abu Dawood and Ibn Mâjah.

[54] This hadith is *ṣaḥeeḥ*. See Shaykh al-Albâni, *Ṣaḥeeḥ Sunan Abi Dawood*, no. 2129. Recorded by Abu Dawood and Nasâ'i.

The Days on Which it is Forbidden to Fast

1. The days of *'Eid*

Abu 'Ubayd, the ex-slave of Ibn Azhar, said: "I performed the *'Eid* prayer with 'Umar ibn al-Khaṭṭâb (رضي الله عنه) and he said, 'The Messenger of Allah (ﷺ) forbade fasting on these two days: The day you break your fast after your fasting and the day on which you eat from your sacrifice.'"[55]

2. The days of *Tashreeq*[56]

Abu Murrah, the ex-slave of Umm Hâni, went with 'Abdullâh ibn 'Amr to his father 'Amr ibn al-'Âṣ. The father brought some food for them and said, "Eat." The son replied, "I am fasting." 'Amr then said, "These are the days in which the Prophet (ﷺ) ordered us to eat and prohibited us from fasting." Mâlik said, "Those were the days of *Tashreeq*."[57] 'Â'ishah and Ibn 'Umar both said, "It is not exempted for anyone to fast on the Days of *Tashreeq* except for the person who does not have a sacrificial animal."[58]

---

[55] Recorded by Bukhari, Muslim, Abu Dawood, Tirmidhi and Ibn Mâjah.

[56] [The word *tashreeq* is related to sunrise.] The Days of *Tashreeq* are the days after the Day of Sacrifice [on the tenth of Dhul-Ḥijjah] and the scholars differ as to whether they are two or three days. They are called the days of *tashreeq* because the meat of the sacrificial animals are laid out in the sun on those days. It is also said that it has this name because the sacrificial animal is not sacrificed until the sun rises. Others say that they are called such because the *'Eid* prayer is not performed until after sunrise. Some have even said that *tashreeq* here stands for the saying of *takbeer* after very prayer. See *Fatḥ al-Bâri*, vol. 4, p. 285.

[57] This hadith is *ṣaḥeeḥ*. See Shaykh al-Albâni, *Ṣaḥeeḥ Sunan Abi Dawood*, no. 2113. Recorded by Abu Dawood

[58] This hadith is *ṣaḥeeḥ*. See Shaykh al-Albâni, *Mukhtasar Ṣaḥeeḥ al-Bukhari*, no. 978. Recorded by Bukhari.

3. Fasting Friday by itself

Abu Hurayrah narrated that he heard the Prophet (ﷺ) say, "None of you should fast Friday unless you also fast the day before it or the day after it."[59]

4. Fasting Saturday by itself

'Abdullâh ibn Busr as-Salami narrated from his sister, aṣ-Ṣamâ', that the Prophet (ﷺ) said, "Do not fast Saturdays except for when Allah has made it obligatory upon you. If you do not find anything except the bark of a grapevine or the bark of a tree, then chew on it."[60]

5. The latter half of the Month of Sha'bân for those who do not regularly fast at that time

Abu Hurayrah reported that the Messenger of Allah (ﷺ) said, "If the first half of the month of Sha'bân has passed, do not fast."[61] He also reported that the Messenger of Allah (ﷺ) said, "Do not precede Ramaḍân by fasting a day or two ahead of it unless a person regularly fasted on those days, in which case he can fast."[62]

6. The "Day of Doubt"

'Ammâr ibn Yâsir said, "Whoever fasts the day concerning which there is doubt (as to whether Ramaḍân has begun or not) has disobeyed Abu al-Qâsim [meaning, the Prophet (ﷺ)]."[63]

---

[59] Recorded by Bukhari, Muslim, Abu Dawood and Tirmidhi.

[60] This hadith is *ṣaḥeeḥ*. Recorded by Abu Dawood, Tirmidhi, Ibn Mâjah.

[61] This hadith is *ṣaḥeeḥ*. See Shaykh al-Albâni, *Ṣaḥeeḥ Sunan Ibn Mâjah*, no. 1339. Recorded by Abu Dawood and by Tirmidhi and Ibn Mâjah with similar wording.

[62] Recorded by Bukhari, Muslim, Abu Dawood, Tirmidhi, Nasâ'i and Ibn Mâjah.

[63] This hadith is *ṣaḥeeḥ*. See Shaykh al-Albâni, *I'rwâ' al-Ghaleel*, no. 961. Recorded by Tirmidhi, Abu Dawood, Nasâ'i and Ibn Mâjah.

7. Fasting the entire year, even if one breaks the fast during the prohibited days

'Abdullâh ibn 'Amr said, "The Messenger of Allah (ﷺ) said to me, "O' 'Abdullâh ibn 'Amr, you fast perpetually and pray the whole night. If you (continue to) do that, your eyes will become weak and you will become weak. There is no fast for the one who fasts perpetually."[64]

Abu Qatâdah narrated that a man came to the Prophet (ﷺ) and said, "O' Messenger of Allah, how do you fast?" The Messenger of Allah (ﷺ) became upset at his question. When 'Umar saw that, he said, "We are pleased with Allah as Lord, with Islam as religion and with Muhammad as a prophet. We seek refuge in Allah from the anger of Allah and from the anger of His messenger." 'Umar continued to repeat that until the Messenger of Allah's anger left. He then said, "O' Messenger of Allah, what is the state of the one who fasts the entire year?" He replied, "He neither fasted nor did he break his fast."[65]

The prohibition of a woman fasting while her husband is present except with his permission

Abu Hurayrah (رضي الله عنه) narrated that the Messenger of Allah (ﷺ) said, "The woman is not to fast if her husband is present except with his permission."[66]

---

[64] Recorded by Bukhari and Muslim.

[65] This hadith is *ṣaḥeeḥ*. See Shaykh al-Albâni, *Ṣaḥeeḥ Sunan Abi Dawood*, no. 2119. Recorded by Muslim, Abu Dawood and Nasâ'i.

[66] Recorded by Bukhari, Muslim, Abu Dawood, Tirmidhi and by Ibn Mâjah with some additional text.

I'tikâf (Personal "Seclusion" in the Mosque for the Purpose of Worship)

Performing *I'tikâf* in the last ten days of Ramaḍân is a recommended Sunnah. It is to be done seeking goodness and also hoping for the Night of *Qadr*. Allah (ﷻ) says:

﴿إِنَّآ أَنزَلْنَٰهُ فِى لَيْلَةِ ٱلْقَدْرِ ﴿١﴾ وَمَآ أَدْرَىٰكَ مَا لَيْلَةُ ٱلْقَدْرِ ﴿٢﴾ لَيْلَةُ ٱلْقَدْرِ خَيْرٌ مِّنْ أَلْفِ شَهْرٍ ﴿٣﴾ تَنَزَّلُ ٱلْمَلَٰٓئِكَةُ وَٱلرُّوحُ فِيهَا بِإِذْنِ رَبِّهِم مِّن كُلِّ أَمْرٍ ﴿٤﴾ سَلَٰمٌ هِىَ حَتَّىٰ مَطْلَعِ ٱلْفَجْرِ ﴿٥﴾﴾ (سورة القدر: ١-٥)

﴿Verily! We have sent it [this Qur'an] down in the night of *al-Qadr* [Decree]. And what will make you know what the night of *al-Qadr* [Decree] is? The night of *al-Qadr* [Decree] is better than a thousand months. Therein descend the angels and the *Rooḥ* [Gabriel] by Allah's Permission with all Decrees. Peace! [All that night, there is Peace and Goodness from Allah to His believing slaves] until the appearance of dawn.﴾ *(Qur'an 97: 1-5)*

'Â'ishah said, "The Messenger of Allah (ﷺ) would practice *I'tikâf* during the last ten (nights) of Ramaḍân. He said, "Seek the Night of *Qadr* during the last ten (nights) of Ramaḍân."[67] She also narrated that he said, "Seek the Night of *Qadr* during the odd (nights) of the last ten (nights) of Ramaḍân."[68]

He also encouraged and exhorted people to pray during the Night of *Qadr*. He stated, "Whoever prays the Night of *Qadr* out of faith and hope (for Allah's pleasure) will have forgiven for him all of

[67] This hadith is *ṣaḥeeḥ*. See Shaykh al-Albâni, *Mukhtasar Ṣaḥeeḥ Bukhari*, no. 987. Recorded by Bukhari and Tirmidhi.

[68] Recorded by Bukhari and Muslim.

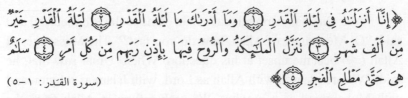

his previous sins."[69]

I'tikâf can only be in a mosque, as Allah (ﷻ) has said:

﴿... وَلَا تُبَٰشِرُوهُنَّ وَأَنتُمْ عَٰكِفُونَ فِى ٱلْمَسَٰجِدِ ... ﴿١٨٧﴾﴾

(سورة البَقـرَة: ١٨٧)

﴾... And do not have sexual relations with them [your wives] while you are in *I'tikâf* in the mosques...﴿ *(Qur'an 2: 187)*

Furthermore, the Prophet (ﷺ) always performed the *I'tikâf* in a mosque.

It is recommended for the one making *I'tikâf* to preoccupy himself with acts of obedience to Allah, such as prayers, reciting the Qur'an, extolling Allah's greatness, praising Allah, declaring Allah's oneness and greatness, seeking His forgiveness, stating prayers for the Prophet (ﷺ), supplications, studying and so on. It is disliked for him to become preoccupied with statements or actions that are not beneficial. It is also disliked for him to refrain from speaking out of belief that such an act will bring him closer to Allah.[70]

It is permissible for him to leave from his place of *I'tikâf* if there some need arises that he must tend to. It is also permissible for him to comb his hair, cut his hair, trim his nails or clean his body. However, the *I'tikâf* is voided if he leaves without any true need or if he has sexual intercourse.

---

[69] Recorded by Bukhari, Muslim, Abu Dawood and Nasâ'i.

[70] Cf., As-Sayyid Sâbiq, *Fiqh as-Sunnah*, vol. 1, p. 404.

Chapter Five — Zakah

The Place of Zakah in the Religion

Zakah is one of the pillars of Islam and one of its obligatory deeds.

Ibn 'Umar narrated that the Messenger of Allah (ﷺ) said, "Islam is built upon five (pillars): testifying that there is none worthy of worship except Allah and that Muhammad is the Messenger of Allah, establishing the prayers, giving the zakah, making the pilgrimage to the House and fasting the month of Ramaḍân."[1]

Zakah has been mentioned alongside the prayers in eighty-two verses of the Qur'an.

The Exhortation to Give Zakah

Allah (ﷻ) says in the Qur'an:

﴿خُذۡ مِنۡ أَمۡوَٰلِهِمۡ صَدَقَةٗ تُطَهِّرُهُمۡ وَتُزَكِّيهِم بِهَا ... ١٠٣﴾ (سورة التوبة: ١٠٣)

﴾Take alms from their wealth in order to purify them and sanctify them with it...﴿ *(Qur'an 9: 103)*

Allah also says:

---

[1] Recorded by Bukhari, Muslim (and this is his wording), Tirmidhi and Nasâ'i.

﴿وَمَآ ءَاتَيْتُم مِّن رِّبًا لِّيَرْبُوَا۟ فِىٓ أَمْوَٰلِ ٱلنَّاسِ فَلَا يَرْبُوا۟ عِندَ ٱللَّهِ ۖ وَمَآ ءَاتَيْتُم مِّن زَكَوٰةٍ تُرِيدُونَ وَجْهَ ٱللَّهِ فَأُو۟لَٰٓئِكَ هُمُ ٱلْمُضْعِفُونَ ﴿٣٩﴾﴾ (سورة الرُّوم: ٣٩)

﴾And that which you give in gift [to others], in order that it may increase [your wealth by expecting to get a better one in return] from other people's property, has no increase with Allah, but that which you give in Zakah seeking Allah's Countenance then those, they shall have manifold increase.﴿ *(Qur'an 30: 39)*

And Abu Hurayrah narrated that the Messenger of Allah (ﷺ) said, "If someone gives in charity the equivalent of a date from his lawful and good earnings — and Allah only accepts what is lawful and good — Allah will take it in His right hand and raise it for its giver, in the same way that one of you raises his small colt, until it becomes similar to a mountain (in size)."[2]

Warning Concerning not Paying Zakah

Allah has said:

﴿وَلَا يَحْسَبَنَّ ٱلَّذِينَ يَبْخَلُونَ بِمَآ ءَاتَىٰهُمُ ٱللَّهُ مِن فَضْلِهِۦ هُوَ خَيْرًا لَّهُم ۖ بَلْ هُوَ شَرٌّ لَّهُمْ ۖ سَيُطَوَّقُونَ مَا بَخِلُوا۟ بِهِۦ يَوْمَ ٱلْقِيَٰمَةِ ۗ وَلِلَّهِ مِيرَٰثُ ٱلسَّمَٰوَٰتِ وَٱلْأَرْضِ ۗ وَٱللَّهُ بِمَا تَعْمَلُونَ خَبِيرٌ ﴿١٨٠﴾﴾ (سورة آل عِمرَان: ١٨٠)

﴾And let not those who covetously withhold of that which Allah has bestowed on them of His Bounty think that it is good for them [and they do not pay the obligatory Zakah]. Nay, it will be worse for them; the things which they covetously withheld shall be tied to their necks like a collar on the Day of Resurrection. And to Allah belongs the

---

[2] Recorded by Bukhari (and this is his wording), Muslim, Tirmidhi and Nasâ'i.

heritage of the heavens and the earth; and Allah is Well-Acquainted with all that you do.» *(Qur'an 3: 180)*

Abu Hurayrah narrated that the Prophet (ﷺ) said, "Whoever is made wealthy by Allah and does not pay Zakah on his wealth, then on Day of Resurrection his wealth will be made like a bald-headed poisonous snake with two poisonous glands. It will encircle his neck and bite his cheeks and say, 'I am your wealth, I am your treasure.' After stating that, the Prophet (ﷺ) then recited the above verse from *Soorah Âli-Imrân*, «And let not those who covetously withhold of that which Allah has bestowed on them of His Bounty think...»"[3]

Allah also says:

﴿ ... وَالَّذِينَ يَكْنِزُونَ الذَّهَبَ وَالْفِضَّةَ وَلَا يُنفِقُونَهَا فِي سَبِيلِ اللَّهِ
فَبَشِّرْهُم بِعَذَابٍ أَلِيمٍ ﴿٣٤﴾ يَوْمَ يُحْمَىٰ عَلَيْهَا فِي نَارِ جَهَنَّمَ فَتُكْوَىٰ بِهَا
جِبَاهُهُمْ وَجُنُوبُهُمْ وَظُهُورُهُمْ ۖ هَٰذَا مَا كَنَزْتُمْ لِأَنفُسِكُمْ فَذُوقُوا مَا كُنتُمْ
تَكْنِزُونَ ﴿٣٥﴾ ﴾ (سورة التوبة: ٣٤-٣٥)

«... Those who hoard up gold and silver, and spend it not in the Way of Allah, announce unto them a painful torment. On the Day when that [wealth] will be heated in the Fire of Hell and with it will be branded their foreheads, thcir flanks, and their backs, [and it will be said to them], 'This is the treasure which you hoarded for yourselves. Now taste of what you used to hoard.'» *(Qur'an 9: 34-35)*

Abu Hurayrah narrated that the Messenger of Allah (ﷺ) said, "If any owner of gold or silver does not pay what is due on him, when the Day of Resurrection would come, pages of fire would be beaten out for him. These would then be heated in the fire of Hell and his

---

[3] This hadith is *ṣaḥeeḥ*. See Shaykh al-Albâni, *Ṣaḥeeḥ Sunan Nasâ'i*, no. 2327. Recorded by Bukhari.

sides, his forehead and his back would be cauterized with them. Whenever these cool down, (the process is) repeated during a day the length of which is fifty thousand years, until the judgment is pronounced among the servants and he sees whether his path is to Paradise or to the Fire." It was said, "O' Messenger of Allah, what about the camel?" He replied, "If any owner of camels does not pay what is due on them, and of his due for them is to milk it on the day when it comes down to water, when the Day of Resurrection comes a soft sandy plain would be set for him, as extensive in length. (He will find) that not a single young one is missing. They will trample him with their hoofs and bite him with their mouths. As often as the first of them passes him, the last of them would be made to return during a day the length of which will be fifty thousand years, until the judgment is pronounced among the servants and he sees whether his path is to Paradise or to the Fire."[4]

The Ruling Concerning the One Who Refuses to Pay Zakah

Zakah is an obligation concerning which the entire Muslim Nation is agreed. It is so well-known that it has become part of the necessary and basic knowledge of Islam, such that anyone who denies its obligatory status falls outside of the fold of Islam and is to be killed as a disbeliever (apostate), unless he is new to Islam and is excused due to his ignorance of its ruling.

If a person refuses to pay it while believing in it and its obligatory status, then he is sinful due to his refusal to pay but that does not take him out of the fold of Islam. However, the authorities

---

[4] This hadith is *ṣaḥeeḥ*. See Shaykh al-Albâni, *Ṣaḥeeḥ al-Jâmi' aṣ-Ṣagheer*, no. 5729. Recorded by Muslim and Abu Dawood.

should take the Zakah from him by force[5] and should also take half of his wealth as a punishment. Bahz ibn Ḥakeem narrated from his father on the authority of his grandfather that he had heard the Messenger of Allah (ﷺ) say, "Upon every forty freely-grazing camels, one young she-camel is to be paid. And all the various camels are considered indistinguishable. The one who pays it seeking its reward shall receive its reward. As for one who refuses, we shall take it from him as well as half of his camels as it is a right from among the rights of our Lord. And none (of the Zakah) is permissible for the family of Muhammad."[6]

If a people refuse to pay it while believing in it and in its obligatory status yet they have some type of militia strength, then those people are to be fought until they pay it. This is based on the statement of the Prophet (ﷺ), "I have been ordered to fight against the people until they testify that there is none worthy of worship except Allah and that Muhammad is the Messenger of Allah, establish the prayer and give the Zakah. Then, if they do that, their blood and wealth will be protected from me — except in accordance with the right of Islam. And their reckoning will be with Allah."[7]

Abu Hurayrah said, "During the time of Abu Bakr (رضي الله عنه) some of the Arabs apostatized. 'Umar (رضي الله عنه) said, 'How are you going to fight the people?' He replied, 'Verily, the Messenger of Allah (ﷺ) said, 'I have been ordered to fight against the people until they testify that there is none worthy of worship except Allah. Whoever says that, will have his wealth and life protected from me — except in accordance with due right. And their reckoning will be with Allah.' By Allah, if they keep from me one female goat that they used to pay

---

5 As-Sayyid Sâbiq, *Fiqh as-Sunnah*, vol. 1, p. 281.

6 This hadith is *ḥasan*. See Shaykh al-Albâni, *Ṣaḥeeḥ al-Jâmi' aṣ-Ṣagheer*, no. 4265. Recorded by Abu Dawood, Nasâ'i and Aḥmad.

7 Recorded by Bukhari, and this is his wording, and Muslim.

to the Messenger of Allah (ﷺ), I will fight them due to their withholding it.' 'Umar then said, 'By Allah, it was only that Allah had opened Abu Bakr's heart to the necessity of fighting. I then realized that it was the correct position.' "[8]

Upon Whom is it Obligatory?

It is obligatory upon every free Muslim who possesses the *nisâb*[9] (minimum amount) and one year has passed since he has possessed that amount of wealth — except it in the case of produce wherein the Zakah is due upon it on the harvest day if it reaches the *nisâb*, as Allah (ﷻ) has said:

﴿... وَءَاتُوا۟ حَقَّهُۥ يَوْمَ حَصَادِهِۦ ... ﴿١٤١﴾﴾ (سورة الأنعام: ١٤١)

﴿... Pay the due thereof on the day of its harvest...﴾ *(Qur'an 6: 141)*

The Types of Wealth Upon Which Zakah is Obligatory

Zakah is obligatory upon money, crops, fruits, livestock and treasures found in the earth.

Zakah on Money, Gold and Silver

The minimum amount upon which Zakah is due upon gold and silver is twenty *dinars*[10] for gold and two hundred *dirhams* for silver.

---

[8] Recorded by Bukhari, Muslim, Abu Dawood, Nasâ'i and Tirmidhi.

[9] [This term is discussed in more detail shortly.]

[10] [*Dinars* and *dirhams* were the currency existing at the time of the Prophet=

'Ali ibn Abu Ṭâlib (ﷺ) narrated that the Prophet (ﷺ) said, "If you have two hundred *dirhams* and you have them for one year, you must pay five *dirhams*. And there is nothing upon it, meaning gold, until you have twenty *dinars*. If you have twenty *dinars* and you have them for one year, you must pay half a *dinar*."[11]

Zakah on Jewellery

Zakah is obligatory on jewellery due to the generality of the verses and hadith. Those who exclude it from the categories of Zakah do not offer any evidence to restrict such generality. In fact, there are some specific texts about it:

Umm Salamah said, "I was wearing jewellery made from *dirhams* of gold. I said, 'O' Messenger of Allah (ﷺ), is this a hoarded treasure?' He replied, 'What reaches the level that you must pay Zakah on and you pay Zakah on it is not a hoarded treasure.' "[12]

'Â'ishah (ﷺ) said, "I came to the Messenger of Allah (ﷺ) wearing silver bracelets. He said, 'What are these, O' 'Â'ishah?' She replied, 'I put them on to beautify myself for you, O' Messenger of Allah.' He replied, 'Did you pay the Zakah on them?' I said, 'No,' or, 'Whatever Allah wills.' He then said, 'It is sufficient for you of the Hell-fire.'[13]

=Muhammad (Blessings and peace of Allah be upon him). Each one of them is equal to a specific amount of gold and silver, respectively.] - Translator

[11] This hadith is *ṣaḥeeḥ*. See Shaykh al-Albâni, *Ṣaḥeeḥ Sunan Abi Dawood*, no. 1291. Recorded by Abu Dawood.

[12] This hadith is *ḥasan*. See Shaykh al-Albâni, *Ṣaḥeeḥ al-Jâmi' aṣ-Ṣagheer*, no. 5582 and *Silsilat al-Aḥâdeeth aṣ-Ṣaḥeeḥah*, no. 559. Recorded by Abu Dawood and ad-Dâraquṭni.

[13] This hadith is *ṣaḥeeḥ*. See Shaykh al-Albâni, *Ṣaḥeeḥ Sunan Abi Dawood*, no. 1384. Recorded by Abu Dawood and ad-Dâraquṭni.

The Zakah on Grains and Fruits

Allah (ﷻ) says:

﴿ ۞ وَهُوَ ٱلَّذِىٓ أَنشَأَ جَنَّٰتٍ مَّعْرُوشَٰتٍ وَغَيْرَ مَعْرُوشَٰتٍ وَٱلنَّخْلَ وَٱلزَّرْعَ مُخْتَلِفًا أُكُلُهُۥ وَٱلزَّيْتُونَ وَٱلرُّمَّانَ مُتَشَٰبِهًا وَغَيْرَ مُتَشَٰبِهٍ ۚ كُلُوا۟ مِن ثَمَرِهِۦٓ إِذَآ أَثْمَرَ وَءَاتُوا۟ حَقَّهُۥ يَوْمَ حَصَادِهِۦ ۖ وَلَا تُسْرِفُوٓا۟ ۚ إِنَّهُۥ لَا يُحِبُّ ٱلْمُسْرِفِينَ ﴿١٤١﴾ ﴾
(سورة الأنعام: ١٤١)

﴾And it is He Who produces gardens trellised and untrellised, and date-palms, and crops of different shape and taste [its fruits and its seeds] and olives, and pomegranates, similar [in kind] and different [in taste]. Eat of their fruit when they ripen, but pay the due thereof on the day of its harvest, and waste not by extravagance. Verily, He likes not those given to extravagance.﴿ *(Qur'an 6: 141)*

What types of crops is zakah due on?

Zakah is only to be paid on four types of crops, as clarified in the following hadith: Abu Burdah narrated from both Abu Moosa and Mu'âdh that the Messenger of Allah (ﷺ) sent them to Yemen to teach the people the matters of their faith. The Prophet (ﷺ) told the two of them not to take Zakah except on the following crops: wheat, barley, dates and raisins.[14]

The minimum required before one pays zakah

In order for Zakah to be obligatory upon the crops and fruits, the amount of the crop must reach the minimum level described in the following hadith. Abu Sa'eed al-Khudri narrated that the Messenger

---

[14] This hadith is *ṣaḥeeḥ*. See Shaykh al-Albâni, *Silsilat al-Aḥâdeeth aṣ-Ṣaḥeeḥah*, no. 879. Recorded by al-Ḥâkim and al-Bayhaqi.

of Allah (ﷺ) said, "Zakah is not due on less than five camels, or on less than five *uqiyâs*[15] or on less than five *wasq*[16]."[17]

The obligatory amount to be paid as zakah

Jâbir narrated that the Prophet (ﷺ) said, "One-tenth is to be given on what is watered by the rivers and rain. One-twentieth is to be given on what is watered by camels (bringing water from the well)."[18]

Ibn 'Umar narrated that the Prophet (ﷺ) said, "One-tenth is to be given on what is watered by rain, springs or whose roots derive its own water underground. One-twentieth is to be given on what is irrigated from streams (by using camels)."[19]

Estimating[20] the dates and grapes

Abu Ḥumayd as-Sâ'idi said, "We went out with the Prophet (ﷺ) for the Battle of Tabook. When we came to Wâdi al-Qurâ, there was a woman in her garden. The Prophet (ﷺ) said to his Companions, "Estimate (how much produce she will have)." The Prophet (ﷺ) estimated that it would be ten *wasq*. He said to the

---

[15] [According to Dr. Muhammad Muhsin Khan, one *uqiya* equals 38.4 grams. See Muhammad Muhsin Khan, trans., *Ṣaḥeeḥ Bukhari* (Beirut, Lebanon: Dar al Arabia, 1985), vol. 2, p. 277.] - Translator

[16] [According to Dr. Muhammad Muhsin Khan, one *wasq* equals 180 kilograms. Ibid.] - Translator

[17] Recorded by Bukhari, and this is his wording, Muslim, Tirmidhi, Nasâ'i and Ibn Mâjah.

[18] This hadith is *ṣaḥeeḥ*. See Shaykh al-Albâni, *Ṣaḥeeḥ al-Jâmi' aṣ-Ṣagheer*, no. 4271. Recorded by Muslim, and this is his wording, Abu Dawood and Nasâ'i.

[19] This hadith is *ṣaḥeeḥ*. See Shaykh al-Albâni, *Ṣaḥeeḥ al-Jâmi' aṣ-Ṣagheer*, no. 4272. Recorded by Bukhari, and this is his wording, Abu Dawood, Tirmidhi, Nasâ'i and Ibn Mâjah.

[20] This is to estimate the amount of dates on the date-palms. Tirmidhi states=

woman, "Reckon your garden's produce." (Later, upon returning,) when they came to Wâdi al-Qurâ, he said to the woman, "How much did your garden produce?" She replied, "Ten *wasq* that the Messenger of Allah (ﷺ) had estimated."[21]

'Â'ishah said, "The Messenger of Allah (ﷺ) used to send 'Abdullâh ibn Rawâḥah to estimate the dates after they appeared but before any are eaten. He would then give the Jews of Khaybar a choice as to whether they would take that estimate or gave that estimate (to the Muslims, as the produce was to be divided in half). This was done so that the Zakah could be estimated before the fruits were eaten and dispersed."[22]

The Zakah on Livestock

Livestock are of three varieties: camels, cattle and sheep.

The Zakah on Camels

Abu Sa'eed al-Khudri narrated that the Messenger of Allah (ﷺ) said, "Zakah is not due on less than five camels."[23]

=that scholars have explained this as saying that when the dates and grapes appear, the governor would send someone to look at them and estimate how much would be the final produce. He would then estimate how much is to be paid and leave them to their crops. When the crop was to be picked, he would come and take the tenth due on it. See *Fatḥ al-Bâri*, vol. 3, p. 403 (Dar ar-Rayyân edition).

[21] This hadith is *ṣaḥeeḥ*. See Shaykh al-Albâni, *Ṣaḥeeḥ Sunan Abi Dawood*, no. 2643. Recorded by Bukhari and Abu Dawood.

[22] This hadith is *ḥasan* due to supporting evidence. See Shaykh al-Albâni, *I'rwâ' al-Ghaleel*, no. 805. Recorded by Abu Dawood.

[23] Recorded by Bukhari, and this is his wording, Muslim, Tirmidhi, Nasâ'i and Ibn Mâjah.

The obligatory amount on camels

Anas narrated: When Abu Bakr (رضي الله عنه) sent me to (collect the Zakah from) the province of Eastern Arabia, he gave me a writing which read, "In the Name of Allah, the Most Gracious, the Most Merciful. Here are the obligatory Zakah payments which Messenger of Allah (ﷺ) prescribed on every Muslim and which Allah ordered His Messenger to observe. Therefore, any Muslim who is asked to pay Zakah accordingly should pay it and whoever is asked to give more than this is not to give it. For a flock of twenty-four camels or less and on every five camels, one sheep is to be given as Zakah. If the flock is between twenty-five and thirty-five camels, a one-year-old she-camel is to be given. If the herd is between thirty-six and forty-five camels, a two-year-old she-camel is to be given. If the herd is between forty-six and sixty camels, a three-year-old she-camel is to be given. If the flock is between sixty-one and seventy-five camels, a four-year-old she-camel is to be given. If the total number of the flock is between seventy-six and ninety camels, two two-year-old she-camels are to be given. If the number of the flock is between ninety-one and a hundred and twenty camels, two three-year-old she-camels are to be given. If the herd is over a hundred and twenty camels, on every forty camels, a two-year-old she-camel is to be given, and on every fifty camels, a three-year-old she-camel is to be given. Whoever has only four camels owes nothing as Zakah, but if the owner of these camels wants to give something, he may do so. If the number of camels is five, the owner has to give one sheep as Zakah."[24]

If one does not possess the required animal to be given

Anas narrated: Abu Bakr (رضي الله عنه) sent me a message, explaining Zakah which Allah had ordered His Messenger to observe. It read,

---

[24] This hadith is *ṣaḥeeḥ*. See Shaykh al-Albâni, *Ṣaḥeeḥ Sunan Abi Dawood*, no. 1385. Recorded by Bukhari, Abu Dawood and Nasâ'i.

"Whoever is supposed to give a four-year-old she-camel from his flock of camels as Zakah but does not have one and only has a three-year-old she-camel, she should be accepted from him along with two sheep if available, or twenty dirhams. Whereas whoever is supposed to give a three-year-old she-camel as Zakah but does not have one but has a four-year-old she-camel, it should be accepted from him, but the Zakah collector should return twenty dirhams or two sheep to him. Moreover, whoever is supposed to give a three-year-old she-camel as Zakah but does not have one and has a two-year-old one, she should be accepted from him along with two sheep or twenty dirhams. Whereas whoever is supposed to give a two-year-old she-camel but has a three-year-old she-camel, it is to be accepted from him, but the Zakah collector should return twenty dirhams or two sheep to him. In addition, whoever is supposed to give a two-year-old she-camel but does not have one and has a one-year-old she-camel instead, she is to be accepted from him along with twenty dirhams or two sheep."[25]

The Zakah on Cattle: The Niṣâb and the Obligatory Amount

Mu'âdh ibn Jabal said, "The Messenger of Allah (ﷺ) sent me to Yemen and he told me to take from every forty cattle, one young two-year old cow. On every thirty, a young bull or a young cow is to be taken."[26]

---

[25] This hadith is *ṣaḥeeḥ*. See Shaykh al-Albâni, *Ṣaḥeeḥ Sunan Abi Dawood*, no. 1385. Recorded by Bukhari, Abu Dawood, Nasâ'i and Ibn Mâjah.

[26] This hadith is *ṣaḥeeḥ*. See Shaykh al-Albâni, *Ṣaḥeeḥ Sunan Abi Dawood*, no. 1394. Recorded by Tirmidhi, Abu Dawood, Nasâ'i and by Ibn Mâjah, and this is his wording as the others have some additional text at the end.

The Zakah on Sheep and Goats: The Niṣâb and the Obligatory Amount

Anas narrated that Abu Bakr wrote for him the obligatory Zakah that Allah obliged upon His messenger (ﷺ). The instructions included: "Concerning the Zakah on a freely-grazing herd of sheep/goats, if it is between forty and a hundred and twenty sheep/goats, one sheep/goat is required as Zakah. If the herd of sheep/goats is between a hundred and twenty and two hundred sheep, two sheep/goats are to be given. If the number of sheep/goats is between two hundred and three hundred sheep/goats, three sheep/goats are to be given; and on every extra hundred sheep/goats, one sheep/goat is to be given as Zakah. If somebody has less than forty freely-grazing sheep/goats, no Zakah is required from him, but if he wants to give something, he may do so."[27]

Prerequisites for the obligation of zakah on livestock

1. Possessing the *nisâb*. This is obvious from the preceding hadith.

2. That they be in the possession of the person for one year. This is based on the hadith, "There is no Zakah on wealth until one year passes over it (in one's possession)."[28]

3. That the livestock be freely-grazing on pastures (as opposed to fodder-fed) for most of the year. This is based on the hadith mentioned earlier, "Concerning the Zakah on a freely-grazing herd of sheep, if it is between forty and a hundred and twenty sheep, one sheep is required as Zakah" and "Concerning freely-grazing camels,

---

[27] This hadith is *ṣaḥeeḥ*. See Shaykh al-Albâni, *Ṣaḥeeḥ Sunan Abi Dawood*, no. 1385. Recorded by Bukhari, Abu Dawood and Nasâ'i.

[28] This hadith is *ṣaḥeeḥ*. See Shaykh al-Albâni, *Ṣaḥeeḥ al-Jâmi' aṣ-Ṣagheer*, no. 7497. Recorded by Ibn Mâjah, ad-Dâraquṭni and al-Bayhaqi.

for every forty, one should give a young she-camel."[29]

What is Not to be Taken as Zakah

Ibn 'Abbâs said, "When the Messenger of Allah (ﷺ) sent Mu'âdh to Yemen, he told him, 'Avoid taking the best of their wealth.'"[30]

Anas narrated that Abu Bakr wrote to him concerning the obligatory Zakah that Allah obligated upon His Messenger (ﷺ) and he stated, "Neither an old nor a blemished animal nor a male goat may be taken as Zakah unless the Zakah collector accepts it."[31]

Co-Owned Wealth

If two or more people share in some wealth upon which Zakah is due and it is not possible to distinguish one's wealth from the other, then they are to pay one Zakah payment if Zakah is obligatory upon them. Anas narrated that Abu Bakr wrote to him the obligatory Zakah that Allah obliged upon His Messenger (ﷺ), saying, "Neither should the property of different people be collected so as to make one whole nor should the whole property be divided for fear of giving more Zakah. If property is possessed by two partners, they should pay Zakah collectively and they will be considered as having paid their Zakah equally."[32]

---

[29] Both of these statements are found in narrations of the writing of Abu Bakr to Anas.

[30] Recorded by Bukhari, Muslim, Tirmidhi, Abu Dawood and Nasâ'i.

[31] This is found in narrations of the writing of Abu Bakr to Anas. [Note that there are two ways to read this hadith. The one as in the translation above and the second as, "unless the owner wills to do so." In this alternative reading, the exception is referring to the male goat only.] - Translator

[32] This is found in narrations of the writing of Abu Bakr to Anas.

Zakah on Buried Treasures

Buried treasures are those buried in pre-Islamic times which are discovered without expending much wealth or effort. One must pay Zakah immediately upon them, without the prerequisite of it being in one's possession for a year or it reaching the level of the *nisâb*. This point is based on the generality of the Prophet's statement, "One-fifth is (to be paid as Zakah) upon found buried treasures."[33]

The Recipients of Zakah

Allah (ﷻ) has said:

﴿إِنَّمَا ٱلصَّدَقَٰتُ لِلۡفُقَرَآءِ وَٱلۡمَسَٰكِينِ وَٱلۡعَٰمِلِينَ عَلَيۡهَا وَٱلۡمُؤَلَّفَةِ قُلُوبُهُمۡ وَفِي ٱلرِّقَابِ وَٱلۡغَٰرِمِينَ وَفِي سَبِيلِ ٱللَّهِ وَٱبۡنِ ٱلسَّبِيلِۖ فَرِيضَةٗ مِّنَ ٱللَّهِۗ وَٱللَّهُ عَلِيمٌ حَكِيمٞ ٦٠﴾ (سورة التوبة: ٦٠)

﴿The alms are only for the poor, the needy, those employed to collect [the funds], and to attract the hearts of those who have been inclined [towards Islam]; and to free the captives; and for those in debt; and for Allah's Cause, and for the wayfarer [a traveller who is cut off from everything]; a duty imposed by Allah. And Allah is All-Knower, All-Wise.﴾ *(Qur'an 9: 60)*

In his commentary to this verse, Ibn Katheer said, "When Allah mentioned the objection to the Prophet (ﷺ) made by the ignorant hypocrites and their ridiculing of him with respect to the

---

[33] Recorded by Bukhari, Muslim, Tirmidhi, Nasâ'i, Ibn Mâjah and Abu Dawood. Some of these record a lengthy hadith while the others record a shorter version.

division of the charity, Allah made it clear that He was the One Who established these categories and rulings. He did not leave the categories to anyone other than Him."

Is it obligatory to give to all of the categories of people mentioned in the verse? Ibn Katheer stated, "The scholars differ concerning these eight categories of people. Is it obligatory to give to all categories or can one give only to those feasible. One view is that it is obligatory to give to all. This is the view of ash-Shâfi'ee and a number of scholars. The second opinion is that it is not obligatory to give to all the categories. In fact, according to this view, it is permissible to give all of it to just one category all the alms even though the other categories are present. This is the view of Mâlik and a number of early and later scholars, including 'Umar, Ḥudhayfah, Ibn 'Abbâs, Abu al-'Âliyah, Sa'eed ibn Jubayr and Maymoon ibn Mahrân. Ibn Jareer said, 'This is the view of the majority of the scholars.' In this case, the mentioning of these categories is in order to explain who should receive the Zakah but does not mean to imply that all of them must be given." Ibn Katheer then said, "We shall mention some hadith related to each of the eight categories:

1. The poor

Ibn 'Amr narrated that the Messenger of Allah (ﷺ) said, "Charity is not permissible for a person of wealth or a person of sound limbs and strength."[34] 'Ubaydullâh ibn 'Adi ibn al-Khiyâr narrated, "Two men informed me that they went to the Prophet (ﷺ) during the Farewell Pilgrimage while he was distributing charity and asked him for some. He looked at them up and down and found them to be strong. He then said, 'If you two wish, (I will give you) but there

---

[34] This hadith is *ṣaḥeeḥ*. See Shaykh al-Albâni, *Ṣaḥeeḥ al-Jâmi' aṣ-Ṣagheer*, no. 7251. Recorded by Tirmidhi and Abu Dawood. Ibn Mâjah and Nasâ'i have recorded it from Abu Hurayrah.

is no share in it for a rich man or one strong and able to earn a living.' "[35]

2. The needy

Abu Hurayrah narrated that the Messenger of Allah (ﷺ) said, "The needy person is not the one who goes around to the people and is dispensed with by a morsel or two of food or one or two dates." They asked, "Who then is the needy, O' Messenger of Allah?" He said, "He does not find enough to satisfy him, and he is not reckoned as needy so people do not give to him while he does not ask anything of the people."[36]

3. Those employed to collect the funds

They are the collectors and messengers who are deserving of a portion due to their efforts. However, it is not allowed to give them anything if they are relatives of the Prophet (ﷺ) for whom it is not allowed to accept charity. It is confirmed in *Ṣaḥeeḥ Muslim* from 'Abdul Muṭalib ibn Rabee'ah ibn al-Ḥârith that he and al-Faḍl ibn al-'Abbâs asked the Prophet (ﷺ) to employ them in collecting the alms. He told them, "Alms are not permissible for Muhammad or for the family of Muhammad, as they are only the dirt of the people."[37]

---

[35] This hadith is *ṣaḥeeḥ*. See Shaykh al-Albâni, *Ṣaḥeeḥ Sunan Abi Dawood*, no. 1438. Recorded by Abu Dawood and Nasâ'i.

[36] Recorded by Bukhari, Muslim (and this is his wording), Nasâ'i and Abu Dawood.

[37] This hadith is *ṣaḥeeḥ*. See Shaykh al-Albâni, *Ṣaḥeeḥ al-Jâmi' aṣ-Ṣagheer*, no. 1664. Recorded by Muslim, Abu Dawood and Nasâ'i.
[Note: This translator could not find this hadith with this exact wording in Muslim. Here, the author is taking the text from Ibn Katheer's Qur'anic commentary while the reference he gives, *Ṣaḥeeḥ al-Jâmi' aṣ-Ṣagheer*, no. 1664, has the exact and proper wording from *Ṣaḥeeḥ Muslim*. And Allah alone knows best.] - Translator
An-Nawawi explained the meaning of, "the filth of the people," by noting,=

4. Those whose hearts have been inclined (towards Islam)

Some are to be given so that they will accept Islam. For example, the Prophet (ﷺ) gave Ṣafwân ibn Umayyah from the booty of Ḥunayn as he had participated in that battle while he was a polytheist. Ṣafwân said, "He continued to give me until he become the most beloved person to me after he had been the most hated person to me."[38]

Some are to be given in order to improve their Islam and make their hearts firm. For example, also after Ḥunayn, the Prophet (ﷺ) gave one hundred camels to some of the nobles of those who embraced Islam in Makkah after it was conquered. He stated, "I give to one person while another is more beloved to me out of fear that Allah may throw him on his face into the Hell-fire."[39]

Bukhari and Muslim record from Abu Sa'eed that 'Ali sent to the Prophet (ﷺ) a gold nugget still in its dirt from Yemen. He distributed it among four people: al-Aqara' ibn Ḥâbis, 'Uyainah ibn Badr, 'Alqamah ibn 'Ulâthah and Zayd al-Khayr. The Prophet said, "It was to reconcile (their hearts)."[40]

Some people are given out of hopes that their peers will embrace Islam. Others are given to collect alms from his surrounding areas. And some may be given in order to fend off any harm to the Muslims from the border areas. And Allah alone knows best.

="It purifies their wealth and souls, as Allah has said, 'Take from their wealth alms to cleanse and purify them by it.' Thus, it is like the filth that results from cleaning." See *Muslim bi-Sharḥ an-Nawawi*, vol. 7, p. 251.

[38] This hadith is *ṣaḥeeḥ*. See Shaykh al-Albâni, *Mukhtasar Ṣaḥeeḥ Muslim*, no. 1588. Recorded by Muslim, Abu Dawood and Nasâ'i.

[39] Recorded by Bukhari, Muslim, Abu Dawood and Nasâ'i.

[40] Recorded by Bukhari, Muslim and Abu Dawood.

Is the Zakah still to be given to those whose hearts are to be reconciled after the time of the Prophet (ﷺ)? Ibn Katheer states that on this point there is a difference of opinion. It is narrated from 'Umar, 'Âmir, ash-Sh'abi and a group of scholars that they are no longer to be given after the death of the Prophet (ﷺ). This is because Allah has strengthened Islam and its people, has established it in the land and has made the people subservient to it. Others say that they are still to be given from the Zakah because the Prophet (ﷺ) gave to such people after the victory over Makkah and the defeat of Hawâzin. Thus, it could still be needed and such people are still to be given.

5. To free the captives

It is narrated from al-Ḥasan al-Baṣri, Muqâtil ibn Ḥayyân, 'Umar ibn 'Abdul 'Azeez, Sa'eed ibn Jubayr, an-Nakha'ee, az-Zuhri and Ibn Zayd that this is in reference to the slaves who have made an agreement to pay for their freedom. Similar has been narrated from Abu Moosa al-Ash'ari. This is also the opinion of ash-Shafi'ee and al-Layth. Ibn 'Abbâs and al-Ḥasan also stated that there is no harm in freeing slaves with the Zakah. This is the view of Aḥmad, Mâlik and Isḥâq. "Slaves" is a more general category than those slaves who have contracted to pay for their freedom. Hence, one can purchase slaves and free them independently. There are many hadith that speak about thc virtues of freeing and releasing slaves. For example, Allah will rescue for him every limb due to the limbs that he set free, even down to the private parts.[41]

---

[41] This hadith is *ṣaḥeeḥ*. See Shaykh al-Albâni, *Ṣaḥeeḥ al-Jâmi' aṣ-Ṣagheer*, no. 6051. Tirmidhi recorded from Abu Hurayrah that he heard the Messenger of Allah (Blessings and peace of Allah be upon him) say, "Whoever sets free the neck of a believing Muslim, Allah will rescue every limb for limb from the Hell-fire, even including the private parts."
[Note: This hadith is actually recorded by Bukhari and Muslim as well and it is more befitting to attribute it to these two sources.] - Translator

6. Those in debt

These fall into different categories. These include those who incurred expenses in solving disputes among others, those who have guaranteed a loan that has now become due, those who cannot pay their debts and those who committed sin but then repented. All of these may be given to as part of this category.

The basis for this is the hadith of Qabeeṣah ibn Mukhâriq al-Hilâli who said, "I incurred a debt (resolving a dispute between people) and went to the Messenger of Allah (ﷺ) asking him to help pay it. The Messenger of Allah (ﷺ) said, 'Wait until some charity is brought to us so that we give it to you.' He then said, 'O' Qabeeṣah! Begging is not allowed except in three cases: a man who incurred debts solving disputes — he is allowed to ask until he collects its amount and then must stop. A man who was inflicted by a disaster that consumed his wealth, he is allowed to ask until he collects what suffices for his livelihood. And a man who was overcome by poverty, such that three knowledgeable relatives of his stand up and proclaim, 'So-and-so was overcome by poverty.' This man is allowed to ask until he collects what sustains his livelihood. Other than these cases, begging is an unlawful amount that one illegally consumes.' "

7. For Allah's Cause

This refers to the fighters who have no right to receive money from the public treasury. According to Aḥmad, al-Ḥasan and Isḥâq, it also includes the pilgrimage to Makkah, based on a hadith.

I (the author) add that Ibn Katheer is referring to the following hadith narrated by Ibn 'Abbâs: "The Messenger of Allah (ﷺ) was intending to perform the pilgrimage. A woman said to her husband, 'Let me make the pilgrimage with the Messenger of Allah (ﷺ).' He replied, 'I have nothing for you to make the pilgrimage on.' She said, 'Let me ride on such and such camel of yours.' He replied, 'It is being kept for the sake of Allah.' He then went to the Messenger of Allah (ﷺ) and said, 'My wife conveys her greetings to you. She has asked me to make the pilgrimage with you. I told her that I have nothing for her to make the pilgrimage on and she requested such and such camel. I told her that it was being kept for the sake of Allah.' The Prophet (ﷺ) then told him, 'If you let her make the pilgrimage upon it, it would be for Allah's cause.' "[42]

8. For the wayfarer

This refers to the traveller who is cut off in a foreign land and has nothing to help him along in his journey. He is to be given from the Zakah until he is able to reach his homeland, even if he be a person of wealth. This is also the ruling for a person who starts a journey from his land and has no money, he is to be given sufficient money from the Zakah until he is able to go and return. The evidence for this position is in the verse above as well as the following hadith recorded by Abu Dawood and Ibn Mâjah from the hadith of Ma'mar from Yazeed ibn Aslam from 'Aṭâ' ibn Yasâr from Abu Sa'eed who said that the Messenger of Allah (ﷺ) said, "It is not permissible to give charity to a rich person except in five cases: one employed to collect the Zakah, a fighter for the sake of Allah, a rich person who bought an item of charity with his wealth, a poor person who is given charity and then he gives it as a gift to a rich person and a debtor."[43]

---

[42] This hadith is *ḥasan ṣaḥeeḥ*. See Shaykh al-Albâni, *Ṣaḥeeḥ Sunan Abi Dawood*, no. 1753. Recorded by Abu Dawood, al-Ḥâkim and al-Bayhaqi.

[43] This hadith is *ṣaḥeeḥ*. See Shaykh al-Albâni, *Ṣaḥeeḥ al-Jâmi' aṣ-Ṣagheer*, no. 2750. Recorded by Abu Dawood and Ibn Mâjah.

Zakât al-Fiṭr (Paid at the End of Ramaḍân)

Its Ruling

Zakât al-Fiṭr is an obligation upon every Muslim. Ibn 'Umar said, "The Messenger of Allah (ﷺ) obligated *Zakât al-Fiṭr* as one *ṣ'â*[44] of dates or barley. It is a must upon every slave and free person, male and female, young or old of the Muslims. He ordered that it should be given before going out to perform the *'Eid* prayer."[45]

Its Wisdom

Ibn 'Abbâs said, "The Messenger of Allah (ﷺ) obligated *Zakât al-Fiṭr* as purification for the fasting person from foul or vain speech and to feed the poor. If someone gives it before the (*'Eid*) prayer, it is an accepted Zakah. If someone gives it after the (*'Eid*) prayer it is simply a type of charity."[46]

Upon Whom is it Obligatory?

It is obligatory upon every free Muslim who possesses enough to support himself and his family for one day and night. It is obligatory for him to be on behalf of himself and all whom he

---

[44] [A *ṣ'â* is four times the amount an average size person can hold in his hands when they are cupped together.] - Translator

[45] Recorded by Bukhari, Muslim, Tirmidhi, Abu Dawood, Nasâ'i and by Ibn Mâjah who does not have the second portion of the hadith.

[46] This hadith is *ḥasan*. See Shaykh al-Albâni, *Ṣaḥeeḥ Sunan Ibn Mâjah*, no. 1480. Recorded by Ibn Mâjah and Abu Dawood.

supports, such as his wife, children and servants, if they are Muslims. Ibn 'Umar said, "The Messenger of Allah (ﷺ) ordered that *Zakât al-Fiṭr* be given on behalf of the young, old, free, slave and those whom you support."[47]

Its Amount

Obligatory upon every individual is half a *ṣ'â*[48] of wheat or a *ṣ'â* of dates, raisins, barley or dried yoghurt, or other kinds of food that can take their place, such as rice and other staple foods. The evidence for the obligation of a half *ṣ'â* of wheat is in the hadith of 'Urwah ibn az-Zubayr who said, "Asmâ' bint Abu Bakr, during the time of the Messenger of Allah (ﷺ), used to give the Zakah on behalf of her family, the free and the slaves among them. She would give half a *ṣ'â* of wheat or a *ṣ'â* of dates, according to the measures and *ṣ'â* that would support them." The evidence that for other than wheat one must give a *ṣ'â* is in the hadith of Abu Sa'eed al-Khudri who said, "We used to give *Zakât al-Fiṭr* as a *ṣ'â* of meal, barley, dates, dried yoghurt or raisins."[49]

"According to most of the jurists, it is not allowed to give its value (in money). However, Abu Ḥaneefah allows it." This was stated by an-Nawawi in *Sharḥ Ṣaḥeeḥ Muslim* (vol. 7, p. 60). I say that Abu Ḥaneefah's view is to be rejected because ﴾your Lord is not forgetful﴿ and had giving its value been permissible, Allah or His Messenger would have made that clear. Hence, it is obligatory to stop

---

[47] This hadith is *ṣaḥeeḥ*. See Shaykh al-Albâni, *I'rwâ' al-Ghaleel*, no. 835. Recorded by ad-Dâraquṭni and al-Bayhaqi.

[48] [A *ṣ'â* is four times the amount an average size person can hold in his hands when they are cupped together.] - Translator

[49] Recorded by Bukhari, Muslim, Tirmidhi, Abu Dawood, Nasâ'i and Ibn Mâjah.

at the apparent and clear meaning of the text without distorting or reinterpreting it.

The time at which it is to be given

Ibn 'Umar stated, "The Messenger of Allah (ﷺ) ordered that it should be given before going out to perform the *'Eid* prayer."[50]

It is permissible to give it to a recipient a day or two before the day of *'Eid al-Fitr*. Nâfi' said, "Ibn 'Umar used to give it to those who would accept it. He would give it a day or two before the day of *'Eid al-Fitr*."[51]

However, it is forbidden to delay it beyond its time without a valid excuse. Ibn 'Abbâs said, "The Messenger of Allah (ﷺ) obligated *Zakât al-Fiṭr* as purification for the fasting person from foul or vain speech and to feed the poor. If someone gives it before the (*'Eid*) prayer, it is an accepted Zakah. If someone gives it after the (*'Eid*) prayer it is simply a type of charity."[52]

Its recipients

Zakât al-Fiṭr is only to be given to the poor. This is clear in the statement just quoted from Ibn 'Abbâs, "to feed the poor."

---

[50] Recorded by Bukhari, Muslim, Tirmidhi, Abu Dawood, Nasâ'i and by Ibn Mâjah who does not have the second portion of the hadith.

[51] This hadith is *ṣaḥeeḥ*. Recorded by Bukhari.

[52] This hadith is *ḥasan*. See Shaykh al-Albâni, *Ṣaḥeeḥ Sunan Ibn Mâjah*, no. 1480. Recorded by Ibn Mâjah and Abu Dawood.

Voluntary Charity

It is recommended to give often as voluntary charity.

Allah (ﷻ) says:

﴿مَّثَلُ ٱلَّذِينَ يُنفِقُونَ أَمْوَٰلَهُمْ فِى سَبِيلِ ٱللَّهِ كَمَثَلِ حَبَّةٍ أَنۢبَتَتْ سَبْعَ سَنَابِلَ فِى كُلِّ سُنۢبُلَةٍ مِّا۟ئَةُ حَبَّةٍ ۗ وَٱللَّهُ يُضَٰعِفُ لِمَن يَشَآءُ ۗ وَٱللَّهُ وَٰسِعٌ عَلِيمٌ ۝٢٦١﴾

(سورة البَقـرَة: ٢٦١)

﴾The likeness of those who spend their wealth in the Way of Allah is as the likeness of a grain [of corn]; it grows seven ears, and each ear has a hundred grains. Allah gives manifold increase to whom He pleases. And Allah is All-Sufficient for His creatures' needs, All-Knower.﴿ *(Qur'an 2: 261)*

Furthermore, the Prophet (ﷺ) said, "In the morning of every day, two angels descend from Heaven. One of them says, 'O' Allah! Compensate whoever spends (in Your cause),' and the other says, 'O' Allah! Destroy whoever withholds.' "[53]

Among the people, priority should be given to one's family and relatives. The Messenger of Allah (ﷺ) said, "Giving charity to the poor is an act of charity while giving charity to a relative is two acts of charity and keeping the ties of kinship."[54]

---

[53] Recorded by Bukhari and Muslim.

[54] This hadith is *ṣaḥeeḥ*. See Shaykh al-Albâni, *Ṣaḥeeḥ al-Jâmi' aṣ-Ṣagheer*, no. 3858. Recorded by Tirmidhi.

Chapter Six — The Pilgrimage (al-Ḥajj)

The Virtues of the Ḥajj and 'Umrah[1]

Abu Hurayrah reported that the Messenger of Allah (ﷺ) said, "One 'Umrah until the next 'Umrah is an expiation for what is between them. And the Ḥajj that is accepted by Allah and performed properly has no reward other than Paradise."[2]

Ibn Mas'ood narrated that the Prophet (ﷺ) said, "Follow up the Ḥajj and 'Umrah (by performing them together) for they remove poverty and sins like the blacksmith's bellows removes impurities from iron, gold and silver. And there is no reward for an accepted Ḥajj other than Paradise."[3]

Abu Hurayrah also related that the Prophet (ﷺ) said, "Whoever performs the Ḥajj for the sake of Allah and does not commit any lewdness or sins returns like the day in which his mother gave him birth."[4]

---

[1] [The 'Umrah can be described as the "minor pilgrimage." It is an act that is performed throughout the year and it has fewer rites than the Ḥajj or "major pilgrimage".] - Translator

[2] Recorded by Bukhari, Muslim, Tirmidhi, Ibn Mâjah and Nasâ'i.

[3] This hadith is *ṣaḥeeḥ*. See Shaykh al-Albâni, *Ṣaḥeeḥ al-Jâmi' aṣ-Ṣagheer*, no. 2899. Recorded by Tirmidhi and Nasâ'i.

[4] Recorded by Bukhari, Muslim, Ibn Mâjah, Nasâ'i and by Tirmidhi who also adds, "His previous sins will be forgiven."

Ibn 'Umar narrated that the Prophet (ﷺ) said, "The fighter for the sake of Allah, the pilgrim and the minor pilgrim are Allah's 'delegation.' He called them and they responded. They ask of Him and He gives to them."[5]

Ḥajj with 'Umrah is obligatory at least once in the life of every adult, sane, free Muslim who has the capability to perform it. Allah (ﷻ) says:

﴿إِنَّ أَوَّلَ بَيْتٍ وُضِعَ لِلنَّاسِ لَلَّذِى بِبَكَّةَ مُبَارَكًا وَهُدًى لِّلْعَٰلَمِينَ ﴿٩٦﴾ فِيهِ ءَايَٰتٌۢ بَيِّنَٰتٌ مَّقَامُ إِبْرَٰهِيمَ ۖ وَمَن دَخَلَهُۥ كَانَ ءَامِنًا ۗ وَلِلَّهِ عَلَى ٱلنَّاسِ حِجُّ ٱلْبَيْتِ مَنِ ٱسْتَطَاعَ إِلَيْهِ سَبِيلًا ۚ وَمَن كَفَرَ فَإِنَّ ٱللَّهَ غَنِىٌّ عَنِ ٱلْعَٰلَمِينَ ﴿٩٧﴾﴾

(سورة آل عِمرَان: ٩٦-٩٧)

﴾Verily, the first House [of worship] appointed for mankind was that at Makkah, full of blessing, and a guidance for the worlds. In it are manifest signs [for example], the place of Abraham; whosoever enters it, he attains security. And Ḥajj to the House is a duty that mankind owes to Allah, those who can afford the expenses; and whoever disbelieves, then Allah stands not in need of any of humankind and jinn.﴿ *(Qur'an 3: 96-97)*

The Ruling of the Ḥajj

On the authority of Abu Hurayrah (رضي الله عنه): "The Prophet (ﷺ) once addressed us saying, "O' people, Allah has made the Ḥajj obligatory upon you." A man said, "Every year, O' Messenger of Allah (ﷺ)?" The Prophet (ﷺ) remained quiet. The man repeated the

---

[5] This hadith is *ḥasan*. See Shaykh al-Albâni, *Ṣaḥeeḥ al-Jâmi' aṣ-Ṣagheer*, no. 2339. Recorded by Ibn Mâjah.

question three times. Finally, the Prophet (ﷺ) said, "If I were to say, 'Yes,' it would become obligatory upon you and you would not be able to do it." Then he said, "Leave me with what I have left you with. Verily, the people before you were destroyed because of their excessive questioning and their opposition to their prophets. If I order you to do something, do what you can. If I prohibit you something, leave it."[6]

Ibn 'Umar narrated that the Messenger of Allah (ﷺ) said, "Islam is built upon five (pillars): testifying that there is none worthy of worship except Allah and that Muhammad is the Messenger of Allah, establishing the prayers, giving the Zakah, making the pilgrimage to the House and fasting the month of Ramaḍân."[7]

Ibn 'Abbâs narrated that the Messenger of Allah (ﷺ) said, "This is an 'Umrah that we are performing together (with the Ḥajj). Whoever does not have a sacrificial animal should leave the inviolable state of pilgrimage completely. Verily, the 'Umrah shall be combined with the Ḥajj until the Day of Resurrection."[8]

Aṣ-Ṣubi ibn Ma'bad said, "I came to 'Umar and said, 'O' Commander of the Faithful, I have embraced Islam and have seen that the Ḥajj and 'Umrah are both obligatory upon me. Therefore, I entered the inviolable state intending both of them.' He replied, 'You have been guided to the Sunnah of your Prophet.'"[9]

---

[6] This hadith is *ṣaḥeeḥ*. See Shaykh al-Albâni, *Mukhtasar Ṣaḥeeḥ Muslim*, no. 639. Recorded by Muslim and Nasâ'i.

[7] Recorded by Bukhari, Muslim (and this is his wording), Tirmidhi and Nasâ'i.

[8] This hadith is *ṣaḥeeḥ*. See Shaykh al-Albâni, *I'rwâ' al-Ghaleel*, no. 982. Recorded by Muslim.

[9] This hadith is *ṣaḥeeḥ*. See Shaykh al-Albâni, *I'rwâ' al-Ghaleel*, no. 983. Recorded by Nasâ'i, Abu Dawood and Ibn Mâjah.

The Ḥajj of a Youth or a Slave

The Ḥajj is not obligatory upon a youth or an insane person. The Prophet (ﷺ) has said, "The pen (recording the deeds) has been raised (and is not recording) for three: the one who is sleeping until he awakens, the child until he reaches the age of puberty and the insane one until he becomes sane."[10]

The Ḥajj is also not obligatory upon the slave as he is not able to perform it due to his being preoccupied with serving his master.

However, if a youth or slave does perform the Ḥajj, their Ḥajj is considered valid but it does not suffice for the obligatory Ḥajj that is obligatory upon them after they reach puberty or are freed. Ibn 'Abbâs narrated that a woman lifted her child to the Prophet (ﷺ) and said, "Can this one make Ḥajj?" He replied, "Yes, and for you will be a reward."[11] He also narrated that the Prophet (ﷺ) said, "Any youth who makes the Ḥajj and then reaches puberty must perform another Ḥajj. Any slave who makes the Ḥajj and is later freed must make another Ḥajj."[12]

What is the Meaning of "Having the Means to Perform the Ḥajj"?

"Having the means" implies being of sound health and possessing what is sufficient for one to make the trip and return from

---

[10] This hadith is *ṣaḥeeḥ*. See Shaykh al-Albâni, *Ṣaḥeeḥ al-Jâmi'*, no. 3513. Recorded by Abu Dawood.

[11] This hadith is *ṣaḥeeḥ*. See Shaykh al-Albâni, *Mukhtasar Ṣaḥeeḥ Muslim*, no. 648. Recorded by Muslim, Abu Dawood and Nasâ'i.

[12] This hadith is *ṣaḥeeḥ*. See Shaykh al-Albâni, *I'rwâ' al-Ghaleel*, no. 986. Recorded by al-Bayhaqi.

the trip, in addition to being able to meet one's needs, the needs of one's dependents and safety along the journey.

The evidence for having sound health is in the narration from Ibn 'Abbâs who said, "A woman from the tribe of Khath'am said, 'O' Messenger of Allah, my father still has to perform the obligation due to Allah of the Ḥajj but he is an old man who is not able to ride a mount. Can I perform the Ḥajj on his behalf?' He replied, 'Perform the Ḥajj on his behalf.' "[13]

The condition of owning what is sufficient for the journey in addition to one's needs and the needs of one's dependents is based on the statement of the Prophet (ﷺ), "It is sufficient of a sin for a person to neglect those who are dependent on him."[14]

As for the condition of safety, this is based on the fact that if a person makes Ḥajj without such safety it will be a cause for harm, which is something that the Shari'ah seeks to avoid.

The Woman's Ḥajj

If the conditions of "having the means" described above are met by a woman, then the Ḥajj is obligatory upon her exactly like it is upon a man. However, in her case there is one additional condition: That she be accompanied by her husband or a male relative. If she cannot meet this condition, she does not "have the means" to perform the Ḥajj. Ibn 'Abbâs narrated that he heard the Messenger of Allah (ﷺ) say, "A man should not be alone with a woman unless there is a male relative present. And a woman should not travel except when accompanied by a male relative." Then a man stood and said, "O'

[13] Recorded by Bukhari, Muslim, Tirmidhi, Abu Dawood and Nasâ'i.

[14] This hadith is *ṣaḥeeḥ*. See Shaykh al-Albâni, *I'rwâ' al-Ghaleel*, no. 989. Recorded by Abu Dawood.

Messenger of Allah (ﷺ), my wife has left to make Ḥajj while I am recorded to participate in such and such military expedition." The Prophet (ﷺ) told him, "Go and make Ḥajj with your wife."[15]

Not Delaying to Perform the Ḥajj

It is obligatory on one who has the means to perform the Ḥajj without delay. The Messenger of Allah (ﷺ) said, "Whoever intends to perform the Ḥajj should do so without delay for a person may get sick, may get lost or encounter some need."[16]

Time and locale restrictions

There are time and locale restrictions, known as *mawâqeet* (plural of *meeqât*) for the performance of the Ḥajj.[17]

Time restrictions (or the specific time of the year that one performs Ḥajj)

Allah (ﷻ) says:

﴿يَسْـَٔلُونَكَ عَنِ ٱلْأَهِلَّةِ ۖ قُلْ هِىَ مَوَٰقِيتُ لِلنَّاسِ وَٱلْحَجِّ ... ﴿١٨٩﴾﴾

(سورة البقرة: ١٨٩)

﴿They ask you [O' Muhammad] about the new moons. Say, 'These are signs to mark fixed periods of time for mankind and for the pilgrimage...'﴾ *(Qur'an 2: 189)*

Allah also says:

---

[15] Recorded by Bukhari and Muslim (and this is his wording).

[16] This hadith is *ṣaḥeeḥ*. See Shaykh al-Albâni, *Ṣaḥeeḥ Sunan Ibn Mâjah*, no. 2331. Recorded by Ibn Mâjah.

[17] *Fiqh as-Sunnah*, vol. 1, p. 549.

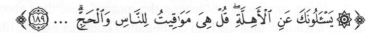

﴿ٱلْحَجُّ أَشْهُرٌ مَّعْلُومَٰتٌ ... ﴿١٩٧﴾﴾ (سورة البَقَرَة: ١٩٧)

﴿The Ḥajj is [in] the well-known [lunar year] months...﴾

(Qur'an 2: 197)

Ibn 'Umar said, "The months of the Ḥajj are Shawwâl (the tenth month of the year), Dhu al-Qa'idah (the eleventh month of the year) and the (first) ten days of Dhu al-Ḥijjah (the twelfth month of the year)."[18] And Ibn 'Abbâs said, "It is from the Sunnah not to enter the inviolable state of Ḥajj except during the months of the Ḥajj."[19]

Locale restrictions[20]

Ibn 'Abbâs said, "The Messenger of Allah (ﷺ) specified Dhu al-Ḥulayfah the *meeqât* for the People of Madeenah; al-Juḥfah for the people of Greater Syria, Yalamlam for the people of Yemen, and Qarn al-Manâzil for the people of Najd. These *meeqâts* are for the people who live in those places and for whoever comes through them intending to perform Ḥajj and 'Umrah. However, someone who lives in the area between one of these *meeqâts* and Makkah can assume the inviolable state from the place where he lives. The people of Makkah can also assume the inviolable state from Makkah."[21] 'Â'ishah (رضي الله عنها) said, "The Prophet (ﷺ) designated Dhât 'Irq as the *meeqât* for the people of Iraq."[22]

---

[18] Its chain is *ṣaḥeeḥ*. See Shaykh al-Albâni, *Mukhtasar Ṣaḥeeḥ Bukhari*, no. 311, p. 372. Recorded by Bukhari without its complete chain.

[19] Its chain is *ṣaḥeeḥ*. See Shaykh al-Albâni, *Mukhtasar Ṣaḥeeḥ Bukhari*, no. 311, p. 372. Recorded by Bukhari without its complete chain.

[20] [The "locale restrictions" or *meeqât* designate the places at which the pilgrims must enter into the inviolable state of the pilgrimage.]

[21] Recorded by Bukhari (and this is his wording), Muslim, Abu Dawood and Nasâ'i.

[22] This hadith is *ṣaḥeeḥ*. See Shaykh al-Albâni, *I'rwâ' al-Ghaleel*, no. 998.=

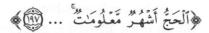

Whoever is intending to go to Makkah to perform the Ḥajj or 'Umrah is not allowed to go beyond these points without assuming the inviolable state of the pilgrimage. Furthermore, it is disliked to assume the inviolable state before one reaches these places. "Everything that is narrated encouraging one to enter the inviolable state before reaching the *meeqât* is not authentic. In fact, the opposite is narrated (in a more sound fashion)." For a discussion of the defects of those narrations, see (Shaykh al-Albâni's) *Silsilat al-Aḥâdeeth ad-Ḍa'eefah*, numbers 210 and 212.

Imam Mâlik made an excellent statement on this point. Imam Mâlik said to a person who wanted to enter the inviolable state before reaching Dhu al-Ḥulayfah, "Do not do so for I fear that you will be put to trial (*fitnah*)." The man asked, "What kind of *fitnah* could occur from that? It is just some distance that I am added." Mâlik told him, "What *fitnah* can be greater than you thinking that you are performing a virtuous deed that the Messenger of Allah (ﷺ) failed to do? (As for me,) I have heard Allah's words:

﴿... فَلْيَحْذَرِ ٱلَّذِينَ يُخَالِفُونَ عَنْ أَمْرِهِۦٓ أَن تُصِيبَهُمْ فِتْنَةٌ أَوْ يُصِيبَهُمْ عَذَابٌ أَلِيمٌ ﴿٦٣﴾﴾

(سورة النّور: ٦٣)

﴿... Let those who oppose the Messenger's commandment beware, lest some *fitnah* [trial or affliction] befall them or a painful torment be inflicted on them.﴾ *(Qur'an 24: 63)*."

Passing the Meeqât without entering the inviolable state

If a person passes the *meeqât* without entering the inviolable state, while he has intended to perform the Ḥajj or 'Umrah, has

---

=Recorded by Abu Dawood in this shortened for while Nasâ'i has a longer narration.

thereby committed a sin and that sin cannot be removed except by going back to the *meeqât*, entering the inviolable state from there and then completing the rest of the rites. If he does not return to that location, his rites are valid but he has committed a sin. However, he is not required to sacrifice an animal. This is based on the following hadith: Ṣafwân ibn Ya'la narrated that Ya'la said to 'Umar (رضي الله عنه), "Show me when the Prophet (ﷺ) is receiving revelation." While the Prophet (ﷺ) was at Ji'rânah with some of his Companions, a man came and asked, "O' Messenger of Allah (ﷺ), what do you say about a person who entered the inviolable state for the 'Umrah while wearing perfume?" The Prophet (ﷺ) remained silent for a little while. Then the revelation came. 'Umar signalled to Ya'la and he came (to see). The Prophet (ﷺ) was being shaded with a garment. Ya'la poked his head in and the Messenger of Allah's face was red and he was breathing audibly. Then that state left him. The Prophet (ﷺ) then said, "Where is the man who asked about the 'Umrah?" The man was then brought and the Prophet (ﷺ) told him, "Wash the perfume off of your body three times and remove your garment. And do what you do in your 'Umrah also in your Ḥajj."[23]

This hadith explicitly indicates that if someone acts contrary to the rules or does something prohibited for the inviolable state, then the only thing he must do is stop that act, as the Messenger (ﷺ) did not order the man who was wearing a garment that have woman's perfume on it to do anything except remove that garment and wash off the perfume. He did not order him to sacrifice an animal as expiation. If such were obligatory, he would have ordered him to do so as it is not allowed to delay the ruling of something beyond the time it is needed, and here the need was present.[24]

---

[23] Recorded by Bukhari, Muslim, Abu Dawood and Nasâ'i.

[24] From *Irshâd as-Sâri al-Muwâlid* by Shaykh Muhammad Ibrâheem Shaqrah.

Entering the inviolable state at the Meeqât

If the person intends to enter the inviolable state and he intended to combine the Ḥajj and 'Umrah, having along with him the sacrificial animal, he should say, "At your service, O' Allah, for both Ḥajj and 'Umrah." If he does not have a sacrificial animal with him, and that is preferred, then he should intend to make the 'Umrah only, by saying, "At your service, O' Allah, for 'Umrah." If he had made the intention for the Ḥajj only (and he is not bringing a sacrificial animal with him), he should negate that intention and make it for 'Umrah only (first and then re-enter the inviolable state to perform the Ḥajj).[25] The Prophet (ﷺ) ordered his Companions to exit from the inviolable state and to make their *sa'ee* and circumambulation that of an 'Umrah, except for those who had brought a sacrificial animal along with them. In fact, he was upset with those who did not respond to his order quickly. He emphasized this point by saying, "Verily, the 'Umrah shall be combined with the Ḥajj until the Day of Resurrection."[26] This text also shows that the 'Umrah forms part of the Ḥajj and is not to be separated from it. The Prophet (ﷺ) also said, "Had I known beforehand what I came to know later, I would not have brought my sacrificial animal with me."[27] In this hadith, the Prophet (ﷺ) was not simply stating his desire to get what he had missed by combining the Ḥajj and 'Umrah into one. Instead, this was an announcement on his part that *at-tamattu'* (making the Ḥajj and 'Umrah separately but on the same visit) is preferable to *al-qirân* (combining the Ḥajj and 'Umrah into one act).

---

[25] Shaykh al-Albâni, *Manâsik al-Ḥajj wa al-'Umrah*.

[26] This hadith is *ṣaḥeeḥ*. See Shaykh al-Albâni, *I'rwâ' al-Ghaleel*, no. 982. Recorded by Muslim.

[27] [Recorded by Bukhari and others.]

Every pilgrim must perform the 'Umrah with his Ḥajj, either by performing the 'Umrah first if he did not have a sacrificial animal with him — which is *at-tamattu'* — or by combining them together if he brought a sacrificial animal with him — which is *al-qirân*. By either that he chooses, he will be following the guidance of the Prophet (ﷺ), even though, as just explained, *at-tamattu'* is preferred over *al-qirân*.

Although it is obligatory on the one performing Ḥajj alone or Ḥajj combined with 'Umrah, if he has not brought a sacrificial animal with him, to leave the inviolable state after the circumambulation and the *sa'ee*, a pilgrim may find that he has does not have the time to do that and to re-enter the inviolable state of Ḥajj without missing the stopping at 'Arafah. In that case, it is permissible for one who has intended to perform the Ḥajj alone or in combination with 'Umrah (*al-qirân*) and who does not have a sacrificial animal with him to continue in the inviolable state and not to exit from it until after he has thrown the pebbles at al-'Uqbah on the Day of Sacrifice. For example, suppose someone comes to Makkah on the eve of the Ninth and he fears that he will miss the "Stay at 'Arafah". In that case, he must proceed immediately to 'Arafah in order not to miss the basic pillar of the Ḥajj by which he will miss the entire Ḥajj, which is the case with the "Stay at 'Arafah". Thus, the Ḥajj done by itself alone is permissible under very strict circumstances. However, if a person performs the Ḥajj alone and avoids making *at-tamattu'* or *al-qirân*, giving preference to performing the Ḥajj alone, then he is sinful because he has not responded properly to the command of the Prophet (ﷺ) when he ordered his Companions to change their Ḥajj into an 'Umrah (to be performed first followed by the Ḥajj). However, his Ḥajj will still be sound.[28]

---

[28] From *Irshâd as-Sâri al-Muwâlid* by Shaykh Muhammad Ibrâheem Shaqrah.

Permissibility of making the intention conditional upon not becoming ill or something of this nature

'Â'ishah (﵂) said, "The Messenger of Allah (ﷺ) came to Ḍuba'ah bint az-Zubayr and said to her, 'Perhaps you have desire to make Ḥajj?' She replied, 'By Allah, but I do feel sick.' So the Prophet (ﷺ) told her, 'Make the Ḥajj but lay down a condition by saying, 'O' Allah, I will finish my inviolable state wherever you refrain me (from going further).' ' "[29] If someone lays down such a condition, then if disease, an enemy or any other causes prevents him from going further, he leaves the inviolable state of pilgrimage and he does not have to sacrifice an animal (as a penalty). However, if someone does not make such a condition and is unable to continue for some reason, he must sacrifice an animal, as Allah has said:

﴿... فَإِنْ أُحْصِرْتُمْ فَمَا ٱسْتَيْسَرَ مِنَ ٱلْهَدْيِ ... ﴿١٩٦﴾﴾ (سورة البقرة: ١٩٦)

﴾... But if you are prevented [from completing the rites], sacrifice an animal such as you can afford...﴿ *(Qur'an 2: 196)*

The sacrificial animal must be a camel, cow or sheep. If a person can only afford a sheep, that will suffice. A camel or a cow would be preferred as expiation. If a person cannot afford to sacrifice an animal, he should fast ten days, analogous to the case of the one who made *at-tamattu'* but was not able to get a sacrificial animal.

"Take Your Pilgrimage Rites from Me": The Ḥajj of the Prophet (ﷺ)

Muslim recorded on the authority of Ja'far ibn Muhammad from his father who narrated: "We went to Jâbir ibn 'Abdullâh and he

---

[29] Recorded by Bukhari, Muslim and Nasâ'i.

began inquiring about the people until it was my turn. I said, 'I am Muhammad ibn 'Ali ibn al-Ḥusayn.' He placed his hand upon my head, opened by upper button and lower one and placed his palm on my chest (to bless me). During those days, I was a young boy. He said, 'Welcome, my nephew. Ask whatever you want to ask.' I asked him but he was blind (and did not respond immediately). The time for prayer came. He stood, covering himself in his mantle. When he would place its end on his shoulders, it would slip down due to it being short. Another mantle was lying on a rack nearby. He led us in the prayer. I said to him, 'Tell me about the Ḥajj of the Messenger of Allah (ﷺ).' He pointed with his hand and made a 'nine' and then said, 'The Messenger of Allah (ﷺ) stayed in (Madeenah) for nine years but did not perform Ḥajj. He then made a public announcement in the tenth year that the Messenger of Allah (ﷺ) was going to perform the Ḥajj. A large number of persons came to Madeenah and all were anxious to follow the Messenger of Allah (ﷺ) and act according to his actions. We set out with him until we reached Dhu al-Ḥulayfah. Asmâ', the daughter of 'Umays, gave birth then to Muhammad ibn Abu Bakr. She sent a message to the Messenger of Allah (ﷺ), asking him as to what she should do. The Prophet (ﷺ) said, 'Take a bath, bandage your private parts and enter into the inviolable state.' The Messenger of Allah (ﷺ) prayed in the mosque and then mounted his she-camel. The camel stoop tall and the Prophet (ﷺ) was one its back at al-Baydâ'. As far as I could see in front of me, behind me, to the right and to the left there nothing but people riding or walking. The Messenger of Allah (ﷺ) was prominent among us and the Qur'an was being revealed to him. It is the Prophet (ﷺ) who knows its meaning. Whatever he did, we also did. He pronounced Allah's Oneness, saying, 'At your service, O' Allah, at your service, at your service. You have no partner. To You belongs the praise, the grace and the dominion. You have no partner.' The people also pronounced this expression (known as *talbiyah*) which they still do today. The Prophet (ﷺ) did not object to any of what was being said but adhered to his own statement. We did not have any intention but that of Ḥajj only, being unaware of the permissibility of performing 'Umrah. However, when we came with him to the House, he touched the pillar, circumambulated (the House) seven times, running on three of them and walking four. Then going to the Place of Abraham, he recited:

﴿... وَٱتَّخِذُواْ مِن مَّقَامِ إِبْرَٰهِـۧمَ مُصَلًّى ... ﴿١٢٥﴾﴾ (سورة البقرة: ١٢٥)

﴿... And take the place of Abraham as a place of prayer...﴾
(Qur'an 2: 125)

The Place was between him and the House. (Ja'far said,) 'My father said, 'I do not know of him stating that except from the Prophet (ﷺ).'' In the two *rak'ahs*, he would recite, ﴿Say: He is Allah, [the] One,﴾ and, ﴿Say: O' you disbelievers﴾. He then returned to the pillar (of the House) and touched and kissed (the black stone). Then he went to (the hillock of) aṣ-Ṣafâ and recited:

﴿۞ إِنَّ ٱلصَّفَا وَٱلْمَرْوَةَ مِن شَعَآئِرِ ٱللَّهِ ... ﴿١٥٨﴾﴾ (سورة البقرة: ١٥٨)

﴿Verily! Aṣ-Ṣafâ and al-Marwah [two hills in Makkah] are of the Symbols of Allah...﴾ *(Qur'an 2: 158)*

(He then said,) 'I begin with what Allah has began with.' So he started at aṣ-Ṣafâ. He went up (the hill) until he could see the House. Facing the *qiblah*, he pronounced the Oneness of Allah and stated His greatness. He said, 'There is none worthy of worship except Allah, alone, with no partner. To Him belongs the dominion and the praise. He has power over all things. There is none worthy of worship except Allah, alone, who fulfilled His promise, gave victory to His servant and alone routed the confederates.' Then he supplicated during that time. He repeated this statement three times. Then he descended towards al-Marwah. When he reached the bottom of the valley, he ran, and when he began the ascent towards al-Marwah, he walked until he reached al-Marwah. Upon al-Marwah, he did the same as he did at aṣ-Ṣafâ. When it was his last circuit to al-Marwah, he said, 'Had I known beforehand what I came to know later, I would not have brought my sacrificial animal with me and I would have made it an 'Umrah. Whoever of you does not have a sacrificial animal with him should leave the inviolable state of pilgrimage and make it an 'Umrah.' Surâqah ibn Mâlik ibn Ju'sham stood and said, 'O' Messenger of Allah, is this just for this year of ours or forever.' The Messenger of Allah (ﷺ) intertwined his fingers and said, 'Verily, the 'Umrah shall be combined with the Ḥajj until the Day of Resurrection.' He said that twice and said, 'No, but forever, forever.' 'Ali then came from Yemen with sacrificial animals for the Prophet. He found Fâṭimah (his wife) having had left the inviolable state, put on dyed clothing and applied kohl. 'Ali objected to that. She said, 'It was my father [that is, the Prophet (ﷺ)] who ordered me to do this.' 'Ali used to say in Iraq, 'I went to the Messenger of Allah (ﷺ) showing annoyance with Fâṭimah for what she had done and asked the Messenger of Allah (ﷺ) about what she had stated to be from him. I told him that I had objected to that. He replied, 'She has told the truth; she has told the truth. What did you say (as your intention) when you began your Ḥajj?'' I ('Ali) replied, 'O' Allah, I enter the inviolable state with the same intent as Your messenger.' He then said, 'I have with me sacrificial animals. So do not leave the inviolable state.' (Jâbir) continued: The total number of those sacrificial animals brought by 'Ali from Yemen and of those brought by the Prophet (ﷺ) was one hundred. Then all the people except the Messenger (ﷺ) and those who had sacrificial animals with them left the inviolable state and had their hair trimmed. When it was the day of *Tarwiyah* (the 8th of Dhu al-Ḥijjah), they went to Mina and re-entered the inviolable state for the Ḥajj. The Messenger of Allah (ﷺ)

rode (to Mina) and led them in the Noon, Afternoon, Sunset, Night and Dawn prayers. He then waited a little until the sun rose. He then commanded that a fur tent be pitched at Namirah. The Messenger of Allah (ﷺ) then set out and the Quraysh were certain that he would halt at al-Mash'ar al-Ḥarâm as the Quraysh would do in pre-Islamic days. However, the Messenger of Allah (ﷺ) went right passed it and rode until he arrived at 'Arafah, where he found the tent had been set up for him at Namirah. He stayed there until after high noon. He asked for his she-camel to be brought and saddled. He came to the bottom of the valley and addressed the people, saying: 'Verily, your blood and wealth are inviolable to you all like the sacredness of this day of yours in this month of yours in this land of yours. Everything pertaining to the Days of Ignorance are hereby abolished under my feet. The blood-money of the Days of Ignorance is abolished. The first blood-money I abolish is our blood-money, the blood-money of Rabee'ah ibn al-Ḥârith, who was being nursed by the tribe of S'ad and was killed by Hudhayl. The interest payments of the Days of Ignorance are abolished. The first interest payment that I abolish is the interest payment due 'Abbâs ibn 'Abdul-Muṭṭalib. It is all abolished. Fear Allah concerning women. You have taken them on a security from Allah and they have been made permitted to you by the words of Allah. However, upon them is not to allow anyone to sit on your bed who you disapprove of. If they should do that, you can beat them but not bruisingly. Upon you, they have the right of food and clothing according to what is customary. I have left something among you concerning which, if you adhere to it, you shall never stray: the Book of Allah. You will be questioned about me and what shall you say?' The people said, 'We bear witness that you have conveyed the message, discharged your duty and advised sincerely.' He then raised his index finger toward the sky and pointed it toward the people and said, 'O' Allah, bear witness. O' Allah, bear witness,' three times. Then the call to prayer and the pronouncement of the beginning of the prayer were made. He then prayed the Noon prayer. Then the pronouncement of the beginning of the prayer was made and he prayed the Afternoon prayer. He did not pray anything in between them. He then rode until he reached his site. He made his she-camel face the side where there were rocks, the path of those who sent on foot in front of him, and then he faced the *qiblah*. He kept standing there until the sun set completely, with its yellow light gone. He placed Usâmah behind him on his animal. He pulled the nose string of the camel so forcefully that its head touched the saddle and he pointed to the people with his right hand, indicating, 'O' people, have calmness, have calmness.' When he came to an elevated portion of sand, he would loosen (the nose string) until the camel climbed it. That is how he reached al-Muzdalifah. Then he led the Sunset and Night prayers, with one call to prayer and two pronouncements of the beginning of the prayer. He did not pray anything in between them. The Messenger of Allah (ﷺ) then lay down until dawn and prayed the Dawn prayer when it was clear that it was dawn, with one call to prayer and one pronouncement of the beginning of the prayer. He again rode the she-camel and when he came to al-Mash'ar al-Ḥarâm, he faced the *qiblah*, supplicated to God, exalted Him and pronounced His oneness. He remained stopping there until the daylight was very clear. He then went quickly before the sun rose. Al-Faḍl ibn 'Abbâs was seated behind him on the she-camel. He had beautiful hair, a fair complexion and a handsome face. As the Messenger of Allah (ﷺ) was moving along, there was a group of women to his side. Al-Faḍl began to look at them. The Messenger of Allah (ﷺ) put his hand on his face to turn it to the other side. He again began to see and the Messenger of Allah (ﷺ) again pushed his face to the other way until he came to the bottom of Muḥassir (on the road between Muzdalifah and Mina). He urged the she-camel on, following the middle road, until he came to the Greater Jamrah (place of casting stones). He came to the Jamrah which is near the tree (known as Jamrah 'Aqabah).

He threw seven pebbles at it, each time saying, 'Allah is greatest.' He threw them from the bottom of the valley. He then went to the place of the sacrifice and sacrificed sixty-three camels by his hand. He then gave the remaining animals to 'Ali to sacrifice. Thus, he joined with him in the sacrifice. He then asked that a piece of flesh from each animal sacrificed be put into a pot. When it was cooked, they both (the Prophet and 'Ali) took some meat out of it and ate its soup. The Messenger of Allah (ﷺ) again rode and came to the House. In Makkah, he prayed the Noon prayer. He came to the Tribe of 'Abdul-Muṭṭalib, who were supplying the water of Zamzam. He said, 'Draw water, O' Tribe of 'Abdul-Muṭṭalib. Were it not that people would take this right of supplying water from me, I also would draw water with you.' So they handed him a pitcher and he drank from it."

In his commentary to *Ṣaḥeeḥ Muslim* (vol. 8, p. 170), Imam an-Nawawi wrote, "This is a great hadith. It contains many beneficial points and the substance of many important principles. Al-Qâḍi ('Iyâḍ) said, 'The people have spoken about its points of jurisprudence and have mentioned many points. Abu Bakr ibn al-Mundhir has compiled a large volume on this hadith and has derived some one hundred and fifty points. An additional similar amount could be added to that.'"

The Essential Components, Obligatory Acts and Sunnah Acts of this Act of Worship

Sunnah Acts of the Ḥajj

The Sunnah related to entering the inviolable state are the following:

1. Making *ghusl* (the complete washing) at the time of entering the inviolable state

Zayd ibn Thâbit narrated that he saw the Prophet (ﷺ) remove (his sewn) clothing to enter the inviolable state and he made *ghusl*.[30]

2. Applying perfume to one's body before entering the inviolable state

'Â'ishah said, "I would perfume the Messenger of Allah (ﷺ) for his inviolable state when he was about to enter into it and when he exited from the inviolable state before circumambulating the House."[31]

3. To wear a white waistwrapper and loose outer garment

Ibn 'Abbâs said, "The Prophet (ﷺ) left from Madeenah after he combed his hair, applied oil and wore a waistwrapper and loose outer garment. His Companions did the same."[32] As for preference for white, it is based on the hadith of Ibn 'Abbâs who narrated that the Messenger of Allah (ﷺ) said, "Wear of your clothing the white clothing for it is the best of your clothing. Also shroud your deceased in it."[33]

4. To pray in the valley of al-'Aqeeq for those who pass by that land

'Umar (رضي الله عنه) narrated that he heard the Messenger of Allah (ﷺ) while in the valley of al-'Aqeeq say, "Tonight, a visitor from my

---

[30] This hadith is *ṣaḥeeḥ*. See Shaykh al-Albâni, *Ṣaḥeeḥ Sunan Tirmidhi*, no. 664. Recorded by Tirmidhi.

[31] Recorded by Bukhari, Muslim, Tirmidhi (with additional text), Abu Dawood, Nasâ'i and Ibn Mâjah.

[32] This hadith is *ṣaḥeeḥ*. Recorded by Bukhari.

[33] This hadith is *ṣaḥeeḥ*. See Shaykh al-Albâni, *Ṣaḥeeḥ al-Jâmi' aṣ-Ṣagheer*, no. 3236 and *al-Janâ'iz*, p. 62. Recorded by Tirmidhi and Abu Dawood.

Lord came to me and said, 'Pray in this blessed valley and say, '(I intend) to put the 'Umrah with the Ḥajj.' ' "[34]

5. Raising one's voice while repeating the *talbiyah*[35]

"Jibreel came to me and ordered me to order my Companions to raise their voices while saying the *talbiyah*."[36] Because of this, the Companions of the Messenger of Allah (ﷺ) used to yell this. Abu Ḥâzim said, "The Companions of the Messenger of Allah (ﷺ), after they entered the inviolable state, would not reach ar-Rawḥâ' before their voices would be hoarse."[37]

6. Repeating the phrases *al-Ḥamdulillâh*, *Subḥânallâh* and *Allâhu akbar* before saying the *talbiyah*

Anas said, "The Messenger of Allah (ﷺ) prayed the Noon prayer four units (*rak'ahs*) while we were in Madeenah and prayed the Afternoon prayers two units at Dhu al-Ḥulayfah. Then he spent the night there until the morning. Then he rode until he was upon al-Baydâ' praising Allah, extolling His perfection and extolling His greatness. Then he made the *talbiyah* for Ḥajj and 'Umrah."[38]

7. To say the *talbiyah* while facing the *qiblah*

Nâfi' said, "When Ibn 'Umar would pray the Morning prayer

---

[34] This hadith is *ṣaḥeeḥ*. See Shaykh al-Albâni, *Ṣaḥeeḥ Sunan Ibn Mâjah*, no. 2410. Recorded by Bukhari, Abu Dawood and Ibn Mâjah.

[35] [This is the statement, "At your service, O' Allah"]

[36] This hadith is *ṣaḥeeḥ*. See Shaykh al-Albâni, *Ṣaḥeeḥ Sunan Tirmidhi*, no. 663. Recorded by Tirmidhi, Abu Dawood, Ibn Mâjah and Nasâ'i.

[37] Its chain is *ṣaḥeeḥ*. Abu Manṣoor recorded it, as state in *al-Muḥalla* (vol. 7, p. 94) with a good chain. Ibn Abu Shaybah also recoded it with a sound chain from al-Muṭalib ibn 'Abdullâh, as stated iṇ *al-Fatḥ* (vol. 3, p. 324) and that chain is broken (*mursal*). See Shaykh al-Albâni, *Manâsik al-Ḥajj*, p. 17.

[38] This hadith is *ṣaḥeeḥ*. See Shaykh al-Albâni, *Ṣaḥeeḥ Sunan Abi Dawood*, no. 1558. Recorded by Bukhari and Abu Dawood has similar to it.

at Dhu al-Ḥulayfah, he would get his mount ready and then get on it. He used to face the *qiblah* saying the *talbiyah* as he sat on his mount setting off to Makkah... He said that the Messenger of Allah (ﷺ) also did that."[39]

Sunnah acts related to entering Makkah

8. 9. and 10. Spending the night at Dhu Ṭuwâ, performing *ghusl* to enter Makkah and to enter it during the daytime

Nâfi' said, "When Ibn 'Umar would enter the limits of the inviolable mosque, he would refrain from making the *talbiyah*. He would then spend the night at Dhu Ṭuwâ, pray the morning prayer there and make *ghusl*. He narrated that the Prophet (ﷺ) would do that."[40]

11. Entering Makkah through the higher ravine

Ibn 'Umar said, "The Prophet (ﷺ) entered Makkah through the higher ravine and left it through the lower passage."[41]

12. To step first with the right foot upon
entering the mosque and to say,

أَعُوذُ بِاللَّهِ الْعَظِيمِ وَبِوَجْهِهِ الْكَرِيمِ وَسُلْطَانِهِ الْقَدِيمِ مِنَ الشَّيْطَانِ الرَّجِيمِ
بِسْمِ اللَّهِ اللَّهُمَّ صَلِّ عَلَى مُحَمَّدٍ وَسَلِّمِ اللَّهُمَّ افْتَحْ لِي أَبْوَابَ رَحْمَتِكَ

"I seek refuge in Allah, the Great, by His Noble Face and Ancient Authority, from the accursed Satan. In the name of Allah, O' Allah, shower blessings and peace upon Muhammad. O' Allah, open for me

---

[39] This hadith is *ṣaḥeeḥ*. Recorded by Bukhari.

[40] Recorded by Bukhari (and this is his wording) while Muslim and Abu Dawood have similar narrations.

[41] Recorded by Bukhari (and this is his wording), Muslim, Nasâ'i and Ibn Mâjah.

the doors of Your mercy."[42]

13. Upon seeing the House

Upon seeing the House one may raise one's hands if so desired, as such is confirmed from Ibn 'Abbâs.[43] Furthermore, if one wishes to make the following supplication, it is good as it has been confirmed from 'Umar, "O' Allah, You are the Source of Peace and from You comes Peace, Our Lord, give us life with peace."[44]

Sunnah acts related to circumambulating the House

14. Putting the ends of the upper loose garment under the right armpit, exposing the right shoulder

Ya'la ibn Umayyah narrated that the Prophet (ﷺ) circumambulated while exposing his right shoulder.[45]

15. Touching the Black Stone

Ibn 'Umar said, "I saw the Messenger of Allah (ﷺ), upon arriving in Makkah, touching and kissing the black stone while beginning the circumambulation. He walked quickly in the first three of the seven circumambulations."[46]

16. Kissing the Black Stone

Zayd ibn Aslam narrated from his father who said, "I saw 'Umar kiss the (Black) Stone. He then said, 'If it were not that I had

---

[42] This hadith is *ṣaḥeeḥ*. *Al-Kalam aṭ-Ṭayyib*, p. 65.

[43] Its chain is *ṣaḥeeḥ*. See Shaykh al-Albâni, *Manâsik al-Ḥajj*, p. 20. Recorded by Ibn Abu Shaybah.

[44] Its chain is *ḥasan*. See Shaykh al-Albâni, *Manâsik al-Ḥajj*, p. 20. Recorded by al-Bayhaqi.

[45] This hadith is *ḥasan*. See Shaykh al-Albâni, *Ṣaḥeeḥ Sunan Ibn Mâjah*, no. 2391. Recorded by Abu Dawood, Tirmidhi and Ibn Mâjah.

[46] Recorded by Bukhari, Muslim and Nasâ'i.

seen the Messenger of Allah kissing you, I would not have kissed you.' "[47]

17. Prostrating upon it

Ibn 'Umar said, "I saw 'Umar ibn al-Khaṭṭâb kiss the (Black) Stone and prostrate upon it. Then he returned and kissed it and prostrated upon it. Then he said, 'This is what I saw the Messenger of Allah doing.' "[48]

18. Saying the *takbeer* upon passing the corner (wherein is the Black Stone)

Ibn 'Abbâs said, "The Prophet (ﷺ) circumambulated the House riding his camel and every time he came to the corner (with the Black Stone), he would point to it with anything he had and say the *takbeer*."[49]

19. Walking quickly during the first three rounds of the first circumambulation of the House

Ibn 'Umar narrated, "When the Messenger of Allah (ﷺ) would make his first circumambulation of the House, he would walk quickly during the three rounds from the (Black) Stone until the Stone, and walk on the other four rounds."[50]

---

[47] Recorded by Bukhari, Muslim, Abu Dawood, Ibn Mâjah, Tirmidhi and Nasâ'i.

[48] This hadith is *ḥasan*. See Shaykh al-Albâni, *I'rwâ' al-Ghaleel*, vol. 4, p. 312. Recorded by al-Bazzâr.

[49] This hadith is *ṣaḥeeḥ*. See Shaykh al-Albâni, *I'rwâ' al-Ghaleel*, no. 1114. Recorded by Bukhari.

[50] This hadith is *ṣaḥeeḥ*. See Shaykh al-Albâni, *Ṣaḥeeḥ Sunan Ibn Mâjah*, no. 2387. Recorded by Ibn Mâjah, this being his wording. Bukhari, Muslim, Abu Dawood and Nasâ'i have something similar.

20. Touching the Yemeni corner

Ibn 'Umar said, "I did not see the Prophet (ﷺ) touching any part of the House except for the two Yemeni corners."[51]

21. Making the following supplication between the two corners

"O' Allah, grant us the good of this life and the good of the Hereafter and save us from the torment of the Hell-fire."[52]

22. After completing the circumambulation, performing a two-*rak'ah* prayer behind the Place of Abraham

Ibn 'Umar said, "The Messenger of Allah (ﷺ) came and made seven rounds around the House. Then he prayed a two-*rak'ah* prayer behind the Place (of Abraham). Then he made the circuits between aṣ-Ṣafâ and al-Marwah." Then Ibn 'Umar recited:

﴿لَّقَدْ كَانَ لَكُمْ فِي رَسُولِ ٱللَّهِ أُسْوَةٌ حَسَنَةٌ ... ﴿٢١﴾﴾ (سورة الأحزاب: ٢١)

﴾Indeed in the Messenger of Allah you have a good example...﴿
(Qur'an 33: 21).[53]

23. To recite at the Place of Abraham, before praying:

﴿... وَٱتَّخِذُواْ مِن مَّقَامِ إِبْرَٰهِـۧمَ مُصَلًّى ... ﴿١٢٥﴾﴾ (سورة البقرة: ١٢٥)

﴾... And take the place of Abraham as a place of prayer...﴿
(Qur'an 2: 125)

— and to recite *Soorah al-Kâfiroon* and *Soorah al-Ikhlâs* in the two-*rak'ah* prayer. This is based on the hadith of Jâbir who said, "When

---

[51] Recorded by Bukhari, Muslim, Abu Dawood and Nasâ'i.

[52] This hadith is *ḥasan*. See Shaykh al-Albâni, *Ṣaḥeeḥ Sunan Abi Dawood*, no. 1666. Recorded by Abu Dawood.

[53] This hadith is *ṣaḥeeḥ*. See Shaykh al-Albâni, *Ṣaḥeeḥ Sunan Ibn Mâjah*, no. 2394. Recorded by Bukhari and Ibn Mâjah.

the Prophet (ﷺ) came to the Place of Abraham, he recited, ﴿... And take the place of Abraham as a place of prayer...﴾ *(Qur'an 33: 21).* In the two *rak'ahs*, he would recite, ﴿Say: He is Allah, [the] One,﴾ and, ﴿Say: O' you disbelievers.﴾"[54]

24. To supplicate between the Black Stone corner and the door of the Ka'bah, by putting one's chest, face and forearms against the Ka'bah

'Amr ibn Shu'ayb narrated from his father on the authority of his grandfather who said, "I circumambulated with 'Abdullâh ibn 'Amr. When we finished the seven rounds, we prayed behind the Ka'bah. I said, 'Shall we not seek refuge in Allah from the Fire.' He said, 'I seek refuge in Allah from the Fire.' Then he touched the (Black Stone) corner and then he put his chest, hands and check up against (the Ka'bah) between the Black Stone and the door (to the Ka'bah). Then he said, 'This is what I saw the Messenger of Allah (ﷺ) doing.'"[55]

25. Drinking from the water of Zamzam and washing one's head with it. In the hadith of Jâbir it states that the Prophet (ﷺ) did this.[56]

Sunnah acts related to the circuits of as-sa'ee

26. Touching the corner as mentioned earlier.

27. Reading the verse:

﴿ ۞ إِنَّ ٱلصَّفَا وَٱلْمَرْوَةَ مِن شَعَآئِرِ ٱللَّهِ ۖ فَمَنْ حَجَّ ٱلْبَيْتَ أَوِ ٱعْتَمَرَ فَلَا جُنَاحَ

---

[54] Recorded by Muslim.

[55] This was mentioned earlier in the hadith of Jâbir. [This is obviously a mistake in the Arabic text. This does not form part of the earlier quoted hadith of Jâbir. This hadith was recorded by Ibn Mâjah.] - Translator

[56] [Actually, in the hadith of Jâbir presented earlier, there is only mention of the Prophet (peace and blessings of Allah be upon him) drinking such water. And Allah alone knows best.]

عَلَيْهِ أَن يَطَّوَّفَ بِهِمَاۚ وَمَن تَطَوَّعَ خَيْرًا فَإِنَّ ٱللَّهَ شَاكِرٌ عَلِيمٌ ﴿١٥٨﴾﴾

(سورة البَقَرَة: ١٥٨)

﴿Verily! Aṣ-Ṣafâ and al-Marwah (two hillocks in Makkah) are of the Symbols of Allah. So it is not a sin on him who perform Ḥajj or 'Umrah of the House to perform the going between them. And whoever does good voluntarily, then verily, Allah is All-Recogniser, All-Knower.﴾ *(Qur'an 2: 158)*

Then one says, "We begin from where Allah began." This is to be done when one gets close to aṣ-Ṣafâ to begin the circuits.[57]

28 Facing the *qiblah* while upon aṣ-Ṣafâ and saying,

اللَّه أكبر اللَّه أكبر اللَّه أكبر لاَ إِلَهَ إِلاَّ اللَّهُ وَحْدَهُ لاَ شَرِيكَ لَهُ لَهُ الْمُلْكُ وَلَهُ الْحَمْدُ وَهُوَ عَلَى كُلِّ شَيْءٍ قَدِيرٌ لاَ إِلَهَ إِلاَّ اللَّهُ وَحْدَهُ أَنْجَزَ وَعْدَهُ وَنَصَرَ عَبْدَهُ وَهَزَمَ الأَحْزَابَ وَحْدَهُ

"Allah is greatest, Allah is greatest, Allah is greatest. There is none worthy of worship except Allah, alone, with no partner for Him. To Him belongs the dominion and the praise. And He has power over everything. There is none worthy of worship except Allah, alone, who fulfilled His promise, gave victory to His servant and alone routed the confederates." Then the person supplicates what he wishes to supplicate. He does this three times.

29. Running quickly between the two green markers

30. Doing the same at al-Marwah that one did on aṣ-Ṣafâ with respect to facing the House and the words of remembrance and supplications

---

57 These acts are based on the hadith of Jâbir.

Sunnah acts related to leaving to Mina

31. Entering the inviolable state for the Ḥajj on the eighth of Dhu al-Ḥijjah from where one is staying there.[58]

32. Praying the Noon, Afternoon, Sunset and Night prayers at Mina, staying overnight at Mina until one prays the Dawn prayer and sun has risen.

33. Praying the Noon and Afternoon prayers, together and in shorter form, at Namirah on the Day of 'Arafah.

34. Not leaving 'Arafah before the sun sets.

The Essential Components of the Ḥajj

1. Having the proper intention

Allah (ﷻ) says:

﴿وَمَآ أُمِرُوٓا۟ إِلَّا لِيَعْبُدُوا۟ ٱللَّهَ مُخْلِصِينَ لَهُ ٱلدِّينَ ... ۝٥﴾ (سورة البيّنة : ٥)

﴾And they were commanded not, but that they should worship Allah, and worship none but Him Alone, sincerely...﴿ *(Qur'an 98: 5)*

The Prophet (ﷺ) also said, "Verily, all actions are based on intention."[59]

2. Staying at 'Arafah

The Prophet (ﷺ) said, "The (essence of the) Ḥajj is 'Arafah."[60] There is also the hadith of 'Urwah aṭ-Ṭâ'ee who said, "I

---

[58] One should keep in mind the Sunnah related to entering the inviolable state, as discussed earlier.

[59] Recorded by Bukhari, Muslim, Tirmidhi, Ibn Mâjah and Nasâ'i.

[60] This hadith is *ṣaḥeeḥ*. See Shaykh al-Albâni, *Ṣaḥeeḥ Sunan Ibn Mâjah*, no. 2441. Recorded by Tirmidhi, Nasâ'i, Ibn Mâjah and Abu Dawood.

came to the Messenger of Allah (ﷺ) at the place of halting, that is, Muzdalifah. I said, 'I have come from the mountains of Ṭayy'. I fatigued my mount and fatigued myself. By Allah, I found no hill but I halted there. Have I completed my Ḥajj?' The Messenger of Allah (ﷺ) said, 'Anyone who offers this prayer along with us, stays with us until we leave and had stopped in 'Arafah before it by night or day will have completed his Ḥajj, and he may wash away the dirt (off of his body).' "[61]

3. Spending the night at Muzdalifah until dawn and praying the Dawn prayer there

This is based on the previously cited hadith of 'Urwah, "Anyone who offers this prayer along with us, stays with us until we leave and had stopped in 'Arafah before it by night or day will have completed his Ḥajj, and he may wash away the dirt (off of his body)."[62]

4. Performing the circumambulation after returning from Mina (known as *tawâf al-ifâḍah*)

Allah has said:

﴿... وَلْيَطَّوَّفُوا۟ بِٱلْبَيْتِ ٱلْعَتِيقِ ﴿٢٩﴾﴾ (سورة الحج: ٢٩)

﴾... [Then let them] circumambulate the Ancient House [the Ka'bah at Makkah].﴿ *(Qur'an 22: 29)*

'Âishah (رضي الله عنها) said, "Ṣafiyyah bint Ḥuyyay had her menses after she had performed the *ifâḍah* circumambulation." The Prophet (ﷺ) was informed of that and he said, "Is she going to delay us?" 'Âishah

---

[61] This hadith is *ṣaḥeeḥ*. See Shaykh al-Albâni, *Ṣaḥeeḥ Sunan Ibn Mâjah*, no. 2442. Recorded by Tirmidhi, Abu Dawood, Ibn Mâjah and Nasâ'i.

[62] This hadith is *ṣaḥeeḥ*. See Shaykh al-Albâni, *Ṣaḥeeḥ Sunan Ibn Mâjah*, no. 2442. Recorded by Tirmidhi, Abu Dawood, Ibn Mâjah and Nasâ'i.

said, "She has already performed the *ifâḍah* and circumambulated the House. Her menses then came after the *ifâḍah.*" The Prophet (ﷺ) said, "Let us go then."[63] The Prophet's statement, "Is she going to delay us?" indicates that one must perform the *ifâḍah* circumambulation and that it will keep one who has not performed it from leaving.

5. Performing the circuits (*as-sa'ee*)
between aṣ-Ṣafâ and al-Marwah

The Prophet (ﷺ) performed this act and also said, "Perform the *sa'ee* for Allah has obligated the *sa'ee* upon you."[64]

The Obligatory Acts of the Ḥajj

1. Entering the inviolable state at the *meeqât*, removing one's clothing and entering into the clothing of the inviolable state and then making the intention by saying, "At your service, O' Allah, for an 'Umrah," or, "At your service, O' Allah, for Ḥajj and 'Umrah."

2. Spending the night at Mina during the Days of *Tashreeq*

The Messenger of Allah (ﷺ) stayed there during these days. However, the Prophet (ﷺ) "exempted the camel herders, allowing them to throw the pebbles on the day of *'Eid*, and to combine the other two throwing of pebbles on the next day."[65] The fact that the Prophet (ﷺ) exempted them means that it is obligatory upon others.

---

[63] Recorded by Bukhari, Muslim, Abu Dawood, Nasâ'i, Tirmidhi and Ibn Mâjah.

[64] This hadith is *ṣaḥeeḥ*. See Shaykh al-Albâni, *I'rwâ' al-Ghaleel*, no. 1072. Recorded by Aḥmad and al-Ḥâkim.

[65] This hadith is *ṣaḥeeḥ*. See Shaykh al-Albâni, *Ṣaḥeeḥ Sunan Ibn Mâjah*, no. 2463. Recorded by Abu Dawood, Tirmidhi, Ibn Mâjah and Nasâ'i.

3. Throwing the pebbles in the proper order

On the Day of the Sacrifice, one throws seven pebbles at Jamrah al-'Aqabah. Every day, on the days of *Tashreeq*, after high noon, one throws seven pebbles at each of the three places of throwing pebbles, starting with the first one, then the middle and then al-'Aqabah.

4. Performing the farewell circumambulation

Ibn 'Abbâs said, "The people were ordered to make the final circumambulation of the House at the end, but the menstruating women are exempted from this."[66]

5. Shaving off or cutting one's hair

Shaving off or cutting one's hair is confirmed by the Qur'an, Sunnah and consensus. As for the Qur'an, Allah says:

﴿لَّقَدْ صَدَقَ ٱللَّهُ رَسُولَهُ ٱلرُّءْيَا بِٱلْحَقِّ لَتَدْخُلُنَّ ٱلْمَسْجِدَ ٱلْحَرَامَ إِن شَآءَ ٱللَّهُ ءَامِنِينَ مُحَلِّقِينَ رُءُوسَكُمْ وَمُقَصِّرِينَ لَا تَخَافُونَ ... ﴿٢٧﴾﴾ (سورة الفتح: ٢٧)

﴾Indeed Allah shall fulfill the true vision which He showed to His Messenger in very truth. Certainly, you shall enter al-Masjid al-Ḥarâm, if Allah wills, secure, [some] having your heads shaved, and [some] having your head hair cut short, having no fear...﴿

(Qur'an 48: 27)

As for the Sunnah, 'Abdullâh ibn 'Umar narrated: "The Messenger of Allah (ﷺ) said, 'O' Allah, have mercy on those who shaved off their hair." They (the people) said, "And those who trimmed it, O' Messenger of Allah?" The Messenger of Allah (ﷺ) again said, "O' Allah, have mercy on those who shaved off their hair." They (the people) said, "And those who trimmed it, O' Messenger of Allah?"

---

[66] Recorded by Bukhari and Muslim.

The Messenger of Allah (ﷺ) again said, "O' Allah, have mercy on those who shaved off their hair." They (the people) said, "And those who trimmed it, O' Messenger of Allah?" Finally, the Messenger of Allah (ﷺ) said, "And those who trimmed it."[67]

The scholars differ concerning the ruling of this act. The majority say it is obligatory while the Shâfi'ees say it is one on the essential acts of the Ḥajj. The reason they differ, as our Shaykh al-Albâni has informed me, is that there is no clear evidence for either view.

The conditions for the validity of the circumambulation[68]

Ibn 'Abbâs narrated that the Messenger of Allah (ﷺ) said, "Circumambulation about the House is like the prayer except that you can speak during it. Whoever does speak during it should only speak what is good."[69]

Since it is like the prayer, the following conditions apply to it:

1. Being free of both types of impurities (discussed earlier)

The Prophet (ﷺ) said, "The prayer is not accepted without purification."[70] Furthermore, the Prophet (ﷺ) told 'Â'ishah, when she received her menses while on the Ḥajj, "Do what the pilgrim does except do not circumambulate the house until you are purified."[71]

---

[67] [With this exact wording, this is narrated by Aḥmad. However, the gist of the report is found in Bukhari and Muslim.] - Translator

[68] Cf., *Fiqh as-Sunnah*, vol. 1, p. 588; *Manâr as-Sabeel*, vol. 1, p. 263.

[69] This hadith is *ṣaḥeeḥ*. See Shaykh al-Albâni, *I'rwâ' al-Ghaleel*, no. 121. Recorded by Tirmidhi, Ibn Khuzaymah, Ibn Ḥibbân, ad-Dârimi, al-Ḥâkim and al-Bayhaqi.

[70] This hadith is *ṣaḥeeḥ*. See Shaykh al-Albâni, *Mukhtasar Ṣaḥeeḥ Muslim*, no. 104. Recorded by Muslim and Tirmidhi.

[71] Recorded by Bukhari and Muslim.

2. Covering one's private parts

Allah (ﷻ) says:

﴿ يَٰبَنِيٓ ءَادَمَ خُذُواْ زِينَتَكُمۡ عِندَ كُلِّ مَسۡجِدٖ ... ﴾ (سورة الأعراف: ٣١)

﴾O' Children of Adam! Take your adornment [by wearing your clean clothes], at every mosque...﴿ *(Qur'an 7: 31)*

Abu Hurayrah narrated that the Messenger of Allah (ﷺ) assigned Abu Bakr to lead the pilgrims who went to perform Ḥajj the year before the Farewell Ḥajj. On the Day of Sacrifice, Abu Bakr sent me along with a group of people in order to announce, "No polytheist will perform Ḥajj after this year, and no naked person will circumambulate the Ka'bah."[72]

3. Fully completing the seven rounds about the House

The Prophet (ﷺ) made seven rounds. Ibn 'Umar said, "The Messenger of Allah (ﷺ) arrived and circumambulated the House seven times, prayed behind the Place (of Abraham) two *rak'ahs* and made the seven circuits between aṣ-Ṣafâ and al-Marwah.

﴿ لَّقَدۡ كَانَ لَكُمۡ فِي رَسُولِ ٱللَّهِ أُسۡوَةٌ حَسَنَةٞ ... ﴾ (سورة الأحزاب: ٢١)

﴾Indeed in the Messenger of Allah you have a good example...﴿ *(Qur'an 33: 21)*"[73]

The Prophet (ﷺ) did that act demonstrating the meaning of the verse:

﴿ ... وَلۡيَطَّوَّفُواْ بِٱلۡبَيۡتِ ٱلۡعَتِيقِ ﴾ (سورة الحج: ٢٩)

﴾... [Then let them] circumambulate the Ancient House [the Ka'bah at Makkah].﴿ *(Qur'an 22: 29)*

---

[72] Recorded by Bukhari, Muslim, Abu Dawood and Nasâ'i.

[73] This hadith is *ṣaḥeeḥ*. See Shaykh al-Albâni, *Ṣaḥeeḥ Sunan Ibn Mâjah*, no. 2394. Recorded by Bukhari and Ibn Mâjah.

If a person leaves any part of the seven circumambulations, even a small part, it does not suffice. If a person has a doubt as to how much he completed, he must act upon the lesser that he thinks is possible, which is that portion that he is certain of.

4. and 5. Beginning the circumambulation from the Black Stone and ending it with the Black Stone, putting the House on one's right side

This is based on the hadith of Jâbir which states, "When the Messenger of Allah (ﷺ) came to Makkah, he went to the Black Stone, touched it and then put it to his right and circumambulated (the House) seven times, running on three of them and walking four." If someone circumambulates the House with the House on his right side, his circumambulation is not valid.

6. The circumambulation has to be outside the house (as opposed to inside any portion of it)

Allah (ﷻ) says, ﴿... [Then let them] circumambulate the Ancient House [the Ka'bah at Makkah].﴾ *(Qur'an 22: 29)* which implies circumambulating the entire House. If someone makes the circumambulation from within the *ḥijr* (the empty space separating the new foundation from the original foundation), his circumambulation is not valid because the Prophet (ﷺ) said, "The *ḥijr* is part of the House."[74]

7. Performing the rounds immediately after one another

This is the manner in which the Prophet (ﷺ) performed the circumambulation. He said, 'Take your rites of pilgrimage from me.'[75]

---

[74] [The author does not ascribe this "hadith" to any source. This translator was not able to find it in any well-known hadith source. However, it was recorded by a number of sources as a statement of Ibn 'Abbâs. It is also the view of the majority of the scholars. And Allah alone knows best.] - Translator

[75] *Ṣaḥeeḥ*, (*I'rwâ' al-Ghaleel*, no. 1074).

If the person stops to make ablution, perform an obligatory prayer that has commenced or to rest a little, he may continue from where he left off. However, if he breaks for a long time, he has to start over.

The conditions for the validity of the circuits between aṣ-Ṣafâ and al-Marwah

The following are conditions for the validity of the *sa'ee* (circuits between aṣ-Ṣafâ and al-Marwah):

1. Performing seven circuits.
2. Beginning with aṣ-Ṣafâ and ending with al-Marwah.
3. Performing along the specified path between aṣ-Ṣafâ and al-Marwah.

These are all according to the manner of the Prophet (ﷺ) who had said, "Take your rites of pilgrimage from me."[76]

Actions that are Prohibited for the Pilgrim

The following are forbidden for the pilgrim

1. Wearing sewn clothing

Ibn 'Umar narrated that a man came and said, "O' Messenger of Allah, what is a pilgrim allowed to wear of clothing?" The Messenger of Allah (ﷺ) said, "He must not wear an undergarment, a turban, trousers, a hooded cloak, or leather socks unless he cannot find slippers. In such a case, he can wear leather socks, which should be cut so as to be below the ankles. It is also forbidden for him to wear clothes scented with saffron or *wars* (a kind of plant used for dyeing)."[77]

---

[76] *Ṣaḥeeḥ*. (*I'rwâ' al-Ghaleel*, no. 1074).

[77] Recorded by Bukhari, Muslim, Abu Dawood and Nasâ'i.

An exemption is made for those who cannot find anything other than trousers or leather socks to wear them without cutting them. Ibn 'Abbâs said, "I heard the Prophet (ﷺ) giving a speech at 'Arafah, saying, "Whoever cannot find sandals can wear leather socks. And whoever cannot find a waist cloth can wear trousers as a pilgrim.""[78]

2. A woman covering her face or hands

Ibn 'Umar narrated that the Prophet (ﷺ) said, "The female pilgrim is not to wear a veil (over her face) or gloves."[79] However, it is permissible for her to cover her face if men pass by her. Hishâm ibn 'Urwah narrated from Fâṭimah bint al-Mundhir that she said, "We used to cover our faces with our headscarves while we were pilgrims. At the time, we were with Asmâ' bint Abu Bakr aṣ-Ṣiddeeq."[80]

3. A man covering his head with a turban or any similar item

This is based on the hadith of Ibn 'Umar in which the Prophet (ﷺ) said, "He must not wear an undergarment, a turban..." It is, though, permissible to seek shade under a tent or something of that nature. This is based on the hadith of Jâbir which states, "The Messenger of Allah (ﷺ) commanded that a fur tent be pitched at Namirah and he stayed there."

4. Wearing perfume

In the hadith narrated by Ibn 'Umar, it states, "Do not wear clothes scented with saffron or *wars* (a kind of plant used for dyeing)."[81] The Prophet (ﷺ) also said about the pilgrim that died

---

[78] Recorded by Bukhari, Muslim, Nasâ'i, Tirmidhi and Abu Dawood.

[79] This hadith is *ṣaḥeeḥ*. See Shaykh al-Albâni, *I'rwâ' al-Ghaleel*, no. 1022. Recorded by Bukhari, Abu Dawood, Nasâ'i and Tirmidhi.

[80] This hadith is *ṣaḥeeḥ*. See Shaykh al-Albâni, *I'rwâ' al-Ghaleel*, no. 1023. Recorded by Mâlik and al-Ḥâkim.

[81] Recorded by Bukhari, Muslim, Abu Dawood and Nasâ'i.

falling from his camel, "Do not scent him with perfume and do not cover his head for he shall be resurrected on the Day of Resurrection reciting the *talbiyah*."[82]

5. and 6. Clipping one's nails or removing, shaving or cutting one's hairs

Allah (ﷻ) says:

﴿... وَلَا تَحْلِقُوا۟ رُءُوسَكُمْ حَتَّىٰ يَبْلُغَ ٱلْهَدْىُ مَحِلَّهُۥ ... ﴿١٩٦﴾﴾ (سورة البقرة: ١٩٦)

﴾... Do not shave your heads until the sacrificial animal reaches the place of sacrifice...﴿ *(Qur'an 2: 196)*

The scholars are all in agreement that it is forbidden for the pilgrim to trim his nails. However, it allowed for one who has some kind of infection or injury to remove his hair and he must perform atonement. Allah says:

﴿... فَمَن كَانَ مِنكُم مَّرِيضًا أَوْ بِهِۦٓ أَذًى مِّن رَّأْسِهِۦ فَفِدْيَةٌ مِّن صِيَامٍ أَوْ صَدَقَةٍ أَوْ نُسُكٍ ... ﴿١٩٦﴾﴾ (سورة البقرة: ١٩٦)

﴾... And whosoever of you is ill or has an ailment in his scalp [necessitating shaving], he must pay a ransom of either observing fast [for three days] or giving charity [feeding six poor persons] or offering a sacrifice [one sheep]...﴿ *(Qur'an 2: 196)*

K'ab ibn 'Ujrah (may Allah be pleased with him) said, "The Messenger of Allah (ﷺ) came to me on the occasion of Ḥudaybiyah while I was kindling a fire under my cooking pot and lice were creeping on my face. He said, 'Are these creatures bothering you?' I replied, 'Yes.' He said, 'Get your head shaved and (as expiation) feed

[82] Recorded by Bukhari, Muslim, Abu Dawood and Nasâ'i.

six needy poor people such and such amount of food, or fast three days or offer a sacrificial animal.' "[83]

7. Having sexual intercourse or any type of foreplay.

8. Committing sins.

9. Disputing improperly with others.

The basis for the prohibition of the last three categories is Allah's statement:

﴿ٱلْحَجُّ أَشْهُرٌ مَّعْلُومَٰتٌ ۚ فَمَن فَرَضَ فِيهِنَّ ٱلْحَجَّ فَلَا رَفَثَ وَلَا فُسُوقَ وَلَا جِدَالَ فِى ٱلْحَجِّ ۗ ... ﴿١٩٧﴾﴾ (سورة البقرة: ١٩٧)

﴿The Ḥajj is [in] the well-known [lunar year] months. So whosoever intends to perform Ḥajj therein [by assuming Ihrâm], then he should not have sexual relations [with his wife], nor commit sin, nor dispute unjustly during the Ḥajj...﴾ *(Qur'an 2: 197)*

10. and 11. Proposing or getting married

'Uthmân (رضي الله عنه) narrated that the Prophet (ﷺ) said, "The pilgrim is not to get married, be married off or propose."[84]

12. Exposing game to be killed or slaughtered, or pointing to or indicating a prey

Allah (سبحانه وتعالى) says:

﴿... وَحُرِّمَ عَلَيْكُمْ صَيْدُ ٱلْبَرِّ مَا دُمْتُمْ حُرُمًا ۗ ... ﴿٩٦﴾﴾ (سورة المائدة: ٩٦)

---

[83] Recorded by Bukhari, Muslim (and this is his wording), Abu Dawood, Nasâ'i, Tirmidhi and Ibn Mâjah.

[84] This hadith is *ṣaḥeeḥ*. See Shaykh al-Albâni, *Mukhtasar Ṣaḥeeḥ Muslim*, no. 814. Recorded by Muslim, Abu Dawood, Tirmidhi and Nasâ'i.

﴾... Forbidden is [the pursuit of] land-game as long as you are in the inviolable state [of Ḥajj or 'Umrah]...﴿ *(Qur'an 5: 96)*

Furthermore, when the Prophet (ﷺ) was asked about the zebra that Abu Qatâdah had hunted down while he was not in the inviolable state although the others were, he said, "Did any of you ask Abu Qatâdah to attack them or did any of you point to them?" They said, "No." He then said, "Then eat."[85]

13. Eating any land-game which one contributed to its hunting by pointing to it or assisting the hunter

This conclusion is understood by the hadith above which states, "Did any of you ask Abu Qatâdah to attack them or did any of you point to them?" They said, "No." He then said, "Then eat."

Invalidators of the Ḥajj[86]

The Ḥajj is invalidated by one of two matters:

First: Sexual intercourse if it were done before the stoning at al-'Aqabah. If it were done after the stoning at al-'Aqabah but before the *ifâḍah* circumambulation, it does not invalidate the Ḥajj although the person has committed a sin. Some scholar, however, opine that sexual intercourse does not invalidate the Ḥajj whatsoever as there is no explicit proof indicating such a position.

Second: Failing to perform one of the essential components of the Ḥajj.

If a person's Ḥajj is invalidated by either of these two, it is obligatory upon him to perform the Ḥajj during the following year if

---

[85] Recorded by Bukhari, Muslim and by Nasâ'i in an abridged form.

[86] Taken from *Irshâd as-Sâri* by Shaykh Muhammad Ibrâheem Shaqrah.

he has the ability to do so, according to what was defined earlier as "having the means to do so." If he cannot perform it in the following year, he must perform it when he has the means to do so as the obligation upon him is immediate whenever he has the means.

Forbidden Acts in the Two Sacred Sanctuaries[87]

In the two *Ṣaḥeeḥs* and other works it is narrated from 'Ubbâd ibn Tameem from his uncle that the Messenger of Allah (ﷺ) said, "Truly, Abraham made Makkah inviolable and prayed for it. I have made Madeenah inviolable as Ibrâheem made Makkah inviolable." The inviolable status was due to revelation from Allah to His two prophets and messengers (Blessings and peace of Allah be upon them). If someone says, "The two inviolable sanctuaries," it is in reference to Makkah and Madeenah. It is not permissible to use such terms except in reference to those two places. It is not even permissible to call al-Aqṣa mosque an inviolable sanctuary or the Mosque of Ibrâheem al-Khaleel, as the revelation has not referred to any place as being inviolable except Makkah and Madeenah. Such an honour must be based on revelation and there is no room for human reasoning on this issue.

There are specific acts that are prohibited in the land of the two sacred sanctuaries, for the resident of those lands as well as for the visitor coming for Ḥajj, 'Umrah and any other purpose. These acts are the following:

1. Hunting or pursuing land game or fowl or helping one to do the same.
2. Uprooting or cutting its plants or shrubs, unless there is a need or necessity for that.

---

[87] Quoted from *Irshâd as-Sâri* by Shaykh Muhammad Ibrâheem Shaqrah.

3. Carrying weapons.
4. Picking up of lost items by a pilgrim; the resident must pick up such lost items as long as he announces them — the difference between the pilgrim and the resident on this point is obvious.[88]

The evidence for the above lies in the statement of the Prophet (ﷺ) on the day of the conquering of Makkah: "Allah has made this city inviolable on the day He created the heavens and the earth. It is sacred by the declaration of Allah until the Day of Resurrection. It was not permissible for anyone to fight herein before me and it was only permissible for me for a portion of the day. It is inviolable by the declaration of Allah until the Day of Resurrection. Therefore its shrubs are not to be uprooted, its game is not to be chased, its lost items should not be picked up except by whoever announces it publicly and its trees are not to be cut." Al-'Abbâs said, "O' Messenger of Allah, except for *al-idhkhir* (a type of grass) for it is used by the blacksmiths and for the houses." So the Prophet (ﷺ) said, "Except for *al-idhkhir.*"[89]

Jâbir narrated that he heard the Prophet (ﷺ) say, "It is not allowed for any of you to carry weapons in Makkah."[90]

'Ali (رضي الله عنه) narrated that the Prophet (ﷺ) said (about Madeenah), "Its shrubs are not to be uprooted, its game is not to be chased and its lost items are not to be picked up except by one who makes it none. It is also not proper for one to carry weapons for fighting therein and it is not proper to cut down any of its trees unless it is man providing fodder for his camel."[91]

---

[88] End of potion taken from Shaqrah.

[89] Recorded by Bukhari, Muslim and Nasâ'i.

[90] This hadith is *ṣaḥeeḥ*. See Shaykh al-Albâni, *Ṣaḥeeḥ al-Jâmi' aṣ-Ṣagheer*, no. 7645. Recorded by Muslim.

[91] This hadith is *ṣaḥeeḥ*. See Shaykh al-Albâni, *Ṣaḥeeḥ Sunan Abi Dawood*, no. 1790. Recorded by Abu Dawood.

Shaykh Shaqrah said, "Whoever does any of these acts has committed a sin. He must repent and seek forgiveness. However, in the case of hunting, the pilgrim must expiate his act by a sacrifice made in addition to repenting and seeking forgiveness."

The recompense for killing game

Allah (ﷻ) says,

﴿يَٰٓأَيُّهَا ٱلَّذِينَ ءَامَنُواْ لَا تَقۡتُلُواْ ٱلصَّيۡدَ وَأَنتُمۡ حُرُمٞۚ وَمَن قَتَلَهُۥ مِنكُم مُّتَعَمِّدٗا فَجَزَآءٞ
مِّثۡلُ مَا قَتَلَ مِنَ ٱلنَّعَمِ يَحۡكُمُ بِهِۦ ذَوَا عَدۡلٖ مِّنكُمۡ هَدۡيَۢا بَٰلِغَ ٱلۡكَعۡبَةِ أَوۡ كَفَّٰرَةٞ طَعَامُ
مَسَٰكِينَ أَوۡ عَدۡلُ ذَٰلِكَ صِيَامٗا لِّيَذُوقَ وَبَالَ أَمۡرِهِۦۗ عَفَا ٱللَّهُ عَمَّا سَلَفَۚ وَمَنۡ عَادَ
فَيَنتَقِمُ ٱللَّهُ مِنۡهُۚ وَٱللَّهُ عَزِيزٞ ذُو ٱنتِقَامٍ ٩٥﴾ (سورة المائدة: ٩٥)

﴾O' you who believe! Do not kill game while you are in the inviolable state [of Ḥajj or 'Umrah]; and whosoever of you kills it intentionally, the penalty is an offering, brought to the Ka'bah, of an eatable animal [i.e. sheep, goat, cow, etc.] equivalent to the one he killed, as adjudged by two just men among you; or, for expiation, he should feed poor persons, or an equivalent in fasting, that he may taste the heaviness of his deed. Allah has forgiven what is past, but whosoever commits it again, Allah will take retribution from him. And Allah is All-Mighty, All-Able of Retribution.﴿ *(Qur'an 5: 95)*

In his commentary to the Qur'an, Ibn Katheer (vol. 2, p. 98) wrote,

> This is a prohibition from Him of hunting by the pilgrim in the inviolable state and forbiddance of taking part in such a deed. This prohibition includes edible animals, mature or otherwise. As for non-edible land animals, ash-Shafi'ee viewed that it is permissible for the pilgrim to kill them. The majority, though, say that such killing is also prohibited. The only exception to this ruling is that

which is confirmed in the two *Ṣaḥeeḥs* from az-Zuhri on the authority of 'Urwah from 'Â'ishah who said that the Messenger of Allah (ﷺ) had said, "Five obnoxious animals may be killed while one is in the inviolable state or not: crows, kites, scorpions, mice and rabid dogs."[92] The majority of the scholars are of the view that the one who intentionally violates this prohibition and the one who does so out of forgetfulness are the same with respect to the obligatory of expiation. Az-Zuhri said, "The Qur'an indicates the one who does it intentionally while the Sunnah indicates the one who does it out of forgetfulness." That is, the Qur'an refers to the sinfulness and obligation of expiation for the one who does the act intentionally in the words, ﴾Allah has forgiven what is past, but whosoever commits it again, Allah will take retribution from him﴿. The Sunnah, in the rulings of the Prophet (ﷺ) as well as those of his Companions, show that this applies to one who does the act mistakenly as well. Furthermore, hunting game (in such a state) is a type of waste and, regardless of whether one causes waste intentionally or unintentionally, one is liable for such waste. However, the one who acted intentionally is sinful while the one who acted mistakenly is not.

(In the verse,) Allah also says, ﴾The penalty is an offering of an eatable animal [i.e. sheep, goat, cow, etc.] equivalent to the one he killed,﴿ which supports Mâlik's, ash-Shâfi'ee's, Aḥmad's and the majority's view that it is obligatory to sacrifice a domesticated animal which is equivalent to the one hunted. If there is no equivalent to the hunted animal, then Ibn 'Abbâs stated that one should give its price (in charity), given in Makkah. Al-Bayhaqi recorded that.[93]

---

[92] Recorded by Bukhari, Muslim and Tirmidhi.

[93] Ibn Katheer, *Tafseer al-Qurân al-'A̲dheem*, vol. 2, p. 99. 'Ikrimah said, "Marwân asked Ibn 'Abbâs while we were at Wâd al-Azraq, 'What is your=

Examples of the Prophet's and his Companions ruling on equivalent animals

Jâbir said, "I asked the Messenger of Allah (ﷺ) about hyenas. He said, 'It is hunted game. One ram should be sacrificed if it is hunted while one is in the inviolable state.' "[94] Jâbir also stated, " 'Umar ibn al-Khaṭṭâb judged concerning a hyena that one must sacrifice a ram. Concerning a deer, one must sacrifice a goat. Concerning a hare, one must sacrifice a well-fed young female goat. Concerning a jerboa, one must sacrifice a four month old female goat."[95]

Ibn 'Abbâs said about the pigeons of the sacred sanctuaries that both the pilgrim and the non-pilgrim must sacrifice one sheep for each pigeon.[96]

Ibn Katheer stated (vol. 2, p. 100), about Allah's words, ﴿Brought to the Ka'bah,﴾ it should be brought to the Ka'bah, meaning it should reach the sacred locale and sacrificed there, with its meat distributed among the poor of the sacred locale. This is agreed upon concerning this issue.

Ibn Katheer continued about Allah's words, ﴿or, for expiation, he should feed poor persons, or an equivalent in fasting,﴾ stating that if the pilgrim cannot find an animal to sacrifice, if there is no

---

=opinion if we hunt and do we find an equivalent of livestock?' He replied, 'See what its price is and give in charity to the poor people of the inhabitants of Makkah.' "

94 This hadith is *ṣaḥeeḥ*. See Shaykh al-Albâni, *Ṣaḥeeḥ Sunan Abi Dawood*, no. 3226. Recorded by Abu Dawood.

95 This hadith is *ṣaḥeeḥ*. See Shaykh al-Albâni, *I'rwâ' al-Ghaleel*, no. 1051. Recorded by Mâlik and al-Bayhaqi.

96 Its chain is *ṣaḥeeḥ*. See Shaykh al-Albâni, *I'rwâ' al-Ghaleel*, no. 1056. Recorded by al-Bayhaqi.

equivalent to the animal in sacrifice or if one argues that the ruling here is one of option among sacrificing an animal, feeding poor people or fasting — because of the use of the word "or" and its apparent meaning — then the person can estimate the value of the animal killed or of a similar animal and use that money to buy food and give that food in charity. He should give every poor person a *mudd* (two hands cupped together's amount of food) to each poor person. If he is not able to do that or, again, if one concludes that the ruling is one of option between the three, he can fast one day for each poor person he would have fed.

Expiation for Sexual Intercourse during the Ḥajj

If a person has sexual intercourse before the first act of exiting from the inviolable state, his Ḥajj has been voided, as described earlier, and he must sacrifice a camel. If he has intercourse after the first exiting from the inviolable state but before the second such exiting, he must sacrifice a sheep and his Ḥajj has not been voided. Ibn 'Abbâs was asked about a man who had intercourse with his wife in Mina before making the *ifâḍah* circumambulation and he said that the man must sacrifice a camel.[97]

'Amr ibn Shu'ayb narrated from his father who said, "A man came to 'Abdullâh ibn 'Amr and asked him about a pilgrim who had intercourse with his wife. He pointed him to 'Abdullâh[98] ibn 'Umar. He said, 'Go to him and ask him.' The person did not know him so I went with him and he asked Ibn 'Umar who said, 'Your Ḥajj has been

---

[97] This report is *ṣaḥeeḥ* as a narration from the Companion Ibn 'Abbâs. See Shaykh al-Albâni, *I'rwâ' al-Ghaleel*, no. 1044. Recorded by al-Bayhaqi.

[98] [The text actually reads 'Ubaydullâh ibn 'Umar. However, the report in al-Bayhaqi and al-Ḥâkim make it clear that it is the Companion 'Abdullâh ibn 'Umar.] - Translator

voided.' The man said, 'What shall I do?' He said, 'Go with the people and do what they do. However, if you are alive next year, make Ḥajj and offer a sacrifice.' He then went back to 'Abdullâh ibn 'Amr while I was with him and informed him of this statement. 'Abdullâh then said, 'Go to Ibn 'Abbâs and ask him as well.' So I went with him to Ibn 'Abbâs and he asked him about the issue. Ibn 'Abbâs said the same as Ibn 'Umar. He went back to 'Abdullâh ibn 'Amr while I was with him and informed him of what Ibn 'Abbâs had said. Then he said (to 'Abdullâh), 'What is your opinion?' He replied, 'I say the same as what those two said.' "[99]

Sa'eed ibn Jubayr stated that a man and his wife together entered the inviolable state for the 'Umrah. They completed all of the rites except for cutting the hair. He had sexual relations with her before she cut her hair. He asked Ibn 'Abbâs about it and said, "She was the lustful one." Ibn 'Abbâs was told that she was listening and therefore he became shy to answer. She said, "Shall you not inform me." So he said to her, "You must sacrifice an animal." She said, "What animal?" He said, "Sacrifice a camel, cow or sheep." She said, "Which is preferred?" He said, "A camel."[100]

If a person cannot find or acquire a camel or sheep, he is to fast three days during the time of Ḥajj and seven upon returning home, as Allah has said:

﴿... فَمَن تَمَتَّعَ بِٱلْعُمْرَةِ إِلَى ٱلْحَجِّ فَمَا ٱسْتَيْسَرَ مِنَ ٱلْهَدْيِ فَمَن لَّمْ يَجِدْ فَصِيَامُ ثَلَٰثَةِ أَيَّامٍ فِى ٱلْحَجِّ وَسَبْعَةٍ إِذَا رَجَعْتُمْ ... ﴿١٩٦﴾﴾ (سورة البَقَـرَة: ١٩٦)

---

[99] This hadith is *ṣaḥeeḥ*. See Shaykh al-Albâni, *I'rwâ' al-Ghaleel*, vol. 4, p. 234. Recorded by al-Bayhaqi.

[100] This hadith is *ṣaḥeeḥ*. See Shaykh al-Albâni, *I'rwâ' al-Ghaleel*, vol. 4, p. 233. Recorded by al-Bayhaqi.

﴾... Whoever performs the 'Umrah in the months of Ḥajj, before [performing] the Ḥajj, he must slaughter a sacrificial animal such as he can afford, but if he cannot afford it, he should observe a fast of three days during the Ḥajj and seven days after his return [to his home]...﴿ *(Qur'an 2: 196)*

It is preferred to fast those three days before the Day Arafah. If one does not do so, then it is permissible to fast them during the Days of *Tashreeq*. Ibn 'Umar and 'Â'ishah (may Allah be pleased with them) both said, "No one is exempted to fast during the Days of *Tashreeq* except for those who cannot find an animal to sacrifice."[101]

Note: "On this point, men and women are exactly equal. However, if the woman was coerced, she does not have to sacrifice an animal and her Ḥajj is valid, in contrast to her husband who had sexual intercourse with her."[102] Sa'eed ibn Jubayr said that a man who had sexual intercourse with his wife came to Ibn 'Abbâs. Ibn 'Abbâs told him, "If she was going along with you, then each of you must sacrifice a quality, excellent camel. If she was assisting you, then you alone must sacrifice a quality, excellent camel."[103]

The Types of Sacrifices Related to the Ḥajj[104]

1. The sacrifice related to *at-tamattu'* and *al-qirân*

This is the sacrifice that is obligated upon the pilgrim when he makes the intention for 'Umrah done in conjunction with Ḥajj (*at-*

---

[101] This hadith is *ṣaḥeeḥ*. See Shaykh al-Albâni, *I'rwâ' al-Ghaleel*, no. 1042. Recorded by Bukhari.

[102] *Irshâd as-Sâri*.

[103] This hadith is *ṣaḥeeḥ*. See Shaykh al-Albâni, *I'rwâ' al-Ghaleel*, no. 1044. Recorded by al-Bayhaqi.

[104] Taken from *Irshâd as-Sâri*, with the relevant Qur'anic verses inserted in the text.

tamattu') or one who makes the intention for 'Umrah joined with the Ḥajj (*al-qirân*). Concerning this, Allah (ﷻ) says: ﴾... Whoever performs the 'Umrah in the months of Ḥajj, before [performing] the Ḥajj [i.e. *Ḥajj at-Tamattu'* and *al-Qirân*] must slaughter a sacrificial animal such as he can afford, but if he cannot afford it, he should observe a fast of three days during the Ḥajj and seven days after his return [to his home]...﴿ *(Qur'an 2: 196)*

2. The sacrifice as a "ransom" (*fidyah*)

This is the sacrifice that is obligatory upon the pilgrim if he has to shave his hair due to a disease or some harm. This is based on Allah's statement:

﴿ ... فَمَن كَانَ مِنكُم مَّرِيضًا أَوْ بِهِۦٓ أَذًى مِّن رَّأْسِهِۦ فَفِدْيَةٌ مِّن صِيَامٍ أَوْ صَدَقَةٍ أَوْ نُسُكٍ ... ﴿١٩٦﴾ ﴾ (سورة البقـرة: ١٩٦)

﴾... And whoever of you is ill or has an ailment in his scalp [necessitating shaving], he must pay a *fidyah* [ransom] of either observing fast [for three days] or giving charity [by feeding six poor persons] or offering a sacrifice [of a sheep]...﴿ *(Qur'an 2: 196)*

3. The sacrifice as expiation

This is the sacrifice that must be made by one who hunts land game while a pilgrim. As for animals caught from the sea, there is no penalty in such a case. (This issued was discussed above.)

4. The sacrifice of the one who is not able to complete the rites of the Ḥajj due to illness, the presence of an enemy or anything of that nature, while the person had not made an exceptive condition for such cases while enter the inviolable state. In this case, Allah says:

﴿ ... فَإِنْ أُحْصِرْتُمْ فَمَا ٱسْتَيْسَرَ مِنَ ٱلْهَدْيِ ... ﴿١٩٦﴾ ﴾ (سورة البقـرة: ١٩٦)

﴾... But if you are prevented [from completing them], sacrifice a sacrificial animal [i.e., a sheep, a cow, or a camel, etc.] such as you can afford...﴿ *(Qur'an 2: 196)*

5. The sacrifice due to sexual intercourse

This is the sacrifice that the pilgrim must make if he has sexual intercourse during this Ḥajj, as was just discussed.

The 'Umrah

The 'Umrah is one of the greatest acts of worship and one of the most virtuous means of getting closer to Allah. By it, Allah raises His servant in rank and removes from him sins. The Prophet (ﷺ) encouraged its performance both by his words and his actions. He said, "One 'Umrah until the next 'Umrah is an expiation for what is between them."[105] The Prophet (ﷺ) also said, "Follow up the Ḥajj and 'Umrah (by performing them together) for they remove poverty and sins like the blacksmith's bellows removes impurities from iron, gold and silver."[106] The Prophet (ﷺ) himself performed the 'Umrah as did his Companions during his lifetime and after his death.[107]

The Essential Components of the 'Umrah

1. Entering the inviolable state, which is inclusive of the intention

The Prophet (ﷺ) said, "Verily, all actions are based on intention."[108]

---

[105] Recorded by Bukhari, Muslim, Tirmidhi, Ibn Mâjah and Nasâ'i.

[106] This hadith is *ṣaḥeeḥ*. See Shaykh al-Albâni, *Ṣaḥeeḥ al-Jâmi' aṣ-Ṣagheer*, no. 2899. Recorded by Tirmidhi and Nasâ'i.

[107] Cf., *Irshâd as-Sâri*.

[108] Recorded by Bukhari, Muslim, Tirmidhi, Ibn Mâjah and Nasâ'i.

2. and 3. The circumambulation of the House (*aṭ-ṭawâf*) and the circuits between aṣ-Ṣafâ and al-Marwâ (*as-sa'ee*)

Allah has said:

﴿... وَلْيَطَّوَّفُوا۟ بِٱلْبَيْتِ ٱلْعَتِيقِ ﴿٢٩﴾﴾ (سورة الحجّ: ٢٩)

﴿... [Then let them] circumambulate the Ancient House [the Ka'bah at Makkah].﴾ *(Qur'an 22: 29)*

Allah has also said:

﴿۞ إِنَّ ٱلصَّفَا وَٱلْمَرْوَةَ مِن شَعَآئِرِ ٱللَّهِ ... ﴿١٥٨﴾﴾ (سورة البقرة: ١٥٨)

﴿Verily! Aṣ-Ṣafâ and al-Marwah [two hills in Makkah] are of the Symbols of Allah...﴾ *(Qur'an 2: 158)*

Furthermore, the Prophet (ﷺ) said, "Perform the *sa'ee* for Allah has obligated the *sa'ee* upon you."[109]

4. Cutting or trimming one's hair

This is based on the hadith of Ibn 'Umar in which the Prophet (ﷺ) said, "Whoever of you does not have a sacrificial animal should circumambulate the House, (go between) aṣ-Ṣafâ and al-Marwah, trim his hair and exit the inviolable state."[110]

The Obligatory Parts of the 'Umrah

It is obligatory upon the one who intends to perform the 'Umrah to enter the inviolable state from one of the *meeqâts*, even if he were already within the confines of Makkah. The visitor inside

---

[109] This hadith is *ṣaḥeeḥ*. See Shaykh al-Albâni, *I'rwâ' al-Ghaleel*, no. 1072. Recorded by Aḥmad and al-Ḥâkim.

[110] Recorded by Bukhari, Muslim, Abu Dawood and Nasâ'i.

Makkah must go outside of the area and enter the inviolable state from a proper location, as can be seen in the Prophet (ﷺ) ordering 'Â'ishah to go to at-Tan'eem to enter the inviolable state there.[111]

The time for making 'Umrah

The 'Umrah may performed at any time during the year. However, it is most virtuous during Ramaḍân. The Prophet (ﷺ) said, "An 'Umrah during Ramaḍân is equivalent to a Ḥajj."[112]

The permissibility of performing it before performing the Ḥajj

'Ikrimah ibn Khâlid asked Ibn 'Umar about performing the 'Umrah before one has ever performed the Ḥajj and he replied that there is no harm in that. He further narrated that Ibn 'Umar said, "The Prophet (ﷺ) made 'Umrah before ever performing the Ḥajj."[113]

Making more than one 'Umrah on a visit[114]

The Prophet (ﷺ) performed four 'Umrahs in four years. In each of his visits, he did not perform more than one 'Umrah. Similarly, his Companions with him also did not perform more than one 'Umrah on each visit. It has not reached us that any of them ever performed two 'Umrahs in one visit, regardless of whether it was during the Prophet's lifetime or after his death. The only except to this was the case of 'Â'ishah (رضي الله عنها), when she had her menses during her Ḥajj with the Prophet. The Prophet told her brother 'Abdur-

---

[111] Recorded by Bukhari, Muslim, Abu Dawood, Tirmidhi and Ibn Mâjah.

[112] This hadith is *ṣaḥeeḥ*. See Shaykh al-Albâni, *Ṣaḥeeḥ al-Jâmi' aṣ-Ṣagheer*, no. 4097. Recorded by Tirmidhi and Ibn Mâjah.

[113] This hadith is *ṣaḥeeḥ*. See Shaykh al-Albâni, *Mukhtasar Ṣaḥeeḥ al-Bukhari*, no. 862. Recorded by Bukhari.

[114] Cf., *Irshâd as-Sâri*.

Raḥmân ibn Abu Bakr to take her to at-Tan'eem for her to enter the inviolable state there for the 'Umrah. However, this was because she thought that her 'Umrah that she performed with the Ḥajj had been voided. She cried due to that and the Messenger of Allah (ﷺ) allowed her to make the 'Umrah, in order to calm her.

This 'Umrah that 'Â'ishah performed was something specific for her. The evidence for that is that it is not known that any of the Companions, men or women, ever made 'Umrah from at-Tan'eem after their Ḥajj, as 'Â'ishah had done. If the Companions knew that what 'Â'ishah did was also sanctioned for them after the Ḥajj, this would have been widely reported. Ash-Shawkâni stated, "The Prophet (ﷺ) did not make 'Umrah going outside of Makkah to enter the inviolable state and then entering Makkah to make 'Umrah like what the people do today. Similarly, it is not affirmed from any of the Companions that they had done that."

It is also not confirmed from any of the Companions that they would repeat an 'Umrah after the Ḥajj. In fact, it is not affirmed that they would repeat the performance of the 'Umrah during any part of the year. They would come upon Makkah for 'Umrah as individual or in groups. They recognized that the 'Umrah is a visit for the purpose of circumambulating the House and making the circuits (*as-sa'ee*) between aṣ-Ṣafâ and al-Marwah. They also knew that circumambulating the House is definitely more virtuous than the *sa'ee*. Instead of busying themselves with going out to at-Tan'eem and doing the acts of a new 'Umrah, they would follow up their 'Umrah that they previously performed by circumambulating the House. It is obvious that in the time that one takes to go out to at-Tan'eem to prepare for a new 'Umrah one can perform hundreds of rounds about the House. Ṭâwoos said, "As for those who prepare for a new 'Umrah from at-Tan'eem, I do not know if they are going to be rewarded or punished." It was said to him, "Punished?" He replied,

"Because they are leaving the circumambulation of the House, going out such and such distance, returning back that same distance while they could have performed two hundred circumambulations. To circumambulate the house is obviously preferred to walking with no purpose."

The view that it is not sanctioned to repeat 'Umrahs in this fashion is supported by the actions of the Prophet (ﷺ) and the actions of the Companions. Our Prophet (ﷺ) has obliged us to follow his Sunnah and the Sunnah of his Successors after him. He said, "So stick to my Sunnah and the Sunnah of the right-principled and rightly-guided Successors. Bite onto that with your molar teeth."[115]

Visiting Illustrious Madeenah[116]

The Virtues of Madeenah

Jâbir ibn Samurah narrated that the Messenger of Allah (ﷺ) said, "Verily, Allah named Madeenah Ṭâbbah (meaning, 'good, pure')."[117] Abu Hurayrah narrated that he heard the Messenger of Allah (ﷺ) say, "Madeenah is like a bellows which eliminates impurities. The Hour will not occur until Madeenah banishes its evil ones like a bellows eliminating the impurities of iron."[118]

---

[115] [Recorded, with slightly different wordings, by Aḥmad, Abu Dawood, Tirmidhi, Ibn Ḥibbân and others. According to Ibn Muhammad, Shaykh al-Albâni, al-Bazzâr, Tirmidhi, al-Ḥâkim, Ibn 'Abdul Barr, Abu Nu'aym and numerous others, this is an authentic hadith.] - Translator

[116] Cf., *Irshâd as-Sâri*.

[117] This hadith is *ṣaḥeeḥ*. See Shaykh al-Albâni, *Ṣaḥeeḥ al-Jâmi' aṣ-Ṣagheer*, no. 1775. Recorded by Muslim.

[118] This hadith is *ṣaḥeeḥ*. See Shaykh al-Albâni, *Mukhtasar Ṣaḥeeḥ Muslim*,=

The Virtues of Its Mosque and Prayers Therein

Abu Hurayrah narrated from the Prophet (ﷺ), "Do not undertake a journey (for religious purposes) except to three mosques: This mosque of mine, the *Masjid al-Ḥarâm* (in Makkah) and *Masjid al-'Aqsa* (in Jerusalem)."[119] He also narrated that the Prophet (ﷺ) said, "A prayer in this mosque of mine is better than a thousand prayers in other mosques, except for the *Masjid al-Ḥarâm* (in Makkah)."[120]

'Abdullâh ibn Zayd narrated that the Messenger of Allah (ﷺ) said, "What is between my house and my pulpit (*minbar*) is a garden from the gardens of Paradise."[121]

Etiquette of Visiting the Noble Mosque and Grave

The virtues that are particular to the Prophet's mosque, the *Masjid al-Ḥarâm* (in Makkah) and the *Masjid al-'Aqsa* (in Jerusalem) and the superiority of the prayers said in those mosques are honours bestowed by Allah upon these three mosques. Whoever goes to those three mosques goes hoping for the special reward and in response to the call from the Prophet (ﷺ) to undertake journeys to these three mosques and to visit them.

In reality, there is no special etiquette for these three mosques as compared to any other mosque. However, some people confuse some issues concerning the Prophet's Mosque and specific etiquette for it. This confusion, though, would not have occurred if it were not for the fact that the Noble Grave is within the confines of the mosque.

=no. 782. Recorded by Muslim.

[119] Recorded by Bukhari, Muslim, Abu Dawood and Nasâ'i.

[120] Recorded by Bukhari, Muslim, Tirmidhi and Nasâ'i.

[121] Recorded by Bukhari, Muslim and Nasâ'i.

So that the Muslim clearly understands what his actions should be when he comes to Madeenah and wants to visit the Mosque of the Prophet, we shall present the etiquette of visiting that mosque:

1. When the person enters the mosque, he should enter with his right foot and say,

بِسْمِ اللَّهِ وَالسَّلامُ عَلَى رَسُولِ اللَّهِ اللَّهُمَّ اغْفِرْ لِي ذُنُوبِي وَافْتَحْ لِي أَبْوَابَ رَحْمَتِكَ

"In the name of Allah and peace be upon the Messenger of Allah. O' Allah forgive me my sins and open for me the doors of Your Mercy."[122] Or, he should say,

أَعُوذُ بِاللَّهِ الْعَظِيمِ وَبِوَجْهِهِ الْكَرِيمِ وَسُلْطَانِهِ الْقَدِيمِ مِنَ الشَّيْطَانِ الرَّجِيمِ

"I seek refuge in Allah, the Great, and in His Noble Face and His ancient rule, from the accursed Satan."[123]

2. Then he should pray a two-*rak'ah* prayer of "greeting the mosque" before he sits.

3. He must be careful to avoid facing the direction of the Noble Grave while praying or facing it while supplicating.

4. Then he goes to the Noble Grave to convey the salutations to the Prophet (ﷺ). He must avoid putting his hand on his chest, bowing his head or doing any act of humility that Allah alone deserves. He must avoid seeking help in the Prophet (ﷺ) as well. He should greet the Prophet (ﷺ) with the words and expressions that the Prophet (ﷺ) used to use when greeting the inhabitants of al-Baqee' cemetery.

---

[122] This hadith is *ṣaḥeeḥ*. See Shaykh al-Albâni, *Ṣaḥeeḥ Sunan Ibn Mâjah*, no. 625. Recorded by Ibn Mâjah and Tirmidhi.

[123] This hadith is *ṣaḥeeḥ*. See Shaykh al-Albâni, *Ṣaḥeeḥ Sunan Abi Dawood*, no. 441. Recorded by Abu Dawood.

Various phrases have been authentically reported from the Prophet, including,

السَّلامُ عَلَى أَهْلِ الدِّيَارِ مِنَ الْمُؤْمِنِينَ وَالْمُسْلِمِينَ وَيَرْحَمُ اللَّهُ الْمُسْتَقْدِمِينَ مِنَّا وَالْمُسْتَأْخِرِينَ وَإِنَّا إِنْ شَاءَ اللَّهُ بِكُمْ لَلاحِقُونَ

"Peace be upon the inhabitants of these places from the believers and the Muslims. May Allah have mercy on those who preceded us and those who will come after. Allah willing, we shall be joining you."[124] One should also greet the Prophet's two Companions, Abu Bakr and 'Umar (who are also buried there) with the same expressions.

5. It is not proper etiquette to raise one's voice in the mosque or at the grave of the Prophet (ﷺ). Etiquette with respect to the Prophet (ﷺ) is the same while he is dead as it was when he was alive.

6. The person should try to pray in the first rows of the congregation, as there are great virtues and rewards in that.

7. His desire to pray in the "garden" (between what was the Prophet's house and his pulpit) should not make him stay back from praying in the first rows. There is no special merit in praying in the "garden" that distinguishes it from any other prayer.

8. It is not from the Sunnah to try to pray forty consecutive prayers in the Prophet's mosque. This practice is based on a popular hadith which states, "Whoever prays forty prayers in my mosque without missing a prayer will have written for him freedom from the Fire, rescue from the punishment and freedom from hypocrisy."[125] This hadith is weak and not authentic.

---

[124] This hadith is *ṣaḥeeḥ*. See Shaykh al-Albâni, *Ṣaḥeeḥ al-Jâmi'*, no. 4421, *al-Janâ'iz*, p. 183. Recorded by Muslim and Nasâ'i.

[125] Shaykh al-Albâni has discussed this in *Silsilat al-Aḥâdeeth aḍ-Ḍa'eefah*, no. 364. He stated that it is recorded by Aḥmad and aṭ-Ṭabarâni in *al-*=

9. It is not sanctioned to continually go back to the Prophet's grave to greet him. In reality, the salutations for the Prophet (ﷺ) reach him wherever the person may be, even if he is at the end of the earth. Such a person and a person standing in front of the grave are the same with respect to receiving rewards for greeting and praying for the Prophet (ﷺ).

10. When the person leaves the mosque, he should not leave by walking backwards (as some people do in order not to turn their backs to the Prophet's grave). Instead, he should step first with his left foot and say,

بِسْمِ اللَّهِ وَالسَّلَامُ عَلَى رَسُولِ اللَّهِ اللَّهُمَّ اغْفِرْ لِي ذُنُوبِي وَافْتَحْ لِي أَبْوَابَ فَضْلِكَ

"In the name of Allah and peace be upon the Messenger of Allah. O' Allah forgive me my sins and open for me the doors of Your Bounty."[126]

Masjid Qubâ'

It is Sunnah for one who comes to Madeenah to visit Masjid Qubâ' and pray there, following the example set by the Messenger of Allah (ﷺ) as "he would regularly visit it, walking or riding. He would visit it on Saturdays and pray two *rak'ahs* therein."[127] The

=*Mu'jam al-Awsaṭ*. In *Zawâ'id al-Mu'jamain* it states that it is from the chain of 'Abdur-Raḥmân ibn Abu ar-Rijâl from Nubayt ibn 'Amr from Anas ibn Mâlik from the Prophet. Aṭ-Ṭabarâni said, "No one but Nubayt has narrated it from Anas and 'Abdur-Raḥmân is the only one who narrated it from Nubayt." Shaykh al-Albâni said, "Its chain is weak. This man Nubait is not known except in this hadith."

[126] This hadith is *ṣaḥeeḥ*. See Shaykh al-Albâni, *Ṣaḥeeḥ Sunan Ibn Mâjah*, no. 625. Recorded by Ibn Mâjah and Tirmidhi.

[127] Recorded by Bukhari, Muslim, Abu Dawood and Nasâ'i.

Prophet (ﷺ) said, "Whoever purifies himself in his house and then goes to Masjid Qubâ' and prayers a prayer therein will have for him like the reward for an 'Umrah."[128]

Al-Baqee' cemetery and Uḥud mountain

Al-Baqee' is the Muslims' cemetery in Madeenah. Many of the Companions are buried there. In fact, to this day, people continue to be buried there. Many come to Madeenah with the hopes of dying there and being buried in that cemetery.

As for Uḥud, [the Prophet (ﷺ) said,] "Uḥud is a mountain which loves us and we love it."[129] Seventy-some odd Companions were buried in this mountain as martyrs. They are the martyrs of the battle that took place in this mountains heart and which has been named after it, the Battle of Uḥud.

If someone comes to Madeenah and wishes to visit the Baqee' Cemetery or the martyrs of Uḥud, there is no prohibition concerning that. The Messenger of Allah (ﷺ) used to forbade visits to graves and then he permitted them, so that one may be reminded of the Hereafter and take a lesson from what has occurred to one's predecessors. However, one must refrain from seeking blessings from those graves, seeking help for them inhabitants, seeking intercession from them with respect to the living or seeking a means of approaching the Lord of all humans through them.

It is not sanctioned for a visitor to Uḥud to intend to visit what is called the "place of prayer of the Prophet" at the foot of the mountain and to pray there. Nor is it sanctioned to climb Uḥud Mountain as a means of getting blessings or the climb "the mountain

---

[128] This hadith is *ṣaḥeeḥ*. See Shaykh al-Albâni, *Ṣaḥeeḥ Sunan Ibn Mâjah*, no. 1160. Recorded by Ibn Mâjah.

[129] Recorded by Bukhari and Muslim.

of the archers" as a means of following in the footsteps of the Companions. Nor are any other actions sanctioned or recommended, other than greeting and making supplications for the martyrs. In fact, all such deeds which are practiced are nothing but innovations that are proscribed. On this point, 'Umar said, "The people before you were destroyed by their (literal) following in the footsteps of their prophets." 'Umar's words should be, for us, both convincing and conclusive.

Other visited places

There are other places in Madeenah which are known as places of visitation, such as the seven mosques close to the battle site of the Battle of Khandaq, the mosque that has markings for both *qiblahs*, some wells, Masjid al-Ghumâmah and mosques which are ascribed to Abu Bakr, 'Umar and 'Â'ishah. There is no special sanction for specifically visiting any of these places. The visitor should not think that he is getting some special blessings for visiting these places. In fact, following in the actual footsteps of the prophets and righteous people was one of the causes for the destruction of the peoples before us. It is not proper for Muslims to go against the guidance of their Prophet Muhammad (ﷺ) or of his Companions. All good is in following his and their guidance and all evil is found in contradicting his and their guidance.

Two important points

<u>Number One</u>:

Many pilgrims seek to spend more days in Madeenah than they do in Makkah, although the prayer in *al-Masjid al-Ḥarâm* in Makkah is equivalent to one hundred thousand prayers in another mosque while prayers said in the Prophet's Mosque in Madeenah are equivalent to only one thousand prayers said in any other mosque.

The big difference in the virtue between the prayers said in the mosque in Makkah and those said in the mosque of Madeenah should convince those pilgrims to stay longer in Makkah than in Madeenah.

Number Two:

Many of the pilgrims believe that visiting the Prophet's Mosque in Madeenah is one of the rites of the pilgrimage. Therefore, they eagerly seek to visit it like they do the rites of the Ḥajj, to the point that if a person person's the Ḥajj but does not visit Madeenah, his Ḥajj is considered deficient. On this point, they quote a number of fabricated hadith, such as, "Whoever makes Ḥajj and does not visit me has dishonoured me." The reality is different from what these people think. Visiting the Prophet's Mosque is a Sunnah that was established by the Prophet's praying therein. However, there is no relationship between visiting it and the Ḥajj. The validity of the Ḥajj is not affected in any way by not visiting the Prophet's Mosque. Nor is the completeness or excellence of the Ḥajj affected by that. This is because visiting the Prophet's Mosque is not one of the rites of the Ḥajj. Instead, it is sanctioned as a separate and distinct act.

Chapter Seven — Marriage

Marriage is one of the most emphasized practices (*Sunan*) of the messengers. Allah (ﷻ) has said:

﴿وَلَقَدْ أَرْسَلْنَا رُسُلًا مِّن قَبْلِكَ وَجَعَلْنَا لَهُمْ أَزْوَاجًا وَذُرِّيَّةً ... ﴿٣٨﴾﴾

(سورة الرّعد: ٣٨)

﴿And indeed We sent Messengers before you [O' Muhammad], and made for them wives and offspring...﴾ *(Qur'an 13: 38)*

It is disliked to leave this practice without a valid excuse. Anas ibn Mâlik narrated that a group of three people came to the houses of the wives of the Prophet (ﷺ) and asked about his acts of worship. When they were told of his actions, it was as if they considered them little. They then said, "Where are we with respect to the Prophet (ﷺ)? Verily, Allah has forgiven for him his past and later sins." One of them then said, "As for me, I shall pray the whole night long." Another said, "I shall fast continuously without breaking my fast." The third said, "I shall remain away from women and will never marry." The Prophet (ﷺ) then came and said, "By Allah, I am most fearful of Allah and most conscious of Him. However, I fast and break my fast, pray and sleep and I marry women. Whoever turns away from my way of life is not from me."[1]

If a person fears that he will commit illegal sexual intercourse and he has the ability to marry, then it becomes obligatory upon him

---

[1] Recorded by Bukhari (and this is his wording), Muslim and Nasâ'i.

to marry. "This is because illegal sexual intercourse is forbidden, as is that which leads to it and which is a precursor to it. If someone fears that he will fall into such an act, he must do what he can to remove it from him. If such an impulse cannot be repelled except by marriage, then marriage is obligatory upon him."[2]

If one is not able to marry, which desiring such, he should then fast. Ibn Mas'ood narrated that the Prophet (ﷺ) said to them, "O' young men, whoever of you has the ability should wed, for it lowers the gaze and protects the private parts. Whoever does not have that ability should fast and that will be his shield."[3]

What Woman is Best to Marry?

If someone wants to get married, he should seek a woman who has the following qualities:

1. She should be religious

Abu Hurayrah narrated that the Prophet (ﷺ) said, "A woman is married for (one of) four reasons: her wealth, her lineage, her beauty or her religiousness. So obtain the one who is religious and may your hands be filled with dust (that is, may you then prosper)."[4]

2. She should be virgin, unless there is some benefit in marrying a non-virgin, mature woman

This principle is based on the hadith of Jâbir who narrated: "I married a woman during the time of the Messenger of Allah (ﷺ). I met the Prophet (ﷺ) and he said, 'O' Jâbir, did you get married?' I

---

[2] Ash-Shawkâni, *as-Sail al-Jarâr*, vol. 2, p. 243.

[3] Recorded by Bukhari, Muslim, Abu Dawood, Tirmidhi, Nasâ'i and Ibn Mâjah.

[4] Recorded by Bukhari, Muslim, Abu Dawood, Ibn Mâjah and Nasâ'i.

replied, 'Yes.' He said, 'A virgin or a non-virgin woman?' I said, 'A non-virgin woman.' He said, 'Why not a virgin whom you could have sported with and she would have sported with you?' I said, 'I have (younger) sisters and I feared that she would come between me and them.' He then said, 'Fine then. A woman is married because of her religiousness, wealth or beauty. So go for the one who is religious and may your hands be filled with dust (that is, may you then prosper).' "[5]

3. She should be child-bearing

Anas narrated that the Prophet (ﷺ) said, "Marry (those women who are) child-bearing and loving for I shall boast about your numbers among the nations (on the Day of Judgment)."[6]

What Man is Best to Marry?

In the same way that men should seek women like those we just described, the guardian of the woman should also seek a pious man to marry the woman he has authority over. Abu Ḥâtim al-Mazani narrated that the Messenger of Allah (ﷺ) said, "If someone whose religion and character you are pleased with comes to you (to marry your daughter or ward), then marry (her off to) him. If you do not do so, there will be commotion on the earth and widespread evil."[7]

There is nothing wrong with a person offering his daughter or sister to a virtuous person. Ibn 'Umar narrated that when Ḥafṣah bint

---

[5] Recorded by Muslim, and this is his wording. Without the last sentence, it is also recorded by Bukhari, Abu Dawood, Tirmidhi, Ibn Mâjah and Nasâ'i.

[6] This hadith is *ṣaḥeeḥ*. See Shaykh al-Albâni, *Ṣaḥeeḥ al-Jâmi' aṣ-Ṣagheer*, no. 2940 and *I'rwâ' al-Ghaleel*, no. 1784. Recorded by Abu Dawood and Nasâ'i.

[7] This hadith is *ṣaḥeeḥ*. See Shaykh al-Albâni, *Ṣaḥeeḥ Sunan Tirmidhi*, no. 866. Recorded by Tirmidhi.

'Umar (ﷺ) was widowed by the death of Khunays ibn Ḥudhâfah al-Sahmi, one of the Companions of the Messenger of Allah (ﷺ), who died in Madeenah, 'Umar ibn al-Khaṭṭâb (ﷺ) said, "I came to 'Uthmân ibn 'Affân (ﷺ) and offered him Ḥafṣah." He said, "I will look into the matter." After some nights he came to him and said, "I decided that I will not get married during these days." 'Umar said, "I then met Abu Bakr and said, 'If you wish, I will marry you to Ḥafṣah bint 'Umar.'" Abu Bakr (ﷺ) remained silent and did not respond at all. I was more upset with him than I was with 'Uthmân. After some nights, the Messenger of Allah (ﷺ) proposed to her and I married her off to him. Abu Bakr then met me, "Perhaps you were upset with me when you offered Ḥafṣah to me and I did not respond at all?" 'Umar said, "Yes, indeed." Abu Bakr then said, "Nothing prevented me from responding to what you offered me except that I knew that the Messenger of Allah (ﷺ) had mentioned her. I though was not about to spread the Messenger of Allah's secret. If the Messenger of Allah (ﷺ) did not marry her, I would have done so."[8]

Looking at the proposed spouse

If someone is considering proposing to a woman, it is sanctioned for him to look at her before he proposes to her. Muhammad ibn Maslamah said, "I proposed to a woman, so I started to conceal myself from her until I saw her in her date palms." It was said to him, "You do that while you are a Companion of the Messenger of Allah (ﷺ)?" He replied, "I heard the Messenger of Allah (ﷺ) say, 'If Allah puts into the heart of a man the idea of proposing to a woman, there is no harm if he takes a look at her.'"[9]

---

[8] This hadith is *ṣaḥeeḥ*. See Shaykh al-Albâni, *Ṣaḥeeḥ Sunan Nasâ'i*, no. 3047. Recorded by Bukhari and Nasâ'i.

[9] This hadith is *ṣaḥeeḥ*. See Shaykh al-Albâni, *Ṣaḥeeḥ Sunan Ibn Mâjah*, no. 1510. Recorded by Ibn Mâjah.

Al-Mugheerah ibn Shu'bah said, "I came to the Prophet (ﷺ) and mentioned to him a woman that I had proposed to. He said, 'Go and look at her as this is more likely to produce affection between the two of you.'"[10]

The Proposal

The proposal is proposal for marriage given to a woman through the means that are well-known among the people. If thc othcr party agrees, this is simply a promise to marry and nothing else. The fiancé and fiancée have no further special relation and there are still considered as not related to each other until they finally do wed.

It does not permissible for a Muslim to make a marriage proposal against that of his brother. Ibn 'Umar said, "The Prophet (ﷺ) forbade selling against one another and making a marriage proposal against one's brother's proposal until he gives up that proposal or gives the proposer permission to do so."[11]

It is not permissible to proposed to a woman who is experiencing a revocable divorce. It is also not allowed to make an explicit statement of proposal to a woman who is experiencing an irrevocable divorce or is in her waiting period after become widowed. However, in these two latter cases, one may make an indirect statement alluding to a proposal. Allah has said:

﴿وَلَا جُنَاحَ عَلَيْكُمْ فِيمَا عَرَّضْتُم بِهِۦ مِنْ خِطْبَةِ ٱلنِّسَآءِ أَوْ أَكْنَنتُمْ فِىٓ أَنفُسِكُمْ ۚ عَلِمَ ٱللَّهُ أَنَّكُمْ سَتَذْكُرُونَهُنَّ وَلَٰكِن لَّا تُوَاعِدُوهُنَّ سِرًّا إِلَّآ أَن تَقُولُوا۟

[10] This hadith is *ṣaḥeeḥ*. See Shaykh al-Albâni, *Ṣaḥeeḥ Sunan Tirmidhi*, no. 868. Recorded by Nasâ'i and Tirmidhi.

[11] This hadith is *ṣaḥeeḥ*. See Shaykh al-Albâni, *Ṣaḥeeḥ Sunan Nasâ'i*, no. 3037. Recorded by Bukhari and Nasâ'i.

قَوۡلٗا مَّعۡرُوفٗاۚ ... ﴿٢٣٥﴾ (سورة البقرة: ٢٣٥)

﴾And there is no sin on you if you make a hint of betrothal or conceal it in yourself, Allah knows that you will remember them, but do not make a promise of contract with them in secret except that you speak an honourable saying...﴿ *(Qur'an 2: 235)*

The Marriage Contract

There are two essential components to the marriage contract: The offer and the acceptance.

In addition, there are some conditions that must be met in order for the contract to be sound. These are the following:

1. The permission of the guardian

'Â'ishah narrated that the Messenger of Allah (ﷺ) said, "If any woman marries without the permission of her guardian, then her marriage is void, then her marriage is void, then her marriage is void. If he has intercourse with her, then she is deserving of the dower that makes her permissible for him. If there is a dispute, then the ruler is the guardian of one who does not have a guardian."[12]

2. The presence of witnesses

'Â'ishah narrated that the Messenger of Allah (ﷺ) said, "There is no marriage except with a guardian and two reputable witnesses."[13]

---

[12] This hadith is *ṣaḥeeḥ*. See Shaykh al-Albâni, *Ṣaḥeeḥ Sunan Ibn Mâjah*, no. 1524. Recorded by Ibn Mâjah, and this is his wording, while Abu Dawood and Tirmidhi have something similar.

[13] This hadith is *ṣaḥeeḥ*. See Shaykh al-Albâni, *Ṣaḥeeḥ al-Jâmi' aṣ-Ṣagheer*, no. 7557. Recorded by al-Bayhaqi and Ibn Ḥibbân.

The obligation of getting the woman's approval before the marriage

Although there is no marriage without a guardian, it is obligatory upon the guardian to obtain the woman's approval before the marriage. It is not allowed for him to compel the woman to marry if she is not pleased with it. If he concludes a marriage contract that she is not pleased, she has the right to annul the contract. Abu Hurayrah narrated that the Prophet (ﷺ) said, "The non-virgin is not to be married until she requests it. And the virgin is not to be married without her consent." They said, "How is her consent (to be known)." He said, "If she remains silent."[14]

Khansâ' bint Khidâm al-Anṣâriyah said that her father had married her while she was a non-virgin and she disapproved of the marriage. She went to the Prophet (ﷺ) and he annulled her marriage.[15]

Ibn 'Abbâs narrated that a virgin young lady came to the Prophet (ﷺ) and mentioned to him that her father had married her off while she disliked it. The Prophet (ﷺ) then gave her the option (to annul the marriage or remain in the marriage)."[16]

The speech for the wedding ceremony

It is recommended that there be a speech when the contract is made. This speech is known as *khuṭbah al-ḥâjah* and its wording is the following:

---

[14] Recorded by Bukhari, Muslim, Abu Dawood, Tirmidhi, Ibn Mâjah and Nasâ'i.

[15] This hadith is *ṣaḥeeḥ*. See Shaykh al-Albâni, *I'rwâ' al-Ghaleel*, no. 183. Recorded by Bukhari, Abu Dawood, Ibn Mâjah and Nasâ'i.

[16] This hadith is *ṣaḥeeḥ*. See Shaykh al-Albâni, *Ṣaḥeeḥ Sunan Ibn Mâjah*, no. 1520. Recorded by Abu Dawood and Ibn Mâjah.

إنَّ الْحَمْدَ لِلَّهِ نَحْمَدُهُ وَنَسْتَعِينُهُ وَنَسْتَغْفِرُهُ وَنَعُوذُ بِاللَّهِ مِنْ شُرُورِ أَنْفُسِنَا وَسَيِّئَاتِ أَعْمَالِنَا مَنْ يَهْدِهِ اللَّهُ فَلا مُضِلَّ لَهُ وَمَنْ يُضْلِلْ فَلا هَادِيَ لَهُ أَشْهَدُ أَنْ لا إِلَهَ إِلاَّ اللَّهُ وَحْدَهُ لا شَرِيكَ لَهُ وَأَشْهَدُ أَنَّ مُحَمَّدًا عَبْدُهُ وَرَسُولُهُ

﴿يَٰٓأَيُّهَا ٱلَّذِينَ ءَامَنُوا۟ ٱتَّقُوا۟ ٱللَّهَ حَقَّ تُقَاتِهِۦ وَلَا تَمُوتُنَّ إِلَّا وَأَنتُم مُّسْلِمُونَ ﴿١٠٢﴾﴾

(سورة آل عمران: ١٠٢)

﴿يَٰٓأَيُّهَا ٱلنَّاسُ ٱتَّقُوا۟ رَبَّكُمُ ٱلَّذِى خَلَقَكُم مِّن نَّفْسٍ وَٰحِدَةٍ وَخَلَقَ مِنْهَا زَوْجَهَا وَبَثَّ مِنْهُمَا رِجَالًا كَثِيرًا وَنِسَآءً ۚ وَٱتَّقُوا۟ ٱللَّهَ ٱلَّذِى تَسَآءَلُونَ بِهِۦ وَٱلْأَرْحَامَ ۚ إِنَّ ٱللَّهَ كَانَ عَلَيْكُمْ رَقِيبًا ﴿١﴾﴾

(سورة النِّساء: ١)

﴿يَٰٓأَيُّهَا ٱلَّذِينَ ءَامَنُوا۟ ٱتَّقُوا۟ ٱللَّهَ وَقُولُوا۟ قَوْلًا سَدِيدًا ﴿٧٠﴾ يُصْلِحْ لَكُمْ أَعْمَٰلَكُمْ وَيَغْفِرْ لَكُمْ ذُنُوبَكُمْ ۗ وَمَن يُطِعِ ٱللَّهَ وَرَسُولَهُۥ فَقَدْ فَازَ فَوْزًا عَظِيمًا ﴿٧١﴾﴾

(سورة الأحزاب: ٧٠-٧١)

أمَّا بَعْدُ

فَإِنَّ أَصْدَقَ الْحَدِيثِ كِتَابُ اللَّهِ وَخَيْرُ الْهُدَى هُدَى مُحَمَّدٍ وَشَرُّ الأُمُورِ مُحْدَثَاتُهَا وَكُلُّ بِدْعَةٍ ضَلالَةٌ وَكُلُّ ضَلالَةٍ فِي النَّارِ

"All praises are to Allah alone. We praise Him, and seek His Help, and ask for His forgiveness. We seek refuge in Allah from the evil in our souls and from our sinful deeds. Whoever Allah guides, no one can mislead. And whoever Allah sends astray, no one can guide. I bear witness that there is none worthy of worship except Allah, One, without any partner. And I bear witness that Muhammad is His servant and messenger.

﴾O' you who have believed, fear Allah as He should be feared and die not except as Muslims.﴿[17]

﴾O' mankind, fear your Lord, Who created you from one soul and created from it its mate and dispersed from both of them many men and women. And fear Allah, through Whom you ask one another, and the wombs. Indeed Allah is ever, over you, an Observer.﴿[18]

﴾O' you who have believed, fear Allah and speak words of appropriate justice. He will [then] amend for you your sins. And whoever obeys Allah and His Messenger has certainly attained a great attainment.﴿[19]

> To proceed: Verily, the truest speech is the Book of Allah. The guidance is the guidance of Muhammad. The worst affairs are the newly-introduced matters. And every heresy is misguidance. And every misguidance is in the Fire (of Hell)."

It is recommend to offer congratulations for a marriage

Abu Hurayrah narrated that when the Prophet (ﷺ) wanted to express marital harmony for the one who got married, he would say,

بَارَكَ اللَّهُ لَكُم وَبَارَكَ عَلَيْكُم وَجَمَعَ بَيْنَكُمَا فِي خَيْرٍ

"Allah's blessing for you and blessings upon you. May you be joined together in goodness."[20]

The dower

Allah has said:

---

[17] This is verse 102 of *Soorah Âli-Imrân.*

[18] This is verse 1 of *Soorah an-Nisâ.*

[19] These are verses 70-71 of *Soorah al-Ahzâb.*

[20] This hadith is *ṣaḥeeḥ*. See Shaykh al-Albâni, *Ṣaḥeeḥ Sunan Ibn Mâjah*, no. 1546. Recorded by Ibn Mâjah (and this is his wording), Abu Dawood and Tirmidhi, with the wording being in the singular.

﴿وَءَاتُوا۟ ٱلنِّسَآءَ صَدُقَـٰتِهِنَّ نِحْلَةً ۚ فَإِن طِبْنَ لَكُمْ عَن شَىْءٍ مِّنْهُ نَفْسًا فَكُلُوهُ هَنِيٓـًٔا مَّرِيٓـًٔا ﴿٤﴾﴾ (سورة النِّساء: ٤)

﴿And give to the women [whom you marry] their dowers with a good heart, but if they, of their own good pleasure, remit any part of it to you, take it, and enjoy it without fear of any harm [as Allah has made it lawful].﴾ *(Qur'an 4: 4)*

The dower is the right of the woman upon the man. She is the sole owner of it. No one, not even her father, may take any of it unless she consents to such taking out of her own free will.

Islamic Law has neither set a minimum nor a maximum for the dower. However, it has encouraged the lightening of this burden and an avoidance of extravagance so that it will be easier for marriage to take place, so that the young men are not burdened with a great expense.

Allah (ﷻ) says:

﴿وَإِنْ أَرَدتُّمُ ٱسْتِبْدَالَ زَوْجٍ مَّكَانَ زَوْجٍ وَءَاتَيْتُمْ إِحْدَىٰهُنَّ قِنطَارًا فَلَا تَأْخُذُوا۟ مِنْهُ شَيْـًٔا ... ﴿٢٠﴾﴾ (سورة النِّساء: ٢٠)

﴿But if you intend to replace a wife by another and you have given one of them a great amount (of gold) as dower, do not take the least bit of it back...﴾ *(Qur'an 4: 20)*

Anas (may Allah be pleased with him) narrated that the Prophet (ﷺ) saw 'Abdur-Raḥmân ibn 'Awf wearing dyed clothing. He asked him, "What is this?" He answered, "I married a woman with a *nawâh* amount of gold[21] (as the dower)." The Messenger of Allah (ﷺ) told

[21] [This amount is equivalent to five *dirhams* or five gold pieces at that time.]

him, “Give a wedding party, even if with just a sheep.”[22]

Sahl ibn S‘ad said, “While I was (sitting) among the people in the company of Allah’s Messenger (ﷺ) a woman stood and said, ‘O’ Allah’s Messenger! She[23] has given herself (in marriage) to you, so give your opinion about her.’ The Prophet (ﷺ) did not give her any reply. She again stood up and said, ‘O’ Allah’s Messenger! She has given herself (in marriage) to you; please give your opinion about her.’ The Prophet (ﷺ) did not give her any reply. She again stood up for the third time and said, ‘O’ Allah’s Messenger! She has given herself in marriage to you; so give your opinion about her.’ So a man stood up and said, ‘O’ Allah’s Messenger! Marry her to me.’ The Prophet (ﷺ) asked him, ‘Have you got anything?’ He said, ‘No.’ The Prophet said, ‘Go and search for something, even if it were an iron ring.’ The man went and searched and then returned saying, ‘I could not find anything. Not even an iron ring.’ Then the Prophet (ﷺ) said, ‘Do you know some of the Qur’an?’ He replied, ‘I know such *Soorah* and such *Soorah*.’ The Prophet (ﷺ) said, ‘Go! I have married her to you for what you know of the Qur’an.’ ”[24]

It is permissible to pay the entire dower in advance or to delay all of its payment or to pay some in advance and to delay the rest. It is permissible for the man to consummate the marriage without having had given the woman anything. It is obligatory upon him to give her a dower that is usually given to women similar to her if the two had not agreed upon a particular amount for the dower. If they had agreed on a specific amount, then he must give that specific amount. One should be very cautious and must beware of not fulfilling this

---

[22] Recorded by Bukhari, Muslim, Abu Dawood, Tirmidhi, Ibn Mâjah and Nasâ’i.

[23] [The woman was actually speaking about herself.]

[24] Recorded by Bukhari (and this is his wording), Muslim, Abu Dawood, Tirmidhi, Ibn Mâjah (in abridged form) and Nasâ’i.

important condition, for the Prophet (ﷺ) has said,"The conditions that you have the most duty to fulfill are those that make permissible for the private parts (of your wives)."[25]

If the husband after the marriage contract yet before consummating the marriage, the woman is entitled to her complete dower. 'Alqamah said, " 'Abdullâh (Ibn Mas'ood) was brought the issue of a woman who was married to a man and then he died before consummation and before agreeing upon a dower. 'Abdullâh said, 'In my view, she should receive the dower of women who are similar to her, she inherits from him and she enters the waiting period.' Ma'qil ibn Sinân al-Ashja'ee then bore witness that the Prophet (ﷺ) gave the same decision (as 'Abdullâh did) in the (similar) case of Birwa' bint Wâshiq."[26]

What month is preferred to begin cohabiting with one's wife

'Â'ishah said, "The Messenger of Allah (ﷺ) married me in the month of Shawwâl and took me to his house as a bride during Shawwâl, and who among the Prophet's wives was dearer to him than I?" And 'Â'ishah preferred that the women of her family would enter the houses of their husbands as brides during the month of Shawwâl.[27]

---

[25] By Bukhari, Muslim, Abu Dawood, Ibn Mâjah, Tirmidhi and Nasâ'i.

[26] This hadith is *ṣaḥeeḥ*. See Shaykh al-Albâni, *I'rwâ' al-Ghaleel*, no. 1939. Recorded by Tirmidhi, Abu Dawood, Ibn Mâjah and Nasâ'i.

[27] This hadith is *ṣaḥeeḥ*. See Shaykh al-Albâni, *Ṣaḥeeḥ Sunan Ibn Mâjah*, no. 1619. Recorded by Muslim and Tirmidhi, and without the middle sentence by Nasâ'i and without the final sentence by Ibn Mâjah.

What is recommended to be done when one first goes to one's wife

It is recommended for the husband to be very kind to her. Thus, he should present a drink or something of that nature to her. Asmâ' bint Zayd said, "I beautified 'Â'ishah for the Messenger of Allah (ﷺ). Then I came to him and called him to come and be with her. He came and sat next to her. He brought a large cup of milk. He drank some and then gave it to her. She lowered her head and was shy." Asmâ' then said, "I encouraged her and said, 'Take it from the hand of the Prophet (ﷺ).' She then took it and drank some of it."[28]

He should put his hand on her forehead, mention the name of Allah and pray for blessings. He should make the statement that is in accord with this hadith from the Prophet (ﷺ): "If one of you marries a woman or buys a servant, he should take her by her forelock, mention Allah's name (saying, 'In the name of Allah') and pray for blessings by saying, 'O' Allah, I ask you for her good and the good of what you have dispositioned her toward and I seek refuge from her evil and the evil you have dispositioned her toward.'"[29]

It is also recommended that they pray two *rak'ahs* together as this has been narrated from some of the early scholars. There are two reports of nature.

First: Abu Sa'eed, the ex-slave of Abu Usayd said, "I married while I was a slave. I invited a number of the Companions of the Prophet, including Ibn Mas'ood, Abu Dharr and Ḥudhayfah (may Allah be pleased with them all). The call of the commencement of the prayer

---

[28] Recorded by al-Ḥumaydi and by Aḥmad, with longer and shorter versions having two separate chains that support one another. Shaykh al-Albâni has mentioned such in *Âdâb az-Zafâf*.

[29] This hadith is *ḥasan*. See Shaykh al-Albâni, *Ṣaḥeeḥ Sunan Ibn Mâjah*, no. 1557. Recorded by Abu Dawood and Ibn Mâjah.

was given and Abu Dharr stepped forward to lead the prayer. They said, 'No.' He said, 'Is it like this?' They said, 'Yes.' So I led them in the prayer while I was an owned slave. They taught me by saying, 'When your wife comes to you, pray two *rak'ahs* and then ask for the good of what has come to you and seek refuge from its evil. Then, it is your affair and your wife's affair.' "[30]

Second: Shaqeeq narrated that a man named Abu Ḥareez said, "I have married a young virgin girl and I am afraid that she will dislike me." 'Abdullâh (that is, Ibn Mas'ood) then said, "Bonding is from Allah and such dislike is from Satan, who desires to make you dislike something that Allah has made permissible for you. Thus, when she comes to you, tell her to pray two *rak'ahs* behind you." In another narration, Ibn Mas'ood further said, "Say, 'O' Allah, bless me via my family and bless my family via me. O' Allah bring us together as what You brought together in goodness and separate between us, if we separate, in goodness.' "[31]

When having intercourse with his wife, he should say, "In the name of Allah, O' Allah, ward off Satan from us and ward off from Satan what You grant us." Concerning this supplication, the Prophet (ﷺ) said,"Then if Allah decrees that they should have a child, Satan will never harm him."[32]

He may approach his wife for sexual intercourse from any position he wishes, from behind her or in front of her. Allah has said:

﴿نِسَآؤُكُمْ حَرْثٌ لَّكُمْ فَأْتُوا۟ حَرْثَكُمْ أَنَّىٰ شِئْتُمْ ... ﴿٢٢٣﴾﴾ (سورة البقرة: ٢٢٣)

﴿Your wives are a tilth for you, so go to your tilth when or how you

[30] Its chain is *ṣaḥeeḥ*. See Shaykh al-Albâni, *Âdâb az-Zafâf*, p. 22. Recorded by Ibn Abi Shaybah.
[31] Ibid, p. 23.
[32] Recorded by Bukhari, Muslim, Abu Dawood, Tirmidhi and Ibn Mâjah.

will...❳ *(Qur'an 2: 223)*

That means, have sexual intercourse with her in any posture you wish, from in front or behind.

Jâbir said, "The Jews would say that if a man came to his wife from behind but through the vagina, the child would be cross-eyed. Then the verse was revealed, ❲Your wives are a tilth for you, so go into your tilth when and how you please❳ *(Qur'an 2: 223)*."[33]

Ibn 'Abbâs said, "The district of the Anṣâr were idol worshippers and lived with the district of the Jews, who were people of a book. The (Anṣâr) used to consider them as having superior knowledge. Therefore, they would imitate them in many of their acts. It was the practice of the People of the Book that they would not approach their wives except from the side. In this way, the woman is most concealed. Thus, those Ansâr took this practice from them. The Quraysh on the other hand would put the woman on their backs and approach their wives in any fashion, from in front, behind or on their backs. When the *Muhâjiroon* came to Madeenah, one of them married a woman from the Anṣâr and he began to approach her in one of the other fashions and she objected to it. She said, 'We only have intercourse on the side. Do that or stay away from me.' This event reached the Messenger of Allah (ﷺ) and Allah then revealed, ❲Your wives are a tilth for you, so go into your tilth when and how you please❳ *(Qur'an 2: 223)*, that is, from in front, behind or on one's back, as long as it is the place of impregnating (that is, the vagina)."[34]

Sodomy is, however, prohibited. The Prophet (ﷺ) said, "Whoever has intercourse with a menstruating woman or commits

---

[33] Recorded by Bukhari, Muslim, Abu Dawood and Ibn Mâjah.

[34] Its chain is *ḥasan*. See Shaykh al-Albâni, *Âdâb az-Zafâf*, p. 28. Recorded by Abu Dawood.

sodomy with a woman has committed disbelief in what has been revealed to Muhammad."[35]

The couple should intend by their marriage to live a chaste life and to protect themselves from falling into what Allah has forbidden. By doing so, even their intimate relations with one another will be recorded as an act of charity for them, as the following hadith demonstrates:

On the authority of Abu Dharr (ﷺ): Some of the Companions of the Messenger of Allah said to the Prophet (ﷺ), "O' Messenger of Allah, the affluent have made off with the rewards. They pray like we pray, fast like we fast and they also give in charity from their extra wealth." He [the Prophet (ﷺ)] said, "Has not Allah made things for you to do in charity? Verily, every saying of *Subḥânallâh* is a charitable act, every saying of *Allâhu Akbar* is a charitable act, every saying of *al-Ḥumdu lilâh* is a charitable act, every saying of *Lâ ilâha illa-Allâh* is a charitable act, ordering good is a charitable act, forbidding evil is a charitable act, and you having sexual intercourse (with your wife) is a charitable act." They said, "O' Messenger of Allah, when one of us fulfills his desire, he will have a reward for that?" He said, "Tell me, if he were to fulfill it unlawfully, would he bear that sin? Similarly, if he fulfills it lawfully, he will have a reward."[36]

The obligation of a wedding feast (Waleemah)

One must have a wedding feast after the consummation of the marriage, as the Prophet (ﷺ) ordered 'Abdur-Raḥmân ibn 'Awf to do

---

[35] This hadith is *ṣaḥeeḥ*. See Shaykh al-Albâni, *I'rwâ' al-Ghaleel*, no. 2006. Recorded by Ibn Mâjah, Tirmidhi and Abu Dawood.

[36] This hadith is *ṣaḥeeḥ*. See Shaykh al-Albâni, *Ṣaḥeeḥ al-Jâmi' aṣ-Ṣagheer*, no. 2588. Recorded by Muslim.

so, as was mentioned earlier. In addition, Buraydah ibn al-Ḥaṣeeb said, "When 'Ali proposed to Fâṭimah, the Messenger of Allah said, 'A wedding must have a wedding feast.' "[37]

The following points must also be kept in mind:

First: The wedding feast should be for three days after consummation. This is what has been narrated from the Prophet (ﷺ). Anas said, "The Prophet (ﷺ) married Ṣafiyah and made her freedom her dower and made the wedding feast three days long."[38]

Second: The righteous people should be invited to it, whether they are rich or poor. The Prophet (ﷺ) said, "Do not be a companion except to a believer and do not have anyone eat your food except a pious person."[39]

Third: A sheep or more, of one has the means, should be offered as a meal. The Prophet (ﷺ) told 'Abdur-Raḥmân ibn 'Awf, "Give a wedding feast, even if with just a sheep."[40] Furthermore, Anas said, "I never saw the Messenger of Allah (ﷺ) give a wedding feast for one of his wives like he did for Zaynab (رضي الله عنها); (in her case,) he slaughtered a sheep."[41]

It is permissible to give the feast with whatever food is within one's means, even if no meat is offered. Anas stated, "The Prophet

---

[37] This hadith is *ṣaḥeeḥ*. See Shaykh al-Albâni, *Ṣaḥeeḥ al-Jâmi' aṣ-Ṣagheer*, no. 2419. Recorded by Aḥmad.

[38] Its chain is *ṣaḥeeḥ*. See Shaykh al-Albâni, *Âdâb az-Zafâf*, p. 74. It is recorded by Abu Ya'la, with his chain, as mentioned by Ibn Ḥajar in *Fatḥ al-Bâri*, (vol. 9, p. 199). Its meaning can also be found in *Ṣaḥeeḥ Bukhari*, as Shaykh al-Albâni mentioned.

[39] Its chain is *ḥasan*. See Shaykh al-Albâni, *Ṣaḥeeḥ al-Jâmi' aṣ-Ṣagheer*, no. 7341. Recorded by Abu Dawood and Tirmidhi.

[40] Recorded by Bukhari, Muslim, Abu Dawood, Tirmidhi, Ibn Mâjah and Nasâ'i.

[41] Recorded by Bukhari, Muslim (and this is his wording) and Ibn Mâjah.

(ﷺ) stayed between Khaybar and Madeenah for three days, beginning his marriage with Ṣafiyyah bint Ḥayy. He invited the Muslims to the wedding feast. However, there was no bread or meat. He asked the people to gather food and they brought dates, dried yoghurt and ghee. That was his wedding feast."[42]

It is not allowed to invite only the rich, excluding the poor

The Prophet (ﷺ) said, "The worst food is the food of the wedding feast. The rich are invited to it while the poor are avoided. Whoever does not respond to the invitation has disobeyed Allah and His Messenger."[43]

The one who is invited to the wedding feast must attend it, as demonstrated by the previous hadith as well as the hadith in which the Prophet (ﷺ) said, "If one of you is invited to the wedding feast, he should go to it."[44] Even if the person is fasting, he should respond to the invitation. The Prophet (ﷺ) said, "If one of you is invited to a meal, he should respond. If he were not fasting, he should eat. If he were fasting, he should pray," that is, invoke blessings (on the people).[45] He may even break his fast if he were voluntarily fasting, especially if the host insists. The Prophet (ﷺ) said, "Whoever is

---

[42] Recorded by Bukhari (and this is his wording), Muslim and Nasâ'i.

[43] [Recorded by Bukhari and others. From the subject matter, it seems that the original Arabic text has the wrong hadith. The original Arabic text has the following from *Ṣaḥeeḥ Muslim*: "The worst food is the food of the wedding feast. Those who come to it are prevented from partaking while those who are invited to it refuse to come. The one who does not respond to the invitation has disobeyed Allah and His Messenger." And Allah alone knows best.] - Translator

[44] Recorded by Bukhari, Muslim and Abu Dawood.

[45] This hadith is *ṣaḥeeḥ*. See Shaykh al-Albâni, *Ṣaḥeeḥ al-Jâmi' aṣ-Ṣagheer*, no. 539. Recorded by al-Bayhaqi, and this is his wording, Muslim and Abu Dawood.

invited should respond to the invitation. If he wishes, he may eat; and if he wishes, he may abstain (from eating)."[46]

It is recommended for the guest to abide by the following two issues

First: After eating, the guest should supplicate for the host, using words that have come from the Prophet (ﷺ). These include any of the following:

اللَّهُمَّ بَارِكْ لَهُمْ فِيمَا رَزَقْتَهُمْ وَاغْفِرْ لَهُمْ وَارْحَمْهُمْ

"O' Allah, bless them in what you have provided them, forgive them and have mercy on them."[47]

اللَّهُمَّ أَطْعِمْ مَنْ أَطْعَمَنِي وَأَسْقِ مَنْ أَسْقَانِي

"O' Allah, feed him who fed me and give him to drink who gave me to drink."[48]

أَكَلَ طَعَامَكُمْ الأَبْرَارُ وَصَلَّتْ عَلَيْكُمْ الْمَلائِكَةُ وَأَفْطَرَ عِنْدَكُمْ الصَّائِمُونَ

"May the righteous eat of your food, the angels pray for you and the fasting person break his fast with you."[49]

Second: The guest should pray for the husband and the wife, asking for goodness and blessings for them, as stated earlier in the section on giving congratulations upon a marriage.

---

[46] This hadith is *ṣaḥeeḥ*. See Shaykh al-Albâni, *I'rwâ' al-Ghaleel*, no. 1955. Recorded by Muslim and Abu Dawood.

[47] This hadith is *ṣaḥeeḥ*. See Shaykh al-Albâni, *Mukhtasar Ṣaḥeeḥ Muslim*, no. 1316. Recorded by Muslim and Abu Dawood.

[48] This hadith is *ṣaḥeeḥ*. Recorded by Muslim.

[49] This hadith is *ṣaḥeeḥ*. See Shaykh al-Albâni, *Ṣaḥeeḥ al-Jâmi' aṣ-Ṣagheer*, no. 1226. Recorded by Abu Dawood.

However, it is not permissible to respond to such an invitation if the gathering involves sinful acts, unless one has the intention to remove them and put a stop to them. If he puts an end to them, that is fine. If not, he must leave. On this point, there are the following narrations:

'Ali said, "I prepared some food and invited the Messenger of Allah (ﷺ). When he came, he saw pictures in my house, so he left. (I said, 'O' Messenger of Allah, by my father and mother, what made you leave?' He said, 'In the house, there was a curtain containing pictures. The angels do not enter a house containing pictures.')"[50] Such was the customary practice of the pious predecessors. Thus, Abu Mas'ood 'Uqbah ibn 'Amr invited by a man for a meal and he said, "Are there pictures in the house?" The man said, "Yes," and Abu Mas'ood refused to enter until the pictures were destroyed, and then he entered.[51]

Bukhari recorded, "Ibn 'Umar invited Abu Ayyoob and he saw a sheet covering the wall. Ibn 'Umar said, 'The women have overpowered us.' Abu Ayyoob said, 'If I were to fear that this would happen to anyone, I would not have feared that it would happen to you. By Allah, I will not partake of your meal.' And then he left."

The women may be permitted to make the wedding known by beating on a hand drum only. They also may sing permissible songs that do not describe people's beauty or lewd matters. There are also some hadith on this point. The Prophet (ﷺ) said, "Announce (and

---

[50] This hadith is *ṣaḥeeḥ*, hadith no. 2708. [Note: This is how the original Arabic text reads, without mentioning the source that the author was referring to.] Recorded by Ibn Mâjah. The additional part in the brackets is recorded by Abu Ya'la in his *Musnad*.

[51] Its chain is *ṣaḥeeḥ*. See Shaykh al-Albâni, *Âdâb az-Zaffâf,* p. 93. Recorded by al-Bayhaqi.

make known) the wedding."[52] The Prophet (ﷺ) also said, "The distinction between what is permissible and forbidden in marriage is the playing of the bangle-less tambourine (or hand drum) and the voice (singing)."[53]

Khâlid ibn Dhakwân narrated that al-Rubayyi' bint Mu'awwidh ibn 'Afrâ' said, "After the consummation of my marriage, the Prophet (ﷺ) came and sat on my bed as far from me as you are now sitting. Our young girls started beating the hand drum and singing chants about our fathers who died at Badr. One of them then said, 'In our midst is a prophet who knows what will happen tomorrow.' The Prophet (ﷺ) told her, 'Leave that statement and say what you were saying.' "[54]

The Sunnah is that if someone marries a virgin while already married to a non-virgin, he will stay with the new wife for seven days and then distribute his time among his wives. If the new wife is a non-virgin, he will stay with her for three days and then distribute his time among his wives. This is what Abu Qilâbah has narrated from Anas. Abu Qilâbah further said, "If I will so, I can also add the fact that Anas related this from the Prophet (ﷺ)."[55]

It is obligatory upon the husband to treat his wife well and to try to please her concerning matters that Allah has made permissible for her, especially if she is still young in age. On this point, there are numerous hadith. For example, the Prophet (ﷺ) said, "The best of

---

[52] This hadith is *ḥasan*. See Shaykh al-Albâni, *Ṣaḥeeḥ Sunan Ibn Mâjah*, no. 1537. Recorded by Ibn Ḥibbân.

[53] This hadith is *ḥasan*. See Shaykh al-Albâni, *Ṣaḥeeḥ Sunan Ibn Mâjah*, no. 1538. Recorded by Nasâ'i, Ibn Mâjah and by Tirmidhi without the words, "in marriage."

[54] This hadith is *ṣaḥeeḥ*. See Shaykh al-Albâni, *Âdâb az-Zaffâf*, p. 108. Recorded by Bukhari, Abu Dawood and Tirmidhi.

[55] Recorded by Bukhari, Muslim, Abu Dawood and Tirmidhi.

you is the one who is best to his family (wife) and I am the best of you to my family."[56] The Prophet (ﷺ) also said, "The believers with the most complete faith are the ones with the best behavior. And the best of you is the one who treats his wives with the best manners."[57]

The Messenger of Allah (ﷺ) also said, "A believing man should never hate a believing woman. If he dislikes one of her characteristics, he will be pleased with another of her characteristics."[58] During his speech of his farewell pilgrimage, the Prophet (ﷺ) said, "Verily, I advise you to treat women well. They are like prisoners under your authority. You have no rights over them other than that unless they come with a clear illicit act. If they do that, then avoid them in their beds and beat them in a non-violent manner. If they then obey you, do not seek any means of regress against them. Truly, you have rights over your wives and your wives have rights over you. As for your rights over your wives, they are that they do not allow anyone to come to your seating that you dislike and that they do not allow anyone into your houses that you dislike. And their rights over you are that you treat them kindly with respect to their clothing and food."[59]

(If a man has more than one wife,) it is obligatory upon him to be just and equitable to them with respect to food, housing, clothing, spending nights with them and any other material issues. If he shows favour to one over the others, he will be falling under the warning set out by the Prophet (ﷺ) in the following hadith: "Whoever has two

---

[56] This hadith is *ṣaḥeeḥ*. See Shaykh al-Albâni, *Ṣaḥeeḥ al-Jâmi' aṣ-Ṣagheer*, no. 3266. Recorded by Tirmidhi.

[57] Ibid, no. 3265.

[58] This hadith is *ṣaḥeeḥ*. See Shaykh al-Albâni, *Ṣaḥeeḥ al-Jâmi' aṣ-Ṣagheer*, no. 7741. Recorded by Muslim.

[59] This hadith is *ḥasan*. See Shaykh al-Albâni, *Ṣaḥeeḥ Sunan Ibn Mâjah*, no. 1501. Recorded by Tirmidhi.

wives and shows favouritism to one of them will come on the Day of Judgment with one of his sides hanging down."[60] However, there is no sin if he inclines to one in his heart only. This is something that he cannot control. Thus, Allah has said:

﴿وَلَن تَسْتَطِيعُوٓا۟ أَن تَعْدِلُوا۟ بَيْنَ ٱلنِّسَآءِ وَلَوْ حَرَصْتُمْ ۖ فَلَا تَمِيلُوا۟ كُلَّ ٱلْمَيْلِ فَتَذَرُوهَا كَٱلْمُعَلَّقَةِ ... ﴿١٢٩﴾﴾ (سورة النِّساء: ١٢٩)

﴿You will never be able to do perfect justice between wives even if it is your ardent desire, so do not incline too much to one of them [by giving her more of your time and provision] so as to leave the other hanging [i.e. neither divorced nor married]...﴾ *(Qur'an 4: 129)*

The Messenger of Allah (ﷺ) used to be just and equitable to his wives concerning material matters, not preferring anyone over the others; however, even though, 'Â'ishah was still his most beloved wife. 'Amr ibn al-'Âṣ narrated that the Prophet (ﷺ) sent him at the head of an expedition to Dhât as-Salâsil. He came to the Prophet (ﷺ) and said, "What person is most beloved to you?" The Prophet (ﷺ) replied, " 'Â'ishah." He then asked, "Among the men?" He then replied, "Her father." 'Amr then asked, "Then whom?" He said, "Then 'Umar ibn al-Khaṭṭâb," and he mentioned a number of men.[61]

How many women can a free man marry?

It is not permissible to be married to more than four wives. Allah has said:

---

[60] This hadith is *ṣaḥeeḥ*. See Shaykh al-Albâni, *Ṣaḥeeḥ al-Jâmi' aṣ-Ṣagheer*, no. 1603. Recorded by Ibn Mâjah, and this is his wording, and by Abu Dawood, Tirmidhi and Nasâ'i.

[61] This hadith is *ṣaḥeeḥ*. See Shaykh al-Albâni, *Ṣaḥeeḥ Sunan Tirmidhi*, no. 3046. Recorded by Tirmidhi.

$$\text{﴿ ... فَٱنكِحُواْ مَا طَابَ لَكُم مِّنَ ٱلنِّسَآءِ مَثْنَىٰ وَثُلَٰثَ وَرُبَٰعَ ... ۝ ﴾}$$

(سورة النِّسَاء: ٣)

❴... Then marry women of your choice, two or three, or four...❵

(Qur'an 4: 3)

Additionally, when Ghaylân ibn Salamah embraced Islam, he had ten wives. The Prophet (ﷺ) told him, "Retain four of them and separate from the rest."[62] Qays ibn al-Ḥârith also said, "I embraced Islam while having eight wives. I came to the Prophet (ﷺ) and told him that and he said, 'Choose four of them.' "[63]

Women that one is prohibited to wed

Allah (ﷻ) says:

$$\text{﴿وَلَا تَنكِحُواْ مَا نَكَحَ ءَابَآؤُكُم مِّنَ ٱلنِّسَآءِ إِلَّا مَا قَدْ سَلَفَ إِنَّهُ}$$

$$\text{كَانَ فَٰحِشَةً وَمَقْتًا وَسَآءَ سَبِيلًا ۝ حُرِّمَتْ عَلَيْكُمْ أُمَّهَٰتُكُمْ}$$

$$\text{وَبَنَاتُكُمْ وَأَخَوَٰتُكُمْ وَعَمَّٰتُكُمْ وَخَٰلَٰتُكُمْ وَبَنَاتُ ٱلْأَخِ وَبَنَاتُ ٱلْأُخْتِ}$$

$$\text{وَأُمَّهَٰتُكُمُ ٱلَّٰتِيٓ أَرْضَعْنَكُمْ وَأَخَوَٰتُكُم مِّنَ ٱلرَّضَٰعَةِ وَأُمَّهَٰتُ}$$

$$\text{نِسَآئِكُمْ وَرَبَٰٓئِبُكُمُ ٱلَّٰتِي فِي حُجُورِكُم مِّن نِّسَآئِكُمُ ٱلَّٰتِي دَخَلْتُم بِهِنَّ}$$

$$\text{فَإِن لَّمْ تَكُونُواْ دَخَلْتُم بِهِنَّ فَلَا جُنَاحَ عَلَيْكُمْ وَحَلَٰٓئِلُ أَبْنَآئِكُمُ}$$

$$\text{ٱلَّذِينَ مِنْ أَصْلَٰبِكُمْ وَأَن تَجْمَعُواْ بَيْنَ ٱلْأُخْتَيْنِ إِلَّا مَا قَدْ سَلَفَ}$$

$$\text{إِنَّ ٱللَّهَ كَانَ غَفُورًا رَّحِيمًا ۝ ۝ وَٱلْمُحْصَنَٰتُ مِنَ ٱلنِّسَآءِ إِلَّا مَا}$$

---

[62] This hadith is ṣaḥeeḥ. See Shaykh al-Albâni, *Ṣaḥeeḥ Sunan Ibn Mâjah*, no. 1589. Recorded by Tirmidhi and Ibn Mâjah.

[63] This hadith is ḥasan ṣaḥeeḥ. See Shaykh al-Albâni, *Ṣaḥeeḥ Sunan Ibn Mâjah*, no. 1588. Recorded by Ibn Mâjah and Abu Dawood.

مَلَكَتْ أَيْمَٰنُكُمْۖ كِتَٰبَ ٱللَّهِ عَلَيْكُمْۚ وَأُحِلَّ لَكُم مَّا وَرَآءَ ذَٰلِكُمْ أَن تَبْتَغُوا۟
بِأَمْوَٰلِكُم مُّحْصِنِينَ غَيْرَ مُسَٰفِحِينَۚ ... ﴿٢٤﴾ (سورة النِّسَاء: ٢٢-٢٤)

﴾And marry not women whom your fathers married, except what has already passed; indeed it was shameful and most hateful, and an evil way. Forbidden to you [for marriage] are: your mothers, your daughters, your sisters, your father's sisters, your mother's sisters, your brother's daughters, your sister's daughters, your foster mother who gave you suck, your foster milk suckling sisters, your wives' mothers, your step daughters under your guardianship, born of your wives to whom you have gone in — but there is no sin on you if you have not gone in them [to marry their daughters], — the wives of your sons who [spring] from your own loins, and two sisters in wedlock at the same time, except for what has already passed; verily, Allah is Oft-Forgiving, Most Merciful. Also [forbidden are] women already married, except those [captives and slaves] whom your right hands possess. Thus has Allah ordained for you. All others are lawful, provided you seek [them in marriage] with a dower from your property, desiring chastity, not committing illegal sexual intercourse...﴿ *(Qur'an 4: 22-24)*

In this verse Allah has mentioned the women one is not allowed to marry. Upon further inspection, we can see that the ineligible women are of two categories:

1. Perpetually ineligible

Such a woman is forbidden for a man to marry during all times.

2. Temporarily ineligible

Such a woman is forbidden for a man to marry as long as she is in her present particular state. If her state changes, the prohibition ceases and she becomes eligible as a wife for the man.

The causes for perpetual ineligibility are: blood relations, marriage ties and breastfeeding ties.

First: Those perpetually forbidden due to blood relations are mothers, daughters, sisters, paternal aunts, maternal aunts, nieces via one's brother and nieces via one's sister.

Second: Those perpetually forbidden due to marriage are:

1. The mother-in-law: It is not necessary that the marriage is consummated. The mother-in-law becomes perpetually forbidden due to the conclusion of the contract itself.
2. Stepdaughters from a wife with whom one has consummated a marriage — if a marriage contract is concluded but the man does not consummate the marriage, then (if there is a divorce or the woman dies) the stepdaughter is still eligible for the man. Allah has stated in the above quoted verse, ﴿but there is no sin on you if you have not gone in them﴾.
3. The daughter-in-law: She becomes perpetually forbidden at the conclusion of the marriage contract.
4. Stepmother: She becomes forbidden for the man as soon as the contract is concluded.

Third: Those perpetually forbidden due to breastfeeding relationships are include what is mentioned in the verse above, ﴿your foster mother who gave you suck, your foster milk suckling sisters﴾. Furthermore, the Prophet (ﷺ) said, "Breastfeeding makes forbidden what is forbidden through blood relations."[64] Based on this, the breastfeeding "foster" mother has the same place as the mother. The one she breastfeeds is forbidden for her and all of the relations to her will also be forbidden for the child, as in the case of the birth mother. Thus, a man cannot marry:

---

[64] Recorded by Bukhari, Muslim, Tirmidhi, Abu Dawood and Nasâ'i.

1. His breastfeeding "foster" mother,
2. The mother of the breastfeeding "foster" mother,
3. The mother-in-law of the breastfeeding "foster" mother,
4. The sister of the breastfeeding "foster" mother,
5. The sister of the husband of the breastfeeding "foster" mother,
6. The daughters and grand-daughters of the breastfeeding "foster" mother and
7. "Sisters" due to breastfeeding from the same breastfeeding "foster" mother.

The breast-feeding that makes one ineligible for marriage

'Â'ishah said that the Prophet (ﷺ) said, "One suckling and two sucklings do not establish the (relationship) that forbids (the two from marrying and so forth)."[65] Umm al-Faḍl narrated that the Prophet of Allah (ﷺ) said, "One breastfeeding or two or one suckling or two do not establish the (relationship) that forbids (the two from marrying and so forth)."[66] 'Â'ishah said, "It was revealed in the Qur'an, ﴿Ten sucklings make the child forbidden﴾, and then it was abrogated to five sucklings and the Prophet (ﷺ) died and that was what was recited of the Qur'an."[67]

However, it is a condition that the breastfeeding take place during the first two years, as Allah has said:

﴿ وَٱلْوَٰلِدَٰتُ يُرْضِعْنَ أَوْلَـٰدَهُنَّ حَوْلَيْنِ كَامِلَيْنِ ۖ لِمَنْ أَرَادَ أَن يُتِمَّ ٱلرَّضَاعَةَ ... ﴾

---

[65] This hadith is *ṣaḥeeḥ*. See Shaykh al-Albâni, *I'rwâ' al-Ghaleel*, no. 2148. Recorded by Muslim, Tirmidhi, Abu Dawood, Ibn Mâjah and Nasâ'i.

[66] This hadith is *ṣaḥeeḥ*. See Shaykh al-Albâni, *Mukhtasar Ṣaḥeeḥ Muslim*, no. 878. Recorded by Muslim, and this is his wording, and Nasâ'i.

[67] This hadith is *ṣaḥeeḥ*. See Shaykh al-Albâni, *Mukhtasar Ṣaḥeeḥ Muslim*, no. 879. Recorded by Muslim, Abu Dawood, Tirmidhi, Ibn Mâjah (in meaning only) and Nasâ'i.

(سورة البَقـرَة: ٢٣٣)

﴿The mothers shall give suck to their children for two whole years, [that is] for those [parents] who desire to complete the term of suckling...﴾ *(Qur'an 2: 233)*

Umm Salamah narrated that the Messenger of Allah (ﷺ) said, "Breastfeeding does not make one ineligible (for marriage) unless it is such that it provides the nutrients to the stomach (of the child) at the breast and is before it is weaned."[68]

Women that one is "temporarily" forbidden to marry

(Such women include the following:)

1. Having two sisters as wives at one time

Allah says in the previously quoted verse:

﴿... وَأَن تَجْمَعُوا۟ بَيْنَ ٱلْأُخْتَيْنِ إِلَّا مَا قَدْ سَلَفَ ... ﴿٢٣﴾﴾

(سورة النِّسَاء: ٢٣)

﴿... Two sisters in wedlock at the same time, except for what has already passed...﴾ *(Qur'an 4: 23)*

2. Having a woman and a her maternal or paternal aunt as wives at one time

Abu Hurayrah narrated that the Prophet (ﷺ) said, "A woman and her paternal aunt nor a woman and her maternal aunt are to be together (as wives of one man at the same time)."[69]

---

68 This hadith is *ṣaḥeeḥ*. See Shaykh al-Albâni, *I'rwâ' al-Ghaleel*, no. 2150. Recorded by Tirmidhi.

69 Recorded by Bukhari, Muslim, Abu Dawood, Tirmidhi, Ibn Mâjah (in meaning only) and Nasâ'i.

3. The wife of another man or one going through a waiting period

In the above quoted verse, Allah (ﷻ) says, ﴾Also [forbidden are] women already married, except those [captives and slaves] whom your right hands possess﴿ *(Qur'an 4: 24)*. Thus, a person cannot marry married women — with the exception of slave-captives (taken in war) who become permissible after remaining a period to make sure they are not pregnant, even if they were married. This is based on the hadith Abu Sa'eed who said, "The Messenger of Allah (ﷺ) sent an expedition to Awṭâs. They met the enemy and fought them. They were victorious over them and took some captives. Some of the Companions of the Messenger of Allah (ﷺ) were refraining from having intercourse with them due to their husbands from the polytheists. Then Allah revealed the verse, ﴾Also [forbidden are] women already married, except those [captives and slaves] whom your right hands possess﴿, that is, they are permissible for them after they finish the waiting period."[70]

4. The woman that one has divorced three times

Such a woman is not permissible for the man until she marries another man in a valid, true marriage. Allah has said:

﴿فَإِن طَلَّقَهَا فَلَا تَحِلُّ لَهُۥ مِنۢ بَعْدُ حَتَّىٰ تَنكِحَ زَوْجًا غَيْرَهُۥ ۗ فَإِن طَلَّقَهَا فَلَا جُنَاحَ عَلَيْهِمَآ أَن يَتَرَاجَعَآ إِن ظَنَّآ أَن يُقِيمَا حُدُودَ ٱللَّهِ ... ﴿٢٣٠﴾﴾ (سورة البقرة: ٢٣٠)

﴾And if he has divorced her [the third time], then she is not lawful unto him thereafter until she has married another husband. Then, if the other husband divorces her, it is no sin on both of them that they reunite, provided they feel that they can keep the limits ordained by Allah...﴿ *(Qur'an 2: 230)*

---

[70] This hadith is *ṣaḥeeḥ*. See Shaykh al-Albâni, *Mukhtasar Ṣaḥeeḥ Muslim*, no. 837. Recorded by Muslim, Tirmidhi, Nasâ'i and Abu Dawood.

5. Marrying a fornicatress

It is not permissible for a man to marry a fornicatress or for a woman to marry a fornicator, unless they have repented, as Allah (ﷻ) has said:

﴿ٱلزَّانِى لَا يَنكِحُ إِلَّا زَانِيَةً أَوْ مُشْرِكَةً وَٱلزَّانِيَةُ لَا يَنكِحُهَآ إِلَّا زَانٍ أَوْ مُشْرِكٌ ۚ وَحُرِّمَ ذَٰلِكَ عَلَى ٱلْمُؤْمِنِينَ ۝٣﴾ (سورة النور : ٣)

﴿The adulterer marries not but an adulteress or a polytheist and the adulteress none marries her except an adulterer or a polytheist, such a thing is forbidden to the believers.﴾ *(Qur'an 24: 3)*

'Amr ibn Shu'ayb narrated from his father on the authority of his grandfather that Marthad ibn Abi Marthad al-Ghanawi would bring the captives (from Makkah to Madeenah) and in Makkah there was a prostitute named 'Anâq who was his friend. He said, "I came to the Prophet and said, 'O' Messenger of Allah, can I marry 'Anâq.' He did not say anything and then the verse was revealed, ﴿The adulterer marries not but an adulteress or a polytheist...﴾. He called for me and read that verse to me. Then he said, 'Do not marry her.'"[71]

Void marriages

1. The *Shighâr* marriage

This is where a man marries off his daughter, sister or any woman under his guardianship in exchange for him getting married to the man's daughter, sister or other relative. This contract, in this fashion, is void, regardless of whether an actual dower is stipulated or not. This conclusion is based on the fact that the Prophet (ﷺ)

---

[71] Its chain is *ḥasan*. See Shaykh al-Albâni, *Ṣaḥeeḥ Sunan Nasâ'i*, no. 3027. Recorded by Abu Dawood, Nasâ'i and Tirmidhi.

prohibited such a practice and warned against it — and Allah has said:

﴿... وَمَآ ءَاتَىٰكُمُ ٱلرَّسُولُ فَخُذُوهُ وَمَا نَهَىٰكُمْ عَنْهُ فَٱنتَهُوا۟ ... ﴿٧﴾﴾

(سورة الحَشر : ٧)

﴿... And whatsoever the Messenger gives you, take it, and whatsoever he forbids you, abstain [from it]...﴾ *(Qur'an 59: 7)*

In *Ṣaḥeeḥ Muslim*, it is recorded on the authority of Abu Hurayrah that the Prophet (ﷺ) forbade the *shighâr* marriage. He said, "*Shighâr* is for a man to say to another man, 'Marry your daughter to me and I will marry my daughter to you,' or, 'Marry your sister to me and I will marry my sister to you.'"[72] The Prophet (ﷺ) also said, "There is to be no *shighâr* in Islam."[73]

These authentic hadith indicate the prohibition of *shighâr* marriage and its voided legal nature. It goes against the Law of Allah. The Prophet (ﷺ) did not distinguish between the case when the dower was stated and when the dower is not stated. As for what was narrated in the hadith of Ibn 'Umar, in which *shighâr* is explained as a man marrying his daughter off to another man in exchange for his daughter without there being any dower between them, this explanation, as the scholars have stated, was from the words of the

---

[72] This hadith is *ṣaḥeeḥ*. See Shaykh al-Albâni, *Mukhtasar Ṣaḥeeḥ Muslim*, no. 808. Recorded by Muslim. [It should be noted that there is nothing explicit in *Ṣaḥeeḥ Muslim* that the sentence, "*Shighâr* is for a man to say to another man, 'Marry your daughter to me and I will marry my daughter to you,' or, 'Marry your sister to me and I will marry my sister to you,'" actually comes from the Prophet (Blessings and peace of Allah be upon him). This is an important point because the author shall explicitly claim that this is the Prophet's own definition of *shighâr*.] - Translator

[73] This hadith is *ṣaḥeeḥ*. See Shaykh al-Albâni, *Ṣaḥeeḥ al-Jâmi' aṣ-Ṣagheer*, no. 7501. Recorded by Muslim.

narrator Nâfi' from Ibn 'Umar and were not the words of the Prophet (ﷺ). The Prophet (ﷺ) explained it in the hadith of Abu Hurayrah as presented above, it is where a man marries his daughter or sister to another man in exchange for his daughter or sister.[74] He did not mention anything about the dower between them. This indicates that mention or non-mention of the dower has no affect on the ruling. What renders this marriage void is the agreement to exchange the two. This in itself is a great evil as it may lead to women being forced to wed men they do not desire to wed, out of giving preference to the needs of their guardians instead of the needs of the women. This is evil and a great wrongdoing to women. Furthermore, this practice may lead to the women not receiving the dower that is usually given to women who are similar to them, as is common among those who actually practice this rejected type of contract — except for those whom Allah wills to guide aright. In addition, it can also lead to many disputes and arguments after the marriage. These are the immediate punishments for the one who goes against the Law of Allah.[75]

2. Marriage solely for the purpose of making a woman once again permissible for her ex-husband

This is where a man marries a thrice-divorced woman after she finishes her menses and then he divorces her so that she can remarry for former husband. This type of marriage is a grave sin and indecency. It is impermissible, regardless of whether its goal or action is stated in the marriage contract, if there was agreement upon it before the marriage or if one of them intended it in his heart only. The

---

[74] [See the earlier note where it is explained that the narration of Abu Hurayrah also does not explicitly state this explanation as the words of the Prophet (Blessings and peace of Allah be upon him).] - Translator

[75] See the treatise *Ḥukm as-Safoor wa al-Ḥijâb wa Nikâḥ ash-Shighâr* by Shaykh 'Abdul-'Azeez ibn Bâz.

one who does such an act is accursed. 'Ali (ﷺ) stated, "The Messenger of Allah (ﷺ) accursed the one who marries to make a woman permissible (for her previous husband) and the one for whom it is done."[76]

'Uqbah ibn 'Âmir narrated: "The Messenger of Allah (ﷺ) said, 'Shall I not inform you of the borrowed billy goat?' They said, 'Certainly, O' Messenger of Allah.' He said, 'He is the one who makes the divorced woman permissible. Allah has cursed the one who marries to make a woman permissible (for her previous husband) and the one for whom it is done."[77]

'Umar ibn Nâfi' narrated from his father that a man came to Ibn 'Umar and asked about a man who had divorced his wife thrice and then his brother marries her, without any preconceived plan from the original husband, in order to make her permissible for him. He asked, "Is she permissible for the first man?" Ibn 'Umar replied, "No, not without a marriage that is desired (and done intentionally). We used to consider that fornication during the time of the Messenger of Allah (ﷺ)."[78]

3. "Marriage of pleasure"

This is a temporary or non-perpetual marriage in which a man contracts with a woman for one day, one week, one month or any other specified period. There is agreement that this type of marriage is forbidden and that such a contract is void. Samurah said, "The Prophet (ﷺ) permitted us marriages of pleasure during the year of the

---

[76] This hadith is *ṣaḥeeḥ*. See Shaykh al-Albâni, *Ṣaḥeeḥ al-Jâmi' aṣ-Ṣagheer*, no. 5101. Recorded by Abu Dawood, Tirmidhi and Ibn Mâjah.

[77] This hadith is *ḥasan*. See Shaykh al-Albâni, *Ṣaḥeeḥ Sunan Ibn Mâjah*, no. 1572. Recorded by Ibn Mâjah, al-Ḥâkim and al-Bayhaqi.

[78] This hadith is *ṣaḥeeḥ*. See Shaykh al-Albâni, *I'rwâ' al-Ghaleel*, vol. 6, p. 311. Recorded by al-Bayhaqi.

Conquest of Makkah while we were entering Makkah. However, we did not even leave Makkah before he prohibited it for us."[79]

Concluding a marriage contract while having the intention to (later) divorce

In *Fiqh al-Sunnah* (vol. 2, p. 38), as-Sayyid Sâbiq stated: The jurists agree that if a man marries a woman without stipulating a certain time period but he in fact intends to divorce her after a period of time or after he finishes his business in a certain land that he is residing in, then his marriage if valid. Al-Awzâ'ee different on this point and considered this a marriage of pleasure. Shaykh Rasheed Riḍâ commented in his *Tafseer al-Manâr*,

> "The strictness of the early and later scholars in prohibited marriages of pleasure required that they also forbade marriage with the intention of divorce, even though the jurists have said that the marriage contract is valid if the groom intends only a specific time but he has not stipulated that in the contract. However, his concealing of that intention is a type of deception and deceit. It is more deserving of being voided then a contract in which they stipulate a time period with the agreement of the groom, bride and her guardian. The only evil resulting from this is making sport of the great bonds of marriage, which are supposed to be the greatest bonds of humans, and turning it into a filed of lusts between those who wish to have multiple partners and the evils that this produces. However, when that is not stipulated (but intended) it is a type of cheating and deception that produces another type of evil: hatred and enmity. Trust will be lost between those who sincerely want a true marriage wherein they protect the

[79] This hadith is *ṣaḥeeḥ*. See Shaykh al-Albâni, *Mukhtasar Ṣaḥeeḥ Muslim*, no. 812. Recorded by Muslim.

chastity of each other and sincerely wish to support one another to build a pious household in the Nation."[80]

Shaykh Rasheed's view is supported by the narration of 'Umar ibn Nâfi' from his father that a man came to Ibn 'Umar and asked about a man who had divorced his wife thrice and then his brother marries her, without any preconceived plan from the original husband, in order to make her permissible for him. He asked, "Is she permissible for the first man?" Ibn 'Umar replied, "No, not without a marriage that is desired (and done intentionally). We used to consider that fornication during the time of the Messenger of Allah (ﷺ)."[81]

The Rights of Spouses

The family is the first building block of the society. If it is in a good state, the society as a whole will be in a good state. If it is in a rotten state, the society as a whole will be in a rotten state. For this reason, Islam has paid a great deal of attention to the make up of the family and has made requirements in it that produce soundness and happiness.

Islam considers the family to be a structure that is built upon the union of two people. The most responsible person is the husband. Allah has said:

﴿ٱلرِّجَالُ قَوَّٰمُونَ عَلَى ٱلنِّسَآءِ بِمَا فَضَّلَ ٱللَّهُ بَعۡضَهُمۡ عَلَىٰ بَعۡضٖ وَبِمَآ
أَنفَقُواْ مِنۡ أَمۡوَٰلِهِمۡۚ فَٱلصَّٰلِحَٰتُ قَٰنِتَٰتٌ حَٰفِظَٰتٞ لِّلۡغَيۡبِ بِمَا حَفِظَ ٱللَّهُۚ

---

[80] [Apparently, this ends the quote from Rasheed Riḍâ as well as the portion from *Fiqh as-Sunnah*.]

[81] This hadith is *ṣaḥeeḥ*. See Shaykh al-Albâni, *I'rwâ' al-Ghaleel*, vol. 6, p. 311. Recorded by al-Bayhaqi.

... ﴿٣٤﴾ (سورة النِّساء: ٣٤)

﴿Men are the protectors and maintainers of women, because Allah has made one of them to excel the other, and because they spend [to support them] from their means. Therefore the righteous women are devoutly obedient [to Allah and to their husbands], and guard in the husband's absence what Allah orders them to guard...﴾ *(Qur'an 4: 34)*

Islam has given each spouse rights upon their partners. By fulfilling these rights, this structure will become secure and will continue. Islam has exhorted each of the partners to fulfill their responsibilities. It also encourages one to overlook temporary shortcomings that may occur in receiving one's rights.

The Rights of the Woman upon the Husband

Allah (ﷻ) says in the Qur'an:

﴿وَمِنْ ءَايَـٰتِهِۦٓ أَنْ خَلَقَ لَكُم مِّنْ أَنفُسِكُمْ أَزْوَٰجًا لِّتَسْكُنُوٓا۟ إِلَيْهَا وَجَعَلَ بَيْنَكُم مَّوَدَّةً وَرَحْمَةً ... ﴿٢١﴾ (سورة الرُّوم: ٢١)

﴿And among His Signs is this, that He created for you wives from among yourselves, that you may find repose in them, and He has put between you affection and mercy...﴾ *(Qur'an 30: 21)*

The kind of affection and mercy that is found among spouses cannot be found among any other two. Allah has created for the spouses a continual form of affection and mercy. Thus, the Law has laid down rights that, when adhered to, further protects that affection and mercy from coming to an end or being lost. Allah says:

﴿... وَلَهُنَّ مِثْلُ ٱلَّذِى عَلَيْهِنَّ بِٱلْمَعْرُوفِ ... ﴿٢٢٨﴾ (سورة البَقَرَة: ٢٢٨)

﴿... And they [women] have rights similar [to those of their husbands] over them according to what is customary and good...﴾

(Qur'an 2: 228)

This very concise passage has gathered together wealth that would take great journeys to amass. It is a general principle that states that women are equal to men in all of their rights — except for one matter that Allah has expressed (in the same verse) by saying:

﴿... وَلِلرِّجَالِ عَلَيْهِنَّ دَرَجَةٌ ... ﴿٢٢٨﴾﴾ (سورة البقرة: ٢٢٨)

﴿... But men have a degree [of responsibility] over them...﴾

(Qur'an 2: 228)

In order to understand what rights they have and what rights are upon them, what is good and customary among the people in their relationships and behaviour with one another in the family has been referred to. What is good and customary among a people is that which is consistent with their laws, beliefs, manners and customs. This sentence has given man a balance by which he can weight his actions with his wife concerning all types of matters and affairs. If he thinks about demanding something from her, he should recall that in parallel something similar is obligatory upon him. Thus, Ibn 'Abbâs said, "I beautify myself for my wife as she beautifies herself for me."[82]

The true Muslim recognizes the rights of his wife upon him. Again, Allah has said, ﴿And they [women] have rights similar [to those of their husbands] over them according to what is customary and good﴾. The Prophet (ﷺ) has also said, "Truly, you have rights upon your wives and your wives have rights upon you."[83]

---

[82] Ibn Jareer aṭ-Ṭabari, vol. 2, p. 453.

[83] This hadith is *ḥasan*. See Shaykh al-Albâni, *Ṣaḥeeḥ Sunan Ibn Mâjah*, no. 1501. Recorded by Tirmidhi and Ibn Mâjah.

The aware Muslim always tries to fulfill the rights of his spouse upon him, without considering whether his own rights are fulfilled, as he is desirous of preserving the feeling of affection and mercy between them. Furthermore, he is also very desirous of defeating Satan's opportunity of bringing enmity and disputes between them, in order to separate them.

Since "the religion is sincere advice", I shall mention the rights of the woman upon the man now and follow that with the rights of the man upon the woman. Perhaps the spouses will take the admonition and exhort one another to truth and exhort one another to patience.

1. "Truly, you have rights upon your wives and your wives have rights upon you." The first of those rights is that the man must treat his wife in a good and proper manner. Allah has said:

﴿... وَعَاشِرُوهُنَّ بِٱلْمَعْرُوفِ ... ﴿١٩﴾﴾ (سورة النِّساء: ١٩)

﴿... And live with them honourably...﴾ *(Qur'an 4: 19)*

This is done by providing food for them when the person takes food himself and providing clothing for them when the person provides for himself. This also includes disciplining her in the proper way as ordered by Allah if one fears that she has become recalcitrant. First, one should offer a kind and beautiful admonition and words, free of abusing, cursing and insulting. If the wife obeys, the matter comes to an end. If she does not obey, then he should separate from her in their beddings. Again, if she then obeys, the matter comes to an end. If she remains recalcitrant, her is to beat her a light, non-bruising beating, being careful to avoid the face. This is based on the verse of the Qur'an:

﴿... وَٱلَّـٰتِى تَخَافُونَ نُشُوزَهُنَّ فَعِظُوهُنَّ وَٱهْجُرُوهُنَّ فِى ٱلْمَضَاجِعِ وَٱضْرِبُوهُنَّ

﴿فَإِنۡ أَطَعۡنَكُمۡ فَلَا تَبۡغُواْ عَلَيۡهِنَّ سَبِيلًاۗ إِنَّ ٱللَّهَ كَانَ عَلِيّٗا كَبِيرٗا ﴿٣٤﴾﴾

(سورة النِّساء: ٣٤)

﴿... As to those women on whose part you see ill-conduct, admonish them [first], [next], refuse to share their beds, [and last] beat them [lightly, if it is useful], but if they return to obedience, seek not against them means [of annoyance]. Surely, Allah is Ever Most High, Most Great.﴾ *(Qur'an 4: 34)*

The Prophet (ﷺ) was asked, "What is the right of the wife upon us?" He replied, "It is that when you eat, you feed her; when you get clothing for yourself, you get clothing for her; do not strike the face; do not swear at her; and do not boycott her except in the house."[84]

A manifestation of the perfection of one's manners and the growth of one's faith is that the man is very, very kind with his wife. The Prophet (ﷺ) said, "The believers with the most complete faith are the ones with the best behaviour. And the best of you is the one who treats his wives with the best manners."[85] Honouring the wife is an indication of a full and wholesome personality. Dishonouring her is a sign of one's cheapness and debased personality. Honouring includes being kind and tender with her and sporting with her, in imitation of the Messenger of Allah (ﷺ). The Prophet (ﷺ) was very kind with 'Â'ishah (رضي الله عنها) and even raced her. 'Â'ishah said, "The Messenger of Allah (ﷺ) raced with me and I beat him. After I had put on weight, we raced again and he beat me. He said, 'This was for that one.'"[86]

---

[84] This hadith is *ṣaḥeeḥ*. See Shaykh al-Albâni, *Ṣaḥeeḥ Sunan Ibn Mâjah*, no. 1500. Recorded by Abu Dawood and Ibn Mâjah.

[85] This hadith is *ṣaḥeeḥ*. See Shaykh al-Albâni, *Ṣaḥeeḥ al-Jâmi' aṣ-Ṣagheer*, no. 3265. Recorded by Tirmidhi.

[86] This hadith is *ṣaḥeeḥ*. See Shaykh al-Albâni, *Âdâb az-Zaffâf*, p. 200. Recorded by Abu Dawood.

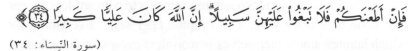

The Prophet (ﷺ) reckoned amusements to be worthless except that done with one's wife. The Prophet (ﷺ) said, "Everything by which humans amuse themselves is worthless except for three things: practicing archery, training one's horse and sporting with one's wife. These are justified."[87]

2. It is the right of the wife upon the husband that he be patient with any harm she does and overlook any of her mistakes. The Prophet (ﷺ) has said, "A believing man should never hate a believing woman. If he dislikes one of her characteristics, he will be pleased with another of her characteristics."[88] The Prophet (ﷺ) also said, "I advise you to treat women well for they have certainly been created from the upper part of the rib and the most crooked part of the rib is the upper part. If you then try to make it straight, you will break it off; if you leave it, it will remain crooked. So, I advise you to treat women well."[89] One of the pious predecessors said, "You should realize that behaving properly towards one's wife does not simply mean not harming her. In fact, it means bearing her harm and being patient with her rashness and anger, in emulation of the Messenger of Allah (ﷺ). His wives would sometimes speak back to him or avoid him from the day until nightfall."[90]

3. It is the right of the wife upon the husband that he protects her and guards her from anything that may damage her reputation and honour. He also must keep her from going out displaying her beauty and not dressing properly. It must also keep her from mixing with

---

[87] This hadith is *ṣaḥeeḥ*. See Shaykh al-Albâni, *Ṣaḥeeḥ al-Jâmi' aṣ-Ṣagheer*, no. 4534. Recorded by Nasâ'i in *al-'Ishrah*, aṭ-Ṭabarâni in *al-Mu'jam al-Kabeer* and Abu Nu'aym in *Aḥâdeeth Abi al-Qâsim al-Aṣam*.

[88] This hadith is *ṣaḥeeḥ*. See Shaykh al-Albâni, *Ṣaḥeeḥ al-Jâmi' aṣ-Ṣagheer*, no. 7741. Recorded by Muslim.

[89] Recorded by Bukhari and Muslim.

[90] *Mukhtaṣar Minhâj al-Qâṣideen*, Pp. 78-79.

men who are not related to her. He must provide her with a complete means for her protection and well-being. He should not permit her to ruin her manners or religion. He should not open opportunities for her to disobey the commands of Allah and His Messenger or commit evil acts. He is the guardian who will be asked about his ward and he has been given the job of protecting and guarding her. Allah has said:

﴿ٱلرِّجَالُ قَوَّٰمُونَ عَلَى ٱلنِّسَآءِ ... ﴿٣٤﴾﴾ (سورة النِّسَاء: ٣٤)

﴾Men are the protectors and maintainers of women...﴿ *(Qur'an 4: 34)*

Furthermore, the Prophet (ﷺ) said, "The man is the shepherd of his family and he will be asked about his ward."[91]

4. It is the right of the wife upon the husband that he teaches her what she needs to know of her religion or that he permits her to attend the sessions of learning. Her need to improve her religion and purify her soul is no less than her need for food and drink. Both of these types of needs must be offered to her. Allah has said:

﴿يَٰٓأَيُّهَا ٱلَّذِينَ ءَامَنُوا۟ قُوٓا۟ أَنفُسَكُمْ وَأَهْلِيكُمْ نَارًا وَقُودُهَا ٱلنَّاسُ وَٱلْحِجَارَةُ ... ﴿٦﴾﴾ (سورة التّحْريم: ٦)

﴾O' you who believe! Ward off from yourselves and your families a Fire [Hell] whose fuel is men and stones...﴿ *(Qur'an 66: 6)*

The wife is a member of one's family. Protecting her from the Hell-fire is via faith and righteous deeds — however, righteous deeds require knowledge and understanding to ensure that they are performed and practiced in the manner prescribed by the Shari'ah.

5. It is also a right of the wife upon her husband that the husband orders her to abide by the religion of Allah and regularly perform the

[91] Recorded by Bukhari and Muslim.

prayer. Allah (ﷻ) says:

﴿وَأْمُرْ أَهْلَكَ بِالصَّلَوٰةِ وَاصْطَبِرْ عَلَيْهَا ... ﴿١٣٢﴾﴾ (سورة طه: ١٣٢)

﴾And enjoin the prayer on your family, and be patient in offering them...﴿ *(Qur'an 20: 132)*

6. It is also a right of the wife upon the husband that he permit her to leave the house whenever there is a need to do so, such as to attend the congregational prayers or to visit her family, relatives and neighbours. However, this is conditioned upon her weighting the Islamic dress and not going out and displaying her beauty. He almost must prevent her from going out perfumed. He also should warn her about mixing with men and shaking their hands. He should also warn her about watching television or listening to songs.

7. It is a right of the wife upon the husband that he not spread about her private matters and that he not mention her shortcomings, as he is like a private secretary to her who is meant to protect and defend her. The most important among the private matters are those that have to do with the bedroom. Thus, the Prophet (ﷺ) warned about spreading such information. Asmâ' bint Yazeed narrated that she was with the Messenger of Allah (ﷺ) and the men and women were sitting. "Perhaps some men speak about what they do with their wives and some women speak about what they do with their husbands." The people were silent. Asmâ' then said, "Yes, by Allah, O' Messenger of Allah (they do it)." The Prophet (ﷺ) then said, "Do not do that. That is like a male devil who met a female devil in the street and he had intercourse with her with the people looking on."[92]

8. It is a right of the wife that the husband seeks her advice in matters, especially in matters that particularly concern her and their children,

---

[92] This hadith is *ṣaḥeeḥ*. See Shaykh al-Albâni, *Âdâb az-Zaffâf*, p. 72. [Recorded by Aḥmad.] - Translator

thereby emulating the Messenger of Allah (ﷺ). The Prophet (ﷺ) would seek the advice of his wives and would follow their views. An example of that nature is what happen on the Day of al-Ḥudaybiyah when, after the treaty was made, the Prophet (ﷺ) told his Companions, "Go and slaughter the animals and then cut your hairs." Not one of the people did that, even though he said it three times. When none of them did what he said, he went to his wife Umm Salamah and mentioned what the people did to her. She said, "O' Prophet of Allah, if you would like them to do that then go, do not speak with anyone of them any word until you slaughtered your sacrificial animal and call your barber to shave your hair." He went and did not speak to anyone of them and did those acts. When the people saw that, they also went and slaughtered their animals and began to shave one another's hairs, to the point that they were almost killing each other due to the rush.[93] Thus, the Prophet (ﷺ) found a lot of good in the opinion of his wife Umm Salamah. This is in contrast to the unjust, dictatorial approach of those who prohibit consulting with women and warn people against it. They say, in colloquial speech, "As for consulting women, if it is beneficial advice, it ruins a year. If it is not beneficial, it ruins a lifetime."

9. It is the right of the wife that the husband returns home immediately after finishing the Night prayer and does not stay out talking until the late hours of thc night. This late-night absence greatly disturbs the wife. It can also build up in her soul distrust and doubts if the husband stays very late or does so repeatedly. In fact, it is the right of the wife that the husband does not spend the night in his house away from his wife in order to fulfill her rights, even if it is for the sake of prayer. Thus, the Prophet (ﷺ) objected to 'Abdullâh ibn 'Amr spending his entire night away from his wife (in prayer) and he

---

.[93] This hadith is *ṣaḥeeḥ*. Recorded by Bukhari.

said to him, "Truly, your wife has a right upon you."[94]

10. It is a right of the wife upon the husband that he treat co-wives, if any, in a just and equitable manner. He must be equitable and equal with respect to food, drink, clothing, housing and spending the nights in their beds. It is not permissible for him to be unfair, unjust or wrongful in any of these matters, as such is forbidden by Allah. The Prophet (ﷺ) said, "Whoever has two wives and shows favouritism to one of them will come on the Day of Judgment with one of his sides hanging down."[95]

Dear brothers in Islam, these are the rights of your wives upon you. It is obligatory upon you to strive to fulfill these rights of theirs. You should not spare any effort in that as fulfilling these rights is one of the causes for your happiness in married life. It is also one of the causes for the peace and security of your household and the key to keeping it free of domestic problems that rob the household of serenity, tranquillity, affection and mercy.

We also remind the women of the necessity of overlooking some of the shortcomings of their husbands with respect to these rights and that they respond to the shortcomings of the men by striving to serve and help them, as they will contribute to the overall happiness of marital life.

The Rights of the Husband upon the Wife

1. The right of the husband upon the wife is great. The Prophet (ﷺ) pointed out its greatness in the hadith recorded by al-Ḥâkim and

---

[94] Recorded by Bukhari, Muslim and Nasâ'i.

[95] This hadith is *ṣaḥeeḥ*. See Shaykh al-Albâni, *I'rwâ' al-Ghaleel*, no. 2017 and *Ṣaḥeeḥ Sunan Ibn Mâjah*, no. 1603. Recorded by Abu Dawood, Tirmidhi, Nasâ'i and Ibn Mâjah with similar wordings.

others from Abu Sa'eed, "The right of the husband over his wife (is so great) that even if she were to lick his wound, she would not have fulfilled his right."[96] The intelligent woman is the one magnifies whatever Allah and His Messenger have magnified. She is the one who respects the magnitude of the right of her husband. Thus, she strives to obey him as obeying him is one of the acts that can lead one to Paradise. The Prophet (ﷺ) said, "If a woman prayers her five (daily prayers), fasts her month (of Ramaḍân), protects her chastity and obeys her husband, it will be said to her, 'Enter Paradise through any of the doors of Paradise you wish.'"[97] Consider, dear Muslim sister, how the Prophet (ﷺ) made obedience to one's spouse as one of the acts that lead to Paradise, like the prayers and fasts. Therefore, adhere to obeying him and refrain from disobeying him, for in disobedience to the husband lies the anger of the Lord. The Prophet (ﷺ) said, "By the One in Whose hand is my soul, no man calls his wife to her bed and she refuses except that the One in the heaven is angry with her until he (her husband) becomes pleased with her."[98]

It is obligatory upon you, dear Muslim women, to behave toward your husband by listening and obeying everything that he asks you to do that is not in contradiction to Islamic Law. However, be completely aware of going to an extreme with respect to such obedience to the point that you obey him in sinful matters. If you do

---

[96] This hadith is *ṣaḥeeḥ*. See Shaykh al-Albâni, *Ṣaḥeeḥ al-Jâmi' aṣ-Ṣagheer*, no. 3147. Recorded by Aḥmad. [In the text, it states "recorded by Aḥmad." This translator believes that this is a mistake as he could not find it in *Musnad Aḥmad* and the source that the author mentions, *Ṣaḥeeḥ al-Jâmi' aṣ-Ṣagheer*, also does not ascribe it to Aḥmad. Instead it was recorded by al-Ḥâkim. Allah knows best.] - Translator

[97] This hadith is *ṣaḥeeḥ*. See Shaykh al-Albâni, *Ṣaḥeeḥ al-Jâmi' aṣ-Ṣagheer*, no. 660. Recorded by Aḥmad.

[98] This hadith is *ṣaḥeeḥ*. See Shaykh al-Albâni, *Ṣaḥeeḥ al-Jâmi' aṣ-Ṣagheer*, no. 7080. Recorded by Muslim.

that, then you will (also) be sinful. An example of this nature would be obeying him in removing hair from one's face as a means of beautification while the Prophet (ﷺ) cursed the one who removes eyebrow hairs and the one who asks for it to be done.[99] Another example would be obeying him in removing the head scarf while going out of one's house because he likes to boast about his wife's beauty in front of others. The Prophet (ﷺ) has said, "Two classes of people are from the inhabitants of Hell that I have not seen: People who have whips like the tails of cows with which they whip the people; women who are dressed but naked, inclining (to evil) and making their husbands incline towards it. Their heads would be like humps of the camel inclined to one side. They will not enter Paradise nor will they smell its scent until its scent can be experienced for such and such a distance."[100]

Another example would be obeying him in having sexual intercourse while on one's period or other acts that Allah has not permitted. The Prophet (ﷺ) said, "Whoever has intercourse with a menstruating woman or commits sodomy with a woman has committed disbelief in what has been revealed to Muhammad."[101] Another example is obeying him in appearing in front of men and shaking their hands. Allah has said:

﴿... وَإِذَا سَأَلْتُمُوهُنَّ مَتَٰعًا فَسْـَٔلُوهُنَّ مِن وَرَآءِ حِجَابٍ ... ﴿٥٣﴾﴾

(سورة الأحزاب: ٥٣)

---

[99] Recorded by Bukhari, Muslim, Abu Dawood, Nasâ'i, Tirmidhi and Ibn Mâjah.

[100] This hadith is *ṣaḥeeḥ*. See Shaykh al-Albâni, *Ṣaḥeeḥ al-Jâmi' aṣ-Ṣagheer*, no. 3799 and *Mukhtasar Ṣaḥeeḥ Muslim*, no. 1388. Recorded by Muslim.

[101] This hadith is *ṣaḥeeḥ*. See Shaykh al-Albâni, *I'rwâ' al-Ghaleel*, no. 2006. Recorded by Ibn Mâjah, Tirmidhi and Abu Dawood.

﴾... And when you ask [his wives] for anything you want, ask them from behind a screen...﴿ *(Qur'an 33: 53)*

The Prophet (ﷺ) also said, "Do not enter upon women." It was said, "O' Messenger of Allah (ﷺ) what do you say about the (male) in-law?" He replied, "The (male) in-law is death."[102] All other acts of disobedience to the Lord may be treated as analogous to these cases. Do not let the obligation of obeying your husband deceive you into thinking that you must obey your husband even in sinful acts. Obedience is only in matters that are lawful. There is no obedience to a created being of something which involves disobedience to the Creator.

2. A right of the husband upon his wife is that she guard her honour and also guard his honour. She should also look after his wealth, children and other household affairs. Allah (ﷻ) has said:

﴿... فَٱلصَّٰلِحَٰتُ قَٰنِتَٰتٌ حَٰفِظَٰتٌ لِّلْغَيْبِ بِمَا حَفِظَ ٱللَّهُ ... ﴿٣٤﴾﴾

(سورة النِّسَاء: ٣٤)

﴾... Therefore the righteous women are devoutly obedient [to Allah and to their husbands], and guard in the husband's absence what Allah orders them to guard [e.g. their chastity, their husband's property, etc.]...﴿ *(Qur'an 4: 34)*

The Prophet (ﷺ) also said, "The woman is a guardian over the household of her husband and she will be asked about her responsibility."[103]

3. It is the right of the husband to have the wife beautify herself for him and that she have a pleasant smile on her face, instead of

---

[102] Recorded by Bukhari, Muslim and Tirmidhi.

[103] This is part of the hadith, "The man is the shepherd of his family". Recorded by Bukhari and Muslim.

frowning and appearing in manners that he dislikes. Aṭ-Ṭabarâni has recorded from the narration of 'Abdullâh ibn Salâm that the Prophet (ﷺ) said, "The best of women is she who pleases you when you look at her, obeys you when you tell to do something and guards in your absence what she is obliged to concerning herself and your wealth."[104] It is most amazing to see women 'letting themselves go' in their house in front of their spouses and then taking utmost care to beautify themselves upon going out of the house. The famous statement has actually become true, "Like an ape in the house and like a deer in the streets." Beware of Allah, O' servant of Allah, concerning yourself and your spouse. The person who has the most right for you to beautify yourself is your husband. Beware of beautifying yourselves for those concerning whom it is not permissible for you to even show yourself. This is from the forbidden display of one's attributes.

4. A right of the husband is that the wife should remain in her house and not leave her house, even to go to the mosque, except with his permission. Allah has said (addressing women):

﴿وَقَرْنَ فِي بُيُوتِكُنَّ ... ﴿٣٣﴾﴾ (سورة الأحزاب: ٣٣)

﴾Stay in your houses...﴿ *(Qur'an 33: 33)*

5. It is also the right of the husband that the wife does not allow anyone into his house except by his permission. The Prophet (ﷺ) said, "As for your rights over your wives, they are that they do not allow anyone to come to your seating that you dislike and that they do not allow anyone into your houses that you dislike."[105]

---

[104] This hadith is *ṣaḥeeḥ*. See Shaykh al-Albâni, *Ṣaḥeeḥ al-Jâmi' aṣ-Ṣagheer*, no. 3299.

[105] This hadith is *ḥasan*. See Shaykh al-Albâni, *Ṣaḥeeḥ Sunan Ibn Mâjah*, no. 1501. Recorded by Tirmidhi.

6. From the rights of the husband over his wife is for her to protect his wealth and not to spend any of it except by his permission. The Prophet (ﷺ) said, "A woman is not to spend anything from the house of her husband except with his permission." It was asked, "O' Messenger of Allah, not even food?" The Prophet (ﷺ) replied, "That is the best of our wealth."[106]

In fact, it is the right of the husband unpin his wife that she not spend any of her own wealth except with his permission, as the Prophet (ﷺ) has said, "It is not allowed for a woman to consume anything of her wealth except by her husband's permission."[107]

7. It is the right of the husband that his wife does not perform voluntary fasts while he is present (that is, not travelling) except with his permission. The Prophet (ﷺ) said, "It is not allowed for a woman to fast and her husband is present except with his permission."[108]

8. It is the right of the husband that he not be bothered by reminders of what the wife spent from her wealth on the house and family. Actually, such reminders void the reward for charity. Allah has said:

$$ \text{﴾يَـٰٓأَيُّهَا ٱلَّذِينَ ءَامَنُواْ لَا تُبْطِلُواْ صَدَقَـٰتِكُم بِٱلْمَنِّ وَٱلْأَذَىٰ ... ﴿} $$

(سورة البَقَرَة: ٢٦٤)

﴿O' you who believe! Do not render in vain your charity by

---

[106] This hadith is *ḥasan*. See Shaykh al-Albâni, *Ṣaḥeeḥ Sunan Ibn Mâjah*, no. 1859. Recorded by Tirmidhi, Abu Dawood and Ibn Mâjah.

[107] Shaykh al-Albâni has discuss this hadith in *Silsilat al-Aḥâdeeth aṣ-Ṣaḥeeḥah*, no. 775. He said, "It was recorded by Tamâm in *al-Fawâ'id* from the chain of 'Anbasah ibn Sa'eed on the authority of Ḥammâd, the client of the Tribe of Umayyah, on the authority of Junâḥ, the client of al-Waleed, from Wâthilah who said that the Prophet (Blessings and peace of Allah be upon him) said... This chain is weak but it has supporting evidence that indicates that it is confirmed.

[108] Recorded by Bukhari and Muslim.

reminders of your generosity or by injury...﴾ *(Qur'an 2: 264)*

9.[109] It is the right of the husband upon his wife that she be satisfied with little and content with what they possess and not overburden the husband by spending beyond his means. Allah (ﷻ) says:

﴿لِيُنفِقْ ذُو سَعَةٍ مِّن سَعَتِهِۦ وَمَن قُدِرَ عَلَيْهِ رِزْقُهُۥ فَلْيُنفِقْ مِمَّآ ءَاتَىٰهُ ٱللَّهُ ۚ لَا يُكَلِّفُ ٱللَّهُ نَفْسًا إِلَّا مَآ ءَاتَىٰهَا ۚ سَيَجْعَلُ ٱللَّهُ بَعْدَ عُسْرٍ يُسْرًا ۞﴾

(سورة الطّلاق : ٧)

﴾Let the rich man spend according to his means, and the man whose resources are restricted, let him spend according to what Allah has given him. Allah puts no burden on any person beyond what He has given him. Allah will grant ease after hardship.﴾ *(Qur'an 65: 7)*

10. It is the right of the husband upon his wife that she bring up her children from him in a good manner, with patience and not being angered with her children in front of him and without supplicating against them or abusing them. All of that would harm the husband and the Prophet (ﷺ) said, "A woman does not harm her husband except that his wife of the *Ḥoor al-'Ain* says, 'Do not harm him, may Allah destroy you. He is just a guest with you and soon he will be departing you to come to us.'"[110]

11. Among the husband's rights is that the wife must treat his parents and relatives well. One who is unkind to a man's parents and relatives is not treating the husband well.

---

[109] [Note that the original Arabic numbers' this as ten and is missing the number nine. Hence, from here onwards the numbering of the rights in English does not match the numbering in the original Arabic text.] - Translator

[110] Recorded by Tirmidhi. [According to Shaykh al-Albâni, this hadith is *ṣaḥeeḥ*. See Shaykh al-Albâni, *Ṣaḥeeḥ al-Jâmi' aṣ-Ṣagheer*, no. 7192.] - Translator

12. The husband's rights include the woman not keeping herself from him whenever he desires her. The Prophet (ﷺ) said, "If a man calls his wife to his bed and she does not come while he spends the night angry with her, then the angels curse her until the morning."[111] The Prophet (ﷺ) also said, "When a man calls his wife to satisfy his desire, let her come to him although she is occupied at the oven."[112]

13. It is a husband's right that the wife keep his affairs and the affairs of his household private, not spreading to others anything of these matters. Of course, the gravest of those issues that women sometimes tell others about has to do with the bedroom and the intimate relations of the spouses. The Prophet (ﷺ) has prohibited such behaviour. Asmâ' bint Yazeed narrated that she was with the Messenger of Allah (ﷺ) and the men and women were sitting. "Perhaps some men speak about what they do with their wives and some women speak about what they do with their husbands." The people were silent. Asmâ' then said, "Yes, by Allah, O' Messenger of Allah (they do it)." The Prophet (ﷺ) then said, "Do not do that. That is like a male devil who met a female devil in the street and he had intercourse with her with the people looking on."[113]

14. It is the right of the husband over his wife that she covet him and try to remain with him, not asking for divorce without any due reason. Thawbân narrated that the Prophet (ﷺ) said, "For any woman who asks her husband for divorce without anything wrong being done the scent of Paradise will be forbidden for her."[114] The

---

[111] Recorded by Bukhari, Muslim and Abu Dawood.

[112] This hadith is *ṣaḥeeḥ*. See Shaykh al-Albâni, *Ṣaḥeeḥ al-Jâmi' aṣ-Ṣagheer*, no. 534. Recorded by Tirmidhi.

[113] This hadith is *ṣaḥeeḥ*. See Shaykh al-Albâni, *Âdâb az-Zaffâf*, p. 72. Recorded by Aḥmad.

[114] This hadith is *ṣaḥeeḥ*. See Shaykh al-Albâni, *I'rwâ' al-Ghaleel*, no. 2035. Recorded by Tirmidhi, Abu Dawood and Ibn Mâjah.

Prophet (ﷺ) also said, "Those women who seek to pay for a divorce (from their husbands[115]) are hypocrites."[116]

Dear Muslim sister, these are the rights of your husband upon you. You must strive to fulfill these rights and overlook your husband's shortcomings with respect to your rights. In this way, affection and mercy will survive, the homes will be set in order and society as a whole will also be set in order.

Mothers must realize that it is an obligation upon them to teach their daughters these rights of the husband and should remind their daughters of these rights before they join with their husbands. This was the practice of the pious women of the early generations. 'Umar ibn Ḥajar, the king of Kindah, proposed to Umm Iyâs bint 'Awf al-Shaybâni. On the wedding night, her mother, Umâmah bint al-Ḥârith gave her an advice that lays out the foundation for a blissful married life and what is obligatory upon her with respect to her husband. She said,

> "My dear daughter, if advice were left for the virtue of etiquette, I would leave this for you. However, this is a reminder for the negligent and support for the intelligent one. If there ever were a woman who was not in need of a spouse due to the wealth of her parents and their strong need for her, I was indeed the most not in need of it. But women were created for men and men were created for women. My dear daughter, you are leaving the environment that you came from and the life that you grew up in to an unfamiliar setting and a companion you have not bonded with. You have become, by his authority over you, a watched person and a servant. Be a servant to him and he will soon be a servant as

---

[115] [Meaning: without due cause.] - Translator

[116] This hadith is *ṣaḥeeḥ*. See Shaykh al-Albâni, *Ṣaḥeeḥ al-Jâmi' aṣ-Ṣagheer*, no. 6681 and *Silsilat al-Aḥâdeeth aṣ-Ṣaḥeeḥah*, no. 633. Recorded by Tirmidhi.

well. Adhere to ten characteristics for him and he will be a treasure for you.

First and second, be submissive to him with satisfaction and listen well to him and obey.

Third and fourth, be aware of what he sees and smells. Never let him see you looking ugly and never let him smell anything but a good scent from you.

Fifth and sixth, be aware of his times for sleeping and eating. Being continually hungry makes one burn and lacking sleep makes one cantankerous.

Seventh and eighth, be prudent with respect to his wealth and guard over his servants and dependents and manage well issues of money and arrange well issues of dependents.

Ninth and tenth, do not disobey him in any matter and do not expose any of his secrets. If you go against his wishes, you will have created malice in his heart against you. And if you spread his secrets, you will not be safe from his betrayal. Finally, never have joy in his presence while he is depressed or be gloomy when he is happy."[117]

"Our Lord! Bestow on us from our wives and our offspring who will be the comfort of our eyes, and make us leaders for the pious."

Marital Disputes

Virtually no family is free of any problems or disputes. However, families differ in the magnitude of such problems. Islam encourages the spouses to try to solve and bring an end to their disputes among themselves. It guides each spouse to the proper steps

[117] Quoted from *Fiqh as-Sunnah*, vol. 2, p. 200.

to be used in dealing with the other spouse. It also encourages them move quickly in taking the steps to solve whenever the first signs of a problem appear. Allah (ﷻ) has said:

﴿... وَٱلَّٰتِي تَخَافُونَ نُشُوزَهُنَّ فَعِظُوهُنَّ وَٱهۡجُرُوهُنَّ فِي ٱلۡمَضَاجِعِ وَٱضۡرِبُوهُنَّۖ ... ﴿٣٤﴾﴾ (سورة النِّساء: ٣٤)

﴿... As to those women on whose part you see ill-conduct, admonish them [first], [next], refuse to share their beds, [and last] beat them [lightly, if it is useful]...﴾ *(Qur'an 4: 34)*

Allah (ﷻ) also says:

﴿وَإِنِ ٱمۡرَأَةٌ خَافَتۡ مِنۢ بَعۡلِهَا نُشُوزًا أَوۡ إِعۡرَاضًا فَلَا جُنَاحَ عَلَيۡهِمَآ أَن يُصۡلِحَا بَيۡنَهُمَا صُلۡحًاۚ وَٱلصُّلۡحُ خَيۡرٌۗ ... ﴿١٢٨﴾﴾ (سورة النِّساء: ١٢٨)

﴿And if a woman fears cruelty or desertion on her husband's part, there is no sin on them both if they make terms of peace between themselves; and making peace is better...﴾ *(Qur'an 4: 128)*

The Islamic approach does not wait until marital discord actually takes place and the banner of disobedience is raised, violating the respect of authority and dividing the structure into battle troops.[118] When the matter reaches such a state, it is very rare that it can ever be resolved. The cure must be resorted to as soon as the signs of recalcitrance start to appear and before it is allowed to fester, as it is very dangerous to leave it and allow it to produce its evil for this foundation. There can be no stability or tranquillity with such recalcitrance. In addition, one cannot properly raise a family in such a setting, especially during the critical times for the youngsters. It, after

---

118 [From this point starts a lengthy section quoted from Sayyid Quṭb, *Fee Dhilâl al-Qur'ân*.]

that, can only lead to the destruction of the entire edifice. Growing up in such an environment results in psychological and physical harm, as well as estrangement. Thus, the issue is very serious. Thus, one must take the curing steps in the proper manner to bring an end to the first signs of recalcitrant, from the moment they are first noticed.

Solving Recalcitrance on the Part of the Wife

Allah has said:

﴿ ... وَٱلَّٰتِي تَخَافُونَ نُشُوزَهُنَّ فَعِظُوهُنَّ وَٱهْجُرُوهُنَّ فِي ٱلْمَضَاجِعِ وَٱضْرِبُوهُنَّ فَإِنْ أَطَعْنَكُمْ فَلَا تَبْغُوا۟ عَلَيْهِنَّ سَبِيلًا إِنَّ ٱللَّهَ كَانَ عَلِيًّا كَبِيرًا ﴿٣٤﴾ ﴾

(سورة النِّساء: ٣٤)

﴿... As to those women on whose part you see ill-conduct, admonish them [first], [next], refuse to share their beds, [and last] beat them [lightly, if it is useful], but if they return to obedience, seek not against them means [of annoyance]. Surely, Allah is Ever Most High, Most Great.﴾ *(Qur'an 4: 34)*

"Admonish them." This is the first measure: to admonish them. This is the first obligation of the one who is the head and maintainer of the family and the one who works to refine the family. Under all circumstances, he is ordered by Allah (ﷻ):

﴿يَٰٓأَيُّهَا ٱلَّذِينَ ءَامَنُوا۟ قُوٓا۟ أَنفُسَكُمْ وَأَهْلِيكُمْ نَارًا وَقُودُهَا ٱلنَّاسُ وَٱلْحِجَارَةُ ... ﴿٦﴾ ﴾

(سورة التّحريم: ٦)

﴿O' you who believe! Ward off from yourselves and your families a Fire [Hell] whose fuel is men and stones...﴾ *(Qur'an 66: 6)*

But in the particular case of a wife's recalcitrance, the husband is guided to a particular direction for the purpose of a particular goal, which is the curing of the disease of recalcitrance before takes root and develops.

However, admonition may not always produce beneficial results. One's passions may overrule one's thoughts, reactions may be uncontrolled, one's egotistic views of ones wealth, family status or other perspectives may make the wife forget that she is a partner in an institution and not an adversary in a battle or in a boasting contest. Thus, the second measure enters the picture. This is a gesture of dignity on the part of the man in which he demonstrates that all those values that the woman uses to state her superiority or to put her above the partner in authority in this institution, things such as beauty and status, are not of greatest importance to the man. Thus, he is instructed, "refuse to share their beds". It is in the bed that the woman's temptations are the greatest, which she can use to override his authority. If the man is able to demonstrate that he can overcome the impulses pushing him to succumb to this, he can remove from the recalcitrant woman her strongest seducing weapon.

This measure is supposed to be done in a very specific way. He avoids her in the bed. It is not supposed to be an open, visible boycotting of the partner. It only occurs where the two spouses are alone. Thus, he does not avoid her in front of the children, which would have a great negative effect on them. He also does not boycott her in front of dangers, which would humiliate the woman or dishonour her. This would create greater recalcitrance. The goal is to rectify the problem of recalcitrance. The goal is not to humiliate the wife or harm the children.

However, even this step may not be successful. Should the institution then be left to collapse? There is yet another measure which is harsher — but it is less harsh and less grave than destroying the entire institution through recalcitrance.

(Allah says,) ﴾[and last] beat them [lightly, if it is useful]﴿. Continuing with the meaning of all of the above and the goals of these measures — these points highlight that this beating is not meant to be a punishment out of revenge or seeking to bring misery. It cannot be not meant to humiliate or belittle. It also cannot be meant to force the wife to accept life under any conditions. No, instead, it must be a measured disciplinary beating. It is to be accompanied with the mercy of the teaching disciplinarian, like the father has with respect to his child or the teacher with respect to his student.

These are prevented measures permitted to counter recalcitrance — before it takes root. However, these measures are also accompanied with stern warnings to ensure that they are not abused. The practical example has been given by the Prophet (ﷺ) in his own household with his wives and via his statements. His directives serve as restraints from going to extremes on either side. He has laid out the correct views in many of his statements.

Mu'âwiyah ibn Ḥaydah asked, "O' Messenger of Allah, what is the right of the wife upon us?" He replied, "It is that when you eat, you feed her; when you get clothing for yourself, you get clothing for her; do not strike the face; do not swear at her; and do not boycott her except in the house."[119]

Iyâs ibn 'Abdullâh ibn Abi Dhubâb (رضي الله عنه) narrated that the Messenger of Allah (ﷺ) said, "Do not strike the female servants of Allah." 'Umar then came to the Messenger of Allah (ﷺ) and said, "The women are becoming rebellious against their husbands. Give them permission to strike them." After that, many women gathered at the houses the Messenger of Allah's wives to complain about the husbands. The Prophet (ﷺ) then said, "Many women have

---

[119] This hadith is *ṣaḥeeḥ*. See Shaykh al-Albâni, *Ṣaḥeeḥ Sunan Ibn Mâjah*, no. 1500. Recorded by Abu Dawood and Ibn Mâjah.

congregated around the family of Muhammad complaining about their husbands. Those mean are not the best among you."[120]

'Abdullâh ibn Zam'ah narrated that he heard the Messenger of Allah (ﷺ) say, "You should not beat your wife like you would beat a slave for perhaps you will then have intercourse with her at the end of your day."[121]

In any case, all of the above measures have limits to them that one must not violate. If the goal is met by any of the measures, it is impermissible to go beyond it and move to the next level, ﴾If they then obey you, do not seek any means of regress against them﴿. When the goal is met, the means are to be stopped, indicating that the goal — the goal of obedience — is the purpose. But it is an obedience based on a positive response and not a forced obedience — such forced obedience is not the kind of obedience that is suitable to establish the institution of the family, which is the basis for the entire society.

The text of the verse alludes to the fact that continuing in those measures after the goal of obedience is met is transgressing the limits, arbitrary action and injustice. ﴾Do not seek any means of regress against them﴿. After this prohibition, Allah reminds the individual that He is Ever Most High, Most Great, so that the hearts will become submissive, the heads lowered and the feelings of arrogance and greatness extinguished. This is the method of the Qur'an in exhorting them to do what is right and intimidating them against evil.[122]

---

[120] This hadith is *ḥasan ṣaḥeeḥ*. See Shaykh al-Albâni, *Ṣaḥeeḥ Sunan Ibn Mâjah*, no. 1615. Recorded by Abu Dawood and Ibn Mâjah.

[121] Recorded by Bukhari, Muslim and Tirmidhi.

[122] [The end is the portion from Sayyid Quṭb,] *Fee Dhilâl al-Qurân*, vol. 2, Pp. 358-362.

Curing Improper Behaviour on the Part of the Husband

Allah (ﷻ) has said:

﴿وَإِنِ ٱمْرَأَةٌ خَافَتْ مِنۢ بَعْلِهَا نُشُوزًا أَوْ إِعْرَاضًا فَلَا جُنَاحَ عَلَيْهِمَآ أَن يُصْلِحَا بَيْنَهُمَا صُلْحًا ۚ وَٱلصُّلْحُ خَيْرٌ ۗ وَأُحْضِرَتِ ٱلْأَنفُسُ ٱلشُّحَّ ۚ وَإِن تُحْسِنُوا۟ وَتَتَّقُوا۟ فَإِنَّ ٱللَّهَ كَانَ بِمَا تَعْمَلُونَ خَبِيرًا ﴿١٢٨﴾﴾ (سورة النِّسَاء: ١٢٨)

﴿And if a woman fears cruelty or desertion on her husband's part, there is no sin on them both if they make terms of peace between themselves; and making peace is better. And human inner-selves are swayed by greed. But if you do good and keep away from evil, verily, Allah is Ever Well-Acquainted with what you do.﴾ *(Qur'an 4: 128).*[123]

Earlier (in *Soorah an-Nisâ'*) the Law dealt with the situation of recalcitrance on the part of the wife and the proper measures that would preserve the sound structure of the family. Now the discussion is concerning abuse or desertion on the part of the husband, threatening the security and honour of the women as well as the sanctity of the family as a whole. Hearts and feelings change over time. Islam is a system for life that deals with every detail of life and discusses every eventuality within the general framework of the values and structure of the society it creates.

If the woman fears being abandoned and that this abandonment may lead to divorce — which is the most hated of the permissible in Allah's sight[124] — or if she fears being left in a

---

[123] [This begins a second lengthy portion taken from Sayyid Quṭb, *Fee Dhilâl al-Qurân*.]

[124] [It is somewhat strange to see the author quoting these words from Sayyid Quṭb without commenting upon them. The statement that Sayyid Quṭb made is=

suspended state, not being truly married nor divorced, then there is no harm on her or on her husband if she gives up some of her financial or other rights. For example, she could give up a portion or all of her maintenance rights or she could give up the nights that she spends with her husband, if he has other wives.

This, though, must be the convulsion made by the woman based on her complete freedom and choice. She may come to this conclusion if she feels that such a situation would be better for her than divorce. This is what is meant by "terms of peace" in the verse saying, ﴿And if a woman fears cruelty or desertion on her husband's part, there is no sin on them both if they make terms of peace between themselves﴾. Then the verse gives the judgment that such ﴿terms of peace﴾, in general, are better than quarrels, disputes, desertion or divorce, as Allah (ﷻ) says, ﴿And making peace is better﴾.[125]

Then the Qur'an encourages the man to do goodness to this woman who still wishes to be with him and is willing to sacrifices some of her rights to remain as his wife. Allah states that He is aware of any goodness he does and Allah will reward him for it. Allah (ﷻ) says, ﴿And human inner-selves are swayed by greed. But if you do good and keep away from evil, verily, Allah is Ever Well-Acquainted with what you do﴾.

The occasion behind the revelation of this verse has been recorded in *Sunan Abi Dawood* from the hadith of Hishâm ibn 'Urwah from his father who reported that 'Â'ishah said (to him), "O' my nephew, the Messenger of Allah (ﷺ) did not show any preference to any of us concerning the spending of nights with each wife. It was

---

=based on a hadith that Shaykh al-Albâni has convincingly argued is a false hadith. (See Shaykh al-Albâni, *I'rwâ' al-Ghaleel*, no. 2040.) Hence there is no basis for making such a statement. And Allah alone knows best.] - Translator

[125] Sayyid Quṭb, *Fee Dhilâl al-Qurân*, vol. 2, p. 539.

very rare that he would not visit every wife each night, spending time with them and sitting close to them but without sexual intercourse, until he reaches the wife whose night it is that he should spend with her. Sawdah bint Zam'ah said, when she got older and feared that the Messenger of Allah (ﷺ) was going to separate from her, 'O' Messenger of Allah, I give my night to 'Â'ishah.' The Prophet (ﷺ) accepted that from her. We think that it was for this occasion and others like it that Allah revealed, ﴿And if a woman fears cruelty or desertion on her husband's part, there is no sin on them both if they make terms of peace between themselves; and making peace is better. And human inner-selves are swayed by greed. But if you do good and keep away from evil, verily, Allah is Ever Well-Acquainted with what you do﴾ *(Qur'an 4: 128)*.[126]

What should be done if the discord between the spouses grows stronger

Allah says:

﴿وَإِنْ خِفْتُمْ شِقَاقَ بَيْنِهِمَا فَابْعَثُوا حَكَمًا مِّنْ أَهْلِهِۦ وَحَكَمًا مِّنْ أَهْلِهَآ إِن يُرِيدَآ إِصْلَـٰحًا يُوَفِّقِ ٱللَّهُ بَيْنَهُمَآ ۗ إِنَّ ٱللَّهَ كَانَ عَلِيمًا خَبِيرًا ﴿٣٥﴾﴾

(سورة النِّساء: ٣٥)

﴿If you fear a breach between the two of them [the man and his wife], appoint [two] arbitrators, one from his family and the other from her's; if they both wish for peace, Allah will cause their reconciliation. Indeed Allah is Ever All-Knower, Well-Acquainted with all things.﴾ *(Qur'an 4: 35)*

The measures that we have mentioned so far are concerned with

---

[126] This hadith is *ḥasan ṣaḥeeḥ*. See Shaykh al-Albâni, *Ṣaḥeeḥ Sunan Abi Dawood*, no. 1868. Recorded by Abu Dawood.

situations wherein the rebellion is not yet great and only the beginning stages of discord are occurring.[127] However, if the recalcitrance is clearly out in the open, then one does not follow the previous measures as they will not produce any benefit in this new climate. This new climate is more like a war between two parties, each wishing to destroy the head of the other. To use those measures in this climate is neither the purpose nor the goal. Similarly, if one finds that those measures are counterproductive, increasing the discord and virtually breaking the last cord holding the two together, then, again, they are not to be used. Under these harsher circumstances, the wise Islamic approach calls for other methods to save the great institution from destruction, before one's hand is raised from it and it is left to be destroyed. This other measure is described in the verse (quoted above,) ﴾If you fear a breach between the two of them [the man and his wife], appoint [two] arbitrators, one from his family and the other from her's; if they both wish for peace, Allah will cause their reconciliation. Indeed Allah is Ever All-Knower, Well-Acquainted with all things﴿ *(Qur'an 4: 35).*

The Islamic approach does not call upon the parties to resign themselves to the first stages of discord and dislike. Nor does it call for a quick dissolution of the marriage contract and quick demolishing of the family institution over the heads of the old and young involved with the family — those who did not commit any sin but yet have no power or escape from the issue. The institution of the family is very dear to Islam due to its great importance in building the society and its bringing forth new bricks for the societal structure, to make it grow and prosper.

---

[127] [This starts another lengthy passage from Sayyid Quṭb, *Fee Dhilâl al-Qur'ân*.]

Islam resorts to this final measure when separation is feared. This should be resorted to before the actual separation takes place. One arbiter from her family, with whom she is pleased, and one arbiter from his family, with him he is pleased, should come together in a peaceful setting, far away from the commotion, emotions and living circumstances that are contributing to their problems. Each of the arbiters should be close to the spouses and have their best interest at heart, seeking to protect their honour and also having compassion and mercy for the young children who are involved. They should desire what is best for the spouses, their children and the institution that is being threatened. At the same time, they must keep the family secrets hidden. Since they are both from the spouses' families, they should have no interest in spreading such secrets as it will eventually cause harm to themselves as well.

The two arbiters meet together to try to bring about reconciliation. If both spouses truly desire reconciliation and anger alone was the cause for them not seeing this desire on each part, then, with the strong desires on the part of the arbiters to help them, Allah may decree that their hearts be reconciled and they come back to one another. Allah has said, ﴾if they both wish for peace, Allah will cause their reconciliation﴿. In other words, if they both desire reconciliation, Allah will respond to this desire and support them. ﴾Indeed Allah is Ever All-Knower, Well-Acquainted with all things﴿.[128]

Why do you forbid what Allah has made permissible for you?

Anas said, "The Messenger of Allah (ﷺ) had a concubine that he had sexual relations with. However, 'Â'ishah and Ḥafṣah kept harassing him about her until he banned her for himself. So then

---

[128] Sayyid Quṭb, *Fee Dhilâl al-Qur'an*, vol. 2, Pp. 263-264.

Allah (ﷻ) revealed the verse:

﴿يَٰٓأَيُّهَا ٱلَّذِينَ ءَامَنُواْ قُوٓاْ أَنفُسَكُمۡ وَأَهۡلِيكُمۡ نَارٗا وَقُودُهَا ٱلنَّاسُ وَٱلۡحِجَارَةُ عَلَيۡهَا مَلَٰٓئِكَةٌ غِلَاظٞ شِدَادٞ لَّا يَعۡصُونَ ٱللَّهَ مَآ أَمَرَهُمۡ وَيَفۡعَلُونَ مَا يُؤۡمَرُونَ ۝٦﴾

(سورة التحريم: ٦)

﴾O' Prophet! Why do you ban [for yourself] that which Allah has made lawful to you, seeking to please your wives? And Allah is Oft-Forgiving, Most Merciful.﴿ *(Qur'an 66: 1).*"[129]

Ibn 'Abbâs said, "If a man makes an oath that his wife is forbidden for him, it is nothing but an oath that he can expiate." Then he recited the verse:

﴿لَّقَدۡ كَانَ لَكُمۡ فِي رَسُولِ ٱللَّهِ أُسۡوَةٌ حَسَنَةٞ ... ۝٢١﴾ (سورة الأحزاب: ٢١)

﴾Indeed in the Messenger of Allah you have an excellent example...﴿ *(Qur'an 33: 21).*[130]

If someone says to his wife, "You are forbidden for me", he must make the expiation for the breaking of an oath. This expiation is mentioned in the following verse:

﴿لَا يُؤَاخِذُكُمُ ٱللَّهُ بِٱللَّغۡوِ فِيٓ أَيۡمَٰنِكُمۡ وَلَٰكِن يُؤَاخِذُكُم بِمَا عَقَّدتُّمُ ٱلۡأَيۡمَٰنَۖ فَكَفَّٰرَتُهُۥٓ إِطۡعَامُ عَشَرَةِ مَسَٰكِينَ مِنۡ أَوۡسَطِ مَا تُطۡعِمُونَ أَهۡلِيكُمۡ أَوۡ كِسۡوَتُهُمۡ أَوۡ تَحۡرِيرُ رَقَبَةٖۖ فَمَن لَّمۡ يَجِدۡ فَصِيَامُ ثَلَٰثَةِ أَيَّامٖۚ ذَٰلِكَ كَفَّٰرَةُ أَيۡمَٰنِكُمۡ إِذَا حَلَفۡتُمۡۚ ... ۝٨٩﴾

(سورة المائدة: ٨٩)

﴾Allah will not punish you for what is unintentional in your oaths, but

---

[129] Its chain is *ṣaḥeeḥ*. See Shaykh al-Albâni, *Ṣaḥeeḥ Sunan Nasâ'i*, no. 3695. Recorded by Nasâ'i.

[130] Recorded by Bukhari and Muslim (and this is his wording).

He will punish you for your deliberate oaths; for its expiation feed ten poor persons, on a scale of the average of that with which you feed your own families; or clothe them; or manumit a slave. But whosoever cannot afford [that], then he should fast for three days. That is the expiation for the oaths when you have sworn...》

(Qur'an 5: 89)

Al-Eelâ' (Making an Oath to Abstain from One's Wife)

If a person swears that he will not have intercourse with his wife for a specific period, which must be less than four months, then it is best for him to simply break that to expiate for that oath and to have intercourse with his wife. The Prophet (ﷺ) said, "If a person swears an oath and then finds that something is better (than what he swore to), then he should do that better thing and expiate for his oath."[131]

If he does not break his oath, then he must have patience until the period of time that he declared comes to an end. The Messenger of Allah (ﷺ) made an oath that he would not approach his wives during the time that his leg was injured. He stayed twenty-nine days in an upper level room. When he came down, they said, "O' Messenger of Allah! You took an oath for a month!" He replied, "The month is twenty-nine days."[132]

If the husband takes an oath that he will never have intercourse again with his wife or if he takes an oath of over four months, then he may break his oath and return to relations with her. Otherwise, the

---

[131] This hadith is *ṣaḥeeḥ*. See Shaykh al-Albâni, *Ṣaḥeeḥ al-Jâmi' aṣ-Ṣagheer*, no. 6208. Recorded by Muslim, Nasâ'i and Ibn Mâjah.

[132] This hadith is *ṣaḥeeḥ*. See Shaykh al-Albâni, *Ṣaḥeeḥ Sunan Nasâ'i*, no. 3233. Recorded by Bukhari, Nasâ'i and Tirmidhi.

wife should wait for the completion of four months and then even demand that he have intercourse with her or divorce her. Concerning this point, Allah (ﷻ) says:

﴿لِّلَّذِينَ يُؤْلُونَ مِن نِّسَآئِهِمْ تَرَبُّصُ أَرْبَعَةِ أَشْهُرٍ فَإِن فَآءُو فَإِنَّ ٱللَّهَ غَفُورٌ رَّحِيمٌ ﴿٢٢٦﴾ وَإِنْ عَزَمُوا۟ ٱلطَّلَٰقَ فَإِنَّ ٱللَّهَ سَمِيعٌ عَلِيمٌ ﴿٢٢٧﴾﴾ (سورة البقرة: ٢٢٦-٢٢٧)

﴿Those who take an oath not to have sexual relation with their wives must wait four months, then if they return [change their idea in this period], verily, Allah is Oft-Forgiving, Most Merciful. And if they decide upon divorce, then Allah is All-Hearer, All-Knower.﴾

(Qur'an 2: 226-227)

Nâfi' narrated that Ibn 'Umar said about this oath of abstinence from one's wife mentioned by Allah in the Qur'an, "Neither of them is permissible to each other after that time period unless he retains her in the proper, customary manner or he intends to divorce, as Allah has ordered."[133]

A<u>dh</u>-<u>Dh</u>ihâr

If a man says to his wife, "You are to me like my mother's back," then he has committed *a<u>dh</u>-<u>Dh</u>ihâr* and his wife becomes forbidden for him — he cannot have intercourse with her or enjoy her in any fashion — until he expiates in the manner described by Allah in His Book:

﴿وَٱلَّذِينَ يُظَٰهِرُونَ مِن نِّسَآئِهِمْ ثُمَّ يَعُودُونَ لِمَا قَالُوا۟ فَتَحْرِيرُ رَقَبَةٍ مِّن قَبْلِ أَن يَتَمَآسَّا ۚ ذَٰلِكُمْ تُوعَظُونَ بِهِۦ ۚ وَٱللَّهُ بِمَا تَعْمَلُونَ خَبِيرٌ ﴿٣﴾ فَمَن لَّمْ يَجِدْ فَصِيَامُ

---

133 This hadith is *ṣaḥeeḥ*. See Shaykh al-Albâni, *I'rwâ' al-Ghaleel*, no. 2080. Recorded by Bukhari.

شَهْرَيْنِ مُتَتَابِعَيْنِ مِن قَبْلِ أَن يَتَمَآسَّا فَمَن لَّمْ يَسْتَطِعْ فَإِطْعَامُ سِتِّينَ مِسْكِينًا ذَٰلِكَ
لِتُؤْمِنُوا بِاللَّهِ وَرَسُولِهِۦ وَتِلْكَ حُدُودُ اللَّهِ وَلِلْكَٰفِرِينَ عَذَابٌ أَلِيمٌ ﴿٤﴾

(سورة المجادلة: ٣-٤)

﴿And those who make unlawful to them [their wives] by *adh-Dhihâr* and wish to free themselves from what they uttered, [the penalty] in that case [is] the freeing of a slave before they touch each other. That is an admonition to you [so that you may not return to such an ill thing]. And Allah is All-Aware of what you do. And he who finds not [the money for freeing a slave] must fast two successive months before they both touch each other. And for him who is unable to do so, he should feed sixty poor. That is in order that you may have perfect Faith in Allah and His Messenger. These are the limits set by Allah. And for disbelievers, there is a painful torment.﴾

(Qur'an 58: 3-4)

Khuwaylah bint Mâlik ibn Tha'labah said, "My husband Aws ibn aṣ-Ṣâmit made *adh-Dhihâr* for me. I went to the Messenger of Allah (ﷺ) to complain to him and he debated with me. He said, 'Fear Allah, for he is your cousin.' I continued my dispute until Allah revealed (the first four verses of *Soorah al-Mujâdilah*), ﴿Indeed Allah has heard the statement of her that disputes with you concerning her husband...﴾. He then said, 'He should free a slave.' I (Khuwaylah) said, 'He does not have the means.' He then said, 'Let him fast two consecutive months.' I said, 'O' Messenger of Allah, he is an old man and he cannot fast.' He then said, 'Let him feed sixty poor.' I said, 'He does not have anything to give in charity.' Then an *araq* amount of dates was brought. I said, 'O' Messenger of Allah, I shall help him with another *araq*.' He said, 'You have done well. Go and feed with it sixty poor. And go back to your cousin.'" And an *araq* is equal to sixty *ṣâ'*.

'Urwah ibn az-Zubayr narrated that 'Â'ishah said, "Blessed is the One Whose hearing encompasses everything. I heard part of what Khawlah[134] bint Thalabah said and I could not hear part of it. She was complaining to the Messenger of Allah (ﷺ) about her husband. She was saying, 'O' Messenger of Allah! I used up my youth and gave him many children until now that I am old and barren, he makes *adh-Dhihâr* for me. O' Allah, I complain to you.' She continued until Jibreel descended with these verses:

﴿قَدْ سَمِعَ ٱللَّهُ قَوْلَ ٱلَّتِى تُجَٰدِلُكَ فِى زَوْجِهَا وَتَشْتَكِىٓ إِلَى ٱللَّهِ ... ۝١﴾

(سورة المجادلة : ١)

﴿Indeed Allah has heard the statement of her that disputes with you concerning her husband and complains to Allah...﴾

(Qur'an 58: 1)."[135]

If someone makes *dhihâr* for a specific period, such as for a day, month and so forth, saying to his wife, "You are like my mother's back to me for one month," this is also *dhihâr*. If he fulfills this oath, there is no expiation upon him. If he, however, has intercourse with her before said period is up, he must expiate for his oath of *dhihâr*.

Salamah ibn Ṣakhr al-Bayâḍi said, "I was a man who had great desire of women, such that I do not think anyone did so more than I. Thus, when Ramaḍân came, I made *dhihâr* to abstain from my wife until the month finished. When she was speaking to me one night, part of her body became uncovered in front of me and I ended up having intercourse with her. In the morning, I informed my people as

---

[134] [Note that in some narrations, like the previous narration, the diminutive form of her name is given, Khuwaylah.] - Translator

[135] This hadith is *ṣaḥeeḥ*. See Shaykh al-Albâni, *Ṣaḥeeḥ Sunan Ibn Mâjah*, no. 1678. Recorded by Ibn Mâjah.

to what had occurred. I said to them, 'Ask the Messenger of Allah (ﷺ) about it.' They said, 'We are not about to do that as Allah may reveal a portion of the Book about us or the Messenger of Allah (ﷺ) may say something about us and we would remain deprived due to it. But go, you with your sin, and mention your case to the Messenger of Allah (ﷺ).' So I went to him and informed him of what had happened. The Messenger of Allah (ﷺ) asked, 'You actually did that?' I said, 'I actually did that. And here I am waiting for the ruling of Allah concerning me.' He then said, 'Then free a slave.' I said, 'By the One Who sent you with the truth, I have no wealth except this servant of mine.' He then said, 'Then fast two consecutive months.' I said, 'O' Messenger of Allah, it is from nothing but the fast that I am facing this trial.' He said, 'Give charity to or feed sixty poor.' I said, 'By the One Who sent you with the truth, we spent this night without even having a dinner.' He then said, 'Go to the charity collector of the Tribe of Zurayq and tell them to give you the charity and feed sixty poor with it and use what remains for yourself.'"[136] The point here is that the Prophet (ﷺ) did not object to him making *adh-Dhihâr*. What he objected to was his touching his wife before its expiration.

The ruling of adh-Dhihâr

Dhihâr is forbidden, as Allah (سبحانه وتعالى) has described it as a false and evil statement and has condemned the one who commits it. Allah says:

﴿ٱلَّذِينَ يُظَٰهِرُونَ مِنكُم مِّن نِّسَآئِهِم مَّا هُنَّ أُمَّهَٰتِهِمْۖ إِنْ أُمَّهَٰتُهُمْ إِلَّا ٱلَّٰٓـِٔي
وَلَدْنَهُمْۚ وَإِنَّهُمْ لَيَقُولُونَ مُنكَرًا مِّنَ ٱلْقَوْلِ وَزُورًاۚ وَإِنَّ ٱللَّهَ لَعَفُوٌّ غَفُورٌ ٢﴾

(سورة المجادلة : ٢)

[136] This hadith is *ṣaḥeeḥ*. See Shaykh al-Albâni, *Ṣaḥeeḥ Sunan Ibn Mâjah*, no. 1677. Recorded by Ibn Mâjah, Abu Dawood and Tirmidhi.

﴿Those among you who make their wives unlawful to them by saying to them, 'You are like my mother's back,' they cannot be their mothers. None can be their mothers except those who gave them birth. And verily, they utter an ill word and a lie. And verily, Allah is Oft-Pardoning, Oft-Forgiving.﴾ *(Qur'an 58: 2)*

Divorce

We demonstrated previously that Islam is very keen upon preserving, safeguarding and protecting married life. We have seen the measures that have been offered to solve marital disputes that can arise, regardless if the cause be one or both of the spouses.

However, those measures may turn out to be unsuccessful, especially if the differences of opinion have become rooted and the disputes strong. In such cases, a stronger measure must be resorted to. This is divorce.

When one studies the laws of divorce, one once again finds Islam's keenness on trying to maintain the institution of the family and its desire to keep the two partners together. This can be seen by the fact that although Islam allows divorce, it does not make it all at once, such that the relationships are immediately cut off between the spouses and the two are never in contact again. Instead, divorce is permitted but it is to occur twice:

﴿ٱلطَّلَٰقُ مَرَّتَانِۖ فَإِمۡسَاكُۢ بِمَعۡرُوفٍ أَوۡ تَسۡرِيحُۢ بِإِحۡسَٰنٖۗ ... ﴿٢٢٩﴾﴾

(سورة البقـرة: ٢٢٩)

﴿The divorce is twice, after that, either you retain her on reasonable terms or release her with kindness...﴾ *(Qur'an 2: 229)*

After the first or second divorce, the man is not permitted to expel the woman from the house until her waiting period is finished. In fact, she cannot leave the house. The purpose behind this is the hope that the anger that produced the divorce will vanish and to encourage them to return to the way things were before. This is what Allah says concerning the matter:

﴿يَٰٓأَيُّهَا ٱلنَّبِىُّ إِذَا طَلَّقْتُمُ ٱلنِّسَآءَ فَطَلِّقُوهُنَّ لِعِدَّتِهِنَّ وَأَحْصُوا۟ ٱلْعِدَّةَ ۖ وَٱتَّقُوا۟ ٱللَّهَ رَبَّكُمْ ۖ لَا تُخْرِجُوهُنَّ مِنۢ بُيُوتِهِنَّ وَلَا يَخْرُجْنَ إِلَّآ أَن يَأْتِينَ بِفَٰحِشَةٍ مُّبَيِّنَةٍ ۚ وَتِلْكَ حُدُودُ ٱللَّهِ ۚ وَمَن يَتَعَدَّ حُدُودَ ٱللَّهِ فَقَدْ ظَلَمَ نَفْسَهُۥ ۚ لَا تَدْرِى لَعَلَّ ٱللَّهَ يُحْدِثُ بَعْدَ ذَٰلِكَ أَمْرًا ①﴾ (سورة الطّلاق: ١)

﴾O' Prophet! When you divorce women, divorce them at their *'Iddah* [prescribed periods], and count [accurately] their periods. And fear Allah your Lord, and turn them not out of their [husband's] homes, nor shall they [themselves] leave, except in case they are guilty of some open illegal sexual intercourse. And those are the set limits of Allah. And whosoever transgresses the set limits of Allah, then indeed he has wronged himself. You [the one who divorces his wife] know not, it may be that Allah will afterward bring some new thing to pass [i.e. to return her back to you if that was the first or second divorce].﴿ *(Qur'an 65: 1)*

In other words, the husband may feel sorry that he divorced her and Allah may put in his heart the desire to have her return to him, which would be simpler and easier.

The Types of Divorce with Respect to the Wording Used

With respect to the wording or expression used, divorce can be divided in to two types: explicit and figurative.

Explicit is that which is understood directly from the words being used and cannot imply anything else. Examples would include, "You are divorced", and any other word that is derived from the word divorced.

When an explicit word is used, divorce takes place, whether the person was joking or playing. Abu Hurayrah narrated that the Prophet (ﷺ) said, "Three are the matters that when said seriously are taken seriously and when said jokingly are also taken seriously: marriage, divorce and returning to one's divorce wife."[137]

Figurative is that which can imply divorce or something else. For example, one could say to one's wife, "Go back to your family". In this case, divorce does not occur unless it was intended. If it was intended, then it is divorce but if it were not intended, it is not divorce. 'Â'ishah (رضي الله عنها) said, "When the Messenger of Allah (ﷺ) went to the daughter of al-Jaun (to consummate his marriage), she said, 'I seek refuge in Allah from you.' He then said to her, 'You have sought refuge in a great One. Go and rejoin your family.' "[138]

In the hadith of K'ab ibn Mâlik, concerning when the Prophet (ﷺ) and his Companions boycotted him for remaining behind the expedition to Tabook, the Messenger of Allah (ﷺ) sent a message to him to separate from his wife. He asked, "Should I divorce her or what should I do?" The reply was, "Just separate from her and do not approach her." So he said to his wife, "Go and rejoin your family."[139]

---

[137] This hadith is *ḥasan*. See Shaykh al-Albâni, *I'rwâ' al-Ghaleel*, no. 1826. Recorded by Ibn Mâjah, Abu Dawood and Tirmidhi.

[138] This hadith is *ṣaḥeeḥ*. See Shaykh al-Albâni, *Ṣaḥeeḥ Sunan Nasâ'i*, no. 3199. Recorded by Bukhari and by Nasâ'i, who stated, "When the woman from the Kalbi tribe..."

[139] Recorded by Bukhari, Muslim, Abu Dawood and Nasâ'i.

The Types of Divorce with Respect to the Conditionality

The wording of the divorce could imply immediacy or it could be conditional.

If it means immediacy, it means that he intends that the divorce takes place from the moment that he stated the divorce. This would be like a husband telling his wife, "You are divorced". The ruling concerning this type of divorce is that it takes place immediately upon the husband stating it.

As for a conditional divorce, this is where the husband lays down a condition upon making the pronouncement of divorce. For example, he may say, "If you go to such and such place, you are divorced." The ruling concerning this type of statement is that if the husband intended by it a statement of divorce, then the divorce takes effect when the condition is met. If he simply meant by his statement a means of encouraging his wife to do something or to refrain from something, then it is simply an oath. If the condition was not fulfilled, then nothing occurred and the husband does not have to do anything about his oath. However, if the condition is fulfilled, then the husband must expiate for breaking his oath. (This is the opinion of Shaykh al-Islam Ibn Taymiyah as expressed in *Majmoo' al-Fatâwâ*, vol. 33, Pp. 44-46, 58-60 and 64-66.)

The Types of Divorce with Respect to if It is Done According to the Sunnah or in an Innovational Manner

Divorce is also divided into the divorce done according to the Sunnah and the divorce done in an innovational manner.

The divorce done according to the Sunnah is wherein the husband divorces his wife, with whom he had consummated the marriage, one time during a time of her purity concerning which the two did not have sexual relations. Allah says, ﴾The divorce is twice, after that, either you retain her on reasonable terms or release her with kindness﴿ *(Qur'an 2: 229)*. Allah also says, ﴾O' Prophet! When you divorce women, divorce them at their *'Iddah* [prescribed periods]﴿ *(Qur'an 65: 1)*. The Prophet (ﷺ) explained this verse when Ibn 'Umar divorced his wife while she was menstruating. 'Umar ibn al-Khaṭṭâb asked the Prophet (ﷺ) about that and the Messenger of Allah (ﷺ) replied, "Order him to take her back and then to keep her until she becomes pure, has her menses again and then becomes pure. Then, if he wills, he may keep her afterwards or he may divorce her before he touches her. That is the period of which Allah has ordered women to be divorced."[140]

An innovational divorce is any divorce that contradicts what is legally sanctioned, such as divorcing one's wife while she is having her menses, during a period of purity in which the two had had sexual relations or to state three divorces in one setting, such as saying, "You are divorced three times", or "You are divorced. You are divorced. You are divorced." This kind of divorce is forbidden and the one who does it is a sinner.

If he divorces her while she is menstruating, the divorce has taken place. If she is qualified to be taken back, she is to be taken back until she becomes pure again, has her menses again and then becomes pure again. At that time, he may keep her as a wife or he may divorce her before touching her. This is how the Prophet (ﷺ) ordered Ibn 'Umar to behave. The proof that such a divorce does occur is in what Bukhari recorded from Sa'eed ibn Jubayr from the same Ibn 'Umar who said, "It was considered one divorce upon me."[141]

---

[140] Recorded by Bukhari, Muslim, Abu Dawood and Nasâ'i.

[141] This hadith is *ṣaḥeeḥ*. See Shaykh al-Albâni, *I'rwâ' al-Ghaleel*, no. 128. Recorded by Bukhari.

Ibn Ḥajar stated in *Fatḥ al-Bâri* (vol. 9, p. 353),

> "It was the Prophet (ﷺ) who ordered Ibn 'Umar to take his wife back and it was he who instructed him what to do afterwards if he wanted to divorce her. When Ibn 'Umar reports that it was considered a divorce on his part, the possibility that it was other than the Prophet (ﷺ) himself who made this conclusion is very distant, especially in the light of the circumstantial evidence in this story. How can it be imagined that Ibn 'Umar would do anything concerning this incident according to his own personal opinion while he was the one who narrated that the Prophet (ﷺ) was unhappy about his actions? How could he not seek his consultation concerning what to do about this incident?"

Ibn Ḥajar further wrote,

> "Ibn Wahb in his *Musnad* recorded from Ibn Abi Dhi'b that Nâfi' informed him that, 'Ibn 'Umar divorced his wife while she was menstruating.' 'Umar then asked the Messenger of Allah (ﷺ) about that. He said, 'Order him to take her back and then remain with her until she becomes pure.'' Ibn Abi Dhi'b said in this hadith from the Prophet (ﷺ), 'It is one (divorce).' Ibn Abi Dhi'b said, 'Ḥandhalah ibn Abi Sufiyân informed me that he heard Sâlim narrate this statement from his father from the Prophet (ﷺ).' Ad-Dâraquṭni recorded with the chain of Yazeed ibn Hâroon from Ibn Abi Dhi'b and Ibn Isḥâq together on the authority of Nâfi' from Ibn 'Umar that the Prophet (ﷺ) said, 'It is one (divorce).'[142] This text concerning this controversial issue must be followed.

Three divorces

If a husband divorces his wife thrice in one sentence or thrice in one setting, it is in fact only one divorce. Muslim recorded that Ibn

[142] Its chain is *ṣaḥeeḥ*. See Shaykh al-Albâni, *I'rwâ' al-Ghaleel*, vol. 7, p.=

'Abbâs said, "During the time of the Messenger of Allah (ﷺ), Abu Bakr and the first two years of 'Umar, three divorces stated at once was considered one divorce. 'Umar ibn al-Khaṭṭâb then said, 'The people are making haste in matter that should take time for them. Maybe we should enforce this upon them.' So he then enforced this upon them." This opinion from 'Umar was his own personal legal reasoning, which he felt was permissible due to a specific benefit he was seeking to achieve. However, it is not allowed to abandon what the Messenger of Allah (ﷺ) ruled and what his Companions were following during his time and during the time of his successor.

The Types of Divorce with Respect to Being Revocable or Irrevocable

Divorce is either revocable or irrevocable. If it is irrevocable, it is either the greater irrevocable divorce or the lesser irrevocable divorce.

The revocable divorce is that divorce which takes place after the marriage has been consummated, was not in exchange for wealth and is preceded by no or only one divorce. Allah has said, ﴿The divorce is twice, after that, either you retain her on reasonable terms or release her with kindness﴾ *(Qur'an 2: 229).*

The woman who is revocably divorced remains the man's wife as long as she is in her waiting period. Her husband has the right to return her as his wife at any time during the waiting period, without her consent or that of her guardian being a precondition. Allah (سبحانه وتعالى) has said:

﴿وَٱلْمُطَلَّقَٰتُ يَتَرَبَّصْنَ بِأَنفُسِهِنَّ ثَلَٰثَةَ قُرُوٓءٍ وَلَا يَحِلُّ لَهُنَّ أَن يَكْتُمْنَ مَا خَلَقَ ٱللَّهُ

=134. Recorded by ad-Dâraquṭni.

فِىٓ أَرْحَامِهِنَّ إِن كُنَّ يُؤْمِنَّ بِٱللَّهِ وَٱلْيَوْمِ ٱلْءَاخِرِ ۚ وَبُعُولَتُهُنَّ أَحَقُّ بِرَدِّهِنَّ فِى ذَٰلِكَ إِنْ أَرَادُوٓا۟ إِصْلَٰحًا ... ﴿٢٢٨﴾ (سورة البَقَرَة: ٢٢٨)

﴿And divorced women shall wait [as regards their marriage] for three menstrual periods, and it is not lawful for them to conceal what Allah has created in their wombs, if they believe in Allah and the Last Day. And their husbands have the better right to take them back in that period, if they wish for reconciliation...﴾ *(Qur'an 2: 228)*

Al-Khula'

Definition of al-Khula'

Khula' comes from a word implying removing one's garment. Recall that the wife is a garment for the man and vice-versa, as Allah has said:

﴿... هُنَّ لِبَاسٌ لَّكُمْ وَأَنتُمْ لِبَاسٌ لَّهُنَّ ... ﴿١٨٧﴾ (سورة البَقَرَة: ١٨٧)

﴿... They are a body cover for you and you are the same for them...﴾ *(Qur'an 2: 187)*

The jurists have defined it as, "A man separates from his wife in exchange for something that he takes from her." It is also sometimes referred to as "ransoming and freeing."[143]

---

[143] *Fiqh as-Sunnah*, vol. 2, p. 253; *Manâr as-Sabeel*, vol. 2, p. 226 and *Fatḥ al-Bâri*, vol. 9, p. 395.

Its legal status

If the discord between the two spouses becomes strong and there is no way to bring about a reconciliation while, at the same time, the wife desires to separate, it is permissible to her to "ransom" herself from her husband by paying him a sum of money in exchange for the harm that he will face due to their separation. Allah says:

﴿... وَلَا يَحِلُّ لَكُمْ أَن تَأْخُذُوا۟ مِمَّآ ءَاتَيْتُمُوهُنَّ شَيْـًٔا إِلَّآ أَن يَخَافَآ أَلَّا يُقِيمَا حُدُودَ ٱللَّهِ ۖ فَإِنْ خِفْتُمْ أَلَّا يُقِيمَا حُدُودَ ٱللَّهِ فَلَا جُنَاحَ عَلَيْهِمَا فِيمَا ٱفْتَدَتْ بِهِۦ ۗ ... ﴿٢٢٩﴾﴾

(سورة البقرة: ٢٢٩)

﴾... And it is not lawful for you [men] to take back [from your wives] any of your dower which you have given them, except when both parties fear that they would be unable to keep the limits ordained by Allah. Then if you fear that they would not be able to keep the limits ordained by Allah, then there is no sin on either of them if she gives back [the dower or a part of it] for her separation...﴿ *(Qur'an 2: 229)*

Ibn 'Abbâs narrated that the wife of Thâbit ibn Qays ibn Shammâs came to the Prophet (ﷺ) and said, "O' Messenger of Allah, I have no complaint against Thâbit with respect to his religion or his character but I fear being ungrateful." The Messenger of Allah (ﷺ) said, "Will you return to him his garden." She said, "Yes." She returned it to him and he ordered him to separate from her.[144]

A warning concerning it

Thawbân narrated that the Messenger of Allah (ﷺ) said, "For any woman who asks her husband for divorce without anything

---

[144] This hadith is *ṣaḥeeḥ*. See Shaykh al-Albâni, *I'rwâ' al-Ghaleel*, no. 2036. Recorded by Bukhari.

wrong being done the scent of Paradise will be forbidden for her."[145] He also narrated that the Prophet (ﷺ) said, "Those women who seek to pay for a divorce (from their husbands[146]) are hypocrites."[147]

Warning to the men about harming the wife

If the husband dislikes the wife and turns away for her for any reason, he should then separate from her in the proper way that Allah has ordered. It is not permissible for him to retain her and harm her until she finally offers to pay something to free herself. Allah says:

﴿وَإِذَا طَلَّقْتُمُ ٱلنِّسَآءَ فَبَلَغْنَ أَجَلَهُنَّ فَأَمْسِكُوهُنَّ بِمَعْرُوفٍ أَوْ سَرِّحُوهُنَّ بِمَعْرُوفٍۚ وَلَا تُمْسِكُوهُنَّ ضِرَارًا لِّتَعْتَدُوا۟ۚ وَمَن يَفْعَلْ ذَٰلِكَ فَقَدْ ظَلَمَ نَفْسَهُۥۚ وَلَا تَتَّخِذُوٓا۟ ءَايَٰتِ ٱللَّهِ هُزُوًاۚ وَٱذْكُرُوا۟ نِعْمَتَ ٱللَّهِ عَلَيْكُمْ وَمَآ أَنزَلَ عَلَيْكُم مِّنَ ٱلْكِتَٰبِ وَٱلْحِكْمَةِ يَعِظُكُم بِهِۦۚ وَٱتَّقُوا۟ ٱللَّهَ وَٱعْلَمُوٓا۟ أَنَّ ٱللَّهَ بِكُلِّ شَىْءٍ عَلِيمٌ ﴿٢٣١﴾﴾ (سورة البقرة: ٢٣١)

﴾And when you have divorced women and they have fulfilled the term of their prescribed period, either take them back on reasonable basis or set them free on reasonable basis. But do not take them back to hurt them, and whoever does that, then he has wronged himself. And treat not the Laws of Allah as a jest, but remember Allah's Favours on you, and that which He has sent down to you of the Book and the Wisdom whereby He instructs you. And fear Allah, and know that Allah is All-Aware of everything.﴿ *(Qur'an 2: 231)*

Allah (ﷻ) also said:

---

[145] This hadith is *ṣaḥeeḥ*. See Shaykh al-Albâni, *Ṣaḥeeḥ Sunan Ibn Mâjah*, no. 1676. Recorded by Tirmidhi, Abu Dawood and Ibn Mâjah.

[146] [Meaning: without due cause.] - Translator

[147] This hadith is *ṣaḥeeḥ*. See Shaykh al-Albâni, *Ṣaḥeeḥ al-Jâmi' aṣ-Ṣagheer*, no. 6681. Recorded by Tirmidhi.

﴿يَا أَيُّهَا الَّذِينَ آمَنُوا لَا يَحِلُّ لَكُمْ أَن تَرِثُوا النِّسَاءَ كَرْهًا ۖ وَلَا تَعْضُلُوهُنَّ
لِتَذْهَبُوا بِبَعْضِ مَا آتَيْتُمُوهُنَّ إِلَّا أَن يَأْتِينَ بِفَاحِشَةٍ مُّبَيِّنَةٍ ۚ وَعَاشِرُوهُنَّ
بِالْمَعْرُوفِ ۚ فَإِن كَرِهْتُمُوهُنَّ فَعَسَىٰ أَن تَكْرَهُوا شَيْئًا وَيَجْعَلَ اللَّهُ فِيهِ خَيْرًا
كَثِيرًا ﴿١٩﴾﴾ (سورة النِّسَاء: ١٩)

﴾O' you who believe! You are forbidden to inherit women against their will, and you should not treat them with harshness, that you may take away part of the dower you have given them, unless they commit open illegal sexual intercourse. And live with them honourably. If you dislike them, it may be that you dislike a thing and Allah brings through it a great deal of good.﴿ *(Qur'an 4: 19)*

Khula' is Dissolution of the Marriage and not a Divorce

If the woman frees herself by *khula'* and separates from her husband, then she is in charge of herself. Her husband has no right to take her back except by her consent. This kind of separation is not a type of divorce, even if it is stated with the same terminology. It is dissolution of the marriage contract in the interest of the woman in exchange for some wealth that she gives up. Ibn al-Qayyim stated,

> "From the things that indicate that this is not a divorce is the fact that Allah (ﷻ) has, concerning less than three divorces after consummation, laid down certain results that are all denied in the case of *khula'*.
>
> First, the husband has the right to bring his wife back (in the case of divorce).
>
> Second, it is limited to three after the last waiting period of which she is not permissible to him except after she marries and consummates with someone else.

Third, the waiting period (in the case of divorce) is three periods. It is confirmed by the texts (of the Book and Sunnah) as well as consensus that one cannot take one's wife back in *khula'*. It is also confirmed by the Sunnah and the statements of the Companions that the waiting period is just one menses (for *khula'*). And it is confirmed by a text that it is permissible after two divorces and that the third divorce could occur after it.

There is a very clear manifestation that it is not a type of divorce. Allah has said, ﴾The divorce is twice, after that, either you retain her on reasonable terms or release her with kindness. And it is not lawful for you [men] to take back [from your wives] any of your dower which you have given them, except when both parties fear that they would be unable to keep the limits ordained by Allah. Then if you fear that they would not be able to keep the limits ordained by Allah, then there is no sin on either of them if she gives back [the dower or a part of it] for her separation...﴿ *(Qur'an 2: 229)*.

Even though that may not be specific for the one who was divorced twice, as it covers her as well as others, it is not permissible that the pronoun refers to an antecedent that was not mention and that is left being free of mention. Either it is to be specified by what precedes it or it will apply to others as well. Then Allah says, ﴾And if he has divorced her [the third time], then she is not lawful unto him thereafter until she has married another husband﴿ *(Qur'an 2: 230)*. This definitely covers anyone who was divorced after she ransomed herself as well as the one who had been divorced twice, as these two have been mentioned as antecedents and must be covered by the texts. This is how (Ibn 'Abbâs,) understood it, he who was the 'translator of the Qur'an', for whom the Prophet (ﷺ) personally prayed for to understand the meaning of the Qur'an — and there is no doubt that such a supplication was responded to. Since the rulings of the woman freeing herself are different from the rulings of divorce, this indicates that it is of a separate genus. This is what the texts, analogy and statements of the Companions call for."[148]

The Waiting Period

Its Definition

The Arabic word for the waiting period (*al-'iddah*) comes from a word meaning to reckon or count. In other words, it refers to the days and period that the women reckon and count. As a legal term, it refers to the period of time that the woman must refrain from marriage after the death of her husband or after separation from her husband. It is reckoned by giving birth, menses or months.

Its Types

The widow whose husband has just died is to enter a waiting period of four months and ten days, regardless of whether the marriage had been consummated. Allah (ﷻ) says:

﴿وَٱلَّذِينَ يُتَوَفَّوْنَ مِنكُمْ وَيَذَرُونَ أَزْوَٰجًا يَتَرَبَّصْنَ بِأَنفُسِهِنَّ أَرْبَعَةَ أَشْهُرٍ وَعَشْرًا ... ﴿٢٣٤﴾﴾

(سورة البقرة: ٢٣٤)

﴾And those of you who die and leave wives behind them, they [the wives] shall wait [as regards their marriage] for four months and ten [days]...﴿ *(Qur'an 2: 234)*

[148] Ibn al-Qayyim, *Zâd al-Ma'ad*, vol. 5, p. 199.

The exception to this is if the woman was pregnant. Then her waiting period is until the time she gives birth. Allah (ﷻ) says:

﴿... وَأُوْلَٰتُ ٱلْأَحْمَالِ أَجَلُهُنَّ أَن يَضَعْنَ حَمْلَهُنَّ ...﴾ (سورة الطّلاق: ٤)

﴾... And for those who are pregnant [whether they are divorced or their husbands are dead], their waiting period is until they deliver [their burdens]...﴿ *(Qur'an 65: 4)*

Al-Miswar ibn Makhramah narrated that Sabiy'ah al-Aslamiyah gave birth one night after her husband's death. She went to the Prophet (ﷺ) and asked him for permission to wed. He gave her permission and so she wedded."[149]

The one who is divorced before consummation has not waiting period. Allah says:

﴿يَٰٓأَيُّهَا ٱلَّذِينَ ءَامَنُوٓاْ إِذَا نَكَحْتُمُ ٱلْمُؤْمِنَٰتِ ثُمَّ طَلَّقْتُمُوهُنَّ مِن قَبْلِ أَن تَمَسُّوهُنَّ فَمَا لَكُمْ عَلَيْهِنَّ مِنْ عِدَّةٍ تَعْتَدُّونَهَا ...﴾ (سورة الأحزاب: ٤٩)

﴾O' you who believe! When you marry believing women, and then divorce them before you have sexual intercourse with them, no waiting period have you to count in respect of them...﴿ *(Qur'an 33: 49)*

The divorced woman after consummation and pregnant will be in her waiting period until the time she gives birth. Allah (ﷻ) says, ﴾And for those who are pregnant [whether they are divorced or their husbands are dead], their waiting period is until they deliver [their burdens]...﴿ *(Qur'an 65: 4)*. Az-Zubayr ibn al-'Awwâm narrated that he was married to Umm Kulthoom bint 'Uqbah. She said to him, "Please me by a divorce." So he divorced her once. He went to the

---

[149] Recorded by Bukhari and Muslim.

prayer and returned to find that she had given birth. He said, "What is wrong with her deceiving me, may Allah then deceive her." Then he went to the Prophet (ﷺ) who said, "Its term (for the waiting period) has come to an end. She is in charge of herself."[150]

If the woman is one who is experiencing menses, then her waiting period is three menstrual periods. Allah has said:

﴿وَٱلْمُطَلَّقَٰتُ يَتَرَبَّصْنَ بِأَنفُسِهِنَّ ثَلَٰثَةَ قُرُوٓءٍ ... ﴿٢٢٨﴾﴾ (سورة البَقَرَة: ٢٢٨)

﴿And divorced women shall wait [as regards their marriage] for three menstrual periods...﴾ *(Qur'an 2: 228)*

The word *quru'* in the verse refers to the menses, as 'Â'ishah had said, "Umm Ḥabeebah had a prolonged flow of blood and the Prophet (ﷺ) told her to leave the prayers during the days of her menses (*quru'*)."[151]

If she is a young woman who does not yet menstruate or an older woman who no longer menstruates, her waiting period is three months. Allah has said:

﴿وَٱلَّٰٓـِٔي يَئِسْنَ مِنَ ٱلْمَحِيضِ مِن نِّسَآئِكُمْ إِنِ ٱرْتَبْتُمْ فَعِدَّتُهُنَّ ثَلَٰثَةُ أَشْهُرٍ وَٱلَّٰٓـِٔي لَمْ يَحِضْنَ ... ﴿٤﴾﴾ (سورة الطَّلَاق: ٤)

﴿And those of your women as have passed the age of monthly courses, for them the waiting periods, if you have doubts [about their periods], is three months, and for those who have no courses their waiting period is three months likewise...﴾ *(Qur'an 65: 4)*

---

[150] This hadith is *ṣaḥeeḥ*. See Shaykh al-Albâni, *Ṣaḥeeḥ al-Jâmi' aṣ-Ṣagheer*, no. 1646. Recorded by Ibn Mâjah.

[151] This hadith is *ṣaḥeeḥ* due to corroborating reports. See Shaykh al-Albâni, *Ṣaḥeeḥ Sunan Abi Dawood*, no. 252. Reported by Abu Dawood.

What is Obligatory upon the Widow During Her Waiting Period

The widow must enter a period of mourning until her waiting period comes to an end. Mourning consists of not beautifying oneself, wearing perfume, wearing jewellery, wearing coloured clothing, applying make-up or applying kohl. Umm 'Aṭiyah said, "We were forbidden to mourn for more than three days for a dead person except in the case of one's husband, for whom we were to mourn for four months and ten days. While mourning, we were not permitted to darken the rim of our eyelids with kohl, apply perfume, or put on any dyed garments except the one made of *'aṣab* (a rough Yemeni cloth). However, at the time of purification, when any of us performed *ghusl* after her menstruation, it was permissible for us to perfume ourselves with the incense from a little fragment of costus. In addition, we were forbidden to follow funeral processions."[152]

Umm Salamah narrated that the Prophet (ﷺ) said, "The widow (in her mourning period) is not to wear garments dyed saffron colour, clothes dyed red or jewellery, nor apply henna to their hairs or apply kohl."[153]

What is Obligatory during the Waiting Period of a Revocable Divorce

During the waiting period of a revocable divorce, the woman must remain in the house of her husband until the waiting period

---

[152] Recorded by Bukhari and Muslim. Abu Dawood, Nasâ'i and Ibn Mâjah have something similar.

[153] This hadith is *ṣaḥeeḥ*. See Shaykh al-Albâni, *Ṣaḥeeḥ Sunan Abi Dawood*, no. 2020. Recorded by Abu Dawood and also by Nasâ'i but without the mention of jewelry.

comes to an end. She may not leave the house and her husband is not allowed to expel from the house. Allah (ﷻ) has stated:

﴿ يَٰٓأَيُّهَا ٱلنَّبِيُّ إِذَا طَلَّقْتُمُ ٱلنِّسَآءَ فَطَلِّقُوهُنَّ لِعِدَّتِهِنَّ وَأَحْصُوا۟ ٱلْعِدَّةَ ۖ وَٱتَّقُوا۟ ٱللَّهَ رَبَّكُمْ ۖ لَا تُخْرِجُوهُنَّ مِنۢ بُيُوتِهِنَّ وَلَا يَخْرُجْنَ إِلَّآ أَن يَأْتِينَ بِفَٰحِشَةٍ مُّبَيِّنَةٍ ... ﴿١﴾ ﴾ (سورة الطّلاق : ١)

﴾O' Prophet! When you divorce women, divorce them at their *'Iddah* [prescribed periods], and count [accurately] their periods. And fear Allah your Lord, and turn them not out of their [husband's] homes, nor shall they [themselves] leave, except in case they are guilty of some open illegal sexual intercourse...﴿ *(Qur'an 65: 1)*

What is Obligatory during the Waiting Period of an Irrevocable Final Divorce

The one who is divorced thrice is not entitled to either housing or maintenance. Fâṭimah bint Qays narrated that the Prophet (ﷺ) said about a thrice-divorced woman, "There is no housing or maintenance for her."[154]

She must go to her household's residence and she is not allowed to go out from there except to meet her needs. Jâbir ibn 'Abdullâh said, "My aunt was divorced. She wanted to go and gather the fruits of her date-palms but a man prevented her from going out. She came to the Prophet (ﷺ) (and informed him of that). He said, "Certainly go and gather the fruits of your date-palms for you may give them in charity or do a good deed.' "[155]

---

[154] This hadith is *ṣaḥeeḥ*. See Shaykh al-Albâni, *Mukhtasar Ṣaḥeeḥ Muslim*, no. 888. Recorded by Muslim.

[155] This hadith is *ṣaḥeeḥ*. See Shaykh al-Albâni, *I'rwâ' al-Ghaleel*, no. 2134.=

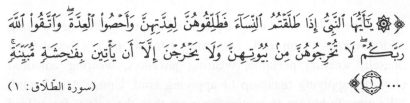

Ensuring that the woman is not pregnant

If a man comes into possession of a slave-girl, it is forbidden for him to enjoy her until it is made certain that she is not pregnant. If she is pregnant, then he remains away from her until she gives birth. If she has her menses, then the waiting period is one menstrual cycle. Ruwaifi' ibn Thâbit narrated that the Prophet (ﷺ) said, "Whoever believes in Allah and the Last Day must not supply his sperm to another's child[156]."[157] Abu Sa'eed narrated that the Prophet (ﷺ) stated about the female captives of Awtâs, "Do not have intercourse with a pregnant woman until she gives birth or a non-pregnant woman until she experiences her menses once."[158] Ibn 'Umar said, "If a slave girl whom one can have intercourse with is given as a gift, sold or set free, then it is to be made clear that she is not pregnant by her experiencing her menses. Virgin girls, however, need not wait such a period."[159]

Custody

Custody means to protect a child from what harms it and to attend to its interest and needs.[160]

If a man separates from his wife while they have a child, she has more right to the child until the child is seven years of age — as

=Recorded by Muslim, Nasâ'i, Abu Dawood and similar by Ibn Mâjah.

156 [That is, by having intercourse with a woman impregnated by another man.]

157 This hadith is *ḥasan*. See Shaykh al-Albâni, *Ṣaḥeeḥ Sunan Abi Dawood*, no. 1890. Recorded by Tirmidhi and by Abu Dawood as part of a lengthy hadith.

158 This hadith is *ṣaḥeeḥ*. See Shaykh al-Albâni, *Ṣaḥeeḥ Sunan Abi Dawood*, no. 1889. Recorded by Abu Dawood.

159 This hadith is *ṣaḥeeḥ*. See Shaykh al-Albâni, *I'rwâ' al-Ghaleel*, no. 2139. Recorded without its complete chain by Bukhari.

160 *Manâr as-Sabeel*, vol. 2, p. 310.

long as she does not remarry. When the child turns seven, he is free to choose between his parents. Whichever one he chooses, he will reside with that parent.

'Amr ibn Shu'ayb narrated from his father on the authority of his grandfather that a woman said, "O' Messenger of Allah! This child of mine was living in my stomach, my breast nourished him, my room is where he was protected and now his father has divorced me and wants to wrest him away from me." The Messenger of Allah (ﷺ) told her, "You have more right to him as long as you do not remarry."[161]

Abu Hurayrah narrated that a woman came to the Prophet (ﷺ) and said, "O' Messenger of Allah! My husband wishes to take my son while he brings me water from the well of Abu 'Inabah and I benefit from him." The Prophet (ﷺ) (said to the youngster), "This is your father and this is your mother. Take the hand of whichever of them you wish." So he took the hand of his mother and left with her.[162]

---

[161] This hadith is *ḥasan*. See Shaykh al-Albâni, *I'rwâ' al-Ghaleel*, no. 2187. Recorded by Abu Dawood.

[162] This hadith is *ṣaḥeeḥ*. See Shaykh al-Albâni, *Ṣaḥeeḥ Sunan Abi Dawood*, no. 1992. Recorded by Nasâ'i, Abu Dawood (as part of a longer story) and by Tirmidhi, in abbreviated form simply mentioning the option given to the child.

Chapter Eight — Business Transactions

The Arabic word *al-bai'* (plural, *al-buyoo'*), or sale, means to transfer possession from one to another in exchange for a price. Purchase (*sharâ'*) is the opposite. However, each term is sometimes used for the other.

Its Legal Sanction

Allah (ﷻ) says:

﴿... وَأَحَلَّ ٱللَّهُ ٱلْبَيْعَ وَحَرَّمَ ٱلرِّبَوٰاْ ... ﴿٢٧٥﴾﴾ (سورة البقرة: ٢٧٥)

﴿... Allah has permitted trading and forbidden interest...﴾

(Qur'an 2: 275)

Allah also says:

﴿يَٰٓأَيُّهَا ٱلَّذِينَ ءَامَنُواْ لَا تَأْكُلُوٓاْ أَمْوَٰلَكُم بَيْنَكُم بِٱلْبَٰطِلِ إِلَّآ أَن تَكُونَ تِجَٰرَةً عَن تَرَاضٍ مِّنكُمْ ... ﴿٢٩﴾﴾ (سورة النساء: ٢٩)

﴿O' you who believe! Do not devour your property among yourselves unjustly except it be a trade amongst you, by mutual consent...﴾ *(Qur'an 4: 29)*

Ḥakeem ibn Ḥizâm (may Allah be pleased with him) narrated that the Prophet (Blessings and peace be upon him) said, "The two parties of a sale[1] still have the option (of cancellation) as long as they have not yet separated."[2]

The Muslims are all in agreement that buying and selling is permissible. Wisdom demands it as the needs of individuals are often in the hands of others and the others may not sacrifice them. By instituting buying and selling, this is a means by which people can meet their needs without hardship.[3]

Encouragement to Earn One's Living

Al-Miqdâm (رضي الله عنه) narrated that the Prophet (ﷺ) said, "No one consumes any food better than that which was earned by his own hands. The Prophet of Allah Dawood (عليه السلام) used to eat what his own hands earned."[4] Abu Hurayrah reported that the Messenger of Allah (ﷺ) said, "It is better for one of you to bring a load of firewood on his back and sell it, than to ask of another who might give him or refuse to give him."[5]

There is No Harm in Wealth as long as One is Still Pious

Mu'âdh ibn 'Abdullâh ibn Khubayb narrated from his father on the authority of his uncle that the Messenger of Allah (ﷺ) said, "There is no harm in riches for the one who has piety (*taqwa*). And

---

[1] [That is, the buyer and the seller or the two parties to a contractual agreement.] - Translator
[2] Recorded by Bukhari, Muslim, Abu Dawood, Tirmidhi and Nasâ'i.
[3] Ibn Ḥajar, *Fatḥ al-Bâri*, vol. 4, p. 287.
[4] This hadith is *ṣaḥeeḥ*. See Shaykh al-Albâni, *Ṣaḥeeḥ al-Jâmi' aṣ-Ṣagheer*, no. 5546. Recorded by Bukhari.
[5] This hadith is *ṣaḥeeḥ*. See Shaykh al-Albâni, *Ṣaḥeeḥ al-Jâmi' aṣ-Ṣagheer*, no. 7069. Recorded by Bukhari, Tirmidhi and Nasâ'i.

health is better for the one who has piety. Tranquillity of the soul is a form of blessing."[6]

Encouragement to Be Moderate in Seeking Livelihood

Jâbir ibn 'Abdullâh narrated that the Messenger of Allah (ﷺ) said, "O' people, fear Allah and act properly and goodly in seeking (wealth) for a soul will not die until it exhausts its sustenance (decreed for it), even if it is slow in coming. Fear Allah and act properly in seeking (wealth by) taking what is permissible and leaving what is forbidden."[7]

Encouragement to be Honest and Warning Concerning Lying

Ḥakeem ibn Ḥizâm narrated that the Prophet (ﷺ) said, "The two parties of a sale[8] still have the option (of cancellation) as long as they have not yet separated. If they are honest with each other they will be blessed in their transaction. If they concealed or lied, then the blessings in their transactions will have been effaced."[9] 'Uqbah ibn 'Âmr narrated that he heard the Messenger of Allah (ﷺ) saying, "A Muslim is a brother to another Muslim. It is not permissible for a Muslim to sell something defective to his brother without pointing that out to him."[10]

---

[6] This hadith is *ṣaḥeeḥ*. See Shaykh al-Albâni, *Ṣaḥeeḥ Sunan Ibn Mâjah*, no. 1741. Recorded by Ibn Mâjah.

[7] Ibid, no. 1743.

[8] [That is, the buyer and the seller or the two parties to a contractual agreement.] - Translator

[9] Recorded by Bukhari, Muslim, Abu Dawood, Tirmidhi and Nasâ'i.

[10] This hadith is *ṣaḥeeḥ*. See Shaykh al-Albâni, *Ṣaḥeeḥ al-Jâmi' aṣ-Ṣagheer*, no. 6705. Recorded by Ibn Mâjah.

Encouragement to be Easygoing and Compromising when Buying or Selling

Jâbir ibn 'Abdullâh narrated that the Messenger of Allah (ﷺ) said, "May Allah have mercy on the one who is easy-going and generous while buying, while selling and when demanding his rights."[11]

The excellence of giving respite to one in straitened circumstances

Abu Hurayrah narrated that the Prophet (ﷺ) said, "There was a trader who used to deal in credit with the people. If he noticed that one was in straitened circumstances, he would tell his boy (working for him), 'Excuse him so that Ạllah may overlook (and forgive our sins) for us.' Therefore, Allah overlooked (his sins) and forgave him."[12]

The prohibition of deception

Abu Hurayrah narrated that one time the Prophet (ﷺ) passed by a man who was selling rains. The Prophet (ﷺ) put his hand into the grains and he found that he was concealing a defect. The Messenger of Allah (ﷺ) then said, "Whoever deceives is not from us."[13]

---

[11] This hadith is *ṣaḥeeḥ*. See Shaykh al-Albâni, *Ṣaḥeeḥ al-Jâmi' aṣ-Ṣagheer*, no. 4454. Recorded by Bukhari.

[12] This hadith is *ṣaḥeeḥ*. See Shaykh al-Albâni, *Ṣaḥeeḥ al-Jâmi' aṣ-Ṣagheer*, no. 3495. Recorded by Bukhari.

[13] This hadith is *ṣaḥeeḥ*. See Shaykh al-Albâni, *I'rwâ' al-Ghaleel*, no. 1319 and *Ṣaḥeeḥ Sunan Ibn Mâjah*, no. 1809. Recorded by Ibn Mâjah (and this is his wording), Abu Dawood, Tirmidhi and Muslim.

Encouragement to Seek One's Livelihood Early in the Morning

Ṣakhr al-Ghâmidi said that the Messenger of Allah (ﷺ) said, "O' Allah, bless my Nation in its early hours."[14]

What one should say upon entering the marketplace

Sâlim ibn 'Abdullâh ibn 'Umar narrated from his father on the authority of his grandfather that the Messenger of Allah (ﷺ) said, "Whoever says (the following) upon entering the marketplace,

لا إِلَهَ إِلاَّ اللَّهُ وَحْدَهُ لا شَرِيكَ لَهُ لَهُ الْمُلْكُ وَلَهُ الْحَمْدُ يُحْيِي وَيُمِيتُ وَهُوَ حَيٌّ لا يَمُوتُ بِيَدِهِ الْخَيْرُ كُلُّهُ وَهُوَ عَلَى كُلِّ شَيْءٍ قَدِيرٌ

'There is none worthy of worship except Allah, alone, without any partner with Him. For Him is the Dominion and to Him is the praise. He gives life and He brings about death; He is living and does not die. In His hand is all good and He has power over all things,' then Allah will record for him one million good deeds and erase from him one million evil deeds and will build for him a house in Paradise."[15]

Allah has Made Trade Permissible

The basic ruling concerning business transactions is that they are all permissible, as long as they are done with the approval of the two parties and they have not been explicitly prohibited by the Lawgiver.

---

[14] This hadith is *ṣaḥeeḥ*. See Shaykh al-Albâni, *Ṣaḥeeḥ Sunan Ibn Mâjah*, no. 1818. Recorded by Ibn Mâjah, Tirmidhi and Abu Dawood.

[15] This hadith is *ḥasan*. See Shaykh al-Albâni, *Ṣaḥeeḥ Sunan Ibn Mâjah*, no. 1817. Recorded by Ibn Mâjah.

Business Transactions Forbidden by the Lawgiver

1. Overly risk transactions

This refers to any transaction containing unknown quantities/ qualities or containing great risk or gambling.

Abu Hurayrah said that the Messenger of Allah (ﷺ) prohibited *bai' al-ḥaṣâh* [16] and overly-risky transactions.[17]

In his commentary to *Ṣaḥeeḥ Muslim* (vol. 10, p. 156), Imam an-Nawawi wrote,

> "The prohibition of overly-risky transactions is a great principle of the principles of business transactions. For this reason, Muslim presented this hadith first. Countless other issues are covered by it, such as the sale of a runaway slave, of something that does not exist, of something unknown, of something that one cannot deliver, of something that is not completely owned by the seller, of the fish in a large body of water, of the milk in an animal's udder, of the fetus in an animal, of unspecified part of a heap, of a piece of clothing among garments, of a sheep among sheep and so on. All of these sales are void as they all constitute a great deal of risk and uncertainty without any called-for need. If, due to some need, people have to venture into risk-bearing transactions, which

---

[16] [This is where one says, for example, "Throw this pebble and whatever merchandise it lands on is yours for such and such price." Again, this type of sale is not valid due to the ignorance and risk involved.] - Translator

[17] This hadith is *ṣaḥeeḥ*. See Shaykh al-Albâni, *Mukhtasar Ṣaḥeeḥ Muslim*, no. 939 and *I'rwâ' al-Ghaleel*, no. 1294. Recorded by Muslim, Tirmidhi, Abu Dawood, Ibn Mâjah and Nasâ'i.

cannot be avoided except with difficulty, and if the amount of risk is miniscule, then the transaction is permissible. Thus, for example, Muslims all agree that it is permissible to buy a stuffed dish even if one does not see what it is stuffed with, while if one were to buy the stuffing by itself, it would not be permissible.

You should realize that the *mulâmasah* transaction[18], the *munâbadhah* transaction[19], the sale of an animal before it is born, the *ḥaṣâh* transaction[20], stud fees and other transactions concerning which there is a particular text are all included under the general category of the prohibition of overly-risky transactions — but they have been mentioned separately and prohibited specifically because they were types of transactions that were well-known in the pre-Islamic days of ignorance.

The mulâmasah transaction and the munâbadhah transaction

Abu Hurayrah said, "Two types of transactions were prohibited: *al-mulâmasah* and *al-munâbadhah*. *Mulâmasah* is where each party touches the garment of the other without inspecting it. *Munâbadhah* is where each flings a garment to the other and neither of them looks at the garment of the other."[21]

Abu Sa'eed al-Khudri said, "The Messenger of Allah (ﷺ) forbade us two types of transactions and two types of garments. He

---

[18] [This is when the seller tells the buyer, for example, "Any garment you touched is yours for such and such."] - Translator

[19] [This is where the seller tells the buyer, "Any garment you fling to me is yours for such and such price."] - Translator

[20] [This is where one says, for example, "Throw this pebble and whatever merchandise it lands on is yours for such and such price." Again, this type of sale is not valid due to the ignorance and risk involved.] - Translator

[21] This hadith is *ṣaḥeeḥ*. See Shaykh al-Albâni, *Mukhtasar Ṣaḥeeḥ Muslim*, no. 938. Recorded by Muslim.

forbade *al-mulâmasah* and *al-munâbadhah* transactions. *Mulâmasah* is for one man to touch another's garment, during the night or day, and not inspect it beyond that. *Munâbadhah* is for one man to fling a garment to the other and vice-versa. That will be the end of their transaction without inspection or approval."[22]

Selling the unborn fetus

Ibn 'Umar said, "The people of the days of ignorance used to sell camel's meat all the way to the extent of *ḥabal al-ḥablah*. And *ḥabal al-ḥablah* is the offspring of the present pregnant camel becoming pregnant (in the future). The Prophet (ﷺ) forbade that."[23]

Al-Ḥaṣâh transaction

Abu Hurayrah said that the Messenger of Allah (ﷺ) prohibited *bai' al-ḥaṣâh*[24] and overly-risky transactions.[25] Imam an-Nawawi wrote in his commentary to *Ṣaḥeeḥ Muslim* (vol. 10, p. 156),

> "There are three interpretations to the meaning of *bai' al-ḥaṣâh*. The first is for a person to say, 'I sell to you the garments upon which these pebbles I throw land on,' or, 'I sell to you the land from here until where the pebbles land.' The second interpretation is that it is for a person to say, 'I have sold this to you but you have

---

[22] Recorded by Bukhari, Muslim (and this is his wording), Abu Dawood and Nasâ'i.

[23] Recorded by Bukhari, Muslim, Abu Dawood, Tirmidhi (in abbreviated form), Nasâ'i and Ibn Mâjah (also in abbreviated form).

[24] [This is where one says, for example, "Throw this pebble and whatever merchandise it lands on is yours for such and such price." Again, this type of sale is not valid due to the ignorance and risk involved.] - Translator

[25] This hadith is *ṣaḥeeḥ*. See Shaykh al-Albâni, *Mukhtasar Ṣaḥeeḥ Muslim*, no. 939 and *I'rwâ' al-Ghaleel*, no. 1294. Recorded by Muslim, Tirmidhi, Abu Dawood, Ibn Mâjah and Nasâ'i.

an option to cancel until I throw these pebbles.' The third is that they allow the throwing of the pebbles to determine the sale, saying, 'If I hit this garment with a pebble, I buy it from you for such and such.' "

Stud fees

Ibn 'Umar said that the Prophet (ﷺ) forbade stud fees.[26]

2. Selling What One Does not Possess

Ḥakeem ibn Ḥâzim said, "I said, 'O' Messenger of Allah, a person comes to me and asks me to sell him something that I do not have, can I still sell it?' The Prophet (ﷺ) replied, 'Do not sell that which you do not have.' "[27]

3. Selling Something Before Taking Possession of It

Ibn 'Abbâs narrated that the Messenger of Allah (ﷺ) said, "Whoever buys foodstuff must not sell them until he takes possession of them." Ibn 'Abbâs further added, "I reckon that everything is analogous to foodstuff."[28]

Ṭâwoos narrated that Ibn 'Abbâs stated that the Messenger of Allah (ﷺ) said, "Whoever buys foodstuff must not sell it until he has weighed it[29]." Ṭâwoos asked Ibn 'Abbâs why that was the case and

---

[26] This hadith is *ṣaḥeeḥ*. See Shaykh al-Albâni, *Mukhtasar Ṣaḥeeḥ Muslim*, no. 1292. Recorded by Bukhari, Abu Dawood and Tirmidhi.

[27] This hadith is *ṣaḥeeḥ*. See Shaykh al-Albâni, *I'rwâ' al-Ghaleel*, no. 1292. Recorded by Ibn Mâjah, Tirmidhi and Abu Dawood.

[28] Recorded by Bukhari, Muslim (and this is his wording), Abu Dawood, Nasâ'i and Tirmidhi.

[29] [Being able to weight it means that it has come into his possession.] - Translator

he replied, "Don't you see that they sell foodstuffs against gold for a specified time."[30]

4. Selling Against One's Brother

Ibn 'Umar narrated that the Prophet (ﷺ) said, "Do not undercut one another in business transactions."[31] Abu Hurayrah also narrated that the Messenger of Allah (ﷺ) said, "A Muslim should not make a purchase (in opposition) to his brother."[32]

5. Al-'Eenah Transaction

Al-'Eenah is when a person buys something from another on credit and takes possession of the item and then turns around and sells it to the original seller for a cash price which is less than the credit price. Ibn 'Umar narrated that the Prophet (ﷺ) stated, "If you begin to participate in *al-'eenah*, take after the tails of cows, become pleased with agriculture and leave jihad in the way of Allah, Allah will inflict upon you a disgrace that will not leave you until you return to their religion."[33]

6. Payments Over Time with an Increase in the Price

These days, purchasing items via payments over time with an increase in the price has become very common. It is known as *bai' al-taqseeṭ*. As is known, this is an item is purchased on credit via

---

[30] Recorded by Bukhari, Muslim (and this is his wording) and Abu Dawood.

[31] Recorded by Bukhari, Muslim and Ibn Mâjah.

[32] This hadith is *ṣaḥeeḥ*. See Shaykh al-Albâni, *I'rwâ' al-Ghaleel*, no. 1298. Recorded by Muslim.

[33] This hadith is *ṣaḥeeḥ*. See Shaykh al-Albâni, *Ṣaḥeeḥ al-Jâmi' aṣ-Ṣagheer*, no. 423. Recorded by Abu Dawood.

payments with an increase in the price of the item due to the delay in paying. An example is buying an item for $1,000 cash or for $1,200 over time. This is one of the forbidden types of transactions. Abu Hurayrah narrated that the Messenger of Allah (ﷺ) said, "Whoever has made a deal with two transactions in one shall receive the lesser of the two or *riba* (interest)."[34]

Items that One is Prohibited to Sell

1. Alcohol

'Â'ishah (رضي الله عنها) said, "When the last verses of *Soorah al-Baqarah* were revealed, the Prophet (ﷺ) went out and said, 'Trade in alcohol has been forbidden.'"[35]

2. Carrion, Swine and Idols

Jâbir ibn 'Abdullâh narrated that he heard the Messenger of Allah (ﷺ) saying in Makkah during the year of the conquering of Makkah, "Allah and His Messenger have forbidden the sale of alcohol, carrion, swine and idols." It was said, "O' Messenger of Allah! What about the fat of carrion for it is used to grease the boats, oil the skins and people use it as lights." He replied, "No, it is forbidden." Then the Messenger of Allah (ﷺ) said, "May Allah

---

[34] This hadith is *ḥasan*. See Shaykh al-Albâni, *Ṣaḥeeḥ al-Jâmi' aṣ-Ṣagheer*, no. 6116. Recorded by Abu Dawood. For my details on this issue, see Shaykh al-Albâni, *Silsilat al-Aḥâdeeth aṣ-Ṣaḥeeḥah*, no. 2326 and *al-Qawl al-Faṣl fee Bai' al-Ajal* by 'Abdur-Raḥmân 'Abdul-Khâliq.

[35] Recorded by Bukhari, Muslim, Abu Dawood and Nasâ'i.

destroy the Jews. Allah forbade them its fat but they collected it together, sold it and devoured its price."[36]

3. Dogs

Abu Mas'ood al-Anṣâri narrated that the Messenger of Allah prohibited the price of a dog, the wages of a prostitute and the earnings of a soothsayer.[37]

4. Pictures or Statues Containing Creatures with Souls

Sa'eed ibn Abu al-Ḥasan said, "I was with Ibn 'Abbâs when a man came and said, 'O' Ibn 'Abbâs! I earn my living from what I make with my hands. I make these pictures.' Ibn 'Abbâs said, 'I will only tell you what I heard from the Messenger of Allah (ﷺ). I heard him say, 'Whoever makes a picture will be punished by Allah until he blows a soul into it and he will never be able to blow a soul into it.'' The man sighed and his face turned pail. Ibn 'Abbâs said, 'What a pity! If you insist on doing such work, then make (things like) this tree. (That is,) everything that does not contain a soul.'"[38]

5. Dates Before they Become Ripe

Anas ibn Mâlik (رضي الله عنه) narrated that the Prophet (ﷺ) forbade the sale of dates until their ripeness had become apparent and the sale of date-palms before their ripeness was clear. It was asked, "What is its

---

[36] Recorded by Bukhari, Muslim, Tirmidhi, Abu Dawood, Ibn Mâjah and Nasâ'i.

[37] Ibid.

[38] Recorded by Bukhari (and this is his wording), Muslim and Nasâ'i in abridged form.

ripeness?" He replied, "When they become red or yellow."[39] He also narrated that the Prophet (ﷺ) forbade the sale of fruits until they ripened. He was asked, "What is its ripeness." He said, "Until they become red." The Messenger of Allah (ﷺ) said, "Don't you see that if Allah keeps the fruits from ripening, how will you take the money from your brother?"[40]

6. Crops Before Grains become Husked

Ibn 'Umar narrated that the Messenger of Allah (ﷺ) forbade the sale of date-palms until they repined and the ears of corn until they were white and free from diseases. He forbade that for both the buyer and the seller.[41]

Options

Option is where one is given a choice between implementing or annulling an action.

The Types of Options

1. The option open to the contracting parties while still at the contractual session (*khiyâr al-majlis*)

The two contracting parties have an option to cancel the contract from the time the contract is concluded until they separate

---

[39] This hadith is *ṣaḥeeḥ*. See Shaykh al-Albâni, *Ṣaḥeeḥ al-Jâmi' aṣ-Ṣagheer*, no. 6928. Recorded by Bukhari.

[40] Recorded by Bukhari (and this is his wording), Muslim and Nasâ'i.

[41] This hadith is *ṣaḥeeḥ*. See Shaykh al-Albâni, *Mukhtasar Ṣaḥeeḥ Muslim*, no. 917. Recorded by Muslim, Abu Dawood, Tirmidhi and Nasâ'i.

from one another, as long as they did not stipulate that there would be no such option, that the option would be dropped, or one of them would drop his right while the other retained it. Ibn 'Umar narrated that the Messenger of Allah (ﷺ) said, "If two people make a sale, then each of them has the option as long as they have not parted. Unless they separate or one of them gives a (further) option to the other, the sale becomes final. If they depart after the sale and none of them cancelled the sale, the sale becomes final."

It is forbidden to hurriedly leave the session out of fear that the other will cancel the transaction. 'Amr ibn Shu'ayb narrated from his father on the authority of his grandfather that the Messenger of Allah (ﷺ) said, "Both parties in a business transaction have a right to annul as long as they have not separated unless it is a bargain with the option to annul is attached to it; and it is not permissible for one of them to separate from the other for fear that one may demand that the bargain be rescinded."[42]

2. The option based on a stipulation

This is where both parties or one of the parties lays down the stipulation that they will have the option for a specified period of time to cancel the agreement. This is a valid condition, even if the time period state is long. Ibn 'Umar narrated that the Messenger of Allah (ﷺ) said, "The two parties to a sales contract have an option as long as they do not depart or if there is a (further) option in the sale."[43]

3. The option due to a defect

Previously it was stated that it is forbidden to conceal a defect. If a person purchases a specific item of merchandise and does not

---

[42] This hadith is *ṣaḥeeḥ*. See Shaykh al-Albâni, *Ṣaḥeeḥ al-Jâmi' aṣ-Ṣagheer*, no. 2895. Recorded by Abu Dawood, Tirmidhi and Nasâ'i.

[43] Recorded by Bukhari, Muslim and Nasâ'i.

realize that it is defective until after they depart, he has the right to return the item to the seller. Abu Hurayrah (رضي الله عنه) reported that the Messenger of Allah (ﷺ) said, "Whoever bought a goat was left unmilked (in order to make it seem like it produces more milk) and then milks the animal (has a choice). If he is pleased with it, he may keep it. If he is displeased with it, he may return it with a *ṣâ'* of dates for the milk (he consumed)."[44] Abu Hurayrah also reported that the Prophet (ﷺ) said, "Do not leave the camels or goats unmilked (to make it seem like they produce more milk). If someone buys them after that, he has the choice after milking them to either keep them or return them with a *ṣâ'* of dates."[45]

Riba (Interest)

The root of the word *riba* means, "an increase", either in the thing itself, as in the verse:

﴿... ٱهۡتَزَّتۡ وَرَبَتۡ ... ۝٥﴾ (سورة الحـَجّ : ٥)

﴾... It is stirred [to life] and swells [*rabat*]...﴿ *(Qur'an 22: 5),*

— or in exchange for something else, like one gold coin for two gold coins.

Its Ruling

Riba or interest is forbidden based on the Qur'an, Sunnah and consensus of the Nation. Allah (سبحانه وتعالى) has said concerning it,

---

[44] By Bukhari (and this is his wording), Muslim, Abu Dawood and Nasâ'i.

[45] This hadith is *ṣaḥeeḥ*. See Shaykh al-Albâni, *Ṣaḥeeḥ al-Jâmi' aṣ-Ṣagheer*, no. 7347. Recorded by Bukhari and by Abu Dawood with an additional portion at the beginning.

﴿يَٰٓأَيُّهَا ٱلَّذِينَ ءَامَنُوا۟ ٱتَّقُوا۟ ٱللَّهَ وَذَرُوا۟ مَا بَقِىَ مِنَ ٱلرِّبَوٰٓا۟ إِن كُنتُم مُّؤْمِنِينَ ﴿٢٧٨﴾ فَإِن لَّمْ تَفْعَلُوا۟ فَأْذَنُوا۟ بِحَرْبٍ مِّنَ ٱللَّهِ وَرَسُولِهِۦ ۖ وَإِن تُبْتُمْ فَلَكُمْ رُءُوسُ أَمْوَٰلِكُمْ لَا تَظْلِمُونَ وَلَا تُظْلَمُونَ ﴿٢٧٩﴾﴾ (سورة البقرة: ٢٧٨-٢٧٩)

﴿O' you who believe! Be afraid of Allah and give up what remains [due to you] from interest [from now onward], if you are [really] believers. And if you do not do it, then take a notice of war from Allah and His Messenger. But if you repent, you shall have your capital sums. Deal not unjustly, and you shall not be dealt with unjustly.﴾ *(Qur'an 2: 278-279)*

Allah also says:

﴿ٱلَّذِينَ يَأْكُلُونَ ٱلرِّبَوٰا۟ لَا يَقُومُونَ إِلَّا كَمَا يَقُومُ ٱلَّذِى يَتَخَبَّطُهُ ٱلشَّيْطَٰنُ مِنَ ٱلْمَسِّ ۚ ... ﴿٢٧٥﴾﴾ (سورة البقرة: ٢٧٥)

﴿Those who consume interest will not stand [on the Day of Resurrection] except like the standing of a person beaten by Satan leading him to insanity...﴾ *(Qur'an 2: 275)*[46]

Allah has also said:

﴿يَمْحَقُ ٱللَّهُ ٱلرِّبَوٰا۟ وَيُرْبِى ٱلصَّدَقَٰتِ ۗ ... ﴿٢٧٦﴾﴾ (سورة البقرة: ٢٧٦)

﴿Allah will destroy interest and will give increase for deeds of charity...﴾ *(Qur'an 2: 276)*

Abu Hurayrah narrated that the Prophet (ﷺ) said,"Avoid the seven

[46] Allah has stated that He will destroy interest. This will be done either by removing that money completely from the hands of the one who has it or forbid him any blessings in his wealth such that he cannot benefit from it. In fact, he will lose it in this life and be punished for it on the Day of Resurrection.

destructive sins." They said, "O' Messenger of Allah, what are they?" He replied, "Associating partners with Allah, committing sorcery, killing a soul with Allah has made inviolable except due to justice, consuming interest, consuming the wealth of orphans, fleeing on the day with the two armies meet and slandering the chaste, naïvely innocent believing women."[47]

Jâbir narrated that the Messenger of Allah (ﷺ) cursed the receiver of interest, the one who gives it, the one who records it and its two witnesses. He said, "They are all the same."[48]

Ibn Mas'ood narrated that the Messenger of Allah (ﷺ) said, "*Riba* has seventy-three varieties, the slightest of which (in sin) is like a man having intercourse with his mother."[49]

'Abdullâh ibn Ḥandhalah narrated that the Prophet (ﷺ) said, "One gold coin of *riba* that a person knowingly consumes is worse than thirty-six acts of fornication."[50]

Ibn Mas'ood also reported that the Prophet (ﷺ) said, "No one is greatly engrossed in *riba* except that his affair will end up in little (wealth)."[51]

---

[47] Recorded by Bukhari, Muslim, Abu Dawood and Nasâ'i.

[48] This hadith is *ṣaḥeeḥ*. See Shaykh al-Albâni, *Mukhtasar Ṣaḥeeḥ Muslim*, no. 955 and *Ṣaḥeeḥ al-Jâmi' aṣ-Ṣagheer*, no. 5090. Recorded by Muslim.

[49] This hadith is *ṣaḥeeḥ*. See Shaykh al-Albâni, *Ṣaḥeeḥ al-Jâmi' aṣ-Ṣagheer*, no. 3539. Recorded by al-Ḥâkim.

[50] This hadith is *ṣaḥeeḥ*. See Shaykh al-Albâni, *Ṣaḥeeḥ al-Jâmi' aṣ-Ṣagheer*, no. 3375. Recorded by Aḥmad.

[51] This hadith is *ṣaḥeeḥ*. See Shaykh al-Albâni, *Ṣaḥeeḥ al-Jâmi' aṣ-Ṣagheer*, no. 5518. Recorded by Ibn Mâjah.

Its Categories

Riba is divided into two categories: *Riba an-Nasee'ah* and *Riba al-Faḍl.*

Riba an-Nasee'ah is a stipulated increase in payments received by the creditor from the debtor due to delaying the payment. This type of *riba* is forbidden by the Qur'an, Sunnah and consensus of the Nation.

Riba al-Faḍl is where money is exchanged for money or food for food in a spot transaction but with unequal values. This is forbidden by the Sunnah and consensus, as it is a means that may lead to *riba an-nasee'ah.*

The Types of Wealth in which Riba Occurs

Riba only occurs with respect to the six categories of wealth that are explicitly stated in the following hadith: 'Ubâdah ibn aṣ-Ṣâmit narrated that the Messenger of Allah (ﷺ) said, "Gold exchanged for gold, silver for silver, wheat for wheat, barley for barley, dates for dates and salt for salt must be for the same amounts, equivalent and hand to hand. If these commodities vary, then sell them in any way you wish as long as it is hand to hand."[52]

If items of the same genus are being exchanged, such as gold for gold or dates for dates it is forbidden to increase any one of them or to pay for them over time. They must be equivalent in weight or amount, regardless of any differences in quality, good or bad. Furthermore, one must take possession of it in the same setting. Abu Sa'eed al-Khudri narrated that the Prophet (ﷺ) said, "Do not sell

---

[52] This hadith is *ṣaḥeeḥ*. See Shaykh al-Albâni, *Mukhtasar Ṣaḥeeḥ Muslim*, no. 939. Recorded by Muslim.

gold for gold unless equivalent in weight, and do not sell a lesser amount for a greater amount or vice-versa. Do not sell silver for silver unless equivalent in weight and do not sell a lesser amount for a greater amount or vice-versa. And do not sell gold or silver that is not present at the moment of exchange for gold or silver that is present."[53]

'Umar ibn al-Khaṭṭâb narrated that the Messenger of Allah (ﷺ) stated, "The selling of gold for gold is *riba* unless it is done hand to hand. The selling of wheat for wheat is *riba* unless it is done hand to hand. The selling of barley for barley is *riba* unless it is done hand to hand. The selling of dates for dates is *riba* unless it is done hand to hand."[54]

Abu Sa'eed said, "We were provided with dates during the lifetime of the Messenger of Allah (ﷺ) and the dates were of different qualities, together. We used to sell two *ṣâ'* for one *ṣâ'* (of a different quality). When that reached the Messenger of Allah (ﷺ) he said, 'Do not exchange two *ṣâ'* of dates for one *ṣâ'* of dates, or two *ṣâ'* of wheat for one *ṣâ'* of wheat, or two gold coins for one gold coin.' "[55]

If one wants to exchange one commodity for another of a different type, such as gold for silver or barley for wheat, this is permissible as long as the exchange takes place at once. This principle is based on the hadith of 'Ubâdah quoted earlier, "If these commodities vary, then sell them in any way you wish as long as it is

---

[53] Recorded by Bukhari, Muslim, Nasâ'i and Tirmidhi has something similar.

[54] Recorded by Bukhari (and this is his wording), Muslim, Tirmidhi and Nasâ'i. They also have it with the wording, "Gold for silver." Abu Dawood has both wordings.

[55] Recorded by Bukhari (in abridged form), Muslim (and this is his wording) and Nasâ'i.

hand to hand."[56] It is also based on the hadith of 'Ubâdah recorded by Abu Dawood and others: "And there is no harm in trading, hand to hand, gold for silver and the silver is more; however, over time is not allowed. And there is no harm in trading, hand to hand, barely for wheat and the wheat is more; however, over time is not allowed."[57]

Thus, if one trades any of these six commodities for another of the six commodities which has a different purpose to it, such as gold for barley or silver for salt, then it is allowed for the quantities to differ as well as for the payment to be made over time. 'Â'ishah (ﷺ) narrated that the Prophet (ﷺ) bought foodstuff from a Jew on credit and he gave him his shield as collateral.[58]

Al-Ameer al-Ṣan'âni wrote in *Subul as-Salâm* (vol. 3, p. 38), "You should realize that the scholars agree that it is allowed to sell one *riba* commodity[59] for another *riba* commodity that does not share it same quality over time and with an increase in the amount, such as buying wheat with gold or barely with silver and others of the weighed items."

It is not permissible to sell fresh dates for dry dates, except for *al-'Arâyâ*, which refers to the poor who do not have date-palms. They are allowed to sell the fresh dates on the trees in exchange for its estimated amount of dried dates. 'Abdullâh ibn 'Umar narrated that the Messenger of Allah (Blessings and peace be upon him) forbade *al-muzâbanah*, which is where fresh dates in the trees are sold against dry dates. He also forbade selling grapes against raisins for an

---

[56] This hadith is *ṣaḥeeḥ*. See Shaykh al-Albâni, *Mukhtasar Ṣaḥeeḥ Muslim*, no. 939. Recorded by Muslim.

[57] This hadith is *ṣaḥeeḥ*. See Shaykh al-Albâni, *I'rwâ' al-Ghaleel,* vol. 5, p. 195. Recorded by Abu Dawood.

[58] This hadith is *ṣaḥeeḥ*. See Shaykh al-Albâni, *I'rwâ' al-Ghaleel*, no. 1393. Recorded by Bukhari.

[59] [A '*riba* commodity' is one of the six mentioned in the earlier quoted hadith.]

estimated weight.[60] Zayd ibn Thâbit (ﷺ) also stated that the Messenger of Allah gave an exemption for the *'Arâyâ* to buy fresh dates according to an estimate of their weight.[61]

The Prophet (ﷺ) forbade the sale of fresh fruits for dried fruits because the fruits lose weight when they dry. S'ad ibn Abi Waqqâṣ narrated that the Prophet (ﷺ) was asked about selling fresh fruit in exchange for dried and he said, "Does the quantity of the fresh decrease when it is dried?" The people answered, "Yes," so he prohibited them that action.[62]

It is not allowed to exchange a *riba* commodity with its own genus, two of them together or with one of the other categories. Faḍâlah ibn 'Ubayd said, "I bought a necklace on the Day of Khaybar for twelve *dinars*. It was made of gold and pearls. I separated (the gold from the gems) and found it to be more than twelve *dinars*. I mentioned that to the Prophet (ﷺ) and he said, 'It should not be sold until its (gold and gems) have been separated.' "[63]

---

[60] Recorded by Bukhari, Muslim and Nasâ'i.

[61] Recorded by Muslim (and this is his wording) while Bukhari, Abu Dawood, Nasâ'i, Tirmidhi and Ibn Mâjah have something similar. *Al-'Ariyah* is where someone gives another the fruit of a date-palm tree but not its ownership. The date-palm owning Arabs used to donate trees to the poor, but only the product and not the tree itself, in the same way that sheep or camel owners would donate the milk but not the animal itself. There is some difference of opinion concerning its meaning in Islamic Law. Mâlik said, "*al-'Ariyah* is where a man lends another a date-palm tree. However, he is then harmed by the other entering into his garden so he buys its estimated product for an amount of dried dates." Yazeed narrated from Sufyân ibn Ḥusayn that *al-'arâyâ* refers to the date-palm trees that were donated to the poor but they would not be able to wait for their product to ripen. Hence, they were allowed to sell the estimated product of those trees for dates. See *Fatḥ al-Bâri*, vol. 4, p. 390.

[62] This hadith is *ṣaḥeeḥ*. See Shaykh al-Albâni, *I'rwâ' al-Ghaleel*, no. 1352. Recorded by Abu Dawood, Ibn Mâjah, Nasâ'i and Tirmidhi.

[63] This hadith is *ṣaḥeeḥ*. See Shaykh al-Albâni, *I'rwâ' al-Ghaleel*, no. 1356.=

Sharecropping

Sharecropping, lexically, refers to working a field in exchange for a portion of its produce. Specifically here it refers to a person giving a piece of land to another for him to farm it on the condition that he will get half, or some other amount, of its produce.

Its Legality

Nâfi' narrated that 'Abdullâh ibn 'Umar informed him that the Prophet (ﷺ) had the people of Khaybar work the fields with each getting half the produce.[64]

Bukhari stated in his *Ṣaḥeeḥ* that Qays ibn Muslim narrated that Abu Ja'far said, "All of the emigrants in Madeenah used to cultivate the land (of the Anṣâr) for a third of fourth of the yield. 'Ali, S'ad ibn Mâlik, 'Abdullâh ibn Mas'ood, 'Umar ibn 'Abdul-'Azeez, al-Qâsim, 'Urwah, the family of Abu Bakr, the family of 'Umar, the family of 'Ali and Ibn Seereen all did sharecropping."

Who Supplies the Capital Needs

There is no harm if the owner of the land, the sharecropper or both of them provide the capital needs. Bukhari states in his *Ṣaḥeeḥ*, " 'Umar would make an agreement with the people that if he provided the seeds, he would get one half of the yield. If they provided the seeds, they would receive such and such amount of the yield. Al-Ḥasan said, 'There is no harm if the land belongs to one of them but they both spend on it and divide the yield between them.'

=Recorded by Muslim, Tirmidhi and Nasâ'i.

[64] Recorded by Bukhari, Muslim, Abu Dawood, Ibn Mâjah and Tirmidhi.

This was also az-Zuhri's view."

Impermissible Forms of Sharecropping

It is not allowed to sharecrop by saying that the owner will receive the yield of a specific portion of the land while the sharecropper receives the yield of another specific portion of the land. It is also not allowed to say to the owner of the land, "I will get such and such produce (regardless of the total produce)."

Ḥandhalah ibn Qays narrated from Râfi' ibn Khadeej who said, "My two uncles told me that during the lifetime of the Prophet (ﷺ) they[65] used to rent out land and would receive the yield on the banks of the river streams (as payment) or from a portion of land stipulated by the owner. The Prophet (ﷺ) though prohibited that." I (Ḥandhalah) said to Râfi', "What if it is for gold or silver coins[66]?" He said, "There is no harm in renting it out for gold or silver." Al-Layth said, "If the intelligent ones study what has been permitted and what has been forbidden they would not allow that (first mentioned) transaction due to the risks involved."[67]

Ḥandhalah also narrated that he asked Râfi' ibn Khadeej about renting out land for gold or silver. He replied, "There is no harm in that. The people used to rent out land during the time of the Prophet (ﷺ) near canals or at the ends of streams or for a portion of the fields. (What would happen sometimes) is that a portion of the produce would be destroyed while another part of the land was fine or vice-versa. Thus, there would be no rent for the people. For that reason, it

---

[65] [Referring to the Companions of the Prophet (Blessings and peace of Allah be upon him).]

[66] [In other words, for money.]

[67] This hadith is *ṣaḥeeḥ*. See Shaykh al-Albâni, *I'rwâ' al-Ghaleel*, vol. 5, p. 299. Recorded by Bukhari and also by Nasâ'i but without al-Layth's statement.

was prohibited. However, there is no harm in renting for something definite and reliable as payment."[68]

Al-Musâqâh

The definition of *al-musâqâh* is wherein a person gives another person some trees to attend to, take care of, water and so on, in exchange for half or a specific portion of their yield.

Its Legality

'Abdullâh ibn 'Umar stated that the Prophet (ﷺ) had the people of Khaybar work the fields with each getting half the produce and yield.[69] Abu Hurayrah also reported that the Anṣâr said to the Prophet (ﷺ), "Divide the palm-trees between us and our brethren." He said, "No." They (the Anṣâr then said to the Emigrants), "Look after the trees and share the fruits with us." They said, "We hear and we obey."[70]

Reviving Dead Lands

This refers to lands that are not being cultivated... Reviving the land is wherein a people cultivates a land concerning which he knows

---

[68] This hadith is *ṣaḥeeḥ*. See Shaykh al-Albâni, *I'rwâ' al-Ghaleel*, vol. 5, p. 302. Recorded by Muslim, Abu Dawood and Nasâ'i.

[69] Recorded by Bukhari, Muslim, Abu Dawood, Ibn Mâjah and Tirmidhi.

[70] Recorded by Bukhari and Muslim. See Shaykh al-Albâni, *I'rwâ' al-Ghaleel*, no. 1471.

of no previous owner. He then waters it or grows crops on it or builds on it, making the land his own (similar to homesteading).

Islam encourages this type of action

'Â'ishah (رضي الله عنها) narrated that the Prophet (ﷺ) said, "Whoever cultivates land that does not belong to anyone has the most right to it." 'Urwah added, " 'Umar gave that ruling during his caliphate."[71] Jâbir reported that the Prophet (ﷺ) said, "If someone revives a dead land, it will be for him."[72] He[73] also narrated that the Prophet (ﷺ) said, "If anyone surrounds a land with a wall, it belongs to him."[74]

Leasing and Hiring (*al-Ijârah*)

Al-Ijârah means to give wages or payment, with or without a time limit. As a technical term, it refers to owning the usufruct of a person (or item) in exchange for compensation.

Its Legal Status

Allah (سبحانه وتعالى) has said:

﴿... فَإِنْ أَرْضَعْنَ لَكُمْ فَـَٔاتُوهُنَّ أُجُورَهُنَّ ... ﴿٦﴾﴾ (سورة الطّلاق: ٦)

[71] This hadith is *ṣaḥeeḥ*. See Shaykh al-Albâni, *Ṣaḥeeḥ al-Jâmi' aṣ-Ṣagheer*, no. 6058. Recorded by Bukhari.

[72] This hadith is *ṣaḥeeḥ*. See Shaykh al-Albâni, *Ṣaḥeeḥ al-Jâmi' aṣ-Ṣagheer*, no. 5975. Recorded by Tirmidhi.

[73] [This is probably a typographical error. It should be, "Samurah narrated".] - Translator

[74] This hadith is *ṣaḥeeḥ*. See Shaykh al-Albâni, *Ṣaḥeeḥ al-Jâmi' aṣ-Ṣagheer*, no. 5952. Recorded by Abu Dawood.

❰... Then if they give suck to the children for you, give them their wages...❱
(Qur'an 65: 6)

Another verse states:

﴾قَالَتْ إِحْدَىٰهُمَا يَٰٓأَبَتِ ٱسْتَـْٔجِرْهُ إِنَّ خَيْرَ مَنِ ٱسْتَـْٔجَرْتَ ٱلْقَوِيُّ ٱلْأَمِينُ ﴿٢٦﴾﴾
(سورة القَصَص: ٢٦)

❰And said one of them [the two women], 'O' my father! Hire him! Verily, the best of men for you to hire is the strong, the trustworthy.❱
(Qur'an 28: 26)

Another verse states:

﴾ ... فَوَجَدَا فِيهَا جِدَارًا يُرِيدُ أَن يَنقَضَّ فَأَقَامَهُۥ قَالَ لَوْ شِئْتَ لَتَّخَذْتَ عَلَيْهِ أَجْرًا ﴿٧٧﴾﴾
(سورة الكهف: ٧٧)

❰... They found therein a wall about to collapse and he [Khidr] set it up straight. [Moses] said, 'If you had wished, surely, you could have taken wages for it.'❱
(Qur'an 18: 77)

Finally, 'Â'ishah (﷠) said, "The Prophet (ﷺ) and Abu Bakr (during their emigration from Makkah to Madeenah) hired a man from the tribe of ad-Dayl and them from the tribe of 'Abd ibn 'Adi to guide them, and he was an expert guide."[75]

What is Allowed to be Hired/Rented

Anything that has a usufruct value while retaining its sound state is permissible to be hired or rented, as long as there is no

---

[75] This hadith is *saheeh*. See Shaykh al-Albâni, *I'rwâ' al-Ghaleel*, no. 1489. Recorded by Bukhari.

specific prohibition against it in Islamic Law. The object that is to be hired must be specified, the payment must be specified and the period of time of hire as well as the nature of the work must also be specified.

Allah (ﷻ) has stated, quoting the words of the companion of Moses:

﴿... إِنِّىٓ أُرِيدُ أَنْ أُنكِحَكَ إِحْدَى ٱبْنَتَىَّ هَٰتَيْنِ عَلَىٰٓ أَن تَأْجُرَنِى ثَمَٰنِىَ حِجَجٍ فَإِنْ أَتْمَمْتَ عَشْرًا فَمِنْ عِندِكَ ... ﴿٢٧﴾﴾ (سورة القصص: ٢٧)

﴿... I intend to wed one of these two daughters of mine to you, on condition that you serve me for eight years, but if you complete ten years, it will be [a favour] from you...﴾ *(Qur'an 28: 27)*

Ḥandhalah also narrated that he asked Râfi' ibn Khadeej about renting out land for gold or silver. He replied, "There is no harm in that. The people used to rent out land during the time of the Prophet (ﷺ) near canals or at the ends of streams or for a portion of the fields. (What would happen sometimes) is that a portion of the produce would be destroyed while another part of the land was fine or vice-versa. Thus, there would be no rent for the people. For that reason, it was prohibited. However, there is no harm in renting for something definite and reliable as payment."[76]

The Workers' Wages

Ibn 'Umar said that the Prophet (ﷺ) said, "Give the wage-earner his wages before his sweat dries."[77]

---

[76] This hadith is *ṣaḥeeḥ*. See Shaykh al-Albâni, *I'rwâ' al-Ghaleel*, vol. 5, p. 302. Recorded by Muslim, Abu Dawood and Nasâ'i.

[77] This hadith is *ṣaḥeeḥ*. See Shaykh al-Albâni, *Ṣaḥeeḥ Sunan Ibn Mâjah*, no. 198. Recorded by Ibn Mâjah.

The sin of one who does not pay the workers' wages

Abu Hurayrah reported that the Prophet (ﷺ) said, "Allah has said, 'I will be a disputant against three persons on the Day of Resurrection: a man who makes a covenant with Me and then commits treachery; a man who sells a free person and consumes his price; and a man who hires a wage-earner and gets the full work from him but he does not give him his wages.'"[78]

What is not Allowed to be Hired/Rented

Allah says in the Qur'an:

﴿... وَلَا تُكْرِهُوا۟ فَتَيَٰتِكُمْ عَلَى ٱلْبِغَآءِ إِنْ أَرَدْنَ تَحَصُّنًا لِّتَبْتَغُوا۟ عَرَضَ ٱلْحَيَوٰةِ ٱلدُّنْيَا ۚ وَمَن يُكْرِههُّنَّ فَإِنَّ ٱللَّهَ مِنۢ بَعْدِ إِكْرَٰهِهِنَّ غَفُورٌ رَّحِيمٌ ﴿٣٣﴾﴾ (سورة النور: ٣٣)

﴾... And force not your maids to prostitution, if they desire chastity, in order that you may make a gain in the goods of this worldly life. But if anyone compels them [to prostitution], then after such compulsion, Allah is Oft-Forgiving, Most Merciful [to those women because they have been forced to do this evil action unwillingly].﴿

(Qur'an 24: 33)

Jâbir said, " 'Abdullâh ibn Ubayy ibn Salool had a slave-girl named Musaykah and another named Umaymah and he forced them into prostitution. They complained about that to the Prophet (ﷺ) and then Allah revealed the verse, ﴾... And force not your maids to prostitution, if they desire chastity, in order that you may make a gain in the goods of this worldly life. But if anyone compels them [to

---

[78] This hadith is *ḥasan*. See Shaykh al-Albâni, *I'rwâ' al-Ghaleel*, no. 1489. Recorded by Bukhari.

prostitution], then after such compulsion, Allah is Oft-Forgiving, Most Merciful [to those women because they have been forced to do this evil action unwillingly]﴿ *(Qur'an 24: 33)*."[79]

Abu Mas'ood al-Anṣâri narrated that the Messenger of Allah prohibited the price of a dog, the wages of a prostitute and the earnings of a soothsayer.[80]

And Ibn 'Umar said that the Prophet (ﷺ) forbade stud fees.[81]

Wages for reciting the Qur'an

'Abdur-Raḥmân ibn Shibl narrated the he heard the Messenger of Allah (ﷺ) say, "Read the Qur'an and do not live off of it nor amass a lot by it. Do not abandon it and do not go beyond its limits."[82]

Jâbir ibn 'Abdullâh stated, "The Messenger of Allah (ﷺ) came out to us while we were reciting the Qur'an. Among us were Bedouins and non-Arabs. The Prophet (ﷺ) said, "Recite and it is all good. A people will come who will recite it exactly (and mechanically) like one straightens an arrow. They will be (seeking the reward) quickly (in this life) and they will not be seeking the later (reward in the Hereafter)."[83]

---

[79] This hadith is *ṣaḥeeḥ*. See Shaykh al-Albâni, *Mukhtasar Ṣaḥeeḥ Muslim*, no. 2155. Recorded by Muslim.

[80] Recorded by Bukhari, Muslim, Abu Dawood, Tirmidhi, Ibn Mâjah and Nasâ'i.

[81] This hadith is *ṣaḥeeḥ*. See Shaykh al-Albâni, *Mukhtasar Ṣaḥeeḥ Muslim*, no. 1292. Recorded by Bukhari, Abu Dawood and Tirmidhi.

[82] This hadith is *ṣaḥeeḥ*. See Shaykh al-Albâni, *Ṣaḥeeḥ al-Jâmi' aṣ-Ṣagheer*, no. 1168. Recorded by Aḥmad.

[83] This hadith is *ṣaḥeeḥ*. See Shaykh al-Albâni, *Silsilat al-Aḥâdeeth aṣ-Ṣaḥeeḥah*, no. 259. Recorded by Abu Dawood. [The translation offered above is based on the interpretation of the hadith from *'Awn al-Ma'bood*, vol. 3, p. 59, as given by the author in a footnote.]

Abu Sa'eed al-Khudri narrated that he heard the Messenger of Allah (ﷺ) say, "Learn the Qur'an and ask of Allah by it for Paradise before there comes a people who learn it and ask by it for this world. Verily, three types of people learn the Qur'an: A person who boasts because of it, a person who lives off of it and a person who reads it for the sake of Allah."[84]

Partnerships

From an Islamic Law perspective, "A partnership is where two or more persons choose to combine together in order to obtain profit. It can even occur without the intent of a person, such as when one inherits such a situation."[85]

Its Legality

Allah (سبحانه وتعالى) says in the Qur'an [quoting Prophet David (عليه السلام)]:

﴿... وَإِنَّ كَثِيرًا مِّنَ ٱلْخُلَطَآءِ لَيَبْغِي بَعْضُهُمْ عَلَىٰ بَعْضٍ إِلَّا ٱلَّذِينَ ءَامَنُوا۟ وَعَمِلُوا۟ ٱلصَّٰلِحَٰتِ وَقَلِيلٌ مَّا هُمْ ... ﴿٢٤﴾﴾ (سورة ص: ٢٤)

﴿... And, verily, many partners oppress one another, except those who believe and do righteous good deeds, and they are few...﴾

(Qur'an 38: 24)

Allah also says:

---

[84] This hadith is *ṣaḥeeḥ*. See Shaykh al-Albâni, *Silsilat al-Aḥâdeeth aṣ-Ṣaḥeeḥah*, no. 463. Recorded by Ibn Naṣr in *Qiyâm al-Layl*, p. 74.

[85] Ibn Ḥajar, *Fatḥ al-Bâri*, vol. 5, p. 129.

﴿... وَإِن كَانَ رَجُلٌ يُورَثُ كَلَٰلَةً أَوِ ٱمْرَأَةٌ وَلَهُۥٓ أَخٌ أَوْ أُخْتٌ فَلِكُلِّ وَٰحِدٍ مِّنْهُمَا ٱلسُّدُسُ ... ﴿١٢﴾﴾ (سورة النِّسَاء: ١٢)

﴾... If the man or woman whose inheritance is in question has left neither ascendants nor descendants, but has left a brother or a sister, each one of the two gets a sixth; but if more than two, they are partners in a third...﴿ *(Qur'an 4: 12)*

As-Sâ'ib said to the Prophet (ﷺ), "You were my partner in the pre-Islamic Days of Ignorance and you were the best of partners. You would never oppose me or argue with me."[86]

The Islamic Partnership

Ash-Shawkâni wrote in *as-Sail al-Jarâr*:

> "The Islamic partnership comes into existence by the approval of two or more who agree that each will contribute a specific amount of wealth seeking by it some earnings and profit. Each will receive from the profits according to the percentage that he contributed. By the same proportion they will also be responsible for the capital of the partnership. It is permissible for the partners to agree that each will receive the same percentage of profit even though the percentage of contributions differed, even with one contributed a little and the other a lot. Something of that nature is considered acceptable in Islamic law, as trade is based on mutual approval and being free to accept whatever is pleasing to the person."[87]

[86] This hadith is *ṣaḥeeḥ*. See Shaykh al-Albâni, *Ṣaḥeeḥ Sunan Ibn Mâjah*, no. 1853. Recorded by Ibn Mâjah.

[87] *As-Sail al-Jarâr*, vol. 3, Pp. 246 and 248.

Silent Partnership (*al-Muḍârabah*)

Its Definition [88]

The word *al-muḍârabah* comes from the expression "*al-ḍarb* on the earth", which means travelling for the purpose of business and trading. Thus, Allah has said in the Qur'an:

﴿... وَءَاخَرُونَ يَضْرِبُونَ فِي ٱلْأَرْضِ يَبْتَغُونَ مِن فَضْلِ ٱللَّهِ ... ﴿٢٠﴾﴾

(سورة المزّمل: ٢٠)

﴿... Others travelling [*yaḍriboona*] through the land, seeking of Allah's Bounty...﴾ *(Qur'an 73: 20)*

It is also called *qarâḍ*, which comes from a word implying "a portion", this is because creditor provides a portion of his wealth for anyone to do business with and he receives a portion of the profits. The exact meaning of it here is: a contract between two parties which states that one will give the other one money in order to trade or do business with it and the profit will be divided between them according to what they agree upon.

Its Legality

Ibn al-Mundhir wrote in his book *al-Ijmâ'* (p. 124), "(The scholars all) agree that *qarâḍ* (a silent partnership) by (contributing only) cash is permissible. They also all agree that the labourer can give any condition (concerning the distribution of profits) that they agree upon, whether it be one-third, one-half or whatever, as long as it is something known and a fixed portion."

---

[88] From as-Sayyid Sâbiq, *Fiqh as-Sunnah*, vol. 3, p. 212.

The Companions of the Messenger of Allah (ﷺ) used to practice this type of business arrangement:

Zayd ibn Aslam narrated that his father said, " 'Abdullâh and 'Ubaydullâh, two sons of 'Umar ibn al-Khaṭṭâb (رضي الله عنه), took part in an army going out to Iraq. On their return they passed by Abu Moosa al-Ash'ari, who was the governor of Baṣrah. He welcomed them and then said, 'If I were able to do something to benefit the two of you I would do so.' Then he said, 'Certainly I can. Here is some wealth from the wealth of Allah. I wish to send it to the Commander of the Faithful ('Umar ibn al-Khaṭṭâb). I will loan it to you and you can buy some merchandise with it from Iraq and then sell it in Madeenah. Then give the principal to the Commander of the Faithful and the profit can be for you two.' They said, 'We would like that.' So they did that. He then wrote to 'Umar ibn al-Khaṭṭâb to take the principal from them. When they came to Madeenah, they made a profit and gave the principal to 'Umar. He said, 'Did everyone in the army receive a loan like the loan you received?' They said, 'No.' 'Umar ibn al-Khaṭṭâb then said, 'Two sons of the Commander of the Faithful are here and I shall give them a loan! Hand over both the principal and the profit!' 'Abdullâh remained silent. But 'Ubaydullâh said, 'This is not necessarily to be, O' Commander of the Faithful. If there were to be any loss to that wealth or if it were destroyed, we would have covered it.' They both repeated their statements again with 'Abdullâh remaining silent. Then a man in 'Umar's gathering said, 'O' Commander of the Faithful, why don't you make it a silent partnership?' He replied, 'Fine, I shall make it a silent partnership.' Thus, 'Umar took the principal and half of the profit. 'Abdullâh and 'Ubaydullâh, the two sons of 'Umar ibn al-Khaṭṭâb, then kept the remaining half of the profit."[89]

---

[89] This hadith is *ṣaḥeeḥ*. See Shaykh al-Albâni, *I'rwâ' al-Ghaleel*, vol. 5, p. 291. Recorded by Mâlik and al-Bayhaqi.

The Labourer is a Trustee

Silent partnerships are permissible whether they are unconditional or conditional. The labourer is not held responsible for the principal used unless he transgresses customary behaviour or contravenes what they had agreed upon. Ibn al-Mundhir stated, "The scholars all agree that the owner of the capital may prohibit the labourer for selling on credit. If he does then sell on credit, he is responsible for that money."[90]

The Companion of the Messenger of Allah (ﷺ), Ḥakeem ibn Ḥizâm used to stipulate upon his labourer upon giving him wealth to trade with, "Do not use my money to purchase any animals, do not carry it over the seas and do not stay with it in a flooded valley. If you do any of those with it, you are then liable for my money."[91]

Advance payment/Forward purchase (*as-Salaf*)

The words *as-salam* and *as-salaf* have the same meaning. In Islamic Law, they refer to the purchasing by an advanced payment of described merchandise that the seller must procure.[92]

Its Legality

Allah (ﷻ) has said in the Qur'an:

---

[90] Ibn al-Mundhir, *al-Ijmâ'*, p. 125.

[91] Its chain is *ṣaḥeeḥ*. See Shaykh al-Albâni, *I'rwâ' al-Ghaleel*, vol. 5, p. 293. Recorded by ad-Dâraquṭni and al-Bayhaqi.

[92] As-Sayyid Sâbiq, *Fiqh as-Sunnah*, vol. 3, p. 171.

﴿يَٰٓأَيُّهَا ٱلَّذِينَ ءَامَنُوٓاْ إِذَا تَدَايَنتُم بِدَيۡنٍ إِلَىٰٓ أَجَلٖ مُّسَمّٗى فَٱكۡتُبُوهُۚ ... ﴿٢٨٢﴾﴾

(سورة البَقَرَة: ٢٨٢)

﴾O' you who believe! When you contract a debt for a fixed period, write it down...﴿ *(Qur'an 2: 282)*

Ibn 'Abbâs stated, "I bear witness that a guaranteed forward payment for a fixed period has been permitted by Allah in His Book." Then he read the verse just quoted.[93] He also stated, "When the Prophet (ﷺ) came to Madeenah, they would deal in future purchases for dates for a period of two and three years. The Prophet then said, 'Whoever makes a forward purchase of anything must do so for a specified measurement, specified weight and for a specified period of time.' "[94]

It is not a Condition that the Seller Actually Possesses the Merchandise

It is not a condition that the seller actually owns the merchandise for which he has received an advance payment. Muhammad ibn Mujâlid said, " 'Abdullâh ibn Shaddâd and Abu Burda sent me to 'Abdullâh ibn Abu Awfâ (may Allah be pleased with them) and told me to ask him whether the people during the lifetime of the Prophet (ﷺ) used to pay in advance for wheat. 'Abdullâh replied, 'We used to pay in advance to the peasants of Greater Syria for wheat, barley and olive oil for a specified measure to be delivered in a known specified time period.' I asked, 'Was the price paid in advance to those who had the merchandise that they

---

[93] This hadith is *ṣaḥeeḥ*. See Shaykh al-Albâni, *I'rwâ' al-Ghaleel*, no. 1369. Recorded by al-Ḥâkim and al-Bayhaqi.

[94] Recorded by Bukhari, Muslim, Tirmidhi, Abu Dawood, Ibn Mâjah and Nasâ'i.

would deliver later?' He replied, 'We did not use to ask them about that.' Then they sent me to 'Abdur-Raḥmân ibn Abzâ and I asked him. He said, 'The Companions of the Prophet (ﷺ) used to practice *as-salam* in the lifetime of the Prophet (ﷺ) and we did not use to ask them whether they had standing crops or not.' "[95]

Loans

The Virtue of Giving Loans

Abu Hurayrah reported that the Prophet (ﷺ) said, "Whoever relieves a believer's distress of the distressful aspects of this world, Allah will rescue him from a difficulty of the difficulties of the Hereafter. Whoever alleviates (the situation of) one in dire straits who cannot repay his debt, Allah will alleviate his lot in both this world and the Hereafter. Allah (ﷻ) is helping the servant as long as the servant is helping his brother."[96]

Ibn Mas'ood narrated that the Prophet (ﷺ) said, "No Muslim gives to another Muslim twice except that it will be like giving him charity once."[97]

---

[95] This hadith is *ṣaḥeeḥ*. See Shaykh al-Albâni, *I'rwâ' al-Ghaleel*, no. 1370. Recorded by Bukhari (and this is his wording), Abu Dawood, Nasâ'i and Ibn Mâjah.

[96] This hadith is *ṣaḥeeḥ*. See Shaykh al-Albâni, *Mukhtasar Ṣaḥeeḥ Muslim*, no. 1888. Recorded by Muslim, Tirmidhi and Abu Dawood.

[97] This hadith is *ḥasan*. See Shaykh al-Albâni, *I'rwâ' al-Ghaleel*, no. 1389. Recorded by Ibn Mâjah.

Strong Warning Concerning Being in Debt

Thawbân, the freed slave of the Messenger of Allah (ﷺ), narrated that the Messenger of Allah (ﷺ) said, "Whosoever's soul leaves his body while he is free of three things will enter Paradise. (The three are:) arrogance, treachery and debt."[98]

Abu Hurayrah narrated that the Prophet (ﷺ) said, "The soul of a believer is suspended due to his debt until someone fulfills it on his behalf."[99]

Ibn 'Umar narrated that the Messenger of Allah (ﷺ) said, "Whoever dies and is in debt a gold or silver coin will have it fulfilled from his good deeds as there will then be no gold or silver coins."[100]

Abu Qatâdah narrated that the Messenger of Allah (ﷺ) stood among them and told them that striving for the sake of Allah and belief in Allah are the most virtuous of deeds. A man stood and said, "O' Messenger of Allah, if I am killed while fighting for the sake of Allah, do you think that it will cancel my sins for me?" The Messenger of Allah (ﷺ) told him, "Yes, if you are killed for the sake of Allah while you were preserving, hoping for reward, facing the enemy and not fleeing." Then he said, "What did you say again?" The man repeated his statement, "O' Messenger of Allah, if I am killed while fighting for the sake of Allah, do you think that it will cancel my sins for me?" The Prophet (ﷺ) then told him, "Yes, if you are killed for the sake of Allah while you were preserving, hoping for

---

[98] This hadith is *ṣaḥeeḥ*. See Shaykh al-Albâni, *Ṣaḥeeḥ Sunan Ibn Mâjah*, no. 1956. Recorded by Ibn Mâjah and Tirmidhi.

[99] This hadith is *ṣaḥeeḥ*. See Shaykh al-Albâni, *Ṣaḥeeḥ al-Jâmi' aṣ-Ṣagheer*, no. 6779 and *Mishkât al-Masâbeeḥ*, no. 2915. Recorded by Tirmidhi.

[100] This hadith is *ṣaḥeeḥ*. See Shaykh al-Albâni, *Ṣaḥeeḥ Sunan Ibn Mâjah*, no. 1958. Recorded by Ibn Mâjah.

reward, facing the enemy and not fleeing — except for debt, as Gabriel just informed me of that."[101]

Taking People's Wealth with the Intention of Repaying Them as Opposed to Intending Simply to Use it Up

Abu Hurayrah (ﷺ) narrated that the Prophet (ﷺ) said, "Whoever takes the wealth of the people intending to repay it, Allah will repay it on his behalf. Whoever takes it intending to destroy it, then Allah will destroy him."[102]

Shu'ayb ibn 'Amr narrated from Ṣuhayb al-Khayr that the Messenger of Allah (ﷺ) said, "Anyone who takes a loan and is not intending to repay it will meet Allah as a thief."[103]

The Command to Repay One's Debt

Allah has said in the Qur'an:

﴿ إِنَّ ٱللَّهَ يَأۡمُرُكُمۡ أَن تُؤَدُّواْ ٱلۡأَمَٰنَٰتِ إِلَىٰٓ أَهۡلِهَا وَإِذَا حَكَمۡتُم بَيۡنَ ٱلنَّاسِ أَن
تَحۡكُمُواْ بِٱلۡعَدۡلِۚ إِنَّ ٱللَّهَ نِعِمَّا يَعِظُكُم بِهِۦٓۗ إِنَّ ٱللَّهَ كَانَ سَمِيعَۢا بَصِيرٗا ۝٥٨ ﴾

(سورة النِّساء : ٥٨)

﴿Verily! Allah commands that you should render back the trusts to those, to whom they are due; and that when you judge between men, you judge with justice. Verily, how excellent is the teaching which He

---

[101] This hadith is *ṣaḥeeḥ*. See Shaykh al-Albâni, *I'rwâ' al-Ghaleel*, no. 1197. Recorded by Muslim, Tirmidhi and Nasâ'i.

[102] This hadith is *ṣaḥeeḥ*. See Shaykh al-Albâni, *Ṣaḥeeḥ al-Jâmi' aṣ-Ṣagheer*, no. 598. Recorded by Bukhari.

[103] This hadith is *ḥasan ṣaḥeeḥ*. See Shaykh al-Albâni, *Ṣaḥeeḥ Sunan Ibn Mâjah*, no. 1954. Recorded by Ibn Mâjah.

[Allah] gives you! Truly, Allah is Ever All-Hearer, All-Seer.﴿
(Qur'an 4: 58)

Repaying the Debt in the Best Manner

Abu Hurayrah (ﷺ) reported that a man had lent the Prophet a camel of a certain age. He came to demand it from the Prophet (ﷺ) and he told the people to give the man a camel. They did not find one of the same age but an older (and better camel). The Prophet (ﷺ) said, "Give that to him." The man said, "You have give me my right in full. May Allah give you in full." The Prophet (ﷺ) then said, "The best among you is he who repays others in the best manner (that is, generously)."[104]

Jâbir ibn 'Abdullâh said, "I came to the Prophet while he was in the most — the subnarrator said that he thought he said at forenoon — and he said, 'Pray two *rak'ahs*.' He owed me something and he paid it back and then some."[105]

Ismâ'eel ibn Ibrâheem ibn 'Abdullâh ibn Abi Rabee'ah al-Makhzoomi narrated from his father on the authority of his grandfather that the Prophet (ﷺ) got a loan from him when he went to fight at Ḥunayn. It was thirty or forty thousand. When he returned, he paid it back. Then the Prophet (ﷺ) said to him, "May Allah bless you in your family and your wealth. Thc recompense for a loan is to pay it back and thanks."[106]

---

[104] This hadith is *ṣaḥeeḥ*. See Shaykh al-Albâni, *I'rwâ' al-Ghaleel*, vol. 5, p. 225. Recorded by Bukhari, Muslim, Tirmidhi and by Nasâ'i in abridged form.

[105] This hadith is *ṣaḥeeḥ*. Recorded by Bukhari and by Abu Dawood, but having the last sentence only.

[106] This hadith is *ḥasan*. See Shaykh al-Albâni, *Ṣaḥeeḥ Sunan Ibn Mâjah*, no. 1968. Recorded by Ibn Mâjah and Nasâ'i.

Seeking One's Due in a Good Manner

Ibn 'Umar and 'Â'ishah (may Allah be pleased with them) both narrated that the Messenger of Allah (ﷺ) said, "Whoever demands a right should demand it with decency, whether it is fulfilled or not fulfilled."[107]

Giving Respite to One in Straitened Circumstances

Allah (ﷻ) says:

﴿وَإِن كَانَ ذُو عُسْرَةٍ فَنَظِرَةٌ إِلَىٰ مَيْسَرَةٍ ۚ وَأَن تَصَدَّقُوا خَيْرٌ لَّكُمْ ۖ إِن كُنتُمْ تَعْلَمُونَ ﴿٢٨٠﴾﴾ (سورة البقرة: ٢٨٠)

﴾And if the debtor is in a hard time [has no money], then grant him time till it is easy for him to repay, but if you remit it by way of charity, that is better for you if you did but know.﴿ *(Qur'an 2: 28)*

Ḥudhayfah (رضي الله عنه) narrated that he heard the Messenger of Allah (ﷺ) say, "A man died and he was spoken to (about his deeds) and he said, 'I used to have business with the people and I would give time to the rich to repay and reduce the debt of the poor.' Therefore, he was forgiven."[108]

The Prophet (ﷺ) also stated, "Whoever would be pleased to have Allah save him from a distress on the Day of Resurrection should then relieve one in straitened circumstances or completely remove his debt."[109]

---

[107] This hadith is *ṣaḥeeḥ*. See Shaykh al-Albâni, *Ṣaḥeeḥ Sunan Ibn Mâjah*, no. 1965. Recorded by Ibn Mâjah.

[108] This hadith is *ṣaḥeeḥ*. See Shaykh al-Albâni, *Ṣaḥeeḥ Sunan Ibn Mâjah*, no. 1963. Recorded by Bukhari.

[109] This hadith is *ṣaḥeeḥ*. See Shaykh al-Albâni, *Ṣaḥeeḥ Sunan Ibn Mâjah*, no. 1963. Recorded by Ibn Mâjah.

Delaying Payment by One who Has Means is a Form of Wrongdoing

Abu Hurayrah (رضي الله عنه) reported that the Prophet (ﷺ) said, "The delaying of repayment by one who has the means is a form of *dhulm* (wrongdoing)."[110]

Imprisoning the One who can but Refuses to Pay

'Amr ibn ash-Shareed narrated from his father that the Messenger of Allah (ﷺ) said, "Delay in payment of debt by one who has means justifies his punishment and defamation."[111]

Every Loan that Entails a Benefit Contains Interest

Abu Burdah said, "I came to Madeenah and met 'Abdullâh ibn Salâm. He said, 'Come with me to my house and I shall give you to drink from a cup from which the Messenger of Allah (ﷺ) drank and you can pray in a mosque in which he prayed in.' So I went with him and he gave me some *suwaiq* to drink, fed me dates and I prayed in his mosque. He then said to me, 'You are in a land in which *riba* has become widespread. One of the varieties of *riba* is for someone to make a loan for a period of time. When that time is reached, he gives him his money with a receptacle containing a gift. Beware of that receptacle and what it contains.'"[112]

---

[110] By Bukhari, Muslim, Abu Dawood, Tirmidhi, Nasâ'i and Ibn Mâjah.

[111] This hadith is *hasan*. See Shaykh al-Albâni, *Saheeh Sunan Nasâ'i*, no. 4373. Recorded by Nasâ'i, Ibn Mâjah and Abu Dawood. Also recorded by Bukhari but without its chain.

[112] This hadith is *saheeh*. See Shaykh al-Albâni, *I'rwâ' al-Ghaleel*, vol. 5, p. 235. Recorded by Bukhari and al-Bayhaqi. [Actually, Bukhari's wording is different from the above quote.] - Translator

Pawning[113]

Lexically, the word *rahn* means "retaining". It is said, "Something is *rahan*", when it is permanent and confirmed. Allah has said:

﴿كُلُّ نَفْسٍۭ بِمَا كَسَبَتْ رَهِينَةٌ ﴿٣٨﴾﴾ (سورة المدَّثِر: ٣٨)

﴿Every person is a pledge [*raheenah*] for what he has earned.﴾ *(Qur'an 74: 38)*

As a technical term, it refers to pawning wherein somebody leaves some form of wealth with another as collateral for a loan that is to be kept by the creditor if the debtor is not able to repay his debt.[114]

Its Legality

Allah has said:

﴿وَإِن كُنتُمْ عَلَىٰ سَفَرٍ وَلَمْ تَجِدُوا۟ كَاتِبًا فَرِهَٰنٌ مَّقْبُوضَةٌ ... ﴿٢٨٣﴾﴾

(سورة البقرة: ٢٨٣)

﴿And if you are on a journey and cannot find a scribe, then let there be a pledge taken...﴾ *(Qur'an 2: 283)*

The verse specifically mentions while on a journey but that is only stated because it is the most common case. It is not meant to imply

---

[113] [An important note on the terminology chosen here: In general, a pawnbroker takes an item as collateral and also charges interest on a loan. Obviously, the charging of interest is not permissible in Islamic law. Hence, a "Muslim pawnbroker" simply makes a loan, takes an item as collateral but does not charge interest.] - Translator

[114] See Ibn Ḥajar, *Fatḥ al-Bâri*, vol. 5, p. 140; *Manâr as-Sabeel*, vol. 1, p. 351.

that if one is not on a journey, one cannot pawn something. There are hadith that prove that pawning is allowed even while not travelling. For example, 'Â'ishah (رضي الله عنها) narrated that the Prophet (ﷺ) bought foodstuff from a Jew on credit and he gave him his shield as collateral.[115]

The pawnbroker using the pawned item

It is not permissible for the pawnbroker to use what has been pawned or pledged with him. Earlier it was shown that any loan that entails benefit is a form of *riba*. However, if the pawned item is an animal that can be ridden or milked, then the pawnbroker can ride the animal or milk it if he feeds it and maintains it while it is with him. Abu Hurayrah (رضي الله عنه) narrated that the Messenger of Allah (ﷺ) said, "The pledged animal can be ridden if it is pledged as long as (the pawnbroker) provides for it and the milk of the milking animals can be drunk as long as (the pawnbroker) provides for it. The one who rides or drinks must provide the expenditures."[116]

Debt Transfer

The lexical meaning of the word *hawâlah* means, "to change, to transfer". As a technical term, the jurists have defined it as, "The transfer of a debt from one person to another". If a person is in debt and can have another who has the means take over the debt, then it is obligatory on the creditor to accept said transfer as long as the new

---

[115] This hadith is *ṣaḥeeḥ*. See Shaykh al-Albâni, *I'rwâ' al-Ghaleel*, no. 1393. Recorded by Bukhari.

[116] This hadith is *ṣaḥeeḥ*. See Shaykh al-Albâni, *Ṣaḥeeḥ al-Jâmi' aṣ-Ṣagheer*, no. 3962. Recorded by Bukhari, Abu Dawood, Tirmidhi and Ibn Mâjah.

debtor has the means to repay the debt. The Prophet (ﷺ) said, "Delay in payment by one of means is a form of wrongdoing. If one of you has his debt transferred to a rich person, let him accept the transfer."[117]

Depositing for Safekeeping

The word *al-wadee'ah* means "to leave something". Here it refers to depositing something with someone for the purpose of safekeeping.

Its Legal Ruling

If a Muslim asks his brother to deposit something with him and to have him safeguard it, it is recommended for him to accept that request if he knows that he has the means to safeguard, as this is a type of assisting one another in piety and righteousness. It is obligatory upon the receiving of the item to return the item whenever the depositor requests it. Allah (ﷻ) has said:

﴿ إِنَّ ٱللَّهَ يَأْمُرُكُمْ أَن تُؤَدُّوا۟ ٱلْأَمَٰنَٰتِ إِلَىٰٓ أَهْلِهَا ... ﴿٥٨﴾ ﴾ (سورة النِّساء: ٥٨)

﴾Verily! Allah commands that you should render back the trusts to those to whom they are due...﴿ *(Qur'an 4: 58)*

The Prophet (ﷺ) also said, "Return the trust to the one who entrusted you."[118]

---

[117] This hadith is *ṣaḥeeḥ*. See Shaykh al-Albâni, *Ṣaḥeeḥ al-Jâmi' aṣ-Ṣagheer*, no. 5876. Recorded by Ibn Mâjah.

[118] This hadith is *ṣaḥeeḥ*. See Shaykh al-Albâni, *Ṣaḥeeḥ al-Jâmi' aṣ-Ṣagheer*, no. 240. Recorded by Tirmidhi and Abu Dawood.

The Responsible Party

The one who is entrusted with a deposit is not responsible for it unless he was negligent. 'Amr ibn Shu'ayb narrated from his father on the author of his grandfather that the Prophet (ﷺ) said, "If one accepts a deposit, there is no liability upon him."[119] He also narrated that the Prophet (ﷺ) said, "There is no liability upon the one who accepts a trust."[120]

Anas ibn Mâlik narrated that 'Umar ibn al-Khattâb (رضي الله عنه) repaid a depositor for a deposit that had been stolen from among his wealth. Al-Bayhaqi said, "This must be understood as meaning that he was negligent concerning it and therefore due to his negligence, he covered it for the other person."[121]

Lending (Items at no Charge)

Its Definition and Legal Ruling

The jurists have defined this as, "The owner of something allowing another to use that item without any payment or compensation".

This is considered a commendable act, as Allah (ﷻ) has stated:

﴿... وَتَعَاوَنُوا۟ عَلَى ٱلْبِرِّ وَٱلتَّقْوَىٰ ... ﴿٢﴾﴾ (سورة المائدة: ٢)

---

[119] This hadith is *ḥasan*. See Shaykh al-Albâni, *Ṣaḥeeḥ Sunan Ibn Mâjah*, no. 1945 and *I'rwâ' al-Ghaleel*, no. 1547. Recorded by Ibn Mâjah.

[120] This hadith is *ḥasan*. See Shaykh al-Albâni, *Ṣaḥeeḥ al-Jâmi' aṣ-Ṣagheer*, no. 7518. Recorded by ad-Dâraquṭni and al-Bayhaqi.

[121] Al-Bayhaqi, *as-Sunan al-Kubra*, vol. 6, p. 289.

﴾... Help you one another in piety and righteousness...﴿ *(Qur'an 5: 2)*

The Prophet (ﷺ) also said, "Allah is helping the servant as long as the servant is helping his brother."[122] Allah (ﷻ) also censures those who are not willing to help others, as He has stated:

﴿فَوَيْلٌ لِّلْمُصَلِّينَ ﴿٤﴾ ٱلَّذِينَ هُمْ عَن صَلَاتِهِمْ سَاهُونَ ﴿٥﴾ ٱلَّذِينَ هُمْ يُرَآءُونَ ﴿٦﴾ وَيَمْنَعُونَ ٱلْمَاعُونَ ﴿٧﴾﴾ (سورة الماعون: ٤-٧)

﴾So woe unto those performers of prayers, Who delay their prayer from their stated fixed times, Those who do good deeds only to be seen [of men], and refuse small kindnesses.﴿ *(Qur'an 107: 4-7)*

It is obligatory to return the borrowed item

Allah (ﷻ) said:

﴿إِنَّ ٱللَّهَ يَأْمُرُكُمْ أَن تُؤَدُّوا۟ ٱلْأَمَـٰنَـٰتِ إِلَىٰٓ أَهْلِهَا ... ﴿٥٨﴾﴾

(سورة النساء: ٥٨)

﴾Verily! Allah commands that you should render back the trusts to those to whom they are due...﴿ *(Qur'an 4: 58)*

The one liable for the borrowed item

The one who borrows something is entrusted with that item and thus there is no liability upon him unless he is negligent or if the owner lays down such a condition of liability. Ṣafwân ibn Ya'la narrated from his father who said that the Messenger of Allah (ﷺ) said to him, "When my messengers come to you, give them thirty coats of mail and thirty camels." He said, "O' Messenger of Allah, is

---

[122] This hadith is *ṣaḥeeḥ*. See Shaykh al-Albâni, *Mukhtasar Ṣaḥeeḥ Muslim*, no. 1888. Recorded by Muslim, Tirmidhi and Abu Dawood.

it a loan with a guarantee on it or a loan simply to be paid back?" He replied, "A loan to be paid back."[123]

In *Subul as-Salâm* (vol. 3, p. 69), al-Ameer aṣ-Ṣan'âni explained,

> "A loan with a guarantee means that if it is destroyed, the person will receive back its price. A loan to be returned means that as long as the object is in tact it will be returned but if it is destroyed, the person is not guaranteed its price back. This hadith is evidence that the borrower does not guarantee the object unless required by the lender. As stated earlier, this is the clearest of the opinions."

Lost and Found

This topic refers to all found items of value concerning which it is not known who the rightful owner is. In general, this topic refers to lost items other than animals. Animals are known by a different name (*ḍâlah*).

What is Obligatory Upon the One who Finds Lost Wealth

If someone finds some wealth, it is obligatory upon him to make known its type and amount. He then takes a trustworthy person as a witness to what he has found. He then safeguards the wealth and announces it for a period of one year. If its rightful owner claims it by identifying its signs properly, he is to be given the wealth even if it is

---

[123] This hadith is *ṣaḥeeḥ*. See Shaykh al-Albâni, *Ṣaḥeeḥ Sunan Abi Dawood*, no. 3045 and *Silsilat al-Aḥâdeeth aṣ-Ṣaḥeeḥah*, no. 630. Recorded by Abu Dawood.

after a year's time. Otherwise, the one who found it can benefit from it. Suwayd ibn Ghaflah said, "I met Ubayy ibn K'ab and he said, "I found a money purse containing one hundred *dinars*. I went to the Prophet (ﷺ) and he said, 'Make a public announcement concerning it for one year.' I did so but nobody claimed it. Then I went to him and he said, 'Make a public announcement concerning it for one year.' I did again but nobody claimed it, so I went to the Prophet (ﷺ) for a third time. He then said, 'Keep the container and its string to tie it. Count it and if its owner comes (give it to him). Otherwise, use it.' " The subnarrator said, "I met (Suwayd) in Makkah and he said, "I do not know if it was three years announcement or just one year."[124]

'Iyâḍ ibn Ḥimâr said that the Messenger of Allah (ﷺ) had said, "Whoever finds a lost item should have one or two trustworthy people witness it. Then he should not change it or conceal it. If its owner comes, he has the most right to it. Otherwise (if the owner does not show), it is the wealth of Allah that He gives to whom He wills."[125]

Lost Sheep or Camels

If one finds a lost goat or sheep, one should take the animal and announce what was found. If its owner comes, it should be returned to him. Otherwise, the finder becomes the owner. However, if one finds a lost camel, one is not to take the camel because there is no reason to fear for the camel.

Zayd ibn Khâlid al-Juhani (رضي الله عنه) said, "A Bedouin came to the Prophet (ﷺ) and asked him about finding lost items. The Prophet (ﷺ) told him, 'Make a public announcement about it for a year.

[124] Recorded by Bukhari, Muslim, Tirmidhi, Ibn Mâjah and Abu Dawood.

[125] This hadith is *ṣaḥeeḥ*. See Shaykh al-Albâni, *Ṣaḥeeḥ Sunan Ibn Mâjah*, no. 2032. Recorded by Ibn Mâjah and Abu Dawood.

Safeguard its container and tie string. If someone comes and describes it to you (give it to him). Otherwise, you may utilize it.' He then said, 'What about a lost goat/sheep?' He replied, 'It is going to be for you, your brother or the wolf.' Then he said, 'And the lost camel?' At this point, the Prophet's face turned red and he said, 'What do you have to do with it? It has its feet, its supply of water and it can reach places of water and it can eat shrubbery.' "[126]

Finding Edible and Insignificant Items

If someone finds something edible along the path, it is permissible for him to eat it. Similarly, if he finds an insignificant item that no one would care about losing, he may take it and own it. Anas narrated that the Prophet (ﷺ) passed by some dates along the path and he said, "If I did not fear that they had been given in charity, I would have eaten them."[127]

Lost items found in the precincts of the inviolable mosques

Lost items found in the precincts of the inviolable most can only be picked up if they are to be announced perpetually and will not be owned by its finder after one year, like other articles. Ibn 'Abbâs narrated that the Messenger of Allah (ﷺ) said, "Allah has made Makkah inviolable. It was not permissible for anyone (to fight) herein before me and it was only permissible for me for a portion of the day. Therefore its shrubs are not to be uprooted, its trees are not to be cut, its game is not to be chased and its lost items should not be picked up except by whoever announces it publicly."[128]

---

[126] Recorded by Bukhari, Muslim, Tirmidhi, Ibn Mâjah and Abu Dawood.

[127] Recorded by Bukhari, Muslim and Abu Dawood.

[128] This hadith is *ṣaḥeeḥ*. See Shaykh al-Albâni, *Ṣaḥeeḥ al-Jâmi' aṣ-Ṣagheer*, no. 1751 and *I'rwâ' al-Ghaleel*, no. 1057. Recorded by Bukhari.

Finding a Lost Child

This refers to finding an underage child on the streets, lost along the way or one whose lineage is not known.

The Ruling of Taking in Such a Child

It is a communal obligation to take in lost children, as Allah (ﷻ) has said, ﴾Help you one another in piety and righteousness﴿ *(Qur'an 5: 2).*

The Child's Islam, Status as a Free Person and Maintenance

If the child is found in an Islamic state, the ruling is that he is considered to be a Muslim. He is also considered to be free regardless of where he may be found, this is because the basic ruling concerning all humans is that they are free unless proven otherwise. If he if found in the possession of some wealth, that wealth may be used to meet his needs. Otherwise, he should be maintained from the public treasury.

Sunayn Abu Jameelah, a man from the Tribe of Sulaym, said, "I found a lost boy. I took him to 'Umar ibn al-Khaṭṭâb. He said that was called 'Urayfah. I said, 'O' Commander of the Faithful, he is a pious man.' 'Umar said, 'Is that so?' He said, 'Yes.' So 'Umar said, 'Take him with you. He is free and his alliance will be with you while his maintenance will be upon us.' "[129]

---

[129] This hadith is *ṣaḥeeḥ*. See Shaykh al-Albâni, *I'rwâ' al-Ghaleel*, no. 1573. Recorded by Mâlik and al-Bayhaqi.

The Inheritance of a Found Child

If the found child should die and leave some wealth but no heirs, the public treasury will inherit from him. Similarly, the state shall receive his blood money if he happened to be killed.

Claiming a Relationship

If a man or woman claims that the child is his or her relative, the child will be joined with them if that were a possibility. If two or more people claim the child, they will have to prove their case. If they are not able to, the child will be taken to an expert on family traits to determine which family the child belongs to. The expert's decision will determine what family the child will go to.

'Â'ishah (رضي الله عنها) said, "The Messenger of Allah (ﷺ) came to me happily, with joy glistening on his face. He said, 'O' 'Â'ishah! Did you know that Mujazziz al-Mudlaji, (who recognizes people's relationships by their features), saw Usâmah ibn Zayd and Zayd with a cloth over them covering their faces but exposing their feet. He then said, 'These feet come one from one another.'"'[130]

Sulaymân ibn Yasâr narrated that a woman had had intercourse with two men during a time of her purity. The expert in the manner said that they both shared in the child, so 'Umar gave the child to both of them.[131]

---

[130] Recorded by Bukhari, Muslim, Abu Dawood, Tirmidhi and Nasâ'i.

[131] This hadith is *ṣaḥeeḥ*. See Shaykh al-Albâni, *I'rwâ' al-Ghaleel*, no. 1578. Recorded by al-Bayhaqi.

Gift-Giving

Gift-giving is where, during one's lifetime, a person gives the ownership of a part of his wealth to another for nothing in return.

Encouragement to Give Gifts

Abu Hurayrah (ﷺ) reported that the Messenger of Allah (ﷺ) said, "O' Muslim women, do not belittle the gift sent by a neighbour, even if it be a hoof of a lamb."[132] He also narrated that the Prophet said, "Give gifts to one another and you will love one another."[133]

Accepting the Smallest of Gifts

Abu Hurayrah narrated that the Prophet (ﷺ) said, "If I were invited to a meal consisting of the hoof of a lamb, I would accept (that invitation). And if I were given the hoof of a lamb, I would accept (that gift)."[134]

Gifts that Should not be Refused

'Azra ibn Thâbit said, "I went to Thumâmah ibn 'Abdullâh. He gave me some perfume and said that Anas would never refuse a gift of perfume. He also said that the Prophet (ﷺ) would not refuse a gift of perfume."[135]

---

[132] Recorded by Bukhari and Muslim.

[133] This hadith is *ṣaḥeeḥ*. See Shaykh al-Albâni, *Ṣaḥeeḥ al-Jâmi' aṣ-Ṣagheer*, no. 3004 and *I'rwâ' al-Ghaleel*, no. 1601. Recorded by al-Bayhaqi.

[134] This hadith is *ṣaḥeeḥ*. See Shaykh al-Albâni, *Ṣaḥeeḥ al-Jâmi' aṣ-Ṣagheer*, no. 5268. Recorded by Bukhari.

[135] This hadith is *ṣaḥeeḥ*. See Shaykh al-Albâni, *Ṣaḥeeḥ Sunan Tirmidhi*, no. 2240. Recorded by Bukhari and Tirmidhi.

Ibn 'Umar narrated that the Prophet (ﷺ) said, "Three are not be refused: a pillow, milk and perfume."[136]

Adequately Reciprocating Gifts

'Â'ishah (رضي الله عنها) said, "The Messenger of Allah (ﷺ) used to accept gifts and give something in return."[137]

Who Should be Given Preference to Receive a Gift

'Â'ishah said, "I said to the Messenger of Allah (ﷺ), 'I have two neighbours, which has more right to a gift?' He replied, '(Give) to the one whose door is closest to you.'"[138]

Kurayb, the freed slave of Ibn 'Abbâs, stated that Maymoonah bint al-Ḥârith (رضي الله عنها) freed a slave but she did not previously seek the Prophet's approval. When it was her day [for the Prophet (ﷺ)] to stay with her, she said, "O' Messenger of Allah, I have freed my slave-girl." He replied, "Have you already done so?" She said, "Yes." The Prophet (ﷺ) then said, "If you have given her to your maternal aunts, your reward would have been greater."[139]

It is forbidden to give preference to some of one's children over others

An-Nu'mân ibn Basheer said, "My father gave me some wealth as a gift. My mother, 'Umrah bint Rawâḥah, said, 'I will not

---

[136] This hadith is *ḥasan*. See Shaykh al-Albâni, *Ṣaḥeeḥ Sunan Tirmidhi*, no. 2241. Recorded by Tirmidhi.

[137] This hadith is *ṣaḥeeḥ*. Recorded by Bukhari, Abu Dawood and Tirmidhi.

[138] This hadith is *ṣaḥeeḥ*. Recorded by Bukhari and Abu Dawood.

[139] Recorded by Bukhari, Muslim and Abu Dawood.

be satisfied until you make the Messenger of Allah (ﷺ) a witness to it.' So my father went to the Prophet (ﷺ) to have witness to my gift. The Messenger of Allah (ﷺ) said to him, 'Did you do that for each of your children?' He replied, 'No.' So he told him, 'Fear Allah and be equitable with respect to your children.' So my father took that gift back." In another narration, it states that the Prophet (ﷺ) told him, "Do not ask me to be witness to it for I do not witness to injustice." In a third narration, he also told him, "Would it please you if they were equally dutiful toward you?" He replied, "Certainly." He then told him, "Then don't (do such an act)."[140]

It is not permissible for anyone to take his gift back or to purchase it

Ibn 'Abbâs said that the Prophet (ﷺ) said, "The bad similitude is not befitting for us. The one who takes back his gift is like a dog who returns to his vomit."[141]

Zayd ibn Aslam narrated from his father that he heard 'Umar ibn al-Khaṭṭâb (رضي الله عنه) said, "I gave a horse for the sake of Allah. The one who received it did not care of it, so I wanted to buy it from him. I thought that he would sell it cheaply. So I asked the Prophet (ﷺ) about that and he said, 'Do not buy it even if he is willing to give it to you for one *dirham*. Truly, the one who takes back what he has given in charity is like a dog who returns to his vomit.' "[142]

The exception to this general rule concerns what a father has given his child. Ibn 'Umar and Ibn 'Abbâs both narrated that the

---

[140] Recorded by Bukhari, Muslim and Abu Dawood.

[141] Recorded by Bukhari (and this is his wording), Muslim, Abu Dawood, Tirmidhi and Nasâ'i.

[142] Recorded by Bukhari, Muslim, Nasâ'i and, in abridged form, by Tirmidhi and Abu Dawood.

Prophet (ﷺ) said, "It is not allowed for a person to give something away and then to take it back, except what a father as given to his child."[143]

Furthermore, if the receiver of the gift returns the gift to the gift giver, it is not disapproved for the gift giver to accept it back. 'Â'ishah (رضي الله عنها) narrated that the Prophet (ﷺ) was praying in a *khamiṣah* (a type of garment) that had patterns on it. He looked at their patterns once (while in prayer). After he finished the prayer, he said, "Go with this *khamiṣ* of mine to Abu Jahm[144] (and give it back to him), and get me his woollen garment that has no pattern, as it distracted me in the prayer."[145]

Aṣ-Ṣa'b ibn Jaththâmah al-Laythi, who was a Companion of the Prophet (ﷺ) said that he gave some meat of an onager to the Messenger of Allah (ﷺ) while he has at al-Abwâ' and in the inviolable state of the pilgrimage. He refused the present though. When the Prophet (ﷺ) saw the sign of sadness on aṣ-Ṣa'b's face, he told him, "We would not refuse your present but we are in the inviolable state of pilgrimage."[146]

Whoever gave something as charity and later inherited it back

'Abdullâh ibn Buraydah narrated from his father who said, "A woman came to the Prophet (ﷺ) and said, 'O' Messenger of Allah, I gave in charity a slave-girl to my mother and now she has died.' He

[143] This hadith is *ṣaḥeeḥ*. See Shaykh al-Albâni, *Ṣaḥeeḥ al-Jâmi' aṣ-Ṣagheer*, no. 7655. Recorded by Abu Dawood, Tirmidhi, Nasâ'i and Ibn Mâjah.

[144] [This is the person who had originally given the garment to the Prophet (Blessings and peace of Allah be upon him) as a present.] - Translator

[145] Recorded by Bukhari, Muslim, Abu Dawood and Nasâ'i.

[146] Recorded by Bukhari, Muslim, Tirmidhi, Ibn Mâjah and Nasâ'i.

stated, 'Allah has rewarded you and returned (her) to you as inheritance.' "[147]

(Government) Workers accepting gifts is a kind of stealing

Abu Ḥumayd as-Sâ'idi said, "The Prophet (ﷺ) employed a man from Azd, called Ibn al-Utbiyah, to collect the alms. When he came back, he said, 'This is for you and this was given as a present to me.' The Prophet then stood upon the pulpit. He praised and thanked Allah and then said, 'What is wrong with the employee whom we send out and then he comes back saying, 'This is for you and this is for me.' Why didn't he sit in the house of his mother and father and see if he will be given gifts or not. By the One in whose Hand is my soul, no one take anything (wrongfully) except that he will come on the Day of Resurrection and it will be on his neck. If it were a camel, he will be grunting. If it were a cow, he will be mooing. And if it were a sheep, he will be bleating.' Then he raised his hands so high that we could see the whiteness of his armpits while saying three times, 'Verily, haven't I conveyed the message?' "[148]

Al-'Umrâ and ar-Ruqbâ

These are two types of conditional gifts. *Al-'Umrâ* comes from the word meaning lifetime while *ar-ruqbâ* comes from a word implying watchfulness. These were types of gifts given in Pre-Islamic days. It is where a person would give another person a house, for example, and then say to him, "I have given this as an *'umrâ* present," or something of that nature. It means that the present is for the lifetime of the receiver. This explains the terminology: a present for a lifetime and a present in which the giver is "watching and

---

[147] This hadith is *ṣaḥeeḥ*. See Shaykh al-Albâni, *Ṣaḥeeḥ Sunan Tirmidhi*, no. 535. Recorded by Muslim, Tirmidhi and Abu Dawood.

[148] Recorded by Bukhari, Muslim and Abu Dawood.

waiting" for the death of the recipient.

The Prophet (ﷺ) considered the condition laid down in these types of gifts as void. He made both *al- 'umrâ* and *ar-ruqbâ* as regular gifts belonging to the receiver and passed on to his heirs after his death, without it being returned to the gift giver.

Jâbir ibn 'Abdullâh said that the Messenger of Allah (ﷺ) said, "*Al-'Umrâ* is permissible for the one to whom it was given and *ar-ruqbâ* is permissible for the one to whom it was given." He also narrated that the Prophet (ﷺ) said, "Keep your wealth and do not ruin it. Truly, whoever makes an *'umrâ* gift, then it is for the one who has been given it, alive and dead, and for his descendents."[149]

Usurping Others' Property and Rights

The word *al-ghaṣb* refers to taking the rights of others unduly.

Its Ruling

Usurping others' property and rights is a kind of wrongdoing (*dhulm*) and wrongdoing will be darkness on the Day of Resurrection. Allah (ﷻ) has stated:

﴿وَلَا تَحْسَبَنَّ ٱللَّهَ غَـٰفِلًا عَمَّا يَعْمَلُ ٱلظَّـٰلِمُونَ ۚ إِنَّمَا يُؤَخِّرُهُمْ لِيَوْمٍ تَشْخَصُ فِيهِ ٱلْأَبْصَـٰرُ ﴿٤٢﴾ مُهْطِعِينَ مُقْنِعِى رُءُوسِهِمْ لَا يَرْتَدُّ إِلَيْهِمْ طَرْفُهُمْ ۖ وَأَفْـِٔدَتُهُمْ هَوَآءٌ ﴿٤٣﴾﴾

(سورة إبراهيم: ٤٢-٤٣)

---

[149] This hadith is *ṣaḥeeḥ*. See Shaykh al-Albâni, *Ṣaḥeeḥ al-Jâmi' aṣ-Ṣagheer*, no. 1388. Recorded by Muslim.

﴾Consider not that Allah is unaware of that which the wrongdoers do, but He gives them respite up to a Day when the eyes will stare [in horror]. [They will be] hastening forward with necks outstretched, their heads raised up [towards the sky], their gaze returning not towards them and their hearts empty [from thinking because of extreme fear].﴿ *(Qur'an 14: 42-43)*

Allah has also said:

﴿وَلَا تَأْكُلُوٓا۟ أَمْوَٰلَكُم بَيْنَكُم بِٱلْبَٰطِلِ ... ﴿١٨٨﴾﴾ (سورة البَقـَرة: ١٨٨)

﴾And eat up not one another's property unjustly [in any illegal way]...﴿ *(Qur'an 2: 188)*

In his Farewell Speech, the Prophet (ﷺ) said, "Verily, your blood, wealth and honour are inviolable to all of you like the sacredness of this day of yours in this land of yours in this month of yours."[150]

Abu Hurayrah (رضي الله عنه) narrated that the Prophet (ﷺ) said, "A fornicator while committing illegal sexual intercourse is not a (true) believer. A drinker while drinking alcohol is not a (true) believer. A thief while committing theft is not a (true) believer. And a robber when robbing and the people are looking at him is not a (true) believer."[151]

It is forbidden to use what one has usurped

It is forbidden upon the usurper to use or benefit from what he has usurped. Instead, it is obligatory upon him to return it. 'Abdullâh ibn as-Sâ'ib ibn Yazeed narrated from his father on the authority of

---

[150] This hadith is *ṣaḥeeḥ*. See Shaykh al-Albâni, *Ṣaḥeeḥ al-Jâmi' aṣ-Ṣagheer*, no. 2068. [Recorded by Muslim.]

[151] Recorded by Bukhari and Muslim. See Shaykh al-Albâni, *Ṣaḥeeḥ al-Jâmi' aṣ-Ṣagheer*, no. 7707.

his grandfather who said that he heard the Messenger of Allah (ﷺ) say, "No one should take the possession of his brother, jokingly or seriously. If one has taken the staff of his brother, he should return it to him."[152]

Abu Hurayrah narrated that the Messenger of Allah (ﷺ) said, "Whoever has wronged another concerning his reputation or anything else should beg him to forgive him before the Day of Resurrection when there will be no money (to compensate for wrong deeds), but, if he has good deeds, those good deeds will be taken from him according to the wrong he has done. And if he has no good deeds, the sins of the wronged person will be loaded on him."[153]

The one who is killed defending his wealth is a martyr

It is permissible for a person to defend his life and wealth if someone is attempting to kill him or take his wealth. Abu Hurayrah (رضي الله عنه) narrated that a man came to the Messenger of Allah (ﷺ) and said, "O' Messenger of Allah, what if a man should come wanting to take my wealth." The Messenger of Allah (ﷺ) replied, "Do not give him your wealth." He then said, "What if he fights me." He replied, "Then fight him." The man then asked, "What do you think will be the case if he should kill me?" He replied, "You will be a martyr." He then asked, "What if I should happen to kill him?" "He will be in the Fire," the Prophet (ﷺ) replied.[154]

---

[152] This hadith is *ḥasan*. See Shaykh al-Albâni, *Ṣaḥeeḥ al-Jâmi' aṣ-Ṣagheer*, no. 7578. Recorded by Abu Dawood (and this is his wording). Tirmidhi has recorded it with the wording, "No one should take the staff of his brother".

[153] This hadith is *ṣaḥeeḥ*. See Shaykh al-Albâni, *Ṣaḥeeḥ al-Jâmi' aṣ-Ṣagheer*, no. 6511. Recorded by Bukhari and Tirmidhi.

[154] This hadith is *ṣaḥeeḥ*. See Shaykh al-Albâni, *Mukhtasar Ṣaḥeeḥ Muslim*, no. 1086. Recorded by Muslim and Nasâ'i.

Usurping land

Sa'eed ibn Zayd said that he heard the Messenger of Allah (ﷺ) say, "Whoever wrongfully takes a piece of land, (on the Day of Judgment) his neck will be encircled with it throughout the seven earths."[155]

Sâlim narrated from his father that the Prophet (ﷺ) said, "Whoever takes a piece of land without due right will be sunk down through the seven earths on the Day of Resurrection."[156]

If someone usurps another's land and grows something or builds something on it, he will be required to root out what he planted or tear down what he built. The Prophet (ﷺ) said, "What the wrongdoer has planted, he has no rights for it."[157] If he did actually plant any crops there, he may receive what he spent on it and the produce is for the rightful owner. Râfi' ibn Khadeej narrated that the Prophet (ﷺ) said, "Whoever farms in a land of a people without their permission shall not be due what he farmed but for him is what he expended."[158]

Preemption

Ash-Shufa' comes from the word *shaf'*, which means spouse. As a legal term, it refers to the transfer of the portion of a partner to his partner that would have gone to another party, paying its value in exchange.

---

[155] Recorded by Bukhari and Muslim.

[156] This hadith is *ṣaḥeeḥ*. See Shaykh al-Albâni, *Ṣaḥeeḥ al-Jâmi' aṣ-Ṣagheer*, no. 6385. Recorded by Bukhari.

[157] This hadith is *ṣaḥeeḥ*. See Shaykh al-Albâni, *Ṣaḥeeḥ Sunan Tirmidhi*, no. 1113. Recorded by Tirmidhi and al-Bayhaqi.

[158] This hadith is *ṣaḥeeḥ*. See Shaykh al-Albâni, *Ṣaḥeeḥ al-Jâmi' aṣ-Ṣagheer*,=

On What Types of Wealth is the Law of Preemption Enforced

Jâbir ibn 'Abdullâh said, "The Prophet (ﷺ) judged by the rule of preemption on every property that had not been subdivided. If the boundaries are demarcated and the roadways are fixed, then there is no preemption."[159]

If a person is a partner in a piece of land, a wall or a house, then it cannot be sold until it is first offered to the partner. If it is sold before offered to the partner, he still has more right to buy it. Jâbir narrated that the Messenger of Allah (ﷺ) said, "If a person owns date-palms or a piece of land, then he is not to sell it until he offers it to his partner."[160]

Abu Râfi' said that the Messenger of Allah (ﷺ) said, "The partner has more right due to his closeness regardless of what is involved."[161]

The neighbour has the right of preemption if they have some common rights

If two neighbours share some rights, such as to a roadway or water, then they each have the right of preemption and one cannot sell without seeking the permission of his neighbour (by offering it to him first). If he sells without his neighbours permission, his

=no. 6272. Recorded by Tirmidhi and Ibn Mâjah.

[159] This hadith is *ṣaḥeeḥ*. See Shaykh al-Albâni, *Ṣaḥeeḥ Sunan Ibn Mâjah*, no. 2028. Recorded by Bukhari (and this is his wording), Abu Dawood and Ibn Mâjah; also by Tirmidhi but without the first sentence.

[160] This hadith is *ṣaḥeeḥ*. See Shaykh al-Albâni, *Ṣaḥeeḥ Sunan Ibn Mâjah*, no. 2021. Recorded by Ibn Mâjah and Nasâ'i.

[161] This hadith is *ṣaḥeeḥ*. See Shaykh al-Albâni, *Ṣaḥeeḥ Sunan Ibn Mâjah*, no. 2027. Recorded by Ibn Mâjah.

neighbour has the first right to what was sold. Jâbir narrated that the Prophet (ﷺ) said, “The neighbour has the most right for preemption with his neighbour. One should wait for him if he is absent. This applies if their roadway is one.”[162] Abu Râfi‘ also narrated that the Prophet (ﷺ) said, “The neighbour has more right to that which is close to him.”[163]

Agency and Power of Attorney

Wikâlah is to entrust an affair to another and have it guarded. In legal terms, it refers to appointing another to represent oneself, either unconditionally or conditionally.

Its Legal Status

Wikâlah is sanctioned by the Qur’an, Sunnah and consensus. For example, Allah says:

﴿وَكَذَٰلِكَ بَعَثْنَٰهُمْ لِيَتَسَآءَلُوا۟ بَيْنَهُمْ ۚ قَالَ قَآئِلٌ مِّنْهُمْ كَمْ لَبِثْتُمْ ۖ قَالُوا۟ لَبِثْنَا
يَوْمًا أَوْ بَعْضَ يَوْمٍ ۚ قَالُوا۟ رَبُّكُمْ أَعْلَمُ بِمَا لَبِثْتُمْ فَٱبْعَثُوٓا۟ أَحَدَكُم بِوَرِقِكُمْ
هَٰذِهِۦٓ إِلَى ٱلْمَدِينَةِ فَلْيَنظُرْ أَيُّهَآ أَزْكَىٰ طَعَامًا فَلْيَأْتِكُم بِرِزْقٍ مِّنْهُ وَلْيَتَلَطَّفْ
وَلَا يُشْعِرَنَّ بِكُمْ أَحَدًا ﴿١٩﴾﴾ (سورة الكهف: ١٩)

﴾Likewise, We awakened them [from their long deep sleep] that they might question one another. A speaker from among them said, ‘How

---

[162] This hadith is *ṣaḥeeḥ*. See Shaykh al-Albâni, *Ṣaḥeeḥ Sunan Ibn Mâjah*, no. 2023. Recorded by Abu Dawood, Tirmidhi and Ibn Mâjah.

[163] This hadith is *ḥasan ṣaḥeeḥ*. See Shaykh al-Albâni, *Ṣaḥeeḥ Sunan Ibn Mâjah*, no. 2024. Recorded by Bukhari, Abu Dawood and Nasâ’i.

long have you stayed [here]?' They said, 'We have stayed [perhaps] a day or part of a day.' They said, 'Your Lord [Alone] knows best how long you have stayed [here]. So send one of you with this silver coin of yours to the town, and let him find out which is the good lawful food, and bring some of that to you. And let him be careful and let no man know of you.'﴾ *(Qur'an 18: 19)*

Abu Râfi' said, "The Messenger of Allah (ﷺ) married Maymoonah (رضي الله عنها) while he was not in the inviolable state of pilgrimage and consummated with her while he was not in the inviolable state of pilgrimage. And I was the messenger between the two of them."[164] The Prophet (ﷺ) also gave someone authority to act on his behalf when it came to repaying a debt[165], implementing fixed prescribed punishments[166] and other acts.

The Muslims all agree that it is permissible — in fact, it is a recommend act as it is a form of aiding one another in acts of piety and righteousness. This is so because not everyone is able to directly fulfill all of his affairs and one sometimes needs to delegate others to act on his behalf.

Matters Concerning Which Power of Attorney is Permissible

Power of attorney is permissible in any kind of dealing or disposition that an individual is allowed to conclude on his own

---

164 Its chain is *ṣaḥeeḥ*. See Shaykh al-Albâni, *I'rwâ' al-Ghaleel*, vol. 6, p. 252. Recorded by ad-Dârimi and Aḥmad.

165 See the hadith of Abu Hurayrah presented earlier in the section on "Repaying debts in a goodly manner".

166 Such as the hadith, "O' Unays, go to that woman and if she confesses, have her stoned." This hadith will be presented in the section on "Fixed prescribed punishments".

behalf. It is permissible for him to delegate authority to others or to accept the delegation from others.

The agent is a trustee

The agent who is given the power of attorney is considered a trustee concerning what he receives from the one doing the entrusting and the actions he takes, meaning he is not liable for anything unless he himself was negligent. The Prophet (ﷺ) has said, "There is no liability upon the one who accepts a trust."[167]

[167] This hadith is *ḥasan*. See Shaykh al-Albâni, *Ṣaḥeeḥ al-Jâmi' aṣ-Ṣagheer*, no. 7518. [Recorded by ad-Dâraquṭni and al-Bayhaqi.]

Chapter Nine — Oaths and Vows

Oaths and Swearing

Definition

The word for oath is *yameen* (pl., *aimân*). It originally refers to one's hand, because when swearing to an oath, they would take each other's right hand.

In Islamic Law, it refers to emphasizing something by mentioning the name of Allah or an attribute of Allah.

How is an Oath Made

An oath is not made except by swearing by Allah, one of His Names or one of His Attributes. 'Abdullâh ibn 'Umar narrated that the Messenger of Allah (ﷺ) came to 'Umar ibn al-Khaṭṭâb (رضي الله عنه) while he was riding his mount and swearing by his fathers. The Messenger of Allah (ﷺ) said, "Certainly Allah has forbidden you from swearing by your fathers. Whoever is to swear an oath must swear by Allah or remain silent."[1]

Anas ibn Mâlik narrated that the Prophet (ﷺ) said, "The Hell-fire will continue to say, 'Is there more?' until the Lord of Power puts

[1] Recorded by Bukhari, Muslim, Abu Dawood and Tirmidhi.

his foot over it. Then it will say, 'Enough, enough, by Your Power.' Then its sides will be brought close to one another."[2]

Swearing by Other than Allah is a Form of Associating Partners with Allah

Ibn 'Umar narrated that he heard the Messenger of Allah (ﷺ) saying, "Whoever has sworn by other than Allah has truly committed disbelief or associated partners (with Allah)."[3] Additionally, Abu Hurayrah narrated that the Messenger of Allah (ﷺ) said, "If one of you swore and said while swearing, 'I swear by al-Lât[4],' he should then say, 'I testify that there is none worthy of worship except Allah.' If someone says to his companion, 'Come, let us gamble,' he should then give charity."[5]

A source of confusion and its clarification

Some people do not swear by Allah and as they fear that they would be lying, while Allah has said:

﴿وَلَا تَجْعَلُوا۟ ٱللَّهَ عُرْضَةً لِّأَيْمَٰنِكُمْ أَن تَبَرُّوا۟ ...﴾ (سورة البقرة: ٢٢٤)

﴾And make not Allah's [Name] an excuse in your oaths...﴿

(Qur'an 2: 224)

The response to this is found in what Mis'ar ibn Kidâm narrated from

---

[2] Recorded by Bukhari, Muslim and Tirmidhi.

[3] This hadith is *ṣaḥeeḥ*. See Shaykh al-Albâni, *Ṣaḥeeḥ al-Jâmi' aṣ-Ṣagheer*, no. 6204. Recorded by Tirmidhi.

[4] [An idol from pre-Islamic times.]

[5] Recorded by Muslim and Nasâ'i; also by Abu Dawood with the words, "Let him give something in charity"; also by Bukhari with the words, "by (the idol) al-Lât and (the idol) al-'Uzzâ."

Wabarah ibn 'Abdur-Raḥmân: 'Abdullâh (Ibn Mas'ood) said, "For me to falsely swear by Allah is more beloved to me than truthfully swearing by other than Allah."[6]

On the other hand, the meaning of the verse, as Ibn Katheer has mentioned, is explained by Ibn 'Abbâs who said, "Do not make your swearing an excuse not to do what is good. Instead, expiate for your oath and do that which is good." Ibn Katheer then noted, "This is the view of Masrooq, ash-Sha'bi, Ibrâheem an-Nakha'ee, Mujâhid, Ṭâwoos, Sa'eed ibn Jubayr, 'Aṭâ', 'Ikrimah, Makḥool, az-Zuhri, al-Ḥasan, Qatâdah, Muqâtil ibn Ḥayyân, ar-Rabee' ibn Anas, aḍ-Ḍaḥḥâk, 'Aṭâ' al-Khurasâni and as-Suddi, may Allah have mercy on them."[7]

Whoever swears by a religion other than Islam

Thâbit ibn aḍ-Ḍaḥḥâk said that the Messenger of Allah (ﷺ) had said, "Whoever intentionally and falsely swears by a religion other than Islam, then he is as he has said."[8]

'Abdullâh ibn Buraydah narrated from his father that the Messenger of Allah (ﷺ) said, "As for whoever says, 'I am innocent of Islam,' if he said it falsely, it is still as he has said. If he said it truthfully, then he will not return to Islam flawless."[9]

---

[6] Recorded by aṭ-Ṭabarâni in *al-Kabeer.*

[7] *Tafseer Ibn Katheer*, vol. 1, p. 266.

[8] Recorded by Bukhari, Muslim (and this is his wording), Abu Dawood, Tirmidhi, Nasâ'i and Ibn Mâjah.

[9] This hadith is *ṣaḥeeḥ*. See Shaykh al-Albâni, *I'rwâ' al-Ghaleel*, no. 2576. Recorded by Abu Dawood, Nasâ'i and Ibn Mâjah. [Note that the original Arabic text states, "Islam will not return to him wholly." The text explicitly points out that the word Islam is in the nominative by adding the *ḍammah* at the end of the word. However, this translator could find this wording only in copy of *Sunan Ibn Mâjah*. It seems - and Allah alone knows best - that it is not the correct wording and that the correct wording is that which is=

One who is asked to swear by Allah should be satisfied with that

Ibn 'Umar narrated that the Messenger of Allah (ﷺ) once heard a man swearing by his father. The Prophet (ﷺ) then said, "Do not swear by your fathers. If someone swears by Allah, he must speak truthfully. Whoever is asked to swear by Allah should be satisfied with that as whoever is not satisfied with Allah is not from (the true servants of) Allah."[10]

Abu Hurayrah narrated that the Prophet (ﷺ) said, "Jesus son of Mary, peace be upon him, saw a man stealing. He said to him, 'Did you steal.' The man said, 'No, by Him other than whom there is none worthy of worship.' Jesus (عليه السلام), then said, 'I believe in Allah and I belie my sight.'"[11]

The Types of Oaths

Oaths may be divided into three types:

1. An unintentional oath,
2. A false oath, and
3. An enacted oath

An unintentional oath and its ruling

What is meant here by an "unintentional oath" is wherein a person swears but he actually did not intend to make an oath. It is like

=presented in the translation. At the very least, it seems certain that the narrations of Abu Dawood and Nasâ'i are those presented in the translation above.] - Translator

[10] This hadith is *ṣaḥeeḥ*. See Shaykh al-Albâni, *Ṣaḥeeḥ Sunan Ibn Mâjah*, no. 1708. Recorded by Ibn Mâjah.

[11] Recorded by Bukhari, Muslim, Nasâ'i and Ibn Mâjah.

when a person says to another, "By Allah, you shall eat," or, "By Allah, you shall drink," while, in reality, he does not mean to be swearing an oath but such statements.

Oaths of this nature are not to be enacted and the one who made the oath is not required to take any action. Allah (ﷻ) has clearly said:

﴿لَّا يُؤَاخِذُكُمُ اللَّهُ بِاللَّغْوِ فِيٓ أَيْمَٰنِكُمْ وَلَٰكِن يُؤَاخِذُكُم بِمَا كَسَبَتْ قُلُوبُكُمْ ... ﴿٢٢٥﴾﴾

(سورة البقرة: ٢٢٥)

﴿Allah will not call you to account for that which is unintentional in your oaths, but He will call you to account for that which your hearts have earned...﴾ *(Qur'an 2: 225)*

Allah has also said:

﴿لَا يُؤَاخِذُكُمُ اللَّهُ بِاللَّغْوِ فِيٓ أَيْمَٰنِكُمْ وَلَٰكِن يُؤَاخِذُكُم بِمَا عَقَّدتُّمُ الْأَيْمَٰنَ ... ﴿٨٩﴾﴾

(سورة المائدة: ٨٩)

﴿Allah will not punish you for what is unintentional in your oaths, but He will punish you for your deliberate oaths...﴾ *(Qur'an 5: 89)*

'Âishah (ﷺ) said about the words, "Allah will not call you to account for that which is unintentional in your oaths," "They were revealed about a person saying, 'No, by Allah,' or, 'Certainly, by Allah.'"[12]

A false oath and its ruling

Al-Yameen al-Ghamoos refers to the false oath by which rights are harmed or by which one intends evil and treachery. The false oath

---

[12] This hadith is *ṣaḥeeḥ*. See Shaykh al-Albâni, *Ṣaḥeeḥ Sunan Abi Dawood*, no. 2789. Recorded by Bukhari.

is known in Arabic as the *ghamoos* oath, which implies "submerged". This is because the one who does it is first submerged in sin and then he will be submerged in the Hell-fire.

To make a false oath is one of the greatest of the great sins for which there is no expiation, as Allah has said:

﴿... وَلَٰكِن يُؤَاخِذُكُم بِمَا عَقَّدتُّمُ ٱلْأَيْمَٰنَ ... ﴿٨٩﴾﴾ (سورة المائدة: ٨٩)

﴾... He will punish you for your deliberate oaths...﴿ *(Qur'an 5: 89)*

This oath is not implemented as an implemented oath is one that can be resolved while there can be no righteousness involved in relation to a false oath.

Allah says in the Qur'an:

﴿وَلَا تَتَّخِذُوٓا۟ أَيْمَٰنَكُمْ دَخَلًۢا بَيْنَكُمْ فَتَزِلَّ قَدَمٌۢ بَعْدَ ثُبُوتِهَا وَتَذُوقُوا۟ ٱلسُّوٓءَ بِمَا صَدَدتُّمْ عَن سَبِيلِ ٱللَّهِ ۖ وَلَكُمْ عَذَابٌ عَظِيمٌ ﴿٩٤﴾﴾ (سورة النحل: ٩٤)

﴾And make not your oaths, a means of deception among yourselves, lest a foot may slip after being firmly planted, and you may have to taste the evil [punishment in this world] of having hindered [men] from the Path of Allah, and yours will be a great torment [i.e. the Fire of Hell in the Hereafter].﴿ *(Qur'an 16: 94)*

Aṭ-Ṭabari stated, "The meaning of this verse is that you are not to make your oaths by which you entered into a covenant with others a means to deceive and commit betrayal, such that they feel safe with you while you have a hidden intent to betray them."[13]

'Abdullâh ibn 'Amr narrated that the Prophet (ﷺ) said, "The great sins are associating partners with Allah, being disobedient to

[13] *Tafseer aṭ-Ṭabari*, vol. 14, p. 166.

parents, killing a soul and making a false oath."[14] Abu Hurayrah narrated that the Messenger of Allah (ﷺ) said, "There are five that have no (acceptable) expiation for them: associating partners with Allah, killing a soul without due right, robbing a believer, fleeing on the day the armies meet and swearing a solemn oath by which one takes wealth without due right."[15]

An enacted oath and its ruling

An enacted oath refers to that oath which was intended by the one who made it and he is determined to fulfill it as a way of emphasizing that he is going to do or not do a specific act.

If he fulfills his oath, there is nothing further upon him. However, if he breaks his oath, he must expiate it, as Allah has said (with respect to oaths):

﴿... وَلَٰكِن يُؤَاخِذُكُم بِمَا كَسَبَتْ قُلُوبُكُمْ ... ﴿٢٢٥﴾﴾ (سورة البقرة: ٢٢٥)

﴿... He will call you to account for that which your hearts have earned...﴾ *(Qur'an 2: 225)*

And:

﴿... وَلَٰكِن يُؤَاخِذُكُم بِمَا عَقَّدتُّمُ ٱلْأَيْمَٰنَ ... ﴿٨٩﴾﴾ (سورة المائدة: ٨٩)

﴿... He will punish you for your deliberate oaths...﴾ *(Qur'an 5: 89)*

Oaths are determined by intention

'Umar ibn al-Khaṭṭâb (رضي الله عنه) narrated that he heard the Messenger of Allah (ﷺ) say, "Verily, all actions are based on

---

[14] This hadith is *ṣaḥeeḥ*. See Shaykh al-Albâni, *Ṣaḥeeḥ al-Jâmi' aṣ-Ṣagheer*, no. 4601. Recorded by Bukhari, Nasâ'i and Tirmidhi.

[15] This hadith is *ḥasan*. See Shaykh al-Albâni, *Ṣaḥeeḥ al-Jâmi' aṣ-Ṣagheer*, no. 3247. Recorded by Aḥmad.

intention."[16] If someone swears by something but inside he is concealing something different, then the determining factor is his intention and not his wording. Suwayd ibn Ḥandhalah said, "We went out intending to go the Messenger of Allah (ﷺ). With us was Wâ'il ibn Ḥujr. (Along the way,) an enemy of his grabbed him. The people found it very difficult to make an oath (stating that he was with them). Therefore, I swore that he was my brother and therefore he let him go. We came to the Messenger of Allah and I informed him that the people felt very uncomfortable about making this oath but I swore that he was my brother. The Prophet (ﷺ) then said, 'You have told the truth. A Muslim is a brother to another Muslim.'"[17]

Thus, the intention of the one making the oath is taken into consideration — unless he is asked to swear to something (by, for example, a judge in a court of law). If he is asked to swear to something, then it is the intention of the one doing the requesting that is the overriding factor. Abu Hurayrah reported that the Messenger of Allah (ﷺ) said, "The oath is according to the intention of the one who requested it."[18] He also narrated that the Prophet (ﷺ) said, "Your oath is on what your companion is telling you to affirm."[19]

Forgetting or doing something by mistake does not break one's oath

If a person makes an oath not to do something and then out of forgetfulness or mistakenly he does that act, then, in such a case, he

[16] Recorded by Bukhari, Muslim, Tirmidhi, Ibn Mâjah and Nasâ'i.

[17] This hadith is *ṣaḥeeḥ*. See Shaykh al-Albâni, *Ṣaḥeeḥ Sunan Ibn Mâjah*, no. 1722. Recorded by Ibn Mâjah and Abu Dawood.

[18] This hadith is *ṣaḥeeḥ*. See Shaykh al-Albâni, *Ṣaḥeeḥ Sunan Ibn Mâjah*, no. 1723. Recorded by Muslim and Ibn Mâjah.

[19] This hadith is *ṣaḥeeḥ*. See Shaykh al-Albâni, *Ṣaḥeeḥ Sunan Ibn Mâjah*, no. 1724. Recorded by Muslim, Ibn Mâjah, Abu Dawood and Tirmidhi.

has not broken his oath. In the Qur'an, Allah has stated (the following supplication):

﴿... رَبَّنَا لَا تُؤَاخِذْنَآ إِن نَّسِينَآ أَوْ أَخْطَأْنَا ... ﴿٢٨٦﴾﴾ (سورة البقرة: ٢٨٦)

﴿... Our Lord! Punish us not if we forget or fall into error...﴾ *(Qur'an 2: 286)*

A hadith states that Allah, the Exalted, the Almighty has answered positively to this supplication.[20]

Making an exception while stating the oath

If one makes an oath and says, "If Allah wills", he has made an exception and, as such, there is no such thing as breaking such an oath. Abu Hurayrah (رضي الله عنه) narrated that the Prophet of Allah Solomon (عليه السلام) the son of David (عليه السلام) said, "Tonight I will go to all one hundred wives and every one of them will deliver a male child who will fight for the sake of Allah." An angel said to him, "Say, 'If Allah wills.' " But Solomon did not say it and forgot to say it. Then he had relations with them and none of them gave birth except one who delivered half a person. The Prophet (ﷺ) said, "If he would have said, 'If Allah wills,' he would not have broken his oath and it would have made him more hopeful of fulfilling his need."[21]

Ibn 'Umar also said that the Messenger of Allah (ﷺ) said, "Whoever makes and oath and says, 'If Allah wills', then he may fulfill if he wishes or discard without violating the oath."[22]

---

[20] This hadith is *ṣaḥeeḥ*. See Shaykh al-Albâni, *Ṣaḥeeḥ Sunan Nasâ'i*, no. 3588. Recorded by Muslim.

[21] Recorded by Bukhari, Muslim and Nasâ'i.

[22] This hadith is *ṣaḥeeḥ*. See Shaykh al-Albâni, *Ṣaḥeeḥ Sunan Ibn Mâjah*, no. 1711. Recorded by Ibn Mâjah, Abu Dawood and Nasâ'i.

Whoever swears to do something and then finds a better thing to do

Abu Hurayrah (ﷺ) narrated that the Messenger of Allah (ﷺ) said, "If a person swears an oath and then finds that something is better (than what he swore to), then he should do that better thing and expiate for his oath."[23]

Prohibition to insist on one's oath

Allah (ﷻ) says:

﴿وَلَا تَجْعَلُوا اللَّهَ عُرْضَةً لِأَيْمَانِكُمْ أَن تَبَرُّوا وَتَتَّقُوا وَتُصْلِحُوا بَيْنَ النَّاسِ ۗ وَاللَّهُ سَمِيعٌ عَلِيمٌ ﴿٢٢٤﴾﴾ (سورة البقرة: ٢٢٤)

﴾And make not Allah's [Name] an excuse in your oaths against your doing good and acting piously, and making peace among mankind. And Allah is All-Hearer, All-Knower.﴿ *(Qur'an 2: 224)*

Ibn 'Abbâs said, "Do not make your swearing an excuse not to do what is good. Instead, expiate for your oath and do that which is good."

Abu Hurayrah narrated that the Messenger of Allah (ﷺ) said, "By Allah, it is more sinful in Allah's sight for one to you to persist[24]

---

[23] This hadith is *ṣaḥeeḥ*. See Shaykh al-Albâni, *I'rwâ' al-Ghaleel*, no. 2084. Recorded by Muslim and Tirmidhi.

[24] The word in the hadith implies continuing an act even after its error has been made clear. An-Nawawi stated that the meaning of the hadith is that a person makes an oath whose continual pursuance is harmful to his family by and thus he should break his oath and expiate for it. Instead, the person insists that he will not break the oath out of fear that he will be committing a sin. In reality, his continuance of his act, his not breaking his oath and his bring harm to his family is much worse than him violating his oath. Of course, this is all to be understood in relation to an oath that does not contain any type of disobedience to Allah.

in an oath regarding his family than giving the expiation which Allah has obligated."[25]

Expiating for a violated oath

If an oath is violated, the expiation is one of three acts:

1. Feeding ten poor people an average meal that one's family eats.
2. Clothing ten poor people.
3. Freeing a slave.

If a person is not able to perform any of those acts, his expiation will be a three day fast. It is, however, not allowed for him to resort to fasting if he has the ability to perform one of the above stated acts. Allah has said:

﴿لَا يُؤَاخِذُكُمُ ٱللَّهُ بِٱللَّغْوِ فِيٓ أَيْمَٰنِكُمْ وَلَٰكِن يُؤَاخِذُكُم بِمَا عَقَّدتُّمُ ٱلْأَيْمَٰنَ ۖ
فَكَفَّٰرَتُهُۥٓ إِطْعَامُ عَشَرَةِ مَسَٰكِينَ مِنْ أَوْسَطِ مَا تُطْعِمُونَ أَهْلِيكُمْ أَوْ كِسْوَتُهُمْ
أَوْ تَحْرِيرُ رَقَبَةٍ ۖ فَمَن لَّمْ يَجِدْ فَصِيَامُ ثَلَٰثَةِ أَيَّامٍ ۚ ذَٰلِكَ كَفَّٰرَةُ أَيْمَٰنِكُمْ إِذَا
حَلَفْتُمْ ... ﴿٨٩﴾﴾ (سورة المائدة : ٨٩)

﴾Allah will not punish you for what is unintentional in your oaths, but He will punish you for your deliberate oaths; for its expiation [a deliberate oath] feed ten poor persons, on a scale of the average of that with which you feed your own families; or clothe them; or manumit a slave. But whosoever cannot afford [that], then he should fast for three days. That is the expiation for the oaths when you have sworn...﴿ *(Qur'an 5: 89)*

---

25 Recorded by Bukhari and Muslim.

Swearing to forbid something

If someone says, "My food is forbidden for me", "Entering the house of so and so is forbidden for me", and the like, then those acts do not become forbidden for him but if he does them he must expiate his oath. Allah (ﷻ) has said:

﴿ يَٰٓأَيُّهَا ٱلنَّبِىُّ لِمَ تُحَرِّمُ مَآ أَحَلَّ ٱللَّهُ لَكَ تَبْتَغِى مَرْضَاتَ أَزْوَٰجِكَ وَٱللَّهُ غَفُورٌ رَّحِيمٌ ۝١ قَدْ فَرَضَ ٱللَّهُ لَكُمْ تَحِلَّةَ أَيْمَٰنِكُمْ ... ۝٢ ﴾ (سورة التّحريم: ١-٢)

﴿O' Prophet! Why do you ban [for yourself] that which Allah has made lawful to you, seeking to please your wives? And Allah is Oft-Forgiving, Most Merciful. Allah has already ordained for you [O' men], the dissolution of your oaths...﴾ *(Qur'an 66: 1-2)*

'Â'ishah (رضي الله عنها) said, "The Messenger of Allah (ﷺ) used to have honey when he was staying at the house of Zaynab bint Jaḥsh. Ḥafṣah and I, therefore, secretly agreed that when he comes to either of us, she should say, 'Have you eaten *mughâfir* (which has a bad smell to it)? I can smell *mughâfir* on your breath.' He said, 'No but I had honey with Zaynab bint Jaḥsh. I will not have it again. I have taken an oath to that and do not inform anyone about this.' "[26]

Ibn 'Abbâs said concerning expiating an oath in which one has forbidden himself something permissible that it is to be expiated. Then he stated the verse:

﴿لَّقَدْ كَانَ لَكُمْ فِى رَسُولِ ٱللَّهِ أُسْوَةٌ حَسَنَةٌ ... ۝٢١﴾ (سورة الأحزاب: ٢١)

﴿Indeed in the Messenger of Allah you have an excellent example to follow...﴾ *(Qur'an 33: 21)*.[27]

---

[26] This hadith is *ṣaḥeeḥ*. See Shaykh al-Albâni, *Ṣaḥeeḥ Sunan Nasâ'i*, no. 3553. Recorded by Bukhari.

[27] [This was quoted earlier as the following: Ibn 'Abbâs said, "If a man=

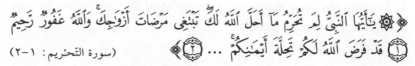

Vows

Definition

The Arabic word for vow is *nadhr* (pl., *nudhoor*). Its root has the meaning of "intimidation, frightening". As a legal term, ar-Râghib has defined it as making a non-obligatory act obligatory upon oneself due to (an originally future incident) coming to pass.

Its Legality

Allah (ﷻ) says in the Qur'an:

﴿وَمَآ أَنفَقْتُم مِّن نَّفَقَةٍ أَوْ نَذَرْتُم مِّن نَّذْرٍ فَإِنَّ ٱللَّهَ يَعْلَمُهُۥ ... ﴿٢٧٠﴾﴾ (سورة البَقـرَة: ٢٧٠)

﴾And whatever you spend for spendings [for Allah's Cause] or whatever vow you make, be sure Allah knows it all...﴿ *(Qur'an 2: 270)*

Allah also says:

﴿ثُمَّ لْيَقْضُواْ تَفَثَهُمْ وَلْيُوفُواْ نُذُورَهُمْ وَلْيَطَّوَّفُواْ بِٱلْبَيْتِ ٱلْعَتِيقِ ﴿٢٩﴾﴾ (سورة الحَجّ: ٢٩)

﴾Then let them complete the prescribed duties [of Ḥajj] for them, and perform their vows, and circumambulate the Ancient House [the Ka'bah at Makkah].﴿ *(Qur'an 22: 29)*

=makes an oath that his wife is forbidden for him, it is nothing but an oath that he can expiate." Then he recited the verse, ﴾Indeed in the Messenger of Allah you have an excellent example﴿ (*al-Aḥzâb*: 21). Recorded by Bukhari and Muslim (and this is his wording).]

Additionally, Allah (ﷻ) says:

﴿يُوفُونَ بِٱلنَّذۡرِ وَيَخَافُونَ يَوۡمٗا كَانَ شَرُّهُۥ مُسۡتَطِيرٗا ٧﴾ (سورة الإنسان: ٧)

﴾They [are those who] fulfill [their] vows, and they fear a Day whose evil will be wide-spreading.﴿ *(Qur'an 76: 7)*

'Â'ishah (رضي الله عنها) narrated that the Prophet (ﷺ) said, "Whoever makes an oath to obey Allah should obey Him. Whoever makes an oath to disobey Allah must not disobey Him."[28]

Prohibition of conditional vows

'Abdullâh ibn 'Umar said, "The Prophet (ﷺ) forbade vows and said, 'It will not avert anything. It is only means by which the miserly person is forced to give (some wealth).' "[29]

Sa'eed ibn al-Ḥârith narrated that he heard Ibn 'Umar saying, "Weren't they prohibited from making vows? The Prophet (ﷺ) said, 'A vow neither hastens nor delays anything. Vows simply extract something from the miserly person.' "[30]

When is a vow valid and when it is not valid

A vow is valid if it is to do an act of devotion taking one closer to Allah. In that case, it is obligatory to fulfill such a vow, based on the earlier quoted hadith from 'Â'ishah, "Whoever makes an oath to obey Allah should obey Him." A vow is not valid if it is to do a sinful act. In such a case, one must (not fulfill the vow and) expiate in the

---

[28] This hadith is *ṣaḥeeḥ*. See Shaykh al-Albâni, *Ṣaḥeeḥ al-Jâmi' aṣ-Ṣagheer*, no. 6565. Recorded by Bukhari, Abu Dawood, Tirmidhi, Nasâ'i and Ibn Mâjah.

[29] Recorded by Bukhari, Muslim, Abu Dawood and Nasâ'i.

[30] Recorded by Bukhari and by Muslim but without Ibn 'Umar's statement.

same manner as one does for violating an oath. 'Â'ishah narrated that the Messenger of Allah (ﷺ) said, "There is no vow (to be fulfilled) for an act of disobedience. Its expiation is the same as the expiation for violating an oath."[31]

As for a vow to do something that is usually permissible, for example a vow to make *Ḥajj* walking or to stand in the sun, such a vow is not to be fulfilled and there is no obligatory expiation. Abu Hurayrah narrated that the Messenger of Allah (ﷺ) saw an old man walking while leaning on his two sons. The Prophet (ﷺ) asked about him and his two sons said, "O' Messenger of Allah, he had made a vow." The Messenger of Allah (ﷺ) told him, "Ride (an animal), old man, for Allah is not in need of you (behaving this way) or of your vow."[32]

Ibn 'Abbâs narrated that the Messenger of Allah (ﷺ) passed by a man in Makkah who was standing in the sunshine. The Prophet (ﷺ) asked him and they said, "He has made a vow to fast, not to seek shade until nightfall, not to speak and to remain standing." The Prophet then said, "Let him speak, seek shade and sit. Let him also complete his fast."[33]

Making a vow and not being able to fulfill it

If someone makes a vow to do an act of obedience but then is not able to fulfill that vow, he should perform the same expiation as that for violating an oath. 'Uqbah ibn 'Âmir narrated that the

---

[31] This hadith is *ṣaḥeeḥ*. See Shaykh al-Albâni, *I'rwâ' al-Ghaleel*, no. 2590. Recorded by Abu Dawood, Tirmidhi, Nasâ'i and Ibn Mâjah.

[32] This hadith is *ṣaḥeeḥ*. See Shaykh al-Albâni, *Mukhtasar Ṣaḥeeḥ Muslim*, no. 1005. Recorded by Muslim.

[33] This hadith is *ṣaḥeeḥ*. See Shaykh al-Albâni, *I'rwâ' al-Ghaleel*, no. 2591. Recorded by Bukhari and Abu Dawood. [Actually, the wording the author presented above is from Ibn Mâjah.] - Translator

Messenger of Allah (ﷺ) said, "The expiation for a vow is (the same as) the expiation for violating an oath."[34]

Whoever makes a vow and then dies (before fulfilling it)

If a person makes a vow and then dies before fulfilling it, his heirs should fulfill it on his behalf. Ibn 'Abbâs narrated that S'ad ibn 'Ubâdah asked the Messenger of Allah (ﷺ) about an unfulfilled vow by his mother who died before she fulfilled it. The Messenger of Allah (ﷺ) said, "Fulfill it on her behalf."[35]

---

[34] This hadith is *ṣaḥeeḥ*. See Shaykh al-Albâni, *Ṣaḥeeḥ al-Jâmi' aṣ-Ṣagheer*, no. 4488. Recorded by Muslim and Nasâ'i.

[35] Recorded by Bukhari, Muslim (and this is his wording), Abu Dawood, Tirmidhi, Nasâ'i and Ibn Mâjah.

Chapter Ten — Foods

Foods refer to what humans consume and get nourished by of staple foods and other types of foods. The basic ruling concerning foods is that they are permissible. Allah (ﷻ) has said:

﴿يَٰٓأَيُّهَا ٱلنَّاسُ كُلُوا۟ مِمَّا فِى ٱلْأَرْضِ حَلَٰلًا طَيِّبًا ...﴿١٦٨﴾﴾ (سورة البقرة: ١٦٨)

﴿O' mankind! Eat of that which is lawful and good on the earth...﴾

(Qur'an 2: 168)

In another verse, Allah states:

﴿... وَكُلُوا۟ وَٱشْرَبُوا۟ وَلَا تُسْرِفُوٓا۟ ۚ إِنَّهُۥ لَا يُحِبُّ ٱلْمُسْرِفِينَ ﴿٣١﴾ قُلْ مَنْ حَرَّمَ زِينَةَ ٱللَّهِ ٱلَّتِىٓ أَخْرَجَ لِعِبَادِهِۦ وَٱلطَّيِّبَٰتِ مِنَ ٱلرِّزْقِ ۚ ...﴿٣٢﴾﴾ (سورة الأعراف: ٣١-٣٢)

﴿... Eat and drink but waste not by extravagance, certainly He [Allah] likes not those who waste by extravagance. Say [O' Muhammad]: Who has forbidden the adoration with clothes given by Allah, which He has produced for his slaves, and the good and lawful foods?...﴾

(Qur'an 7: 31-32)

No food is forbidden except for what Allah has forbidden in His book or upon the tongue of His Messenger. To forbid something that Allah has not forbidden is to forge a lie against Allah. Allah has said:

﴿قُلْ أَرَءَيْتُم مَّآ أَنزَلَ ٱللَّهُ لَكُم مِّن رِّزْقٍ فَجَعَلْتُم مِّنْهُ حَرَامًا وَحَلَٰلًا قُلْ ءَآللَّهُ أَذِنَ لَكُمْ ۖ أَمْ عَلَى ٱللَّهِ تَفْتَرُونَ ﴿٥٩﴾ وَمَا ظَنُّ ٱلَّذِينَ يَفْتَرُونَ عَلَى ٱللَّهِ

ٱلْكَذِبَ يَوْمَ ٱلْقِيَٰمَةِ ۗ إِنَّ ٱللَّهَ لَذُو فَضْلٍ عَلَى ٱلنَّاسِ وَلَٰكِنَّ أَكْثَرَهُمْ لَا يَشْكُرُونَ ﴿٦٠﴾ (سورة يونس: ٥٩-٦٠)

﴾Say [O' Muhammad to these polytheists], 'Tell me, what provision Allah has sent down to you! And you have made of it lawful and unlawful.' Say [O' Muhammad], 'Has Allah permitted you [to do so], or do you invent a lie against Allah?' And what think those who invent lies against Allah, on the Day of Resurrection? Truly, Allah is full of Bounty to mankind, but most of them are ungrateful.﴿ *(Qur'an 10: 59-60)*

Allah has also said:

﴿وَلَا تَقُولُوا لِمَا تَصِفُ أَلْسِنَتُكُمُ ٱلْكَذِبَ هَٰذَا حَلَٰلٌ وَهَٰذَا حَرَامٌ لِّتَفْتَرُوا عَلَى ٱللَّهِ ٱلْكَذِبَ ۚ إِنَّ ٱلَّذِينَ يَفْتَرُونَ عَلَى ٱللَّهِ ٱلْكَذِبَ لَا يُفْلِحُونَ ﴿١١٦﴾ مَتَٰعٌ قَلِيلٌ وَلَهُمْ عَذَابٌ أَلِيمٌ ﴿١١٧﴾﴾ (سورة النحل: ١١٦-١١٧)

﴾And say not concerning that which your tongues put forth falsely, 'This is lawful and this is forbidden,' so as to invent lies against Allah. Verily, those who invent lies against Allah will never prosper. A passing brief enjoyment [will be theirs], but they will have a painful torment.﴿ *(Qur'an 16: 116-117).*

Forbidden Foods

Allah (ﷻ) says:

﴿وَمَا لَكُمْ أَلَّا تَأْكُلُوا مِمَّا ذُكِرَ ٱسْمُ ٱللَّهِ عَلَيْهِ وَقَدْ فَصَّلَ لَكُم مَّا حَرَّمَ عَلَيْكُمْ إِلَّا مَا ٱضْطُرِرْتُمْ إِلَيْهِ ۗ ... ﴿١١٩﴾﴾ (سورة الأنعام: ١١٩)

﴾And why should you not eat of that [meat] on which Allah's Name has been pronounced [at the time of slaughtering the animal], while He has explained to you in detail what is forbidden to you, except under compulsion of necessity?...﴾ *(Qur'an 6: 119)*

Allah has made sufficiently clear and in detail what is forbidden for us to eat. Allah (ﷻ) says:

﴿حُرِّمَتْ عَلَيْكُمُ ٱلْمَيْتَةُ وَٱلدَّمُ وَلَحْمُ ٱلْخِنزِيرِ وَمَآ أُهِلَّ لِغَيْرِ ٱللَّهِ بِهِۦ وَٱلْمُنْخَنِقَةُ وَٱلْمَوْقُوذَةُ وَٱلْمُتَرَدِّيَةُ وَٱلنَّطِيحَةُ وَمَآ أَكَلَ ٱلسَّبُعُ إِلَّا مَا ذَكَّيْتُمْ وَمَا ذُبِحَ عَلَى ٱلنُّصُبِ وَأَن تَسْتَقْسِمُوا۟ بِٱلْأَزْلَٰمِ ۚ ذَٰلِكُمْ فِسْقٌ ... ﴿٣﴾﴾ (سورة المائدة: ٣)

﴾Forbidden to you [for food] are: carrion, blood, the flesh of swine, and the meat of that which has been slaughtered as a sacrifice for others than Allah, or has been slaughtered for idols, or on which Allah's Name has not been mentioned while slaughtering, and that which has been killed by strangling, or by a violent blow, or by a headlong fall, or by the goring of horns — and that which has been [partly] eaten by a wild animal — unless you are able to slaughter it [before its death] — and that which is sacrificed on altars. [Forbidden] also is to use arrows seeking luck or decision, [all] that is disobedience of Allah and sin...﴾ *(Qur'an 5: 3)*

Allah has also said:

﴿وَلَا تَأْكُلُوا۟ مِمَّا لَمْ يُذْكَرِ ٱسْمُ ٱللَّهِ عَلَيْهِ وَإِنَّهُۥ لَفِسْقٌ ... ﴿١٢١﴾﴾

(سورة الأنعام: ١٢١)

﴾Eat not of that [meat] on which Allah's Name has not been pronounced [at the time of the slaughtering of the animal], for surely it is a sin and disobedience of Allah...﴾ *(Qur'an 6: 121)*

In another verse, Allah has said:

﴿قُل لَّآ أَجِدُ فِى مَآ أُوحِىَ إِلَىَّ مُحَرَّمًا عَلَىٰ طَاعِمٍ يَطْعَمُهُۥٓ إِلَّآ أَن يَكُونَ مَيْتَةً أَوْ دَمًا مَّسْفُوحًا أَوْ لَحْمَ خِنزِيرٍ فَإِنَّهُۥ رِجْسٌ أَوْ فِسْقًا أُهِلَّ لِغَيْرِ ٱللَّهِ بِهِۦ ... ﴿١٤٥﴾﴾ (سورة الأنعام: ١٤٥)

﴾Say [O' Muhammad], 'I find not in that which has been inspired to me anything forbidden to be eaten by one who wishes to eat it, unless it be carrion or blood poured forth [by slaughtering or the like], or the flesh of swine, for that surely is impure, or impious [unlawful] meat [of an animal] which is slaughtered as a sacrifice for others than Allah...﴿ *(Qur'an 6: 145)*

Additionally, Allah (ﷻ) says:

﴿... وَحُرِّمَ عَلَيْكُمْ صَيْدُ ٱلْبَرِّ مَا دُمْتُمْ حُرُمًا ... ﴿٩٦﴾﴾ (سورة المائدة: ٩٦)

﴾... Forbidden is [the pursuit of] land-game as long as you are in a state of pilgrimage...﴿ *(Qur'an 5: 96)*

What is Included as Carrion

Included in the prohibition of carrion is any part of an animal that is cut off from the animal while it is still alive. Abu Wâqid al-Laythi narrated that the Messenger of Allah (ﷺ) said, "What is cut off of an animal while it is living is considered carrion."[1]

Exceptions to the law of carrion and blood

Ibn 'Umar narrated that the Messenger of Allah (ﷺ) said, "Two types of carrion and two types of blood have been made permissible for you. As for the two types of carrion, they are fish and

[1] This hadith is *ṣaḥeeḥ*. See Shaykh al-Albâni, *Ṣaḥeeḥ Sunan Ibn Mâjah*, no. 2606. Recorded by Ibn Mâjah and Abu Dawood.

locust. As for the two types of blood, they are the liver and the spleen."[2]

The Prohibition of Consuming Donkeys

Anas ibn Mâlik narrated that a man came to the Messenger of Allah (ﷺ) and said, "The donkeys have been eaten." Another came and said, "The donkeys have been eaten." Another came and said, "The donkeys have perished." The Prophet (ﷺ) then told a caller to announce to the people, "Verily, Allah and His Messenger have forbidden you from donkey meat, as it is a filth." So then the cooking pots were overturned while they were boiling with (the donkey) meat.[3]

The Prohibition of Consuming Fanged Beasts of Prey and Birds with Talons

Ibn 'Abbâs narrated that the Messenger of Allah (ﷺ) forbade every fanged beast of prey and every bird with talons.[4]

The Prohibition of Consuming al-Jallâlah

Al-Jallâlah is an animal the majority of whose diet is made up of impure things. It is forbidden to eat such animals, drink their milk or ride them. Ibn 'Umar narrated that the Messenger of Allah (ﷺ)

---

[2] This hadith is *ṣaḥeeḥ*. See Shaykh al-Albâni, *Ṣaḥeeḥ al-Jâmi' aṣ-Ṣagheer*, no. 210 and *Silsilat al-Aḥâdeeth aṣ-Ṣaḥeeḥah*, no. 1118. [With the wording reproduced above, it was recorded by Ibn Mâjah.] - Translator

[3] Recorded by Bukhari and Muslim.

[4] This hadith is *ṣaḥeeḥ*. See Shaykh al-Albâni, *Mukhtasar Ṣaḥeeḥ Muslim*, no. 1332. Recorded by Muslim, Abu Dawood and by Nasâ'i with the additional words, "He forbade them the Day of Khaybar."

forbade the meat and milk of *al-jallâlah*.[5] He also said that the Messenger of Allah (ﷺ) forbade *al-jallâlah* camels, including riding them or drinking their milk.[6]

When do jallâlah animals become permissible

If such an animal is retrained and kept for three days, eating only pure foods, then it is permissible to slaughter it and eat it. It is narrated that Ibn 'Umar used to restrain and keep *jallâlah* chickens for three days.[7]

The Permissible of Eating Anything that is Forbidden Due to Necessity

Allah has said:

﴿... فَمَنِ ٱضْطُرَّ غَيْرَ بَاغٍ وَلَا عَادٍ فَلَآ إِثْمَ عَلَيْهِ ۚ إِنَّ ٱللَّهَ غَفُورٌ رَّحِيمٌ ﴿١٧٣﴾﴾

(سورة البقرة: ١٧٣)

﴿... But if one is forced by necessity without willful disobedience nor transgressing due limits, then there is no sin on him. Truly, Allah is Oft-Forgiving, Most Merciful.﴾ *(Qur'an 2: 173)*

Allah has also said:

﴿... فَمَنِ ٱضْطُرَّ فِى مَخْمَصَةٍ غَيْرَ مُتَجَانِفٍ لِّإِثْمٍ ۙ فَإِنَّ ٱللَّهَ غَفُورٌ رَّحِيمٌ ﴿٣﴾﴾

(سورة المائدة: ٣)

---

[5] This hadith is *ṣaḥeeḥ*. See Shaykh al-Albâni, *Ṣaḥeeḥ Sunan Ibn Mâjah*, no. 2582. Recorded by Ibn Mâjah, Abu Dawood and Tirmidhi.

[6] This hadith is *ḥasan ṣaḥeeḥ*. See Shaykh al-Albâni, *Ṣaḥeeḥ Sunan Abi Dawood*, no. 3217. Recorded by Abu Dawood.

[7] This hadith is *ṣaḥeeḥ*. See Shaykh al-Albâni, *I'rwâ' al-Ghaleel*, no. 2504. Recorded by Ibn Abi Shaybah.

﴾... But as for him who is forced by severe hunger, with no inclination to sin [such can eat these above-mentioned meats], then surely, Allah is Oft-Forgiving, Most Merciful.﴿ *(Qur'an 5: 3)*

Ibn Katheer wrote in his Commentary to the Qur'an (vol. 2, p. 14),

"(This verse means) that if one is in need of partaking of any of those forbidden foods mentioned by Allah due to an immediate necessity, then he is allowed to eat them and Allah is Forgiving and Merciful for him. Allah is knowledgeable of the need of His servant who is in a state of necessity and is in dire need to those foods and, thus, He overlooks that from them and forgives them. In the *Musnad* (of Aḥmad) and in *Ṣaḥeeḥ Ibn Ḥibbân* it is recorded on the authority of Ibn 'Umar that the Messenger of Allah (ﷺ) said, 'Verily Allah loves that one resorts to His exemptions in the same way that He dislikes for one to resort to disobeying Him.'[8] Thus, the jurists say that eating carrion could, under some circumstances, be obligatory, such as if the person fears for his life and finds no other food. It could also be recommended or permissible, depending on the circumstances. The jurists differ over the question of whether the person is to eat only as little as meets his hunger or if he is allowed to fill his stomach or if he is allowed to fill his stomach and keep extra food as provisions. There are different views on these questions as discussed in the law books. It is not a precondition for eating carrion that one must first go three days without finding any food, as many of the masses and others erroneously believe. Instead, whenever is forced by necessity, it becomes permissible for him."

---

[8] This hadith is *ṣaḥeeḥ*. See Shaykh al-Albâni, *Ṣaḥeeḥ al-Jâmi' aṣ-Ṣagheer*, no. 1886. Recorded by Aḥmad. Also see Shaykh al-Albâni, *I'rwâ' al-Ghaleel*, vol. 3, p. 9, no. 564.

Islamic Manner of Slaughtering Animals

The word *adh-dhakkâh*, lexically speaking, has the meaning of "purifying something, making something good". Thus, one says that there is a '*dhakkiyah* smell", meaning there is a pleasant, good smell. Islamic Law has borrowed this term for the slaughtered animal because its being made permissible by the Law implies it has been made good.

Thus, the purport of the discussion here is the manner in which animals are slaughtered, as animals that one is permitted to eat cannot be eaten unless there are slaughtered properly — with the exception of fish and locust.

Whose Slaughtering is Acceptable

Meat is made permissible by the slaughtering done by any Muslim or one from the People of the Book, whether male or female. Allah (ﷻ) has said:

﴿... وَطَعَامُ ٱلَّذِينَ أُوتُوا۟ ٱلْكِتَٰبَ حِلٌّ لَّكُمْ ... ٥﴾ (سورة المائدة : ٥)

﴾... The food of the people of the Book [Jews and Christians] is lawful to you...﴿ *(Qur'an 5: 5)*

Ibn 'Abbâs said, "Their food refers to their slaughtered animals."[9] K'ab ibn Mâlik stated that a woman slaughtered a sheep with a stone. The Prophet (ﷺ) was asked about that and he said, "Tell her to eat it."[10]

---

[9] This hadith is *ṣaḥeeḥ*. See Shaykh al-Albâni, *I'rwâ' al-Ghaleel*, no. 2528. Recorded by Bukhari.

[10] This hadith is *ṣaḥeeḥ*. See Shaykh al-Albâni, *I'rwâ' al-Ghaleel*, no. 2527. Recorded by Bukhari.

Instruments Used for Slaughtering

It is permissible to slaughter with any instrument that will cut the throat except for teeth or claws. 'Abâyah ibn Rifâ'ah narrated from his grandfather that he had said, "O' Messenger of Allah, we do not have a knife." The Prophet (ﷺ) then said, "Whatever causes the blood to flow and has had Allah's name mentioned (upon it), you may eat, as long as it were not a claw or a tooth. The claw is the knife of the Ethiopians and the tooth is a bone."[11]

Shaddâd ibn Aws said, "Two statements I remember exactly from the Messenger of Allah (ﷺ): 'Verily, Allah has prescribed excellence in all things. Thus, if you kill, kill in a good manner. If you slaughter, slaughter in a good manner. Each of you should sharpen his blade and spare suffering to the animal he is slaughtering.' "[12]

The Manner of Slaughtering

Animals are of two types: those that can be slaughtered and those that one cannot have the capacity to slaughter. Those animals that can be slaughtered must be slaughtered by cutting the windpipe and the throat. Ibn 'Abbâs said, "Slaughtering is at the windpipe and the throat." Ibn 'Umar, Ibn 'Abbâs and Anas all said that there is no harm if one cuts off the head.

Râfi' ibn Khadeej said, "I said, 'O' Messenger of Allah, we are going to face the enemy tomorrow and we have no knives.' He said, 'Hurry (in killing the animal). Whatever causes the blood to flow and

---

[11] Recorded by Bukhari, Muslim, Abu Dawood, Tirmidhi, Nasâ'i and Ibn Mâjah.

[12] This hadith is *ṣaḥeeḥ*. See Shaykh al-Albâni, *I'rwâ' al-Ghaleel*, no. 2540. Recorded by Muslim, Tirmidhi, Abu Dawood, Nasâ'i and Ibn Mâjah.

has had Allah's name mentioned (upon it), you may eat, as long as it were not a claw or a tooth. I shall inform you about that: The tooth is a bone and the claw is the knife of the Ethiopians.' As war booty, we got camels and sheep. One of the camels ran away. A man shot it with an arrow and it stopped. The Messenger of Allah (ﷺ) then said, 'Some of these camels are as wild as the other wild animals. If one them overcomes you like this (and you cannot restrain it to slaughter it), then deal with it in this fashion.'"[13]

The Status of the Fetus

If the fetus comes out of the belly of its mother and is alive on its own, one must slaughter it as well. If however it comes out dead, then the slaughtering of the mother is considering the slaughtering of the fetus. Abu Sa'eed said, "We asked the Messenger of Allah (ﷺ) about the fetus and he said, 'Eat it if you wish for its slaughtering was the slaughtering of its mother.'"[14]

Mention the Name of Allah upon Slaughtering

Mentioning the name of Allah upon slaughtering is a condition for its permissibility. If someone intentionally does not mention the name of Allah, the slaughtered animal is not permissible for consumption. Allah has said:

﴿فَكُلُوا۟ مِمَّا ذُكِرَ ٱسْمُ ٱللَّهِ عَلَيْهِ إِن كُنتُم بِـَٔايَـٰتِهِۦ مُؤْمِنِينَ ﴿١١٨﴾﴾

(سورة الأنعام: ١١٨)

---

[13] Recorded by Bukhari and Muslim. See Shaykh al-Albâni, *Ṣaḥeeḥ al-Jâmi' aṣ-Ṣagheer*, no. 2185.

[14] This hadith is *ṣaḥeeḥ*. See Shaykh al-Albâni, *Ṣaḥeeḥ Sunan Abi Dawood*, no. 2451. Recorded by Abu Dawood.

﴿So eat of that [meat] on which Allah's Name has been pronounced [while slaughtering the animal], if you are believers in His revelations.﴾ *(Qur'an 6: 118)*

Allah also says:

﴿وَلَا تَأْكُلُوا۟ مِمَّا لَمْ يُذْكَرِ ٱسْمُ ٱللَّهِ عَلَيْهِ وَإِنَّهُۥ لَفِسْقٌ ۗ وَإِنَّ ٱلشَّيَـٰطِينَ لَيُوحُونَ إِلَىٰٓ أَوْلِيَآئِهِمْ لِيُجَـٰدِلُوكُمْ ۖ وَإِنْ أَطَعْتُمُوهُمْ إِنَّكُمْ لَمُشْرِكُونَ ﴿١٢١﴾﴾

(سورة الأنعام: ١٢١)

﴿Eat not of that [meat] on which Allah's Name has not been pronounced [at the time of the slaughtering of the animal], for surely it is a sin and disobedience of Allah. And certainly, the devils do inspire their friends [from mankind] to dispute with you, and if you obey them, then you would indeed be polytheists.﴾ *(Qur'an 6: 121)*

And Râfi' ibn Khadeej narrated that the Prophet (ﷺ) said, "Whatever causes the blood to flow and has had Allah's name mentioned (upon it), you may eat."[15]

Facing the Animal Toward the Qiblah

It is recommended to direct the animal toward the *qiblah* and to say what the Prophet (ﷺ) said as mentioned in the following hadith: Jâbir ibn 'Abdullâh said, "On the day of Sacrifice, the Prophet (ﷺ) slaughtered two castrated horned rams having more white than black colour. When he faced them toward (the *qiblah*), he said, 'I am directed my face towards the One Who created the heavens and the earth, upon the religion of Abraham, the pure monotheist, and I am

[15] Recorded by Bukhari and Muslim. See Shaykh al-Albâni, *Ṣaḥeeḥ al-Jâmi' aṣ-Ṣagheer*, no. 2185.

not from among the polytheists. Verily, my prayers, rites, life and death are for Allah, the Lord of the Worlds, having no partner. Thus have I been commanded and I am the first of those who submit. O' Allah, this is from You and for You on behalf of Muhammad and his Nation. In the name of Allah and Allah is the Greatest.' Then he slaughtered (them)."[16]

Hunting

Allah (ﷻ) says:

﴿... وَإِذَا حَلَلْتُمْ فَاصْطَادُوا ... ﴿٢﴾﴾ (سورة المائدة: ٢)

﴿... But when you finish the inviolable state [of Ḥajj or 'Umrah], you may hunt...﴾ *(Qur'an 5: 2)*

Allah also says:

﴿يَسْأَلُونَكَ مَاذَا أُحِلَّ لَهُمْ قُلْ أُحِلَّ لَكُمُ الطَّيِّبَاتُ وَمَا عَلَّمْتُم مِّنَ الْجَوَارِحِ مُكَلِّبِينَ تُعَلِّمُونَهُنَّ مِمَّا عَلَّمَكُمُ اللَّهُ فَكُلُوا مِمَّا أَمْسَكْنَ عَلَيْكُمْ وَاذْكُرُوا اسْمَ اللَّهِ عَلَيْهِ ... ﴿٤﴾﴾

(سورة المائدة: ٤)

﴿They ask you [O' Muhammad] what is lawful for them [as food]. Say, 'Lawful unto you are good foods which Allah has made lawful. And [what is caught by] those beasts and birds of prey which you have trained as hounds, training and teaching them [to catch] in the manner as directed to you by Allah; so eat of what they catch for you, but pronounce the Name of Allah over it...﴾ *(Qur'an 5: 4)*

---

[16] This hadith is *ṣaḥeeḥ*. See Shaykh al-Albâni, *Ṣaḥeeḥ Sunan Abi Dawood*, no. 2425. Recorded by Abu Dawood.

Fishing and seeking animals from the sea is permissible at all times. Hunting land game is also permissible at all times unless one is in the inviolable state of the Ḥajj or 'Umrah. Allah has said:

﴿أُحِلَّ لَكُمْ صَيْدُ ٱلْبَحْرِ وَطَعَامُهُۥ مَتَٰعًا لَّكُمْ وَلِلسَّيَّارَةِ ۖ وَحُرِّمَ عَلَيْكُمْ صَيْدُ ٱلْبَرِّ مَا دُمْتُمْ حُرُمًا ... ﴿٩٦﴾﴾ (سورة المائدة: ٩٦)

﴿Lawful to you is [the pursuit of] water-game and its use for food — for the benefit of yourselves and those who travel, but forbidden is [the pursuit of] land-game as long as you are in the inviolable state of Ḥajj or 'Umrah...﴾ *(Qur'an 5: 96)*

Whose Hunting will Make the Game Permissible

Hunted animals caught by anyone whose slaughtering is acceptable will be permissible.

The Instruments of Hunting

Hunting is done by instruments that will cause death, such as a sword, knife or arrows. It can also be with the use of hunting animals. Allah (ﷻ) says:

﴿يَٰٓأَيُّهَا ٱلَّذِينَ ءَامَنُوا۟ لَيَبْلُوَنَّكُمُ ٱللَّهُ بِشَىْءٍ مِّنَ ٱلصَّيْدِ تَنَالُهُۥٓ أَيْدِيكُمْ وَرِمَاحُكُمْ ... ﴿٩٤﴾﴾ (سورة المائدة: ٩٤)

﴿O' you who believe! Allah will certainly make a trial of you with something in [the matter of] the game that is well within reach of your hands and your lances...﴾ *(Qur'an 5: 94)*

Again, Allah says:

﴿يَسْـَٔلُونَكَ مَاذَآ أُحِلَّ لَهُمْۖ قُلْ أُحِلَّ لَكُمُ ٱلطَّيِّبَٰتُ ۙ وَمَا عَلَّمْتُم مِّنَ ٱلْجَوَارِحِ مُكَلِّبِينَ تُعَلِّمُونَهُنَّ مِمَّا عَلَّمَكُمُ ٱللَّهُۖ ... ﴿٤﴾﴾ (سورة المائدة: ٤)

﴾And [what is caught by] those beasts and birds of prey which you have trained as hounds, training and teaching them [to catch] in the manner as directed to you by Allah...﴿ *(Qur'an 5: 4)*

The instrument used must pierce the body of the hunted animal and penetrate into it (and cannot simply be a glancing strike).

If a hunting animal is used, it must be a trained animal and it cannot actually eat any of the caught animal. Furthermore, there cannot be another animal with it at the site (as then one would not know which animal caught the prey).

Mentioning the name of Allah is also a condition for the permissibility of hunted game. One must mention the name of Allah when shooting the arrow or when releasing the trained animal.

'Adi ibn Ḥâtim (رضي الله عنه) said: "I asked the Messenger of Allah (ﷺ) about hunting with an arrow that has no feathers and no arrowhead. He said, 'If you hit the game with its sharp edge, then eat it. If you hit it with the shaft and it is killed, then it is like an animal killed with a piece of wood. In that case, do not eat it.' I then said, 'I send my dog for game. (What is the ruling concerning that?)' He stated, 'If you sent your dog and you mention the name of Allah, then eat the prey.' I said, 'What if he ate a part of the prey?' He said, 'In that case, do not eat it for he did not catch it for you but he caught it for himself.' I then said, 'I send my dog and then I find another dog with it at the site.' He said, 'Do not eat (that prey), for you have mentioned the name of Allah over your dog but you did not mention it in the case of the other dog.'"[17]

---

[17] Recorded by Bukhari, Muslim and Nasâ'i.

Untrained hunting dogs

What is caught by untrained hunting dogs is not permissible unless one finds the animal still alive and slaughters it. Abu Tha'labah al-Khushani said, "I said, 'O' Prophet of Allah, we are in the lands of the People of the Book. Can we eat from their plates? We are also in a land in which people hunt with bows and with trained as well as untrained dogs. What is then proper for me?' He said, 'As for what you mentioned about the People of the Book: If you can find other plates to eat from, do not from their. If you cannot find others, then wash them and you can eat from them. As for what you caught with a bow and had mention the name of Allah, you may eat of it. As for you, you caught with a trained dog and had mentioned the name of Allah, you may eat of that as well. As for what you caught with an untrained dog and you found it alive and slaughtered it, you may eat from that also.'"[18]

When the prey falls into water

If the prey falls into water, it is forbidden to eat it. The Prophet (ﷺ) told 'Adi ibn Ḥâtim, "When you shoot your arrow, mention the name of Allah. If you find the animal dead, you may eat it — unless you find it in water, as in that case you do not know of the water killed it or your arrow."[19]

---

[18] Recorded by Bukhari, Muslim and Ibn Mâjah. Nasâ'i recorded it without the mention of the People of the Book.

[19] This hadith is *ṣaḥeeḥ*. See Shaykh al-Albâni, *I'rwâ' al-Ghaleel*, no. 2556.

Prey that is Not Found for Two or Three Days and then Found

If a person shoots his arrow and hits and animal but then he is not able to find that prey for two or three days, after which he finds it, it is permissible for him to eat it as long as it has not become smelly. 'Adi ibn Ḥâtim narrated that the Prophet (ﷺ) told him, "If you hit an animal and find it after a day or two with no marks on it other than your arrow, you may eat it."[20]

Sacrificial Animals

This refers to those animals that are slaughtered on the Day of Sacrifice and the Days of *Tashreeq* as a means of getting closer to Allah.

Their Ruling

The sacrifice is obligatory upon one who has the means. The Prophet (ﷺ) said, "Whoever has the means but did not make the sacrifice should not approach our place of prayer."[21]

> "The reasoning here is that since he prohibited the one with the means to perform the sacrifice from coming close to the place of prayer if he did not make the sacrifice, that means that he has left something which is obligatory. It is as if there is no benefit for

[20] This hadith is *ṣaḥeeḥ*. See Shaykh al-Albâni, *Mukhtasar Ṣaḥeeḥ Muslim*, no. 1239. Recorded by Muslim.

[21] This hadith is *ḥasan*. See Shaykh al-Albâni, *Ṣaḥeeḥ Sunan Ibn Mâjah*, no. 2533. Recorded by Ibn Mâjah.

coming closer to Allah by means of the prayer for the one who did not perform this obligation. Mikhnaf ibn Sulaym said, 'We were staying with the Prophet (ﷺ) at 'Arafah and he said, 'O' people, every household must make a sacrifice and *'ateerah* every year. Do you know what *'ateerah* is? It is what the people call the sacrifice of the month of Rajab.''[22] The *'ateerah* sacrifice has been abrogated, as the Prophet (ﷺ) said, 'There is no *fara'* [23] or *'ateerah* (in Islam).'[24] The abrogation of *'ateerah* does not mean that the sacrifice is also abrogated. Jundab ibn Sufiyân al-Bajali said, 'I witnessed the Prophet (ﷺ) on the Day of Sacrifice and he said, 'Whoever sacrificed before the prayer must repeat it with another in its place. One who has not sacrificed yet should perform the sacrifice.' The apparent meaning implies obligation, especially since there is an order to repeat the act.'"[25]

What Animals Qualify for the Sacrifice

The sacrificial animal can only be a camel, sheep/goat or a cow. Allah has said:

﴿وَلِكُلِّ أُمَّةٍ جَعَلْنَا مَنسَكًا لِّيَذْكُرُوا اسْمَ اللَّهِ عَلَىٰ مَا رَزَقَهُم مِّن بَهِيمَةِ الْأَنْعَامِ ... ﴿٣٤﴾﴾

(سورة الحجّ : ٣٤)

﴾And for every nation We have appointed religious ceremonies, that

---

[22] This hadith is *ḥasan*. See Shaykh al-Albâni, *Ṣaḥeeḥ Sunan Ibn Mâjah*, no. 2532. Recorded by Tirmidhi, Abu Dawood, Ibn Mâjah and Nasâ'i.

[23] [*Fara'* refers to specific offspring of camels or sheep with which they used to offer to their idols, a sacrifice made when the number of their herd reached its desired number or a meal given on the occasion of the birth of camels.] - Translator

[24] Recorded by Bukhari, Muslim, Abu Dawood, Tirmidhi and Nasâ'i.

[25] Ash-Shawkâni, *As-Sail al-Jarâr*, vol. 4, Pp. 74-75, with some abridgement.

they may mention the Name of Allah over the beast of cattle that He has given them for food...﴿ *(Qur'an 22: 34)*

A camel or cow suffices for how many people?

Ibn 'Abbâs said, "We were travelling with the Messenger of Allah (ﷺ) and the time of the Sacrifice came. Ten of us would share in one camel and seven would share in one cow."[26]

A sheep/goat suffices for one man and his household

'Aṭâ' ibn Yasâr said, "I asked Abu Ayyoob al-Anṣâri, 'How was the sacrifice among you during the lifetime of the Messenger of Allah?' He said, 'During the lifetime of the Messenger of Allah (ﷺ), a man would sacrifice a sheep on his behalf and on behalf of his household. He would eat from it and feed others. Then the people started to boast and things became as you see them now.' "[27]

What is Not Permissible as a Sacrificial Animal

'Ubayd ibn Fayrooz said, "I said to al-Barâ' ibn 'Âzib, 'Tell me about what is disliked or prohibited by the Messenger of Allah (ﷺ) for the sacrificial animal.' He said, 'The Messenger of Allah (ﷺ) went like this with his hand — and my hand is smaller than his — and said, 'Four types of animals are not sufficient for the sacrifice: a one-eyed animal that is obviously one-eyed; a sick animal which is obviously ill; a lame animal with an obvious limp; and an old animal that has no marrow and is extremely lean and skinny.' And he said, 'I

---

[26] This hadith is *ṣaḥeeḥ*. See Shaykh al-Albâni, *Ṣaḥeeḥ Sunan Ibn Mâjah*, no. 2536. Recorded by Ibn Mâjah, Tirmidhi and Nasâ'i.

[27] This hadith is *ṣaḥeeḥ*. See Shaykh al-Albâni, *Ṣaḥeeḥ Sunan Ibn Mâjah*, no. 2546. Recorded by Ibn Mâjah and Tirmidhi.

hate that there should be some shortcoming in the ear.' He said, 'What I dislike of them, leave them but I do not make them forbidden for anyone.' '"[28]

A small milking goat of less than one year is not suitable for the sacrifice. Al-Barâ' ibn 'Âzib said, "One of my maternal uncles, called Abu Burdah, sacrificed before the prayer. The Messenger of Allah (ﷺ) told him, 'The sheep you slaughtered is just the sheep for meat.' He say, 'O' Messenger of Allah, I have a small milking goat of less than one year.' The Prophet (ﷺ) told him, 'Slaughter it and it will not be appropriate for anyone other than you.' Then he said, 'Whoever slaughtered before the prayer has slaughtered for himself. Whoever slaughtered after the prayer has completed the rites and was in accord with the practice of the Muslims.' "[29]

The *'Aqeeqah* (Slaughtering an Animal due to the Birth of a Child)

'Aqeeqah refers to what is slaughtered due to the birth of a child.

Its Ruling

'Aqeeqah is obligatory upon the one who the child was born to. For a boy, it is two sheep of similar age and for a girl it is one

---

[28] This hadith is *ṣaḥeeḥ*. See Shaykh al-Albâni, *Ṣaḥeeḥ Sunan Ibn Mâjah*, no. 2545. Recorded by Ibn Mâjah, Abu Dawood, Nasâ'i and by Tirmidhi in abbreviated form.

[29] Recorded by Bukhari and Muslim. Its meaning is also recorded by Tirmidhi, Abu Dawood and Nasâ'i.

sheep. Salmân ibn 'Âmir aḍ-Ḍabbi narrated that he heard the Messenger of Allah (ﷺ) say, "An *'aqeeqah* is to be offered for a boy. So spill the blood (by slaughtering an animal) on his behalf and remove him of his suffering."[30] 'Â'ishah (رضي الله عنها) said, "The Messenger of Allah (ﷺ) told us to have an *'aqeeqah*, for a boy two sheep and for a girl one sheep."[31] Al-Ḥasan narrated from Samurah[32] that the Prophet (ﷺ) said, "Every boy is a pledge for his *'aqeeqah*, to be slaughtered on the seventh day, his hair is to be shaved and he is be given a name."[33]

Its Timing

The Sunnah is to slaughter on the seventh day after the birth. If that is missed, it should be on the fourteenth day. If that is missed as well, it should be on the twenty-first day. Buraydah narrated that the Prophet (ﷺ) said, "The *'aqeeqah* is to be slaughtered on the seventh or the fourteenth or the twenty-first."[34]

---

[30] This hadith is *ṣaḥeeḥ*. See Shaykh al-Albâni, *Ṣaḥeeḥ Sunan Ibn Mâjah*, no. 2562. Recorded by Bukhari, Abu Dawood, Tirmidhi and Nasâ'i.

[31] This hadith is *ṣaḥeeḥ*. See Shaykh al-Albâni, *Ṣaḥeeḥ Sunan Ibn Mâjah*, no. 2561. Recorded by Ibn Mâjah and Tirmidhi.

[32] [The Arabic text has, "Al-Ḥasan ibn Samurah." That is obviously simply a typographical error.] - Translator

[33] This hadith is *ṣaḥeeḥ*. See Shaykh al-Albâni, *Ṣaḥeeḥ al-Jâmi' aṣ-Ṣagheer*, no. 2563. Recorded by Ibn Mâjah, Abu Dawood, Tirmidhi and Nasâ'i.

[34] This hadith is *ṣaḥeeḥ*. See Shaykh al-Albâni, *Ṣaḥeeḥ al-Jâmi' aṣ-Ṣagheer*, no. 4132. Recorded by al-Bayhaqi.

What is Recommended to be Done for the Child

1. *Taḥneek*

Abu Moosa (ﷺ) said, "I had a son, so I went to the Prophet (ﷺ). He named him Ibrâheem. He did *taḥneek* [35] with a date. He prayed for blessings for him and gave him to me." That was Abu Moosa's eldest son.[36]

2. Shaving the head on the seventh day and to give in charity an equivalent weight (of the baby's hair) in silver.

Al-Ḥasan narrated from Samurah[37] that the Prophet (ﷺ) said, "Every boy is a pledge for his *'aqeeqah*, to be slaughtered on the seventh day, his hair is to be shaved and he is be given a name."[38] Abu Râfi' narrated that the Prophet (ﷺ) said to Fâṭimah when she gave birth to al-Ḥasan, "Shave his head and give in silver the weight of his hair in charity to the poor."[39]

3. Circumcising on the seventh day

Aṭ-Ṭabarâni recorded in *al-Mu'jam aṣ-Ṣagheer* from Jâbir that the Messenger of Allah (ﷺ) had an *'aqeeqah* for al-Ḥasan and al-Ḥusayn and he circumcised them on the seventh day.[40] Aṭ-Ṭabarâni

---

[35] [This is where a person chews something sweet, like a date, and places it into the baby's mouth.]

[36] Recorded by Bukhari (and this is his wording) and by Muslim without the words, "prayed for blessings for him."

[37] [Once again, the Arabic text has, "Al-Ḥasan ibn Samurah." That is obviously simply a typographical error.] - Translator

[38] This hadith is *ṣaḥeeḥ*. See Shaykh al-Albâni, *Ṣaḥeeḥ al-Jâmi' aṣ-Ṣagheer*, no. 2563. Recorded by Ibn Mâjah, Abu Dawood, Tirmidhi and Nasâ'i.

[39] This hadith is *ḥasan*. See Shaykh al-Albâni, *I'rwâ' al-Ghaleel*, no. 1175. Recorded by Aḥmad and al-Bayhaqi.

[40] Recorded by aṭ-Ṭabarâni in *al-Mu'jam aṣ-Ṣagheer* and al-Bayhaqi.

also recorded in *al-Mu'jam al-Awsaṭ* that Ibn 'Abbâs said, "Seven are from the Sunnah on the seventh day of the child: he is to be named, he is to be circumcised and have the harm removed from him, his ear is to be pierced, he is to have an *'aqeeqah* on his behalf, his head is to be shaved, the blood of the slaughtered animal is wiped on him and the weight of his hair in gold or silver is to be given in charity."[41]

[41] Recorded by aṭ-Ṭabarâni in *al-Mu'jam al-Awsaṭ*. Shaykh al-Albâni has mentioned these reports in *Tamâm al-Minnah* (p. 68). The two hadiths, although each having some weakness, strengthen each other as they come via different sources and neither of them contains narrators accused of lying or forging hadith.
Note that wiping the blood of the slaughtered animal on the baby has been prohibited.

Chapter Eleven — Bequests

The Arabic word for bequests comes from a term implying, "connecting". The one who makes a bequest connects what is in his life with what is after his death.

As a legal term, it refers to a person bestowing upon another an item, credit or use of something to another as a gift after his death.

Its Ruling

To make a bequest is obligatory upon the one who has wealth that he wishes to bequest. Allah (ﷻ) says:

﴿كُتِبَ عَلَيۡكُمۡ إِذَا حَضَرَ أَحَدَكُمُ ٱلۡمَوۡتُ إِن تَرَكَ خَيۡرًا ٱلۡوَصِيَّةُ لِلۡوَٰلِدَيۡنِ وَٱلۡأَقۡرَبِينَ بِٱلۡمَعۡرُوفِۖ حَقًّا عَلَى ٱلۡمُتَّقِينَ ١٨٠﴾ (سورة البقرة: ١٨٠)

﴾It is prescribed for you, when death approaches any of you, if he leaves wealth, that he make a bequest to parents and next of kin, according to reasonable manners [This is] a duty upon the pious.﴿

(Qur'an 2: 180)

'Abdullâh ibn 'Umar narrated that the Messenger of Allah (ﷺ) said, "It is not right for a Muslim who wishes to bequest something to spend two nights except that he has his written bequest with him."[1]

---

[1] Recorded by Bukhari, Muslim, Abu Dawood, Tirmidhi, Ibn Mâjah and Nasâ'i.

The amount of wealth recommended for a bequest

S'ad ibn Abi Waqqâṣ said, "The Prophet (ﷺ) came to visit me while I was in Makkah — and he disliked for one to die in the land from which one had emigrated. He said, 'May Allah have mercy of Ibn 'Afrâ' (who had died in the land from which he had emigrated).' I said, 'O' Messenger of Allah, shall I bequest all of my wealth?' He said, 'No.' I said, 'Half?' He said, 'No.' Then I said, 'A third?' He replied, 'One-third (is permissible but even) one-third is a lot. For you to leave your heirs wealthy is better than to leave them dependent on what the people give them (via begging). Whatever you spend (properly) will be an act of charity, even the morsel of food that you raise to your wife's mouth. Perhaps Allah may lengthen your life so that some people may benefit from you while others will be harmed due to you.'" At that time, S'ad had only one daughter.[2]

There is no bequests for the pre-determined heirs

Abu Umâmah al-Bâhily said that he heard the Messenger of Allah (ﷺ) say during his speech of the Farewell Pilgrimage, "Verily Allah has given each his due right. Thus, there is no bequest for the predetermined heir."[3]

What should be written at the beginning of the bequest

Anas said, "They used to write the following at the beginning of their bequests:

---

[2] Recorded by Bukhari (and this is his wording), Muslim, Abu Dawood and Nasâ'i.

[3] This hadith is *ṣaḥeeḥ*. See Shaykh al-Albâni, *Ṣaḥeeḥ Sunan Ibn Mâjah*, no. 2194. Recorded by Ibn Mâjah, Abu Dawood and Tirmidhi. [In Islamic law, the law has automatically stated certain shares for predetermined heirs. These heirs shall receive their fixed shares and are not allowed to receive any further bequest beyond that amount.] - Translator

'In the name of Allah, the Most Compassionate, the Most Merciful. This is the bequest of so and so, who bears witness that there is none worthy of worship except Allah, alone without any partners, and that Muhammad is His servant and messenger. He also bears witness that the Hour is coming without any doubt and that Allah shall resurrect those in the graves. I advise those whom I have left behind from my family to fear Allah and make matters proper between them. I also advise them to obey Allah and His Messenger if they are truly believers. I advise them with what Prophet Ibrâheem (ﷺ) advised his two sons and Jacob, 'O' my sons, Allah has chosen for you the religion and therefore do not die except as Muslims'.'"[4]

When does the person receive what he was bequeathed

The one receiving a bequest is not entitled to it until after the bequeather has died and after his debts have been paid. If his debts consume all of his estate, nothing is to be given as a bequest. 'Ali (رضي الله عنه) said, "The Messenger of Allah (ﷺ) used to settle the debts before fulfilling the bequests, even though you recite (in the Qur'an), ﴾After any bequests made or debts to be paid﴿."[5]

An Important Note

Given that the majority of the people today are engaged in innovations in their religion, especially in matters related to the funeral, it becomes obligatory upon a Muslim to write a bequest demanding that he be prepared and buried according to the Sunnah. This act would be in implementation of the verse in the Qur'an:

---

[4] This hadith is *ṣaḥeeḥ*. See Shaykh al-Albâni, *I'rwâ' al-Ghaleel*, no. 1647. Recorded by ad-Dâraquṭni and al-Bayhaqi.

[5] This hadith is *ḥasan*. See Shaykh al-Albâni, *Ṣaḥeeḥ Sunan Ibn Mâjah*, no. 2195 and *I'rwâ' al-Ghaleel*, no. 1667. Recorded by Ibn Mâjah and Tirmidhi.

﴿يَٰٓأَيُّهَا ٱلَّذِينَ ءَامَنُوا۟ قُوٓا۟ أَنفُسَكُمْ وَأَهْلِيكُمْ نَارًا وَقُودُهَا ٱلنَّاسُ وَٱلْحِجَارَةُ عَلَيْهَا مَلَٰٓئِكَةٌ غِلَاظٌ شِدَادٌ لَّا يَعْصُونَ ٱللَّهَ مَآ أَمَرَهُمْ وَيَفْعَلُونَ مَا يُؤْمَرُونَ ﴿٦﴾﴾

(سورة التحريم : ٦)

﴿O' you who believe! Ward off from yourselves and your families a Fire whose fuel is men and stones, over which are [appointed] angels stern [and] severe, who disobey not the Commands they receive from Allah, but do that which they are commanded.﴾ *(Qur'an 66: 6)*

Thus, the Companions of the Messenger of Allah (ﷺ) used to leave such a bequest. Many reports of this nature can be found. Thus, for example, 'Âmir ibn S'ad ibn Abi Waqqâṣ told his son during his final illness, "Make the grave with a niche to the side and erect a brick over it, as they had done for the Messenger of Allah (ﷺ)."[6]

A Second Important Note

If a man has a descendent (such as his son) who is an heir but who dies during the man's lifetime, he then must make a bequest on behalf of the children of that descendent (that is, his own grandchildren) to the amount that the descendent would have inherited-up to one-third of one's wealth and one-third itself is a lot. If the man dies without making such a bequest for the children of his son, then they are to be given the amount that they had a right to, as this is considered a type of debt on the man. If the man dies without making such a bequest, the debt is not done away with and these days the issue can be taken to court.

---

[6] Quoted from Shaykh al-Albâni, *Ahkâm al-Janâ'iz*, p. 8.

Chapter Twelve — Inheritance[1]

The Arabic word for inheritance, *farâ'iḍ* (pl., *fareeḍah*), comes from a word implying specified or determined amount, as in the verse:

﴿... فَنِصۡفُ مَا فَرَضۡتُمۡ ... ﴿٢٣٧﴾﴾ (سورة البَقَرَة: ٢٣٧)

﴿... Then pay half of what you specified...﴾ *(Qur'an 2: 237)*

In Islamic Law, it refers to the determined proportion that an inheritor receives.

Warning Concerning Misappropriating Estates

In Pre-Islamic times among the Arabs, only men would inherit and women would not. Furthermore, only older children would inherit and not the younger ones. Islam then came and gave each its due right. This right is termed by Allah (ﷻ) in the Qur'an as:

﴿... وَصِيَّةً مِّنَ ٱللَّهِ ... ﴿١٢﴾﴾ (سورة النِّسَاء: ١٢)

﴿... A Commandment from Allah...﴾ *(Qur'an 4: 12)*

And:

﴿... فَرِيضَةً مِّنَ ٱللَّهِ ... ﴿١١﴾﴾ (سورة النِّسَاء: ١١)

﴿... Ordained by Allah...﴾ *(Qur'an 4: 11)*

[1] Cf., as-Sayyid Sâbiq, *Fiqh as-Sunnah*, vol. 3, p. 424.

After using those terms, then comes a very strong and emphasized warning concerning any kind of violation of Allah's laws concerning inheritance. Allah (ﷻ) says:

﴿تِلْكَ حُدُودُ ٱللَّهِ ۚ وَمَن يُطِعِ ٱللَّهَ وَرَسُولَهُۥ يُدْخِلْهُ جَنَّٰتٍ تَجْرِى مِن تَحْتِهَا ٱلْأَنْهَٰرُ خَٰلِدِينَ فِيهَا ۚ وَذَٰلِكَ ٱلْفَوْزُ ٱلْعَظِيمُ ﴿١٣﴾ وَمَن يَعْصِ ٱللَّهَ وَرَسُولَهُۥ وَيَتَعَدَّ حُدُودَهُۥ يُدْخِلْهُ نَارًا خَٰلِدًا فِيهَا وَلَهُۥ عَذَابٌ مُّهِينٌ ﴿١٤﴾﴾ (سورة النِّسَاء: ١٣-١٤)

﴿These are the limits [set by] Allah, and whosoever obeys Allah and His Messenger will be admitted to Gardens under which rivers flow [in Paradise], to abide therein, and that will be the great success. And whosoever disobeys Allah and His Messenger and transgresses His limits, He will cast him into the Fire, to abide therein; and he shall have a disgraceful torment.﴾ *(Qur'an 4: 13-14)*

What is Inherited from the Wealth of the Deceased

When a person dies, the first use for his wealth is to pay for his shroud and burial. After that, any debts he may still have must also be paid. This will be followed by the distribution of any bequests that he may have made, as Allah has said:

﴿... مِنۢ بَعْدِ وَصِيَّةٍ يُوصِى بِهَآ أَوْ دَيْنٍ ... ﴿١١﴾﴾ (سورة النِّسَاء: ١١)

﴿... After the payment of legacies he may have bequeathed or debts...﴾ *(Qur'an 4: 11)*

And 'Ali (رضي الله عنه) said, "The Messenger of Allah (ﷺ) used to settle the debts before fulfilling the bequests."[2]

---

[2] This hadith is *ḥasan*. See Shaykh al-Albâni, *Ṣaḥeeḥ Sunan Ibn Mâjah*, no. 2195 and *I'rwâ' al-Ghaleel*, no. 1667. Recorded by Ibn Mâjah and Tirmidhi.

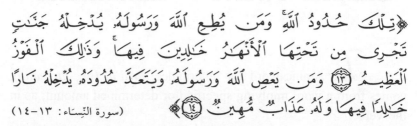

Causes Entitling One to Be an Heir

The causes entitling one to be an heir are three:

1. Blood relationship

Allah (ﷻ) has said:

﴿... وَأُوْلُواْ ٱلْأَرْحَامِ بَعْضُهُمْ أَوْلَىٰ بِبَعْضٍ ... ﴿٦﴾﴾ (سورة الأحزاب: ٦)

﴾... And blood relations among each other have closer personal ties in the Decree of Allah [regarding inheritance]...﴿ *(Qur'an 33: 6)*

2. *Al-Walâ'* (Clientage[3])

Ibn 'Umar narrated that the Prophet (ﷺ) said, "*Al-Walâ'* is kinship like the kinship of blood."[4]

3. Marriage

Allah has said:

﴿ وَلَكُمْ نِصْفُ مَا تَرَكَ أَزْوَٰجُكُمْ ... ﴿١٢﴾﴾ (سورة النِّساء: ١٢)

﴾In that which your wives leave, your share is a half...﴿ *(Qur'an 4: 12)*

Factors Preventing one from Inheriting

1. Murder

Abu Hurayrah (رضي الله عنه) reported that the Messenger of Allah (ﷺ) said: "The murderer (of the deceased) does not inherit."[5]

---

[3] [The most common example of this type of special relationship is that which exists between the slave owner and his freed slave.] - Translator

[4] This hadith is *ṣaḥeeḥ*. See Shaykh al-Albâni, *Ṣaḥeeḥ al-Jâmi' aṣ-Ṣagheer*, no. 7157. Recorded by al-Ḥâkim and al-Bayhaqi.

[5] This hadith is *ṣaḥeeḥ*. See Shaykh al-Albâni, *Ṣaḥeeḥ al-Jâmi' aṣ-Ṣagheer*, no. 4436 and *I'rwâ' al-Ghaleel*, no. 1672. Recorded by Ibn Mâjah and Tirmidhi.

2. Being of a different religion

Usâmah ibn Zayd narrated that the Prophet (ﷺ) said, "The Muslim does not inherit from a disbeliever nor does the disbeliever inherit from a Muslim."[6]

3. Slavery

The slave and everything that he possesses actually belong to his owner. Thus, if he were to inherit from a relative, that inheritance would go to his master and not him.

Males who Inherit

The categories of males who inherit are ten in number:

1. and 2. The son and his son and so on, no matter how distant

Allah (سبحانه وتعالى) says:

﴿يُوصِيكُمُ ٱللَّهُ فِىٓ أَوْلَـٰدِكُمْ ۖ لِلذَّكَرِ مِثْلُ حَظِّ ٱلْأُنثَيَيْنِ ... ﴿١١﴾﴾

(سورة النِّساء: ١١)

﴾Allah commands you as regards your children's [inheritance]; to the male, a portion equal to that of two females...﴿ *(Qur'an 4: 11)*

3. and 4. The father and his fathers
and so on, no matter how distant

Allah (سبحانه وتعالى) says:

﴿... وَلِأَبَوَيْهِ لِكُلِّ وَٰحِدٍ مِّنْهُمَا ٱلسُّدُسُ ... ﴿١١﴾﴾ (سورة النِّساء: ١١)

﴾... For parents, a sixth share of inheritance to each...﴿
(Qur'an 4: 11)

---

[6] Recorded by Bukhari, Muslim, Tirmidhi, Ibn Mâjah and Abu Dawood.

The grandfather is considered a father, as the Prophet (ﷺ) said, "I am the son of 'Abdul-Muṭṭalib."[7]

5. and 6. The brother and his sons even if distant

Allah (ﷻ) says:

﴿... وَهُوَ يَرِثُهَآ إِن لَّمْ يَكُن لَّهَا وَلَدٌ ... ﴾ (سورة النِّساء: ١٧٦)

﴾... A woman, who left no child, her brother takes her inheritance...﴿ *(Qur'an 4: 176)*

7. and 8. The maternal uncle and his son, even if distant

The Prophet (ﷺ) said, "Give the inheritance to its rightful recipients. Whatever remains is to be given to the closest male relative."[8]

9. The husband

Allah says:

﴿وَلَكُمْ نِصْفُ مَا تَرَكَ أَزْوَاجُكُمْ ... ﴾ (سورة النِّساء: ١٢)

﴾In that which your wives leave, your share is a half...﴿ *(Qur'an 4: 12)*

10. The male who has free a slave

The Prophet (ﷺ) said, "The *walâ'* (clientage) is for the one who did the freeing."[9]

Females who Inherit

The categories of females who inherit are nine in number:

---

[7] [Recorded by Bukhari, Muslim, Tirmidhi and Abu Dawood.]

[8] Recorded by Bukhari, Muslim and Tirmidhi.

[9] Recorded by Bukhari, Muslim and Tirmidhi. Abu Dawood and Ibn Mâjah have something similar.

1. and 2. The daughter and the daughter of the son, no matter how far done

Allah (ﷻ) says:

﴿يُوصِيكُمُ ٱللَّهُ فِيٓ أَوۡلَٰدِكُمۡۖ ... ﴾ (سورة النِّسَاء: ١١)

﴿Allah commands you as regards your children's [inheritance]; to the male, a portion equal to that of two females...﴾ *(Qur'an 4: 11)*

3. and 4. The mother and the grandmother

Allah says:

﴿... وَلِأَبَوَيۡهِ لِكُلِّ وَٰحِدٖ مِّنۡهُمَا ٱلسُّدُسُ ... ﴾ (سورة النِّسَاء: ١١)

﴿... For parents, a sixth share of inheritance to each...﴾ *(Qur'an 4: 11)*

5. The sister

﴿... إِنِ ٱمۡرُؤٌاْ هَلَكَ لَيۡسَ لَهُۥ وَلَدٞ وَلَهُۥٓ أُخۡتٞ فَلَهَا نِصۡفُ مَا تَرَكَۚ ... ﴾

(سورة النِّسَاء: ١٧٦)

﴿... If it is a man that dies, leaving a sister, but no child, she shall have half the inheritance...﴾ *(Qur'an 4: 176)*

6. The wife

Allah says:

﴿... وَلَهُنَّ ٱلرُّبُعُ مِمَّا تَرَكۡتُمۡ ... ﴾ (سورة النِّسَاء: ١٢)

﴿... In that which you leave, their [your wives] share is a fourth...﴾ *(Qur'an 4: 12)*

7. The woman who has freed a slave

Again, the Prophet (Blessings and peace be upon him) said, "The *walâ'* (clientage) is for the one who did the freeing."[10]

Those who have the Right to the Estate

Those who have the right to the estate are of three categories: those with predetermined shares, *al-'aṣibah* (to be explained below) and relatives through the womb of the mother.

The portions that have been stated in the Book of Allah are six: One-half, one-fourth, one-eighth, two-thirds, one-third and one-sixth. Those who can possibly receive one-half are five categories:

1. The husband if his wife did not have any children

Allah (ﷻ) says:

﴿ وَلَكُمْ نِصْفُ مَا تَرَكَ أَزْوَاجُكُمْ إِن لَّمْ يَكُن لَّهُنَّ وَلَدٌ ... ﴿١٢﴾ ﴾

(سورة النِّساء: ١٢)

﴾In that which your wives leave, your share is a half if they have no child...﴿ *(Qur'an 4: 12)*

2. The daughter

Allah says:

﴿ ... وَإِن كَانَتْ وَاحِدَةً فَلَهَا ٱلنِّصْفُ ... ﴿١١﴾ ﴾ (سورة النِّساء: ١١)

﴾... If only one [daughter], her share is half...﴿ *(Qur'an 4: 11)*

3. The granddaughter via one's son

By consensus, she takes the same place as the daughter. Ibn al-Mundhir said, "All the scholars agree that the sons of the son and the

[10] Recorded by Bukhari, Muslim and Tirmidhi. Abu Dawood and Ibn Mâjah have something similar.

daughters of the son take the same place as one's sons and daughters, the males the same as the males and the females the same as the females, if the deceased did not leave behind a son from his loin."[11]

4. and 5. The full sister and the half sister from one's father

Allah (ﷻ) says:

﴿... إِنِ ٱمۡرُؤٌاْ هَلَكَ لَيۡسَ لَهُۥ وَلَدٌ وَلَهُۥٓ أُخۡتٌ فَلَهَا نِصۡفُ مَا تَرَكَۚ ... ﴿١٧٦﴾﴾

(سورة النساء: ١٧٦)

﴿... If it is a man that dies, leaving a sister, but no child, she shall have half the inheritance...﴾ *(Qur'an 4: 176)*

A <u>one-quarter</u> (one-fourth) share is for the following two categories:

1. The husband if the wife has a child

Allah says:

﴿... فَإِن كَانَ لَهُنَّ وَلَدٌ فَلَكُمُ ٱلرُّبُعُ مِمَّا تَرَكۡنَۚ ... ﴿١٢﴾﴾

(سورة النساء: ١٢)

﴿... In that which your wives leave, your share is a half if they have no child; but if they leave a child, you get a fourth of that which they leave...﴾ *(Qur'an 4: 12)*

2. The wife if the husband does not have a child

Allah says:

﴿... وَلَهُنَّ ٱلرُّبُعُ مِمَّا تَرَكۡتُمۡ إِن لَّمۡ يَكُن لَّكُمۡ وَلَدٌۚ ... ﴿١٢﴾﴾

(سورة النساء: ١٢)

﴿... In that which you leave, their [your wives] share is a fourth if you leave no child...﴾ *(Qur'an 4: 12)*

---

[11] Ibn al-Mundhir, *al-Ijmâ'*, p. 79.

Those who may receive one-eighth is only one category, the wife if the husband has a child. Allah (ﷻ) says:

﴿... فَإِن كَانَ لَكُمْ وَلَدٌ فَلَهُنَّ ٱلثُّمُنُ مِمَّا تَرَكْتُمْ ... ﴿١٢﴾﴾

(سورة النِّساء: ١٢)

﴿... But if you leave a child, they get an eighth of that which you leave...﴾ *(Qur'an 4: 12)*

Two-thirds can possibly go to four categories:

1. and 2. Two daughters or two granddaughters from one's son Allah says:

﴿... فَإِن كُنَّ نِسَآءً فَوْقَ ٱثْنَتَيْنِ فَلَهُنَّ ثُلُثَا مَا تَرَكَ ... ﴿١١﴾﴾ (سورة النِّساء: ١١)

﴿... If [there are] only daughters, two or more, their share is two thirds of the inheritance...﴾ *(Qur'an 4: 11)*

3. and 4. Two full sisters or two half-sisters from one's father Allah says:

﴿... فَإِن كَانَتَا ٱثْنَتَيْنِ فَلَهُمَا ٱلثُّلُثَانِ مِمَّا تَرَكَ ... ﴿١٧٦﴾﴾ (سورة النِّساء: ١٧٦)

﴿... If there are two sisters, they shall have two-thirds of the inheritance...﴾ *(Qur'an 4: 176)*

One-third can possible go to one category:

1. The mother if there is no category blocking her inheritance Allah (ﷻ) says:

﴿... فَإِن لَّمْ يَكُن لَّهُۥ وَلَدٌ وَوَرِثَهُۥٓ أَبَوَاهُ فَلِأُمِّهِ ٱلثُّلُثُ ... ﴿١١﴾﴾

(سورة النِّساء: ١١)

﴿... If no children, and the parents are the [only] heirs, the mother has a third...﴾ *(Qur'an 4: 11)*

2. Two or more siblings from the mother's side

Allah (ﷻ) says:

﴿... وَإِن كَانَ رَجُلٌ يُورَثُ كَلَٰلَةً أَوِ ٱمْرَأَةٌ وَلَهُۥٓ أَخٌ أَوْ أُخْتٌ فَلِكُلِّ وَٰحِدٍ مِّنْهُمَا ٱلسُّدُسُ ۚ فَإِن كَانُوٓا۟ أَكْثَرَ مِن ذَٰلِكَ فَهُمْ شُرَكَآءُ فِى ٱلثُّلُثِ ۚ ... ﴿١٢﴾﴾ (سورة النِّسَاء: ١٢)

﴾... If the man or woman whose inheritance is in question has left neither ascendants nor descendants, but has left a brother or a sister, each one of the two gets a sixth; but if more than two, they share in a third...﴿ *(Qur'an 4: 12)*

<u>One-sixth</u> may go to seven categories of people:

1. The mother with the existence of a child or brethren

Allah says:

﴿... وَلِأَبَوَيْهِ لِكُلِّ وَٰحِدٍ مِّنْهُمَا ٱلسُّدُسُ مِمَّا تَرَكَ إِن كَانَ لَهُۥ وَلَدٌ ۚ فَإِن لَّمْ يَكُن لَّهُۥ وَلَدٌ وَوَرِثَهُۥٓ أَبَوَاهُ فَلِأُمِّهِ ٱلثُّلُثُ ۚ فَإِن كَانَ لَهُۥٓ إِخْوَةٌ فَلِأُمِّهِ ٱلسُّدُسُ ۚ ... ﴿١١﴾﴾ (سورة النِّسَاء: ١١)

﴾For parents, a sixth share of inheritance to each if the deceased left children; if no children, and the parents are the [only] heirs, the mother has a third; if the deceased left brothers or [sisters], the mother has a sixth﴿ *(Qur'an 4: 11)*

2. The grandmother if the mother is no longer alive

Ibn al-Mundhir said, "The scholars agree that the grandmother gets one-sixth and if the deceased did not have a (living) mother."[12]

[12] Ibn al-Mundhir, *al-Ijmâ'*, p. 84.

3. The child of one's mother, male or female when no other heirs are left

Allah (ﷻ) says:

﴿... وَإِن كَانَ رَجُلٌ يُورَثُ كَلَـٰلَةً أَوِ ٱمْرَأَةٌ وَلَهُۥٓ أَخٌ أَوْ أُخْتٌ فَلِكُلِّ وَٰحِدٍ مِّنْهُمَا ٱلسُّدُسُ ... ﴿١٢﴾﴾ (سورة النِّسَاء: ١٢)

﴿... If the man or woman whose inheritance is in question has left neither ascendants nor descendants, but has left a brother or a sister, each one of the two gets a sixth...﴾ *(Qur'an 4: 12)*

4. The granddaughter via one's son with one's own daughter

This is based on the hadith of Abu Qays which states: Huzayl ibn Sharaḥbeel said, "Abu Moosa was asked about a daughter, a son's daughter and a sister. He said, 'The daughter receives one-half and the sister receives one-half. Go to Ibn Mas'ood and he will tell you the same.' So Ibn Mas'ood was asked about it and was informed of what Abu Moosa had said. Ibn Mas'ood then stated, 'If I give the same decision, I would have gone wrong and would not be of the rightly-guided. I shall decide in the manner that the Prophet (ﷺ) decided: the daughter receives one-half and the son's daughter will receive one sixth, totally two-thirds. The remainder is for the sister.' We then came to Abu Moosa and informed him of what Ibn Mas'ood stated. He then said, 'Do not ask me anymore as long as this deeply knowledgeable one is among you.'"[13]

5. The half-sister from the father in the presence of the full sister

The half-sister (will receive one-sixth) to total two-thirds

[13] This hadith is *ṣaḥeeḥ*. See Shaykh al-Albâni, *I'rwâ' al-Ghaleel*, no. 1683. Recorded by Bukhari and without the last sentence it is also recorded by Abu Dawood and Tirmidhi.

between the two as the case is analogous to the previous son's daughter in the presence of one's own daughter.

6. The father in the presence of a son

Allah (ﷻ) says:

﴿... وَلِأَبَوَيْهِ لِكُلِّ وَٰحِدٍ مِّنْهُمَا ٱلسُّدُسُ مِمَّا تَرَكَ إِن كَانَ لَهُۥ وَلَدٌ ... ﴿١١﴾﴾ (سورة النِّساء: ١١)

﴿... For parents, a sixth share of inheritance to each if the deceased left children...﴾ *(Qur'an 4: 11)*

7. The grandfather if the father is no longer alive

Ibn al-Mundhir said, "The scholars all agree that the rule for the grandfather is the same as that for the father."[14]

Al-'Aṣibah

Al-'Aṣibah (plural of *'Âṣib*, like *Ṭâlib* "student" and *Ṭalibah* "students") are the tribe and relatives of the man from his father's side.

The purport of it here is the person to whom the remainder of the estate will go to after the predetermined inheritors receive their shares. If there is nothing left of the estate, the *'âṣib* will receive nothing — unless he happens to be the son, in which case him also being the *'âṣib* will not prevent him from his inheritance.

Furthermore, *al-'aṣibah* are entitled to all of the estate if none of the predetermined inheritors exist. Ibn 'Abbâs narrated that the Prophet (ﷺ) said, "Give the inheritance to its rightful recipients. Whatever remains is to be given to the closest male relative."[15]

---

[14] Ibn al-Mundhir, *al-Ijmâ'*, p. 84.

[15] Recorded by Bukhari, Muslim and Tirmidhi.

Allah (ﷻ) has said:

﴿... وَهُوَ يَرِثُهَآ إِن لَّمْ يَكُن لَّهَا وَلَدٌ ... ﴿١٧٦﴾﴾ (سورة النِّساء: ١٧٦)

﴾... If [such a deceased was] a woman, who left no child, her brother takes her inheritance...﴿ *(Qur'an 4: 176)*

Thus, all of the inheritance has been ascribed to the brother when he is the sole heir. The remainder of the *'aṣibah* are to be dealt with in an analogous manner.

Its categories [16]

Al-'Aṣibah can be divided into two categories: *'Aṣibah* of blood relations and *'aṣibah* due to a specific cause.

The *'aṣibah* due to a specific cause is that which results from setting a slave free. The Prophet (ﷺ) said, "The *walâ'* (clientage) is for the one who did the freeing."[17] The Prophet (ﷺ) also said, "*Al-Walâ'* is kinship like the kinship of blood."[18]

The freed slave inherits only if none of the related *'aṣibah* are present. It makes no difference whether the freed slave is a male or female. 'Abdullâh ibn Shaddâd narrated from the daughter of Ḥamzah who said, "My ex-master died and left behind a daughter. The Messenger of Allah (ﷺ) divided up his wealth between me and his daughter. He gave me half and gave her half."[19]

---

[16] Cf., as-Sayyid Sâbiq, *Fiqh as-Sunnah*, vol. 3, p. 437.

[17] Recorded by Bukhari, Muslim and Tirmidhi. Abu Dawood and Ibn Mâjah have something similar.

[18] This hadith is *ṣaḥeeḥ*. See Shaykh al-Albâni, *Ṣaḥeeḥ al-Jâmi' aṣ-Ṣagheer*, no. 7157. Recorded by al-Ḥâkim and al-Bayhaqi.

[19] This hadith is *ḥasan*. See Shaykh al-Albâni, *Ṣaḥeeḥ Sunan Ibn Mâjah*, no. 221. Recorded by Ibn Mâjah and al-Ḥâkim.

The *'aṣibah* of blood relations can also be divided into three categories:

1. *'Aṣibah* due to one's own relationship

This refers to the men who inherit from a person, save for the husband and the child of the mother (half-brothers).

2. *'Aṣibah* due to another person

This refers to the daughters and daughters of one's sons, full sisters and half-sisters from one's father. Each of them, in the presence of a brother, is an *'aṣibah*. She will receive half of what the brother receives, based on the words of Allah:

﴿... وَإِن كَانُوٓا۟ إِخْوَةً رِّجَالًا وَنِسَآءً فَلِلذَّكَرِ مِثْلُ حَظِّ ٱلْأُنثَيَيْنِ ... ﴿١٧٦﴾﴾

(سورة النّساء: ١٧٦)

﴿... If there are brothers and sisters, the male will have twice the share of the female...﴾ *(Qur'an 4: 176)*

3. *'Aṣibah* in conjunction with another person

This refers to the sisters with the daughters, based on the report from Ibn Mas'ood presented earlier, "The remainder is for the sister."[20]

[20] This hadith is *ṣaḥeeḥ*. See Shaykh al-Albâni, *I'rwâ' al-Ghaleel*, no. 1683. Recorded by Bukhari and without the last sentence it is also recorded by Abu Dawood and Tirmidhi.

Blocking and Preventing

What is meant by "blocking" is where a specific individual is completely or partially blocked from his share due to the presence of another heir.

Preventing refers to a specific person being prevented from his share due to a cause that denies him the right of inheritance, such as murdering the deceased and so forth.

Blocking is of two types, partial and complete. Partial blocking refers to the cases in which the share of the heir is reduced due to the presence of another heir. This occurs to five groups of people:

1. The husband's share is reduced from one-half to one-fourth in the presence of a child.

2. The wife's share is reduced from one-fourth to one-eighth in the presence of a child.

3. The mother's share is reduced from one-third to one-sixth if the deceased had descendents.

4. The granddaughter from the son.

5. A sister from the father.

The complete blocking means that a person loses his share completely due to the presence of another heir, such as the brother losing all of his right to inheritance in the presence of a child. The complete blocking does not occur with respect to six categories of heirs, although they are susceptible to partial blocking. These six are the following:

1. and 2. The parents (both mother and father)

3. and 4. Children (sons and daughters)

5. and 6. Husband and wife

Other than these, a person could possibly be completely blocked from his share of the inheritance.

Complete blocking is based on two principles:

1. People connected to the deceased through another person do not inherit if the other person is still present, thus the grandson via a son does not inherit if the son is present. The exception is the children of the mother who inherit along with her although they are connected to the deceased through her.

2. The closer relative takes precedence over the more distant relative. Thus, the son blocks the nephew. If they are equal in degree, the one stronger in closeness takes precedence. Thus, the full brother blocks the half-brother from the father.

Chapter Thirteen — Fixed Prescribed Punishments

The word *ḥudood* (plural of *ḥadd*) originally means, "The barrier between two things." Lexically, it implies, "prevention".[1] As a technical term, it means, "The legally prescribed punishments for sinful acts implemented to prevent such acts from occurring."[2]

The Crimes that Call for Fixed Prescribed Punishments

The Qur'an and Sunnah have laid down specific punishments for specific crimes. These are known as "the crimes invoking fixed prescribed punishments". They are fornication/adultery, slander, theft, consuming alcohol, brigandry, apostasy and rebellion.

The excellence of implementing the fixed prescribed punishments

Abu Hurayrah narrated that the Messenger of Allah (ﷺ) said, "A legal punishment that is implemented on earth is better for the inhabitants of the earth than if it were to rain for forty mornings."[3]

---

[1] As-Sayyid Sâbiq, *Fiqh as-Sunnah*, vol. 2, p. 302.

[2] *Manâr as-Sabeel*, vol. 2, p. 360.

[3] This hadith is *ḥasan*. See Shaykh al-Albâni, *Ṣaḥeeḥ Sunan Ibn Mâjah*, no. 2057. Recorded by Ibn Mâjah and Nasâ'i.

It is obligatory to implement the law upon relatives and non-relatives, upper classes and lower classes

Ubâdah ibn aṣ-Ṣâmit said that the Messenger of Allah (ﷺ) said: "Implement the fixed prescribed punishments of Allah upon the relatives and non-relatives — and do not fear, for the sake of Allah, the blame of any reproacher."[4]

'Â'ishah (رضي الله عنها) said, "Usâmah spoke to the Prophet (ﷺ) about a woman (who had committed theft). The Prophet (ﷺ) said, 'Those before you were destroyed simply because they would implement the fixed prescribed punishments upon the weak and they would leave the rich. By the One in whose hand is my soul, if Fâṭimah had done that act, I would have her hand cut off.' "[5]

Disapproval of interceding in such crimes after it has been taken to the authorities

'Â'ishah (may Allah be pleased with her) said, "The Quraysh were worried about a woman from the Tribe of Makhzoom who had committed theft. They said, 'Who can speak to the Messenger of Allah (ﷺ) and who can dare to except Usâmah ibn Zayd, the beloved of the Messenger of Allah (ﷺ).' So Usâmah spoke to the Messenger of Allah (ﷺ) and he said, 'Do you intercede in one of the prescribed punishments from Allah?' Then he stood and said, 'O' people, those before you went astray because if a noble among them would steal, they would let him go while if a poor person among them stole, they would implement the punishment upon him. By Allah, if Fâṭimah, the daughter of Muhammad were to steal, Muhammad would have

---

[4] This hadith is *ḥasan*. See Shaykh al-Albâni, *Ṣaḥeeḥ Sunan Ibn Mâjah*, no. 2058. Recorded by Ibn Mâjah.

[5] This hadith is *ṣaḥeeḥ*. See Shaykh al-Albâni, *I'rwâ' al-Ghaleel*, no. 2319. Recorded by Bukhari.

her hand cut off.' "[6]

It is Preferred to Conceal the Faults of a Believer

Abu Hurayrah reported that the Messenger of Allah (ﷺ) said, "Whoever conceals (the faults of) a Muslim, Allah will conceal (his faults) in this life and the Hereafter."[7]

It is also recommended that the individual keep his own faults concealed. The Prophet (ﷺ) said, "Everyone of my Nation is apt to be forgiven except for those who commit sins openly. Included among those who commit sins openly is where a person performs a deed during the night and, although Allah had concealed that sin, in the morning he says, 'O' so and so, last night I did such and such.' He spent the night being concealed by Allah and in the morning he uncovered Allah's concealment from himself."[8]

The Fixed Prescribed Punishment is Expiation

Ubâdah ibn aṣ-Ṣâmit said, "We were with the Prophet (ﷺ) in a gathering and he said, 'Make the oath of allegiance to me that you will not associate anything with Allah, you will not steal, you will not commit fornication...' And he mentioned everything in the verse. Then he said, 'Whoever fulfills it among you will have his reward upon Allah. If anyone falls into any of those things and is punished for it, that will be the expiation. If anyone falls into any of them and Allah conceals it for him, then it is up to Allah, if He wills He will

---

[6] Recorded by Bukhari, Muslim, Abu Dawood, Nasâ'i, Tirmidhi and Ibn Mâjah.

[7] This hadith is *ṣaḥeeḥ*. See Shaykh al-Albâni, *Mukhtasar Ṣaḥeeḥ Muslim*, no. 1888. Recorded by Muslim, Tirmidhi, Ibn Mâjah and Abu Dawood.

[8] Recorded by Bukhari and Muslim.

forgive him and if He wills He will punish him.'"[9]

Who is to implement the fixed prescribed punishments[10]

The fixed prescribed punishments are not to be implemented except by the ruler or his representative, as the Prophet (ﷺ) used to implement them during his lifetime and his successors did the same afterwards. He would also appoint someone to carry out the punishment, as when he said, "Go, O' Unays, to that woman and if she confesses, stone her to death."[11]

It is permitted for the slave-owner to execute the legal punishment upon his slaves. The Prophet (ﷺ) said, "If a slave-girl fornicates and it is proven, (her owner) should lash her and should not reproach her (after that). Then if she fornicates again, he should lash her and not reproach her. If she does it a third time, he should sell her even if it be for a rope of hair."[12]

The Punishment for *Zinâ* (Adultery/Fornication)

Zinâ (unlawful sexual intercourse) is forbidden and is one of the greatest of the great sins. Allah has said:

﴿وَلَا تَقْرَبُوا۟ ٱلزِّنَىٰٓ ۖ إِنَّهُۥ كَانَ فَٰحِشَةً وَسَآءَ سَبِيلًا ﴿٣٢﴾﴾ (سورة الإسراء: ٣٢)

﴾And come not near to the unlawful sexual intercourse. Verily, it is immoral and an evil way.﴿ *(Qur'an 17: 32)*

---

[9] Recorded by Bukhari, Muslim and Nasâ'i.

[10] *Manâr as-Sabeel*, vol. 2, p. 361.

[11] This story shall be presented shortly.

[12] Recorded by Bukhari and Muslim.

'Abdullâh ibn Mas'ood said, "I asked the Messenger of Allah (ﷺ), 'What is the greatest sin?' He replied, 'That you make a partner with Allah while He created you.' I then said, 'Then what?' He said, 'Then is that you should kill your child out of fear that he will eat with you.' I said, 'Then what?' He said, 'That you should commit *zinâ* with your neighbour's wife.' "[13]

Allah (ﷻ) says:

﴿وَٱلَّذِينَ لَا يَدْعُونَ مَعَ ٱللَّهِ إِلَٰهًا ءَاخَرَ وَلَا يَقْتُلُونَ ٱلنَّفْسَ ٱلَّتِي حَرَّمَ ٱللَّهُ إِلَّا بِٱلْحَقِّ وَلَا يَزْنُونَ ۚ وَمَن يَفْعَلْ ذَٰلِكَ يَلْقَ أَثَامًا ﴿٦٨﴾ يُضَٰعَفْ لَهُ ٱلْعَذَابُ يَوْمَ ٱلْقِيَٰمَةِ وَيَخْلُدْ فِيهِۦ مُهَانًا ﴿٦٩﴾ إِلَّا مَن تَابَ وَءَامَنَ وَعَمِلَ عَمَلًا صَٰلِحًا فَأُوْلَٰٓئِكَ يُبَدِّلُ ٱللَّهُ سَيِّـَٔاتِهِمْ حَسَنَٰتٍ ۗ وَكَانَ ٱللَّهُ غَفُورًا رَّحِيمًا ﴿٧٠﴾﴾

(سورة الفرقان: ٦٨-٧٠)

﴾And those who invoke not any other god along with Allah, nor kill such life as Allah has forbidden, except for just cause, nor commit illegal sexual intercourse and whoever does this shall receive the punishment. The torment will be doubled to him on the Day of Resurrection, and he will abide therein in disgrace; Except those who repent and believe, and do righteous deeds, for those, Allah will change their sins into good deeds, and Allah is Oft-Forgiving, Most Merciful.﴿ *(Qur'an 25: 68-70)*

In the lengthy hadith of Samurah ibn Jundub concerning the vision of the Prophet (ﷺ), the Prophet (ﷺ) said, "We proceeded until we came to a baking oven. — Samurah said, 'I think the Prophet (ﷺ) said that there were noises and voices therein.' — We looked into and found naked men and women and then there was a flame of fire reaching them from underneath. When the flame reached them, they

[13] Recorded by Bukhari, Muslim, Abu Dawood and Tirmidhi.

cried out loud. I said, 'Who are they?'... (Later the Prophet recounted that he was told,) 'As for those naked men and women you saw in a building like an oven, they were the male and female fornicators.' "[14]

Ibn 'Abbâs narrated that the Messenger of Allah (ﷺ) said, "A fornicator while committing illegal sexual intercourse is not a (true) believer. A thief while committing theft is not a (true) believer. A drinker while drinking alcohol is not a (true) believer." 'Ikrimah said, "I asked Ibn 'Abbâs, 'How does the faith remove itself from him?' He replied, 'Like this,' and he intertwined his fingers and then released them. He continued, 'If he repents it returns to him like this,' and he intertwined his fingers again."[15]

The Categories of Zinâ

The one who committed *zinâ* could be either a virgin or a non-virgin (via a legal relationship).

If a free, adult, legally responsible, non-virgin (via a legal relationship)[16] willingly commits *zinâ*, he or she is to be stoned unto death. Jâbir ibn 'Abdullâh al-Anṣâri said, "A man from the Tribe of Aslam came to the Messenger of Allah (ﷺ) and informed him that he had committed *zinâ*. He testified to it four times. The Messenger of Allah (ﷺ) ordered that he be stoned. He was a non-virgin."[17]

---

[14] This hadith is *ṣaḥeeḥ*. See Shaykh al-Albâni, *Ṣaḥeeḥ al-Jâmi' aṣ-Ṣagheer*, no. 3462. Recorded by Bukhari.

[15] This hadith is *ṣaḥeeḥ*. See Shaykh al-Albâni, *Ṣaḥeeḥ al-Jâmi' aṣ-Ṣagheer*, no. 7708. Recorded by Bukhari and also by Nasâ'i but without the quote from Ibn 'Abbâs.

[16] There is no such set legal punishment on a youth or an insane person, based on the hadith that has been mentioned previously on a number of occasions, "The pen has been raised from three."

[17] This hadith is *ṣaḥeeḥ*. See Shaykh al-Albâni, *Sunan Abi Dawood*, no. 3725. Recorded by Tirmidhi and Abu Dawood.

Ibn 'Abbâs narrated that 'Umar ibn al-Khaṭṭâb (رضي الله عنه) addressed the people saying, "Verily, Allah sent Muhammad (ﷺ) with the truth and revealed to him the Book. The verse of stoning was part of what was revealed to him. We read it, understood it and memorized it. The Prophet (ﷺ) had people stoned and we did so after him. I fear that, after some time, someone may say, 'By Allah, I do not find the verse of stoning in the Book of Allah.' They will then go astray by leaving an obligation that Allah revealed. Stoning is correct in the Book of Allah for the non-virgin (through a legal relationship) who commits *zinâ*, whether male or female, if the proof is established or there is pregnancy or a confession."[18]

The penalty for a slave

If a male or female slave commits *zinâ*, there is no stoning in that case. However, they are to be lashed fifty times. Allah says:

﴿... فَإِذَآ أُحْصِنَّ فَإِنْ أَتَيْنَ بِفَٰحِشَةٍ فَعَلَيْهِنَّ نِصْفُ مَا عَلَى ٱلْمُحْصَنَٰتِ مِنَ ٱلْعَذَابِ ... ﴿٢٥﴾﴾ (سورة النِّساء: ٢٥)

﴿... And after they have been taken in wedlock, if they commit illegal sexual intercourse, their punishment is half that for free [unmarried] women...﴾ *(Qur'an 4: 25)*

'Abdullâh ibn 'Ayyâsh al-Makhzoomi said, " 'Umar ibn al-Khaṭṭâb (رضي الله عنه) gave me instructions about the slave-girls of the Quraysh. Thus, we flogged some of the slave-girls in the Muslim lands fifty lashes each."[19]

---

[18] Recorded by Bukhari, Muslim, Abu Dawood and Tirmidhi.

[19] This hadith is *ḥasan*. See Shaykh al-Albâni, *I'rwâ' al-Ghaleel*, no. 2345. Recorded by Mâlik and al-Bayhaqi.

One who is Forced into Zinâ is not to be Punished

'Abdur-Raḥmân as-Salami said, " 'Umar ibn al-Khaṭṭâb was brought a woman about to die from thirst. A shepherd passed by and she asked him for water. He refused to give her water unless he could have his way with her and she did so. 'Umar consulted with the people about stoning her. 'Ali said, 'She was compelled to do so, so I think she should be let go.' So 'Umar did so."[20]

The Punishment for a Virgin

Allah (ﷻ) says:

﴿ٱلزَّانِيَةُ وَٱلزَّانِى فَٱجْلِدُوا۟ كُلَّ وَٰحِدٍ مِّنْهُمَا مِا۟ئَةَ جَلْدَةٍ ۖ وَلَا تَأْخُذْكُم بِهِمَا رَأْفَةٌ فِى دِينِ ٱللَّهِ إِن كُنتُمْ تُؤْمِنُونَ بِٱللَّهِ وَٱلْيَوْمِ ٱلْءَاخِرِ ۖ وَلْيَشْهَدْ عَذَابَهُمَا طَآئِفَةٌ مِّنَ ٱلْمُؤْمِنِينَ ﴿٢﴾﴾

(سورة النُّور: ٢)

﴾The woman and the man guilty of illegal sexual intercourse, flog each of them with a hundred stripes. Let not pity withhold you in their case, in a punishment prescribed by Allah, if you believe in Allah and the Last Day. And let a party of the believers witness their punishment.﴿

(Qur'an 24: 2)

Zayd ibn Khâlid al-Juhhani said that he heard the Messenger of Allah (ﷺ) order that the one who committed *zinâ* who was a virgin should be flogged one hundred times and banished for one year.[21] 'Ubâdah ibn aṣ-Ṣâmit said that the Messenger of Allah (ﷺ) said, "Take (the

[20] This hadith is *ṣaḥeeḥ*. See Shaykh al-Albâni, *I'rwâ' al-Ghaleel*, no. 2313. Recorded by al-Bayhaqi.

[21] This hadith is *ṣaḥeeḥ*. See Shaykh al-Albâni, *I'rwâ' al-Ghaleel*, no. 2347. Recorded by Bukhari.

guidance) from me; take from me. Allah has made a way for them. The virgin with the virgin shall be lashed one hundred times and banished for a year. The non-virgin with the non-virgin shall be lashed one hundred times and stoned (to death)."[22]

How is the Punishment Affirmed

"The punishment is affirmed by one of two means: confession or witnesses."[23]

As for confession, one finds in the case of the Prophet (ﷺ) stoning Mâ'iz and the woman from the Tribe of Ghâmdi after he confessed to their sin. Ibn 'Abbâs said, "When Mâ'iz came to the Prophet (ﷺ) (to confess), the Prophet (ﷺ) said to him, 'Perhaps you just kissed her, winked at her or looked at her.' He replied, 'No, O' Messenger of Allah (ﷺ).' Then the Prophet (ﷺ) asked him using no euphemism, 'Did you have intercourse with her?' (When he replied in the affirmative,) at that time the Prophet (ﷺ) ordered for him to be stoned."[24]

Sulaymân ibn Buraydah narrated from his father who said, "A woman from the Tribe of Ghâmid of the Azd came to the Prophet (ﷺ) and said, 'O' Messenger of Allah, purify me!' He said, 'Woe to you. Go and seek Allah's forgiveness and repent to Him.' She said, 'Perhaps you are going to try to turn me back like you did with Mâ'iz ibn Mâlik.' He said, 'What has happened to you?' She said, 'I am pregnant from *zinâ*.' He said, 'Was it you?' She said, 'Yes.' He then told her, '(You will not be punished) until you deliver what is in your

---

[22] This hadith is *ṣaḥeeḥ*. See Shaykh al-Albâni, *Mukhtasar Ṣaḥeeḥ Muslim*, no. 1036. Recorded by Muslim, Abu Dawood, Tirmidhi and Ibn Mâjah.

[23] As-Sayyid Sâbiq, *Fiqh as-Sunnah*, vol. 3, p. 352.

[24] This hadith is *ṣaḥeeḥ*. See Shaykh al-Albâni, *Sunan Abu Dawood*, no. 3724. Recorded by Bukhari and Abu Dawood.

womb.' One of the Anṣâr was responsible for her until she delivered. He later came to the Prophet (ﷺ) and said, 'The woman from the Ghâmdi tribe has delivered (her baby).' The Prophet (ﷺ) then said, 'Thus, we shall not stone her and leave her child small with no one to suckle him.' One of the Anṣâr got up and said, 'The responsibility for its suckling shall be upon me, O' Prophet of Allah.' So then he had her stoned."[25]

If the person withdraws their confession, they are to be let free. Nu'aym ibn Huzzâl said, "Mâ'iz ibn Mâlik was an orphan living in the house of my father. At one time, he committed *zinâ* with a slave-girl belonging to the clan." The hadith continues stating, "He [the Prophet (ﷺ)] ordered to have him stoned. He was taken out to Ḥarrah (near Madeenah). While he was being stoned, he could not bear the pain of the stones and fled. 'Abdullâh ibn Unays came across him when those who were throwing the stones and could not catch him threw a camel's foreleg at him. This struck him and killed him. They then went to the Prophet (ﷺ) and informed him about that. In response, he stated, 'Why didn't you leave him? Perhaps he would have repented and Allah would have turned to him with forgiveness.' "[26]

Ruling Concerning One who Says, "I Committed Zinâ with such and such Woman"

If a person confesses to have committed *zinâ* with a specific woman, the punishment is to be applied to him. If the woman also confesses, she is also to be taken and punished. If she does not

---

[25] This hadith is *ṣaḥeeḥ*. See Shaykh al-Albâni, *Mukhtasar Ṣaḥeeḥ Muslim*, no. 1039. Recorded by Muslim.

[26] This hadith is *ṣaḥeeḥ*. See Shaykh al-Albâni, *Ṣaḥeeḥ Sunan Abi Dawood*, no. 3716. Recorded by Abu Dawood.

confess, she is not punished.

Abu Hurayrah and Zayd ibn Khâlid narrated the following: Two disputants came to the Messenger of Allah (ﷺ). One of them said, "Judge between us according to the Book of Allah." The other — the more intelligent one — said, "Certainly, O' Messenger of Allah (ﷺ), judge between us according to the Book of Allah and allow me to speak." The Prophet said, "Speak." He said, "This son of mine was working for this man and committed *zinâ* with his wife. They told me that my son was to be stoned so I ransomed him from them by paying them one hundred sheep and a slave-girl of mine. Then I asked the people of knowledge and they informed me that my son was to be lashed one hundred times and banished for a year while the woman is to be stoned." The Messenger of Allah (ﷺ) said, "By the One in whose hand is my soul, I shall judge between you by the Book of Allah. As for your sheep and slave-girl, they are to be returned to you." He then had his son lashed one hundred times and banished for one year. He then told Unays al-Aslami to go to the other woman and, if she confesses, to stone her. She confessed and was stoned to death.[27]

Affirming the Act Via Witnesses

Allah (سُبْحَانَهُ وَتَعَالَى) says:

﴿وَالَّذِينَ يَرْمُونَ الْمُحْصَنَاتِ ثُمَّ لَمْ يَأْتُوا بِأَرْبَعَةِ شُهَدَاءَ فَاجْلِدُوهُمْ ثَمَانِينَ جَلْدَةً وَلَا تَقْبَلُوا لَهُمْ شَهَادَةً أَبَدًا ... ﴿٤﴾﴾ (سورة النّور: ٤)

﴿And those who accuse chaste women, and produce not four witnesses, flog them with eighty stripes, and reject their testimony

---

[27] Recorded by Bukhari, Muslim, Abu Dawood, Tirmidhi, Ibn Mâjah and Nasâ'i.

forever, they indeed are the evildoers...❯ *(Qur'an 24: 4)*

If four free and respectable men witness that they actually saw a man entering his private part into that of a woman, then both the man and the woman are to receive the legal punishment.

If three bear witness and the fourth refuses, then the three are to be given the punishment for slander, as the above verse demonstrates. Furthermore, Qasâmah ibn Zuhayr said, "When the issue concerning Abu Bakrah and al-Mugheerah occurred" — and he mentioned the story and continued by saying, "The witnesses were called forth. Abu Bakrah, Shibl ibn Ma'bad and Abu 'Abdullâh Nâfi' all bore witness. When these three gave their testimony, the issue became very difficult for 'Umar (رضي الله عنه). When Ziyâd came he said to him, 'Do not bear testimony, Allah willing, except to the truth.' He stated, 'As for *zinâ*, I do not bear witness to that. However, I saw something very disgusting.' 'Umar said, 'Allah is greatest.' He gave the three the legal punishment and had them flogged. After being punished, Abu Bakrah said, 'I bear witness that he committed *zinâ*.' 'Umar understood from this that he had repeated his calumny and that he should be punished again. 'Ali (رضي الله عنه) prevented him, saying, 'If you flog him, you should stone your companion.' So 'Umar left him and did not flog him."[28]

Ruling Concerning One who Had Intercourse with a Close Relative (within the Prohibited Degrees of Marriage)

If someone commits *zinâ* with a relative that is within the prohibited degrees of marriage, he is to be killed regardless of

[28] Its chain is *ṣaḥeeḥ*. See Shaykh al-Albâni, *I'rwâ' al-Ghaleel*, vol. 8, p. 29. Recorded by al-Bayhaqi.

whether he is a virgin or a non-virgin. If he marries the woman, he is to be killed and have his wealth taken from him. Al-Barâ' said, "I met my maternal uncle and with him was a banner. I said, 'Where are you going?' He replied, 'The Messenger of Allah (ﷺ) sent me to a man who had married his father's wife after his death. He sent me to strike his neck and take his wealth.' "[29]

Whoever Commits Animal Bestiality

Ibn 'Abbâs narrated that the Messenger of Allah (ﷺ) said, "Whoever commits sodomy with an animal is to be killed and the animal is to be killed as well."[30]

The Punishment for Homosexual Sodomy

If a male commits sodomy with another male the punishment is death, whether they be virgins or non-virgins. Ibn 'Abbâs narrated that the Messenger of Allah (ﷺ) said, "For whoever you find doing the acts of the people of Lot, kill the one doing the sodomy and the one being sodomized."[31]

---

[29] This hadith is *ṣaḥeeḥ*. See Shaykh al-Albâni, *I'rwâ' al-Ghaleel*, no. 2351 and *Ṣaḥeeḥ Ibn Mâjah*, no. 2111. Recorded by Abu Dawood and Nasâ'i. Tirmidhi and Ibn Mâjah have also recorded it but without the portion that states that half of his wealth is to be taken.

[30] This hadith is *ḥasan ṣaḥeeḥ*. See Shaykh al-Albâni, *Ṣaḥeeḥ Sunan Tirmidhi*, no. 1176. Recorded by Tirmidhi, Abu Dawood and Ibn Mâjah.

[31] This hadith is *ṣaḥeeḥ*. See Shaykh al-Albâni, *Ṣaḥeeḥ Sunan Ibn Mâjah*, no. 2075. Recorded by Tirmidhi, Abu Dawood and Ibn Mâjah.

Slandering Another with a False Accusation of *Zinâ*

Al-Qadhaf is to accuse or slander another with the implication of *zinâ*, such as saying to the person, "O' you fornicator" or any words which are clearly understood to mean that the person is being accused of committing *zinâ*.

Its Ruling

Such a slander is one of the greater sins. Allah (ﷻ) has said:

﴿إِنَّ ٱلَّذِينَ يَرْمُونَ ٱلْمُحْصَنَٰتِ ٱلْغَٰفِلَٰتِ ٱلْمُؤْمِنَٰتِ لُعِنُوا۟ فِى ٱلدُّنْيَا وَٱلْءَاخِرَةِ وَلَهُمْ عَذَابٌ عَظِيمٌ ﴿٢٣﴾﴾ (سورة النور: ٢٣)

﴿Verily, those who accuse chaste women, who never even think of anything touching their chastity and are good believers, are cursed in this life and in the Hereafter, and for them will be a great torment.﴾ *(Qur'an 24: 23)*

Abu Hurayrah (رضي الله عنه) narrated that the Messenger of Allah (ﷺ) said, "Avoid the seven destructive sins." They said, "O' Messenger of Allah, what are they?" He replied, "Associating partners with Allah, committing sorcery, killing a soul with Allah has made inviolable except due to justice, consuming interest, consuming the wealth of orphans, fleeing on the day with the two armies meet and slandering the chaste, naïvely innocent believing women."[32]

If a person commits such a slander, he is to be flogged eighty times, as Allah (ﷻ) has said: ﴿And those who accuse chaste women,

[32] Recorded by Bukhari, Muslim, Abu Dawood and Nasâ'i.

and produce not four witnesses, flog them with eighty stripes, and reject their testimony forever, they indeed are the evildoers❩ *(Qur'an 24: 4).*

Al-Li'ân

If a man slanders his own wife by accusing her of *zinâ* and she denies it, then the punishment will be executed upon him unless he can present evidence (that is, other witnesses) or he makes *al-li'ân* toward her. *Li'ân* is the practice described in the following verses of the Qur'an:

﴿وَٱلَّذِينَ يَرْمُونَ أَزْوَٰجَهُمْ وَلَمْ يَكُن لَّهُمْ شُهَدَآءُ إِلَّا أَنفُسُهُمْ فَشَهَٰدَةُ أَحَدِهِمْ أَرْبَعُ شَهَٰدَٰتٍۭ بِٱللَّهِ إِنَّهُۥ لَمِنَ ٱلصَّٰدِقِينَ ۝ وَٱلْخَٰمِسَةُ أَنَّ لَعْنَتَ ٱللَّهِ عَلَيْهِ إِن كَانَ مِنَ ٱلْكَٰذِبِينَ ۝ وَيَدْرَؤُاْ عَنْهَا ٱلْعَذَابَ أَن تَشْهَدَ أَرْبَعَ شَهَٰدَٰتٍۭ بِٱللَّهِ إِنَّهُۥ لَمِنَ ٱلْكَٰذِبِينَ ۝ وَٱلْخَٰمِسَةَ أَنَّ غَضَبَ ٱللَّهِ عَلَيْهَآ إِن كَانَ مِنَ ٱلصَّٰدِقِينَ ۝﴾ (سورة النُّور: ٦-٩)

❨And for those who accuse their wives, but have no witnesses except themselves, let the testimony of one of them be four testimonies [i.e. testifies four times] by Allah that he is one of those who speak the truth. And the fifth [testimony] [should be] the invoking of the Curse of Allah on him if he be of those who tell a lie [against her]. But it shall avert the punishment [of stoning to death] from her, if she bears witness four times by Allah, that he [her husband] is telling a lie. And the fifth [testimony] should be that the Wrath of Allah be upon her if he [her husband] speaks the truth.❩ *(Qur'an 24: 6-9)*

Ibn 'Abbâs narrated: To the Prophet (ﷺ), Hilâl ibn Umayyah accused his wife of committing adultery with Shareek ibn Saḥmâ'. The Prophet (ﷺ) said to him, "Present the evidence or you shall receive the punishment (of flogging) upon your back." He replied,

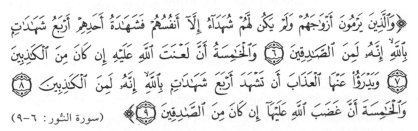

"O' Messenger of Allah, if somebody sees his wife with another man, will he go and try to bring witnesses?" The Prophet (ﷺ) continue to say, "Present the evidence as otherwise you shall receive the punishment (of flogging) upon your back." Hilâl then said, "By the One who sent you with the truth, I am being truthful and Allah will reveal that which will make my back free of any punishment." Then Jibreel (ﷺ) came down and revealed to the Prophet: ﴿And for those who accuse their wives, but have no witnesses except themselves... And the fifth [testimony] should be that the Wrath of Allah be upon her if he [her husband] speaks the truth﴾ *(Qur'an 24: 6-9)*. The Prophet read those verses till the end and then left and sent for the woman. Hilâl came and bore witness. The Prophet (ﷺ) told them, "Allah knows that one of you is a liar. Would any of you two like to repent?" Then the woman stood to make her claim. When it came to the fifth oath, the people stopped her and said, "This oath will definitely bring (Allah's curse on you if you are guilty)." Ibn 'Abbâs noted, "She hesitated and recoiled until we thought that she would withdraw. Then she said, 'I will not disgrace my people for the remainder of the days,' and she continued with the fifth oath." The Prophet (ﷺ) then said, 'Watch her. If she gives birth to a black-eyed child with large hips and fat shins, then it is that of Shareek ibn Saḥmâ'." Later, she gave birth to such a child. The Prophet (ﷺ) then said, "If it were not for what has transpired from the Book of Allah, I would certainly have dealt with her (by punishing her for adultery)."[33]

The effects of al-Li'ân

If *al-li'ân* occurs between two spouses, the following rulings then result:

---

[33] This hadith is *ṣaḥeeḥ*. See Shaykh al-Albâni, *I'rwâ' al-Ghaleel*, no. 2098. Recorded by Bukhari, Abu Dawood, Tirmidhi and Ibn Mâjah.

1. The two are to be separated

Ibn 'Umar said, "The Prophet executed the *li'ân* between a man and woman from the Anṣâr and he separated them."[34]

2. The two are forever forbidden to marry again

Sahl ibn S'ad said, "Concerning the two who make *li'ân*, the Sunnah has been that the two are separated and may never be reunited."[35]

3. The woman of the *li'ân* is still entitled to her dower

Ayyoob narrated from Sa'eed ibn Jubayr who said, "I said to Ibn 'Umar, 'What happens if a man slanders his wife?' He said, 'The Prophet (ﷺ) separated two from the Tribe of al-'Ijlân.' He told them, 'Allah knows that one of you is a liar. Would any of you two like to repent?' They both refused. He then said, 'Allah knows that one of you is a liar. Would any of you two like to repent?' They both refused again. Finally, he said, 'Allah knows that one of you is a liar. Would any of you two like to repent?' They both refused again and he separated between them." Ayyoob further said, " 'Amr ibn Deenâr said to me, 'There is something in that hadith that I do not find you narrating.' The man said, 'What about my wealth (that is, the dower)?' He was told, 'There is no wealth for you. If you are speaking the truth, you had consummated the marriage with her. If you are lying, you more so do not deserve it.' "[36]

4. The child will be attributed to the mother only in the case of *li'ân*

Ibn 'Umar said, "The Prophet (ﷺ) executed the *li'ân* between a man and his wife. He denied it was his child. He separated the two

---

[34] Recorded by Bukhari and Muslim.

[35] This hadith is *ṣaḥeeḥ*. See Shaykh al-Albâni, *I'rwâ' al-Ghaleel*, no. 2104. Recorded by Abu Dawood and al-Bayhaqi.

[36] Recorded by Bukhari, Muslim, Abu Dawood and Nasâ'i.

and joined the child to the mother."[37]

5. The woman involved in the *li'ân* and her child will still continue to inherit from one another

Ibn Shihâb stated concerning the hadith of Sahl ibn S'ad (quoted above), "The Sunnah was that after the two parties were separated and she was pregnant, the child would be attributed to her and called by her name (only)." He also said, "The Sunnah also continued that the child would inherit from her and she would inherit from him according to the shares that Allah has determined."[38]

The Punishment for Consuming Alcohol (*Khamr*)

Allah (ﷻ) says:

﴿يَٰٓأَيُّهَا ٱلَّذِينَ ءَامَنُوٓاْ إِنَّمَا ٱلۡخَمۡرُ وَٱلۡمَيۡسِرُ وَٱلۡأَنصَابُ وَٱلۡأَزۡلَٰمُ رِجۡسٞ مِّنۡ عَمَلِ ٱلشَّيۡطَٰنِ
فَٱجۡتَنِبُوهُ لَعَلَّكُمۡ تُفۡلِحُونَ ٩٠ إِنَّمَا يُرِيدُ ٱلشَّيۡطَٰنُ أَن يُوقِعَ بَيۡنَكُمُ ٱلۡعَدَٰوَةَ
وَٱلۡبَغۡضَآءَ فِي ٱلۡخَمۡرِ وَٱلۡمَيۡسِرِ وَيَصُدَّكُمۡ عَن ذِكۡرِ ٱللَّهِ وَعَنِ ٱلصَّلَوٰةِ فَهَلۡ أَنتُم مُّنتَهُونَ
٩١﴾

(سورة المائدة: ٩٠-٩١)

﴿O' you who believe! Intoxicants, gambling, idols and arrows for seeking luck or decision are an abomination from Satan's handiwork. So avoid [strictly all] that [abomination] in order that you may be successful. Satan wants only to excite enmity and hatred between you with intoxicants and gambling, and hinder you from the

---

[37] Recorded by Bukhari, Muslim, Abu Dawood, Tirmidhi, Nasâ'i and Ibn Mâjah.

[38] Recorded by Bukhari, Muslim and Abu Dawood.

remembrance of Allah and from the prayer. So, will you not then abstain?﴿ *(Qur'an 5: 90-91)*

Abu Hurayrah reported that the Messenger of Allah (ﷺ) said, "A fornicator while committing illegal sexual intercourse is not a (true) believer. A drinker while drinking alcohol is not a (true) believer."[39]

'Abdullâh ibn 'Amr narrated that the Prophet (ﷺ) said, "Alcohol is the mother of all evils. If one drinks it, his prayer will not be accepted for forty days. If he dies with it in his stomach, he will die a death of the Days of Ignorance."[40]

Ibn 'Abbâs narrated that the Prophet (ﷺ) said, "Alcohol is the mother of the lewd acts and the greatest of the great sins. Whoever drinks it could have intercourse with his mother, his maternal aunt and his paternal aunt."[41]

Abu Hurayrah said that the Messenger of Allah (ﷺ) said, "The alcoholic is like one who worships idols."[42] In addition, Abu ad-Dardâ' narrated that the Prophet (ﷺ) said, "The alcoholic shall not enter Paradise."[43] Ibn 'Umar stated that the Prophet (ﷺ) said, "Alcohol has been cursed in ten ways: its essence, the one who squeezes it, the one who has it squeezed, the one who sells it, the one who buys it, the one who carries it, the one to whom it is carried, the

---

[39] Recorded by Bukhari and Muslim. See Shaykh al-Albâni, *Ṣaḥeeḥ al-Jâmi' aṣ-Ṣagheer*, no. 7707.

[40] This hadith is *ḥasan*. See Shaykh al-Albâni, *Ṣaḥeeḥ al-Jâmi' aṣ-Ṣagheer*, no. 3344. Recorded by aṭ-Ṭabarâni in *al-Mu'jam aṣ-Ṣagheer.*

[41] This hadith is *ḥasan*. See Shaykh al-Albâni, *Ṣaḥeeḥ al-Jâmi' aṣ-Ṣagheer*, no. 3345. Recorded by aṭ-Ṭabarâni in *al-Mu'jam al-Kabeer.*

[42] This hadith is *ḥasan*. See Shaykh al-Albâni, *Ṣaḥeeḥ Sunan Ibn Mâjah*, no. 2720 and *Silsilat al-Aḥâdeeth aṣ-Ṣaheeḥah*, no. 677. Recorded by Ibn Mâjah.

[43] This hadith is *ṣaḥeeḥ*. See Shaykh al-Albâni, *Ṣaḥeeḥ Sunan Ibn Mâjah*, no. 2721. Recorded by Ibn Mâjah.

one who profits from it, the one who drinks it and the one who pours it."[44]

What is Khamr?

Ibn 'Umar narrated that the Prophet (ﷺ) said, "Every intoxicant is *khamr* and every *khamr* is forbidden."[45] 'Â'ishah (رضي الله عنها) narrated that the Messenger of Allah (ﷺ) was asked about fruit nectar made from dates that the people of Yemen would drink. The Messenger of Allah (ﷺ) replied, "Every drink that intoxicates is forbidden."[46]

Ibn 'Umar narrated that 'Umar stood at the pulpit and said, "The prohibition of *khamr* has been revealed. And *khamr* is made from five sources: grapes, dates, honey, wheat and barley. *Khamr* is anything which seizes the mind."[47]

An-Nu'mân ibn Basheer narrated that the Messenger of Allah (ﷺ) said, "There is alcohol made from wheat; there is alcohol made from barley; there is alcohol made from grapes; there is alcohol made from dates; and there is alcohol made from honey."[48]

---

[44] This hadith is *ṣaḥeeḥ*. See Shaykh al-Albâni, *Ṣaḥeeḥ Sunan Ibn Mâjah*, no. 2725. Recorded by Ibn Mâjah (and this is his wording) and Abu Dawood.

[45] This hadith is *ṣaḥeeḥ*. See Shaykh al-Albâni, *Ṣaḥeeḥ Sunan Ibn Mâjah*, no. 2734. Recorded by Muslim and Ibn Mâjah.

[46] Recorded by Bukhari (and this is his wording), Muslim, Abu Dawood, Tirmidhi and Nasâ'i.

[47] Recorded by Bukhari, Muslim, Abu Dawood and Nasâ'i.

[48] This hadith is *ṣaḥeeḥ*. See Shaykh al-Albâni, *Ṣaḥeeḥ Sunan Ibn Mâjah*, no. 2724. Recorded by Ibn Mâjah, Abu Dawood and Tirmidhi.

There is no difference between consuming a small or large amount of alcohol

'Abdullâh ibn 'Umar said that the Messenger of Allah (ﷺ) said, "Every intoxicant is forbidden. If a large amount of something intoxicates, then (even) a small amount of it is forbidden."[49]

'Â'ishah (رضي الله عنها) also said that the Prophet (ﷺ) said, "Every intoxicant is forbidden. If many gallons[50] of something intoxicates, then even a handful of it is forbidden."[51]

The legal punishment for consuming alcohol

If a legally responsible, non-coerced person knowingly drinks alcohol, he is to be flogged forty lashes. If the ruler sees that more should be added, he may increase it to eighty. Al-Ḥuṣayn ibn al-Mundhir said, " 'Ali had al-Waleed ibn 'Uqbah flogged forty lashes for drinking alcohol. Then he said, 'The Prophet (ﷺ) and Abu Bakr flogged forty lashes. 'Umar lashed them eighty times. They are all Sunnah and this one is most beloved to me.' "[52]

If a person repeatedly drinks and is repeatedly flogged, then the ruler can give him the death penalty if he so wills. Abu Hurayrah reported that the Messenger of Allah (ﷺ) said, "If someone consumes alcohol, flog him. If he does it again, flog him. If he does it

---

[49] This hadith is *ṣaḥeeḥ*. See Shaykh al-Albâni, *Ṣaḥeeḥ Sunan Ibn Mâjah*, no. 2736. Recorded by Ibn Mâjah. Nasâ'i has recorded these two sentences as two separate hadith.

[50] [The actual word used in the hadith is *faraq*, which is a measure used in Madeenah and is equivalent to some sixteen *raṭl*, with each *raṭl* equaling some 400 or 500 grams.]

[51] This hadith is *ṣaḥeeḥ*. See Shaykh al-Albâni, *Ṣaḥeeḥ al-Jâmi' aṣ-Ṣagheer*, no. 4552. Recorded by Tirmidhi and Abu Dawood.

[52] This hadith is *ṣaḥeeḥ*. See Shaykh al-Albâni, *Mukhtasar Ṣaḥeeḥ Muslim*, no. 1047. Recorded by Muslim.

again, flog him." Then on the fourth time, he said, "If he does it again, strike his neck."[53]

How the punishment is affirmed

The punishment for drinking alcohol is affirmed by one of two means: 1. confession or 2. the witness of two reputable witnesses.[54]

It is not allowed to supplicate against one who has consumed alcohol

'Umar ibn al-Khaṭṭâb (ﷺ) narrated: During the time of the Prophet (ﷺ), a man named 'Abdullâh and nicknamed "donkey" used to make the Messenger of Allah (ﷺ) laugh. But the Messenger of Allah used to have him flogged for drinking. One time he was brought and the Prophet (ﷺ) commanded that he be flogged. A man among the people said, "O' Allah, curse him for how often he is brought (to be punished)." The Prophet (ﷺ) then said, "Do not curse for, by Allah, I know that he loves Allah and His Messenger."[55]

Abu Hurayrah said, "The Prophet (ﷺ) was brought a drunk person. He commanded that he be beaten. Some people hit him with their hands, others with their sandals and some with their garments. When it finished, a man said, 'May Allah disgrace him.' At that the Messenger of Allah (ﷺ) said, 'Do not be Satan's helper against your brother.'"[56]

---

[53] This hadith is *ḥasan ṣaḥeeḥ*. See Shaykh al-Albâni, *Ṣaḥeeḥ Sunan Ibn Mâjah*, no. 2085. Recorded by Ibn Mâjah, Abu Dawood and Nasâ'i.

[54] As-Sayyid Sâbiq, *Fiqh as-Sunnah*, vol. 2, p. 336.

[55] This hadith is *ṣaḥeeḥ*. See Shaykh al-Albâni, *Mishkât al-Maṣâbeeḥ*, no. 2621. Recorded by Bukhari.

[56] This hadith is *ṣaḥeeḥ*. See Shaykh al-Albâni, *Ṣaḥeeḥ al-Jâmi' aṣ-Ṣagheer*, no. 7442. Recorded by Bukhari and Abu Dawood.

The Punishment for Theft

Wealth is one of the necessities of life that Islam seeks to safeguard and preserve. Islam has ordered that wealth by earned through legal means — and the basic ruling concerning all matters is that of permissibility. Islam has also prohibited that wealth be earned through forbidden means, while clarifying what are the forbidden means.

﴿... وَقَدْ فَصَّلَ لَكُم مَّا حَرَّمَ عَلَيْكُمْ ... ﴿١١٩﴾﴾ (سورة الأنعام: ١١٩)

﴾... He has explained to you in detail what is forbidden to you...﴿ *(Qur'an 6: 119)*

One of the forbidden means to gaining wealth is theft. Theft is defined as, "the taking of wealth that belongs to others in a manner involving stealth and secrecy."[57]

Stealing is one of the great sins. Its legal punishment has been stipulated in the Qur'an, Sunnah and consensus of the Nation. Allah (ﷻ) has said:

﴿وَٱلسَّارِقُ وَٱلسَّارِقَةُ فَٱقْطَعُوٓا۟ أَيْدِيَهُمَا جَزَآءًۢ بِمَا كَسَبَا نَكَٰلًا مِّنَ ٱللَّهِ ۗ وَٱللَّهُ عَزِيزٌ حَكِيمٌ ﴿٣٨﴾﴾ (سورة المائدة: ٣٨)

﴾Cut off [from the wrist joint] the [right] hand of the thief, male or female, as a recompense for that which they committed, a punishment by way of example from Allah. And Allah is All-Powerful, All-Wise.﴿ *(Qur'an 5: 38)*

'Abdullâh ibn 'Umar said, "The Messenger of Allah (ﷺ) cut (the hand) of a thief for (stealing a) shield worth three *dirhams*."[58]

---

[57] Ibn Qudâmah, *al-Mughni*, vol. 8, p. 240.

[58] Recorded by Bukhari, Muslim, Tirmidhi, Abu Dawood and Nasâ'i.

Ibn al-Mundhir said, "The scholars all agree that the cutting of the hand of the thief is obligated once two free, righteous Muslim men bear witness to the theft."[59]

If an adult, non-coerced, sane person steals, it is obligatory to implement the legal punishment if he confesses to it or if two acceptable witnesses testify to his act. However, there are two further conditions that must be met before the legal punishment is implemented: the value of the item stolen must be above the level of the *niṣâb* and the stolen item must have been safeguarded in a normal fashion.

'Â'ishah (ﷺ) narrated that the Messenger of Allah (ﷺ) said, "Do not cut the hand of a thief except for something worth a quarter of a *dinar* or more."[60]

Ibn al-Mundhir stated, "The scholars all agree that amputation is obligatory when the thief steals something safeguarded (or protected in a normal fashion) that requires amputation."[61] What is meant by safeguarded or protected in a normal fashion is that the item was kept in a way that one safeguards similar items, such as in a gated house, in a safe, in a locked location and so forth. (Thus, the valuable item was not left out in the open tempting anyone to take it.)

The author of *ar-Rawḍah an-Nadiyah* (vol. 2, p. 277) stated, "Safeguarded refers to what the people would usually consider safeguarding of that type of wealth. Thus, a warehouse is where seeds and straw are safeguarded. A stable is where animals are kept. A pen is where sheep are kept. A *jareen* is where the fruits are stored."

---

[59] Ibn al-Mundhir, *al-Ijmâ'*, p. 140.

[60] Recorded by Bukhari, Muslim (and this is his wording), Tirmidhi, Abu Dawood, Nasâ'i and Ibn Mâjah.

[61] Ibn al-Mundhir, *al-Ijmâ'*, p. 139.

'Abdullâh ibn 'Amr ibn al-'Âṣ narrated that the Messenger of Allah (ﷺ) was asked about fruits hung up to dry. He replied, "If a person in need takes some in his mouth without filling his clothing, there is nothing to be done to him. If someone carries off something, he is to be fined twice the value and punished. And if anyone steals something after it has been moved to the place where dried fruits are stored (*al-jareen*) and the amount stolen reaches the value of a shield, then he is (to have his hand) amputated."[62]

The person who has had his property stolen may forgive the thief if this is done before the case is taken to the authorities. Ṣafwân ibn Umayyah said, "I was sleeping in the mosque on a garment of mine which cost thirty *dirhams*. A man came and stole it from me. The man was caught and taken to the Prophet (ﷺ) who ordered his (hand to be) amputated. I went to him and said, 'Are you going to cut his hand simply because of thirty *dirhams*? I hereby sell it to him and allow him to pay me over time.' The Prophet (ﷺ) then said, 'Why didn't you do that before he was brought to me?' "[63]

The author of *ar-Rawḍah an-Nadiyah* (vol. 2, p. 279) stated, "The scholars agree that if a thief steals once, his right hand should be amputated. If he steals a second time, his right foot should be amputated. However, they differ concerning his stealing a third time after having had his right hand and right foot amputated. Most say that his left hand should then be amputated." At this point, Shaykh al-Albâni stated in his notes to *ar-Rawḍah*, "This has been authentically narrated from Abu Bakr and 'Umar (may Allah be pleased with them), as recorded by al-Bayhaqi." The *Rawḍah* continues, "Then if he steals again, his right foot is to be amputated.

---

[62] This hadith is *ḥasan*. See Shaykh al-Albâni, *Ṣaḥeeḥ Sunan Abi Dawood*, no. 3689. Recorded by Abu Dawood, Ibn Mâjah and Nasâ'i.

[63] This hadith is *ṣaḥeeḥ*. See Shaykh al-Albâni, *Ṣaḥeeḥ Sunan Abi Dawood*, no. 3695. Recorded by Abu Dawood and Ibn Mâjah.

If he steals after that, he is to be punished in a manner decided by a judge and imprisoned."

Brigandry

Brigandry refers to a band of Muslims within in an Islamic state wreaking havoc, causing bloodshed, destroying wealth, disgracing people's honour and destroying crops, thereby threatening the religion, culture, system and law.[64]

Its Ruling

Brigandry is one of the greatest of crimes and therefore its punishment is one of the most far-reaching. Allah (ﷻ) has stated:

﴿إِنَّمَا جَزَٰٓؤُاْ ٱلَّذِينَ يُحَارِبُونَ ٱللَّهَ وَرَسُولَهُۥ وَيَسْعَوْنَ فِى ٱلْأَرْضِ فَسَادًا أَن يُقَتَّلُوٓاْ أَوْ يُصَلَّبُوٓاْ أَوْ تُقَطَّعَ أَيْدِيهِمْ وَأَرْجُلُهُم مِّنْ خِلَٰفٍ أَوْ يُنفَوْاْ مِنَ ٱلْأَرْضِ ۚ ذَٰلِكَ لَهُمْ خِزْىٌ فِى ٱلدُّنْيَا ۖ وَلَهُمْ فِى ٱلْءَاخِرَةِ عَذَابٌ عَظِيمٌ ﴿٣٣﴾﴾

(سورة المائدة: ٣٣)

﴿The recompense of those who wage war against Allah and His Messenger and do mischief in the land is only that they shall be killed or crucified or their hands and their feet be cut off on the opposite sides, or be exiled from the land. That is their disgrace in this world, and a great torment is theirs in the Hereafter.﴾ *(Qur'an 5: 33)*

---

64 Cf., As-Sayyid Sâbiq, *Fiqh as-Sunnah*, vol. 2, p. 393.

Anas (رضي الله عنه) said, "A group of people from the Tribe of 'Ukl came and embraced Islam. They got ill from the climate in Madeenah. The Prophet (ﷺ) told them to go to the camels collected from the alms and to drink their milk and urine. They did so and were cured. But then they apostatized, killed the camel shepherd and took the camels. The Prophet (ﷺ) sent some people to pursue them and they were brought before him. He had their hands and feet amputated and their eyes put out with heated iron and then they were not cauterized until they died."[65]

The Repentance of a Rebel before the Authorities Catch Him

Allah (سبحانه وتعالى) says (after the above quoted verse):

﴿إِلَّا ٱلَّذِينَ تَابُوا۟ مِن قَبْلِ أَن تَقْدِرُوا۟ عَلَيْهِمْ ۖ فَٱعْلَمُوٓا۟ أَنَّ ٱللَّهَ غَفُورٌ رَّحِيمٌ ﴿٣٤﴾﴾ (سورة المائدة: ٣٤)

﴿Except for those who [having fled away and then] came back [as Muslims] with repentance before they fall into your power; in that case, know that Allah is Oft-Forgiving, Most Merciful.﴾

(Qur'an 5: 34)

---

[65] Recorded by Bukhari and Muslim.

Chapter Fourteen — Criminal Offenses[1]

Criminal offenses refer to all of the crimes that one commits towards others. They are various but all combined under this general heading. They could be crimes against another's life or limb. They could have occurred intentionally or mistakenly.[2] In Islamic Law, it refers to, "aggressions against another's person that require retaliation or the payment of money."[3]

The Great Sanctity of Muslim Lives

Allah (ﷻ) says:

﴿... وَلَا تَقْتُلُوٓا۟ أَنفُسَكُمْ ۚ إِنَّ ٱللَّهَ كَانَ بِكُمْ رَحِيمًا ﴿٢٩﴾ وَمَن يَفْعَلْ ذَٰلِكَ عُدْوَٰنًا وَظُلْمًا فَسَوْفَ نُصْلِيهِ نَارًا ۚ وَكَانَ ذَٰلِكَ عَلَى ٱللَّهِ يَسِيرًا ﴿٣٠﴾﴾

(سورة النِّساء: ٢٩-٣٠)

﴾... And do not kill yourselves [nor kill one another]. Surely, Allah is Most Merciful to you. And whoever commits that through aggression and injustice, We shall cast him into the Fire, and that is easy for Allah.﴿ *(Qur'an 4: 29-30)*

---

1 This section is based on *Fiqh as-Sunnah* and *Manâr as-Sabeel*, with some abridgement and relying only on the authentic narrations they quoted.

2 Aṣ-Ṣan'âni, *Subul as-Salâm*, vol. 3, p. 231.

3 *Manâr as-Sabeel*, vol. 2, p. 315.

Allah (ﷻ) also says:

﴿وَمَن يَقْتُلْ مُؤْمِنًا مُّتَعَمِّدًا فَجَزَآؤُهُۥ جَهَنَّمُ خَٰلِدًا فِيهَا وَغَضِبَ ٱللَّهُ عَلَيْهِ وَلَعَنَهُۥ وَأَعَدَّ لَهُۥ عَذَابًا عَظِيمًا ﴿٩٣﴾﴾

(سورة النِّساء: ٩٣)

﴾And whoever kills a believer intentionally, his recompense is Hell to abide therein, and the Wrath and the Curse of Allah are upon him, and a great punishment is prepared for him.﴿ *(Qur'an 4: 93)*

Additionally, Allah says:

﴿مِنْ أَجْلِ ذَٰلِكَ كَتَبْنَا عَلَىٰ بَنِىٓ إِسْرَٰٓءِيلَ أَنَّهُۥ مَن قَتَلَ نَفْسًۢا بِغَيْرِ نَفْسٍ أَوْ فَسَادٍ فِى ٱلْأَرْضِ فَكَأَنَّمَا قَتَلَ ٱلنَّاسَ جَمِيعًا وَمَنْ أَحْيَاهَا فَكَأَنَّمَآ أَحْيَا ٱلنَّاسَ جَمِيعًا ... ﴿٣٢﴾﴾

(سورة المائدة: ٣٢)

﴾Because of that We ordained for the Children of Israel that if anyone killed a person not in retaliation of murder, or [and] to spread mischief in the land — it would be as if he killed all mankind, and if anyone saved a life, it would be as if he saved the life of all mankind...﴿ *(Qur'an 5: 32)*

Abu Hurayrah narrated that the Prophet (ﷺ) said, "Avoid the seven destructive sins." They said, "O' Messenger of Allah, what are they?" He replied, "Associating partners with Allah, committing sorcery, killing a soul with Allah has made inviolable except due to justice, consuming interest, consuming the wealth of orphans, fleeing on the day with the two armies meet and slandering the chaste, naïvely innocent believing women."[4]

---

[4] Recorded by Bukhari, Muslim, Abu Dawood and Nasâ'i.

'Abdullâh ibn 'Umar ibn al-Khaṭṭâb narrated that the Messenger of Allah (ﷺ) said, "The perishing of this world is lighter in Allah's sight than the killing of a Muslim man."[5]

Abu Sa'eed al-Khudri and Abu Hurayrah narrated that the Messenger of Allah (ﷺ) said, "If the inhabitants of the heaven and the inhabitants of the earth joined together in the taking of the blood of a believer, Allah would throw them into the Hell-Fire."[6]

'Abdullâh ibn Mas'ood said that the Prophet (ﷺ) said, "The first issue that will be decided among the people is that of blood."[7] He also narrated that the Messenger of Allah (ﷺ) said, "A man will come holding the hand of another man and he said, 'O' my Lord, this man killed me.' He will say to him, 'Why did you kill him?' The man will say, 'I killed him so that the honour and authority will belong to You.' Allah will then say, 'It was for Me.' A second man will come holding the hand of another man and will say, 'O' my Lord, this man killed me.' Allah will say to him, 'Why did you kill him?' He will say, 'So that the honour and authority will belong to so and so.' Allah will say, 'It was not for so and so,' and he will cast his sin upon him."[8]

The Prohibition of Suicide

Abu Hurayrah narrated that the Prophet (ﷺ) said, "Whoever throws himself off a mountain and kills himself will be in Hell throwing himself down into it perpetually in such a state therein.

---

[5] This hadith is *ṣaḥeeḥ*. See Shaykh al-Albâni, *Ṣaheeḥ al-Jâmi' aṣ-Ṣagheer*, no. 5077. Recorded by Tirmidhi and Nasâ'i.

[6] This hadith is *ṣaḥeeḥ*. See Shaykh al-Albâni, *Ṣaheeḥ al-Jâmi' aṣ-Ṣagheer*, no. 5247. Recorded by Tirmidhi.

[7] Recorded by Bukhari, Muslim, Tirmidhi and Nasâ'i.

[8] This hadith is *ṣaḥeeḥ*. See Shaykh al-Albâni, *Ṣaheeḥ Sunan Nasâ'i*, no. 3732. Recorded by Nasâ'i.

Whoever drinks poison and kills himself with it will have in his hand poison and drinking it in the Hell-fire perpetually in such a state therein. Whoever kills himself with an iron weapon will have the weapon in his hand stabbing his abdomen in the Hell-fire perpetually in such a state therein."[9]

Jundub ibn 'Abdullâh said that the Messenger of Allah (ﷺ) said, "Among the people before you there was a man who was injured. He suffered from the pain and therefore took a knife and cut his hand with it, bleeding to death. Allah said, 'My servant has hurried his soul to Me so I shall forbid for him Paradise.' "[10]

Jâbir narrated that aṭ-Ṭufayl ibn 'Amr al-Dawsi came to the Prophet (ﷺ) and said, "Do you need a strong, fortified protection?" — The Tribe of Daws had a fort in the pre-Islamic days. — The Prophet (ﷺ) declined this offer because Allah had already reserved that privilege for the Anṣâr. When the Prophet (ﷺ) finally emigrated to Madeenah, aṭ-Ṭufayl ibn 'Amr emigrated to him. Another man from his tribe also emigrated with him. The climate of Madeenah was not good for him and he fell ill. He felt very discomforted so he took an iron arrowhead and he cut his knuckles. He then bled to death. Aṭ-Ṭufayl ibn 'Amr say him in a dream and saw him in a good state but with his hands wrapped. Aṭ-Ṭufayl asked him, "What did your Lord do with you?" He replied, "He forgave me due to my emigration to the Prophet (ﷺ)." He then said, "Why do I see your hands wrapped?" He replied, "I was told, 'We would not set right anything of your which you yourself damaged.'" Aṭ-Ṭufayl then told the Messenger of Allah (ﷺ) about that story and the Messenger of Allah (ﷺ) said, "O' Allah, pardon his hands as well."[11]

---

[9] Recorded by Bukhari, Muslim, Tirmidhi, Abu Dawood (mentioning just the portion about poison) and Nasâ'i.

[10] Recorded by Bukhari and Muslim.

[11] This hadith is *ṣaḥeeḥ*. See Shaykh al-Albâni, *Mukhtasar Ṣaḥeeḥ Muslim*,=

Who May Be Killed

Allah (ﷻ) says:

﴿وَلَا تَقْتُلُوا النَّفْسَ الَّتِي حَرَّمَ اللَّهُ إِلَّا بِالْحَقِّ ... ﴿٣٣﴾﴾ (سورة الإسراء: ٣٣)

﴾And do not kill anyone which Allah has forbidden, except for a just cause...﴿ *(Qur'an 17: 33)*

Ibn 'Umar narrated that the Messenger of Allah (ﷺ) said, "I have been ordered to fight against the people until they testify that there is none worthy of worship except Allah and that Muhammad is the Messenger of Allah, establish the prayer and give the Zakah. Then, if they do that, their blood and wealth will be protected from me — except in accordance with the right of Islam. And their reckoning will be with Allah, the Exalted."[12] The Prophet (ﷺ) explained the categories of people who may be killed when he said, "It is not legal (to spill) the blood of a Muslim except in one of three cases: the fornicator who has previously experienced legal sexual intercourse, a life for a life and one who forsakes his religion and separates from the community."[13]

The Categories of Killing

Killing is of three categories: deliberate, quasi-deliberate and unintentional.

Deliberate is where a legally responsible person intends to kills a person whose life is protected by law by taking steps that he

---

=no. 97. Recorded by Muslim.

[12] Recorded by Bukhari and Muslim.

[13] Recorded by Bukhari, Muslim, Abu Dawood, Tirmidhi, Nasâ'i and Ibn Mâjah.

believes would lead to his death.

Quasi-deliberate is where a person intends to strike another person in a way that usually does not lead to death.

Unintentional is where a legally responsible person does an act which is permissible for him, such as hunting, that ends in the death of another person.

The Legal Ramifications of Killing

For the latter two categories of killing stated above, there is expiation upon the one who brought about the death and blood money to be paid by the clan of the one who brought about the death. Allah (ﷻ) has said:

﴿وَمَا كَانَ لِمُؤْمِنٍ أَن يَقْتُلَ مُؤْمِنًا إِلَّا خَطَـًٔا ۚ وَمَن قَتَلَ مُؤْمِنًا خَطَـًٔا فَتَحْرِيرُ رَقَبَةٍ مُّؤْمِنَةٍ وَدِيَةٌ مُّسَلَّمَةٌ إِلَىٰٓ أَهْلِهِۦٓ إِلَّآ أَن يَصَّدَّقُوا۟ ۚ فَإِن كَانَ مِن قَوْمٍ عَدُوٍّ لَّكُمْ وَهُوَ مُؤْمِنٌ فَتَحْرِيرُ رَقَبَةٍ مُّؤْمِنَةٍ ۖ وَإِن كَانَ مِن قَوْمٍۭ بَيْنَكُمْ وَبَيْنَهُم مِّيثَـٰقٌ فَدِيَةٌ مُّسَلَّمَةٌ إِلَىٰٓ أَهْلِهِۦ وَتَحْرِيرُ رَقَبَةٍ مُّؤْمِنَةٍ ۖ فَمَن لَّمْ يَجِدْ فَصِيَامُ شَهْرَيْنِ مُتَتَابِعَيْنِ تَوْبَةً مِّنَ ٱللَّهِ ۗ وَكَانَ ٱللَّهُ عَلِيمًا حَكِيمًا ﴿٩٢﴾﴾

(سورة النِّساء: ٩٢)

﴿It is not for a believer to kill a believer except [that it be] by mistake, and whosoever kills a believer by mistake, [it is ordained that] he must set free a believing slave and a compensation [blood money] be given to the deceased's family, unless they remit it. If the deceased belonged to a people at war with you and he was a believer; the freeing of a believing slave [is prescribed], and if he belonged to a people with whom you have a treaty of mutual alliance, compensation [blood money] must be paid to his family, and a believing slave must be freed. And whoso finds this [the penance of freeing a slave] beyond his means, he must fast for two consecutive months in order to seek repentance from Allah. And Allah is Ever All-Knowing, All-Wise.﴿ *(Qur'an 4: 92)*

However, in the case of murder, the relative or guardian of the affairs of the deceased has the option between retaliation and forgiving him with a payment of the blood money. Allah (ﷻ) says:

﴿يَٰٓأَيُّهَا ٱلَّذِينَ ءَامَنُواْ كُتِبَ عَلَيۡكُمُ ٱلۡقِصَاصُ فِي ٱلۡقَتۡلَىۖ ٱلۡحُرُّ بِٱلۡحُرِّ وَٱلۡعَبۡدُ بِٱلۡعَبۡدِ وَٱلۡأُنثَىٰ بِٱلۡأُنثَىٰۚ فَمَنۡ عُفِيَ لَهُۥ مِنۡ أَخِيهِ شَيۡءٞ فَٱتِّبَاعُۢ بِٱلۡمَعۡرُوفِ وَأَدَآءٌ إِلَيۡهِ بِإِحۡسَٰنٖۗ ذَٰلِكَ تَخۡفِيفٞ مِّن رَّبِّكُمۡ وَرَحۡمَةٞۗ فَمَنِ ٱعۡتَدَىٰ بَعۡدَ ذَٰلِكَ فَلَهُۥ عَذَابٌ أَلِيمٞ ١٧٨﴾

(سورة البَقَرَة: ١٧٨)

﴾O' you who believe! The Law of Equality in punishment is prescribed for you in case of murder: the free for the free, the slave for the slave, and the female for the female. But if the killer is forgiven by the brother [or the relatives] of the killed against blood money, then adhering to it with fairness and payment of the blood money, to the heir should be made in fairness. This is alleviation and a mercy from your Lord. So after this whoever transgresses the limits [i.e. kills the killer after taking the blood money], he shall have a painful torment.﴿ *(Qur'an 2: 178)*

Abu Hurayrah reported that the Prophet (ﷺ) said, "If someone is killed, his relatives have a choice between two options: the blood-money or retaliation (via the death penalty)."[14]

The blood money is not an absolute obligation with respect to murder. It is in lieu of the death penalty. However, they may come to an agreement on any amount other than the stipulated blood money,

---

[14] Recorded by Bukhari and Muslim.

even if it is more than the regular blood money. The Prophet (ﷺ) said, "Whoever kills a believer intentionally shall be handed over to the relatives of the victim. If they wish, they may have him killed. Or, if they wish, they may take the blood money from him, which is thirty four-year old camels, thirty *jadha'ah*[15] and forty pregnant camels. Whatever reconciliation they come to will be for them, due to the harshness of the blood money requirement."[16]

However, the most virtuous path to follow is freely pardoning the murderer. Allah (ﷻ) has said:

﴿... وَأَن تَعْفُوٓا۟ أَقْرَبُ لِلتَّقْوَىٰ ... ﴿٢٣٧﴾﴾ (سورة البقرة: ٢٣٧)

﴿... And to forego and give is nearer to piety...﴾ *(Qur'an 2: 237)*

The Prophet (ﷺ) said, "When pardoning others, Allah increases one's honour."[17]

Requirements for the obligating of the law of retaliation

The law of retaliation is not obligatory unless the following requirements are met:

1. The murderer must be a legally responsible person. There is no retaliation via the death penalty upon a minor, an insane person or one who was sleeping. The Prophet (Blessings and peace be upon him) has said, "The pen (recording the deeds) has been raised (and is not recording) for three: the one who is sleeping until he awakens, the

---

[15] This term can imply a two-year old sheep, a three-year old cow or a five-year old camel.

[16] This hadith is *ḥasan*. See Shaykh al-Albâni, *Ṣaheeḥ Sunan Tirmidhi*, no. 1121. Recorded by Tirmidhi and Ibn Mâjah.

[17] This hadith is *ṣaḥeeḥ*. See Shaykh al-Albâni, *Ṣaḥeeḥ Sunan Tirmidhi*, no. 1894. Recorded by Muslim and Tirmidhi.

child until he reaches the age of puberty and the insane one until he becomes sane."[18]

2. The victim must have been one whose life was protected by the law and could not have been one whose blood was liable to be taken based on the hadith presented earlier, "It is not legal (to spill) the blood of a Muslim except in one of three cases: the fornicator who has previously experienced legal sexual intercourse, a life for a life and one who forsakes his religion and separates from the community."[19]

3. The murderer cannot have been the father of the victim, as the Prophet (ﷺ) had said, "The father is not to be killed due to (his killing) his child."[20]

4. The victim could not have been a disbeliever while the murderer was a Muslim, as the Prophet (ﷺ) said, "A Muslim is not to be killed due to (the killing) of a disbeliever."[21]

5. The victim could not have been a slave while the murderer was a free person, as al-Ḥasan has said, "A free person is not to be killed due to (the killing) of a slave."[22]

---

[18] This hadith is *ṣaḥeeḥ*. See Shaykh al-Albâni, *Ṣaḥeeḥ al-Jâmi'*, no. 3513. Recorded by Abu Dawood.

[19] Recorded by Bukhari, Muslim, Abu Dawood, Tirmidhi, Nasâ'i and Ibn Mâjah.

[20] This hadith is *ṣaḥeeḥ*. See Shaykh al-Albâni, *I'rwâ' al-Ghaleel*, no. 2214. Recorded by Tirmidhi.

[21] This hadith is *ḥasan ṣaḥeeḥ*. See Shaykh al-Albâni, *Ṣaḥeeḥ Sunan Tirmidhi*, no. 1141. Recorded by Bukhari, Tirmidhi and Nasâ'i.

[22] This is an authentic narration from al-Ḥasan. See Shaykh al-Albâni, *Ṣaḥeeḥ Sunan Abi Dawood*, no. 3787. Recorded by Abu Dawood. This is the opinion of the majority of the scholars. They present a great deal of pieces of evidence but all of them have some weakness to them. Ash-Shanqeeṭi has presented them in *Aḍwâ' al-Bayân* and stated, "These numerous reports - although none=

A Group of People can Be Executed for Participating in Murdering One Person

If a group of people band together to kill one individual, they can all be executed. Mâlik recorded that Sa'eed ibn al-Musayyab said, " 'Umar ibn al-Khaṭṭâb put to death a group of people, five or seven in number, due to their killing one person by deceiving him to go to a remote location and killing him there. 'Umar said, 'If all of the people of San'a had taken part in the plot to kill this person, I would have had them all executed.' "[23]

How the penalty of retaliation is confirmed

The penalty of retaliation is confirmed via one of two ways: confession or the witness of two reputable witnesses.

=of them are free from some weakness - strengthen one another and support one another to the point that they taken together can be considered an acceptable proof. What further supports these pieces of evidence showing that a free person is not killed due to a slave is the fact that in laws of retaliation for injury and not life there is no retaliation against a free person due to injuries to a slave. If this is the case with respect to injuries, it must more so be the case without respect to killing. The only ones who differ with the opinion concerning injuries are Dawood and Ibn Abi Layla. The stance of the majority is also strengthened by the fact that if one mistakenly kills a slave, one pays the value of the slave and not the blood money and a group of scholars put a further condition that the value of the slave not be in excess of the blood money value. Their position is also supported by the fact that if a free person slanders a slave, the punishment for slander is not applied to the free person according to the majority of the scholars, except for what has been narrated from Ibn 'Umar, al-Ḥasan and the Literalist school who say that the punishment is required if the free person slanders the slave who is the mother of a child."

[23] This hadith is *ṣaḥeeḥ*. See Shaykh al-Albâni, *I'rwâ' al-Ghaleel*, no. 2201. Recorded by Mâlik, ash-Shafi'ee in *al-Umm* and al-Bayhaqi.

As for confession, Anas stated, "A Jew crushed the head of a slave-girl between two rocks. (As she was dying), she was asked, 'Who did this to you? Was it so and so?' They kept stating different names until they came to the name of the Jew and she motioned with her head. The Jew was brought and he confessed to the act. The Prophet (ﷺ) commanded that his head be crushed between two stones."[24]

As for the testimony of two reputable witnesses, Râfi' ibn Khadeej said, "One of the Anṣâr was killed at Khaybar. His relatives went to the Prophet (ﷺ) and mentioned that to him. He told them, 'Do you have two witnesses who can testify that your relative was killed?' They said, 'No Muslims were there, as only Jews are there and they would be willing to do even a greater act that this.' The Prophet (ﷺ) then said, 'Choose fifty from among them and ask them to swear an oath (that none of them were involved in the killing).' They refused to do so, so the Prophet (ﷺ) paid the blood money from what he had."[25]

Conditions for implementing the law of retaliation

The following conditions must be met before the law of retaliation may be implemented:

1. The relative who has the right to make the decision has to be a legally responsible person. If the person is a child or insane, the murderer is to be imprisoned until the relative becomes legally responsible.

2. The relatives who have a say in the matter have to all be in agreement. If one or some of them do not request that the law of

---

[24] Recorded by Bukhari, Muslim, Abu Dawood, Tirmidhi, Nasâ'i and Ibn Mâjah.

[25] This hadith is *ṣaḥeeḥ* due to corroborating reports. See Shaykh al-Albâni, *Ṣaḥeeḥ Sunan Abi Dawood*, no. 3793. Recorded by Abu Dawood.

retaliation is implemented, the retaliation is dropped. Zayd ibn Wahb stated, "A case of a man killing another man was brought to 'Umar. The relatives of the victim wanted the murderer to be put to death. However, the sister of the victim, who was also the wife of the murderer, said that she has pardoned her share for her husband. 'Umar then said, 'The man has been rescued from the death penalty.' "[26] He also narrated, "A man found his wife with another man and killed her. That case was taken to 'Umar ibn al-Khaṭṭâb (رضي الله عنه). One of the victim's sisters gave up her right to have him put to death. Thus 'Umar told the rest of the relatives to accept the blood money."[27]

3. The punishment cannot extend to anyone beyond the guilty party: Thus, for example, if the law of retaliation is to be meted out to a woman who is pregnant, she is not to be killed until she gives birth and first breastfeeds the child.[28] 'Abdullâh ibn Buraydah narrated from his father who said, "A woman from the Tribe of Ghamd told the Prophet (ﷺ), 'I have committed adultery.' He said to her, 'Return (home).' She returned (to her home) and the next day she came and said, 'Perhaps you are going to turn me away like you did Mâ'iz ibn Mâlik. By Allah, I am pregnant.' He again said, 'Return.' On the following day she came again. He then told her, 'Return (home) until you give birth.' When she gave birth she came back with her child.

---

[26] This hadith is *ṣaḥeeḥ*. See Shaykh al-Albâni, *I'rwâ' al-Ghaleel*, no. 2222. Recorded by 'Abdur-Razzâq.

[27] This hadith is *ṣaḥeeḥ*. See Shaykh al-Albâni, *I'rwâ' al-Ghaleel*, no. 2225. Recorded by al-Bayhaqi.

[28] The first breastfeeding from the mother is a necessity. Executing the mother before that would harm the child. After that, if one can find someone to foster the child, he will be given the child and the criminal will be executed, based on the hadith of Muslim [presented earlier]. If no one is to be found, the mother will be left to breastfeed the child for two entire years, based on the hadith of Abu Dawood above.

He then told her, 'Return (home) and breastfeed him until he is weaned.' She returned again after he was weaned, having in his hand some food that he was eating. The Prophet (ﷺ) ordered that the child be given over to one of the Muslims and he had a put dug for her. Then he gave the command to have her stone. Khâlid was one of those who stoned her. He threw a stone at her and a drop of her blood fell on his cheek and he cursed her. The Prophet (ﷺ) said to him, 'Be gentle, Khâlid. By the One in whose hand is my soul, she has performed such an act of repentance that if a wrongful tax collector were to perform it, he would be forgiven.' He then had the prayer performed her and had her buried."[29]

How is the retaliation to be carried out

The basic principle concerning the law of retaliation is that the murderer is to be killed in the same manner in which he committed his murder. This is the requirement of equity and reciprocity. Allah (ﷻ) has said:

﴿... فَمَنِ ٱعْتَدَىٰ عَلَيْكُمْ فَٱعْتَدُوا۟ عَلَيْهِ بِمِثْلِ مَا ٱعْتَدَىٰ عَلَيْكُمْ ... ﴿١٩٤﴾﴾

(سورة البقرة: ١٩٤)

﴾... Then whoever transgresses the prohibition against you, you transgress likewise against him...﴿ *(Qur'an 2: 194)*

Allah also says:

﴿وَإِنْ عَاقَبْتُمْ فَعَاقِبُوا۟ بِمِثْلِ مَا عُوقِبْتُم بِهِۦ ... ﴿١٢٦﴾﴾ (سورة النحل: ١٢٦)

﴾And if you punish [your enemy, O' you believers in the Oneness of

---

[29] This hadith is *ṣaḥeeḥ*. See Shaykh al-Albâni, *Ṣaḥeeḥ Sunan Abi Dawood*, no. 3733. Recorded by Muslim and by Abu Dawood, and the context here is from him.

Allah], then punish them with the like of that with which you were afflicted...﴿

(Qur'an 16: 126)

Furthermore, the Prophet (ﷺ) crushed the head of the Jew with a stone in the same way that he murdered the girl by crushing her head with a stone.[30]

Retaliation is from the duties of the ruler

Al-Qurṭubi stated:

> "There is no difference of opinion concerning the fact that the law of retaliation is to be carried out by those in authority. It is obligatory upon them to implement the law of retaliation, the required punishments and other laws, as Allah has demanded all of the believers to fulfill the law of retaliation while at the same time the believers are all not in a position to implement the law of retaliation. Hence, the ruler stands in the place of the believers in implementing the law of retaliation and other required punishments."[31]

Aṣ-Ṣâwi, in his notes to the Qur'anic commentary known as *al-Jalâlayn*, has explained this point in the following manner:

> "When it is confirmed that the murder was deliberate and intentional, it becomes obligatory upon the Islamic ruler to give power to the relatives of the victim over the murderer. The ruler is to enact whatever the relative chooses, be it retaliation, pardon or blood money. It is not permissibility for the relative on his own to inflict a punishment on the murderer without the permission of the ruler, as this would cause great harm and chaos. If the guardian

---

[30] Recorded by Bukhari, Muslim, Abu Dawood, Tirmidhi, Nasâ'i and Ibn Mâjah.

[31] Al-Qurṭubi, *Al-Jâmi' li-Aḥkâm al-Qurân*, vol. 2, Pp. 245-6.

does kill him before he receives the authority of the ruler, he is to face a discretionary punishment."[32]

Retaliation for injuries less than loss of life

In the same way that there is retaliation for loss of life, there is also retaliation for injuries that are less than that. Allah (ﷻ) has said:

﴿وَكَتَبْنَا عَلَيْهِمْ فِيهَآ أَنَّ ٱلنَّفْسَ بِٱلنَّفْسِ وَٱلْعَيْنَ بِٱلْعَيْنِ وَٱلْأَنفَ بِٱلْأَنفِ وَٱلْأُذُنَ بِٱلْأُذُنِ وَٱلسِّنَّ بِٱلسِّنِّ وَٱلْجُرُوحَ قِصَاصٌ ... ﴿٤٥﴾﴾

(سورة المائدة: ٤٥)

﴾And We ordained therein for them: Life for life, eye for eye, nose for nose, ear for ear, tooth for tooth, and wounds equal for equal...﴿

(Qur'an 5: 35)

This ruling, although it is in relation to the nations before us, also applies to us as the Prophet (ﷺ) approved of it. Bukhari and Muslim record on the authority of Anas ibn Mâlik (رضي الله عنه) that ar-Rubayyi' bint an-Naḍr ibn Anas broke an incisor tooth of a slave-girl. They asked them to accept compensation but they would not accept anything except retaliation. Her brother Anas ibn an-Naḍr came and said, "O' Messenger of Allah, is ar-Rubayyi's tooth to be broken? By the One who sent you with the truth, her incisor tooth will not be broken." The Prophet (ﷺ) told him, "O' Anas, the Book of Allah obligates retaliation." But then (her) people were satisfied and forgave (ar-Rubayyi'). The Messenger of Allah (ﷺ) then said, "Among Allah's servants there are some whom if they swear by Allah, Allah will fulfill what they swore to."[33]

---

[32] Quoted in as-Sayyid Sâbiq, *Fiqh as-Sunnah*, vol. 2, p. 453.

[33] This hadith is *ṣaḥeeḥ*. See Shaykh al-Albâni, *Ṣaḥeeḥ al-Jâmi' aṣ-Ṣagheer*, no. 2228. Recorded by Bukhari, Abu Dawood, Nasâ'i and Ibn Mâjah.

The prerequisites for implementing the law of retaliation for injuries and wounds[34]

The following conditions must be met before the law of retaliation for injuries is implemented:

1. The one who caused the injury must be a legal responsible (adult, insane) person.

2. The incident must have been intentional. This is because there is no retaliation if a person mistakenly kills another person. Therefore, this ruling must be even more so true in the case of injuries caused by mistakes.

3. The "blood" of the victim must be comparable to that of the perpetrator. Thus, one does not implement retaliation upon a Muslim due to an injury caused to a *dhimmi* (non-Muslim resident of an Islamic state), nor to a free person due to an injury to a slave, nor to the father due to an injury to his son.

The law of retaliation concerning extremities

There are three conditions that must be met before implementing the law of retaliation upon the extremities:

1. It must be possible to perform the retaliation without causing harm (beyond the retaliation). Thus, it would be possible to amputate from joints or that which has a clear end, such as the nose cartilage, which is the soft portion. There is no retaliation for a deep, internal wound or for cutting off one of the forearm or for bones in general other than teeth.

2. The injured part must have an equivalent with respect to what is

---

[34] [These refer to injuries to other than the head or face. Those fall under a separate category that shall be discussed later.] - Translator

called and its side of the body. Thus, one cannot amputate the right hand due to an injury caused to the left or vice-versa. One cannot take retaliation against the little finger due to an injury caused to (what is known in the West as) the "ring finger" or vice-versa. In this case, the two parts do not share the same name. One cannot amputate a primary part for an extraneous one, since they are not equal in their place and importance.

3. The part of the injured person and of the one who caused the injury must be equivalent with respect to health and quality. One cannot amputate a sound limb due to injury caused to an already crippled limb. Nor does one amputate a complete hand for an injury done to a hand that was already missing some fingers — however, in this case, the reverse is permissible.

Retaliation for intentional wounds

As for intentional wounds, there is no retaliation obligatory unless it is possible, such that the injury done to the perpetrator is exactly equal to the original injury, with no increase or decrease to the injury. If equity and reciprocity can only be achieve by going beyond the amount of the original injury, with great possible danger or with further harm caused, then there is no retaliation in such cases. In such cases, one has to pay the blood money.

The Blood Money

The *diyah* is the money that is obligated due to an assault upon another. This money is to be given to the victim or to his relatives. It can occur where there is a possibility of retaliation or when there is no such possibility.

The *diyah* is also called *'aql*. The source for that is that a murderer used to pay the blood money in camels and he would tie them (*'aqalahâ*) up at the courtyard of the relatives of the deceased or he would tie them down with his cord (*'iqâl*) in order to hand them over to the relatives of the deceased. One would say, "*'aqaltu* from so and on" if he paid off his blood money.

The basis for this practice is the Qur'anic verse:

﴿وَمَا كَانَ لِمُؤْمِنٍ أَن يَقْتُلَ مُؤْمِنًا إِلَّا خَطَـًٔا ۚ وَمَن قَتَلَ مُؤْمِنًا خَطَـًٔا فَتَحْرِيرُ رَقَبَةٍ مُّؤْمِنَةٍ وَدِيَةٌ مُّسَلَّمَةٌ إِلَىٰٓ أَهْلِهِۦٓ إِلَّآ أَن يَصَّدَّقُوا۟ ۚ فَإِن كَانَ مِن قَوْمٍ عَدُوٍّ لَّكُمْ وَهُوَ مُؤْمِنٌ فَتَحْرِيرُ رَقَبَةٍ مُّؤْمِنَةٍ ۖ وَإِن كَانَ مِن قَوْمٍۭ بَيْنَكُمْ وَبَيْنَهُم مِّيثَـٰقٌ فَدِيَةٌ مُّسَلَّمَةٌ إِلَىٰٓ أَهْلِهِۦ وَتَحْرِيرُ رَقَبَةٍ مُّؤْمِنَةٍ ۖ فَمَن لَّمْ يَجِدْ فَصِيَامُ شَهْرَيْنِ مُتَتَابِعَيْنِ تَوْبَةً مِّنَ ٱللَّهِ ۗ وَكَانَ ٱللَّهُ عَلِيمًا حَكِيمًا ﴿٩٢﴾﴾ (سورة النِّسَاء: ٩٢)

﴾It is not for a believer to kill a believer except [that it be] by mistake, and whosoever kills a believer by mistake, [it is ordained that] he must set free a believing slave and a compensation [blood money] be given to the deceased's family, unless they remit it. If the deceased belonged to a people at war with you and he was a believer; the freeing of a believing slave [is prescribed], and if he belonged to a people with whom you have a treaty of mutual alliance, compensation [blood money] must be paid to his family, and a believing slave must be freed. And whoso finds this [the penance of freeing a slave] beyond his means, he must fast for two consecutive months in order to seek repentance from Allah. And Allah is Ever All-Knowing, All-Wise.﴿ *(Qur'an 4: 92)*

'Amr ibn Shu'ayb narrated from his father on the authority of his grandfather that the Messenger of Allah (ﷺ) judged in a case of an unintentional killing that the blood money was to be one hundred camels, thirty of which were six months to two years old, thirty which were two years old, thirty which were three plus years old and ten which were male three plus years old.[35]

He also said, "The value of the *diyah* during the time of the Messenger of Allah (ﷺ) was eight hundred *dinars* or eight thousand *dirhams*. The *diyah* of the People of the Book at that time was half that of the Muslims. This continued until 'Umar became the caliph. He stood and addressed the people, saying, 'Camels have become expensive.' So then 'Umar set the rate for those whose wealth was in gold at one thousand *dinars*, for the people of silver twelve thousand *dirhams*. For the people whose wealth was in cows, it was two hundred cows. For the people who owned sheep, it was two thousand sheep. For those who owned garments, it was two hundred garments. However, he left the *diyah* of the People of the Book same and did not raise it."[36]

Killing that Obligates Blood Money

The scholars agree that the blood money is obligatory in cases of mistaken killings and quasi-deliberate killings. It is also obligatory in the case of intentional murder wherein the perpetrator does not fulfill the requirements for having the punishment meted out to them, such as death caused by a minor or an insane person. The blood money is also obligatory when the victim is not of the same level of inviolability as the murderer, such as when a slave is killed by a free person. The blood money is also obligatory if a sleeping person's

---

[35] This hadith is *ḥasan*. See Shaykh al-Albâni, *Ṣaḥeeḥ Sunan Ibn Mâjah*, no. 2128. Recorded by Abu Dawood, Ibn Mâjah and Nasâ'i.

[36] This hadith is *ḥasan*. See Shaykh al-Albâni, *I'rwâ' al-Ghaleel*, no. 2247. Recorded by Abu Dawood.

movement caused the death of another person or who falls upon another while sleeping and kills the other person.

The Types of Blood Money

The blood money can be either "heavier" or "lighter". The "lighter" is required in the case of a mistaken killing. The "heavier" is required in the case of a quasi-deliberate killing. In the case of murder, if the relative of the deceased pardons the murderer and they agree upon some compensation, whatever they agree upon will be acceptable, as previously quoted from 'Amr ibn Shu'ayb on the authority of his father from his grandfather that the Prophet (ﷺ) said, "Whoever kills a believer intentionally shall be handed over to the relatives of the victim. If they wish, they may have him killed. Or, if they wish, they may take the blood money from him, which is thirty four-year old camels, thirty *jadha'ah* [37] and forty pregnant camels. Whatever reconciliation they come to will be for them, due to the harshness of the blood money requirement."[38]

The "heavier" blood money is equivalent to one hundred camels, which forty of them being pregnant. The Prophet (ﷺ) said, "The accidental semi-deliberate killing by a whip or a staff (has a blood money of) one hundred camels, forty of which already have her offspring in her belly."[39] This blood money can come from the money of the one who committed the act.

---

[37] This term can imply a two-year old sheep, a three-year old cow or a five-year old camel.

[38] This hadith is *ḥasan*. See Shaykh al-Albâni, *Ṣaḥeeḥ Sunan Tirmidhi*, no. 1121. Recorded by Tirmidhi and Ibn Mâjah.

[39] This hadith is *ṣaḥeeḥ*. See Shaykh al-Albâni, *Ṣaḥeeḥ Sunan Ibn Mâjah*, no. 2126. Recorded by Abu Dawood, Ibn Mâjah and Nasâ'i.

The blood money due to a mistaken or quasi intentional killing is upon the clan of the perpetrator. This refers to his male relatives from his father side. It includes the adult, wealthy, sane males. Also included among them are the blind, the aged and the senile — if they possess wealth. However, females, poor, underage and insane members are not included. Also, the relative of a different religion than the perpetrator is also not included. This is because this principle is based on who it is that must come to the aid and support of the person and all of these categories are excluded from the requirement of giving the individual aid and support.

The basis for requiring the clan to pay the blood money is in the hadith narrated by Abu Hurayrah (رضي الله عنه) who said, "Two women from the tribe of Hudhayl fought and one of them threw a stone at the other and killed her and what was in her womb. The Prophet (ﷺ) judged that the blood money for the fetus was a male or female slave and he judged that the blood money upon the woman was to be upon her clan."[40]

The Blood Money for the Parts of the Body

Humans have body parts that are singular, such as nose, tongue and private part, and others that come in pairs, such as eyes, ears and hands. Yet other parts are even more in number.

If a person destroys another person's singular body parts or both body parts that come in pairs, the injured party is entitled to the complete blood money. If a person destroys one of a body part that comes in pairs, then the injured party is entitled to half of the complete blood money. Thus, the complete blood money will be paid for the nose or both eyes. However, if one eye is destroyed, the

[40] Recorded by Bukhari, Muslim and Nasâ'i.

person is entitled to half of the complete blood money. For both eyelids of one eye, the person is entitled to half but for one eyelid on one eye, the person is entitled to one-quarter of the complete blood money. For all of the fingers or all of the toes, the person is entitled to the complete blood money. However, for each finger or toe, the person is entitled to ten camels. If all of the teeth are knocked out, the person is entitled to the complete blood money. For each individual tooth, a person receives five camels.

Abu Bakr ibn 'Ubaydullâh ibn 'Umar narrated from 'Umar that the Messenger of Allah (ﷺ) said, "For the nose, if it is completely removed, the blood money is one hundred camels. For one hand, it is fifty camels. For one leg, it is fifty camels. For one eye, it is fifty. For a wound that falls just short of reaching the brain, it is one-third of the complete blood money. For a deep wound, it is one third of the complete blood money. For an injury that causes a bone to be dislocated, it is fifteen camels. For a wound that reaches the bone, it is five camels. For a tooth, it is five camels. For every finger/toe there it is ten camels."[41]

Abu Bakr ibn Muhammad ibn 'Amr ibn Ḥazm narrated from his father on the authority of his grandfather that the Prophet (ﷺ) sent to the people of Yemen a document containing the laws of Zakah, *Sunan* and blood money. It contained the following instructions: "The blood money for a life is one hundred camels. For the nose, if it is removed completely, it is the complete amount of the blood money. For the tongue, it is the complete blood money. For both lips, it is the complete blood money. For both testicles, it is the complete blood money. For the male private part, it is the complete blood money. For the spinal column, it is the complete blood money. For both eyes, it is

---

[41] This hadith is *ṣaḥeeḥ* due to supporting evidence. See Shaykh al-Albâni, *Ṣaḥeeḥ Sunan Nasâ'i*, no. 4513. Recorded by al-Bazzâr and al-Bayhaqi.

the complete blood money. For one leg, it is half the complete blood money. For a wound that falls just short of reaching the brain, it is one-third of the complete blood money. For a deep wound, it is one third of the complete blood money. For an injury that causes a bone to be dislocated, it is fifteen camels. For every finger of the hand or toe of the feet it is ten camels. For a tooth, it is five camels. For a wound that reaches the bone, it is five camels."[42]

The Blood Money for the Losing the Use of One's Limbs

If a person strikes another person and the victim loses his mind or one of his senses, such as hearing, seeing, smell or taste, or being able to speak by pronouncing all of the letters then, concerning all of these cases, the blood money is the complete blood money (that is, one hundred camels).

'Awf said, "I heard an old man speaking before the civil war of Ibn al-Ash'ath. I described the old man and they said, 'That was Abu al-Muhallab, the uncle of Abu Qulâbah.' A person threw a stone and hit his head and he lost his hearing, speech, sanity, memory and he no longer has relations with women. 'Umar judged that he should receive the total of four complete blood moneys."[43]

If a person has only one good eye and somebody knocks that out, he receives the complete blood money. 'Umar, his son 'Abdullâh and 'Ali ibn Abi Ṭâlib (may Allah be pleased with them) each made

---

[42] This hadith is *ṣaḥeeḥ* due to supporting evidence. See Shaykh al-Albâni, *I'rwâ' al-Ghaleel*, no. 2275 and *Ṣaḥeeḥ Sunan Nasâ'i*, no. 4513. Recorded by Mâlik and Nasâ'i.

[43] This hadith is *ḥasan*. See Shaykh al-Albâni, *I'rwâ' al-Ghaleel*, no. 2289. Recorded by ibn Abi Shaybah and al-Bayhaqi.

this judgment. Qatâdah said, "I heard Abu Mijlaz say, 'I asked 'Abdullâh about a one-eyed person who has his good eye knocked out.' 'Abdullâh ibn Ṣafwân then said, ' 'Umar judged that he should received the complete blood money.' I said, 'I asked Ibn 'Umar.' He (Ibn 'Umar) said, 'Isn't he narrating to you from 'Umar?' "[44]

Qatâdah narrated from Khilâs that 'Ali stated concerning a one-eyed man who had his good eye poked out, "If he wishes he can take the complete blood money or he can take half of the blood money and have one eye poked out from the one who poked his eye out."[45]

Head and Face Wounds

Ash-Shajjâj refers to wounds that occur on the head and face. There are ten varieties of such:

1. *Al-Khâriṣah* — this peels the skin but does not cause bleeding
2. *Al-Dâmiyah* — this causes bleeding
3. *Al-Bâḍi'ah* — this greatly rips open the flesh
4. *Al-Mutalâḥimah* — this goes deeply into the flesh
5. *Al-Samḥâq* — this is where only a light layer of skin remains covering the bone

There is no retaliation for these five types of head wounds[46] nor is there any fixed compensation. Instead, the mattered is to be judged by a competent person.[47]

---

[44] Its chain is *ṣaḥeeḥ*. See Shaykh al-Albâni, *I'rwâ' al-Ghaleel*, no. 2270. Recorded by al-Bayhaqi and by Ibn Abi Shaybah but without the part, "I am asking...".

[45] Recorded by Ibn Abi Shaybah and al-Bayhaqi.

[46] As it would not be possible to carry out an equivalent wound.

[47] Ibn al-Mundhir said, "All the people whose opinion I know say that the=

6. *Al-Mooḍiḥah* — this is a wound that reaches the bone. For this, one receives five camels.

7. *Al-Hâshimah* — this is an injury wherein a bone is broken. For this, one receives ten camels.

8. *Al-Munaqqilah* — this is where the bone is dislocated. For this, one receives fifteen camels.

9. *Al-Ma'moomah* or *al-Âmmah* — this is an injury such that only a thin layer remains over the brain. For this, one receives one-third of the complete blood money.

10. *Al-Dâmighah* — this is an injury that reaches the brain. For this as well, one receives one-third of the complete blood money.

Blood money for a deep, penetrating wound

A deep, penetrating wound is one which reaches the internal parts of the body, such as the stomach, back, chest, windpipe and bladder. For these, one receives one-third of the complete blood money, as the written document of 'Amr ibn Ḥazm (referred to earlier) states, "For deep wounds, it is one-third of the complete blood money."

=meaning of 'being judged' is as follows: If a person is inflicted with an injury for which there is no fixed blood money, then one asks how much his value would be if he were a slave before suffering such an injury or being struck in such a way. Suppose the value is one hundred *dinars*. Then one asks what his value is after that injury and his recovery. Suppose it is ninety-five *dinars*. In that case, the one who caused the injury must pay one-twentieth of the complete blood money to the injured person. If the value afterwards were ninety *dinars*, then he is to receive one-tenth of the complete blood money. Anything less or more can be figured in the same manner." Ibn al-Mundhir, *al-Ijmâ'*, p. 151.

The Blood Money of a Woman

If a woman is accidentally killed, her blood money is half that of a man. Similarly, her bodily parts and wounds will also carry a blood money value half of that for men. Shurayḥ said, " 'Urwah al-Bâriqi came to me from 'Umar saying that the blood money for the wounds of men and women are the same in the case of teeth and injuries that reach the bone. However, for anything greater than that, the blood money for the woman is half of that for the man."[48]

The Blood Money of the People of the Book

If a person from the People of the Book is mistakenly killed, the blood money will be half of that for a Muslim. The male from the People of the Book has half the blood money of a Muslim male while a female from the People of the Book has half the blood money of a Muslim woman. 'Amr ibn Shu'ayb narrated from his father on the authority of his grandfather that the Messenger of Allah (ﷺ) judged that the blood money of the People of the Two Books is to be half of the blood money of the Muslims — and they are the Jews and the Christians.[49]

The Blood Money of the Fetus

If the fetus dies due to an intentional or unintentional assault on its mother wherein the mother survives, then a *ghurrah* becomes

---

[48] Its chain is *ṣaḥeeḥ*. See Shaykh al-Albâni, *I'rwâ' al-Ghaleel*, vol. 7, p. 307. Recorded by Ibn Abi Shaybah.

[49] This hadith is *ḥasan*. See Shaykh al-Albâni, *I'rwâ' al-Ghaleel*, no. 2251. Recorded by Ibn Mâjah, Tirmidhi and Nasâ'i with similar wordings. Abu Dawood records, "The blood money of a protected [non-Muslim] citizen is half that of a free male," that is a free Muslim male.

obligatory (which is a male or female slave). This is regardless if the fetus comes out of the mother dead or if it dies within the womb. It is also regardless of whether the fetus was a male or female. If the woman also dies, then there is also her complete blood money as well. Abu Hurayrah (رضي الله عنه) narrated, "Two women from the tribe of Hudhayl fought and one of them threw a stone at the other and killed her and what was in her womb. They took the case to the Prophet (ﷺ) and he judged that the blood money for the fetus was a male or female slave and he judged that the blood money upon the woman was to be upon her clan, her hairs, her child and those with her."[50]

If the child comes out alive and then dies, there is a complete blood money. If it were a male, it would be one hundred camels and if it were a female, it would be fifty camels. This is because we are certain that it died due to the assault but it is more similar to a non-fetus in this case.

[50] Recorded by Bukhari and Muslim.

Chapter Fifteen — Judicial Proceedings

Their Legality

Judicial proceedings are sanctioned by the Qur'an, Sunnah and consensus of the Muslim Nation. Allah (ﷻ) says in the Qur'an:

﴿وَأَنِ ٱحْكُم بَيْنَهُم بِمَآ أَنزَلَ ٱللَّهُ ... ﴿٤٩﴾﴾ (سورة المائدة: ٤٩)

﴿And so judge [you O' Muhammad] between them by what Allah has revealed...﴾ *(Qur'an 5: 49)*

Allah also says:

﴿يَٰدَاوُۥدُ إِنَّا جَعَلْنَٰكَ خَلِيفَةً فِى ٱلْأَرْضِ فَٱحْكُم بَيْنَ ٱلنَّاسِ بِٱلْحَقِّ ... ﴿٢٦﴾﴾

(سورة ص: ٢٦)

﴿O' David! Verily! We have placed you as a successor on earth, so judge you between men in truth [and justice]...﴾ *(Qur'an 38: 26)*

'Amr ibn al-'Âṣ narrated that he heard the Messenger of Allah (ﷺ) say, "If a judge (or ruler) decided a case and strove (to determine the correct ruling), then if he were correct, he receives two rewards. And if he strove and was incorrect, he receives just one reward."[1] The

---

[1] Recorded by Bukhari, Muslim, Abu Dawood and Ibn Mâjah.

Muslims have all agreed concerning the sanctioning of judicial proceedings.

Its Ruling

Judicial proceedings are a communal obligation. The ruler, given the ability to do so, must appoint judges in the land to judge between the people. The Prophet (ﷺ) judged between the people and he sent 'Ali as a judge to Yemen. The rightly-guided caliphs judged between the people and also appointed judges in the different lands.[2]

Its Merit

'Abdullâh ibn Mas'ood said that the Messenger of Allah (ﷺ) said, "There is no jealousy except with respect to two people: A man whom Allah has given wealth and he uses it up for the sake of the Truth and a man whom Allah has given wisdom and he decides by it and acts accordingly."[3]

Its Perils

Abu Hurayrah narrated that the Prophet (ﷺ) said, "Whoever has been appointed a judge has truly been slaughtered without a knife!"[4]

Abu Buraydah reported that the Prophet (ﷺ) said, "Judges are of three categories: one in Paradise and two in the Hell-fire. As for the one in Paradise, it is a man who recognizes the truth and judges in

---

[2] *Manâr as-Sabeel*, vol. 2, p. 453.

[3] Recorded by Bukhari, Muslim and Ibn Mâjah.

[4] This hadith is *ṣaḥeeḥ*. See Shaykh al-Albâni, *Ṣaḥeeḥ al-Jâmi' aṣ-Ṣagheer*, no. 6190. Recorded by Abu Dawood, Tirmidhi and Ibn Mâjah.

accordance with it. As for the man who recognizes the truth but is unjust in his ruling, he is in the Hell-fire. And the man who judges among the people with ignorance, he is also in the Hell-fire."[5]

The Prohibition of Seeking a Judgeship

'Abdur-Raḥmân ibn Samurah said, "The Prophet (ﷺ) said to me, 'O' 'Abdur-Raḥmân ibn Samurah, do not ask for the position of authority. If you are given it due to your request, you will be entrusted with it on your own. If you are given it without asking for it, you will be helped in it."[6]

When is the Role of Judge Demanded upon a Person

Ibn Ḥajar wrote in *Fatḥ al-Bâri* (vol. 13, p. 146):

> "Abu 'Ali al-Karâbeesi, the companion of ash-Shafi'ee, wrote in his book, *Kitâb Âdâb al-Quḍâ'*, 'I do not know of any difference of opinion among the previous scholars that the one who has the most right to judge between the Muslims is the one whose virtues, honesty, knowledge and piety are established; a reader of the Book of Allah and knowledgeable of most of its rulings; knowledgeable of the Sunnah of the Messenger of Allah (ﷺ) and memorizing most of it; having similar knowledge of the statements of the Companions; knowledgeable of where there is agreement and disagreement and knowledge of the statements of the jurists among the Followers; able to distinguish what is authentic from what is defective; follower in new issues the Book of Allah, if he finds to solution there then the Sunnah, if not there

---

[5] This hadith is *ṣaḥeeḥ*. See Shaykh al-Albâni, *Ṣaḥeeḥ al-Jâmi' aṣ-Ṣagheer*, no. 4446. Recorded by Abu Dawood and Ibn Mâjah.

[6] Recorded by Bukhari, Muslim, Abu Dawood, Tirmidhi and Nasâ'i.

then he acts in accord with what the leading Companions acted upon; he often goes over points with the people of knowledge and consults with them, with politeness and piety; he guards his tongue, stomach and private parts from what is forbidden; he understands the words of the claimants; finally he must be intelligent and staying way from following desires. Although we know that no one on the face of the earth combines together all of these attributes, it is still a must that the people of every place seek the one who is most complete and virtuous.'"

Women are not to be Judges

Abu Bakrah said, "On the Day of the Battle of Jamal, Allah benefited me by words (that I had heard). When it reached the Prophet (ﷺ) that the Persians had crowned the daughter of Kisra their ruler, he said, 'A people will not prosper if they are ruled by a woman.' "[7]

A Judge's Etiquette

It is obligatory upon the judge to be just between the two disputants with respect to his look, his words, his seating arrangements and his entering upon decision.[8] Abu al-Maleeḥ al-Hudhali said, " 'Umar ibn al-Khaṭṭâb wrote to Abu Moosa al-Ash'ari, saying, 'Judging is truly an unequivocal obligation and a followed practice. You must understand if (the case) comes to you, as there is no benefit to speaking the truth if it is not implemented. And be equal to the people with respect to your facing them, our seating and your

---

[7] This hadith is *ṣaḥeeḥ*. See Shaykh al-Albâni, *Ṣaḥeeḥ al-Jâmi' aṣ-Ṣagheer*, no. 5225. Recorded by Bukhari, Tirmidhi and Nasâ'i.

[8] *Manâr as-Sabeel*, vol. 2, p. 460.

justice. A noble person should not have hope in your wrongful behaviour."[9]

It is Forbidden for a Judge to Accept Bribes or Gifts

'Abdullâh ibn 'Amr narrated that the Messenger of Allah (ﷺ) said, "The curse of Allah is upon the one who gives a bribe and the one who takes a bribe."[10] Abu Ḥumayd as-Sâ'idi narrated that the Messenger of Allah (ﷺ) said, "Gifts for the (state) employees is theft."[11]

It is Forbidden to Give a Judgment While Angered

'Abdul-Mâlik ibn 'Umar said that he heard 'Abdur-Raḥmân ibn Abi Bakrah say, "Abu Bakrah wrote to his son, who was in Sijistân, saying, 'You should not judge between two people while you are angered, for I have heard the Prophet (ﷺ) say, 'A judge should not decide between two people while he is angered.''"[12]

A Ruling by a Judge Does not Alter the Truth Whatsoever

Whoever is given a judgment wherein he is given the right of his brother must not accept that judgment for the ruling of a judge

---

[9] This report is *ṣaḥeeḥ*. See Shaykh al-Albâni, *I'rwâ' al-Ghaleel*, no. 2619. Reported by ad-Dâraquṭni.

[10] This hadith is *ṣaḥeeḥ*. See Shaykh al-Albâni, *Ṣaḥeeḥ Sunan Ibn Mâjah*, no. 1871. Recorded by Ibn Mâjah and Tirmidhi.

[11] This hadith is *ṣaḥeeḥ*. See Shaykh al-Albâni, *I'rwâ' al-Ghaleel*, no. 2622. Recorded by Aḥmad and al-Bayhaqi.

[12] Recorded by Bukhari, Muslim, Tirmidhi, Abu Dawood, Nasâ'i and Ibn Mâjah.

does not make what is impermissible, permissible or vice-versa. Umm Salamah, the wife of the Prophet (ﷺ), narrated that the Prophet (ﷺ) heard a dispute outside the door to his apartment. He went out to the disputants and said, "I am but a human being. You come to me with a dispute and one of you may be more convincing than the other, so I think he has spoken truthfully and grant him the judgment due to that. But whoever is granted a judgment taking the right of another Muslim, then that is actually a portion of the Hell-fire which he can take or he can leave."[13]

The Claims and Proofs

The *da'âwâ* (pl. of *da'wâ*) are the claims is that someone is seeking. Thus, Allah has said:

﴿... وَلَكُمْ فِيهَا مَا تَدَّعُونَ ﴿٣١﴾﴾ (سورة فصّلت: ٣١)

﴿... Therein you shall have [all] for which you ask for [*tadda'oon*].﴾ *(Qur'an 41: 31)*,

— meaning all that you seek or request.

As a legal term, it is the claim that someone makes for himself that he has the right over something in the possession or control of another. The *mudda'ee* is the plaintiff or the one who is seeking his right. If he were to remain silent, the case would be dropped. The *mudd'â 'alayh* is the defendant from whom a right is being sought. If he were to remain silent, the case would not be dropped. The *bayinât* (pl. of *bayinah*) are the signs or evidence, such as witness and so on. The fundamental principles of such procedures are based on the hadith of Ibn 'Abbâs who narrated that the Messenger of Allah (ﷺ)

---

[13] Recorded by Bukhari, Muslim, Abu Dawood, Tirmidhi, Nasâ'i and Ibn Mâjah.

said, "Were people to be given according to their claims, men would claim the wealth and blood of the people. But the taking of an oath is upon the one against whom the claim is being made."[14] And 'Amr ibn Shu'ayb narrated from his father on the authority of his grandfather that the Messenger of Allah (ﷺ) said, "The burden of proof is upon the plaintiff and the taking of an oath is upon the one against whom the claim is being made."[15]

The sin of one who claims something that does not belong to him

Abu Dharr narrated that he heard the Messenger of Allah (ﷺ) say, "Whoever claims something that does not belong to him is not from among us and he shall take his own seat in the Hell-fire."[16]

The sin of one who swears a false oath in order to take wealth that belongs to another

'Abdullâh ibn Mas'ood said that the Messenger of Allah (ﷺ) said, "Whoever makes an oath as a defendant which is a false oath done to take the wealth of a Muslim will meet Allah on the Day of Resurrection while He is angered with him."[17]

Abu Umâmah al-Ḥârithi narrated that he heard the Messenger of Allah (ﷺ) say, "A person does not take the right of another Muslim via a false oath except that Allah will forbid for him Paradise and obligate for him the Hell-fire." A man from the people asked,

---

[14] Recorded by Bukhari, Muslim (along with a story related to it) and Ibn Mâjah.

[15] This hadith is *ṣaḥeeḥ*. See Shaykh al-Albâni, *Ṣaḥeeḥ al-Jâmi' aṣ-Ṣagheer*, no. 2896. Recorded by Tirmidhi.

[16] This hadith is *ṣaḥeeḥ*. See Shaykh al-Albâni, *Ṣaḥeeḥ al-Jâmi' aṣ-Ṣagheer*, no. 1877. Recorded by Muslim and Ibn Mâjah.

[17] Recorded by Bukhari, Muslim, Abu Dawood, Tirmidhi and Ibn Mâjah.

"O' Messenger of Allah, even if it is an insignificant thing?" The Prophet (ﷺ) replied, "Even if it were a toothstick from the Arâk tree."[18]

The means by which a claim is affirmed

The means by which a claim is affirmed are three: confession/ admission, witness testimony and an oath.[19]

Admission/confession

An admission is where one accepts the opponents claim. It is obligatory to act upon such an admission as long as the one doing the admitting is a non-coerced legally responsible individual. The Prophet (ﷺ) had Mâ'iz, the woman from the Tribe of Ghâmid and the woman from the Tribe of Juhan each stoned based on their confessions. The Prophet (ﷺ) said, "Go, O' Unays, to that woman and if she confesses, stone her to death."[20]

Witness Testimony

Concerning the rights of human beings, bearing witness is a communal obligation. Allah (ﷻ) has said:

﴿... وَلَا يَأْبَ ٱلشُّهَدَآءُ إِذَا مَا دُعُوا۟ ... ﴿٢٨٢﴾﴾ (سورة البقرة: ٢٨٢)

﴾... And the witnesses should not refuse when they are called on...﴿ *(Qur'an 2: 282)*

[18] This hadith is *ṣaḥeeḥ*. See Shaykh al-Albâni, *Ṣaḥeeḥ Sunan Ibn Mâjah*, no. 1882. Recorded by Ibn Mâjah. Muslim and Nasâ'i have something similar.
[19] Cf., as-Sayyid Sâbiq, *Fiqh as-Sunnah*, vol. 3, p. 328.
[20] This story shall be presented shortly.

Providing witness testimony is an individual obligation, as Allah (ﷻ) has said:

﴿... وَلَا تَكْتُمُوا۟ ٱلشَّهَـٰدَةَ ۚ وَمَن يَكْتُمْهَا فَإِنَّهُۥٓ ءَاثِمٌ قَلْبُهُۥ ... ﴿٢٨٣﴾﴾

(سورة البقرة: ٢٨٣)

﴿... And conceal not the evidence for he, who hides it, surely his heart is sinful...﴾ *(Qur'an 2: 283)*

It is obligatory upon the witness to speak the truth, even if it be against his own interest. Allah has said:

﴿۞ يَـٰٓأَيُّهَا ٱلَّذِينَ ءَامَنُوا۟ كُونُوا۟ قَوَّٰمِينَ بِٱلْقِسْطِ شُهَدَآءَ لِلَّهِ وَلَوْ عَلَىٰٓ أَنفُسِكُمْ أَوِ ٱلْوَٰلِدَيْنِ وَٱلْأَقْرَبِينَ ۚ إِن يَكُنْ غَنِيًّا أَوْ فَقِيرًا فَٱللَّهُ أَوْلَىٰ بِهِمَا ۖ فَلَا تَتَّبِعُوا۟ ٱلْهَوَىٰٓ أَن تَعْدِلُوا۟ ۚ وَإِن تَلْوُۥٓا۟ أَوْ تُعْرِضُوا۟ فَإِنَّ ٱللَّهَ كَانَ بِمَا تَعْمَلُونَ خَبِيرًا ﴿١٣٥﴾﴾

(سورة النساء: ١٣٥)

﴿O' you who believe! Stand out firmly for justice, as witnesses to Allah, even though it be against yourselves, or your parents, or your kin, be he rich or poor, Allah is a Better Protector to both [than you]. So follow not the lusts [of your hearts], lest you may avoid justice, and if you distort your witness or refuse to give it, verily, Allah is Ever Well-Acquainted with what you do.﴾ *(Qur'an 4: 135)*

It is forbidden for a person to bear testimony that is not based on knowledge. Allah (ﷻ) says: ﴿Except those who bear witness to the truth while they know﴾ *(Qur'an 43: 86).*

Bearing false witness is one of the greatest of the great sins. Abu Bakrah said, "The Prophet (ﷺ) said three times, 'Shall I not inform you of the greatest of the great sins?' They said, 'Certainly, O' Messenger of Allah.' He said, 'Associating partners with Allah, being undutiful to one's parents,' and then he sat up while before he was reclining and said, 'And certainly giving false witness,' and he continued to say that until we said, 'If only he would be silent.' "[21]

Whose testimony is to be accepted

Testimony is only to be accepted from an adult, sane, righteous/reputable Muslim.

The testimony of a disbeliever is not to be accepted, even if it be against one of his own, as Allah (ﷻ) has said:

﴿... وَأَشْهِدُوا۟ ذَوَىْ عَدْلٍ مِّنكُمْ ... ﴿٢﴾﴾ (سورة الطّلاق: ٢)

﴿... And take for witness two just persons from among you...﴾ *(Qur'an 65: 2)*

Allah also says:

﴿... مِمَّن تَرْضَوْنَ مِنَ ٱلشُّهَدَآءِ ... ﴿٢٨٢﴾﴾ (سورة البَقـرَة: ٢٨٢)

﴿... From those you approve of as witnesses...﴾ *(Qur'an 2: 282)*

"A disbeliever is not reputable, he is not approved of and he is not from among us."[22]

The testimony of a youngster is also not accepted. Allah says:

﴿... وَٱسْتَشْهِدُوا۟ شَهِيدَيْنِ مِن رِّجَالِكُمْ ... ﴿٢٨٢﴾﴾ (سورة البَقـرَة: ٢٨٢)

﴿... And get two witnesses out of your own men...﴾ *(Qur'an 2: 282)*

— and a youngster is not from "our own men".

---

[21] Recorded by Bukhari and Muslim.

[22] *Manâr as-Sabeel*, vol. 2, p. 486.

The witness of an imbecile, insane person and the likes is not accepted. Their witness cannot be accepted against themselves and, therefore, certainly cannot be accepted against others.

The testimony of an evildoer is not acceptable as Allah (ﷻ) has said:

﴿... وَأَشْهِدُوا ذَوَىْ عَدْلٍ مِّنكُمْ ... ﴿٢﴾﴾ (سورة الطّلاق: ٢)

﴿... And take for witness two just persons from among you...﴾ *(Qur'an 65: 2)*

The Prophet (ﷺ) also said, "The testimony of a deceitful man, a deceitful woman, a fornicator, a fornicatress or one who harbours ill feelings towards his brothers is not permissible."[23]

The minimum number of witnesses

Rights of are two types, what are known as the "right of Allah" and the right of humans.[24]

As for the rights of humans, they can be subdivided into three categories:

1. Those concerning which only the witness of two men is accepted

These are matters not concerning financial issues and which are attended by men, such as marriage and divorce.

Allah (ﷻ) says:

---

[23] This hadith is *ḥasan*. See Shaykh al-Albâni, *Ṣaḥeeḥ Sunan Ibn Mâjah*, no. 1916. Recorded by Abu Dawood and Ibn Mâjah. Ibn Mâjah has a statement in the middle saying, "One who has had the legal punishment applied to him in Islam."

[24] The text of *al-Ghâyah* and *at-Taqreeb*.

﴿فَإِذَا بَلَغْنَ أَجَلَهُنَّ فَأَمْسِكُوهُنَّ بِمَعْرُوفٍ أَوْ فَارِقُوهُنَّ بِمَعْرُوفٍ وَأَشْهِدُواْ ذَوَىٰ

عَدْلٍ مِّنكُمْ ... ﴿٢﴾﴾   (سورة الطَّلَاق: ٢)

❲Then when they are about to fulfill their term appointed, either take them back in a good manner or part with them in a good manner. And take for witness two just men from among you [Muslims]...❳

(Qur'an 65: 2)

The Prophet (ﷺ) said, "There is no marriage except with a guardian and two reputable witnesses."[25] In this verse and hadith, witnesses have been mentioned in the masculine form only.

2. Those concerning which the witness of two men or one man and two women or one man and an oath are accepted

These are matters concerning wealth, such as buying, selling, renting, pawning and the like. Allah says:

﴿ ... وَٱسْتَشْهِدُواْ شَهِيدَيْنِ مِن رِّجَالِكُمْ فَإِن لَّمْ يَكُونَا رَجُلَيْنِ فَرَجُلٌ

وَٱمْرَأَتَانِ مِمَّن تَرْضَوْنَ مِنَ ٱلشُّهَدَآءِ أَن تَضِلَّ إِحْدَىٰهُمَا فَتُذَكِّرَ إِحْدَىٰهُمَا

ٱلْأُخْرَىٰ ... ﴿٢٨٢﴾﴾   (سورة الْبَقَرَة: ٢٨٢)

❲... And get two witnesses out of your own men. And if there are not two men [available], then a man and two women, such as you agree for witnesses, so that if one of them [two women] errs, the other can remind her...❳

(Qur'an 2: 282)

Ibn 'Abbâs narrated that the Messenger of Allah (ﷺ) decided a case based on an oath and one witness.[26]

---

[25] This hadith is *ṣaḥeeḥ*. See Shaykh al-Albâni, *Ṣaḥeeḥ al-Jâmi' aṣ-Ṣagheer*, no. 7557. Recorded by al-Bayhaqi and Ibn Ḥibbân.

[26] This hadith is *ṣaḥeeḥ*. See Shaykh al-Albâni, *Ṣaḥeeḥ Sunan Ibn Mâjah*, no. 1920. Recorded by Muslim, Ibn Mâjah and Abu Dawood.

3. Those concerning which two men, a man and two women or four women are accepted

These are matters that men, in general, are not witness to, such as breastfeeding, pregnancy and non-obvious diseases and conditions of women.

As for the "rights of Allah", (which herein refers mostly to the fixed prescribed punishments), the testimony of women are not accepted. Az-Zuhri said, "No one is to be flogged due to any of the fixed prescribed punishments except due to the witness of two men." This can be further subdivided into three categories:

1. Those concerning which not less than four witnesses will be accepted

This concerns the case of *zinâ*. Allah (ﷻ) says:

﴿وَالَّذِينَ يَرْمُونَ الْمُحْصَنَاتِ ثُمَّ لَمْ يَأْتُوا بِأَرْبَعَةِ شُهَدَاءَ فَاجْلِدُوهُمْ ثَمَانِينَ جَلْدَةً ... ﴿٤﴾﴾

(سورة النّور: ٤)

﴾And those who accuse chaste women, and produce not four witnesses, flog them with eighty stripes...﴿ *(Qur'an 24: 4)*

2. Those concerning which two witnesses will be accepted

This concerns the fixed prescribed punishments other than *zinâ*, based on the statement of az-Zuhri quoted above.

3. Those concerning which one witness is accepted

This concerns the sighting the new moon for the beginning of the month of Ramaḍân.[27]

---

[27] See the earlier section on the fast of Ramaḍân.

Taking an oath

If the plaintiff is not able to present any proof and the defendant denies his charge, then the claimant can only ask the defendant to make an oath (freeing himself from the claim). The Prophet (ﷺ) said, "The burden of proof is upon the plaintiff and the taking of an oath is upon the one against whom the claim is being made."[28]

Al-Ash'ath ibn Qays al-Kindi said, "There was a dispute between me and another man concerning a well. We took our dispute to the Messenger of Allah (ﷺ) and he said (to me), '(Present your) two witnesses or his oath (can be made as his defense).' I said, 'He will then go ahead and take an oath and not care.' The Messenger of Allah (ﷺ) then said, 'If someone makes an oath receiving thereby some wealth while he was being deceitful, then he will meet Allah while Allah is angered with him.' Then, in affirmation of this, Allah (سبحانه وتعالى) revealed the verses:

﴿إِنَّ ٱلَّذِينَ يَشۡتَرُونَ بِعَهۡدِ ٱللَّهِ وَأَيۡمَٰنِهِمۡ ثَمَنٗا قَلِيلًا أُوْلَٰٓئِكَ لَا خَلَٰقَ لَهُمۡ فِي ٱلۡأٓخِرَةِ وَلَا يُكَلِّمُهُمُ ٱللَّهُ وَلَا يَنظُرُ إِلَيۡهِمۡ يَوۡمَ ٱلۡقِيَٰمَةِ وَلَا يُزَكِّيهِمۡ وَلَهُمۡ عَذَابٌ أَلِيمٞ ٧٧﴾ (سورة آل عِمرَان: ٧٧)

﴾Verily, those who purchase a small gain at the cost of Allah's Covenant and their oaths, they shall have no portion in the Hereafter. Neither will Allah speak to them, nor look at them on the Day of Resurrection, nor will He purify them, and they shall have a painful torment.﴿ *(Qur'an 3: 77)*."[29]

---

[28] This hadith is *ṣaḥeeḥ*. See Shaykh al-Albâni, *Ṣaḥeeḥ al-Jâmi' aṣ-Ṣagheer*, no. 2896. Recorded by Tirmidhi.

[29] Recorded by Bukhari.

Chapter Sixteen — Jihad[1]

Definition[2]

Jihad comes from the word *juhd*, meaning ability and toil. One says *jâhada* (perfect tense), *yujâhidu* (imperfect tense), *jihâd* and *mujâhadah* (verbal nouns) when one exerts all of one's efforts and uses all of one's ability, bearing extraordinary effort when fighting and repelling the enemy.

An exertion is not called a jihad in its true sense unless it is done for the sake of Allah, seeking to elevate His word, raise the standard of truth, repel falsehood and exerting oneself for the Allah's pleasure. If someone is intending something less than that of the pleasures of this world, then his actions cannot be called a jihad in the true sense. The one who fights to gain a position, to receive the spoils of war, to demonstrate his bravery or to gain some fame will receive no portion of reward or recompense. Abu Moosa narrated that a man came to the Prophet (ﷺ) and said, "A man fights for the bounty, another man fights to be mentioned (among those who fought) and another fights for show. Which is the one who fights for the cause of Allah?" He answered, "The one who fights to make the word of Allah supreme is the one who (fights) for the cause of Allah."[3]

---

[1] For more details, see my thesis which I prepared for my Master's degree, entitled *al-Ḥarb wa as-Salâm fee al-Islâm fee Dhau' Soorah Muhammad*.

[2] As-Sayyid Sâbiq, *Fiqh as-Sunnah*, vol. 3, Pp. 27 and 40.

[3] Recorded by Bukhari, Muslim, Abu Dawood, Tirmidhi and Ibn Mâjah.

Exhortation to Take Part in Jihad

Abu Hurayrah (⬤) narrated that the Messenger of Allah (⬤) stated, "Whoever believes in Allah and His Messenger, establishes the prayer and fasts Ramaḍân has a right upon Allah that He shall enter him into Paradise, whether he strove for the sake of Allah or simply sat in the land in which he was born." They (around him) said, "Shall we not give the people this good news?" He replied, "In Paradise there are one-hundred grades that Allah has prepared for those who strive for the sake of Allah. Between each grade is the distance between the sky and the earth. If you ask Allah, ask Him for *al-Firdaws*, it is the best part of Paradise and the highest part." (The subnarrator said,) "I think he said, 'Above it is the Throne of the Merciful and from it flow the rivers of Paradise.' "[4]

He also narrated that the Messenger of Allah (⬤) said, "The similitude of the one who makes jihad for the sake of Allah is like a fasting and praying person who is reading the verses of Allah and does not stop fasting and praying until the one who made jihad for the sake of Allah returns."[5]

He also narrated that the Messenger of Allah (⬤) said, "Allah has guaranteed that whoever fights in His cause, and is motivated by nothing except belief in Me and affirmation of My messengers, either will be recompensed with reward or booty (if he survives), or will be admitted to Paradise (if he is killed)."[6]

---

[4] This hadith is *ṣaheeḥ*. See Shaykh al-Albâni, *Ṣaheeḥ al-Jâmi' aṣ-Ṣagheer*, no. 2126 and *Silsilat al-Aḥâdeeth aṣ-Ṣaheeḥah*, no. 921. Recorded by Bukhari.

[5] This hadith is *ṣaheeḥ*. See Shaykh al-Albâni, *Ṣaheeḥ al-Jâmi' aṣ-Ṣagheer*, no. 2126. Recorded by Muslim and Tirmidhi.

[6] Recorded by Bukhari and Muslim.

The Excellence of Martyrdom

Masrooq said, "We asked 'Abdullâh ibn Mas'ood about the verse:

﴿وَلَا تَحْسَبَنَّ ٱلَّذِينَ قُتِلُوا۟ فِى سَبِيلِ ٱللَّهِ أَمْوَٰتًۢا ۚ بَلْ أَحْيَآءٌ عِندَ رَبِّهِمْ يُرْزَقُونَ ﴿١٦٩﴾﴾

(سورة آل عمران: ١٦٩)

﴿Think not of those who are killed in the Way of Allah as dead. Nay, they are alive, with their Lord, and they have provision.﴾

(Qur'an 3: 169)

He said, 'We asked the Messenger of Allah (ﷺ) about that.' He replied, 'Their souls are in the bodies of green birds that have nests hanging onto the Throne. They go about freely and eat from Paradise wherever they like and then return to those nests. Their Lord glanced at them and said, 'Do you desire anything?' They say, 'What thing can we desire when we go about freely in Paradise wherever we wish.' He asked them that three times. When they saw that He would continue to ask them, they said, 'O' Lord, we wish that our souls would be returned to our bodies so that we could fight for Your sake again.' When He saw that they were not in need, they were left (to enjoy their stay in Paradise).' "[7]

Anas narrated that ar-Rubayyi' bint al-Barâ', who was the mother of Ḥârithah ibn Surâqah, came to the Prophet (ﷺ) and said, "O' Prophet of Allah, will you not tell me about Ḥârithah, — and he had been killed on the Day of Badr, shot by an arrow coming from an unknown archer — for if he is in Paradise, I shall be patient but it is other than that, I shall exert myself in crying for him." The Prophet (ﷺ) said, "O' Umm Ḥârithah, there are (many) gardens in Paradise

---

[7] This hadith is *ṣaḥeeḥ*. See Shaykh al-Albâni, *Mukhtasar Ṣaḥeeḥ Muslim*, no. 1068. Recorded by Muslim and Tirmidhi.

and your son received the highest garden, *al-Firdaws*."[8]

Al-Miqdâm ibn M'adi Karib said that the Messenger of Allah (ﷺ) said, "The martyr will have six traits with Allah: He will be forgiven at the first moment (he bleeds); he will see his seat in Paradise (while in the grave); he will be protected from the punishment of the grave; he will be safe from the Great Frightening (on the Day of Judgment); on his head will be place a crown of glory a ruby of which will be better than the world and what it contains; he will be wed to seventy maidens with large black eyes; and he will intercede for seventy of his relatives."[9]

Abu Hurayrah (رضي الله عنه) stated that the Messenger of Allah (ﷺ) said, "The martyr does not feel any of the pain of being killed except like what one of you feels as the pain of a pinch."[10]

Intimidation Concerning Abandoning Jihad

Allah (سبحانه وتعالى) says:

﴿يَـٰٓأَيُّهَا ٱلَّذِينَ ءَامَنُوا۟ مَا لَكُمْ إِذَا قِيلَ لَكُمُ ٱنفِرُوا۟ فِى سَبِيلِ ٱللَّهِ ٱثَّاقَلْتُمْ
إِلَى ٱلْأَرْضِ ۚ أَرَضِيتُم بِٱلْحَيَوٰةِ ٱلدُّنْيَا مِنَ ٱلْـَٔاخِرَةِ ۚ فَمَا مَتَـٰعُ ٱلْحَيَوٰةِ
ٱلدُّنْيَا فِى ٱلْـَٔاخِرَةِ إِلَّا قَلِيلٌ ﴿٣٨﴾ إِلَّا تَنفِرُوا۟ يُعَذِّبْكُمْ عَذَابًا أَلِيمًا
وَيَسْتَبْدِلْ قَوْمًا غَيْرَكُمْ وَلَا تَضُرُّوهُ شَيْـًٔا ۗ وَٱللَّهُ عَلَىٰ كُلِّ شَىْءٍ قَدِيرٌ
﴿٣٩﴾﴾ (سورة التوبة: ٣٨-٣٩)

---

[8] This hadith is *ṣaḥeeḥ*. See Shaykh al-Albâni, *Ṣaḥeeḥ al-Jâmi' aṣ-Ṣagheer*, no. 7852. Recorded by Bukhari and Tirmidhi.

[9] This hadith is *ṣaḥeeḥ*. See Shaykh al-Albâni, *Ṣaḥeeḥ Sunan Ibn Mâjah*, no. 2257. Recorded by Tirmidhi and Ibn Mâjah.

[10] This hadith is *ḥasan ṣaḥeeḥ*. See Shaykh al-Albâni, *Ṣaḥeeḥ al-Jâmi' aṣ-Ṣagheer*, no. 2260. Recorded by Tirmidhi, Ibn Mâjah and Nasâ'i.

﴾O' you who believe! What is the matter with you, that when you are asked to march forth in the Cause of Allah [i.e. Jihâd] you cling heavily to the earth? Are you pleased with the life of this world rather than the Hereafter? But little is the enjoyment of the life of this world as compared with the Hereafter. If you march not forth, He will punish you with a painful torment and will replace you by another people, and you cannot harm Him at all, and Allah is Able to do all things.﴿ *(Qur'an 9: 38-39)*

In another verse, Allah states:

﴿وَأَنفِقُوا فِي سَبِيلِ اللَّهِ وَلَا تُلْقُوا بِأَيْدِيكُمْ إِلَى التَّهْلُكَةِ ... ﴿١٩٥﴾﴾

(سورة البقرة: ١٩٥)

﴾And spend in the Cause of Allah and do not throw yourselves into destruction...﴿ *(Qur'an 2: 195)*

While commenting on this verse, Ibn Katheer wrote:

> "Al-Layth ibn S'ad narrated from Yazeed ibn Abi Ḥabeeb on the authority of Aslam Abu 'Imrân who said, 'One of the *Muhajireen* went up against the rows of the enemy at Constantinople until he broke through it. At the time, Abu Ayyoob al-Anṣâri was with us. Some people said, 'He led himself to his destruction by his own hands (referring to the above verse).' Abu Ayyoob then said, 'We are most aware of the meaning of this verse. It was revealed with respect to us. We accompanied the Messenger of Allah and we participated in battles with him and were given victory. When Islam spread and became dominant, we, the Anṣâr, met and said to each other, 'We have been honoured by Allah by being companions to His prophet and He helped him until Islam spread and its adherents became many. We have given it preference over our wives, wealth and children. Now the war has put down its burden and we can go back to our wives and children and stay

with them.' Then Allah revealed concerning us, ﴾And spend in the Cause of Allah and do not throw yourselves into destruction﴿. Thus, 'destruction' refers to staying with one's family and wealth while abandoning the jihad.' This was recorded by Abu Dawood, Tirmidhi, Nasâ'i, 'Abd ibn Ḥumaid in his *Tafseer*, Ibn Abi Ḥâtim, Ibn Jareer, Ibn Marduwaih, al-Ḥâfidh Abu Ya'la al-Muṣali in his *Musnad*, Ibn Ḥibbân in his *Ṣaḥeeḥ* and al-Ḥâkim in his *Mustadrak*. All of them record it from the hadith of Yazeed ibn Abi Habeeb. Tirmidhi said, 'It is *hasan ṣaḥeeḥ ghareeb*.' Al-Ḥâkim says that it meets the conditions of Bukhari and Muslim although they did not record it.' "[11]

Ibn 'Umar narrated that the Prophet (ﷺ) said, "If you begin to participate in *al-'eenah*[12], take after the tails of cows, become pleased with agriculture and leave jihad in the way of Allah, Allah will inflict upon you a disgrace that will not leave you until you return to their religion."[13]

Its Ruling

Allah (ﷻ) has said:

﴿كُتِبَ عَلَيْكُمُ ٱلْقِتَالُ وَهُوَ كُرْهٌ لَّكُمْ وَعَسَىٰٓ أَن تَكْرَهُوا۟ شَيْـًٔا وَهُوَ خَيْرٌ لَّكُمْ وَعَسَىٰٓ أَن تُحِبُّوا۟ شَيْـًٔا وَهُوَ شَرٌّ لَّكُمْ وَٱللَّهُ يَعْلَمُ وَأَنتُمْ لَا تَعْلَمُونَ ﴿٢١٦﴾﴿

(سورة البقرة: ٢١٦)

---

[11] Tafseer ibn Katheer, vol. 1, p. 228. This hadith is *ṣaḥeeḥ*. See Shaykh al-Albâni, *Ṣaḥeeḥ Sunan Abi Dawood*, no. 2187. Recorded by Abu Dawood, Tirmidhi and al-Ḥâkim.

[12] [A business transaction involving interest.] - Translator

[13] This hadith is *ṣaḥeeḥ*. See Shaykh al-Albâni, *Ṣaḥeeḥ al-Jâmi' aṣ-Ṣagheer*, no. 423. [Recorded by Aḥmad, Abu Dawood and others.]

﴾Fighting is ordained for you [Muslims] though you dislike it, and it may be that you dislike a thing which is good for you and that you like a thing which is bad for you. Allah knows but you do not know.﴿ *(Qur'an 2: 216)*

Jihad is a communal obligation, as Allah has said:

﴿لَّا يَسْتَوِى ٱلْقَٰعِدُونَ مِنَ ٱلْمُؤْمِنِينَ غَيْرُ أُو۟لِى ٱلضَّرَرِ وَٱلْمُجَٰهِدُونَ فِى سَبِيلِ ٱللَّهِ بِأَمْوَٰلِهِمْ وَأَنفُسِهِمْ ۚ فَضَّلَ ٱللَّهُ ٱلْمُجَٰهِدِينَ بِأَمْوَٰلِهِمْ وَأَنفُسِهِمْ عَلَى ٱلْقَٰعِدِينَ دَرَجَةً ۚ وَكُلًّا وَعَدَ ٱللَّهُ ٱلْحُسْنَىٰ ۚ وَفَضَّلَ ٱللَّهُ ٱلْمُجَٰهِدِينَ عَلَى ٱلْقَٰعِدِينَ أَجْرًا عَظِيمًا ﴿٩٥﴾﴿

(سورة النِّسَاء: ٩٥)

﴾Not equal are those of the believers who sit [at home], except those who are disabled, and those who strive hard and fight in the Cause of Allah with their wealth and their lives. Allah has preferred in grades those who strive hard and fight with their wealth and their lives above those who sit [at home]. Unto each, Allah has promised good [Paradise], but Allah has preferred those who strive hard and fight, above those who sit [at home] by a huge reward.﴿ *(Qur'an 4: 95)*

"Allah has informed that there is greater virtue for those who strive for His sake while both they and those who sit at home shall receive what is good. If those who sat at home were failing to perform an obligation, they would then receive what is evil and not what is good."[14]

You should realize that it is recommended to make jihad often, based on the verses and the reports concerning it. The minimum that is obligatory in a year is once, as the Prophet (ﷺ) did not leave any year after being obliged to make jihad except that he made it at least once. Following his example is obligatory. Furthermore, this is a

---

[14] *Tafseer aṭ-Ṭabari*, vol. 2, p. 345.

recurring obligation and the minimum required to meet the recurring obligation is once per year, like fasting and Zakah. If need requires more than once in a year, more than once is obligatory, as it is a communal obligation and must be determined according to its need. And Allah alone knows best.[15] However, we must understand and the people as well must understand that there is no fighting in Islam until after the announcement of the beginning of hostilities. Furthermore, the enemy must first receive a choice between accepting Islam, paying the *jizyah*[16] or fighting. Additionally, agreed upon pacts, if any, must be openly repudiated, in the case of fearing betrayal. The final pact will be with the non-Muslim citizens accepting the authority of Islam and paying the *jizyah*. This is the only pact that is acceptable — unless the Muslims are in a state of weakness and therefore the ruler decides in their specific circumstances to agree, during that stage, to accept a treaty of some sort.[17]

The Etiquette of Fighting

Buraydah said, "Whenever the Messenger of Allah (ﷺ) appointed anyone as leader an army or detachment he would especially exhort him to fear Allah and to be good to the Muslims who were with him. He would say, 'Fight in the name of Allah and for the sake of Allah. Fight against those who disbelieve in Allah. Go in warfare and do not embezzle the spoils; do not break your pledge; and do not mutilate (the dead) bodies; do not kill the children. When

---

[15] [At this point in the original, the author makes a mark signifying that this is the end of a quote. However, there was no sign as to a beginning of a quote nor as to where this quote was from.] - Translator

[16] [The *jizyah* is the poll-tax paid by non-Muslim citizens of the Islamic state in lieu of military service.]

[17] Sayyid Quṭb, *adh-Dhilâl*. [No volume or page number was given in the reference.]

you meet your enemies who are polytheists, invite them to three courses of action. If they respond to any one of these, accept it and refrain from (fighting) them. Invite them to (accept) Islam; if they respond to you, accept it from them and desist from fighting against them. Then invite them to migrate from their lands to the land of Emigrants (in Madeenah) and inform them that, if they do so, they shall have all the privileges and obligations of the Emigrants. If they refuse to migrate, tell them that they will have the status of Bedouin Muslims and will be subjected to the Commands of Allah that are enforced upon the believers, but they will not get any share from the spoils of war or *fai'*[18] except when they actually fight with the Muslims. If they refuse to accept Islam, demand from them the *jizyah*. If they agree to pay it, accept that from them and refrain from (fighting) them. If they refuse to pay the *jizyah*, seek Allah's help and fight them.'"[19]

Ibn 'Umar said, "A woman was found dead after one of battles of the Messenger of Allah (ﷺ). Therefore, the Messenger of Allah (ﷺ) forbade the killing of women and children."[20]

The Prophet (ﷺ) sent Mu'âdh ibn Jabal (رضي الله عنه) as a teacher to the people of Yemen. He advised with the following, "You are coming to a people from the People of the Book. Invite them to testify that there is none worthy of worship except Allah and that I am the Messenger of Allah. If they obey you in that, inform them that Allah has obligated five prayers upon them in every day and night. If they obey you in that, inform them that Allah has obligated a charity upon them that is to be taken from their rich and returned to their poor. If they obey you in that, beware of taking the best of their

---

[18] [*Fai'* refers to wealth surrendered to Muslims without any fighting.]

[19] This hadith is *ṣaḥeeḥ*. See Shaykh al-Albâni, *Mukhtasar Ṣaḥeeḥ Muslim*, no. 1111. Recorded by Muslim and by Tirmidhi is abridged form.

[20] Recorded by Bukhari, Muslim, Abu Dawood, Tirmidhi and Ibn Mâjah.

wealth and fear the supplication of the oppressed for there is no barrier between it and Allah."[21]

Upon Whom is Jihad Obligatory

Jihad is obligatory upon ever adult, sane, free, male Muslim who has the ability to fight and has the financial means to support himself and his family in his absence.

As for the requirement of being a Muslim, this is obvious as jihad is fighting against the disbelievers.

As for the requirement of being an adult and not a child, it is based on the statement of Ibn 'Umar, "I was presented to the Messenger of Allah (ﷺ) for the Battle of Uḥud while I was fourteen years old and he did not permit me. I was then presented for the Battle of Khandaq while I was fifteen and he permitted me."[22]

As for the requirement of being sane and not otherwise, it is based on the hadith presented earlier, "The pen (recording the deeds) has been raised (and is not recording) for three: the one who is sleeping until he awakens, the child until he reaches the age of puberty and the insane one until he becomes sane."[23]

As for the requirement of being male, this is based on the hadith of 'Â'ishah (رضي الله عنها) who said, "O' Messenger of Allah, is there any jihad upon women?" He replied, "Yes, upon them is a type of jihad that does not include in it fighting: the Ḥajj and 'Umrah."[24]

---

[21] Recorded by Bukhari and Muslim.

[22] Recorded by Bukhari, Muslim, Tirmidhi, Nasâ'i and Abu Dawood.

[23] This hadith is *ṣaḥeeḥ*. See Shaykh al-Albâni, *Ṣaḥeeḥ al-Jâmi'*, no. 3513. Recorded by Abu Dawood.

[24] This hadith is *ṣaḥeeḥ*. See Shaykh al-Albâni, *Ṣaḥeeḥ Sunan Ibn Mâjah*, no. 2345. Recorded by Ibn Mâjah, Aḥmad and ad-Dâraquṭni.

As for jihad not being obligatory upon the will and those without financial means, this is based on Allah's words:

﴿لَّيْسَ عَلَى ٱلضُّعَفَآءِ وَلَا عَلَى ٱلْمَرْضَىٰ وَلَا عَلَى ٱلَّذِينَ لَا يَجِدُونَ مَا يُنفِقُونَ حَرَجٌ إِذَا نَصَحُوا۟ لِلَّهِ وَرَسُولِهِۦ ... ﴿٩١﴾﴾ (سورة التوبة: ٩١)

﴾There is no blame on those who are weak or ill or who find no resources to spend [for Jihad], if they are sincere and true [in duty] to Allah and His Messenger...﴿ *(Qur'an 9: 91)*

As for jihad not being obligatory upon non-free people, it is because the slave is the property of his owner and cannot perform jihad without his owner's permission.

When Does Jihad Become an Individual Obligation

Jihad is not an individual obligation except under the following circumstances:

1. When the legally responsible person finds himself in the rows of the battle

Allah (ﷻ) says:

﴿يَـٰٓأَيُّهَا ٱلَّذِينَ ءَامَنُوٓا۟ إِذَا لَقِيتُمْ فِئَةً فَٱثْبُتُوا۟ ... ﴿٤٥﴾﴾ (سورة الأنفال: ٤٥)

﴾O' you who believe! When you meet [an enemy] force, take a firm stand against them...﴿ *(Qur'an 8: 45)*

Allah also says:

﴿يَـٰٓأَيُّهَا ٱلَّذِينَ ءَامَنُوٓا۟ إِذَا لَقِيتُمُ ٱلَّذِينَ كَفَرُوا۟ زَحْفًا فَلَا تُوَلُّوهُمُ ٱلْأَدْبَارَ ﴿١٥﴾﴾ (سورة الأنفال: ١٥)

﴾O' you who believe! When you meet those who disbelieve, in a battlefield, never turn your backs to them.﴿ *(Qur'an 8: 15)*

2. When the enemy invades any land of the Muslim lands

3. When the ruler calls for a general enlistment and participation upon those legally capable

The Prophet (ﷺ) said, "There is no emigration (to Madeenah) after the conquering of Makkah. However, there is still jihad and (proper) intention. If you are all called to go out (for jihad), then you should all go out (for jihad)."[25]

Prisoners of war

Disbelievers who are captured are of two types. One type can be made slaves due to their being captured. These are the women and the children, as the Prophet (ﷺ) forbade the killing of women and children.[26] The Prophet (ﷺ) used to distribute such prisoners in the same way that he would distribute wealth.

The second type refers to those that do not become slaves due to their being captured. These are the adult males. The Muslim leader has the option of having them killed, enslaving them, setting them free or ransoming them for wealth or men (such as Muslim prisoners held by the enemy). He does any of these according to the interests of the Muslim state. Allah (ﷻ) has said:

﴿مَا كَانَ لِنَبِيٍّ أَن يَكُونَ لَهُۥٓ أَسْرَىٰ حَتَّىٰ يُثْخِنَ فِي ٱلْأَرْضِ ... ﴿٦٧﴾﴾

(سورة الأنفال: ٦٧)

﴾It is not for a Prophet that he should have prisoners of war [and free

[25] Recorded by Bukhari, Muslim, Tirmidhi and Abu Dawood.

[26] Recorded by Bukhari, Muslim, Abu Dawood, Tirmidhi and Ibn Mâjah.

them with ransom] until he had made a great slaughter [among his enemies] in the land...❵ *(Qur'an 8: 67)*

The Prophet (ﷺ) had the mean of thc Tribe of Quray<u>dh</u>ah killed, he enslaved the men from the Tribe of Muṣṭalaq, he freed Abu al-'Âṣ ibn ar-Rabee' and Thumâmah ibn Athâl, he ransomed the prisoners of Badr for money and he also freed a polytheist from the Tribe of 'Uqayl in exchange for two of his Companions. Allah (ﷻ) has said:

﴿فَإِذَا لَقِيتُمُ ٱلَّذِينَ كَفَرُوا۟ فَضَرْبَ ٱلرِّقَابِ حَتَّىٰٓ إِذَآ أَثْخَنتُمُوهُمْ فَشُدُّوا۟ ٱلْوَثَاقَ فَإِمَّا مَنًّۢا بَعْدُ وَإِمَّا فِدَآءً حَتَّىٰ تَضَعَ ٱلْحَرْبُ أَوْزَارَهَا ... ﴿٤﴾﴾ (سورة محمد: ٤)

❴So, when you meet [in fighting] those who disbelieve smite at their necks till when you have killed and wounded many of them, then bind a bond firmly [on them, i.e. take them as captives]. Thereafter [is the time] either for generosity [i.e. free them without ransom], or ransom [according to what benefits Islam], until the war lays down its burden...❵ *(Qur'an 47: 4)*

The Salb

[The Prophet (ﷺ) said,] "If a person kills an opponent (in battle), for him is his *salb*."[27] The *salb* refers to what the enemy has on his body at the time of being killed, including his clothing, jewellery, weaponry and even his mount if he was killed while riding one.

The war booty

The war booty is distributed after the *salb*. Four-fifths of the war booty goes to those who took part in the battle. The foot soldier

---

[27] Recorded by Bukhari, Muslim, Tirmidhi and Abu Dawood. [Actually, all of these record it with the wording, "If a person kills an opponent (in battle)=

receives one share while the horseman receives three shares.

Allah has said:

﴿وَاعْلَمُوٓا۟ أَنَّمَا غَنِمْتُم مِّن شَىْءٍ فَأَنَّ لِلَّهِ خُمُسَهُۥ وَلِلرَّسُولِ وَلِذِى ٱلْقُرْبَىٰ وَٱلْيَتَٰمَىٰ وَٱلْمَسَٰكِينِ وَٱبْنِ ٱلسَّبِيلِ ... ﴿٤١﴾﴾ (سورة الأنفال: ٤١)

﴿And know that whatever of war-booty that you may gain, verily one-fifth of it is assigned to Allah, and to the Messenger, and to the near relatives [of the Messenger], [and also] the orphans, the poor and the wayfarer...﴾ *(Qur'an 8: 41)*

Ibn 'Umar said, "I saw the war booty divided into five parts and then distributed via their shares. What was given to the Messenger of Allah (ﷺ) he was free to decide how to divide it."[28] He also said, "The Messenger of Allah (ﷺ) distributed the shares on the Day of Khaybar: the horseman receiving three shares, for the horse two shares and for the soldier one share."[29] Ibn 'Abbâs said, "The Prophet (ﷺ) gave three shares to the horsemen and two shares to the footmen."[30]

The shares are only apportioned to those who meet five requirements: being a Muslim, adult, sane, free, and male. If any of these conditions is not met, then the person is given a small portion but he is not given a full share as the jihad is not obligatory on him or her.

=and he has evidence for that, for him is his *salb*."] - Translator

[28] [Recorded by Aḥmad.]

[29] This hadith is *ṣaḥeeḥ*. See Shaykh al-Albâni, *Ṣaḥeeḥ Sunan Ibn Mâjah*, no. 2303. Recorded by Ibn Mâjah. Without mentioning Khaybar, it is also recorded by Bukhari, Muslim and Abu Dawood.

[30] This hadith is *ṣaḥeeḥ*. See Shaykh al-Albâni, *I'rwâ' al-Ghaleel*, no. 1227. Recorded by al-Bayhaqi.

'Umayr, the ex-slave of Abi al-Laḥm, said, "I participated with my masters on the Day of Khaybar while I was a slave. I was not given a share of the war booty but I was given some household items. I would carry a sword, dragging it on the ground due to its weight."[31]

Ibn 'Abbâs said, "The Messenger of Allah (ﷺ) would go to war having women with him to attend to the injured. He gave them some amount from the war booty but he would not apportion for them actual shares."[32]

The distribution of al-Khumus

Al-Khumus (which is the one-fifth share out of the war booty) remaining is to be distributed as five shares: one share for the Messenger of Allah (ﷺ) — which after his time is to be used for the public interest — one share for his relatives, which are the Tribes of Hâshim and al-Muṭalib, one share for orphans, one share for poor and one share for travellers. Allah (ﷻ) has said: ﴿And know that whatever of war-booty that you may gain, verily one-fifth of it is assigned to Allah, and to the Messenger, and to the near relatives [of the Messenger], [and also] the orphans, the poor and the wayfarer...﴾ *(Qur'an 8: 41).*

The Fai'

As a legal term, this refers to everything that is taken from the disbelievers without any fighting, such as the wealth that they leave behind out of fear from the Muslims, the *jizyah*, the land-tax, wealth left behind by a non-Muslim citizen who has not legal heirs.

---

[31] This hadith is *ḥasan*. See Shaykh al-Albâni, *Ṣaḥeeḥ Sunan Ibn Mâjah*, no. 2304. Recorded by Tirmidhi, Abu Dawood and Ibn Mâjah.

[32] This hadith is *ṣaḥeeḥ*. See Shaykh al-Albâni, *Mukhtasar Ṣaḥeeḥ Muslim*, no. 1151. Recorded by Muslim, Abu Dawood and Tirmidhi.

The dhimmah pact

Dhimmah means a pact, security and protection. The *dhimmah* pact is where a ruler or his representative accepts for the People of the Book or other disbelievers to remain in their disbelief while adhering to the following two conditions:

1. They will pay the *jizyah* and
2. will adhere to the laws of Islam in general.[33]

The basis for this pact is in the words of Allah:

﴿قَـٰتِلُوا۟ ٱلَّذِينَ لَا يُؤْمِنُونَ بِٱللَّهِ وَلَا بِٱلْيَوْمِ ٱلْـَٔاخِرِ وَلَا يُحَرِّمُونَ مَا حَرَّمَ ٱللَّهُ وَرَسُولُهُۥ وَلَا يَدِينُونَ دِينَ ٱلْحَقِّ مِنَ ٱلَّذِينَ أُوتُوا۟ ٱلْكِتَـٰبَ حَتَّىٰ يُعْطُوا۟ ٱلْجِزْيَةَ عَن يَدٍ وَهُمْ صَـٰغِرُونَ ﴿٢٩﴾﴾ (سورة التوبة: ٢٩)

﴿Fight against those who believe not in Allah, nor in the Last Day, nor forbid that which has been forbidden by Allah and His Messenger and those who acknowledge not the religion of truth among the people of the Scripture [Jews and Christians], until they pay the *jizyah* with willing submission, and feel themselves subdued.﴾ *(Qur'an 9: 29)*

The obligations of this pact

If the *dhimmah* pact is concluded it means that it is forbidden to fight them, their wealth must be protected, their honour is to be respected, their freedom is guaranteed and they are not to be harmed.[34] The Prophet (ﷺ) said, "When you meet your enemies who are polytheists, invite them to three courses of action. If they respond to any one of these, accept it and refrain from (fighting) them. Invite

[33] Al-Sayyid Sâbiq, *Fiqh as-Sunnah*, vol. 3, p. 64.

[34] Ibid, p. 65.

them to (accept) Islam; if they respond to you, accept it from them and desist from fighting against them. Then invite them to migrate from their lands to the land of Emigrants (in Madeenah) and inform them that, if they do so, they shall have all the privileges and obligations of the Emigrants. If they refuse to migrate, tell them that they will have the status of Bedouin Muslims and will be subjected to the Commands of Allah that are enforced upon the believers, but they will not get any share from the spoils of war or *fai'*[35] except when they actually fight with the Muslims. If they refuse to accept Islam, demand from them the *jizyah*. If they agree to pay it, accept that from them and refrain from (fighting) them."[36]

The laws that the non-Muslim citizens must abide by

The laws of Islam are applied to the non-Muslim citizens with respect to the rights of humans, that is, with respect to contracts and dealings, compensation for injuries and damages and fixed prescribed punishments.[37] Anas narrated, "A Jew crushed the head of a slave-girl between two rocks. (As she was dying), she was asked, 'Who did this to you? Was it so and so?' They kept stating different names until they came to the name of the Jew and she motioned with her head. The Jew was brought and he confessed to the act. The Prophet (ﷺ) commanded that his head be crushed between two stones."[38] Ibn 'Umar said, "The Prophet (ﷺ) was brought two Jews who had committed adultery after being non-virgins and he had them both stoned."[39]

---

[35] [*Fai'* refers to wealth surrendered to Muslims without any fighting.]

[36] This hadith is *ṣaḥeeḥ*. See Shaykh al-Albâni, *Mukhtasar Ṣaḥeeḥ Muslim*, no. 1111. Recorded by Muslim and by Tirmidhi is abridged form.

[37] *Manâr as-Sabeel*, vol. 2, p. 298.

[38] By Bukhari, Muslim, Abu Dawood, Tirmidhi, Nasâ'i and Ibn Mâjah.

[39] This hadith is *ṣaḥeeḥ*. See Shaykh al-Albâni, *I'rwâ' al-Ghaleel*, no. 1253. [Recorded by Ibn Ḥibbân and al-Bayhaqi.]

When is the pact violated and negated

If anyone of the *dhimmis* refuse to pay the *jizyah* or abide by the laws of Islam, he has violated his pact as he is not fulfilling the conditions of the pact. Similarly, committing acts of aggression against the Muslim or cursing Allah and His Messenger will also negate the pact.

It is narrated that a man was brought to 'Umar who had tried to coerce a Muslim woman into committing *zinâ* with him. 'Umar (رضي الله عنه) said, "It is not upon this that we have made an agreement with you." He then ordered that he be crucified in Jerusalem.[40] 'Ali (رضي الله عنه) said, "A Jewish woman use to curse the Prophet (ﷺ) and abuse him. A man strangled her until she died and the Messenger of Allah (ﷺ) denied any blood money for her."[41]

The ramifications of negating the pact

If the *dhimmah* pact is negated, then the ruling concerning those that violated the pact is that they become like prisoners of war. If they accept Islam, it is forbidden to kill them. If they do not embrace Islam, the Muslim ruler has a choice between having them killed, releasing them freely or ransoming them, as mentioned in the section on prisoners of war.

From whom is the jizyah to be taken

Nâfi' narrated from Aslam that 'Umar (may Allah be pleased with him) wrote to his military commanders, "Do not levy the *jizyah* upon women and children. And do not levy it except upon those who

---

[40] This report is *ḥasan*. See Shaykh al-Albâni, *I'rwâ' al-Ghaleel*, no. 1278. Recorded by Ibn Abi Shaybah and al-Bayhaqi.

[41] Its chain is *ṣaḥeeḥ*. See Shaykh al-Albâni, *I'rwâ' al-Ghaleel*, vol. 5, p. 91. Recorded by Abu Dawood and al-Bayhaqi.

have the means."[42]

The amount of the jizyah

Mu'âdh said that when the Prophet (ﷺ) sent him to Yemen, he told him to take from every adult male one *dinar* or its equivalent in a type of Yemeni garment.[43] It is permissible to increase this amount, based on the report of Aslam who said, " 'Umar ibn al-Khaṭṭâb set the *jizyah* upon the people who deal in gold at four *dinars*, those who deal in silver at forty *dirhams* while at the same time obliging them to supply food and hospitality for three days to the Muslims."[44]

Actually, the Muslim leader should take into considerations the level of ease or hardship of the people. Ibn Abi Najeeḥ said, "I said to Mujâhid, 'Why is it that the people of ash-Shâm pay four *dinars* while those of Yemen pay only one *dinar*?' He said, 'It has to do with how well off they are.' "[45]

---

[42] This report is *ṣaḥeeḥ*. See Shaykh al-Albâni, *I'rwâ' al-Ghaleel*, no. 1255. Recorded by al-Bayhaqi.
[43] This hadith is *ṣaḥeeḥ*. See Shaykh al-Albâni, *I'rwâ' al-Ghaleel*, no. 1254. Recorded by Abu Dawood.
[44] This report is *ṣaḥeeḥ*. See Shaykh al-Albâni, *I'rwâ' al-Ghaleel*, no. 1261. Recorded by al-Bayhaqi.
[45] This hadith is *ṣaḥeeḥ*. See Shaykh al-Albâni, *I'rwâ' al-Ghaleel*, no. 1260. Recorded by Bukhari without its complete chain.

Chapter — Seventeen
Emancipating Slaves

Emancipation means to remove the state of being owned...

Encouragement to Emancipate Slaves and Its Merit

Allah (ﷻ) has said:

﴿فَلَا ٱقْتَحَمَ ٱلْعَقَبَةَ ﴿١١﴾ وَمَآ أَدْرَىٰكَ مَا ٱلْعَقَبَةُ ﴿١٢﴾ فَكُّ رَقَبَةٍ ﴿١٣﴾﴾

(سورة البَلَد: ١١-١٣)

﴾But he has made no effort to pass on the path that is steep. And what will make you know the path that is steep? [It is] freeing a neck [a slave].﴿ *(Qur'an 90: 11-13)*

Abu Hurayrah (ﷺ) narrated that the Prophet (ﷺ) said, "Any man who emancipates a Muslim will have Allah rescue each limb of his from the Hell-fire due to every limb of he (who he emancipated)."[1] And Abu Moosa al-Ash'ari (ﷺ) narrated that the Prophet (ﷺ) said, "Three will be given their reward twice: A man from the People of the Book who believed in his prophet and then found out about the Prophet (ﷺ) and believed in him, followed him and attested to him, for him there are rewards twice. An owned slave who fulfills the right of Allah and the right of his owner, for him there are rewards twice. A

---

[1] Recorded by Bukhari and Muslim.

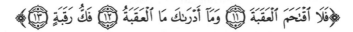

man who had a female slave and fed her well and taught her well and then freed her and married her, for him there are rewards twice."[2]

What is the Best Slave (to Free)

Abu Dharr (ﷺ) said, "I asked the Messenger of Allah (ﷺ), 'What is the best deed?' He replied, 'Belief in Allah and jihad for his sake.' I then asked, 'What is the best slave?' He replied, 'The one with the highest price and who is dearest to his owners.' "[3]

When is it Preferred to Free Slaves?

Asmâ' bint Abi Bakr (ﷺ) said, "The Prophet (ﷺ) ordered the freeing of slaves during an eclipse."[4]

Causes of Emancipation[5]

Emancipation can be via the owner voluntarily freeing the slave out of a desire to please Allah, driven by the aforementioned hadith that point to the virtues of such an act.

Emancipation can also occur through ownership — that is, if anyone comes into possession of a relative within the prohibited degrees of marriage, that slave becomes free. Samurah ibn Jundub narrated that the Prophet (ﷺ) said, "If anyone owns a relative within the prohibited degrees of marriage, he is free."[6]

---

[2] Recorded by Bukhari, Muslim (and this is his wording), Tirmidhi and Nasâ'i.

[3] Recorded by Bukhari and Muslim.

[4] This hadith is *ṣaḥeeḥ*. See Shaykh al-Albâni, *Mukhtasar Ṣaḥeeḥ al-Bukhari*, no. 118. Recorded by Bukhari.

[5] *Manâr as-Sabeel*, vol. 2, p. 110.

[6] This hadith is *ṣaḥeeḥ*. See Shaykh al-Albâni, *Ṣaḥeeḥ Sunan Ibn Mâjah*, no. 2046. Recorded by Abu Dawood, Tirmidhi and Ibn Mâjah.

A slave can be emancipated if part of his ownership is freed. In other words, if a slave is co-owned by partners and one of them frees his shares and he is a person of means, then the remaining value of the slave is to be estimated and he should give that money to his partner(s) and free the slave completely. 'Abdullâh ibn 'Umar narrated that the Messenger of Allah (ﷺ) said, "Whoever emancipates his share in a slave and he has the money for the rest of the price of the slave, the slave should be fairly evaluated and he should give his partners their share and free the slave completely. Otherwise, he has freed only the portion he has freed."[7]

If the emancipator does not have the means to free the slave completely, he has only freed the portion he freed. However, the slave should then try to work to pay off the remainder of his freedom so that the owners may receive his complete value. Abu Hurayrah narrated that the Prophet (ﷺ) said, "Whoever frees his portion of a slave should free the slave completely by paying the rest of his price if he has the means to do so. Otherwise, the value of the slave is to be estimated and he should be helped to work, without hardship, to pay the rest of his value."[8]

Freeing a slave upon one's death

A slave can be freed upon one's death by being told, "If I die, you are free after my death." In such a case, when the person dies, the slave will become free as long as the value of the slave is less than one-third of the deceased's property.[9] 'Imrân ibn Ḥuṣayn said, "A man died while having six slaves and no other wealth and he had freed them upon his death. The Messenger of Allah (ﷺ) divided them into three groups and drew lots between them, freeing two of

---

[7] Recorded by Bukhari, Muslim, Abu Dawood and Tirmidhi.

[8] Recorded by Bukhari, Muslim, Abu Dawood, Tirmidhi and Ibn Mâjah.

[9] *Manâr as-Sabeel*, vol. 2, p. 116.

them and keeping four of them as slaves. He then had harsh words for what (the deceased) had done."[10]

It is valid to sell or give away a slave who was declared free upon one's death

Jâbir ibn 'Abdullâh said, "The Prophet (ﷺ) found out about a man from his Companions who had declared the setting free of his slave upon his death. However, the man had no other wealth than that. (But before the man's death) the Prophet (ﷺ) sold him for eight hundred *dirhams* and sent that money to him (the owner)."[11]

Making an agreement to work for one's freedom

Al-Kitâbah is a contract whereby the slave is given his freedom in exchange for some agreed upon remuneration.[12]

Its ruling

If the slave asks his owner for such a contract, it is obligatory upon his owner to respond positively to his request if he knows that the slave has the means to earn his freedom. Allah has said:

﴿... وَالَّذِينَ يَبْتَغُونَ الْكِتَابَ مِمَّا مَلَكَتْ أَيْمَانُكُمْ فَكَاتِبُوهُمْ إِنْ عَلِمْتُمْ فِيهِمْ خَيْرًا ... ﴿٣٣﴾﴾ (سورة النّور: ٣٣)

﴾... And such of your slaves as seek a writing [of emancipation], give them such writing, if you know that they are good and trustworthy...﴿ *(Qur'an 24: 33)*

---

[10] This hadith is *ṣaḥeeḥ*. See Shaykh al-Albâni, *Mukhtasar Ṣaḥeeḥ Muslim*, no. 895. Recorded by Muslim, Abu Dawood, Tirmidhi and Nasâ'i.

[11] Recorded by Bukhari, Muslim and Abu Dawood.

[12] Ibn Ḥajar, *Fatḥ al-Bâri*, vol. 5, p. 184.

Moosa ibn Anas said, "Seereen asked Anas for a contract for freedom — and he owns lots of wealth — but Anas refused. He went to 'Umar who told him, 'Write the contract for him.' He again refused. 'Umar beat him with his stick and read the verse, ﴾Give them such writing, if you know that they are good and trustworthy﴿, so write the contract.' "[13]

When does he become free

When the slave fulfills the conditions of the contract or when the owner releases him from its obligation, he becomes free. Otherwise, he remains a slave until he fully satisfies the contract. 'Amr ibn Shu'ayb narrated from his father on the authority of his grandfather that the Messenger of Allah (ﷺ) said, "The slave who has contracted to pay for his freedom remains a slave as long as even a *dirham* is left according to his contract."[14]

Selling a slave who has contracted to work for his freedom

It is valid to sell such a slave if he accepts the slave. 'Amrah bint 'Abdur-Raḥmân said, "Bareerah went to 'Â'ishah, the Mother of the Believers, to seek her help (in being freed). 'Â'ishah said to her, 'If your people want the remainder of price all at once and I free you, I shall do so.' Bareerah mentioned that to her people and they said, 'No, unless the relationship of *walâ'* (clientage) is for us.' " Mâlik said that Yaḥya said, " 'Amrah then said that 'Â'ishah mentioned that to the Messenger of Allah (Blessings and peace be upon him) and he said, 'Buy her and set her free as the relationship of *walâ'* is only for

[13] Its chain is *ṣaḥeeḥ*. See Shaykh al-Albâni, *I'rwâ' al-Ghaleel*, no. 1760. Recorded by Bukhari without its complete chain.

[14] This hadith is *ḥasan*. See Shaykh al-Albâni, *Ṣaḥeeḥ Sunan Abi Dawood*, no. 3323 and *I'rwâ' al-Ghaleel*, no. 1674. Recorded by Abu Dawood.

the one who does the freeing.'"[15]

Al-Walâ'

Al-Walâ' establishes the right of inheritance for the one who does the manumitting from the one who has been manumitted. However, as noted earlier, the one having the relationship of *walâ'* only inherits if the freed slave does not have any male relatives to inherit from him.

It is not allowed to sell the right of *walâ'* nor can one give it away as a gift. Ibn 'Umar said, "The Prophet (ﷺ) forbade the selling or the gifting of *al-walâ'*."[16]

---

[15] Recorded by Bukhari and Muslim.
[16] Ibid.

Final Words

This completes what I wish to compile and arrange in this concise book. If I have been correct and upon the truth, that is what I had intended. If it is otherwise, I ask Allah to forgive me and to pardon me. I have made the section on emancipation the last section out of hopes that it will be a source of my rescue from the Hell-fire and being entered into the mercy of the All-Powerful, the Oft-Forgiving.

I ask Allah to make this book accepted in heaven and earth. I also ask that He record rewards for me due to it, wipe away from me my sins and burdens and store it for me as a treasure on the day in which no wealth or children will avail anyone, except for the one who comes to Allah with a sound heart.

The last of our supplications is: "All praise be to Allah, the Lord of the Worlds."

References

The Noble Qur'an.

Âdâb az-Zafâf: Shaykh al-Albâni, al-Maktabah al-Islâmiyah, 1409 H.

Aḥkâm al-Janâ'iz: Shaykh al-Albâni, al-Maktab al-Islâmi, 1986.

Al-Fatḥ ar-Rabbâni: Aḥmad 'Abdur-Raḥmân al-Banâ, Dâr al-Shihâb.

Al-Ijmâ': Ibn al-Mundhir, Dâr Taybah, 1982.

Al-Majmoo' Sharḥ al-Muhadhab: an-Nawawi, Dâr al-Fikr.

Al-Mughni: Ibn Qudâmah al-Maqdisi, Ri'âsah Idârâj al-Buḥooth al-Ilmiyyah wa al-Iftâ', 1981.

Al-Muhalla: Abu Muhammad ibn Ḥazm, Dâr al-Âfâq al-Jadeedah.

Al-Mu'jam al-Kabeer: aṭ-Ṭabarâni, Ḥamdi as-Salafi ed., Maktabah ibn Taymiyah.

Al-Muqni': Ibn Qudâmah al-Maqdisi, al-Muassasah al-Sa'eediyah.

Al-Mustadrak: al-Ḥâkim Muhammad ibn 'Abdullâh, Dâr al-Kutub al-'Ilmiyah.

Al-Muwâfaqât: Abu Isḥâq ash-Shâṭibi, Dâr al-Ma'rifah.

Ar-Rawḍah an-Nadiyah: Ṣiddeeq Ḥasan Khân, Dâr al-Ma'rifah, 1978.

As-Sail al-Jarâr: ash-Shawkâni, Dâr al-Kutub al-'Ilmiyah, 1985.

As-Silsilat aṣ-Ṣaḥeeḥah: Shaykh al-Albâni, al-Maktab al-Islâmi, 1985.

At-Taqreeb li-Fiqh Ibn Qayyim al-Jawziyah: Bakr Abu Zayd.

Al-Umm: ash-Shâfi'ee, Dâr al-Ma'rifah, 1973.

'Awn al-Ma'bood: Shams al-Haq al-Adheem Abâdi, Dâr al-Fikr, 1979.

Bidâyah al-Mujtahid: Ibn Rushd al-Qurṭubi, Dâr al-Ma'rifah, 1981.

Fatḥ al-Bâri: Ibn Ḥajar al-Asqalâni, Dâr al-Ma'rifah.

Fee Dhilâl al-Qur'an: Sayyid Quṭb.

Fiqh as-Sunnah: Sayyid Sâbiq, Dâr al-Fikr, 1977.

Iḥkâm al-Aḥkâm: Ibn Daqeeq al-'Eid, Dâr al-Kutub al-'Ilmiyah.

Irshâd as-Sâri: Muhammad Ibrâheem Shaqrah.

I'rwâ al-Ghaleel: Shaykh al-Albâni, al-Makbat al-Islâmi, 1985.

Jâmi' al-Bayân: Ibn Jareer aṭ-Ṭabari, Dâr al-Fikr, 1984.

Kashf al-Ustâdhir az-Zawâ'id al-Bazzâr: al-Haythami, Muassasah ar-Risâlah, 1984.

Kifâyah al-Akhyâr, Taqi al-Deen al-Ḥuṣani, Dâr al-Ma'rifah.

Majma' az-Zawâ'id: al-Haythami, Muassasah al-Mâ'rif, 1986.

Majmoo' Fatawâ Ibn Taymiyah: 'Abdur-Raḥmân ibn Muhammad ibn Qâsim, ed., ar-Ri'âsah al-'Âmah li-Shu'oon al-Ḥaramayn al-Shareefayn.

Manâr as-Sabeel: Ibrâheem ibn Ḍoowiyân, al-Maktab al-Islâmi, 1984.

Mawârid adh-Dh'amân ila Zawâ'id Ibn Ḥibbân: Noor ad-Deen al-Haythami, Dâr al-Kutub al-'Ilmiyah.

Mishkâh al-Maṣâbeeḥ: al-Khaṭeeb at-Tabreezi, Shaykh al-Albâni, ed., al-Maktab al-Islâmi, 1985.

Mukhtasar Sunan Abi Dawood: al-Mundhiri. Maktabah as-Sunnah al-Muhammadiyah.

Musannaf Ibn Abi Shaybah: Ibn Abi Shaybah, ad-Dâr as-Salafiyah bi-l-Hind, 1979.

Nail al-Awṭâr: ash-Shawkâni, Dâr al-Jeel, 1973.

Ṣaḥeeḥ al-Jâmi': Shaykh al-Albâni, al-Maktab al-Islâmi, 1969.

Ṣaḥeeḥ Ibn Khuzaymah: Ibn Khuzaymah, al-Maktab al-Islâmi, 1975.

Ṣaḥeeḥ Muslim bi-Sharḥ an-Nawawi: an-Nawawi, Dâr Iḥyâ' at-Turâth al-'Arabi, 1972.

Ṣaḥeeḥ Muslim: Muhammad Fu'âd 'Abdul-Bâqi, ed., Dâr al-Fikr, 1983.

Ṣaḥeeḥ Sunan Abi Dawood: Shaykh al-Albâni, al-Maktab al-Islâmi, 1986.

Ṣaḥeeḥ Sunan Ibn Mâjah: Shaykh al-Albâni, al-Maktab al-Islâmi, 1989.

Sharḥ as-Sunnah: al-Baghawi, al-Maktab al-Islâmi, 1983.

Sharḥ az-Zarqâni 'ala al-Muwaṭṭa, az-Zarqâni, Dâr al-Ma'rifah, 1978.

Sharḥ Ma'âni al-Âthâr: aṭ-Ṭaḥâwi, Dâr al-Kutub al-'Ilmiyah, 1979.

Ṣifah Ṣalât an-Nabi: Shaykh al-Albâni, Maktabah al-Mâ'rif, 1991.

Subul as-Salâm: al-Ameer aṣ-Ṣan'âni, Maktabah ar-Risâlah al-Ḥadeethah, 1971.

Sunan al-Bayhaqi: al-Bayhaqi, Dâr al-Ma'rifah.

Sunan ad-Dârimi: ad-Dârimi, Ḥadeeth Akâdeemi Pakistan, 1984.

Sunan aa-Dâraquṭni: ad-Dâraquṭni, Dâr al-Maḥâsin.

Sunan an-Nasâ'i: an-Nasâ'i, Dâr al-Fikr, 1930.

Sunan at-Tirmidhi: Tirmidhi, Dâr al-Fikr, 1983.

Sunan Ibn Mâjah: Ibn Mâjah, Dâr al-Fikr.

Tafseer al-Qur'ân al-'Adheem: Ibn Katheer, Dâr al-Ma'rifah, 1983.

Tamâm al-Minnah: Shaykh al-Albâni, al-Maktabah al-Islâmiyah, 1408.

Tuhfah al-Aḥwadhi: al-Mubârakfoori, Dâr al-Fikr, 1979.

Zâd al-Ma'âd: Ibn Qayyim al-Jawziyah, Muassasah ar-Risâlah, 1986.

Glossary

'Aqeeqah	عقيقة :	The ceremony of celebrating the birth of a child by cutting the hair of the child on the eight day of its birth and donating its weight in silver/gold and slaughtering animal — goat or sheep, i.e., two for the male and one for the female
'Aṣab	عصب :	A rough Yemeni cloth
'Aṣr	عصر :	Afternoon, Afternoon prayer, name of the 103rd *Soorah* of the Qur'an
Âmeen	آمين :	Lit. Answer our prayer; may Allah sanction the supplication, so be it
Adha	أذى :	Harmful (to have sex with one's wife while she is having her menses)
A<u>dh</u>-<u>Dh</u>ihâr	الظِهار :	Lit. Back; One of the pre-Islamic way of divorce by saying, 'You are to me as the back of my mother'
Al-'Aṣabah	العصبة :	Paternal relations, the tribe and relatives of the man from his father's side
Al-Adhâ	الاذى :	Filth, rocks and thorns (things that harms someone)
Al-Bai'	البيع :	The sale

Al-Ghaṣb	الغصب :	To usurp other's rights, taking the rights of others by force or by fraud
Al-Jallâlah	الجلّاله :	Animal whose majority of diet is of impure things
Al-Jareen	الجرين :	A place where dried fruits are stored
Al-Madhi	المذي :	A thin, clear, sticky fluid emerging from male genital
Al-Muḍârabah	المضاربة :	A commercial term meaning silent partnership
Al-Qadhaf	القذف :	To defame, slander or accuse
Al-Qadr	القدر :	A Divine Decree
Al-Qirân	القِران :	Combining the Ḥajj and 'Umrah simultaneously with one *iḥrâm*, i.e., performing Ḥajj after 'Umrah without coming out of 'Umrah *iḥrâm*
Al-Wadee'ah	الوديعة :	To leave something or depositing something for the purpose of safekeeping
Al-Wadi	الودي :	A white, thick fluid that comes out after urination
Al-Walâ'	الولاء :	Clientage
Al-Waseelah	الوسيلة :	Highest rank in Paradise
Al-Yameen al-Ghamoos	اليمين الغموس :	False oath intending evil and treachery
Aṣ-Ṣa'eed	الصعيد :	The face of the earth, earth, sand, clay, also upperland, plateau
Ash-Shajjâj	الشجّاج :	Skull fracture, wounds of head and face

As-Sa'ee	السعي :	Making the circuits between aṣ-Ṣafâ and al-Marwah in 'Umrah and Ḥajj
As-Sadl	السدل :	Leaving onc's garment down all the way to the ground when in standing position, to pray with the arms at one's sides — the Mâliki and Shi'a way
At-Tammatu'	التمّتُّع :	A kind of Ḥajj where in a man comes out of *iḥrâm* after performing 'Umrah and enters into *iḥrâm* for Ḥajj on 8th of Dhul Hijjah
'Awrah	عورة :	Human private parts (that are to be covered)
Dhimmah	ذِمّة :	A pact, security and protection
Dhimmi	ذِمّي :	Non-Muslim resident of an Islamic state
Dhuhr	ظُهر :	Noon, Noon prayer
Dhulm	ظُلم :	Wrongdoing, oppression, injustice, violence
Diyah	دِية :	Blood money
'Eid	عيد :	Festival of Muslims on 1st Shawwal and 10th Dhul Hijjah every year
Fai'	فئ :	Land surrendered to Muslims without any fighting
Fajr	فجر :	Dawn, Dawn prayer, name of the 89th *Soorah* of the Qur'an
Farâ'iḍ	فرائض :	Sing. *Fareeḍah*; Religious duty, distributive shares in estate, inheritance
Fidyah	فِدْية :	Ransom to get freedom

Fiqh فِقه : Islamic jurisprudence

Fiṭrah فِطرة : Nature, natural inclination

Fitnah فِتنة : Trial, tribulation

Ghusl غُسل : Complete bath

Ḥadath حَدَث : Passing wind with or without sound

Ḥaṣâh حصاة : Lit. Pebble; *Jâhiliyah* commercial terminology where one says, "Throw this pebble and whatever merchandise it lands on is yours for such and such price"

Ḥawâlah حوالة : To change or to transfer

Ḥoor al-'Ayn حور العين : Houris with large and beautiful eyes, i.e., women of Paradise

Ḥudood حُدود : Sing. *Ḥadd*; originally "The barrier between two things"; lexically, "prevention"; technically, "Legally prescribed punishment for the sin committed"

Hadith حديث : The record of the sayings and deeds of and approvals by, the last Prophet

Ḥajj حج : Major pilgrimage in the month of Dhul-Hijjah from 8 to 13, 9th being the main — the day of 'Arafah

'Iddah عِدّة : Prescribed waiting period for the woman to remarry when she is widowed or divorced

Ijtihâd إجتِهاد : Lit. 'Utmost effort'; exercise of reason in order to try to find an appropriate ruling on a matter not directly ruled in the Qur'an

'Illiyeen	عِلّيين :	The place where the register of the righteous is kept
Imam	إمام :	A leader in prayer, ruler of the Muslim state
'Isha'	عشاء :	Night, Night prayer
Istiḥâḍah	إستحاضة :	Metrorrhagia or uterine hemorrhaging
I'tikâf	اعتكاف :	Seclusion in the mosque for the purpose of worship normally in the last ten days of Ramaḍân
Jihad	جهاد :	Striving for the cause of Allah, also holy war
Jizyah	جِزيه :	Tax paid by the non-Muslims to the Islamic state in lieu of military service
Khamiṣah or *Khamiṣ*	خميسة/ خميس :	A type of garment
Khamr	خمر :	Alcohol, intoxicant
Khula'	خُلع :	Dissolution of the marriage sought by woman
Khuṭbah	خُطبة :	Sermon, Speech (on the pulpit)
Kufr	كفر :	Disbelief
Li'ân	لِعان :	A type of slander
Maghrib	مغرب :	Sunset, Sunset prayer
Masjid	مسجد :	Mosque
Meeqât	ميقات :	Pl. *Muwaqeet*; One of the designated places near Makkah for entering into *iḥrâm* to perform Ḥajj or 'Umrah
Mudd	مُدّ :	Measurement equivalent to what a person with average size hands holds when cupped together

Muhâjiroon	مهاجر :	Emigrants from Makkah to Madeenah at the time of the last Prophet
Mulâmasah	مُلامسة :	A *Jâhiliyah* commercial term where the seller says to the buyer "Any garment you touched is yours for such and such price"
Munâbadhah	مُنابذه :	A *Jâhiliyah* commercial term where the seller says to the buyer, "Any garment you fling to me is yours for such and such price"
Mustaḥâḍah	مُستحاضة :	A condition where the woman has a continual blood flow not related to menstruation
Nadhr	نذر :	Vow, votif offering
Niṣâb	نِصاب :	A minimum prescribed amount over which one has to pay Zakah
Qiblah	قبلة :	The direction of Ka'bah in Makkah Muslims face while praying
Qunoot	قنوت :	Special supplication made during praying *witr*
Raheenah	رهينة :	Pledge, mortgage
Rahn	رهن :	Pawning, mortgaging
Rak'ah	ركعة :	A unit of prayer
Riba	رِبا :	Usury, interest
ṣ'â	صاع :	A measurement, it is four times the amount an average person can hold in his hands when they are cupped together

Ṣalât aḍ-Ḍuḥâ	صلاة الضُحى	: A non-obligatory forenoon prayer also known as "Prayer of the Patient"
Ṣaheeḥ	صحيح	: Authentic
Sharâ'	شراء	: Purchase
Shari'ah	شريعة	: Islamic law
Shirk	شرك	: Associating partners with Allah, polytheism
Sijjeen	سِجّين	: The place where the register of the deeds of the disbelievers, polytheists, sinners and evil doers is kept
Soorah	سورة	: Chapter (of the Qur'an)
Sunan	سُنن	: Plural of Sunnah, Books of hadiths collection
Sunan al-Fiṭrah	سنن الفطرة	: The natural practices
Sunnah	سُنّة	: Prophets sayings, ways and deeds
Sutrah	سُترة	: A barrier between one praying and any one who passes in front of him
Suwaiq	سويق	: A drink...
Taḥneek	تحنيك	: A tradition where a person chew something sweet, like a date and places it into the baby's mouth
Ṭahârah	طهارة	: Purity, being free from the impurity
Takbeer	تكبير	: Saying, "Allah is All-Great"
Talbiyah	تلبية	: Recitation said while performing Ḥajj or 'Umrah
Taqwa	تقوى	: Piety
Tashahhud	تشهُّد	: Lit. To make *shahâdah*; Sitting

		position before the end of a two/four units prayer
Tashreeq	تشريق :	The 10th, 11th and, 12th and 13th of Dhul Hijjah
Tayammum	تيمُّم :	Dry ablution with clean earth
Thareed	ثريد :	A dish of soaked bread, meat and broth
Ummah	أُمّة :	Nation, (Islamic) community
'Umrah	عمرة :	Minor pilgrimage to Ka'bah in Makkah performed at any time of the year, comprising of *Iḥrâm*, *ṭawâf*, *sa'ee* and shaving or trimming the head hair
Waleemah	وليمة :	Wedding feast
Wars	ورس :	A kind of plant used for dyeing
Wasq	وسق :	A measurement, one *wasq* equals 180 Kilograms
Witr	وتر :	A non-obligatory prayer prayed in odd numbers after the night prayer and before the *fajr*
Wuḍoo'	وضوء :	Ablution
Zakâh	زكوٰة / زكاة :	Poor due, a pillar of Islam, obligatory on every Muslim possessing wealth over a prescribed limit
Zakât al-Fiṭr	زكاة الفِطر :	Poor due paid at the end of the month of Ramaḍân
Zinâ	زِنا :	Adultery, fornication, unlawful sexual intercourse

List of Contents